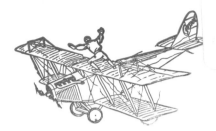

Ex Libris

SiLVER HANRAHAN
B

Sept 11/1998
Purchased AT
MAiN AVE Books
Tillamook, Or.

KNOW AVIATION

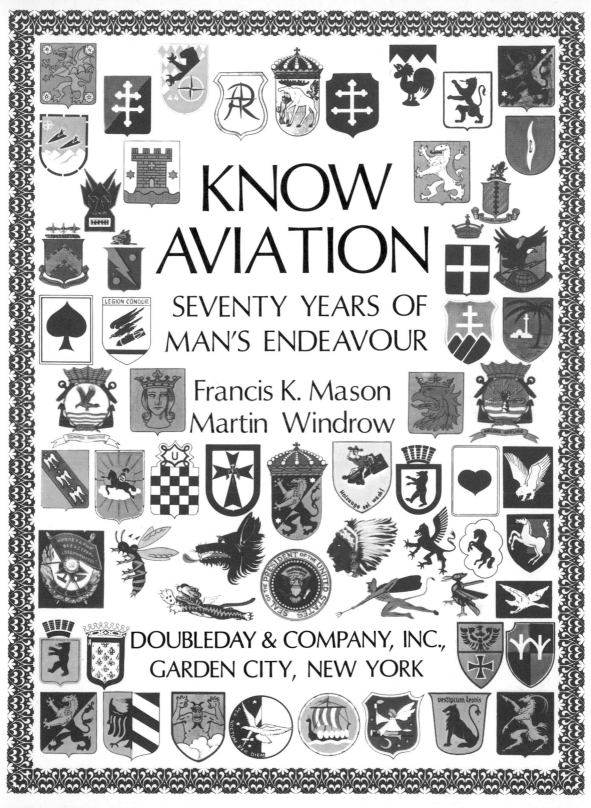

KNOW
AVIATION

SEVENTY YEARS OF MAN'S ENDEAVOUR

Francis K. Mason
Martin Windrow

DOUBLEDAY & COMPANY, INC.,
GARDEN CITY, NEW YORK

This book was designed and produced by
Alban Book Services Limited,
147 London Road, St. Albans, Herts, England

© *Francis K. Mason and Martin Windrow* (*1973*)
  George Philip & Son Limited (*1973*)
  Alban Book Services Limited (*1973*)

ISBN 0-385-0-0550-4

Published in Great Britain by
GEORGE PHILIP & SON LIMITED
12–14 Long Acre, London WC2E 9LP

Filmset in 8/9 pt. Times New Roman 327
Printed in Great Britain on 118 gsm paper by
W. S. COWELL LIMITED
at the Butter Market, Ipswich, England

LIST OF CONTENTS

✦ A PERSONAL INTRODUCTION ✦

Perhaps the most dramatic yet comprehensible manner by which to introduce the subject of this book is to cite the life of my own father who, though seldom an active participant in aviation has lived through it all. And perhaps he, more than many people, has come to understand just what aviation has truly represented; for many years he was a professional geographer, studying and teaching the character of Man's Earth, yet in his lifetime he has seen the horse displaced by the coming of the motor car and then the aeroplane – the means by which this Earth has shrunk from travel-spans of months to mere hours.

To be more specific, my father was born in the eighteen-eighties, at a time when the British Army was still galloping to war and was floating its first hydrogen balloons over Africa. In due course he joined the British Army, in which his duties took him to India; here, in February 1911, he made his one minor excursion into the remoter chronicles of aviation history when he accompanied Henri Pequet in his fragile Humber biplane across the Jumna River, carrying the world's first scheduled air mails.

Whether or not this sombre experience, accompanied by considerable trepidation on the part of my father, discouraged him from further aerial exploits is not relevant to this short note. Suffice it to say that he never again ventured into the air, save much more recently in a pressurised airliner to and from the Channel Isles over a somewhat wider expanse of water than the Jumna.

After a war spent firmly on the ground in France, my father's service in the Army moved to India once again where he became engaged in survey work in the Himalayas, that huge land mass that has for so long provided an almost impenetrable barrier against all comers. Yet in the very year that he left India and the Army to take up the Professorship offered to him at Oxford University, an aeroplane flew over the peak of Mount Everest. It was as if aviation was following his shadow.

My father came home to Oxford where he remained for thirty years. He saw little of his second war at close quarters, although he became an Air Raid Warden! But Oxford was never bombed. During his years in retirement he has watched while jets have come and gone across the broad oceans, joined fireside arguments about the portents of supersonic travel, and marvelled at Man's journeys into space. He has seen the horse-drawn buggy of his youth evolve into a multi-billion dollar buggy ride upon the dusty plains of the moon. He has lived in the age of the hydrogen balloon and that of the hydrogen bomb.

This, then, is what is really meant when one breathlessly observes that Man's conquest of the air has occupied but a single lifetime.

F.K.M.

ACKNOWLEDGEMENTS

The Compilers have received considerable advice and assistance from numerous individuals and organisations both in the United Kingdom and overseas, and from U.K. representatives of foreign nations, their armed forces and commercial interests; the Publishers and Compilers particularly wish to express their appreciation to the following for their contribution to this book:

Air Lingus and Aerlinte Eirann
Aerolineas Argentinas
Air Canada
Air France
Air Inter
Alitalia
Alaska Airlines Inc.
Allegheny Airlines Inc.
The Royal Australian Air Force
Austrian Airlines
American Airlines Inc.
Winyard L. Baggs III
Force Aérienne Belge
Sr. Alberto Bertoni
The Boeing Company
Braniff International Inc.
Britannia Airways Ltd.
British Aircraft Corporation
British Air Ferries Ltd.
British Caledonian Airways Ltd.
British European Airways Corporation
British Island Airways Ltd.
British Midland Airways Ltd.
British Overseas Airways Corporation
The Canadian Armed Forces
Canadian Pacific Air
Cessna Aircraft Company
Channel Airways Ltd.
Fuerza Aérea de Chile
Fuerza Aérea de Colombiana
Condor Flugdienst GmbH
The Confederate Air Force
Continental Air Lines Inc.
Court Line Ltd.
C.S.E. Aviation (Carlisle) Ltd.
Dan-Air Services Ltd.
The Royal Danish Air Force (Flyvevaabnet)
The Ministry of Defence (Air), Great Britain
Delta Air Lines Inc.
Deutsche Lufthansa AG
Eastern Air Lines Inc.
Fairchild Hiller Corporation (Republic Aviation)
Finnair Oy

L'Armée de l'Air, Aéronautique Navale and Aviation Légère de l'Armée de Terre of France
The Finnish Air Force
General Dynamics Corporation
The Luftwaffe and Marineflieger of the Federal German Republic
Grumman Aircraft Engineering Corporation
Hawker Siddeley Aviation
Koninklijke Luchtmacht and Marine Luchtvaardienst of Holland
Leslie Hunt, Esq.
Iberia, Lineas Aereas de Espagna SA
The Indian Air Force
The Israel Defence Force/Air Force, Chel Ha'avir
The Aeronautica Militare Italiano
Japan Air Lines
K.L.M. (Royal Dutch Airlines)
Lockheed Aircraft Corporation
McDonnell Douglas Aircraft Corporation
Monarch Airlines Ltd.
National Air Lines Inc.
Northeast Airlines Ltd.
Northwest Orient Airlines Inc.
Kongelige Norske Luftforsvaret
Novosti
Ozark Air Lines Inc.
Pan American World Airways Inc.
Fuerza Aérea de Peruana
Trevor Robinson, Esq.
SABENA
Scandinavian Airlines System
South African Airways
Ejercito del Aire of Spain
The Flygvapnet (Royal Swedish Air Force)
Swissair
Thurston Aviation Ltd.
Trans World Airlines Inc.
The Türk Hava Kuvvetleri
United Airlines Inc.
The U.S. Department of Defense (All Services)
Angus Welch, Esq.
Western Airlines Inc.
Leonard Williams, Esq.

✒ CHAPTER 1 ✒
A Chronology of Aviation

Although the detailed history of lighter-than-air transportation lies outside the scope of this book, a brief chronological commentary on the development of ballooning is included as a preface to the dawn of heavier-than-air aviation which broke at the turn of the twentieth century. By so doing it can be seen that by the time that the Wright brothers achieved their famous flight in 1903 mankind had already achieved air travel, and had applied air vehicles to many purposes – not least to military demands. Indeed, it was to be many years before the aeroplane achieved journeys whose distances matched those of many of the balloon and airship pioneers.

THE DAWN OF AIR TRAVEL

1783   On 5th June an unmanned Montgolfière hot-air balloon gives the first public demonstration at Annonnay in France. On 19th September a sheep, a duck and a cock are sent aloft at Versailles in a Montgolfière, descending two miles distant after an 8-minute flight. On 21st November **air travel by man is achieved** when François Pilâtre de Rozier and the Marquis d'Arlandes in a 49-ft. diameter Montgolfière ascend from the Chateau La Muette in the Bois de Boulogne and land 5½ miles distant on the Butte-aux-Cailles after 25 minutes. On 1st December **the first voyage by a hydrogen-filled** balloon is made from the Tuileries, Paris, by Jacques Alexandre César Charles and Aîné Robert, alighting 27 miles distant near the town of Nesles.

1784   On 25th February the first manned balloon ascent is made by the Chevalier Paolo Andreani, with the brothers Augustin and Charles Gerli in a Montgolfière at Moncuco near Milan. The **first woman to make a free flight in a balloon** is Madam Thible accompanied by a Monsieur Fleurant in a Montgolfière at Lyons on 4th June. **The first balloon voyage in England** is made by Vincenzo Lunardi (1759–1806), an employee at the Italian Embassy in London, on 15th September from the Honourable Artillery Company's training ground at Moorfields, London, to Standon Green End, Hertfordshire, in a (hydrogen-filled) Charlière. (**The first balloon voyage in Britain** is generally ascribed to James Tytler (1747–1804) who makes his first short flight at Edinburgh on 25th August in a Montgolfière.)

1785   On 7th January **the English Channel is first crossed by air** when the Frenchman Jean-Pierre Blanchard (1753–1809), accompanied by the American Dr. John Jeffries (1744–1819) ascend from Dover at 1 p.m. and alight in the Forêt de Felmores, France, at 3.30 p.m. **The first ballooning fatalities are suffered** when on 15th June de Rozier (see 1783) and Jules Romain are killed in a hydrogen-cum-hot-air balloon at Huitmile Warren, near Boulogne. Blanchard makes **the first balloon ascents in Germany** (at Frankfurt), **in Holland** (The Hague) **and Belgium** (Ghent); he also creates a distance record with a 300-mile voyage from Lille in Belgium, accompanied by the Chevalier de L'Espinard in August.

1788   Jean-Pierre Blanchard makes **the first balloon ascent in Switzerland**, ascending from Basle in a hydrogen balloon.

9

1789	Blanchard makes **the first balloon ascents in Poland** (at Warsaw) **and Czechoslovakia** (at Prague) using a Montgolfière.
1793	On 9th January Blanchard makes **the first balloon ascent in the new world** at Philadelphia, landing in Gloucester County, New Jersey, after a flight of 46 minutes.
1794	On 26th June **a man-carrying balloon is first put to military use** by the French republican army, manned by Capitaine Coutelle at the Battle of Fleurus.
1836	On 7th–8th November **the first long-distance flight by a balloon from England** is made by *The Royal Vauxhall Balloon* manned by Charles Green, Robert Holland M.P. and Monck Mason, from Vauxhall Gardens, London, landing 480 miles (770 km) distant near Weilberg in the Duchy of Nassau.
1847	W. S. Henson (1812–1888) and John Stringfellow (1799–1883) complete **the first model aeroplane powered by a steam engine** at Chard, Somerset, England. Henson later emigrates to America and none of Stringfellow's powered models ever achieves sustained flight.
1852–53	A ten-year-old boy (and shortly afterwards, an adult) are carried aloft in sustained flight by a glider designed and built by Sir George Cayley at Brompton Hall, Yorkshire, England, to become **the first human beings carried aloft in sustained flight by a heavier-than-air craft.**
1858	**Australia's first balloon ascent** is made on 29th March by a hydrogen balloon, *Australasian*, at Melbourne.
1861	**The first American Army Balloon Corps** is formed on 1st October under the command of Thaddeus Sobieski Coulincourt Lowe, Chief Aeronaut of the Army of the Potomac.
1862	**America's first military use of a man-carrying balloon** is that by the Federal Army at the crossing of Rappahannock River on 11th December during the Civil War. Balloons are also used at the Battle of Chancellorsville (30th April to 5th May 1863).
1864–68	**The first military use of balloons in an international war outside Europe** is made by the Brazilian Marquis de Caxias during the appalling Paraguayan War between these dates.
1868	**The first aeronautical exhibition in Great Britain** is staged at the Crystal Palace, London, by the Aeronautical Society, exhibiting model engines driven by steam, oil gas and guncotton.
1871	In collaboration with John Browning, F. H.

	Wenham (1824–1908) builds **the world's first wind tunnel** for the Aeronautical Society of Great Britain. Wenham had been the first scientist to deduce correctly the lift distribution properties of a cambered aerofoil, and built various gliders during the mid-nineteenth century.
1879	Captain J. L. B. Templar of the Middlesex Militia becomes **the first British Air Commander** when appointed to develop balloons for the British Army with Captain H. P. Lee, Royal Engineers. A sum of £150 is allowed by the War Office (as **the first British "Air Estimates"**) for the work, and his own balloon *Crusader* is **the first balloon to be used by the British Army,** in 1879. *Pioneer*, **the first balloon to be constructed for the British Army,** in 1879, costs £71 from the £150 appropriation. **The first balloon ascent in Canada** is made on 31st July by Richard Cowan, Charles Grimley and Charles Page in a hydrogen balloon at Montreal.
1880	**Man-carrying balloons are first used by the British Army** on manoeuvres at Aldershot, Hampshire, on 24th June. Army balloon detachments accompany British military forces sent to Bechuanaland in 1884, and to the Sudan in 1885.
1884	Gottlieb Daimler (1834–1900) invents the light, petrol-fuelled, high-speed engine.
1888	Wölfert's airship is **the first full-size aircraft to be propelled by a petrol engine** (Tissandier's airship of 1883 had been propelled by an electric motor).
1889	The German Otto Lilienthal (1848–1896) publishes his classic *Der Vogelflug als Grundlage der Fliegekunst* ("The Flight of Birds as the Basis of Aviation").
1890	**The first full-size piloted aeroplane,** Clément Ader's (1841–1925) steam-powered *Éole*, leaves the ground on 9th October but fails to fly.
1891–96	Numerous successful piloted flights by gliders are made in this period, and these inspire the eventual phase in aviation which culminates in successful powered, sustained, manned flight.
1894	Sir Hiram Stevens Maxim (1840–1916, inventor of the Maxim gun in 1884), tests his steam-powered biplane test-rig on 31st July which just rises from its rails, but fails to fly.
1895	Lilienthal makes his first successful flights in his biplane glider, achieving sustained gliding flight at the Rhinower Hills, near Stöllen, Germany. Percy Sinclair Pilcher (1866–99) builds his

first manned glider, the *Bat*, and flies from the banks of the River Clyde; he thus becomes **Britain's first true aviator.**

1896 Octave Chanute (1832–1910), French-born American engineer, achieves successful, manned gliding flight with his biplane hang-glider. His Pratt-truss method of rigging is later adopted by the Wright brothers.
9th August. Otto Lilienthal crashes while gliding and dies the following day.
Samuel Pierpont Langley achieves success with steam-powered model tandem-wing aeroplanes.

1897 The Schwartz all-metal airship flies.

1898 The Aéro Club de France is founded in Paris. In America, Langley obtains Government finance to continue his efforts to build full-size versions of his successful models.

1899 On 30th September Percy Pilcher (see 1895) crashes with his *Hawk* glider and dies on 2nd October.

1900 Count Ferdinand von Zeppelin (1838–1917) flies his first large airship over Lake Constance. Wilbur (1867–1912) and Orville Wright (1871–1948) fly their *No. 1* glider at Kitty Hawk, North Carolina, U.S.A. (moving to the nearby Kill Devil Hills the following year to fly their *No. 2* glider).

1901 The Brazilian Alberto Santos-Dumont (1873–1932) flies his *No. 6* airship round the Paris Eifel Tower. Langley achieves faltering flight with **the first petrol-driven model aeroplane.**
Samuel Franklin Cody (1861–1913), who had been experimenting with large kites in England, is drawn across the English Channel in a canoe attached to one of his box-kites. Cody patents his man-lifting box-kites.
In London, the Aero Club of Great Britain is founded.

1902 The Wright brothers invent co-ordinated lateral (rudder) control and roll (by wing-warping). They make almost 1,000 flights in their *No. 3* glider.

THE DAWN BREAKS

1903 8th December. Langley's *Aerodrome*, a manned, full-size (48-ft., 16-m., span), powered aeroplane crashes after fouling its launcher on the Potomac River (its pilot, Charles M. Manley, is rescued), and the American Government withdraws its financial assistance.
17th December. Wilbur and Orville Wright achieve **the world's first powered, sustained and controlled flight by an aeroplane** at Kill Devil Hills, near Kitty Hawk, North Carolina, U.S.A. with their *Flyer I.*

1904 The British Army adopts Cody's man-lifting kites. On 26th May the Wrights start flights in their *Flyer II*, using the weight-and-derrick method of launching for the first time on 7th September. On 9th November Wilbur Wright achieves the first flight of over five minutes' duration.

1905 In June the Wrights complete **the world's first wholly-practical aeroplane,** their *Flyer III.* On 4th October Orville makes the first flight of over half-an-hour's duration, but after 16th October neither brother flies again until 6th May 1908. At this time (1905) no one else in the world has succeeded in emulating the Wright's first flights.

1906
-3-06 **The first tractor monoplane,** designed by the Paris-domiciled Transylvanian, Trajan Vuia (1872–1950), is tested but is unsuccessful; nevertheless it leads the European monoplane tradition and certainly inspired Louis Blériot (1872–1936), the first great and successful advocate.

12-9-06 The Dane, Jacob Christian H. Ellehammer, makes **the first significant "flight" in Europe** with a tethered "hop" of about 140 feet (45 m.), but no free-flight follows immediately.

12-11-06 Santos-Dumont (see 1901) achieves **the first official hop-flight by a manned, powered aeroplane in Europe** of 721 feet (241 m.) in 21·2 seconds in his *14-bis* aeroplane – in effect a box-kite powered by a 50-h.p. *Antoinette* engine.

1907
1-8-07 An Aeronautical Division of the Office of the Chief Signals Officer, U.S. Army, is established "to study the flying machine and the possibility of adapting it to military purposes." The Division comprised Captain Charles Chandler and two other ranks.

12-10-07
13-10-07 **The North Sea is crossed by air for the first time** by the hydrogen balloon *Mammoth,* manned by Mons. A. F. Gaudron (French aeronaut) accompanied by two others. Ascending from Crystal Palace, London, they land at Brackan, Lake Vänern, 720 miles (1,160 km.) distant in Sweden.

9-11-07 Henry Farman (1874–1958) makes the **first flight in Europe of over one minute's duration** on a Voisin with a flight of 1,030 metres in 1 min. 14 seconds.

10-11-07 Louis Blériot (see 1906) first flies his *Type VII*, the **world's first tractor monoplane with enclosed fuselage, rear-mounted empennage,** and two-wheel main undercarriage and tail-wheel. The limited success achieved by this aeroplane before Blériot finally crashes it on 18th December convinces him that this basic configuration is sound.

1908

13-1-08 Henry Farman makes **the first official 1-km. closed-circuit flight in Europe** on a modified Voisin at Issy-les-Moulineaux, France.

14-5-08 **The world's first passenger flight in an aeroplane** is made by Charles W. Furnas; his pilot is Wilbur Wright, and the flight is at Kill Devil Hills.

30-5-08 Europe's **first passenger flight in an aeroplane** is made by Henry Farman who takes aloft the Frenchman Ernest Archdeacon (1863–1957) who was co-founder of the *Fédération Aéronautique Internationale* on 14th October 1905.

28-6-08 The Dane, Jacob Ellehammer (see 1906), makes **the first aeroplane flight in Germany** at Kiel in his triplane. The **first German aeroplane pilot**, Hans Grade, flies a development of this aeroplane at Magdeburg in October.

4-7-08 Blériot, in his *No. VIII*, makes **the first monoplane flight of over five minutes.** Glenn Hammond Curtiss (1878–1930) wins the *Scientific American* prize for the first public flight in the U.S.A. (of 1 minute 42½ seconds' duration).

8-7-08 Léon Delagrange (1873–1910) carries aloft **the world's first woman passenger in an aeroplane** – Madame Thérèse Peltier – at Turin, Italy, in the Voisin-Delagrange. It is believed that a few days earlier Delagrange had become the **first aeroplane pilot to fly in Italy.**

8-8-08 Wilbur Wright starts his highly-influential displays of flying in Europe with a flight at Hunaudières, France, with the **world's first practical two-seat aeroplane.** A week later he moves to Camp d'Auvours where he continues to give demonstrations until 31st December.

3-9-08 Orville Wright commences flying at Fort Myer giving demonstrations to the U.S. Army, and on 9th September makes the **first flight of over one hours' duration.** On 17th September he crashes and is injured; his passenger, Lieutenant Thomas Etholen Selfridge, U.S. Signal Corps (1882–1909), is killed and is thus the **world's first powered-aeroplane occupant to be killed while flying.**

8-10-08 **The first Briton to fly as an aeroplane passenger** is Griffith Brewer, taken aloft by Wilbur Wright at Camp d'Auvours; he is followed on the same day by the Hon. Charles Stewart Rolls (1877–1910), Frank Hedges Butler (founder of the Aero Club of Great Britain in 1901), and Colonel B. F. S. Baden-Powell, Secretary of the Aeronautical Society.

1909

23-2-09 **The first aeroplane flight in Canada** is made by John A. Douglas McCurdy over Baddeck Bay, Nova Scotia, in his *Silver Dart* biplane, the first flight of which had been made in the U.S.A. the previous December.

-4-09 **The first aeroplane flight in Austria** is made by the Frenchman Georges Legagneux on a Voisin at Vienna.

30-4-09 **The first aeroplane flight by a resident Englishman in England** is made by J. T. C. Moore-Brabazon (later Lord Brabazon of Tara) on a Voisin at Leysdown, Isle of Sheppey, covering 450 feet (130 m.).

14-5-09 **The first aeroplane flight over one mile in Britain** is made by Samuel Cody (see 1901) in *British Army Aeroplane No. 1* over Laffan's Plain, Hampshire.

-7-09 **The first aeroplane flight in Sweden** is made by the Frenchman Georges Legagneux on his Voisin at Stockholm. **The first aeroplane flight in Russia** is made by Van Den Schkrouff at Odessa, also on a Voisin.

25-7-09 **The first successful aeroplane flight across the English Channel** is made by the Frenchman Louis Blériot in his Type XI monoplane, flying from Calais to a field near Dover.

c. 28-7-09 Mrs. Cody, wife of Samuel Cody, is **the first woman passenger to fly in an aeroplane in Britain** when she accompanies her husband in his aeroplane over Laffan's Plain, Hampshire.

2-8-09 **Canada's first aeroplane passenger,** F. W. "Casey" Baldwin is taken aloft at Petawawa, Ontario, by John McCurdy.

22-8-09
29-8-09 **The world's first international aviation meeting** is held at Rheims, France. At this meeting Henry Farman achieves the **world's first flight of over 100 miles,** and is also the **first to carry aloft two passengers simultaneously.**

7-9-09 Eugene Lefebvre is killed testing a French-built Wright biplane, and is thus **the first aeroplane pilot to be killed flying.**

8-9-09 Cody makes the **first flight of over one hour's duration in Britain.**

22-9-09 Captain Ferdinand Ferber (1862–1909) is the world's second pilot to be killed in an aeroplane. He is killed in a taxying accident at Boulogne in a Voisin.

-10-09 **The first aeroplane flight in Romania** is made

The great French aviation pioneer, Louis Blériot (1872–1936), pilot and aircraft constructor, and conqueror of the English Channel in 1909

by Louis Blériot in his Type XI at Bucharest.

2-10-09   Orville Wright makes **the world's first flight at over 1,000 feet altitude.**

15-10-09
23-10-09   **The first aviation meetings in Britain** are held. At the first, at Doncaster (15th to 23rd October), five of the twelve participating aeroplanes manage to fly. The second, at Squire's Gate, Blackpool (18th to 23rd October), is however officially recognised by the Aero Club, and seven aeroplanes are coaxed into the air.

23-10-09   **The world's first woman pilot,** Mme. la Baronne de la Roche, a Frenchwoman, receives her Pilot's Certificate at Châlons, France, qualifying on a Voisin.

5-12-09   **The first manned-glider flight in Australia** is made by George Augustus Taylor at Narrabeen Beach, NSW. His wife becomes **the world's first woman glider pilot** when she flies his glider later the same month.

9-12-09   **America's first monoplane flight** is made by the Walden III, designed by Dr. Henry W. Walden and powered by a 22-h.p. 3-cylinder Anzani engine, at Mineola, Long Island, N.Y.

By the end of 1909, aviation had progressed to the point where the aeroplane was recognised as a practical vehicle. America's lead had already been eroded away, although the Wright biplane was still widely recognised as the most developed aircraft in the world. Nevertheless, all world records standing at the end of the year had been established by Europeans and in wholly-European aeroplanes. These were: Speed, 47·85 m.p.h. (77 kph) by Blériot in a Blériot XII at Rheims; distance, 145 miles (233 km) by Henry Farman in a Farman at the Camp de Châlons; altitude, 1,486 feet (453 m) by Hubert Latham (1883–1912) in an Antoinette at the Camp de Châlons.

1910

-1-10   **The first aeroplane flights in Egypt** are made this month by two Humber-built Blériot monoplanes flown by Capt. G. W. P. Dawes and J. V. Neale during practice for a meeting at Heliopolis. Both pilots crashed.

-1-10   **The first aeroplane flight in Australia** is made during the month by an imported Wright biplane flown by Colin Defries, the motor-racing driver, at Sydney, NSW. Ehrich Weiss (better known as Harry Houdini, the escapologist) first flies on 18th March at Digger's Rest, Victoria.

15-2-10   The prefix "Royal" is granted by H.M. King Edward VII to the Aero Club of Great Britain.

10-3-10   Emil Aubrun, flying a Blériot, makes **the world's first night flights** at Villalugano, Buenos Aires, Argentine.

13-3-10   **The first aeroplane flight in Switzerland** is made by the German Captain Engelhardt in a Wright A biplane from the ice-covered lake at St. Moritz.

28-3-10   Henri Fabre (b. 1883) makes **the world's first seaplane flight** in a floatplane of his own design at Martigues, near Marseilles, France.

27-4-10
28-4-10   Louis Paulhan wins the *Daily Mail* London-Manchester air race, beating the Englishman Claude Grahame-White. During the race Grahame-White makes **the first night flight in Europe.**

2-6-10   The Hon. Charles Stewart Rolls, flying a Short-built Wright biplane, completes **the first non-stop double-crossing of the English Channel.**

12-7-10   The Hon. C. S. Rolls becomes **the first British pilot to lose his life while flying** when his French-built Wright biplane suffers a structural failure and crashes during the Bournemouth Aviation Week (a flying meeting).

10-8-10   Claude Grahame-White carries **the first British air mail** in a Blériot monoplane from Squires Gate, Blackpool, but fails to reach his destination at Southport.

17-8-10   The Franco-American John B. Moisant makes **the first passenger-carrying aeroplane** crossing of the English Channel, carrying his mechanic in his two-seat Blériot.

11-9-10 Robert Loraine in a Farman biplane makes **the first aeroplane crossing of the Irish Sea** (although he is forced to ditch 60 yards short of the Irish coast).

2-10-10 **The first mid-air collision** occurs at Milan between Captain Bertram Dickson (in a Farman) and the Anglo-French H. J. Thomas (in an Antoinette). Thomas escapes unhurt, but Dickson is badly injured and never flies again.

14-11-10 In America Eugene B. Ely makes **the first aeroplane take-off from a ship,** flying a Curtiss biplane from a platform on the bows of the light cruiser U.S.S. *Birmingham* (3,750 tons) in the Hampton Roads, Virginia.

1911
6-1-11 A crowd of 750,000 Indians attend a flying display by Henri Jullerot in his Military Biplane at Calcutta.

7-1-11 The American pilots Lieut. Myron Sidney Crissy and Philip O. Parmelee **drop the first explosive bombs from an aeroplane** during trials at San Francisco, California.

18-1-11 Eugene B. Ely makes **the first aeroplane landing on a ship,** landing his Curtiss biplane on a 119 ft. 4 in. (40 m) platform on the stern of the cruiser U.S.S. *Pennsylvania* (13,680 tons) anchored in San Francisco Bay.

-2-11 Glenn Curtiss makes **the first premeditated water-landing, water-taxying and water-take-off,** beside the U.S.S. *Pennsylvania* (13,680 tons) anchored in San Diego Bay, California.

5-2-11 Vivian C. Walsh makes **the first aeroplane flight in New Zealand** at Auckland in a Howard-Wright (type) biplane.

18-2-11 **The world's first official air mail** is carried in India by the Frenchman Henri Pequet in a Humber biplane from Allahabad to Naini Junction across the Jumna River.

23-3-11 **The world's first aeroplane flight with eleven passengers** is made by Louis Bréguet in a Bréguet biplane at Douai, France. On the following day **twelve passengers** are carried by Roger Sommer in a Sommer biplane.

12-4-11 The Frenchman Pierre Prier, flying a Blériot, makes **the first non-stop flight from London to Paris.**

29-8-11 Mrs. Hilda B. Hewlett becomes **the first British woman to gain a pilot's certificate** (No. 122), qualifying at Brooklands on a Farman. Her son, Sub. Lt. F. E. T. Hewlett, is taught to fly by her and is one of the first

five pilots of the Naval Wing, R.F.C., in October 1912.

-9-11
-11-11 Calbraith P. Rodger makes a 4,000-mile coast-to-coast air crossing of the U.S.A. in a Wright biplane from Long Island, N.Y., to Long Beach, California, in 82 stages in 82 hours' flying time during 49 days. In the course of the voyage he crashed nineteen times but was followed by a special train carrying spares for his aircraft.

9-9-11 **The first official British air mail** is carried by Gustav Hamel (died 1914) in a Blériot from Hendon to Windsor.

17-10-11 **The first Chinese national to receive a pilot's certificate** is Zee Yee Lee who is granted R.Ae.C. Certificate No. 148 after qualifying in a Bristol Boxkite on Salisbury Plain, England.

23-10-11 The Italians make **the first use of aeroplanes in warfare** in the Italo-Turkish campaign in Libya, their Air Flotilla using two Blériot XIs, two Farmans, three Nieuports and two Etrich Taubes.

18-11-11 Lt. Cdr. O. Schwann, R.N., is **the first British naval pilot to take-off from the water,** but crashes on landing.

1-12-11 **The first British naval pilot to land an aeroplane on the water** is Lt. Arthur Longmore, R.N. (later Air Chief Marshal Sir Arthur Longmore, G.C.B., D.S.O., R.A.F.) who lands his Short S.27 seaplane on the River Medway.

1912
10-1-12 **The first British naval aeroplane pilot to take off from a ship** is Lt. Charles Rumney Samson whose first officially recorded take-off is made on this day from a platform on the bows of the battleship H.M.S. *Africa* (17,500 tons) in a Short S.27.

-2-12 Jules Védrines is **the first to fly at over 100-m.p.h.** in his Monocoque Deperdussin.

1-3-12 **The world's first parachute descent from an aeroplane** is made by Captain Albert Berry, jumping from a Benoist aircraft flown by Anthony Jannus at 1,500 ft. over Jefferson Barracks, St. Louis, U.S.A.

-3-12 Following the death of five French pilots in Blériot monoplanes, the French Government orders the grounding of such aircraft pending their re-building to withstand negative-g forces. The ban lasts only a fortnight.

13-4-12 The Royal Flying Corps is founded by Royal Warrant signed on this day and implemented on 13th May.

16-4-12 **The first American woman to receive a pilot's certificate** is Harriet Quimby. She becomes **the first woman to pilot an aeroplane across**

the English Channel, flying a Blériot from Deal on this day.

-5-12 **The world's first aeroplane to take off from a ship underway** is Cdr. Charles Samson in a Short S.27, taking off from the battleship, H.M.S. *Hibernia* during the Royal Naval Review off Portland.

7-5-12 An American aeroplane is **first armed with a machine gun.** It is a Wright biplane armed with a Lewis gun and flown by Lt. Thomas de Witt Milling (gunner, Charles de Forest Chandler, U.S. Signal Corps) at College Park, Maryland.

30-5-12 Wilbur Wright dies from typhoid.

1-6-12 **The first aeroplane flight in Norway by a Norwegian** is made by Lt. Hans E. Dons, a submarine officer, flying a German *Start* across Oslo Fjord.

17-6-12 **The first American woman pilot to be killed flying** is Julie Clark of Denver, Colorado, when her Curtiss biplane hits a tree at Springfield, Illinois.

-8-12 The first British military aircraft trials are staged and this competition is won by Cody's "Cathedral".

4-8-12 **The first two-passenger cross-Channel aeroplane flight** is made by William Barnard Rhodes-Moorhouse in a Bréguet biplane accompanied by his wife and a friend from Douai to Bethersden, Kent.

9-9-12 Jules Védrines establishes a new world speed record of 108·18 m.p.h. (173·65 kph) at Chicago, Illinois, in his Monocoque Deperdussin.

12-9-12 **The first French naval aeroplane,** a Maurice Farman equipped with pontoons, is purchased.

23-10-12 **The Argentine's first naval aviator,** Teniente de Navio Melchor Z. Escola, is granted his pilot's certificate by the Argentine Aero Club.

1913

-3-13 **China's first military aircraft,** twelve Caudrons, are ordered from France.

15-4-13 **The first Schneider Trophy** (the *Jacques Schneider Air Racing Trophy for Hydro-Aeroplanes*) is contested at Monaco over 28 laps of a 10-km. course. It is won by M. Prévost at 45·75 m.p.h. (73·63 kph) in a 160-h.p. Gnôme-powered Deperdussin.

16/17-4-13 Lt. R. Cholmondeley, No. 3 Sqdn., R.F.C., makes **the first night flight by a British military aeroplane,** flying by moonlight between Larkhill and Upavon.

13-5-13 **The world's first large aeroplane,** the Sikorsky *Bolshoi* (= "The Great") with a span of about 92 ft. 6 in. (28·2 m), is flown by Igor Sikorsky at St. Petersburg. Powered by four 100-h.p. Argus engines, this aircraft is the precursor of the heavy bomber.

21-6-13 **The first woman in the world to parachute from an aeroplane** is Miss Georgia ("Tiny") Broadwick who jumps from an aeroplane flown by Glenn Martin over Griffith Field, Los Angeles, Calif.

-7-13 The Avro 504 (later famous as a trainer with the R.F.C.) makes its first flight and undergoes trials at Brooklands.

16-8-13 **The first major British seaplane competition** is the *Daily Mail* Hydro-Aeroplane Trial for a flight round the coast of Britain. There are only four entrants and Samuel Cody is killed before he can compete. Harry Hawker (1889–1921) is the only starter and he reaches Dublin before crashing. The £5,000 is not awarded, but Hawker receives £1,000 as consolation.

20-8-13 **The first pilot in the world to perform a loop** is Lt. Nesterov of the Imperial Russian Army who performs the feat in a Nieuport monoplane at Kiev.

23-9-13 Roland Garros (1888–1918) makes **the first air crossing of the Mediterranean** flying a Morane-Saulnier monoplane from Saint-Raphaël to Bizerte in 7 hr. 53 min., a distance of 453 miles (700 km).

-9-13 **The first British pilot to perform a loop is** Benjamin C. Hucks who loops a Blériot at Hendon.

-11-13 The Sopwith Tabloid makes its first flight during November and completes its trials at Farnborough on the 29th. It displays a spectacular performance and may be regarded as the origin of the scout aeroplane.

29-11-13
29-12-13 Jules Védrines makes **the first aeroplane flight from France to Egypt** flying a Blériot monoplane. His route is from Nancy to Cairo, *via* Wurtzburg, Prague, Vienna, Belgrade, Sofia, Constantinople, Tripoli (Syria) and Jaffa.

Notwithstanding the early military use of aeroplanes by Italian forces in 1911–12, the year 1913 may be regarded as the end of an era in which the aeroplane had been predominantly a sporting vehicle – albeit something of a plaything for the so-called "middle class". Yet this period of aviation history had seen the seeds sown – almost entirely without substantial assistance from government finances – from which the aeroplane's enormous influence on our lives has grown. International flights had been made. Passengers had been carried. Air displays were frequent. The first Government orders had been placed for the purchase of aeroplanes, and more than a dozen nations had formed air arms of their military forces. Aviation had

The de Havilland D.H.2, widely regarded as the first British "fighter" aircraft, which achieved air superiority over France in 1915 until the appearance of the Fokker monoplane

reached every continent of the globe.

At the end of 1913 the world flying records stood as follows: *Speed, 126·67 m.p.h. (203 kph) by M. Prévost of France in a Deperdussin monoplane at Rheims; distance, 634·54 miles (1021·2 km), by A. Seguin of France in a Henry Farman on a closed circuit between Paris and Bordeaux; and altitude, 20,014 feet (6120 m) by Georges Legagneux of France in a Nieuport at Saint-Raphaël.*

THE AEROPLANE IN A WORLD AT WAR

1914

-1-14   The Sikorsky *Ilya Mourametz* (developed from the *Bolshoi*) makes its first flight at St. Petersburg. It makes a flight on 11th February carrying 16 people on board, and in June makes a flight from St. Petersburg to Kiev (a distance of 1,590 miles, 2560 km).

-2-14   **The world's first scheduled passenger air service** is started in Florida, U.S.A., by P. E. Fansler, employing A. Jannus to fly a Benoist flying-boat the 22 miles between St. Petersburg and Tampa, carrying passengers and freight. The project is shortlived.

23-3-14   Siam forms a military flying corps under H.R.H. the Prince of Piscnoulok, Chief of the Siamese General Staff.

-4-14   **American naval aeroplanes participate in combat for the first time** when five Curtiss A-1s from the U.S.S. *Mississippi* and U.S.S. *Birmingham* are flown on reconnaissance sorties during the Vera Cruz incident. Some of the aircraft come under rifle fire but suffer only minor damage.

9-5-14   **The first parachute descent from an aeroplane over Great Britain** is made by W. Newall at Hendon from a Grahame-White Charabanc flown by R. H. Carr.

15-5-14   **The first city-to-city aeroplane passenger in Canada** is flown between Toronto and Hamilton in a Curtiss flying-boat flown by Theodore Macaulay.

18-7-14   The U.S.A. forms the first Air Service of the Signal Corps, U.S. Army, with an establishment of six aeroplanes, sixty officers and 260 men.

20-7-14   The second Schneider Trophy race, staged between Monaco and Cape Martin, is won for Great Britain by a Sopwith Tabloid seaplane flown by Howard Pixton at a speed of 85·5 m.p.h. (137·6 kph).

28-7-14   Sqdn. Cdr. Arthur Longmore, R.N. (see 1-12-11) **drops a standard naval torpedo from a naval aircraft for the first time** – a 14-inch (35·6 cm) torpedo from a Short seaplane. A few weeks earlier a dummy weapon had been dropped in Italy by Capitano Alessandro Guidoni from a twin-engine monoplane designed by Pateras Pescara.

30-7-14   **The North Sea is first crossed by an aeroplane,** a Blériot flown by the Norwegian, Tryggve Gran.

1-8-14   Germany declares war on Russia, and the following day demands the right of passage through Belgium. On 3rd August Germany declares war on France.

4-8-14   War is declared between Britain and Germany. On the 5th Austria-Hungary declares war on Russia, and on the 10th France declares war on Austria-Hungary, and Britain follows suit on the 12th.

11-8-14   The first ground echelon of the R.F.C. embarks at Southampton for France. *At the outbreak of war the R.F.C.'s aircraft strength is 179 with a mobilised, uniformed strength of 2,073 officers and men, under the command of Brigadier General Sir David Henderson, Argyll and Sutherland Highlanders. In contrast the French strength is 1,500 aircraft, and that of Germany about 1,000.*

12-8-14 **The first British airmen to be killed on active service** are Lt. R. R. Skene and his mechanic (named Barlow) of No. 3 Sqdn., R.F.C., who are killed in their Blériot when flying to Dover prior to flying to France.

13-8-14 The first R.F.C. squadrons start flying to France; the first aeroplane to land there is a B.E.2a, No. *347*, of No. 2 Squadron, flown by Lt. H. D. Harvey-Kelly who lands near Amiens at 08.20 hrs.

19-8-14 The first R.F.C. reconnaissance patrols are flown in France, and on the 22nd a patrol detects General von Kluck's II Army Corps closing with the British front. On this day **the first British aeroplane destroyed in action,** an Avro 504 of No. 5 Sqdn., R.F.C., flown by Lt. V. Waterfall, is shot down by ground rifle fire in Belgium.

25-8-14 **The first German aircraft to be forced down** lands after a confrontation with three unarmed aircraft of No. 2 Sqdn., R.F.C.

26-8-14 **The first aeroplane to be destroyed by ramming** is an Austrian two-seater flown by Leutnant Baron von Rosenthal, rammed over Galicia by Staff Captain P. N. Nesterov (see 20-8-13) of the Imperial Russian XI Corps Air Squadron in an unarmed Morane-Saulnier monoplane. Both pilots are killed.

30-8-14 **The first aerial bombs to fall on a capital city** are those dropped at the Quai de Valmy, Paris, by a German *Taube* flown by Leutnant Ferdinand von Hiddessen, killing two civilians.

6-9-14 The Battle of the Marne opens.

16-9-14 Approval for the formation of the Canadian Aviation Corps is given; initial establishment is two officers and a Burgess-Dunne biplane.

22-9-14 **The first British air raid on Germany** is made by four aircraft of the Eastchurch R.N.A.S. squadron, one of which, flown by Flt. Lt. Collett, drops 20-lb. (9 kg) Hales bombs on the airship sheds at Düsseldorf, but they fail to explode.

5-10-14 **The first aeroplane in the world to be shot down by another** is a German two-seater, possibly an Aviatik, shot down over Rheims by Sergeant Joseph Frantz and Caporal Quénault in a Voisin of *V.B.24* using a Hotchkiss gun.

31-10-14 Following the shelling of Russian ports by Turkish warships, Russia declares war on Turkey, and Britain follows suit on 5th November.

8-10-14 **The first successful air raid on Germany** is made by Sqdn. Cdr. Spenser D. A. Grey and Flt. Lt. R. L. G. Marix in Sopwith Tabloids of the Eastchurch R.N.A.S. squadron. Marix bombs the airship shed at Düsseldorf, destroying Zeppelin Z.IX, and Grey bombs Cologne railway station.

-11-14 **The first Russian woman to serve as a military pilot** (and probably the first in the world) is Princess Eugenie Mikhailovna Shakhovskaya who is posted to the 1st Field Air Squadron, Imperial Russian Air Corps. (The princess survives the War and the Revolution; indeed she becomes chief executioner of the *Cheka* – the Bolshevik secret police – at Kiev.)

21-12-14 **The first German aeroplane raid over Britain,** by one aircraft, is made over Dover; the two bombs dropped, however, land in the sea near Admiralty Pier.

24-12-14 **The first bomb to fall on Britain** is dropped by a German aeroplane over Dover, and explodes near the castle.

1915

19-1-15 **The first airship raid on Britain** is made by the German naval airships *L.3* and *L.4* in the Yarmouth area, flying from Hamburg and Nordholz. A third airship, *L.6,* turns back following engine trouble.

23-1-15 Turkish land forces, advancing to attack the Suez Canal, are revealed by air reconnaissance.

17-2-15 H.M.S. *Ark Royal* – the **first ship completed as an aircraft (seaplane) carrier** – arrives at the entrance to the Dardanelles and sends one of her seaplanes on reconnaissance against the Turks.

3-3-15 The National Advisory Committee for Aeronautics (N.A.C.A., the precursor of today's N.A.S.A.) is established in the U.S.A. by Act of Congress.

10-3-15 **The first British bombing raids in tactical support of ground operations** are made on railways carrying German reinforcements in the Menin and Courtrai area during the Neuve Chapelle offensive.

1-4-15 The French pilot Lt. Roland Garros (see 23-9-13) flying a Morane-Saulnier Type L parasol monoplane fitted with a Hotchkiss gun and armoured propeller, shoots down an Albatros. Four further German aircraft fall to his gun in the next 18 days, but he is forced down on 19th April and his gun gear falls into German hands. A true gun-interrupter gear is quickly developed by German engineers, leading to the installation of a synchronised gun in the Fokker monoplane.

26-4-15 **The first air Victoria Cross** is awarded posthumously to 2nd Lt. W. B. Rhodes-Moorhouse (see 4-8-12), a B.E.2 pilot of No. 2 Sqdn., R.F.C., for gallantry in a low-level bombing raid on Courtrai railway station on this day.

31-5-15 **The first airship raid on London** is made by a German Army airship whose bombs fall on the East End of the capital.

6/7-6-15 **The first airship to be destroyed in air combat** is *LZ.37*, bombed in mid-air over Ghent by Flt. Sub.-Lt. R. A. J. Warneford, No. 1 Sqdn., R.N.A.S., flying a Morane-Saulnier parasol monoplane from Dunkirk. He is awarded the Victoria Cross, but dies twelve days later in a flying accident.

31-7-15 Max Immelmann shoots down his first victim while flying a Fokker monoplane scout equipped with a single synchronised L.M.G.08 machine-gun.

12-8-15 Flt. Cdr. C. H. Edmonds, flying a Short 184 seaplane from H.M.S. *Ben-My-Chree*, attacks a 5,000-ton Turkish ship in the Sea of Marmara with a torpedo; the ship sinks and this incident is widely recorded as the first instance in which a ship is sunk by an aerial torpedo, but a British submarine also claims the same victim. Two days later another Turkish ship is unquestionably sunk by an aerial torpedo attack launched from the *Ben-My-Chree*.

19-8-15 Colonel Hugh M. Trenchard assumes command of the R.F.C. in France.

5-11-15 **An aeroplane is first catapulted from a ship** when an AB-2 flying-boat is thus launched from the stern of the American battleship, U.S.S. *North Carolina*, anchored in Pensacola Bay, Florida.

12-12-15 **The world's first all-metal aeroplane,** the Junkers J.1, a private venture initiated by the *Forschungsansalt Professor Junkers*, is first flown at Dessau, Germany.

1916

21-2-16 The Battle of Verdun opens.

-3-16 **American Army aeroplanes are first used in actual military operations** when eight Curtiss JN-1s of the 1st Aero Squadron, U.S. Army, accompany the punitive expedition to Mexico under General John Pershing.

5-5-16 The formation of an Air Board in London is announced to co-ordinate demands for aircraft by the R.F.C. and R.N.A.S.

17-5-16 **The first air-launching of one aeroplane from another** (i.e. composite aircraft) is carried out during a flight by a Felixstowe Baby flying-boat carrying a Bristol Scout C. Flown by Flt. Lt. M. J. Day, R.N.A.S., the Bristol flies off the flying-boat being flown by John Cyril Porte at 1,000 feet (300 m) over Harwich. Although successful, the experiment is not repeated.

31-5-16 The naval Battle of Jutland is **the first major fleet action in which an aeroplane is used to significant effect.** Flt. Lt. F. J. Rutland with an observer, Asst. Paymaster G. S. Trewin, flying a seaplane from H.M. Seaplane Carrier *Engadine*, spotted and shadowed a force of German light cruisers and destroyers.

18-6-16 **The first American pilot to be shot down in the First World War** is H. Clyde Balsley flying with the *Lafayette Escadrille* near Verdun, France, who is forced down and wounded.

Also on this day the famous German pilot, Max Immelmann, is shot down and killed in combat with 2nd Lieut. G. R. McCubbin of No. 25 Sqdn., R.F.C., near Lens.

23-6-16 **The first American pilot to be killed in the First World War** is Victor Emmanuel Chapman of the *Lafayette Escadrille* operating near Verdun.

1-7-16 The Battle of the Somme opens and continues until late November. During this long campaign the R.F.C. establishes air superiority over and well behind the enemy lines.

27-8-16 Italy declares war on Germany, and Romania declares war on Austria-Hungary; on the following day Germany declares war on Romania, and on 30th August Turkey also declares war on Romania.

1-9-16 Bulgaria declares war on Romania.

2/3-9-16 Lieutenant William Leefe Robinson, No. 39 (Home Defence) Sqdn., R.F.C., and Worcestershire Regiment, destroys **the first German airship to fall on British soil.** A Schutte-Lanz (*L.21*), it falls near Cuffley, Hertfordshire. Leefe Robinson is awarded the Victoria Cross for this action.

12-10-16 **The first British airline company,** Aircraft and Travel Ltd, is registered in London by George Holt Thomas. Owing to the War, it remains dormant until 1919.

28-10-16 Oswald Boelcke, the great German fighter leader, is killed in action as the result of a collision with another German aircraft during combat.

18

28-11-16 **The first aeroplane raid on London** is made by a single German naval aeroplane, an L.V.G. C II, flown by Deck Offizier Paul Brandt and Leutnant Walther Ilges, which drops six light bombs near Victoria Station in broad daylight. In the early hours of the same morning two airships of the Imperial German Navy had been destroyed over the English east coast.

1917

-2-17 No. 100 Squadron, R.F.C., is formed at Hingham, Norfolk, and crosses to France on 21st March. This is the **first British unit specifically formed for night bombing operations** and is equipped with F.E.2Bs.

6-4-17 The United States of America declares war on Germany (and Cuba follows suit on the next day).

7-5-17 Captain Albert Ball, R.F.C., is killed while flying an S.E.5 near Lens, on the Western Front. The cause of his death has never been established, and the award of his Victoria Cross is gazetted on 3rd June.

20-5-17 **The first submarine is sunk by an aeroplane.** The German *U-36* is attacked and sunk in the North Sea by a flying-boat commanded by Flt. Sub.-Lt. C. R. Morrish, R.N.A.S.

25-5-17 **The first large aeroplane raid on Britain in daylight** is carried out by 21 Gotha G IVs of *Kagohl 3* commanded by Hauptmann Ernst Brandenburg. Most of their bombs fall on Folkestone, Kent, killing 95 and injuring 260. Despite reaction by about 70 British fighters, only one bomber is lost (probably following engine failure) and another crashes on landing.

30-5-17 **The first successful dirigible of the U.S. Navy** is the Goodyear F-1, which makes its first flight on this day, flying from Chicago, Illinois, to Wingfoot Lake, near Akron, Ohio.

5-6-17 *Kagohl 3*, again led by Brandenburg, carries out a raid with 22 Gotha G IVs on Sheerness, Kent. One bomber is shot down.

-6-17 **The first aeroplane designed from the outset as a carrier-borne torpedo-bomber** is the Sopwith Cuckoo which makes its first flight this month.

13-6-17 *Kagohl 3* launches its first daylight raid on London with 20 Gotha G IVs. 4·3 tons of bombs are dropped on the capital, killing 162 and injuring 432.

30-6-17 Lt.-Col. William Mitchell succeeds Major T. F. Dodd as Aviation Officer, American Expeditionary Forces in France.

7-7-17 A second raid by *Kagohl 3* penetrates to London in daylight. Of 24 Gothas which set out, only 15 land safely (there being numerous landing accidents). 57 people are killed in the bombing.

11-7-17 A British Cabinet committee, including Lt. Gen. Jan C. Smuts, is formed to examine the co-ordination of air defence (in the light of German daylight raids on South-East England). It recommends the formation of a single Air Ministry to amalgamate all matters connected with air warfare.

2-8-17 **The first landing by an aeroplane on a ship underway** is made by Sqdn. Ldr. E. H. Dunning, R.N.A.S. in a Sopwith Pup on to the deck of H.M.S. *Furious* (22,000 tons). He is killed shortly afterwards when his aircraft

Classic single-seat scout, the Sopwith Pup of 1916–17

is blown over the side of the ship.

12-8-17 The last major daylight raid by *Kagohl 3* on Britain strikes Southend, Essex, killing 32 and injuring 46.

13-8-17 The 1st Aero Squadron, U.S. Air Service, sails from America for Europe under the command of Major Ralph Royce.

21-8-17 **The first enemy airship to be shot down by a ship-launched landplane** is *L.23*, which is shot down off the Danish coast by a Sopwith Pup flown by Flt. Sub.-Lt. B. A. Smart from a platform aboard the light cruiser, H.M.S. *Yarmouth*.

3-9-17 Brig. Gen. William L. Kenly becomes the first Chief of Air Service, American Expeditionary Forces.

11-9-17 The great French ace, Capitaine Georges Guynemer, is missing from a flight over Poelcapelle, France. The cause of his death remains a mystery to this day.

11-10-17 The 41st Wing, R.F.C., is formed to carry out strategic bombing of industrial targets in Germany.

20-11-17 The Battle of Cambrai opens.

27-11-17 Brig. Gen. B. D. Foulis succeeds Brig. Gen. William L. Kenley as the American Chief of Air Service in Europe.

29-11-17 The Air Force (Constitution) Bill, providing for the creation of the Air Ministry and the Royal Air Force, receives the Royal Assent.

7-12-17 The United States of America declares war on Austria-Hungary.

22-12-17 Following the Russian Revolution, which had broken out on 12th March 1917, and the seizure of power in Russia by the Bolsheviks Lenin and Trotsky, peace negotiations are opened between Russia and Germany.

1918

2-1-18 The British Air Council and Air Ministry are created by an Order in Council. The first Secretary of State for Air is Lord Rothermere, and the first Chief of the Air Staff is Maj. Gen. Sir Hugh Trenchard.

18-1-18 Maj. Gen. Sir John Salmond succeeds Maj. Gen. Sir Hugh Trenchard as commander of the R.F.C. in France.

5-2-18 **The first American pilot, serving under American colours, to destroy an enemy aeroplane,** is Lt. Stephen W. Thompson on this day over the Western Front.

20-3-18 The world's first international scheduled air mail service is inaugurated between Vienna and Kiev using Hansa-Brandenburg C I biplanes for military mails, and continues until November.

1-4-18 The Royal Air Force is formed by the amalgamation of the R.F.C. and the R.N.A.S. The Women's Royal Air Force is also formed on this day.

12-4-18 The last airship raid on Britain to inflict casualties is carried out.

13-4-18 **The first air crossing of the Andes** is made by Argentine army pilot Teniente Luis C. Candelaria in a Morane-Saulnier mono-

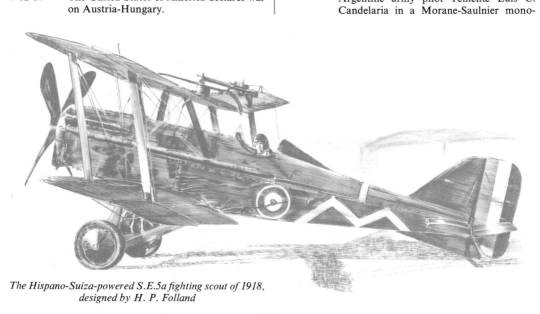

The Hispano-Suiza-powered S.E.5a fighting scout of 1918, designed by H. P. Folland

	plane from Zapala, Argentine, to Cunco, Chile.
14-4-18	Maj. Gen. Sir Hugh Trenchard is succeeded as Chief of the Air Staff by Maj. Gen. Sir Frederick Sykes following disagreements with Lord Rothermere.
21-4-18	The highest-scoring of all First World War pilots, Rittmeister Manfred, Freiherr von Richthofen, is shot down and killed near Sailly-le-Sec, France.
25-4-18	Lord Rothermere resigns as Secretary of State for Air and is succeeded by Sir William Weir.
29-4-18	Lt. Edward V. Rickenbacker, later to become American top ace of the War, shoots down his first enemy aircraft.
20-5-18	American military aviation is detached from the U.S. Army Signal Corps. Two air-departments are established, the Bureau of Military Aeronautics and the Bureau of Aircraft Production. On the following day Maj. Gen. William L. Kenly is appointed Director of Military Aeronautics, and on 29th May John D. Ryan becomes Director of Aircraft Production.
29-5-18	Brig. Gen. Mason M. Patrick is appointed Chief of Air Service, U.S. Expeditionary Forces.
5-6-18	Maj. Gen. Sir Hugh Trenchard is appointed to command the Independent Air Force set up on this day for the strategic bombing of Germany.
12-6-18	The first American day bombing is carried out by the 96th Aero Squadron on the Dommary-Baroncourt railway yards.
26-7-18	Major Edward "Mick" Mannock, V.C., D.S.O. and two Bars, M.C. and Bar, the highest-scoring British pilot of the War is shot down and killed by ground fire over the Western Front.
28-7-18 8-8-18	**The first flight from Britain to Egypt** is made by a Handley Page 0/400 flown by Major A. S. MacLaren, M.C., with Brig. Gen. A. E. Borton, from Cranwell, Lincolnshire, to Heliopolis, Egypt.
-8-18	The fastest operational German scout of the War, the Fokker D VIII monoplane, reaches the Front during this month. A number of accidents following wing failure causes it to be withdrawn from service shortly afterwards.
11-11-18	The Armistice with Germany is signed and hostilities end on the Western Front.

(At the end of the First World War the Royal Air Force is the largest air force in the world, with almost 700 bases and airfields, 22,647 aeroplanes, 27,333 officers and 263,410 other ranks.)

14-11-18	Brig. Gen. William Mitchell is appointed Chief of Air Service, U.S. Third Army.
13-12-18	**The first flight from Britain to India starts.** Sqdn. Ldr. A. C. S. MacLaren, M.C., and Lt. Robert Halley, D.F.C., set out in a Handley Page V/1500 (with Brig. Gen. N. D. K. McEwen as passenger) and reach Cairo on 1st January 1919, and Delhi, India, on the 16th of that month. The aircraft is subsequently used in the Third Afghan War.

1919–1932
AUSTERITY AND ADVENTURE

1919

2-1-19	Major-General C. T. Menoher is appointed the U.S. Director of Air Service.
11-1-19	Major-General Sir Hugh Trenchard is re-appointed Chief of the Air Staff; Winston Churchill becomes Secretary of State for Air.
18-1-19	The Peace Conference assembles in Paris.
12-2-19	A Department of Civil Aviation is estab-lished within the British Air Ministry.
10-3-19	Brig.-Gen. William Mitchell is appointed Director of Aeronautics in the U.S.A. under Major-Gen. C. T. Menoher.
19-4-19	Leslie Leroy Irvin (1895–1965) makes the **first successful use of a free parachute from an aeroplane,** using a parachute he had developed for the U.S. Army in a descent at McCook Field, Dayton, Ohio.
30-4-19	Civil flying in Britain is formally restored with the issue of Air Navigation Regula-tions (1919), and on 1st May such flying is duly authorised.
8-5-19 to 31-5-19	**The first crossing of the Atlantic by air** is made by a Curtiss NC-4 flying boat com-manded by Lieut. Cdr. A. C. Read. The route is from New York, U.S.A. to Ply-mouth, England, via the Azores and Lisbon. Two similar aircraft fail to complete the flight in company with Read.
18-5-19	Harry Hawker and Lt. Cdr. K. F. Mac-kenzie-Grieve fail in an attempt to cross the Atlantic non-stop in a Sopwith biplane. They are picked up at sea about 1,000 miles east of Newfoundland.
14-6-19 15-6-19	**The Atlantic is crossed non-stop for the first time** by a Vickers Vimy flown by Capt. John Alcock and Lt. Arthur Whitten Brown, flying from St. John's, Newfoundland, to Clifden, Co. Galway, Ireland. Both Alcock and Brown are knighted for their achieve-ment.
28-6-19	The Versailles Treaty of Peace is signed pro-hibiting all German military air forces and

2-7-19 to 6-7-19 calling for the destruction of all air material. **The first airship crossing of the Atlantic** is made by the R-34 with a crew of 30 commanded by Sqdn. Ldr. G. H. Scott, flying from East Fortune, Scotland, to New York. It then completes **the first double-crossing** by returning to Pulham, Norfolk, England, between 9th and 13th July.

7-8-19 **The first flight across the Canadian Rockies** (and also the first flight carrying mails) is made by a Curtiss Jenny flown by Capt. Ernest C. Hoy from Vancouver to Calgary *via* Lethbridge.

25-8-19 **The world's first scheduled airline international flight** is made by a D.H.4A of Air Transport and Travel Ltd, flown by Lt. E. H. "Bill" Lawford from Hounslow to Le Bourget, Paris.

7-10-19 K.L.M. (Royal Dutch Airlines) is formed.

11-11-19 The Paris-London air mail service is inaugurated.

21-11-19 to 10-12-19 A Vickers Vimy flown by two Australian brothers, Capt. Ross Smith and Lt. Keith Smith, makes **the first flight from Britain to Australia,** flying from Hounslow, England, to Darwin, Australia. The feat earns them knighthoods and the Australian Government's prize of £10,000.

18-12-19 Sir John Alcock is killed near Rouen, France, when his Vickers Viking crashes in bad weather.

1920

4-2-20 to 20-3-20 **The first flight from Britain to Cape Town** is made by Col. Pierre van Ryneveld, D.S.O., M.C., and Capt. Christopher Quintin Brand. Flying from Brooklands in a Vickers Vimy, they crash on 11th March, but complete the flight in a D.H.9. The feat earns them knighthoods and the Union Government's prize of £5,000.

5-2-20 The R.A.F. College at Cranwell is opened.

18-2-20 Authority is given by Order in Council for the formation of the Canadian Air Force.

5-7-20 **The first R.A.F. Tournament** (later known as the R.A.F. Display) is held at Hendon.

9-8-20 The South African Air Force is formed.

1-11-20 **The first American international scheduled passenger service** is inaugurated by Aeromarine West Indies Airways between Key West, Florida, and Havana, Cuba.

16-11-20 The Queensland and Northern Territory Aerial Services (QANTAS) is formed for air taxi and regular air services in Australia under the chairmanship of Sir Fergus McMaster (1879-1950).

14-12-20 **The first fatal accident occurs on a scheduled British commercial flight** when a Handley Page 0/400 crashes in fog at Cricklewood, London; two crew and two passengers are killed, but four passengers escape.

1921

21-2-21 to 24-2-21 Lt. William D. Coney of the U.S. Air Service makes **the first solo Coast-to-Coast flight in the U.S.A.,** flying from Rockwell Field, San Diego, Calif., to Jacksonville, Florida.

22-2-21 23-2-21 E. M. Allison and Jack Knight make **the first Coast-to-Coast air mail flight in the U.S.A.,** flying from San Francisco, Calif., to Mineola, New York.

31-3-21 The Australian Air Force is established by proclamation, pending the passage of the Air Defence Act.

5-4-21 Capt. the Hon. F. E. Guest is appointed the British Secretary of State for Air.

23-6-21 A Cairo-Baghdad air mail service is inaugurated.

21-7-21 The German warship *Ostfriesland*, 22,800 tons is sunk in bombing trials off the coast of Virginia, U.S.A., by U.S. Army MB-2 bombers commanded by Brig. Gen. William Mitchell.

10-8-21 The U.S. Navy Bureau of Aeronautics is formed under Rear Admiral William A. Moffett.

13-8-21 The Australian Air Force is granted the prefix "Royal" by H.M. King George V.

24-8-21 The British airship R-38 breaks up in the air over Hull, England, with the loss of 44 lives (of whom 32 are American).

5-10-21 Maj. Gen. Mason M. Patrick becomes Chief of Air Service in the U.S.A.

1922

1-4-22 The R.A.F. Staff College is opened at Andover.

7-4-22 **The first collision between commercial aeroplanes on scheduled flights** occurs between a D.H.18 (*G-EAWO*) of Daimler Airways and a Farman Goliath of *Grands Express Aériens* 18 miles north of Beauvais, France. All seven occupants are killed.

4-9-22 **The first Coast-to-Coast crossing of the U.S.A. in a single day** is accomplished by Lt. James H. Doolittle in a D.H.4B flying from Pablo Beach, Florida, to Rockwell Field, San Diego, Calif., in 21 hr. 20 min.

8-9-22 9-9-22 **The first King's Cup Air Race** is flown from Croydon and Glasgow and back, and is won by Capt. Frank Barnard in a D.H.4A (*G-EAMU*).

-9-22 **The first American aircraft carrier,** the U.S.S. *Langley*, 11,050 tons, is completed after conversion from a collier. Cdr. Virgil C. Griffin is the first pilot to take off from

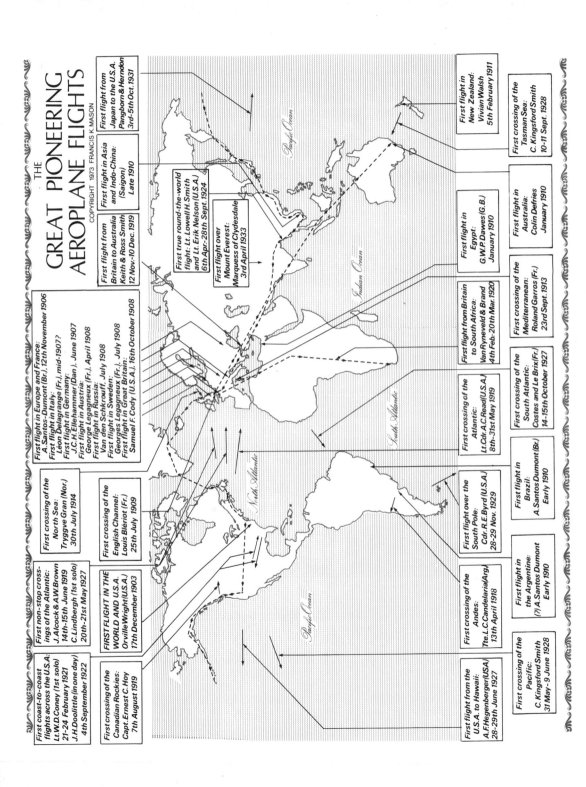

	her deck (on 17th October).
1-10-22	The R.A.F. assumes military control in Iraq. The success of this expedient ensures the continued existence of the young Service.
20-10-22	**The first American to escape by parachute from a disabled aeroplane** is Lt. Harold R. Harris who jumps from a Loening monoplane over North Dayton, Ohio.
2-11-22	Sir Samuel Hoare is appointed Secretary of State for Air.
-12-22	**The first Japanese aircraft carrier,** the *Hoshe*, 7,474 tons, is completed.

1923

13-2-23	H.M. King George V approves the prefix "Royal" for the Canadian Air Force.
10-4-23	Daimler Airways inaugurates **the first scheduled air service between London and Berlin,** with stops at Bremen and Hamburg.
2-5-23 3-5-23	**The first non-stop flight across the U.S.A.** is made by Lt. O. G. Kelley and Lt. J. A. Macready in a Fokker T-2 flying from New York to San Diego in 26 hr. 50 min. 3 sec.
14-6-23	The New Zealand Air Force is formed.
27-6-23	**The first in-flight refuelling of an aeroplane** is successfully achieved at San Diego, Calif., by Capt. Lowell H. Smith and Lt. J. P. Richter. On 27th–28th August they remain airborne in their DH-4B for 37 hr. 15 min. 44 sec., refuelling in flight.
4-9-23	**The first American helium-filled rigid airship,** the *Shenandoah*, makes its first flight at Lakehurst, New Jersey.

1924

23-1-24	Lord Thompson is appointed Secretary of State for Air.
1-4-24	Imperial Airways, the British national airline, is formed by amalgamation of Handley Page Transport, Instone Air Lines, Daimler Airways and British Marine Air Navigation.
6-4-24 to 28-9-24	**The first round-the-world flight (and the first trans-Pacific flight and the first westbound air crossing of the Atlantic)** is made by U.S. airmen. Four Douglas DWC biplanes (captained by Major Frederick Martin, Lt. Lowell H. Smith, Lt. Leight Wade and Lt. Erik Nelson) set out from Seattle and fly westward round the world. Lts. Smith and Nelson complete the circumnavigation after 57 stops.
26-4-24	A daily London–Paris air service is started by Imperial Airways.
3-5-24	A daily London–Cologne air service is started by Imperial Airways.
17-6-24	A daily London–Paris–Basle–Zurich air service is started by Imperial Airways.

1-7-24	The U.S. Post Office commences a transcontinental air mail service across the U.S.A. with 14 intermediate stops. The first westbound flight is flown by Wesley L. Smith; the eastbound pilot from San Francisco is Claire K. Vance.
7-11-24	Sir Samuel Hoare succeeds Lord Thompson as Secretary of State for Air.

1925

1-1-25	Air Marshal Sir John Salmond is appointed to command Air Defences of Great Britain.
2-2-25	President Coolidge of the U.S.A signs the Kelly Bill to authorise air transport of mail under contract.
22-2-25	The famous D.H. **Moth makes its first flight** when Capt. Geoffrey de Havilland flies the prototype *G-EBKT* at Stag Lane, Middlesex.
3-9-25	The U.S. dirigible *Shenandoah* breaks up in a storm over Ava, Georgia. Lt. Cdr. Zachary Landsdowne, the captain, is among the 14 dead.
16-11-25 to 13-3-26	The first flight from London to Cape Town and back is accomplished by a D.H.50 (*G-EBFO*) flown by Alan Cobham, A. B. Elliott and B. W. G. Emmott.
17-12-25	Brig. Gen. William Mitchell is found guilty by court martial of conduct likely to bring discredit on the Service and resigns his commission.

1926

9-5-26	**The first aeroplane flight over the North Pole** is made by a Fokker monoplane flown by Floyd Bennett from Spitzbergen with Cdr. R. E. Byrd as navigator.
11-5-26 to 14-5-26	**The first airship flight over the North Pole** is made by Lincoln Ellsworth and R. Amundsen in the dirigible *Norge* flying from Spitzbergen to Alaska.
20-5-26	President Coolidge of the U.S.A. signs the Air Commerce Act to regulate civil aeronautics in America.
30-6-26 to 1-10-26	The first return flight from Britain to Australia and back is made by the D.H.50J, *G-EBFO*, with Alan Cobham and A. B. Elliott. On the return flight Elliott is killed by a stray Bedouin bullet between Baghdad and Basra. On his return Cobham is knighted for his achievement.
1-7-26	The Royal Swedish Air Force (*Flygvapnet*) is formed.
2-7-26	The U.S. Air Service is re-designated the Air Corps, under the Air Corps Act.

1927

20-5-27 21-5-27	Capt. Charles A. Lindbergh makes the **first solo non-stop crossing of the Atlantic** in the

The Handley Page Heyford was the R.A.F.'s last biplane heavy bomber; the outcome of an Air Ministry requirement issued in 1928. it remained in service until 1939

	single-engine Ryan monoplane *Spirit of St. Louis*, flying from Long Island, New York, to Paris, France.
20-5-27 to 23-5-27	Flt. Lt. C. R. Carr and Flt. Lt. L. E. M. Gillman attempt to fly from Cranwell, England, to India non-stop, but are forced down in the Persian Gulf after a flight of 3,420 miles. Both are rescued unhurt.
28-6-27 29-6-27	**The first non-stop aeroplane flight from the American mainland to Hawaii** is made by a U.S. Air Corps Fokker C-2 flown by Lt. Albert F. Hegenberger and Lt. Lester J. Maitland.
14-10-27	**The first non-stop air crossing of the South Atlantic** is accomplished by a Bréguet aircraft flown by Dieudonné Costes and Lt. Lebrix flying from Senegal to Natal, Brazil.
19-10-27	Pan American Airways starts its first service on a 90-mile route between Key West, Florida, and Havanna, Cuba.
14-12-27	Maj. Gen. J. E. Fechet succeeds Maj. Gen. Mason M. Patrick as Chief of the U.S. Air Corps.

1928

7-2-28	Sqdn. Ldr. H. J. L. ("Bert") Hinkler makes
22-2-28	**the first solo flight from Britain to Australia** flying from London to Darwin in the Avro Avian prototype (*G-EBOV*).
12-2-28 17-5-28	Lady Heath (previously Mrs. Elliott-Flynn) makes the **first solo flight from South Africa to Britain,** flying from Cape Town to Croydon in an Avro Avian III (*G-EBUG*).
9-3-28 30-4-28	Lady Bailey makes the **first solo return flight between Britain and South Africa,** flying from London in de Havilland Moths

	(*G-EBSF* and *G-EBTG*) and reaching Cape Town on 30th April. She starts back from Cape Town on 21st September and reaches home on 16th January 1929.
30-3-28	Maj. Mario de Bernardi of Italy establishes a new world speed record of 318·64 m.p.h. (512·69 kph) at Venice in a Macchi M-52*bis*.
12/13-4-28	Hauptmann Hermann Köhl, Baron von Hünefeld and Cmdt. J. Fitzmaurice, flying a Junkers-W 33, make the **first east-to-west aeroplane crossing of the North Atlantic,** flying from Baldonnel, Ireland, to Greenly Island, Labrador.
15-5-28	The Australian Flying Doctor Service is inaugurated by QANTAS and the Australian Inland Mission at Cloncurry. The first aircraft is a D.H.50 (*G-EBIW/G-AUER*), its first pilot Capt. A. H. Affleck, and the first doctor Dr. K. H. Vincent Welsh.
31-5-28 10-6-28	Capt. Charles Kingsford Smith and C. T. P. Ulm, flying a Fokker F.VIIb-3m *Southern Cross*, make the **first flight from the United States to Australia,** flying from Oakland, California, to Brisbane, Australia, *via* Honolulu and Fiji.
-6-28	First flight of the Hawker Hart prototype, *J9052*, flown by P. W. S. Bulman at Brooklands, England.
25-6-28	First flight of the Boeing Model 83 (forerunner of the F4B-1 fighter of the U.S. Navy).
11-6-28	**The world's first flight by a rocket-powered aeroplane** is made by the *Ente* (= Duck), a sailplane, powered by two Sander slow-burning rockets, built by the *Rhön-Rossitten*

Gesellschaft. It makes a three-quarter-mile flight near the Wässerküppe mountain, Germany. (Fritz von Opel's famous flight at Rebstock takes place on 30th September.)

10-9-28 The Fokker F.VIIb-3m *Southern Cross,*

11-9-28 flown by Kingsford Smith and C. T. P. Ulm (see above), makes the **first air crossing of the Tasman Sea,** flying from Sydney, Australia, to Christ Church, New Zealand.

18-9-28 A Cierva C.8L Mark II (*G-EBYY*), flown by Don Juan de la Cierva, makes the **first crossing of the English Channel by a rotating-wing aircraft,** flying from Croydon to Le Bourget.

19-12-28 The first autogiro to fly in the United States of America is flown by Harold F. Pitcairn at Willow Grove, Philadelphia.

1929

23-12-28 The R.A.F. undertakes to evacuate civilians
5-2-29 from Kabul in Afghanistan during inter-tribal disturbances; between these dates eight Vickers Victoria aircraft of No. 70 Sqdn., R.A.F., and a Handley Page Hinaidi carry 586 people out of the troubled area.

30-3-29 Imperial Airways start the London-Karachi air service using Armstrong Whitworth Argosy, Short Calcutta flying-boats and D.H. 66 Hercules aircraft. The total single fare is £130 (about $300) inclusive of a rail link between Basle, Switzerland, and Genoa, Italy.

24-4-29 Sqdn. Ldr. A. G. Jones Williams, M.C., and
26-4-29 Flt. Lt. N. H. Jenkins, O.B.E., D.F.C., D.S.M., make the **first non-stop aeroplane flight from Britain to India,** flying a Fairey monoplane from Cranwell, England, to Karachi, India, in 50 hr. 48 min.

8-5-29 First production delivery of the Bristol Bulldog II fighter to the Royal Air Force. The first 27 such aircraft are divided between Nos. 3 and 17 Squadrons at Upavon.

8-6-29 Lord Thompson becomes British Secretary of State for Air for the second time.

-6-29 First deliveries are made to the U.S. Navy of the Boeing F4B-1 shipboard fighter.

8-8-29 The German airship, *Graf Zeppelin,* com-
29-8-29 manded by Dr. Hugo Eckener, makes the **first airship flight around the world,** flying eastwards from Lakehurst, New Jersey, *via* Friedrichshafen, Tokyo and Los Angeles, and returning to Lakehurst.

6-9-29 The Schneider Trophy is won for Great Britain by Flt. Lt. H. R. D. Waghorn in a Supermarine S.6 over the Solent, England, at a speed of 328·63 m.p.h. On the 12th September, Sqdn. Ldr. A. H. Orlebar,

A.F.C., flying the S.6, establishes a new world record speed of 357·75 m.p.h. (575·62 kph) at Ryde, Isle of Wight.

14-10-29 The British airship R-101 (*G-FAAW*) makes its first flight at Cardington, England.

28-11-29 Cdr. R. E. Byrd of the United States makes
29-11-29 the **first flight over the South Pole** in a Ford monoplane.

16-12-29 The British airship R-100 (*G-FAAV*) makes its first flight from Howden, Yorkshire, to Cardington.

1930

1-1-30 Air Chief Marshal Sir John Salmond succeeds Marshal of the Royal Air Force Lord Trenchard as Chief of the Air Staff.

-1-30 The first deliveries of the Boeing P-12 biplane fighter are made to the U.S. Army Air Corps.

11-4-30 The British Air Ministry and Imperial Airways complete a survey of the air route between Cairo, Egypt, and Cape Town, South Africa.

5-5-30 Miss Amy Johnson makes the **first solo
24-5-30 flight by a woman from Britain to Australia,** flying D.H.60G Gipsy Moth *Jason* (*G-AAAH*) from Croydon to Darwin.

15-5-30 **The first American air stewardess,** Miss Ellen Church, makes her first duty flight with United Air Lines between San Francisco, California, and Cheyenne, Wyoming.

-6-30 First flight of the prototype Handley Page Heyford (*J9130*) heavy night-bomber, later delivered to the R.A.F.

29-7-30 The British airship R-100 flies from Britain
16-8-30 to Canada (29th July–1st August) and back (13th–16th August) with a crew of 44.

-8-30 First flight of the prototype Short Rangoon flying-boat (*S1433*).

1-9-30 Air Marshal Sir Hugh Dowding is appointed the Air Minister for Supply and Research on the British Air Council.

4-10-30 The British airship R-101, on a flight from Britain to Egypt and India, crashes near Beauvais, France, and is destroyed by fire. Among the 47 passengers killed (out of 54 on board) are Lord Thompson, Secretary of State for Air, and Maj. Gen. Sir Sefton Brancker, Director of Civil Aviation. The disaster ends rigid airship development in Britain.

18-10-30 Lord Amulree succeeds Lord Thompson as British Secretary of State for Air.

25-10-30 **The first through coast-to-coast air service in America** is inaugurated simultaneously by Transcontinental and Western Air Inc., between New York and Los Angeles.

14-11-30	First flight of the first Handley Page 42 Hannibal 4-engine biplane airliner (*G-AAGX*) is made from Radlett, Hertford-shire. These aircraft later brought new standards of luxury and reliability to air travel.
25-11-30	Canadian Airways Ltd begin operations.

1931

6-1-31	Ten Savoia Marchetti S.55 flying-boats, commanded by General Balbo of Italy, make the **first formation air crossing of the South Atlantic,** flying from Portuguese Guinea to Natal, Brazil.
24-2-31	First flight by the first Short S.17 Kent commercial flying-boat is made from the River Medway, Kent, flown by J. Lankaster Parker.
28-2-31	Imperial Airways starts its weekly air passenger and mail service between London and Central Africa.
25-3-31	First flight by the Hawker Fury biplane fighter (*K1926*), flown by P. W. S. Bulman at Brooklands.
1-4-31	C. W. A. Scott takes off from Lympne, England, on a solo flight to Australia. He arrives at Darwin on 9th April.
29-4-31	First flight of the Boeing XB-901 (proto-type of the B-9 bomber) is made by Les Tower at Seattle, Washington.
-5-31	First Service deliveries of the Hawker Fury fighter are made to No. 43 Sqdn., R.A.F. at Tangmere, England.

1-5-31	SABENA opens a daily passenger service be-tween London-Antwerp-Malmö (Sweden) with the Fokker F.VIIb-3m.
11-6-31	The Handley Page H.P.42 *Hannibal* (*G-AAGX*) enters service with Imperial Airways on the London-Paris route.
23-6-31 1-7-31	Wiley Post and Harold Gatty, flying the Lockheed *Winnie Mae*, complete a round-the-world flight. Flying from New York, their route is Chester, Berlin, Irkutsk, Alaska and back to New York – a distance of 15,474 miles, covered in 8 days 15 hr. 51 min.
23-7-31	A non-stop flight of 5,012 miles (8044 km) is made by Russell N. Boardman and John Polando in a Bellanca aircraft from New York to Istanbul, Turkey.
18-9-31	Japan attacks China and begins a long cam-paign which leads to the Japanese occupa-tion of all Manchuria.
29-9-31	The Schneider Trophy is won outright by Flt. Lt. J. N. Boothman of Great Britain flying a Supermarine S.6B near Lee-on-Solent. His average speed is 340·8 m.p.h. Flt. Lt. G. H. Stainforth, A.F.C., of the R.A.F. High Speed Flight, also flying an S.6B, sets up a new world air speed record of 407·02 m.p.h. (654·90 kph) at Ryde, England.
3-10-31 5-10-31	**The first non-stop flight between Japan and the U.S.A.** is made by Clyde Pangborn and Hugh Herndon in a Bellanca aircraft, flying from Japan to Wenatchee, Washington.

R. J. Mitchell's superlative seaplane design, the Supermarine S.6B, winner of the Schneider Trophy outright in 1931
flown by Flt. Lt. J. N. Boothman at 340·8 m.p.h.

27-10-31
28-10-31 Sqdn. Ldr. Oswald Robert Gayford, D.F.C., A.F.C. and Flt. Lt. D. L. G. Bett, flying the Fairey Long-Range Monoplane, make a non-stop flight from Cranwell to Abu Sueir, Egypt.

27-10-31
7-12-31 Sqdn. Ldr. H. J. L. Hinkler, flying solo in a D.H. Puss Moth (*CF-APK*), completes a flight from New York to London *via* Central America and the South Atlantic.

9-11-31 The Marquess of Londonderry becomes the British Secretary of State for Air.

-11-31 First flight of the Fairey Hendon prototype (*K1695*) monoplane heavy bomber, which later served in small numbers with the R.A.F.

22-12-31 Maj. Gen. B. D. Foulis is appointed Chief of the U.S. Army Air Corps.

1932
20-1-32 The Imperial Airways passenger and mail service from London to Central Africa is extended to Cape Town for mails only. The full passenger service to Cape Town opens on 27th April.

2-2-32 The International Conference for Disarmament assembles in Geneva under the auspices of the League of Nations.

24-2-32
28-2-32 J. A. Mollison flies a D.H. Moth solo from Lympne, England, to Cape Town, in 4 days 17 hr. 50 min.

30-3-32 The Boeing XP-936 monoplane fighter (forerunner of the famous P-26A of the U.S. Army Air Corps) makes its first flight.

20-5-32
21-5-32 **The first solo air crossing of the Atlantic by a woman** is accomplished by Miss Amelia Earhart (Mrs. Putnam), flying a Lockheed Vega from Harbour Grace, Newfoundland, to Londonderry, Northern Ireland.

-6-32 First flight of the Armstrong Whitworth XV Atalanta 4-engine monoplane airliner (*G-ABPI*, later *G-ABTI*).

18-8-32
19-8-32 Flying D.H. Puss Moth (*G-ABXY*) from Portmarnock, Dublin, to Pennfield, New Brunswick, J. A. Mollison achieves the **first solo east-west aeroplane crossing of the Atlantic.**

25-8-32 **The first non-stop coast-to-coast crossing of the United States of America by a woman** is made by Miss Amelia Earhart flying from Los Angeles to New York.

14-11-32 A new east-to-west coast-to-coast record for an air crossing of the United States is set up by Roscoe Turner in a Wendall-Williams aircraft, with an elapsed time (including two stops) of 12 hr. 33 min.

THE WAR CLOUDS GATHER AGAIN, 1933–1938

1933
7-1-33 Sqdn. Ldr. H. J. L. Hinkler (see previous years) is killed when his D.H. Puss Moth crashes in the Alps.

6-2-33
8-2-33 **The first non-stop flight from England to South Africa** is made by Sqdn. Ldr. O. R.

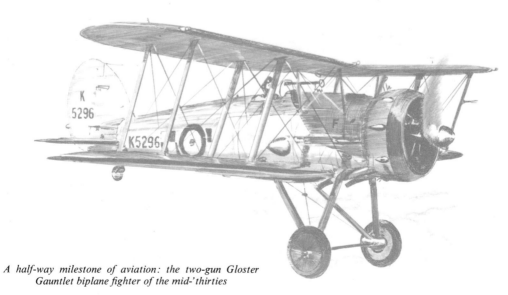

A half-way milestone of aviation: the two-gun Gloster Gauntlet biplane fighter of the mid-'thirties

Gayford, D.F.C., A.F.C., and Flt. Lt. G. E. Nicholetts, A.F.C., in the Fairey Long-Range Monoplane (*K1991*), flying 5,431 miles (8595 km) from Cranwell to Walvis Bay, South-West Africa, in 57 hr. 25 min., and establishing a new world long distance record.

18-2-33 Imperial Airways completes its ten millionth mile of revenue flying.

15-3-33 The air accident insurance premium is reduced from 12 shillings to one shilling per £1,000 for passengers of Imperial Airways, thus bringing air insurance into line with that for surface travel for the first time anywhere in the world.

27-3-33 Japan withdraws from the League of Nations.

1-4-33 The Indian Air Force is formed. Air Chief Marshal Sir Geoffrey Salmond succeeds his brother, Sir John, as Chief of the British Air Staff.

3-4-33 **Aircraft flights are first made over Mount Everest,** the two Westland Wallace aeroplanes being flown by the Marquess of Clydesdale and Flt. Lt. D. F. McIntyre, A.F.C.

4-4-33 The U.S. dirigible *Akron* crashes at sea killing 73 on board, including Rear Admiral A. Moffett, head of the U.S. Navy Bureau of Aeronautics. This is the world's worst air disaster to date.

21-4-33 The U.S. dirigible *Macon* makes its first flight.

22-5-33 Air Chief Marshal Sir Edward Ellington is appointed Chief of the Air Staff in Britain after Sir Geoffrey Salmond died on 27th April.

21-6-33 Indian Trans-Continental Airways is formed to operate the Trans-India route in conjunction with Imperial Airways when the London-to-Karachi service is extended to Calcutta on 1st July.

Also on this date the American Grumman FF-1 naval fighter enters service with U.S. Navy Squadron VF-5B (attached to the carrier U.S.S. *Lexington*) and is the first U.S. Navy aircraft with a retractable undercarriage.

1-7-33 **The first formation air crossing of the North**
15-7-33 **Atlantic** is made by 24 Italian Savoia Marchetti S.55 flying boats commanded by General Balbo, flying from Italy to Chicago, *via* Iceland.

15-7-33 Wiley Post makes the **first round-the-world**
22-7-33 **solo flight** flying a Lockheed monoplane from New York, *via* Berlin, Moscow, Irkutsk, Alaska and back to New York.

The flight covers 15,596 miles (25099 km) and is accomplished in 7 days 18 hr. 49 min.

30-8-33 Air France is formally inaugurated.

23-9-33 The Imperial Airways London-Calcutta air service is extended to Rangoon, Burma.

14-10-33 Germany withdraws from the League of Nations and the International Disarmament Conference.

18-10-33 First flight of the Grumman XF2-1 fighter – later to join the U.S. Navy as the F2F-1.

24-10-33 Winston Churchill gives the first of his famous warnings in the British Parliament on the dangers posed by the growth of Germany's military aviation.

9-12-33 Imperial Airways' London-Rangoon service is extended to Singapore.

31-12-33 First flight by the prototype Polikarpov I-16 *Ishak* (="Little Donkey"). This Russian aircraft becomes the **first monoplane fighter in the world with fully-enclosed cockpit and fully-retractable undercarriage to enter operational service.**

1934

18-1-34 QANTAS Empire Airways is inaugurated under the chairmanship of Sir Fergus McMaster; among the objects of the airline is to combine the interests of QANTAS and Imperial Airways when the London-Singapore route is extended to Australia.

19-2-34 The U.S. Army Air Corps begins flying internal air mail services, but within three weeks nine passengers and pilots are killed and the services are suspended on 10th March. They are restarted on 19th March, only to end finally on 1st June.

-4-34 First flight of the Japanese Mitsubishi G3M prototype twin-engine bomber, forerunner of the type which on 10th December 1941 attacks and sinks the British battleships, H.M.S. *Repulse* and H.M.S. *Prince of Wales*.

10-4-34 A new world speed record is set up by W/O Francesco Agello of Italy at 423·85 m.p.h. (681·97 kph) flying a Macchi-Castoldi 72 at Lago di Garda, Italy.

20-7-34 The British Government proposes an increase in the strength of the R.A.F. by 41 squadrons during the next five years.

8-8-34 **The first non-stop aeroplane flight from**
9-8-34 **Canada to Britain** is made by a D.H. Dragon (*G-ACJM*) "*Trail of the Caribou*" flown by Capt. L. Reid and J. R. Ayling from Georgian Bay, Ontario, to Heston, near London.

20-10-34 The MacRobertson Air Race from Milden-
25-10-34 hall, England, to Melbourne, Australia, is

won by the D.H.88 Comet (*G-ACSS*) "*Grosvenor House*" flown by C. W. A. Scott and Tom Campbell Black. The handicap class is won by a Douglas DC-2 of K.L.M. flown by K. D. Paramentier and J. J. Moll.

22-10-34
4-11-34
The first flight from Australia to the U.S.A. is made by Sir Charles Kingsford Smith and Captain Taylor flying a Lockheed aircraft from Brisbane, Australia, to Oakland, California, *via* Fiji and Hawaii.

23-10-34
Lt. Francesco Agello (see 10-4-34) establishes a new world speed record for Italy in his Macchi-Castoldi 72 at 440·69 m.p.h. (709·69 kph) at Lago di Garda.

10-12-34
The Imperial Airways London-Singapore air service is extended to Brisbane, Australia, QANTAS operating the Darwin-Brisbane leg, and later taking over the Darwin-Singapore section.

1935

11-1-35
12-1-35
Miss Amelia Earhart flies solo from Honolulu to Oakland, California, in her Lockheed Vega in a time of 18 hr. 16 min.

4-2-35
First flight of the Japanese Mitsubishi A5M prototype monoplane fighter.

12-2-35
The U.S. Navy dirigible *Macon* crashes into the sea off California.

9-3-35
The German Government formally confirms for the first time the existence of the new *Luftwaffe*.

28-3-35
First flight of the prototype Consolidated PBY flying-boat – precursor of the Catalina, widely used during the Second World War.

16-4-35
17-4-35
Pan American World Airways starts its trans-Pacific proving flights, flying from Alameda, California, to Honolulu.

21-5-35
Hitler repudiates the military clauses of the Versailles Treaty, and introduces conscription in Germany.

22-5-35
Proposals to strengthen British air forces by 1,500 front-line aircraft by 1937 are laid before Parliament.

7-6-35
Sir Philip Cunliffe Lister (later Viscount Swinton) becomes the British Secretary of State for Air.

23-7-35
The first steps are taken to provide a radar defence screen in Britain with the presentation of a report on "radio direction-finding" to the Air Defence Research Committee.

28-7-35
The Boeing Model 299 (prototype of the famous B-17 Flying Fortress) four-engine heavy bomber makes its first flight, flown by Les R. Tower at Boeing Field, Seattle, Washington.

8-8-35
First flight of the prototype Morane-Saulnier M.S.405, from which the M.S.406

fighter is developed – the first French monoplane fighter with enclosed cockpit and retractable undercarriage.

15-8-35
Wiley Post and Will Rogers are killed in a take-off crash near Point Barrow, Alaska.

-9-35
First flight of Willy Messerschmitt's prototype Messerschmitt Bf 109V1 monoplane fighter. Developments of this superb aircraft remain in service with the *Luftwaffe* until the end of the Second World War.

1-10-35
British Airways is formed by the amalgamation of Highland Airways, Northern and Scottish Airways, Hillman Airways, Spartan Airlines and United Airways.

3-10-35
Italy declares war upon Abyssinia.

6-11-35
The prototype Hawker Hurricane (*K5083*) 8-gun monoplane fighter is first flown by P. W. S. Bulman at Brooklands, England.

11-11-35
A world altitude record for balloons is set up by the American balloon *Explorer II,* manned by Captains O. A. Anderson and A. W. Stevens of the U.S. Army Air Corps, which ascends from Rapid City, South Dakota, to a height of 72,395 feet (22066 m).

11-11-35
13-11-35
Miss Jean Batten of New Zealand makes the **first solo air crossing of the South Atlantic by a woman,** flying a Percival Gull Six (*G-ADPR*) from Lympne, England, to Natal, Brazil, *via* Thies, Senegal.

22-11-35
The first scheduled trans-Pacific air mail flight is started by a Pan American World Airways Martin M.130 flying-boat flown by Capt. Edwin C. Musick from San Francisco to Manila, Philippines, *via* Honolulu, Midway, Wake Island and Guam.

17-12-35
First flight of the first Douglas DC-3 twin-engine monoplane airliner, flown by Carl A. Cover at Clover Field, California. Later famous as the Dakota, it became the standard Allied transport during the Second World War and was to remain in service the world over for more than 35 years.

24-12-35
Maj. Gen. Oscar Westover is appointed Chief of the U.S. Army Air Corps.

1936

19-2-36
Brig. Gen. William Mitchell dies in the Doctor's Hospital, New York.

3-3-36
A Parliamentary Defence White Paper raises from 1,500 to 1,750 aircraft the proposed increase in R.A.F. strength.

5-3-36
The prototype Supermarine Spitfire (*K5054*) 8-gun fighter makes its first flight.

7-3-36
Germany completes an unopposed re-occupation of the Rhineland.

17-3-36
First flight of the Armstrong Whitworth Whitley (*K4586*) four-engine bomber.

A Bristol Blenheim I of No. 139 (Bomber) Squadron, R.A.F. Despite a disappointing performance, the Blenheim came to be widely used the world over by the R.A.F., and was still employed as a night fighter during the Battle of Britain in 1940

-4-36	A complete reorganisation of the Royal Air Force into a functional command structure is announced. Training Command is to be commanded by Air Marshal Sir Charles Burnett (w.e.f. 1-5-36); Fighter Command by Air Chief Marshal Sir Hugh Dowding (w.e.f. 14-7-36); Bomber Command by Air Chief Marshal Sir John Steele (w.e.f. 14-7-36); and Coastal Command by Air Marshal Sir Arthur Longmore (w.e.f. 14-7-36).
5-5-36	Mussolini announces the Italian occupation of Addis Ababa and the end of the Abyssinian War.
15-6-36	First flight of the Vickers Wellington prototype (*K4049*) twin-engine bomber.
21-6-36	First flight of the Handley Page Hampden prototype (*K4040*) twin-engine bomber.
26-6-36	First free flight by the prototype Focke-Wulf Fw 61V1 (*D-EBVU*) twin-rotor helicopter – the **first successful helicopter in the world.**
4-7-36	First flight by the first Short C-Class flying-boat, *Canopus* (*G-ADHL*), flown by John Lankester Parker, O.B.E.
18-7-36	The Civil War breaks out in Spain.
30-7-36	Sir Philip Sassoon announces British plans for an experimental trans-Atlantic air mail service. The Royal Air Force Volunteer Reserve is formed as a means of providing an extra peacetime reserve of officers and men.
1-9-36	Air Marshal Philip Joubert de la Ferté assumes command of R.A.F. Coastal Command.

4-9-36 5-9-36	**The first east-west crossing of the Atlantic by a woman pilot** is made by Mrs. Beryl Markham, flying from Abingdon, England, to Baleine, Nova Scotia, where she crashes (without injury).
5-10-36 16-10-36	**The first solo flight from Britain to New Zealand by a woman** is made by Miss Jean Batten in her Percival Gull Six (*G-ADPR*) "*Jean*", flying from Lympne, Kent, to Auckland, New Zealand (in the fastest-ever time from England of 11 days 45 min.).
13-10-36	The Swiss Air Force is inaugurated by Government Decree as an independent Service.
21-10-36	Pan American World Airways commences an air passenger service between San Francisco, California, and Manila, Philippines.

1937

1-4-37	The formation of the Royal New Zealand Air Force is announced.
12-4-37	The first gas turbine built in Britain as a step towards such an aero-engine, designed by Frank Whittle, is first bench tested.
26-4-37	German aircraft of the Spanish Nationalist Forces fighting in the Civil War bomb Guernaca, seat of the Basque Government.
6-5-37	The German hydrogen-filled airship *Hindenburg*, the world's largest, is destroyed by fire whilst docking at Lakehurst, New Jersey, after flying from Germany. 33 of the 97 on board are killed. The disaster is considered by many at the time as the outcome of American refusal to allow export of inert helium gas to Germany.

29-5-37	The German warship *Deutschland* is attacked off the Balearic Islands, while performing "non-intervention" patrols, by Government aircraft; 28 of the ship's crew are killed.
2-7-37	Miss Amelia Earhart and Capt. Fred Noonan are lost at sea between British New Guinea and Howland Island during a round-the-world flight attempt.
5-7-37 6-7-37	The first North Atlantic flying-boat route survey is carried out by Imperial Airways and Pan American Airways.
29-7-37 2-8-37	The second North Atlantic route survey is flown by an Imperial Airways flying-boat.
15-8-37 17-8-37	The third North Atlantic route survey is flown by an Imperial Airways flying-boat.
18-8-37	Air Chief Marshal Sir Frederick Bowhill is appointed as A.O.C.-in-C., R.A.F. Coastal Command.
27-8-37	The fourth North Atlantic route survey is flown by an Imperial Airways flying-boat.
1-9-37	Air Chief Marshal Sir Cyril Newall succeeds Sir Edward Ellington as Chief of the Air Staff in Britain.
12-9-37	Air Chief Marshal Sir Edgar Ludlow-Hewitt succeeds Sir John Steele as A.O.C.-in-C., R.A.F. Bomber Command.
13-9-37 14-9-37	The fifth North Atlantic route survey is flown by a flying-boat of Imperial Airways.
23-12-37 26-12-37	The Pan American Airways flying-boat *Samoa Clipper* inaugurates the first air mail and freight service between the U.S.A. and New Zealand, flying *via* Honolulu to Auckland. The *Samoa Clipper* crashes in the Samoan Islands, with the loss of the crew of seven, during the second flight on 11th January 1938.

The International Civil Aviation Organisation (ICAO) announces that during 1937 the scheduled airlines of the world carried 2,500,000 passengers – the average number carried by each aircraft being 5·3.

1938

19-1-38	Twenty U.S. Navy aircraft, carrying a total of 127 men, fly from San Diego, California, to Pearl Harbor, Hawaii, in 20 hours.
10-2-38	Sqdn. Ldr. John Woodburn Gillan, A.F.C., commanding No. 111 Squadron, R.A.F. – the first squadron to be equipped with the Hawker Hurricane 8 gun fighter – flies a Hurricane from Edinburgh to London in 48 minutes, at an average ground speed of 408 m.p.h.
23-2-38	The Short-Mayo composite aircraft, consisting of the *Mercury* seaplane atop the *Maia* flying-boat, achieve their first in-flight

	separation near Rochester, Kent.
2-3-38	The operational strength of the R.A.F. is announced as 68 bomber squadrons, 30 fighter squadrons, 15 general reconnaissance squadrons and 10 army co-operation squadrons.
11-3-38	Hitler orders the military occupation of Austria, and the German annexation is completed two days later.
27-3-38 29-3-38	A Dornier Do 18 (*D-ANHR*) flying-boat of *Lufthansa* is catapulted from the German seaplane carrier *Westfalen* off Start Point, England, and flies non-stop to Caravelas, Brazil, establishing a seaplane straight-line distance record of 5,214 miles (8392 km) in 43 hr. 15 min.
31-3-38	Air Marshal John S. T. Bradley is appointed A.O.C.-in-C. of the newly-formed R.A.F. Maintenance Command.
20-4-38	A mission, led by Air Commodore Arthur Harris (later commander of R.A.F. Bomber Command), visits the U.S.A. to examine the possibility of purchasing suitable American aircraft for the R.A.F. Among the aircraft recommended for initial purchase are the Lockheed Hudson and North American Harvard.
21-4-38	The "shadow factory" scheme is announced in Britain for the manufacture of aircraft and aero-engines by companies outside the established aircraft industry.
12-5-38	During a Parliamentary debate the Air Ministry's handling of the R.A.F.'s expansion is criticised, and formation of a Ministry of Supply is proposed; it is rejected however by Prime Minister Neville Chamberlain.
15-5-38	America continues to refuse the export of helium to Germany, as announced on this day by U.S. Secretary of State for the Interior H. L. Ickes.
16-5-38	Sir Kingsley Wood is appointed British Secretary of State for Air.
9-6-38	The British Government announces its decision to purchase 200 Lockheed Hudsons and 200 North American Harvards from the U.S.A. for the R.A.F., at a cost of £5·4 million. This decision is heavily criticised by all Parties.
6-7-38	Imperial Airways flies the entire Britain-Australia route with flying-boats (Short C-Class) for the first time, flying from Southampton to Sydney in 10½ days.
20-7-38 22-7-38	The *Mercury* seaplane, upper component of the Short-Mayo composite aircraft (see 23-2-38) flies non-stop from Foynes, Eire, to Montreal, Canada, the trans-Atlantic

crossing occupying 13 hr. 29 min. from coast to coast.

-8-38   The first production delivery of the Supermarine Spitfire fighter is made to No. 19 Sqdn., R.A.F., at Duxford, but the squadron is not fully operational until 1939.

13-9-38   Hitler threatens Czechoslovakia and demands the right of self-determination for 3½ million Germans living in that country.

14-9-38   The German hydrogen-filled airship LZ.130 *Graf Zeppelin*, makes its first flight at Friedrichshafen.

21-9-38   Maj. Gen. Oscar Westover, Chief of the U.S. Army Air Corps, is killed in an air accident at Burbank airport, California. The following day Maj. Gen. Henry H. ("Hap") Arnold is appointed to succeed him.

30-9-38   The Munich Agreement is signed by Germany, Italy, Britain and France, permitting Germany to occupy Sudetan German areas of Czechoslovakia. Despite the inherent treachery of this Agreement to Czechoslovakia, it serves to buy a year's respite in which the strengthening of French and British forces may be accelerated.

26-10-38   The Armstrong Whitworth Ensign four-engine airliner enters service with Imperial Airways on the London-Paris route.

5-11-38   Two Vickers Wellesley bombers of the
7-11-38   R.A.F. Long Range Development Unit (*L2638* flown by Sqdn. Ldr. Richard Kellett, and *L2680* flown by Flt. Lt. Andrew Combe) fly from Ismailia, Egypt, to Ross Smith Airport, Darwin, Australia, non-stop to establish a new world distance record of 7,157·7 miles (11487 km).

28-11-38   A Focke-Wulf Fw 200 Condor (*D-ACON*)
30-11-38   "*Brandenburg*" four-engine airliner of *Lufthansa* is flown from Berlin to Tokyo by Flugkapitän Henke and Flugkapitän von Moreau in 46 hr. 15 min., with refuelling stops at Basrah, Karachi and Hanoi. On its return flight the aircraft force lands in the sea off Manila.

10-12-38   First flight of the R.A.F.'s first Lockheed Hudson is made at Burbank, California.

-12-38   First deliveries of the North American Harvard are made to the R.A.F.

THE AEROPLANE IN TOTAL WAR, 1939–1945

The Spanish Civil War, which ended in 1939, had been but a dress-rehearsal for one small part of one nation's air force – that of Germany – but the bombing of towns had provided a foretaste of things to come. International war, which few in Europe felt could long be delayed, would bring aeroplanes in their hundreds, even thousands, against towns and cities. Germany, who had tested the claws of her fledgling air force in Spain, would demonstrate to the world how whole campaigns on the land would be won, and nations subjugated, through superiority in the air. The Nazi tyranny ensured that, while other countries moved through the stages of "democratic rearmament", Germany would possess a crushing supremacy. Thus was born of mankind the policy of Blitzkrieg*; the aeroplane was merely the instrument – no more nor less than the tank and torpedo.*

The Focke-Wulf Fw 200 Condor "Brandenburg" of Lufthansa, which was flown from Berlin to Tokyo in November 1938. During the Second World War the Fw 200 was modified for maritime reconnaissance use by the Luftwaffe, and was used extensively against Allied shipping

The Fokker D.XXI fighter, which served with the air forces of Holland, Denmark and Finland and fought in the desperate air battles of 1940; it is shown here in the markings of the Finnish Air Force

F.K.M'73

1939

17-1-39   The formation of the Auxiliary Air Force Reserve is announced to enable ex-members of the Auxiliary Air Force to rejoin their units in an emergency.

26-1-39   The Spanish Nationalist Army captures the Republican capital, Barcelona.

24-2-39   Pan American Airways takes delivery of the first Boeing Model 314 flying-boat at Baltimore and it is named shortly afterwards *Yankee Clipper* by Mrs. Franklin D. Roosevelt.

14-3-39   Hitler announces that Czechoslovakia is to become a German Protectorate, and its military occupation by Germany starts the following day.

26-3-39   Pan American Airways starts a series of trans-Atlantic survey flights with the *Yankee Clipper*, flying from Baltimore to Southampton *via* the Azores, Lisbon, Bordeaux and Marseilles.

30-3-39   A new world speed record is set up by Germany when Flugkapitän Hans Dieterle flies the Heinkel He 100V8 at 463·92 m.p.h. (746·45 kph) at Oranienburg, Germany.

31-3-39   Neville Chamberlain announces in Parliament that France and Britain have given guarantees of aid to Poland in the event of an attack on her independence.

2-4-39   The end of the Spanish Civil War is announced in Madrid.

5-4-39   The British aircraft carrier H.M.S. *Illustrious* (16,000 tons) is launched at Barrow-in-Furness.

20-4-39   The establishment of a Ministry of Supply is announced in the British Parliament, although its immediate responsibility is for supplies to the Army.

26-4-39   Germany betters her own world speed record with Flugkapitän Fritz Wendel's flight at Augsburg, Germany, in the "Messerschmitt Bf 109R" at 469.22 m.p.h. (754·97 kph).

1-7-39   The Women's Auxiliary Air Force is formed under the directorship of Miss J. Trefusis Forbes. Air Chief Marshal Sir Arthur Longmore is appointed A.O.C.-in-C., Training Command.

30-7-39   The first production Boulton-Paul Defiant turret-fighter (*L6950*) flies.

4-8-39   The British Overseas Airways Corporation Bill, amalgamating Imperial Airways with British Airways to form the new Corporation, receives the Royal Assent.

27-8-39   **The world's first jet-propelled aircraft,** the Heinkel He 178V1, makes its first flight at Marienehe, Germany, flown by Flugkapitän Erich Warsitz. It is powered by a single 992 lb.s.t. (450 kg) Heinkel HeS 3B turbojet.

1-9-39   Germany invades Poland and commences to bomb Polish towns and cities, including Warsaw. Britain and France demand the withdrawal of German forces from Polish territory, and Britain mobilises her armed forces.

2-9-39   Ten squadrons of Fairey Battle light

bombers of the R.A.F. Advanced Air Striking Force (AASF) fly to France.

3-9-39 The British ultimatum to Germany expires and a state of war exists between Britain and Germany, and, later in the day, between France and Germany. Australia and New Zealand declare war on Germany. On the first day the **first British aircraft to enter German airspace during the War** is a Blenheim IV (*N6215*) of No. 139 Sqdn., R.A.F., flown by Fg. Off. Andrew McPherson on a photographic mission over German naval units at Wilhelmshaven. On the first night of the War, R.A.F. bombers drop leaflets over Germany.

4-9-39 **The first British bombs to fall on German targets** are dropped this day among German shipping at Wilhelmshaven by a Blenheim IV (*N6204*) of No. 110 Sqdn., R.A.F., flown by Flt. Lt. Kenneth Christopher Doran.

4-9-39
9-9-39 Four squadrons of Hurricanes, five of Lysanders, and four of Blenheims fly to France as the Air Component of the British Expeditionary Force.

10-9-39 **The first British gallantry awards to be gazetted during the War** are two Distinguished Flying Crosses made to Fg. Off. A. McPherson and Flt. Lt. K. C. Doran (see above).

26-9-39 **The first German aeroplane shot down by British forces during the War** is a Dornier Do 18 (*Werke Nr. 731*) of *2 Staffel, Küstenfliegergruppe 506*, forced down in the North Sea by Blackburn Skuas from H.M.S. *Ark Royal*.

28-9-39 Warsaw surrenders, and with the close of the Polish campaign the country is partitioned by Germany and Russia. The Polish Air Force, contrary to current propaganda reports, is only partly destroyed on the ground and during the campaign destroys nearly 200 German aircraft; total recorded *Luftwaffe* combat losses are 203 aircraft, 221 aircrew killed, 133 wounded and 218 missing.

10-10-39 The Empire Air Training Scheme is announced, in which Canada, New Zealand and Australia join to provide training facilities for R.A.F. and Dominion aircrews.

16-10-39 **The first enemy aircraft to be shot down over British soil during the War** are two Heinkel He 111s of *Kampfgeschwader 26*, shot down during an attack on British warships in the Firth of Forth; one is shot down by fighters of Nos. 602 and 603 Sqdn., A.A.F., and the other by ground fire, but both fall into the sea.

28-10-39 **The first enemy aeroplane, shot down by British forces, to fall on British soil during the War** is a Heinkel He 111H-1 (*1H + JA*) of *Stabsstaffel, Kampfgeschwader 26*, is shot down by British fighters and falls on Dalkeith Hills, six miles south of Haddington, near the Firth of Forth.

10-11-39 General H. H. Arnold, Chief of the U.S. Army Air Corps, proposes the development of a bomber with a 2,000-mile radius of action. This proposal, authorised on 2nd December 1939, leads to the development of the Boeing B-29 Superfortress.

13-11-39 **The first German bombs to fall on British soil during the War** are dropped by four German aircraft during an attack on shipping at the Shetland Isles. They cause little damage and no casualties.

18-11-39 German aircraft sow the first magnetic mines in British coastal waters.

26-11-39 British Overseas Airways Corporation is formally established under the chairmanship of Sir John Reith.

30-11-39 The "Winter War" between Russia and Finland breaks out when Russia invades Finland, and her bombers raid Helsinki and other towns. The **first Finnish air loss** is Sgt. Kukkonen, flying a Fokker D.XXI of HLeLv.24 Fighter Squadron, who is shot down by his own anti-aircraft guns. On the same day Lieut. Eino Luukkanen of the same squadron claims the **first aerial victory for Finland,** destroying a Russian SB-2 bomber.

18-12-39 After a number of daylight raids on German shipping by unescorted R.A.F. bombers during the past two months, which had suffered heavily from German fighters, a sortie on this day by 24 Wellingtons results in the loss of 12 bombers and damage to others. Thereafter these fruitless raids are abandoned.

1940

24-2-40 First flight of the prototype Hawker Typhoon (*P5212*) is made by P. G. Lucas.

7-3-40 The Hon. Clive Pearson succeeds Sir John Reith as chairman of B.O.A.C.

13-3-40 The Russo-Finnish War ends with the conclusion of a peace treaty signed in Moscow. Although a British fighter squadron (No. 263 (Gladiator) Squadron) was being prepared to go to Finland's aid, it is forestalled by the peace treaty.

15-3-40 Brig. Gen. James E. Chaney, U.S.A.A.C., is appointed to command the newly-established U.S. Air Defense Command, planned

16-3-40 for the integration of American defences against air attack.
The first British civilian casualties of the War are suffered during a German raid by *KG 26* on Scapa Flow. One man is killed and seven other people are injured.

26-3-40 In **the first substantial air combat over the Western Front,** a Hurricane squadron of the R.A.F. claims to shoot down five Bf 109s; *Luftwaffe* records disclose the loss of four.

3-4-40 Air Marshal Sir Charles Portal is appointed A.O.C.-in-C., R.A.F. Bomber Command.

5-4-40 Sir Samuel Hoare is appointed British Secretary of State for Air.

9-4-40 Germany attacks Denmark and Norway, Denmark being overrun in a single day. German forces land in Norway at Narvik, Trondheim, Bergen and Stavanger.

13-4-40 R.A.F. Hampdens carry out the **first air-mining by British aircraft during the War,** sowing mines off the Danish coast.

15-4-40 Eleven R.A.F. Blenheims attack Trondheim airfield in Norway – the **first R.A.F. Bomber Command raid of the War against an inland target.**

23-4-40
24-4-40 H.M. Aircraft Carrier *Glorious* sails to Norway with No. 263 (Gladiator) Sqdn., R.A.F., aboard, these are successfully flown off and land on the frozen Lake Lesjaskog in Central Norway. The fighters are operated with little success under great difficulties and the expedition is abandoned, the pilots being brought home by merchant ship.

25-4-40 The American aircraft carrier, U.S.S. *Wasp,* is commissioned.

1-5-40 Central Norway is evacuated by Allied forces, principally owing to the lack of adequate air cover in the face of enemy air superiority.

10-5-40 Germany invades Holland, Belgium and Luxembourg, thus ending the so-called "Phoney War" in the West with a ferocious display of *Blitzkrieg.* On this first day the *Luftwaffe* is heavily committed simultaneously against the R.A.F., the French *Armée de l'Air,* and the air forces of Holland and Belgium, and suffers severely, losing 304 aircraft destroyed (including 157 Junkers Ju 52/3m transports) and 51 damaged, 267 aircrew killed, 133 wounded and 340 missing. The **first air victory by a Dutch pilot** is a Junkers Ju 88A-2 of *KG 30* shot down by a pilot of *IeJa.V.A.* The largest single air fight this day is between a formation of Dutch Fokker D.XXIs and fifty-five Junkers Ju 52/3ms of *KGzbV 9*; German records disclose that this unit loses 39 of its aircraft.

In Britain Neville Chamberlain resigns as Prime Minister and Winston Churchill forms a Coalition Government, and assumes the post of Minister of Defence. Sir Archibald Sinclair is appointed Secretary of State for Air.

14-5-40 As the result of a tragic misunderstanding the *Luftwaffe* heavily bombs Rotterdam and reports suggest that about 900 civilians are killed.
In Britain the Ministry of Aircraft Production is formed under the leadership of Lord Beaverbrook.

15-5-40 The Dutch forces capitulate and the Battle of France opens in earnest.

15/16-5-40 The R.A.F. carries out the **first heavy raid (*sic*) on the Ruhr** with 93 Wellingtons and Whitleys. Bombing is scattered, and enemy records report that "only" 22 people are killed.

22-5-40 The R.A.F.'s second expedition to Norway.

4-6-40 H.M.S. *Glorious* carries No. 263 Sqdn. (with a fresh complement of Gladiators) and No. 46 (Hurricane) Sqdn., R.A.F., to Northern Norway where they land at Bardufoss, near Narvik. After a fortnight of successful operations, covering the British ground forces, the situation is regarded as unprofitable and evacuation is ordered. The fighter squadrons land back on H.M.S. *Glorious,* but the carrier is caught and sunk on the 8th June by the German warships *Scharnhorst* and *Gneisenau* with the loss of all but two pilots of the squadrons.

27-5-40 R.A.F. Flying Training Command is formed, and Air Marshal L. A. Pattinson appointed A.O.C.-in-C.

30-5-40
4-6-40 The evacuation of the British Expeditionary Force and elements of the French Army is ordered from Dunkirk. Home-based R.A.F. squadrons of Fighter Command provide air cover over the crowded beaches against German bombing attacks.

9-6-40 Norwegian forces are ordered to capitulate and the campaign in Norway ends.

10-6-40 Italy declares war on the Allies, and Italian aircraft start raiding Malta on the following day.

12-6-40 **The first Victoria Crosses to be awarded to members of the R.A.F. in the War** are announced. They are awarded posthumously to Fg. Off. Donald Edward Garland and Sgt. Thomas Gray, the crew of a No. 12 Sqdn. Fairey Battle who had attacked bridges over the Belgian Albert Canal on 12th May.

17-6-40 Evacuation of the B.E.F. from France is

28-6-40 completed and the last Hurricanes leave Nantes for Tangmere, England.

28-6-40 Marshal Balbo, Italian Governor of Libya and famous for his pre-War formation flights, is killed when his aircraft is shot down by his own anti-aircraft gunners near Tobruk.

30-6-40 It is announced that during May and June the R.A.F. has lost 959 aircraft on operations, of which 477 are fighters lost during the Battle of France.

1-7-40 The Germans complete the occupation of the Channel Islands, and the Battle of Britain opens with *Luftwaffe* attacks against coastal targets in Southern England.

1/2-7-40 The R.A.F. drops the **first 2,000-lb. (908 kg) bomb of the War** in an attack on the *Scharnhorst* at Kiel.

7-7-40
25-7-40 *Luftwaffe* raids increase against Southern England with heavy attacks against coastal convoys, ports and naval installations. R.A.F. fighter squadrons are successful in their interceptions but become involved in wasteful combats with "free chasing" enemy single-seat fighters. The object of the German attacks in this phase of the Battle is to draw British fighters into the air and destroy them as a prelude to a planned invasion across the English Channel. Meanwhile R.A.F. Bomber Command continues to raid targets in Northern and Western Germany.

26-7-40 The first Royal Canadian Air Force Squadron equipped with Canadian-built Hurricanes arrives in Britain. Despite the demands being made on fighter production in Britain, a small number of Hurricanes is supplied to the Middle East during June and July. Losses suffered by the *Luftwaffe* during July amount to 173 bombers and 75 fighters, against a loss of 118 R.A.F. fighters. [1]

1-8-40
7-8-40 There is a discernible pause in the air operations over Britain; this is partly due to the stoppage of coastal convoys in the Channel and also to the regrouping of *Luftwaffe* units in readiness for the main assault in preparation for the invasion.

8-8-40 Heavy attacks re-start against British coastal convoys and R.A.F. airfields.

12-8-40 Widespread attacks, often using dive-bombers, continue against R.A.F. fighter stations and units of the coastal radar defences.

15-8-40 The heaviest fighting of the Battle of Britain takes place with attacks against British airfields by three *Luftflotten* based all round the European coast from Norway to France. British losses on this day amount to 29 fighters and 17 bombers, but the *Luftwaffe* records disclose the loss of 36 fighters and 40 bombers. 16 R.A.F. pilots, 7 of them wounded, are saved.

16-8-40 The heavy German attacks continue, although the losses inflicted upon *Luftflotte 5*

---

[1] All losses quoted for the War period are those recorded in and analysed from contemporary Service returns, and *not* those published in distorted forms for various propaganda purposes.

The Junkers Ju 87 R-2, the notorious German dive-bomber which suffered crippling losses at the hands of the R.A.F. in August 1940

Mainstay of the R.A.F.'s night bombing raids of 1940 was the Vickers Wellington, of which the Rolls-Royce Merlin-powered Mark II is shown here

on the previous day has deterred raids by this Norway- and Denmark-based air fleet. The **first and only Victoria Cross award to a pilot of Fighter Command** is made to Flt. Lt. John Brindley Nicolson of No. 249 (Hurricane) Sqdn., for an action over Southampton.

18-8-40
31-8-40   Heavy air fighting continues over Southern England, but after crippling losses by the *Luftwaffe's Stukageschwader*, the Junkers Ju 87 dive-bomber is virtually withdrawn. British fighter airfields in the South are badly damaged, but owing to the failure of the Messerschmitt Bf 110 as an escort fighter the Bf 109 is allotted this duty, and owing to the partial discontinuation of the "free chases" R.A.F. fighter losses are not critical at this stage. During August the *Luftwaffe* loses 273 bombers and 347 fighters against the loss of 363 fighters. Other R.A.F. commands in other theatres however lose 48 fighters. During this period the first Short Stirling four-engine heavy bombers are delivered to No. 7 Sqdn., R.A.F., at Leeming, Yorkshire.

1-9-40
6-9-40   While R.A.F. aircraft commence bombing attacks on barges concentrating at Channel ports in preparation for the invasion of Britain, *Luftwaffe* fighter sweeps re-impose heavy losses among Hurricane and Spitfire Squadrons in Southern England; and at the heavy rate of attrition suffered in this week it seems likely that Fighter Command must face defeat. During this period the first Bristol Beaufighter night fighters begin to reach British squadrons.

7-9-40   Göring takes personal command of the German operations over Britain and switches his attacks from the R.A.F. on to London. In the evening a two-wave attack is launched up the Thames Estuary and results in **the biggest single air combat in history** involving a clash of about 1,200 aircraft in an area of 15 miles by 30 miles during 35 minutes.

8-9-40
15-9-40   Sporadic raiding continues but British fighter squadrons gain a respite in which losses are made good, so that when heavy attacks are made on London on the 15th the German bomber formations are severely mauled and big losses inflicted.

Although heavy daylight attacks continue to be made against Britain up to the end of October, the big raids on London on 15th September mark the climax of the Battle. The main Luftwaffe bomber offensive is switched to night raids on British cities – raids which continue with no respite until the following May. British night fighters can do little to oppose these raids. Failure to defeat the R.A.F. in the Battle of Britain brings about postponement – and ultimate abandoning – of plans to invade England.

19-9-40   The first convoy, carrying fighter reinforcements for the Middle East, reaches Takoradi in West Africa; the Hurricanes are then flown overland to Egypt.

5-10-40   Air Chief Marshal Sir Charles Portal is appointed Chief of the British Air Staff, and Air Chief Marshal Sir Richard Pierse becomes A.O.C.-in-C., R.A.F. Bomber Command.

-10-40   During October R.A.F. raids are made in growing strength against Berlin.

8-10-40	The formation of the **first "Eagle" squadron** – manned by American volunteer pilots with the R.A.F. – is announced.
11-10-40	The first Beaufighter night fighter squadron, No. 29 Sqdn., R.A.F., becomes operational.
20-10-40	Italian aircraft bomb the outskirts of Cairo.
27/28-10-40	Whitley bombers attack the Skoda works in Czechoslovakia.
28-10-40	Italy attacks Greece through Albania, and Italian aircraft bomb Patras.
5-11-40	Churchill discloses that so far in the War British civilian casualties in air raids on Britain have amounted to 14,000 killed and 20,000 seriously injured. Britain sends three squadrons of Blenheims and one of Gladiators to the aid of Greece.
10-11-40	The air ferrying across the Atlantic of American-built aircraft to Britain starts under the directorship of Capt. D. C. T. Bennett of B.O.A.C., who leads the first formation of seven Lockheed Hudsons to arrive.
11-11-40	Italian aircraft attempt to raid Britain from bases in Belgium but are met and severely mauled by Hurricane squadrons; the venture is shortlived.
14/15-11-40	The *Luftwaffe* carries out a heavy night raid on Coventry, England, by 437 bombers; the attack kills 380 civilians and seriously injures 800.
-11-40	Throughout the month the *Luftwaffe* continues to raid British cities by night, London, Liverpool, Southampton, Bristol and Birmingham all being heavily bombed. Attacks, on a smaller scale, are carried out by R.A.F. bombers on Berlin, Essen, Hamburg, Cologne and Bremen. The first Avro Manchester heavy bombers are delivered to No. 207 Sqdn., R.A.F., at Waddington, Lincolnshire.
25-11-40	Air Chief Marshal Sir Hugh Dowding, victor of the Battle of Britain, is succeeded by Air Marshal Sir W. Sholto Douglas as leader of R.A.F. Fighter Command. The first delivery of the Handley Page Halifax four-engine heavy bomber is made to No. 35 Sqdn., R.A.F., at Leeming, Yorkshire. Also on this day is made the first flight of the prototype de Havilland Mosquito (*E-0234*, later *W4050*), flown by Geoffrey de Havilland, Jr.
-12-40	The night raiding of British and German cities continues throughout the month, culminating in a devastating fire raid on London on 29th/30th December which destroys many historic buildings. Liverpool,

Manchester, Coventry and Birmingham are also raided, while R.A.F. bombers (Wellingtons, Whitleys and Hampdens) repeatedly attack Mannheim and Düsseldorf. Numerous raids on Italy are also made both from Britain and the Middle East.

1941

1-1-41 4-1-41	Three fire raids, each by about 90 R.A.F. bombers, are made in the Bremen area.
5-1-41	Miss Amy Johnson (Mrs. Mollison) is killed while ferrying an aircraft in Britain; her aircraft falls in the Thames Estuary.
6-1-41	German doubts of Italian ability to prevent the passage of British convoys through the Mediterranean lead to the movement of *Luftwaffe* units to Sicily, and on 10th January sixty German aircraft attack the carrier, H.M.S. *Illustrious*, south of Sicily, scoring six hits. On the 11th the British cruiser, H.M.S. *Southampton*, is sunk by air attack. After further hits on *Illustrious* in Malta harbour, the carrier is safely sailed to Alexandria.
9-1-41	The first flight is made of the prototype Avro Lancaster (*BT308*) four-engine heavy bomber.
-1-41	In *Luftwaffe* attacks on British cities, London, Cardiff, Portsmouth, Plymouth and Swansea are heavily raided. British bombers attack Turin, Wilhelmshaven and Hanover.
10/11-2-41	Short Stirling heavy bombers of the R.A.F. operate for the first time, in a raid against Rotterdam. This is the **first combat use of four-engine bombers by the R.A.F.**
-2-41	R.A.F. Fighter Command steps up sweeps over enemy-occupied coasts in Northern Europe attacking enemy coastal shipping, airfields and ports.
24/25-2-41	Avro Manchester heavy bombers of the R.A.F. are first flown on operations in an R.A.F. raid on Brest, France.
1/2-3-41	More than 100 R.A.F. bombers (including 30 Stirlings and Manchesters) attack Cologne.
7-3-41	Increased assistance is given to Greece, including the landing of an expeditionary force and four additional squadrons of aircraft.
10/11-3-41	Handley Page Halifax heavy bombers of the R.A.F. are first flown on operations in an R.A.F. raid on Le Havre, France.
11-3-41	The "Lease-Lend" Bill is signed by President Roosevelt providing for the supply to overseas nations (on loan, transfer or sale) of U.S. war materials considered to be vital

	in the interests of American defence.
19/20-3-41	A heavy raid is made on London by about 370 German bombers.
28-3-41	R.A.F. Blenheims and naval Swordfish torpedo bombers participate in the naval battle off Cape Matapan which results in a British victory and the sinking of several Italian warships.
31-3-41 1-4-41	**The first 4,000-lb. (1,816 kg) bomb** is dropped by an R.A.F. Wellington during an attack on Emden. This is the **heaviest bomb yet dropped by an aircraft.**
3-4-41 31-5-41	An Axis-inspired revolt in Iraq brings about reaction by R.A.F. units based at Habbaniyah which attack the Iraqi Army and German *Luftwaffe* units in the country, and the situation is restored by the end of May.
6-4-41	The German warship *Gneisenau* is attacked and damaged in Brest harbour by a Beaufort torpedo-bomber of No. 22 Sqdn., R.A.F., whose pilot Fg. Off. Kenneth Campbell is awarded a posthumous Victoria Cross. The warships *Scharnhorst* and *Gneisenau* had been constantly attacked throughout February and March by R.A.F. bombers but little damage done.
16/17-4-41	London is attacked by about 460 German bombers.
17/18-4-41	Berlin is attacked by 118 R.A.F. bombers including 60 Manchesters, Stirlings and Halifaxes.
22-4-41	British forces start evacuation from Greece. R.A.F. losses in the Greek campaign during the past four months amount to 92 bombers and 69 fighters.
1-5-41	Lt.-Col. J. T. C. Moore-Brabazon (later Lord Brabazon of Tara) is appointed Minister of Aircraft Production.
10/11-5-41	Rudolf Hess, Deputy Führer of Germany, flies to Scotland in a Messerschmitt Bf 110 in an attempt to negotiate peace terms with Britain. He is confined to the Tower of London. A heavy raid on London, the last severe attack for almost three years, causes the deaths of 1,212 people and serious injuries to a further 1,769.
14-5-41	British forces, evacuated from Greece and concentrated in Crete, come under heavy attack by German bombers now based in Greece.
15-5-41	**The first flight by a British jet-propelled aeroplane,** the Gloster E.28/39, is made by P. E. G. Sayer at Cranwell, Lincolnshire.
20-5-41	The German airborne assault on Crete begins.
23-5-41	B.O.A.C. commences trans-Atlantic flights by three Boeing 314A flying-boats

	(*G-AGBZ*, "*Bristol*"; *G-AGCA* "*Berwick*"; *G-AGCB* "*Bangor*"), the special Flight being formed under Capt. J. C. Kelly Rogers.
24-5-41 27-5-41	The German battleship *Bismarck* is sunk in the Atlantic by British warships after a four-day operation which also involves shadowing and attacks by aircraft – its location by a Catalina of No. 209 Sqdn., flown by Plt. Off. D. A. Briggs, and its crippling by Swordfish torpedo aircraft from the carrier, H.M.S. *Ark Royal*.
1-6-41	Air Vice-Marshal A. W. Tedder is appointed A.O.C.-in-C., R.A.F. Middle East.
12/13-6-41	R.A.F. bombers drop 445 tons of bombs in a raid on the Ruhr – **the heaviest tonnage of bombs yet. dropped in a single night,** and made possible by the activation of four new squadrons of four-engine bombers.
14-6-41	Air Chief Marshal Sir Philip Joubert de la Ferté is appointed A.O.C.-in-C., R.A.F. Coastal Command.
22-6-41	Germany attacks Russia on a front extending from the Baltic to the Black Sea. In the first day's fighting the *Luftwaffe* destroys more than 400 Russian aircraft – a high proportion of them on the ground. Italy and Romania declare war on Russia, while Churchill pledges support for the U.S.S.R.
25-6-41	Finland is attacked by Russia and the "Continuation War" opens.
29-6-41	Lord Beaverbrook is appointed Minister of Supply.
30-6-41	**Handley Page Halifax heavy bombers operate in daylight for the first time** in a raid on Kiel.
21/22-7-41	**Moscow is heavily raided for the first time** by about 200 German bombers. About fifty further raids on the city are made during the next eight weeks.
7/8-8-41	**Berlin is bombed by Russian aircraft for the first time.**
12/13-8-41	The R.A.F. drops 82 tons of bombs on Berlin – the most in a single raid on the German capital. The long distance flown by the R.A.F. bombers severely limits their bombloads.
-9-41	Deliveries of the first Hawker Typhoon fighters are made to Nos. 56 and 609 Sqdns., R.A.F., at Duxford.
11-9-41	R.A.F. Hurricanes of No. 151 Wing, sent by merchant convoy round the North Cape to assist the Russians, make their first combat sorties in the defence of Murmansk.
20-9-41	The first operational sortie – a deep reconnaissance flight over France – is made by a D.H. Mosquito (*W4055*).

30-9-41	Although, since the German attack on Russia when most *Luftwaffe* bomber units moved to the Eastern Front, German raids on Britain dwindled during the summer of 1941, British civilian casualties for air raids to date are announced as 41,254 killed and 51,859 seriously injured. German civilian casualties to date total about 11,400 killed and 21,000 seriously injured.
31-10-41	In the five months since 1st June 1941 enemy shipping totalling 209,000 tons has been sunk in the Mediterranean; of this, about one-third has been sunk by R.A.F. aircraft flying from Malta. On this day the first production Avro Lancaster heavy bomber (*L7527*) makes its first flight.
3-11-41	Maj. Gen. Lewis H. Brereton, U.S.A.A.C., is appointed to command the U.S. Far East Air Forces, at the request of General Douglas MacArthur.
7/8-11-41	In one of the heaviest night raids by over 400 R.A.F. bombers on Berlin, Cologne and Mannheim, 37 British bombers fail to return (partly due to bad weather). Of these, 22 are four-engine Stirlings and Halifaxes.
12-11-41	The British aircraft carrier, H.M.S. *Ark Royal*, is torpedoed by a U-Boat east of Gibraltar and sinks some hours later.
18-11-41	Operation *Crusader* – an advance by the British Eighth Army in Cyrenaica – opens, supported in strength by British aircraft.
6-12-41	Two Japanese troop convoys, steaming towards Northern Malaya, are sighted by Lockheed Hudson crews of No. 1 Squadron, Royal Australian Air Force, flying from Kota Bharu.
7-12-41	Japanese carrier-borne aircraft carry out a surprise attack on the main American base in the Pacific at Pearl Harbor, Hawaii, causing heavy damage on shore and crippling numerous heavy ships of the U.S. Pacific Fleet. On the same day Japan announces a state of war with America and Britain, and in Europe Britain declares war on Finland, Hungary and Romania.
8-12-41	R.A.A.F. Hudsons attack Japanese forces landing at Kota Bharu. Britain and the U.S.A. declare war on Japan. In a raid on Clark Field, Philippines, Japanese aircraft destroy seventeen B-17 Flying Fortress bombers and 45 fighters. On this date the total strength of the U.S.A.A.C. is 12,000 aeroplanes, 23,000 officers and 275,000 men.
10-12-41	The United States of America declares war on Germany and Italy.

13-12-41	Japanese forces invade Burma.
19-12-41	Japanese seaborne forces start landing on the Philippine Islands.
23-12-41	Rangoon is first bombed by Japanese aircraft.
25-12-41	Hong Kong, without any air defences, surrenders to Japanese forces.
30-12-41	Singapore is hit by the first of numerous Japanese air raids.

1942

20-1-42	Hurricane fighters, sent as reinforcements to Singapore, shoot down eight Japanese bombers from a force of 27 bombing the city. On the following day Japanese Mitsubishi Zero-Sen fighters are sent as escort for the bombers and shoot down five Hurricanes without loss. During the period 30th December–15th February Singapore city suffers 18 heavy raids and 25 lesser attacks.
11/12-2-42	The German warships *Scharnhorst*, *Gneisenau* and *Prinz Eugen* make good their escape from Brest up the English Channel to German home ports. In air attacks launched by the R.A.F. and Fleet Air Arm against the ships during their dash, 42 aircraft are lost. An attack by six Swordfish results in the loss of the entire formation – its leader Lt. Cdr. Eugene Esmonde being awarded a posthumous Victoria Cross. The *Scharnhorst* and *Gneisenau* are however damaged by mines.
15-2-42	Singapore surrenders to the Japanese.
22-2-42	Air Marshal Arthur Harris is appointed A.O.C.-in-C., R.A.F. Bomber Command. The first U.S. Air H.Q. is established in England under Brig. Gen. Ira C. Eaker, commanding U.S. Bomber Command.
26-3-42	The first Douglas DC-4 (C-54A Skymaster) is flown by John F. Martin at Santa Monica, California.
-3-42	During March, Malta is heavily raided by German and Italian aircraft flying from Sicily. In the Far East, Darwin, Australia, is frequently raided by the Japanese.
4/5-4-42	A Japanese carrier task force in the Indian Ocean is sighted by a Catalina pilot on the 4th April. On the following morning Japanese carrier aircraft attack bases in Ceylon. Defending Hurricanes and Fulmars destroy 25 attacking aircraft for the loss of 19. Japanese aircraft attack and sink the British cruisers, H.M.S. *Cornwall* and *Dorsetshire*, 300 miles from Ceylon.
9-4-42	In further attacks by Japanese carrier aircraft, heavy damage is done in Ceylon, but

Continued on Page 44

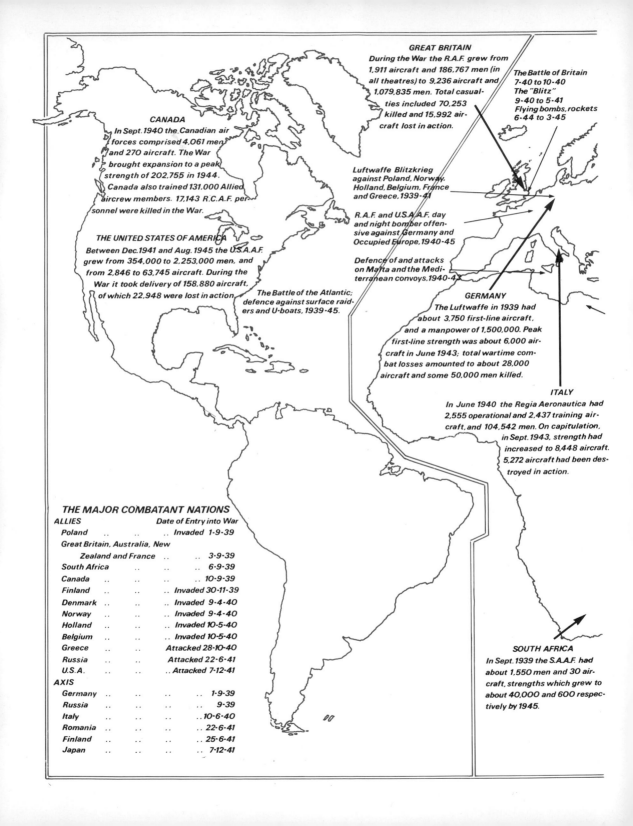

GREAT BRITAIN
During the War the R.A.F. grew from
1,911 aircraft and 186,767 men (in
all theatres) to 9,236 aircraft and
1,079,835 men. Total casualties included 70,253
killed and 15,992 air-
craft lost in action.

The Battle of Britain
7-40 to 10-40
The "Blitz"
9-40 to 5-41
Flying bombs, rockets
6-44 to 3-45

CANADA
In Sept.1940 the Canadian air
forces comprised 4,061 men
and 270 aircraft. The War
brought expansion to a peak
strength of 202,755 in 1944.
Canada also trained 131,000 Allied
aircrew members. 17,143 R.C.A.F. personnel were killed in the War.

Luftwaffe Blitzkrieg
against Poland, Norway,
Holland, Belgium, France
and Greece, 1939-41

R.A.F. and U.S.A.A.F. day
and night bomber offen-
sive against Germany and
Occupied Europe, 1940-45

THE UNITED STATES OF AMERICA
Between Dec.1941 and Aug.1945 the U.S.A.A.F.
grew from 354,000 to 2,253,000 men, and
from 2,846 to 63,745 aircraft. During the
War it took delivery of 158,880 aircraft,
of which 22,948 were lost in action.

The Battle of the Atlantic;
defence against surface raiders and U-boats, 1939-45.

Defence of and attacks
on Malta and the Medi-
terranean convoys, 1940-4

GERMANY
The Luftwaffe in 1939 had
about 3,750 first-line aircraft,
and a manpower of 1,500,000. Peak
first-line strength was about 6,000 aircraft in June 1943; total wartime combat losses amounted to about 28,000
aircraft and some 50,000 men killed.

ITALY
In June 1940 the Regia Aeronautica had
2,555 operational and 2,437 training aircraft, and 104,542 men. On capitulation,
in Sept.1943, strength had
increased to 8,448 aircraft.
5,272 aircraft had been destroyed in action.

THE MAJOR COMBATANT NATIONS

ALLIES

		Date of Entry into War
Poland	..	.. Invaded 1-9-39
Great Britain, Australia, New		
Zealand and France	..	.. 3-9-39
South Africa	..	.. 6-9-39
Canada	..	.. 10-9-39
Finland	..	Invaded 30-11-39
Denmark	..	.. Invaded 9-4-40
Norway	..	.. Invaded 9-4-40
Holland	..	.. Invaded 10-5-40
Belgium	..	.. Invaded 10-5-40
Greece	..	Attacked 28-10-40
Russia	..	Attacked 22-6-41
U.S.A.	..	.. Attacked 7-12-41

AXIS

Germany	..	..	.. 1-9-39
Russia	..	..	.. 9-39
Italy	..	..	..10-6-40
Romania	..	..	.. 22-6-41
Finland	..	..	.. 25-6-41
Japan	..	..	.. 7-12-41

SOUTH AFRICA
In Sept.1939 the S.A.A.F. had
about 1,550 men and 30 aircraft, strengths which grew to
about 40,000 and 600 respectively by 1945.

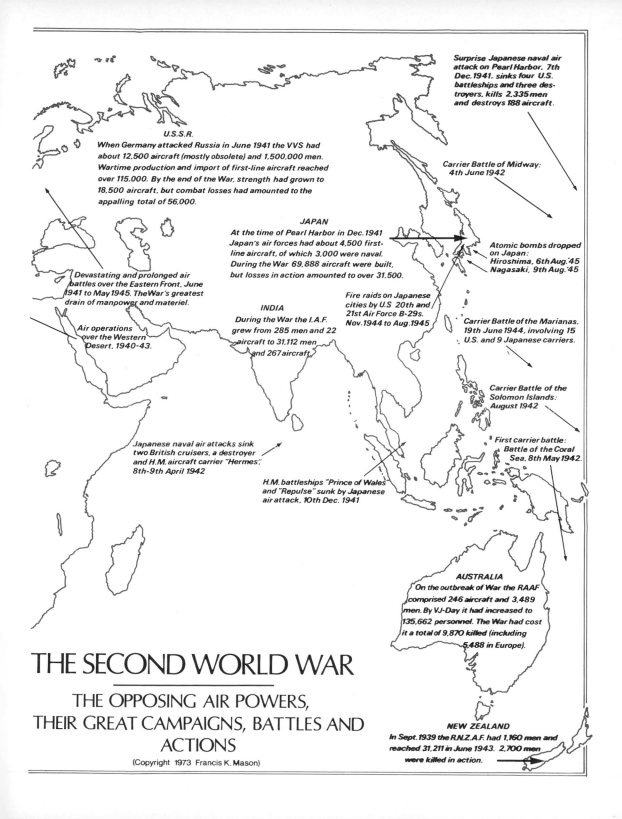

Surprise Japanese naval air attack on Pearl Harbor, 7th Dec.1941, sinks four U.S. battleships and three destroyers, kills 2,335 men and destroys 188 aircraft.

Carrier Battle of Midway: 4th June 1942

U.S.S.R.
When Germany attacked Russia in June 1941 the VVS had about 12,500 aircraft (mostly obsolete) and 1,500,000 men. Wartime production and import of first-line aircraft reached over 115,000. By the end of the War, strength had grown to 18,500 aircraft, but combat losses had amounted to the appalling total of 56,000.

JAPAN
At the time of Pearl Harbor in Dec.1941 Japan's air forces had about 4,500 first-line aircraft, of which 3,000 were naval. During the War 69,888 aircraft were built, but losses in action amounted to over 31,500.

Atomic bombs dropped on Japan:
Hiroshima, 6th Aug.'45
Nagasaki, 9th Aug.'45

Devastating and prolonged air battles over the Eastern Front, June 1941 to May 1945. The War's greatest drain of manpower and materiel.

Fire raids on Japanese cities by U.S. 20th and 21st Air Force B-29s. Nov.1944 to Aug.1945

Air operations over the Western Desert, 1940-43.

INDIA
During the War the I.A.F. grew from 285 men and 22 aircraft to 31,112 men and 267 aircraft.

Carrier Battle of the Marianas, 19th June 1944, involving 15 U.S. and 9 Japanese carriers.

Carrier Battle of the Solomon Islands: August 1942

Japanese naval air attacks sink two British cruisers, a destroyer and H.M. aircraft carrier "Hermes", 8th-9th April 1942

First carrier battle: Battle of the Coral Sea, 8th May 1942.

H.M. battleships "Prince of Wales" and "Repulse" sunk by Japanese air attack, 10th Dec. 1941

AUSTRALIA
On the outbreak of War the RAAF comprised 246 aircraft and 3,489 men. By VJ-Day it had increased to 135,662 personnel. The War had cost it a total of 9,870 killed (including 5,488 in Europe).

THE SECOND WORLD WAR

THE OPPOSING AIR POWERS, THEIR GREAT CAMPAIGNS, BATTLES AND ACTIONS

NEW ZEALAND
In Sept.1939 the R.N.Z.A.F. had 1,160 men and reached 31,211 in June 1943. 2,700 men were killed in action.

24 raiding aircraft are destroyed for the loss of 11 British fighters. The aircraft carrier, H.M.S. *Hermes* and the destroyer H.M.S. *Vampire* are sunk by Japanese aircraft off Ceylon.

17-4-42 Twelve Avro Lancaster heavy bombers carry out a low-level daylight raid on a diesel engine factory at Augsburg. Seven Lancasters are shot down, and the leader of the raid, Sqdn. Ldr. John Dering Nettleton, a South African, survived to be awarded the Victoria Cross. He is killed in a raid on Turin later.

18-4-42 Sixteen North American B-25 Mitchells of the U.S.A.A.F., flying from the carrier, U.S.S. *Hornet*, and led by Lt.-Col. James Doolittle, carry out a daylight raid on Tokyo. Doolittle is promoted to Brig. Gen. on the following day and is awarded the Congressional Medal of Honor.

20-4-42 47 Spitfires are flown off the American carrier, U.S.S. *Wasp*, to reinforce the defences of Malta.

23-4-42
28-4-42 Between these dates R.A.F. Bomber Command raids Rostock on the Baltic Coast. These raids (and one on Lubeck the previous month) prompt a series of reprisal raids by the *Luftwaffe* on British cities of architectural interest only – known as "Baedeker" raids.

24/25-4-42 A Baedeker raid is launched against Exeter, Devon.

25/26-4-42 A Baedeker raid is made on Bath, Somerset (and again the following night).

27-28-4-42 A Baedeker raid is made on Norwich, Norfolk.

28/29-4-42 A Baedeker raid is made on the city of York.

29/30-4-42 A second Baedeker raid is made on Norwich.

3/4-5-42 A third Baedeker raid is made on Bath, Somerset.

7-5-42
9-5-42 **The first naval battle in which reliance is placed wholly on aeroplanes** is the Battle of the Coral Sea. The U.S. Navy loses the carrier U.S.S. *Lexington* and 69 aircraft; the Japanese lose the carrier *Shoho* and 85 aircraft. The Japanese shortage of aircraft thus inflicted is critical in the Battle of Midway (see 4-6-42).

30/31-5-42 **The first "1,000-bomber" raid** is launched by R.A.F. Bomber Command against Cologne. Although more than 300 of the 1,046 bombers sent are from the Command's training units, about 900 crews claim to bomb the city and drop 1,455 tons of bombs, by far the heaviest tonnage yet dropped in a single raid. 39 bombers fail to return.

31-5-42 A reprisal raid by German aircraft is carried out on Canterbury, Kent.

1/2-6-42 A second very heavy raid (by 950 bombers) is made by the R.A.F. on Essen, but thick cloud obscures the target and it is not considered wholly successful. 31 bombers fail to return.

4-6-42 The American Navy wins a great victory at the Battle of Midway. U.S. Navy aircraft from the carriers U.S.S. *Hornet, Yorktown* and *Enterprise* destroy four Japanese carriers, one heavy cruiser and 250 aircraft; American losses are the *Yorktown*, a destroyer and 150 aircraft.

16-6-42 The Italian battleship *Littorio* is torpedoed and badly damaged by an aircraft of No. 38 Sqdn., R.A.F., flown by Plt. Off. O. L. Hawes.

18-6-42 Maj. Gen. Carl Spaatz assumes command of the U.S. Eighth Army Air Force in Britain.

23-6-42 The U.S. 10th Army Air Force, under Maj. Gen. Lewis H. Brereton, is ordered to move from India to Egypt to provide bomber strength in North Africa. From these bomber units is formed the U.S. 9th Army Air Force in November 1942.

25/26-6-42 The third "1,000-bomber" raid by R.A.F. Bomber Command is carried out on Bremen, from which 49 aircraft fail to return.

1-7-42 The first Boeing B-17E Fortress heavy bomber of the U.S. 8th Army Air Force lands in Britain at Prestwick, Scotland. Within a month two Groups of these bombers arrive in Britain.

4-7-42 The first "official" raid by American aircrew in Europe is carried out against enemy airfields in Holland, crews of the 15th Bombardment Squadron, U.S.A.A.F., flying Bostons "loaned" by the R.A.F.

5-7-42 First flight is made by the prototype Avro York (*LV626*) transport aircraft.

10-7-42 First flight is made by the prototype Douglas XA-26 (Invader) attack-bomber.

11-7-42 U.S. fighters start offensive sweeps over Northern France.

17-8-42 A force of B-17 Fortresses, led by Brig. Gen. Ira C. Eaker, bombs railway yards at Rouen, France.

18/19-8-42 R.A.F. Bomber Command raids Flensburg, Schleswig Holstein, **using a Pathfinder Force for the first time.** The force, formed just previously, is commanded by Air Cdre. D. C. T. Bennett (late of B.O.A.C.).

19-8-42 A combined operations raid is made against Dieppe, France, as a rehearsal for major operations against enemy-held coastlines.

The Focke-Wulf Fw 190 A-4 fighter-bomber which commenced daylight sweeps over Southern England late in 1941

	In this operation, which is supported by about 60 squadrons of light bombers, fighters and other aircraft, the Allies lose about 110 aircraft, the *Luftwaffe* only 42.
20-8-42	The U.S. 12th Army Air Force, later based in North Africa, is formed in the U.S.A. and on 23rd September Brig. Gen. James H. Doolittle assumes command.
21-9-42	The prototype Boeing XB-29 (Superfortress) heavy bomber makes its first flight at Seattle, Washington.
25-9-42	R.A.F. Mosquitos make a pin-point bombing attack on a Gestapo H.Q. building in Oslo, Norway.
1-10-42	**The first American jet aircraft,** the Bell XP-59, makes its first flight at Muroc Dry Lake, California.
23/24-10-42	The last great battle of Alamein opens in the Western Desert, and continuous air attacks are made on enemy positions by R.A.F. fighter-bombers and medium bombers.
4-11-42	The German and Italian lines at El Alamein crack under pressure from the British 8th Army, and in the ensuing retreat along the North African coast the enemy columns are constantly attacked by Allied aircraft.
8-11-42	Landings by British, American and Free French forces are made on the coast of French North Africa, supported by carrier-borne aircraft and formations flying from Gibraltar.
22-11-42	Sir Stafford Cripps is appointed Minister of Aircraft Production in Britain.

4-12-42	All nine Blenheim Vs of a raid by No. 18 Sqdn., R.A.F., sent against an airfield in Tunisia, are shot down when intercepted by 50 Messerschmitt Bf 109s. The formation leader, Wg. Cdr. H. G. Malcolm, is awarded a posthumous Victoria Cross.
	On this day American bombers make their first raid on Italy with an attack by 9th Air Force Liberators on Naples.
20/21-12-42	Calcutta is raided by the Japanese for the first time.

1943

1-1-43	No. 6 Group, Royal Canadian Air Force, becomes operational in R.A.F. Bomber Command and three nights later carries out its first operation – a mining sortie off the Frisian Islands.
9-1-43	Maj. Gen. Carl Spaatz is appointed C.-in-C., Allied Air Forces in North-West Africa. The prototype Lockheed Constellation makes its first flight at Burbank, California.
11-1-43	Air Chief Marshal Sir Sholto Douglas succeeds Sir Arthur Tedder as A.O.C.-in-C., R.A.F. Middle East Command.
27-1-43	In the **first U.S.A.A.F. bombing raid on Germany,** Fortresses attack Wilhelmshaven and other towns in north-western Germany.
30-1-43	**The first daylight raid on Berlin** is carried out by R.A.F. Mosquitos.
5-2-43	Air Marshal Sir John Slessor is appointed A.O.C.-in-C., R.A.F. Coastal Command.
10-2-43	The recommendations of a committee led by Lord Brabazon of Tara, set up to make

proposals for British post-War commercial aircraft, are for six distinct designs. These eventually materialise as the Bristol Brabazon, the Airspeed Ambassador, the Bristol Britannia, the de Havilland Comet, the Miles Marathon and the de Havilland Dove.

11-2-43   Air Chief Marshal Sir Arthur Tedder is appointed C.-in-C., Mediterranean Air Command.

4-3-43   In the Battle of the Bismarck Sea, American aircraft destroy a Japanese troop-carrying convoy sailing for the invasion of New Guinea.

5-4-43   The prototype Gloster Meteor twin-jet fighter makes its first flight. This is the only Allied jet fighter to see combat service later in the War.

25-3-43   Air Chief Marshal Sir Frederick Bowhill is appointed A.O.C.-in-C., R.A.F. Transport Command, formed recently.

During March 1943 Air Marshal Sir Arthur Harris' Bomber Command opens the great night bombing offensive against Germany, an offensive which is extended to "round-the-clock" bombing by the American daylight raids which start in earnest in May 1943.

10-4-43 \
22-4-43   In this period large formations of German transport aircraft, carrying fuel and other supplies from Sicily to Tunisia for the trapped German and Italian forces in North Africa, are frequently caught by Allied fighters, and about 130 enemy aircraft are destroyed for the loss of 21 British and American aircraft.

15-4-43   The first information about German experiments with long-range rockets is prepared for the British Cabinet, and a committee of investigation is set up under Mr. Duncan Sandys.

18-4-43   The Japanese Admiral Isoroku Yamamato is shot down and killed while flying from Rabaul to Bougainville. His bomber-transport is shot down by Captain Thomas G. Lanphier flying a P-38 Lightning of the U.S. 13th Army Air Force from Guadalcanal.

16/17-5-43   Specially-trained crews in a force of 19 Avro Lancasters of No. 617 Sqdn., R.A.F., led by Wg. Cdr. Guy Gibson, carrying special mines designed by Barnes Wallis, attack the Mohne, Sorpe and Eder dams in North-West Germany. All three dams are damaged and the Mohne and Sorpe reservoirs flood the Ruhr basin, drowning 1,200 German and foreign workers. Eight of the Lancasters are shot down or otherwise destroyed, and Gibson is awarded the Victoria Cross. He is killed in action on 19th September 1944.

20-5-43   Viscount Knollys is appointed chairman of B.O.A.C.

15-6-43   The 58th Bombardment Wing, U.S.A.A.F., is formed at Marietta, Georgia, Brig. Gen. Kenneth B. Wolfe taking command on 21st June. When fully activated with a force of 162 B-29 Superfortress heavy bombers, the Wing later goes to the Far East for the strategic bombing of Japan.

20/21-6-43   "Shuttle-bombing" operations begin with a raid on Friedrichshafen, the R.A.F. Lancasters flying from Britain, and going on to North Africa; three nights later they return to Britain, bombing the Italian naval base at Spezia *en route*.

9/10-7-43   The invasion of Sicily begins and includes the **first major Allied airborne assault using gliders and paratroops** on enemy-held territory. Owing to inadequate training of many of the glider-tug pilots in night operations, 69 of the 137 gliders released land in the sea.

The North American B-25J Mitchell, an 18-gun version of the famous U.S.A.A.F. light/medium bomber

19-7-43	**Rome is bombed for the first time,** by 158 B-17s and 112 B-24 Liberators of the U.S.A.A.F. after warning leaflets have been dropped.
24/25-7-43	A new phase of bomber operations opens against Germany with a night raid by more than 700 R.A.F. heavy bombers. Metalised strips (known as *Window*) are dropped to confuse German radar and this is so effective that only 12 bombers are lost.
25-7-43 3-8-43	Three further heavy night raids on Hamburg are made by Bomber Command. In the four raids since 24th July more than 3,000 aircraft have been despatched and 87 lost; huge areas of the port are devastated and most of the population evacuated.
1-8-43	177 B-24 Liberators of the U.S.A.A.F. based in North Africa are sent to attack the oil refineries at Ploesti, Romania; considerable damage is done, but 56 bombers fail to return.
17-8-43	Large formations of U.S.A.A.F. B-17 Fortresses and B-24 Liberators attack German ball-bearing factories at Schweinfurt-am-Main and the Messerschmitt factory at Regensburg. 59 bombers are shot down.
17/18-8-43	600 R.A.F. bombers attack the German rocket research establishment at Peenemünde on the Baltic coast in bright moonlight. Forty aircraft are shot down and fifteen others crash on returning to Britain.
3-9-43	An armistice is concluded between the Allies and Italy.
10-9-43	The Italian battleship *Roma*, on its way to Malta after being surrendered under the armistice terms, is sunk by a radio-controlled bomb launched by a German aircraft.
16-9-43	The British warship, H.M.S. *Warspite* is hit and severely damaged by a German radio-controlled bomb.
20-9-43	The first flight is made of the de Havilland Vampire prototype single-jet fighter (*LZ548*).
13-10-43	Italy declares war on Germany.
14-10-43	288 Fortresses and Liberators of the U.S. 8th Army Air Force carry out a successful raid on the Schweinfurt ball-bearing factories, but lose 60 of their number.
1-11-43	U.S. Marine forces land on Bougainville in the Solomon Islands under strong support by carrier-borne fighters and fighter-bombers.
2-11-43	Lt. Gen. Carl Spaatz is appointed to command the U.S. Mediterranean Air Force, which includes the U.S. 12th and 15th Army Air Forces.
18-11-43	A new phase in the bombing offensive against Germany opens with the "first battle of Berlin". Before the end of November five night raids by a total of 1,200 four-engine bombers are made, for the loss of 43 aircraft.
-11-43	Britain collects photographic evidence which confirms German work on "flying bombs", both at Peenemünde and in the building of launching sites in Northern France.
13-12-43	The U.S. 8th and 9th Army Air Forces send 1,462 aircraft – the largest number to date – to attack Kiel, Bremen, Hamburg and Schipol, Amsterdam. Those raiding Kiel are escorted by P-51 Mustang fighters.
20-12-43	The first Allied air attack is carried out on a flying-bomb launching site in Northern France. These attacks are continued for almost a year.
24-12-43 29-12-43	Between these dates a number of important air appointments are made. They include: Air Chief Marshal Sir Arthur Tedder as Deputy Supreme Commander of the North European Forces of Liberation; Lt. Gen. Carl Spaatz to command the U.S. Strategic Bombing of Germany; Maj. Gen. James Doolittle to command the U.S. 8th Army Air Force; Lt. Gen. Ira C. Eaker to command Allied Air Forces, Mediterranean; and Lt. Gen. Nathan F. Twining to command the U.S. 15th Army Air Force, in the Mediterranean.
1944 9-1-44	The first flight is made by the prototype Lockheed XP-80 Shooting Star single-seat fighter (later **the first American operational jet fighter).**
11-1-44	About 800 B-17s and B-24s of the U.S. 8th and 9th Air Forces, escorted by P-51s, attack German fighter factories at Halberstadt, Brunswick and elsewhere. 38 German fighters are shot down, but the American losses are 56 bombers and six fighters.
14-1-44	Air Marshal Sir John Slessor is appointed Deputy C.-in-C., Mediterranean Allied Air Forces; and Air Marshal Sir Keith Park becomes A.O.C.-in-C., R.A.F. Middle East Command.
20-1-44	Air Chief Marshal Sir Sholto Douglas is appointed A.O.C.-in-C., R.A.F. Coastal Command.
21/22-1-44	Beginning of the "Little Blitz" – attacks by up to 100 German bombers against London and other British cities. These continue for about two months, the average loss per raid

	being about 9·5%, a total loss of 132 German bombers being inflicted by British night fighters, rocket, gun and balloon barrages.
10-2-44	In Burma the Japanese surround part of the Indian Seventh Division, but this is sustained by 2,000 tons of supplies dropped by Brig. Gen William D. Old's U.S. Air Transport Command.
15-2-44	In Italy the monastry at Monte Cassino is bombed to rubble by 222 aircraft of the Mediterranean Allied Air Forces. Attempts fail to capture the ruins until the hill is stormed by Polish forces on 18th May.
15/16-2-44	891 R.A.F. bombers raid Berlin, hitting numerous factories; 42 aircraft are lost to the defences and a further 17 crash on return to Britain.
18-2-44	A pin-point raid is carried out by R.A.F., Canadian and Australian Mosquitos on the prison at Amiens, France.
6-3-44	609 B-17s and B-24s, escorted by P-38s, P-47s and P-51s, attack Berlin in daylight. They destroy 53 German fighters but lose 68 bombers and 13 fighters. In this and five following raids on Berlin by escorted bombers of the 8th and 9th Air Forces, 1,479 bomber sorties and 904 fighter sorties are launched; 179 bombers and 47 fighters are lost, and 83 German fighters shot down.
24-4-44	The first Boeing B-29 Superfortress heavy bombers of the 58th Wing, 20th U.S. Bomber Command land at Kwanghan, Chengtu, China.
4-6-44	Rome is occupied by the Allied Fifth Army.
5-6-44	The first raids by the U.S. 58th Wing B-29 Superfortresses are carried out against railway targets at Bangkok, Siam.
6-6-44	D-Day. Allied forces land in Normandy, France, heavily supported by tactical attacks and strategic bombing by aircraft based in Britain. Three airborne divisions are also dropped by parachute and glider, and deception raids are flown in order to draw enemy forces from the beachhead. In the 24 hours of 6th June Allied aircraft fly 14,674 sorties in support of the invasion, but *Luftwaffe* opposition is very light. By the following day engineer units have constructed the first beachhead airstrip for the emergency use of Allied fighters.
12-6-44	**The first German flying-bombs are launched against South-East England** but none of the first ten bombs launched reach Britain.
13-6-44	**The first flying-bomb to reach Britain** falls at Swanscombe, Kent, at 4.18 a.m. Others follow later in the day.
14-6-44	The prototype Avro Tudor I commercial
	airliner flies for the first time.
14/15-6-44	**The first flying-bomb to be shot down by a fighter** is destroyed by a Mosquito of No. 605 Sqdn., R.A.F., flown by Flt. Lt. J. G. Musgrave. The flying-bomb attacks gain momentum and during the first fortnight an average of 97 bombs fall on Britain every 24 hours.
16-6-44	B-29 Superfortresses of the U.S. 20th Bomber Command attack Japan for the first time, raiding iron and steel mills at Yawata, Kyushu.
19-6-44	Two Japanese aircraft carriers, the *Taiho* and *Shokaku*, are sunk by the U.S. submarines *Albacore* and *Cavalla*. On the following day Grumman Avengers torpedo and sink the Japanese carrier, *Hiyo*. All these actions take place in the area of the Mariana Islands.
6-7-44	Winston Churchill announces that up to this day a total of 2,754 flying bombs have been launched against Britain, and that 2,752 people have been killed by them.
12-7-44	No. 616 Sqdn., R.A.F., becomes the first Allied operational jet-equipped squadron, with Gloster Meteor jet fighters, and is subsequently flown in the defences against the flying bombs. The first operational sortie is made on 21st July.
17-7-44	**Napalm ("jellied-petrol" incendiary) bombs are first used** by U.S.A.A.F. P-38 Lightnings in a strafing raid on an enemy fuel depôt at Coutances, France.
13-8-44 18-8-44	As a result of a swift advance by American forces round the German left flank in France, the remains of 16 German divisions are trapped in a pocket near Falaise. R.A.F. rocket-equipped Typhoons fly numerous sorties attacking this army, and by the time the remnants are destroyed or captured German casualties amount to about 80,000 men and all their equipment.
-8-44	Attacks by B-29s are stepped up against Japan after initial difficulties in delivering supplies to the 20th Bomber Command in China.
27/28-8-44	Use of VT-fuzes in anti-aircraft gun ammunition for guns in South-East England brings substantial success against the flying-bombs. Out of 97 bombs launched against Britain in this twenty-four hours, 87 are destroyed – 69 by the guns.
29-8-44	Maj. Gen. Curtiss E. LeMay assumes command of the B-29s of the 20th U.S. Bomber Command.
1-9-44	**The first air-launched flying-bombs** (carried by Heinkel He 111s) fall in East Anglia.

Main weapon of R.A.F. Bomber Command for the last three years of the War, the Avro Lancaster heavy bomber

8-9-44	**The first German V.2 rocket** falls near Paris at about 5 a.m.; nearly two hours later a rocket falls at Chiswick, London, killing two people and injuring ten. A minute or so later a rocket falls at Epping.
10-9-44	First flight of the Fairchild C-82 Packet transport is made.
15-9-44	R.A.F. Lancasters hit the German battleship *Tirpitz* in Altenfjord, Norway, with a 12,000-lb. "Tallboy" bomb. It is not a fatal hit and the ship later moves to Tromsö Fjord.
17-9-44 25-9-44	The Arnhem operation. Three Allied airborne divisions are dropped well forward of advancing Allied armies in Holland to secure bridges. The British First Airborne Division is dropped furthest forward at Arnhem but, coming under heavy enemy pressure, suffers crippling casualties. The survivors are eventually ordered to withdraw.
6-10-44	Following a number of Japanese raids on the B-29 bases in China, Northrop P-61 Black Widow night fighters are delivered to the Chengtu airfields.
12-10-44	The first B-29 of the 21st Bomber Command, under the command of Brig. Gen. Haywood S. Hansell, lands in the Mariana Islands.
27-10-44	The naval battle of Leyte Gulf, Philippine Islands results in the crippling of Japanese naval power, largely through the action of

land- and carrier-based aircraft. The Japanese lose three battleships, four carriers, the *Zuikaku, Chitose, Chiyoda* and *Zuiho* and twenty other warships; the Americans lose three carriers, U.S.S. *Princeton, Gambier Bay* and *St. Lô* and three destroyers. Japanese "suicide" aircraft are widely used.

28-10-44	B-29s of the U.S. 21st Bomber Command launch their first raids on Truk in the Caroline Islands.
1-11-44	**The first sortie over Tokyo by a land-based American aircraft** is made by an F-13, a photo-reconnaissance version of the B-29 Superfortress, flown by Capt. Ralph D. Steakly from the Marianas.
12-11-44	The German battleship *Tirpitz* capsizes in Tromsö Fjord, Norway, after being hit or narrowly missed by three 12,000-lb. "Tallboy" bombs dropped by Lancasters of Nos. 9 and 617 Sqdns., R.A.F., flying from Lossiemouth, Scotland.
14-11-44	Air Chief Marshal Sir Trafford Leigh-Mallory is killed when his York transport aircraft crashes into mountains in France.
29/30-11-44	**The first night attack on Tokyo** is made by 21st Bomber Command B-29s flying from the Marianas. Up to this date B-29 casualties suffered by the 20th and 21st Bomber Commands in action amount to 61 aircraft.
17-12-44	The 509th Composite Group of the U.S. 20th Army Air Force is established at Wendover, Utah. This is to become responsible

for the dropping of the atom bombs in 1945. Its commander is Col. Paul W. Tibbets. The Group's single combat unit is the 393rd Bombardment Squadron.

21-12-44 General Henry H. Arnold becomes General of the Army, the only air officer to hold this "five-star" general's rank.

1945

1-1-45 The *Luftwaffe* launches its last major offensive operation – Operation *Herrmann* – against Allied airfields in Northern Europe. About 800 fighters and fighter-bombers of every available type are assembled and thrown into the attack which destroys a total of 144 British and 76 American aircraft and damages a further 111 (of which 59 are subsequently written off). German losses are 204 aircraft. As a result of the attack four fighter squadrons, one squadron of bombers and one of transports have to be withdrawn to re-equip and re-man. Such has been the enormous build-up of Allied air power in Europe that these losses are considered insignificant.

17-1-45 Brig. Gen. Roger M. Ramey succeeds Curtiss E. LeMay as commander of the U.S. 20th Bomber Command, and the latter takes command of the 21st Bomber Command.

21-1-45 The American carrier, U.S.S. *Ticonderoga*, is severely damaged by Japanese "suicide" pilots.

3-2-45 About 1,000 B-17s and B-24s, escorted by some 400 fighters, raid Berlin.

13/14-2-45
15-2-45 Dresden, which has not previously been bombed, is raided by successive waves of British and American bombers by day and night. The raids, involving a total of 1,800 sorties, are intended to assist the Russians by destroying an important centre of communications behind the Eastern Front. Huge fires rage, more than 1,600 acres of the city are devastated and tens of thousands of people killed (some reports put the figure at 135,000, but higher figures are discounted).

19-2-45 American forces land on Iwo Jima; capture of this deprives the Japanese of air bases from which to attack the B-29 bases in the Marianas, and in turn provides bases for American escort fighters to accompany the raids on Japan.

25-2-45 The heaviest raid to date on Tokyo is carried out by 170 Superfortresses, almost all carrying incendiary bombs. Huge areas are engulfed in fire.

5-3-45 The only American civilians killed by enemy air attack on the American mainland are a woman and five children killed at Lake View, Oregon, by a Japanese bomb-carrying balloon launched from a submarine off the West Coast of America.

9/10-3-45 279 B-29s raid Tokyo from medium altitude at night, it being conceded that high-level precision daylight raids have failed to destroy the Japanese aircraft industry. 14 B-29s are shot down by the defences, but a quarter of Tokyo is laid waste and 83,700 Japanese people are killed. In subsequent night raids, Nagoya, Osaka, Kobe and Yokohama are

Widely egarded as the ultimate in piston-engine fighter design was the Martin-Baker M.B.5. Powered by a Rolls-Royce Griffon 83 and capable of a speed of about 480 m.p.h., it made its first flight on 23rd May 1944, but was deprived of production status by the end of the Second World War

attacked by steadily increasing forces of B-29s.

12-3-45 Over 1,000 R.A.F. Lancasters and Halifaxes drop 4,800 tons of bombs on Dortmund, Germany.

14-3-45 **The first 22,000-lb. "Grand Slam" bomb is** dropped by a Lancaster, flown by Sqdn. Ldr. C. C. Calder, No. 617 Sqdn., R.A.F., on the Bielefeld railway viaduct and destroys two spans.

27-3-45 The last V.2 rocket to fall on Britain drops at Orpington, Kent. This is the last of 1,115 rockets to fall in Britain, of which 500 fall on London. Total casualties caused are 2,855 killed and 6,268 seriously injured.

29-3-45 The last flying-bomb to cross the British coast is destroyed near Sittingbourne, Kent. Of the 9,200 flying-bombs launched against Britain from all sources, about 6,000 have crossed the coast and of these, 3,957 have been destroyed. Total casualties caused are 6,139 killed and 17,239 seriously injured.

10-4-45 The last enemy sortie flown over Britain by an operational aircraft of the *Luftwaffe* is flown by an Arado Ar 234 jet reconnaissance aircraft from Norway or Denmark.

29-4-45
8-5-45 Owing to the ravages of war, there is an acute shortage of food in Holland, and during this period R.A.F. heavy bombers drop more than 6,600 tons of food and clothing to the Dutch in Rotterdam, The Hague and elsewhere.

9-5-45 *Reichsmarschall* Hermann Göring is captured by American troops in Austria.

9-5-45
11-5-45 The German forces surrender and the War in Europe comes to an end. *While American, British and British Commonwealth armed forces continue the War against Japan, it is announced that 60,595 British civilians have been killed and 86,182 severely injured in air raids. German civilian casualties from air raids amount to 597,623 killed, and over one million injured.*

14-5-45 More than 470 B-29s of the 21st Bomber Command carry out a devastating fire raid on Nagoya, Japan. Ten B-29s are lost. A similar raid is made on 17th May.

23/24-5-45 520 B-29s launch a fire raid on Tokyo. Two nights later a similar raid is carried out, and by now almost 17 square miles of the city has been totally burnt out.

17-6-45 Between this date and 14th August the B-29s of the U.S. 20th and 21st Bomber Commands carry out 63 major raids against Japanese towns and cities, involving 9,730 separate sorties. Of the total populated area attacked, more than 40% is burnt out, and

at Toyama, on 1st August, the entire town is razed to the ground. On 2nd July all but 200,000 of Tokyo's six million population are evacuated to escape the bombing.

15-7-45 The 2nd Tactical Air Force is reconstituted as the British Air Forces of Occupation, Germany, and Air Chief Marshal Sir Sholto Douglas is appointed Air C.-in-C. Italy declares war on Japan.

16-7-45 **The first atomic bomb is experimentally and successfully detonated** at Alamogordo, New Mexico, U.S.A. Meanwhile echelons of the 509th Composite Group, responsible for dropping the atomic bombs on Japan, have been arriving by sea at Tinian, Mariana Islands.

20-7-45 B-29s of the 509th Composite Group join in the conventional bombing of Japan to gain operational experience.

25-7-45 A Directive on this date addressed to General Carl A. Spaatz, commanding the strategic bombing forces in the Pacific, orders the dropping of the first atomic bomb on or after the 3rd August on one of the four Japanese cities, Hiroshima, Kokura, Niigata or Nagasaki.

28-7-45 A North American B-25 Mitchell bomber collides with the 79th floor of the Empire State building in fog over New York. A total of 19 people are killed and 26 injured.

6-8-45 **The first air-dropped atomic bomb** is dropped on Hiroshima on Honshu by a B-29 of the 509th Composite Group flown by Colonel Paul W. Tibbets from Tinian, Mariana Islands. The bomb destroys 4·7 square miles of the city and kills 71,000 Japanese, severely injuring a further 68,000.

8-8-45 Russia declares war on Japan.

9-8-45 The second air-dropped atomic bomb falls on Nagasaki from a B-29 flown by Maj. Charles W. Sweeney, commander of the 393rd Bombardment Squadron. Japanese estimates place the casualties from this bomb at 25,680 dead and 23,345 severely injured.

14/15-8-45 President Harry Truman announces the unconditional surrender of Japan at midnight. The instrument of surrender is signed aboard the American battleship, U.S.S. *Missouri* in Tokyo Bay on 2nd September.

THE AEROPLANE BECOMES BIG BUSINESS

20-9-45 **The world's first propjet aeroplane flies.** This is the Gloster Meteor experimentally powered by two Rolls-Royce Trents, Derwent jet engines adapted to drive propellers.

7-11-45   A new world speed record is set up for Britain by a Gloster Meteor IV jet fighter flown by Group Captain H. J. Wilson, A.F.C., at a speed of 606·38 m.p.h. (975·67 kph).

1946

1-1-46   Marshal of the Royal Air Force Sir Arthur Tedder succeeds Lord Portal as Chief of the British Air Staff.

26-1-46   The fastest crossing of the United States and the longest flight of a jet aircraft to date is made by a Lockheed P-80A Shooting Star jet fighter flown by Col. William A. Council, U.S.A.F., from Long Beach, California, to La Guardia, New York. His average speed is 548·6 m.p.h.

4-2-46   Pan American Airways makes its first scheduled passenger-carrying trans-Atlantic flight with a Lockheed Constellation, flying from New York to Hurn, England, *via* Newfoundland and Ireland.

15-3-46   South American Airways Ltd begins its regular air service, flying Avro Lancastrian aircraft between London and Buenos Aires.

12-5-46   B.O.A.C. and QANTAS open their Britain-Australia service, flying Short Hythe flying boats between Southampton and Sydney.

31-5-46   London Airport (previously named Heathrow) is opened to international commercial traffic. Although the airport has still only one runway, and tents are used to provide "terminal facilities", it quickly becomes one of the busiest commercial airports in the world.

1-6-46   The first Pan American trans-Atlantic flight between New York and London lands at the newly-opened London Airport.

1-7-46   At the Bikini Atoll in the Pacific, an atomic bomb, of the same type as that dropped on Nagasaki, is released over a fleet of 73 vessels for experimental purposes. Only five of the ships are sunk.

12-7-46   The R.A.F. High Speed Flight is formed at Tangmere under Gp. Capt. E. M. Donaldson.

27-7-46   The prototype Supermarine Attacker naval jet fighter makes its first flight.

1-8-46   The British Civil Aviation Bill, 1946, receives the Royal Assent. This provides for three British state-owned airline Corporations: British Overseas Airways Corporation, British European Airways Corporation, and British South American Airways Corporation.

8-8-46   **The world's largest bomber to date,** the Convair XB-36, makes its first flight at Forth Worth, Texas. Later, this aircraft enters service as the U.S. Strategic Air Command's first "deterrent bombing force".

1-9-46   The first Vickers Viking twin-engine airliner is introduced into service with B.E.A.

7-9-46   A new world speed record is established for Britain when Gp. Capt. E. M. Donaldson flies an improved Gloster Meteor IV jet fighter at a speed of 615·78 m.p.h. (990·79 kph) over a course near Rustington, Sussex, England.

27-9-46   Geoffrey de Havilland, Jr., is killed in a D.H.108 Swallow high-speed research jet aircraft when it breaks up over the Thames Estuary. It is widely believed that he was probably the first man to exceed the speed of sound.

29-9-46 / 1-10-46   America establishes a new world straight-line distance record with a flight by a Lockheed Neptune, *Truculent Turtle,* flown by Cdr. Thomas D. Davies and a crew of four from Perth, Australia, to Columbus, Ohio, U.S.A., a distance of 11,236 miles (17667 km).

6-10-46   A Boeing B-29, flown by Col. C. S. Irvine, flies from Honolulu to Cairo, non-stop *via* the Magnetic North Pole, a flight of 9,442 nautical miles.

9-12-46   The American Bell XS-1 rocket-propelled research aircraft flies under its own power over Muroc, California, having been dropped from the belly of a Boeing B-29.

31-12-46   *The I.C.A.O. announces that during 1946 the world's scheduled airlines have carried a total of 18,200,000 passengers, and that the average number of passengers per aircraft is 16·5.*

1947

26-1-47   A take-off accident involving a Douglas DC-3 at Kastrup, Denmark, costs the lives of 22 people, including Prince Gustav Adolf of Sweden.

17-3-47   The prototype North American XB-45 four-jet bomber makes its first flight at Muroc, California.

8-6-47   American Airlines inaugurate their coast-to-coast service, flying Douglas DC-6 four-engine airliners between New York and Los Angeles, with a single stop at Chicago. Total scheduled elapsed time is about ten hours in each direction.

15-6-47   Lt. Gen. Ira C. Eaker retires from the U.S.A.F.; Lt. Gen. Hoyt S. Vandenburg is appointed Chief of the U.S. Air Staff.

19-6-47   A new world speed record is set up by

America with a flight by the Lockheed P-80R Shooting Star, flown by Col. Albert Boyd at Muroc, California, at a speed of 623·74 m.p.h. (1003·60 kph).

16-7-47 **The world's first jet-powered flying-boat,** the prototype Saunders-Roe SR/A1 single-seat fighter flying-boat, powered by two Metrovick axial-flow jet engines, makes its first flight.

20-8-47 America establishes a new world speed record with a speed of 640·74 m.p.h. (1030·95 kph), achieved by a Douglas D-558 Skystreak research aircraft flown by Cdr. Turner F. Caldwell, U.S. Navy, at Muroc, California.

23-8-47 The prototype Avro Tudor 2 airliner crashes during a test flight at Woodford, Manchester, killing four of the occupants – including Mr. Roy Chadwick, the aircraft's designer.

25-8-47 America betters her own world speed record with a flight by the Douglas D-558 Skystreak at 650·92 m.p.h. (1047·33 kph) at Muroc, California, flown by Maj. Marion E. Carl of the U.S. Marine Corps.

1-10-47 The prototype North American XF-86 Sabre makes its first flight at Muroc, flown by George Welch. The Sabre becomes the most widely-used fighter in the Western World for the next twenty years.

The Canadair CL-13B Sabre of the R.C.A.F., a Canadian-built version of the North American F-86 Sabre jet fighter

14-10-47 **The first pilot in the world to exceed the speed of sound in level flight is Maj. Charles E. ("Chuck") Yeager.** His flight in the Bell XS-1 does not constitute a world speed record as his aircraft is carried aloft and released by a Boeing B-29.

17-12-47 The prototype Boeing XB-47 Stratojet six-jet bomber makes its first flight at Seattle, Washington.

31-12-47 *The I.C.A.O. announces that during 1947 the world's scheduled airlines have carried a total of 21,000,000 passengers, and that the average number of passengers per aircraft is 16·6.*

1948

30-1-48 The Avro Tudor 4, (*G-AHNP, "Star Tiger"*) of B.S.A.A.C. disappears without trace between the Azores and Bermuda. The 31 on board include Air Marshal Arthur Coningham.

23-3-48 A new world altitude record for aeroplanes is established for Britain by Gp. Capt. John Cunningham at 59,446 feet in a D.H. Vampire near Hatfield, Hertfordshire, England.

5-4-48 A Vickers Viking of B.E.A. collides with a Russian fighter over Berlin and 15 people are killed.

14-5-48 The first Egyptian-Israeli War breaks out
11-6-48 after termination of the British Mandate for Palestine. Egyptian Spitfires raid Tel Aviv.

24-6-48	Following the termination of all road and rail traffic between Berlin and the West by the Russians on this date, the Americans and British organise a massive air supply operation ("the Berlin Airlift") for the city. This operation continues for over a year until 6th October 1949.
12-7-48 14-7-48	**The first Atlantic crossing by jet aircraft** is made by six D.H. Vampire jet fighters of No. 54 Sqdn., R.A.F., flying from Stornoway to Goose Bay, Labrador, *via* Iceland and Greenland.
16-7-48	The first flight by the prototype Vickers Viscount four-propjet airliner (*G-AHRF*) is made at Wisley, Surrey, England, flown by J. Summers. During the next ten years more than 400 Viscounts are built and widely exported to the world airlines.
20-7-48	Sixteen Lockheed P-80A Shooting Star jet fighters of the U.S.A.F. cross the Atlantic *via* Greenland and Iceland, *en route* for Fürstenfeldbruck, Germany.
15-9-48	America establishes a new world speed record with a flight by a North American F-86A Sabre jet fighter flown by Maj. Richard L. Johnson, U.S.A.F., at 670·98 m.p.h. (1079·61 kph), at Muroc, California.
16-10-48	Lt. Gen. Curtiss E. LeMay assumes command of the U.S.A.F. Strategic Air Command.
4-11-48	The fastest flight to date between Britain and Italy is made by a D.H. Vampire flown from Hatfield, England, to Ciampino airport, Rome, in a time of 2 hr. 50 min. 40 sec., at an average speed of 323 m.p.h.
31-12-48	*The I.C.A.O. announces that during 1948 the world's scheduled airlines have carried a total of 23,500,000 passengers, and that the average number of passengers per aircraft is 16·5.*

1949

7-1-49	Czechoslovak-built Messerschmitt Bf 109 fighters, supplied to the Israeli Air Force, attack R.A.F. reconnaissance patrols near the Egyptian frontier and shoot down four Spitfires and one Tempest fighter. Two R.A.F. pilots are killed.
13-1-49	Air Vice-Marshal Sir Basil Embry is appointed A.O.C.-in-C., R.A.F. Fighter Command.
17-1-49	The Avro Tudor 4 (*G-AGRE, "Star Ariel"*) of B.S.A.A.C. disappears without trace with 20 on board between Bermuda and Jamaica. Two days later the Tudor 4 airliner is grounded while an investigation of the type is conducted.
5-2-49	A Lockheed Constellation establishes a new

	airliner coast-to-coast record in the U.S.A. with a flight from Los Angeles to New York in 6 hr. 18 min.
2-3-49	**The first non-stop round-the-world flight** is made by the Boeing B-50 Superfortress *"Lucky Lady II"*, flown from Carswell, A.F.B., Fort Worth, Texas, by Capt. James Gallagher and a crew of 18. It covers a distance of about 22,500 miles at a speed of 239 m.p.h., and is refuelled in the air over the Azores, Saudi Arabia, the Philippines and Hawaii.
4-3-49	A passenger-carrying record is set up by a Martin JRM-2 *"Caroline Mars"* of the U.S. Navy, carrying 269 persons from San Diego to San Francisco, California.
31-3-49	The accounts of the British state-owned airlines, published on this day, disclose a total loss of £11·7 million, by far the largest ever, and the largest loss incurred by the airlines of any nation.
13-5-49	The prototype English Electric Canberra twin-jet bomber (*VN799*) is flown by Wg. Cdr. Roland Beamont at Warton, Lancashire.
30-6-49	Sir Miles Thomas is appointed chairman of B.O.A.C.
27-7-49	The prototype de Havilland Comet airliner (*G-ALVG*) makes its first flight from Hatfield, England, flown by Gp. Capt. John Cunningham. **This is the world's first pure-jet airliner.**
30-7-49	Following widespread criticism of British South American Airways, and the loss of two of its Tudor airliners, the airline is absorbed into B.O.A.C., as provided for in the Airways Corporation Act, 1949.
4-9-49	The first Bristol Brabazon I eight-engine airliner (see 10-2-43) makes its first flight at Filton, England, flown by A. J. Pegg.
15-10-49	B.O.A.C. takes delivery of its first Boeing Stratocruiser (*G-ALSA, "Cathay"*) airliner.
28-10-49	Air Marshal Sir Hugh Lloyd is appointed A.O.C.-in-C., R.A.F. Bomber Command.
18-11-49	**The largest number of persons flown across the Atlantic in an aeroplane to date** is 103 in a U.S.A.F. Douglas C-74 Globemaster flying from Mobile, Alabama, to Marham, Norfolk.
7-12-49	B.O.A.C. commence scheduled trans-Atlantic passenger services with its new Boeing Stratocruisers.
31-12-49	*The I.C.A.O. announces that during 1949 the world's scheduled airlines have carried a total of 26,500,000 passengers, and that the average number of passengers per aircraft is 17·3.*

1950

1-1-50 Air Chief Marshal Sir John Slessor is appointed Chief of the British Air Staff.

15-1-50 General of the Air Force Henry H. Arnold, U.S.A.F., dies at Sonoma, California.

27-1-50 The British Government signs an agreement to purchase 70 Boeing B-29 Superfortress bombers for the R.A.F. The contract, costing £14 million, is widely criticised in Britain as it is considered that the B-29 does not represent any significant advance over the Avro Lincoln, and that the money would be better spent in developing future British jet bombers. As a result, it is estimated that 40,000 jobs are lost in the British aircraft industry.

12-3-50 The Avro Tudor V (*G-AKBY*) owned by Air Marshal D. C. T. Bennett's Airflight Ltd, crashes when approaching to land at Llandow, South Wales. The death roll of 81 makes this the **worst air disaster to date.**

18-3-50 Gp. Capt. John Cunningham flies the prototype D.H. Comet airliner from Hatfield, England, to Ciampino, Rome, in 2 hr. 2 min., and returns in the afternoon in 2 hr. 4 min. The average speed is about 450 m.p.h.

21-3-50 Gp. Capt. John Cunningham flies the Comet from Hatfield to Copenhagen in 1 hr. 18 min. 36 sec., at an average speed of 453·98 m.p.h.

22-3-50 The first Boeing B-29, ordered by the British Government for the R.A.F., and renamed the Washington I, lands in Britain.

4-4-50 John Cunningham's record flight to Copenhagen (see 21-3-50) is bettered by Sqdn. Ldr. Jan Zurakowski who flies a Gloster Meteor 8 jet fighter to Copenhagen in 1 hr. 5 min. 54 sec., at an average speed of 541·43 m.p.h.

8-4-50 A U.S. Navy patrol aircraft is shot down by Russian fighters over the Baltic. Ten American airmen are killed.

13-4-50 A bomb explodes aboard a B.E.A. Vickers Viking airliner flying from Northolt to Paris. The air stewardess, Miss S. M. Cramsie, is the only person injured, and the aircraft is flown back to Northolt by the pilot, Capt. I. R. Harvey, who is awarded the George Medal.

24-4-50 John Cunningham flies the Comet prototype airliner from Hatfield to Khartoum and Nairobi, establishing new F.A.I. records between London and Cairo.

3-5-50 The new British aircraft carrier, H.M.S. *Ark Royal* (36,800 tons) is launched at Birkenhead.

25-6-50 The Korean War starts. North Korean forces invade South Korea and capture Kaesong. On the following day President Truman of the U.S.A. orders the U.S. Air Force to the assistance of South Korea, although it is generally accepted that the U.S.A.F. is at its lowest ebb since 1941.

27-6-50 **The first North Korean Air Force (NKAF) aircraft to be shot down** are three Russian-built Yak-9s destroyed by five North American F-82G Twin Mustangs near Kimpo. The first falls to the guns of Lieut. William G. Hudson of the 68th All-Weather Fighter-Interception Squadron. Shortly afterwards U.S.A.F. Boeing B-29s start bombing targets in North Korea.

29-7-50 A Vickers Viscount 630 four-propjet airliner is experimentally introduced on B.E.A.'s London-Paris route, becoming the **first propjet airliner in the world to carry fare-paying passengers.**

31-7-50 By this date about two-thirds of South Korea has been overrun by the North Koreans.

3-8-50 B.E.A. orders 28 Vickers Viscount airliners.

22-9-50 The first non-stop flight from Britain to the U.S.A. by a jet aircraft is made by a Republic F-84 Thunderjet, flown by Col. D. C. Schilling, U.S.A.F., from Manston, Kent, to Limestone, Maine, and flight-refuelled three times *en route*.

19-10-50 Pyongyang, capital of North Korea, is captured by South Korean and American forces after a month-long offensive.

8-11-50 **The world's first jet-*versus*-jet air combat** takes place in Korea over the Yalu River between Russian-built MiG-15 fighters and four Lockheed F-80C Shooting Stars of the U.S. 51st Fighter-Interception Wing. In this combat Lt. Russel J. Brown becomes the **first jet fighter pilot to shoot down another jet aircraft.**

17-12-50 **The North American F-86A Sabre goes into combat for the first time** over Korea, and the pilot of one, Lt. Col. Bruce H. Hinton, U.S.A.F. of the 336th Squadron, destroys a MiG-15 during the second patrol of the day.

31-12-50 *The I.C.A.O. announces that during 1950 the world's scheduled airlines have carried a total of 31,200,000 passengers, and that the average number of passengers per aircraft is 19·1.*

1951

21-2-51 An English Electric Canberra twin-jet bomber is flown from Aldergrove, Northern Ireland, to Gander, Newfoundland, by Sqdn. Ldr. A. E. Callard, R.A.F., the 2,072 miles being covered in 4 hr. 37 min. at a speed of 449·46 m.p.h.

The North American F-86D. Widely known as the "Sabre-Dog", the F-86D was the world's first true all-weather single-seat fighter and served with the U.S.A.F. during the nineteen-fifties. Despite extensive equipment its afterburning J47 turbojet bestowed a performance similar to that of the F-86 day fighters. A total of 2,506 was built between March 1951 and August 1955

23-2-51	The prototype Dassault Mystère, powered by a Hispano Suiza-built Rolls-Royce Nene turbojet engine, makes its first flight in France.
15-3-51	A Boeing B-47 Stratojet 4-jet bomber of the U.S.A.F. is successfully flight-refuelled by a Boeing KC-97A four-engined tanker.
29-3-51	Lt. Gen. Lauris Norstad, U.S.A.F., is appointed C.-in-C., Allied Air Forces, Central Europe.
13-4-51	Sqdn. Ldr. Neville Duke is appointed Chief Test Pilot of Hawker Aircraft Ltd.
18-5-51	The prototype Vickers Valiant four-jet swept-wing bomber (*WB210*) makes its first flight.
20-5-51	**The world's first "jet ace"** – the first jet fighter pilot to destroy five enemy jet aircraft in air combat – is Capt. James A. Jabara, U.S.A.F., of the 4th Fighter Interceptor Wing in Korea, who shoots down his fifth and sixth MiG-15 on this day.
19-7-51	A small airship, the *Bournemouth*, is completed by the Airship Club of Great Britain organised by Lord Ventry. This is the first airship completed in Britain since the R-101 disaster of 1930.
20-7-51	The prototype Hawker Hunter single-seat jet fighter (*WB188*) is first flown by Sqdn. Ldr. Neville Duke. In due course the Hunter becomes Britain's standard fighter in R.A.F. service for fifteen years, and about 2,000 are built.
1-8-51	The prototype Supermarine Swift single-seat jet fighter (*WJ960*) is first flown by Michael Lithgow.

15-8-51	Maj. William Bridgeman, a Douglas test pilot, achieves an altitude of 79,494 feet in the Douglas D-558-2 Skyrocket experimental aircraft, thereby exceeding the balloon record established on 11th November 1935.
24-8-51	**The first Congressional Medal of Honor to to awarded to an airman during the Korean War,** is awarded to Maj. Louis J. Sebille, U.S.A.F., who crashed his damaged aircraft on enemy positions on 5th August. The award is made posthumously.
31-8-51	A new Belfast-to-Gander point-to-point record is set up by Wg. Cdr. Roland Beamont flying a Canberra jet bomber over the 2,072 miles in 4 hr. 18 min. 24 sec., at an average speed of 483·91 m.p.h.
26-9-51	The prototype de Havilland D.H.110 (later the Sea Vixen) twin-jet all-weather fighter makes its first flight.
26-11-51	The Gloster Javelin prototype delta-wing twin-jet fighter (*WD804*) makes its first flight.
31-12-51	*The I.C.A.O. announces that during 1951 the world's scheduled airlines have carried a total of 39,900,000 passengers, and that the average number of passengers per aircraft is 21·9.*

1952

31-3-52	B.O.A.C. announces that for the first time the airline has succeeded in returning a small surplus (of £274,999); B.E.A., on the other hand, reports a loss of £1,423,611.

15-4-52	The prototype Boeing XB-52 eight-jet heavy bomber makes its first flight. Later, as the Stratofortress, the B-52 is to become the main conventional aeroplane in the U.S. Strategic Air Command's "deterrent force" for more than fifteen years.
2-5-52	B.O.A.C. starts the **world's first scheduled commercial air services with pure-jet airliners,** flying D.H. Comet 1s on the London-Johannesburg route.
15-7-52 31-7-52	**The first helicopter crossing of the North Atlantic** is made by two Sikorsky S-55 helicopters flown by Capt. Vincent H. McGovern and Lt. Harold Moore, U.S.A.F. from Westover, Massachusetts, to Prestwick, Scotland, *via* Maine, Labrador, Greenland and Iceland.
11-8-52	B.O.A.C. introduces the Comet jet airliner on to its London-Ceylon route.
16-8-52	The Bristol Britannia four-propjet airliner (*G-ALBO*) makes its first flight flown by A. J. Pegg.
22-8-52	The prototype Saunders-Roe Princess ten-engine flying-boat airliner makes its first flight flown by Geoffrey Tyson.
30-8-52	The first prototype Avro Vulcan four-jet delta-wing heavy bomber (*VX770*) makes its first flight.
6-9-52	The prototype D.H. 110 twin-engine all-weather fighter prototype breaks up in the air at the S.B.A.C. Display at Farnborough killing the crew, John Derry and Anthony Richards, and 28 spectators on the ground. A further 63 are injured.
3-10-52	Britain makes her first test explosion of an atomic device at the Monte Bello Islands off Australia.
6-10-52	A B.O.A.C. Comet 1 suffers a slight take-off accident and damage at Rome's Ciampino airport.
3-11-52	The Swedish prototype Saab Lansen two-seat all-weather fighter makes its first flight.
19-11-52	America establishes a new world speed record when Capt. J. Slade Nash, U.S.A.F., flying a North American F-86D Sabre all-weather fighter at Salton Sea, California, flies at 698·50 m.p.h. (1123·89 kph).
20-12-52	In the worst air disaster to date, 86 out of 116 men aboard a Douglas C-124 Globemaster are killed when the aircraft crashes on take-off at Moses Lake, Washington.
24-12-52	The prototype Handley Page Victor four-jet "cresent-wing" bomber (*WB771*) makes its first flight.
31-12-52	*The I.C.A.O. announces that during 1952 the world's scheduled airlines have carried a total of 45,000,000 passengers, and that the average number of passengers per aircraft is 23·2.*

1953

1-1-53	Air Chief Marshal Sir William Dickson is appointed Chief of the British Air Staff.
27-1-53	Flt. Lt. L. M. Whittington, flying a Canberra jet bomber from London Airport, sets up a new point-to-point speed record to Maripur, Karachi, covering the 3,921 miles in 8 hr. 52 min. 28 sec. On the following day he lands at Darwin, Australia, setting up a new London-Darwin point-to-point record time of 22 hr. 21·8 sec.
3-3-53	A Comet jet airliner (*CF-CUN, "Empress of Hawaii"*) of Canadian Pacific Airlines crashes on take-off at Karachi, India; all eleven occupants are killed.
5-3-53	A Polish pilot, seeking asylum in the West, lands his MiG-15 jet fighter on the Danish island of Bornholm. He is granted asylum, but his aircraft is returned to Poland.
2-5-53	The B.O.A.C. Comet 1 (*G-ALYV*) crashes in a storm shortly after taking off from Dum Dum, Calcutta, India, with the loss of all 43 lives on board. The subsequent report suggests that the aircraft suffered a structural failure.
4-5-53	An official world altitude record for aeroplanes is established for Britain by a Bristol Olympus-powered Canberra aircraft, which, flown by W. F. Gibb, climbs to 63,668 feet from Filton, Bristol, England.
25-5-53	The North American YF-100 Super Sabre prototype supersonic jet fighter makes its first flight. This is the **first of the American "century" generation of supersonic fighters.**
18-6-53	All 129 occupants of a Douglas C-124 Globemaster military transport are killed when the aircraft crashes near Tokyo. This is the **worst aviation disaster to date.**
5-7-53	A new London-Paris point-to-point record is set up by a Supermarine Swift fighter flown by Michael Lithgow, in a time of 19 min. 14 sec.
16-7-53	A new world's speed record is set up by America with a flight by a North American F-86D Sabre flown by Lt. Col. William F. Barnes at 715·75 m.p.h. (1151·64 kph), at Salton Sea, California.
27-7-53	An armistice agreement brings the war in Korea to an end.
31-8-53	America establishes a new aeroplane altitude record of 83,235 feet by a Douglas D-558-2 Skyrocket of the U.S. Navy, flown by Lt. Col. Marion E. Carl, U.S. Marine Corps. As the aircraft is carried aloft to

34,000 feet by a Boeing B-29 "mother" aircraft the record does not qualify as a world record.

7-9-53 Britain recaptures the world speed record with a flight by the Hawker Hunter prototype at 727·63 m.p.h. (1170·76 kph), flown by Sqdn. Ldr. Neville Duke at Littlehampton, Sussex, England.

21-9-53 A North Korean pilot, Lt. Ro Kum-Suk, defects with his MiG-15 jet fighter, which he lands on Kimpo airfield. The aircraft is shipped to the U.S.A. for detailed examination.

25-9-53 A new world speed record is established by a Supermarine Swift jet fighter flown by Michael Lithgow of Britain at a speed of 735·70 m.p.h. (1183·74 kph) in Libya, Africa. This is beaten on 3rd October by the Douglas XF4D Skyray flown by Lt. Cdr. James Verdin, U.S. Navy, at 752·94 m.p.h. (1211·48 kph) at Salton Sea, California.

24-10-53 The prototype Convair YF-102 Delta Dagger delta-wing fighter makes its first flight.

29-10-53 A new world speed record is set up by America with a flight at 755·15 m.p.h. (1215·04 kph) by Lt. Col. Frank K. Everest, U.S.A.F., in a North American YF-100A Super Sabre.

20-11-53 A speed of 1,327 m.p.h. is achieved by the Douglas D-558-2 Skyrocket flown by Scott Crossfield, after air-launching from a B-29.

17-12-53 A new point-to-point record from London to Cape Town is set up by a Canberra bomber flown by Wg. Cdr. G. G. Petty, who completes the flight in 12 hr. 21 min. 3·8 sec.

29-12-53 *The I.C.A.O. announces that during 1953 the world's scheduled airlines have carried a total of 52,400,000 passengers, and that the average number of passengers per aircraft is 24·8.*

1954

12-1-54 The B.O.A.C. Comet 1 (*G-ALYP*) crashes into the sea off Elba, Italy, killing all 35 on board. The following day B.O.A.C. announces that it is grounding all Comets temporarily pending an investigation.

7-2-54 First flight of the prototype Lockheed XF-104 Starfighter is made by Tony Le Vier at the Edwards A.F.B., Mojave Desert, California.

23-3-54 B.O.A.C. recommences air services using the Comet jet airliner.

1-4-54 The last operational sortie by a Supermarine Spitfire with the R.A.F. is made over the Malayan jungle in operations against Communist terrorists.

2-4-54 General Hoyt S. Vandenburg, previously Chief of Staff, U.S. Air Force, 1948–53, dies.

8-4-54 The B.O.A.C. Comet 1 (*G-ALYY*) crashes into the sea off the Italian coast near Rome, killing all 21 on board. On the following day the British Ministry of Civil Aviation withdraws the Comet's Certificate of Airworthiness, and the aircraft is withdrawn from commercial service.

22-6-54 The prototype Douglas XA4D Skyhawk single-seat naval attack fighter for the U.S. Navy makes its first flight.

15-7-54 The prototype Boeing 707 four-jet airliner makes its first flight at Renton, near Seattle, Washington. This becomes the most widely-used jet airliner in the world between 1960 and 1972.

2-8-54 The Convair XFY-1, "tail-sitting" vertical take-off aircraft makes its first free vertical take-off and landing. So complex is the transition to horizontal flight that its test programme remains purely academic.

3-8-54 The Rolls-Royce "flying bedstead" makes its first free flight. This is a rudimentary step in the progress towards vertical take-off, and consists of two horizontally-mounted Rolls-Royce Nene jet engines with their jet deflected downwards. It is flown by Capt. R. T. Shepherd.

4-8-54 The English Electric P-1 twin-engine fighter prototype is first flown by Roland Beamont. This is later developed to become the Lightning fighter, the R.A.F.'s first aircraft capable of supersonic flight in level flight.

29-9-54 The McDonnell F-101A Voodoo "penetration" fighter makes its first flight. This is later widely used as a reconnaissance fighter by the U.S. Air Force.

6-10-54 The Fairey FD-2 Delta supersonic research aircraft makes its first flight at Boscombe Down, England. It is damaged in a landing on 17th November.

11-12-54 The American aircraft carrier, U.S.S. *Forrestal*, (59,600 tons) is launched at Newport News, Virginia.

31-12-54 *The I.C.A.O. announces that during 1954 the world's scheduled airlines have carried a total of 59,000,000 passengers, and that the average number of passengers per aircraft is 25·8.*

1955

9-2-55 No. 138 Sqdn., R.A.F. is the first bomber squadron of the R.A.F. to receive the Vickers Valiant four-jet bomber, at Gaydon, Warwickshire.

17-3-55	B.O.A.C. announces that it proposes to buy twenty D.H. Comet 4s, of a wholly new design, and that these would in due course be introduced on the North Atlantic route and the London-Johannesburg route.
1-4-55	The German airline, *Lufthansa*, recommences commercial operations, flying a service between Hamburg, Düsseldorf and Frankfurt with a Convair 340 (captained by a British pilot).
27-5-55	The French Sud-Aviation SE.210 Caravelle prototype airliner (*F-WHHH*) makes its first flight at Toulouse. This is progressively developed into one of Europe's most succesful jet airliners of the post-War years.
29-6-55	The first Boeing B-52 eight-jet heavy bomber to enter squadron service is delivered to the 93rd Bomber Wing, Castle A.F.B., Merced. California.
27-7-55	A Lockheed Constellation of the Israel airline El-Al is shot down by Bulgarian fighters near the frontier between Bulgaria and Greece. All 58 occupants are killed.
8-8-55	Recalling the flight by a Hawker Hurricane of No. 111 Sqdn., R.A.F., from Edinburgh to London on 10th February 1938, Sqdn. Ldr. R. L. Topp, commanding officer of No. 111 Sqdn., flies a Hawker Hunter from Edinburgh to Farnborough, Hampshire, at an average speed of 717 m.p.h.
20-8-55	America sets up a new world speed record with a flight by Col. H. A. Hanes, U.S.A.F., at 822·27 m.p.h. (1323·03 kph) in a North American F-100C Super Sabre, at Edwards A.F.B., California.
29-8-55	A new world altitude record is established by Britain with a climb to 65,876 feet by a Canberra bomber, powered by Bristol Olympus turbojets, flown by Wg. Cdr. W. F. Gibb.
28-9-55	Air Marshal Sir Harry Broadhurst is appointed A.O.C.-in-C., R.A.F. Bomber Command.
8-10-55	The American aircraft carrier, U.S.S. *Saratoga* (59,600 tons), is launched at New York navy shipyards. Its cost is estimated to be about $207m.
13-10-55	Pan American Airways announces that in its policy to re-equip entirely with jet airliners it has placed orders for twenty Boeing 707s and twenty-five Douglas DC-8s, at a cost of more than $96m.
16-10-55	The prototype Boeing 707 four-jet airliner crosses the United States from coast-to-coast twice in a single day.
1-11-55	A Douglas DC-6B airliner is destroyed by a bomb, placed aboard by a man who hopes to collect heavy insurance benefits on his mother who was aboard the aircraft. All 44 occupants are killed, and the murderer is traced and later sentenced to death.
16-11-55	K.L.M. (Royal Dutch Airlines), who had been the first European airline to purchase and operate the Douglas DC-3 in 1936, orders eight DC-8 jet airliners – the first European airline to do so.
28-12-55	A D.H. Comet 3 airliner arrives at London Airport, flown by John Cunningham, having completed a round-the-world flight. The last leg, from Montreal to London, is flown at an average speed of 548 m.p.h.
29-12-55	*The I.C.A.O. announces that during 1955 the world's scheduled airlines have carried a total of 69,000,000 passengers, and that the average number of passengers per aircraft is 27·4.*

1956

10-2-56	Marshal of the Royal Air Force Viscount Trenchard, "father of the Royal Air Force", dies at his London home, aged 83.
24-2-56	The Gloster Javelin twin-jet all-weather two-seat fighter enters service with No. 46 Sqdn., R.A.F., at Odiham, Hampshire.
10-3-56	**The world air speed record is taken over the 1,000-m.p.h. mark for the first time** by Britain with a record flight at 1,132 m.p.h. (1821 kph) by the Fairey Delta 2 research aircraft flown by L. Peter Twiss.
16-5-56	A British atomic device is detonated in the Monte Bello Islands off the coast of Northern Australia.
21-5-56	**The first American hydrogen bomb to be air-dropped** is released from a Boeing B-52, flown by Major David Critchlow, over the Bikini atoll test area.
30-6-56	In the **worst air collision to date,** all 128 occupants of a Trans-World Airlines Lockheed Constellation and a United Airlines Douglas DC-7 are killed when the aircraft collide over the Grand Canyon, Arizona, U.S.A.
1-10-56	An Avro Vulcan bomber, in which Air Marshal Sir Harry Broadhurst, A.O.C.-in-C., R.A.F. Bomber Command, had been visiting Australia and New Zealand, crashes while trying to land at London Airport. Sir Harry and the pilot, Sqdn. Ldr. D. R. Howard, escape by ejector seat, but the other four occupants are killed.
11-10-56	**The first British atomic bomb to be dropped by an aircraft** is released over Maralinga, Southern Australia, by a Vickers Valiant of R.A.F. Bomber Command flown by Sqdn.

Ldr. E. J. G. Flavell.

29-10-56
7-11-56
The Suez Crisis. Following Egyptian rejection of an Anglo-French ultimatum to move Egyptian forces back from the Suez Canal, British and French Air Forces went into action to neutralise the Egyptian Air Force. After landings of British troops, ordered to clear Egyptian forces from the area of the Canal, American pressure in the U.N. General Assembly forces a cease-fire, and the eventual withdrawal of British and French forces in the area. Egypt thereafter unilaterally controls the passage of shipping through the Canal.

31-12-56
The I.C.A.O. announces that during 1956 the world's scheduled airlines have carried a total of 78,600,000 passengers, and that the average number of passengers per aircraft is 28·8.

1957

21-3-57
A Boeing C-97 of the U.S. Air Force (MATS) is lost over the Pacific with all 67 persons on board.

-3-57
First deliveries of the Chance-Vought F-8A Crusader supersonic carrier-based fighter are made to a U.S. Navy Squadron (VF-32).

15-5-57
The first British hydrogen bomb to be dropped is released from a Vickers Valiant bomber of No. 49 Sqdn., R.A.F., in the Christmas Island area of the Pacific, flown by Wg. Cdr. K. G. Hubbard.

-6-57
First flight of the Russian Il-18 75/100-seat four-propjet airliner is made.

16-7-57
A Lockheed Super-Constellation of K.L.M. crashes off New Guinea, killing 57 persons on board.

11-8-57
A Douglas DC-4 with 79 people on board crashes into a swamp near Quebec, Canada, with the loss of all occupants.

13-11-57
A point-to-point record is established between Buenos Aires and Washington, U.S.A. by a Boeing KC-135 tanker of the U.S. Air Force, flown by Gen. Curtiss E. LeMay at 472·16 m.p.h. (758·73 kph).

19-12-57
The first jet-powered airliners to enter scheduled passenger service on the North Atlantic are B.O.A.C.'s Bristol Britannia four-propjet aircraft.

1958

26-1-58
First deliveries of the Lockheed F-104A Starfighter are made to the 83rd Fighter-Interception Squadron, U.S. Air Force, at Hamilton Air Force Base.

18-5-58
The first flight by the first production Sud Caravelle twin-jet airliner (*F-BHRA*, "*Alsace*") is made.

27-5-58
The prototype McDonnell F-4 Phantom II shipboard supersonic fighter makes its first flight.
Also on this date the U.S. Air Force (the 335th Tactical Fighter Squadron) takes delivery of the first operational Republic F-105B Thunderchief tactical fighter-bombers.

14-8-58
A second Lockheed Super-Constellation of K.L.M. (see 16-7-57) is lost at sea 130 miles west of Ireland with the loss of all 99 persons on board.

31-8-58
The prototype North American A-5 Vigilante attack aircraft for the U.S. Navy makes its first flight. Capable of a speed of 1,385 m.p.h. (2258 kph), this aircraft later serves as a naval strategic-reconnaissance shipboard aircraft.

19-9-58
The first Kaman H-43 Huskie helicopter is flown for the U.S. Air Force.

4-10-58
The first pure-jet airliners to enter scheduled passenger service on the North Atlantic route are B.O.A.C.'s D.H. Comet 4s, flying non-stop between London and New York.

17-10-58
A Tupolev Tu-104 twin-jet airliner of the Russian airline Aeroflot crashes at Kanash, Chuvashskaya A.S.S.R., in the U.S.S.R., with the loss of 75 lives.

1959

20-1-59
The first flight of the Vickers Vanguard four-propjet airliner is made by G. R. ("Jock") Bryce from Brooklands, England.

11-3-59
The first flight of the Sikorsky YHSS-2 (later SH-3) Sea King helicopter is made.

10-4-59
The first flight of the Northrop T-38A Talon lightweight supersonic trainer for the U.S. Air Force is made by Lew Nelson.

20-4-59
The Ilyushin Il-18 four-propjet airliner first enters service with Aeroflot on a number of internal routes based on Moscow.

12-5-59
Sud Caravelle twin-jet airliners first enter service with Air France on the Paris-Rome-Istanbul route.

-7-59
First deliveries of the Convair F-106 Delta Dart supersonic interceptor fighter are made to the U.S. Air Defense Command.

-10-59
The first round-the-world jet passenger service is opened by Pan American World Airways using Boeing 707s. The first to fly the service is a Boeing 707-321, "*Jet Clipper Windward*".

1960

15-3-60
The first U.S. Air Force unit to be activated with the Convair B-58A Hustler four-jet supersonic delta-wing bomber is the 43rd Bomb Wing at Carswell Air Force Base.

The British Aircraft Corporation TSR-2 supersonic bomber prototype. Arguably the most advanced bomber ever produced in Europe, the TSR-2 was, between 1959 and 1964, the cornerstone of British Air Staff future planning but was finally overcome by repeated political opposition on the grounds of high costs. Despite numerous radical features and advanced equipment it was abandoned after about three prototyyes had been completed; within three years the British Government was obliged to purchase several hundred American combat aircraft – none of which fully performed the TSR-2's rôle

6-4-60	The Short SC.1 experimental vertical take-off aircraft achieves its first transition from vertical to horizontal flight and back.
9-4-60	The first flight of the prototype Grumman A2F-1 (later A-6A) Intruder carrier-based attack bomber for the U.S. Navy is made.
1-5-60	A Lockheed U-2 long-range surveillance aircraft of the U.S. Air Force, flown by Francis Gary Powers, is shot down near Sverdlovsk while on a high-altitude "spy" mission over the U.S.S.R. The publicity which attended Russian indignation reveals that the U.S.A. had been engaged in these flights for some months previously.
-6-60	The first flight of the Russian Tupolev Tu-124 twin-jet, airliner is made.
6-7-60	The first Potez Air Fouga Magister to be assembled by Israeli Aircraft Industries is delivered to the Israeli Defence Force/Air Force.
29-7-60	The first flight of the French Max Holste (Nord) Super Broussard feederliner is made.
19-9-60	A Douglas DC-6B of World Airways bursts into flames shortly after take-off from Guam, and all 78 occupants are killed.
12-10-60	The first tethered hovering trials of the prototype Hawker P.1127 (*XP831*) vertical take-off aircraft start at Dunsfold, Surrey, "flown" by A. W. ("Bill") Bedford, Hawker's Chief Test Pilot.
-12-60	The first McDonnell F4H-1 Phantom II supersonic shipboard fighters are delivered to U.S. Navy squadrons (commencing with VF-101).

16-12-60	**In the worst air disaster to date** a United Air Lines Douglas DC-8 collides with a Trans-World Airlines Super Constellation over Brooklyn, New York. 134 lives are lost.
1961	
24-4-61	The huge Tupolev Tu-114 *Rossiya* first enters Aeroflot service on the Moscow-Khabarovsk route, flying the route non-stop.
9-5-61	The first deliveries of the Boeing B-52H Stratofortress are made to the U.S. Strategic Air Command's 379th Strategic Wing at Wurtsmith Air Force Base.
26-5-61	Flying from New York to Paris in a Convair B-58A Hustler, William R. Payne sets a new point-to-point speed record at 1,090·93 m.p.h. (1,753·07 kph), crossing the Atlantic in 3 hr. 19 min. 44·53 sec.
28-6-61	The Austrian Air Force receives the first of a batch of Swedish SAAB-29F fighter-bombers.
2-7-61	The Indonesian Air Force takes delivery of the first batch of Russian Tupolev Tu-16 bombers.
24-7-61	The Royal Canadian Air Force's No. 412 Sqdn takes the first Canadian deliveries of the McDonnell F-101B Voodoo all-weather interceptor.
10-8-61	The first European-built Lockheed F-104G Super Starfighter (destined for the *Luftwaffe*) makes its first flight at Manching, Bavaria.
14-8-61	The first flight is made of the first Canadair-built CF-104 Starfighter at Montreal by

Robert Kidd; it flies at Mach 2 on its first flight.

12-10-61 The first French pre-production Dassault Mirage IVA twin-jet supersonic strategic bomber is flown at Melun-Villaroche.

1-11-61 The first Avro 748 "Subroto" to be assembled in India is flown at Kanpur.

11-11-61 The first Fokker-built Lockheed F-104G Super Starfighter is flown at Schipol, Amsterdam, by Fokker's Chief Test Pilot, A. P. Moll.

22-11-61 A new world's speed record is established by America when a McDonnell F4H-1F Phantom fighter flies at 1,606·51 m.p.h. (2585·43 kph), flown by Lt. Col. Robert B. Robinson, U.S.A.F., at Edwards Air Force Base, California.

4-12-61 The first Belgian-assembled Lockheed F-104G Super Starfighter is flown at Gosselies.

14-12-61 The second prototype Hawker P.1127 vertical take-off aircraft (*XP836*) crashes, but without injury to the pilot, Bill Bedford, who ejects safely at very low level.

1962

9-1-62 The prototype de Havilland Trident (*G-ARPA*) three-jet medium-range airliner makes its first flight at Hatfield, Hertfordshire.

31-1-62 The Brazilian Air Force receives the first of six ex-U.S.A.F. Fairchild C-119 Packet transports.

23-2-62 The supersonic version of the Bristol Olympus engine makes its first flight in the bomb-bay of an Avro Vulcan bomber.

5-3-62 Flying from Los Angeles to New York in a Convair B-58A Hustler supersonic bomber, Robert G. Sowers establishes a new coast-to-coast record of 1,216·47 m.p.h. (1954 kph), completing the flight in 2 hr. 58·71 sec.

14-4-62 First flight of the Bristol Type 188 research aircraft is made at Boscombe Down, England, flown by Godfrey Auty; this aircraft is constructed almost entirely of stainless steel.

22-4-62 On a flight from the United States to Europe in a Lockheed Jetstar, Miss Jacqueline Cochrane sets up over 30 point-to-point speed records, almost all of which still stand ten years later.

3-6-62 An Air France Boeing 707 crashes on take-off at Paris and 130 lives are lost.

9-6-62 The first Italian-assembled Lockheed F-104G (by Fiat) is flown by Cdr. Vittorio Sanseverino.

22-6-62 A second Air France Boeing 707 (see above) crashes at Guadaloupe in the West Indies during a storm, killing 113 people.

Also on this day, the last Boeing B-52H Stratofortress is completed at Wichita. A total of 744 of these large bombers have been built.

27-6-62 The North American X-15A-2, in the course of ultra-high-speed trials at very high altitude, achieves a speed of 4,104 m.p.h. (6605 kph, Mach 5·92), flown by J. A. Walker.

29-6-62 The first flight of the Vickers VC-10 four-jet airliner is made by G. R. ("Jock") Bryce, from Brooklands to Wisley, Surrey.

7-7-62 Russia establishes a new world speed record with a Sukhoi "Type E-166" aircraft at 1,665·89 m.p.h. (2681·00 kph) flown by Col. Georgiy Mosolov, at Siderovo, Tyumenskaya, U.S.S.R.

-8-62 The first tethered hovering flight trials of the French Dassault-Sud Mirage Balzac V vertical take-off research aircraft start at Melun-Villaroche.

2-10-62 The twin-jet Tupolev Tu-124 airliner first enters service with Aeroflot on the Moscow-Tallinn route.

31-10-62 The Russian Antonov An-24 twin-propjet medium-capacity airliner first enters Aeroflot service on the Kiev-Kherson route.

-11-62 The first squadron of the Japanese Air Self Defence Force (No. 201 Sqdn.) to receive the Lockheed F-104J Starfighter receives its first aircraft (including two F-104DJ trainers).

1963

17-1-63 The prototype Short Skyvan light freight aircraft makes its first flight.

1-2-63 First deliveries are made of the Grumman A-6 Intruder to a U.S. Navy Squadron (VA-42). A Middle East Airlines Vickers Viscount airliner collides with a Turkish Douglas C-47 over Ankara, Turkey, killing 95 people.

14-2-63 The Indian Air Force receives the first of a batch of MiG-21 fighters from Russia.

25-2-63 The first prototype Transall C.160 bi-national transport flies for the first time at Melun-Villaroche, France.

-3-63 The Pakistan Air Force takes delivery of the first two of four Lockheed C-130 Hercules transports being supplied by the U.S.A.

18-3-63 The Dassault Balzac V vertical take-off research aircraft achieves its first transitions between vertical and horizontal flight.

9-4-63 The Royal Australian Air Force takes delivery of its first (French-built) Dassault

	Mirage III0 fighter at Melun-Villaroche, France.
4-5-63	The prototype Dassault Mystère 20 6/10-passenger makes its first flight at Bordeaux-Merignac, France.
19-5-63	A Boeing VC-137 (707) of the U.S. Air Force flies from Washington, D.C., to Moscow, flown by Col. J. B. Swindal, setting up new point-to-point speed records *en route* between Washington, Philadelphia, New York, Boston, Baltimore, Oslo, Stockholm and Moscow. The same aircraft returns two days later.
3-6-63	A chartered Northwest Airlines Douglas DC-7 crashes into the sea off British Columbia, Canada, killing 101 people.
29-6-63	The Swedish prototype SAAB-105 trainer/light attack aircraft is flown for the first time by Karl-Erik Fernberg.
28-7-63	A D.H. Comet airliner of the United Arab Republic Airlines crashes into the sea off Bombay, India, all 62 on board being killed.
2-9-63	A Sud Caravelle of Swissair crashes on take-off at Zurich, Switzerland, killing 80 people.
-9-63	The German VJ 101 C X1 experimental vertical take-off aircraft achieves transitions between vertical and horizontal flight.
16-10-63	Flying a Convair B-58A Hustler bomber from Tokyo to Anchorage, Maj. S. J. Kubesch, U.S.A.F., establishes a new point-to-point speed record of 1,095·08 m.p.h. (1759·73 kph), completing the flight in 3 hr. 9 min. 41·8 sec.
16-11-63	The first Australian-assembled Dassault Mirage III0 fighter flies for the first time at Avalon, near Melbourne.
29-11-63	A Trans-Canada Airlines Douglas DC-8F crashes on take-off at Montreal, Canada, killing 118 on board.
17-12-63	The first Lockheed C-141A StarLifter strategic transport makes its first flight at Atlanta, Georgia.

1964

5-1-64	The first Short Belfast strategic freighter makes its first flight from Sydenham, Belfast, Northern Ireland.
10-1-64	The French Dassault Balzac V vertical take-off research aircraft crashes at Melun-Villaroche, killing the pilot.
1-2-64	The Boeing 727 three-jet airliner first enters passenger-carrying operation, an Eastern Airlines aircraft flying the Miami-Washington route.
7-3-64	The first Hawker Siddeley Kestrel (*XS688*) vertical take-off close-support aircraft makes its first flight at Dunsfold, Surrey,

	flown by Bill Bedford.
-3-64	The Royal Australian Air Force takes delivery of the first of a batch of 15 D.H.C. Caribou transport aircraft from Canada.
9-4-64	The first D.H.C.5 Buffalo STOL transport makes its first flight in Canada.
16-4-64	Greece takes delivery of the first of 36 Lockheed F-104G Super Starfighters for the Royal Hellenic Air Force.
4-6-64	The first flight is made by the French Dassault Mirage IIIT.
31-7-64 1-8-64	A point-to-point speed record is set up between London and Reykjavik by Lord Trefgarne (*et al*) in a D.H. Dragonfly at a speed of 36·07 m.p.h. (57·97.kph). He flies on to New York from Reykjavik to New York at a new record speed of 33·87 m.p.h. (54·43 kph).
2-10-64	A U.T.A. Douglas DC-6 airliner crashes at Granada, Spain, killing 70 people.
15-10-64	A three-nation evaluation squadron is formed at West Raynham, England, with pilots from the R.A.F., U.S.A.F., U.S. Navy, U.S. Army, and the *Luftwaffe*, to evaluate the operational potentialities of the Hawker Siddeley Kestrel vertical take-off close-support aircraft.

1965

-1-65	The first deliveries of a batch of 16 Hawker Siddeley Buccaneer S.Mk. 50 strike aircraft are made to the South African Air Force.
8-2-65	An Eastern Air Lines Douglas DC-7B crashes into the sea off New York killing all 84 on board.
27-2-65	The Russian Antonov An-22 *Antheus* long-range heavy transport makes its first flight.
9-4-65	The BAC One-Eleven twin-fanjet airliner first enters commercial service with British United Airways, and with Braniff International Airways on 20th April.
1-5-65	The United States recaptures the world speed record from Russia (see 7-7-62) with a flight by a Lockheed YF-12A flown by Colonel Robert L. Stephens at 2,070·10 m.p.h. (3331·51 kph) from Edwards A.F.B., California, U.S.A.
7-5-65	First flight of the first BAC Super VC-10 long-range four-fanjet airliner (*G-ASGA*) is made from Brooklands to Wisley, Surrey.
20-5-65	A Pakistan Airlines Boeing 720B crashes at Cairo Airport, Egypt, killing 121 people. The first flight of the DHC-6 Twin Otter STOL light transport is made.
25-6-65	A Boeing C-135 Stratolifter of the U.S. Air Force crashes on take-off at Los Angeles airport, killing 85 people.

The North American OV-10A Bronco

16-7-65	The first flight of the North American OV-10A Bronco counter-insurgency aircraft is made at Columbus, Ohio.
19-7-65	The first production Bréguet Atlantic twin-turboprop maritime patrol aircraft is flown. The maritime air forces of France, Germany, Holland and Italy receive a total of 87 aircraft during the next seven years.
-8-65	The Ghana Air Force takes delivery of the first of seven Italian Aermacchi MB.326F armed two-seat trainers.

1966

20-1-66	The first Service deliveries of the Short Belfast four-turboprop strategic freight transport are made to No. 53 Sqdn., R.A.F., at Brize Norton, England.
4-2-66	In the **worst air disaster to date involving a single aircraft,** an All-Nippon Boeing 727 airliner crashes into Tokyo Bay, killing all 133 persons on board.
5-3-66	A B.O.A.C. Boeing 707 with 124 persons on board crashes on Mount Fuji, Japan, killing all occupants. This is **Britain's worst air disaster to date.**
31-8-66	The first pre-production Hawker Siddeley Harrier V/STOL tactical support aircraft is flown from Dunsfold, England.
24-12-66	A Canadair CL44, chartered by American authorities, crashes into a village in South Vietnam, killing 129 people.
27-12-66	The first flight is made by the Fiat G91Y prototype tactical reconnaissance fighter – a twin-engine development of the successful single-engine G91.

1967

8-2-67	The first prototype of the Swedish Saab-37 *Viggen* (= Thunderbolt) multi-mission combat aircraft makes its first flight.
10-2-67	The prototype Dornier Do 31 E 3 experimental V/STOL transport aircraft makes its first flight. This is powered by two 15,000-lb.s.t. Bristol Pegasus and eight 4,400-lb.s.t. Rolls-Royce RB.164-4D engines.
-3-67	The Brazilian Air Force orders six DHC-5 Buffalo STOL utility transports. This order is later increased to 18.
3-3-67	The Russian Beriev Be-30 twin-turboprop STOL transport makes its first flight.
9-4-67	The prototype Boeing 737 twin-fanjet airliner makes its first flight. Within three years of this date 170 production aircraft are delivered to 24 airlines.
9-5-67	The first Fokker F.28 Fellowship 55/65-seat twin-fanjet airliner (*PH-JHG*) makes its first flight.
23-5-67	The prototype Hawker Siddeley Nimrod four-fanjet maritime reconnaissance aircraft makes its first flight.
18-8-67	The first prototype Handley Page H.P.137 Jetstream twin-jet light transport (*G-ATXH*) makes its first flight at Radlett, Hertfordshire, England.
-9-67	Aeroflot first introduces the Tupolev Tu-134 twin-fanjet airliner on its Moscow-Stockholm route.
5-10-67	The first prototype of the Japanese Shin Meiwa PX-3 (*5801*) anti-submarine four-turboprop flying-boat makes its first flight.
6-11-67	The first U.S. Navy Squadron (VA-147) with Vought Corsair II shipboard attack fighters sails for Vietnam aboard the U.S.S. *Ranger*.
18-11-67	First flight of the Dassault Mirage G swing-wing experimental fighter is made at Istres,

France, and within two months reaches a speed of Mach 2·1 with wings fully-swept to 70°.

28-12-67   The first production Hawker Siddeley Harrier GR.1 vertical take-off aircraft makes its first flight at Dunsfold, Surrey.

1968

28-6-68   The first production Hawker Siddeley Nimrod maritime reconnaissance aircraft for the R.A.F. makes its first flight.

30-6-68   **The world's largest aircraft,** the prototype Lockheed C-5 Galaxy four-turbofan logistic transport, makes its first flight. In little over a year later the first production aircraft is handed over to the U.S. Military Airlift Command.

-7-68   The Swiss Air Force takes delivery of the first Swiss-built Dassault Mirage III-RS supersonic tactical reconnaissance aircraft, the total of 18 aircraft being divided between *Nrs. 16* and *17 Fliegerkompagnie*. In the same month the Russian airline Aeroflot inaugurates the Moscow-New York passenger service with Ilyushin Il-62 long-range four-fanjet 114/168-seat airliners.

8-9-68   The first flight is made by the first SEPECAT Jaguar (E-01, a French-built two-seater).

11-9-68   The prototype Dassault MD 320 Hirondelle (*F-WPXP*) 10/12-seat utility/executive transport is first flown at Bordeaux-Mérignac, France.

4-10-68   The first Russian Tupolev Tu-154 tri-fanjet airliner is flown for the first time.

31-12-68   The first Russian Tupolev Tu-144 supersonic airliner makes its first flight.

1969

9-2-69   The first Boeing 747 "jumbo-jet" high-capacity airliner makes its first flight.

2-3-69   The first prototype of the BAC-Aérospatiale Concorde (French-built, *"001"*) supersonic airliner makes its first flight.

16-3-69   In **the worst air disaster to date,** a Douglas DC-9 of Venezuelan Air Lines crashes on Maracaibo, Venezuela, with the loss of all on board, and many others on the ground. At least 155 deaths are reported.

1-4-69   The first R.A.F. squadron, No. 1 (Fighter) Sqdn., Wittering, takes delivery of the first Hawker Siddeley Harrier GR.1s. It is thus the **first squadron in the world to operate at full combat status with vertical take-off fixed-wing combat aircraft.**

22-4-69   The first Hawker Siddeley Harrier T.Mk. 2 two-seat trainer is flown by Duncan Simpson from Dunsfold, England.

1-10-69   The first prototype Concorde (*001*) flies at supersonic speed for the first time.

-10-69   The Russian Tupolev Tu-144 supersonic airliner flies at supersonic speed for the first time.

14-11-69   The shipboard prototype of the SEPECAT Jaguar M-05 makes its first flight at Melun-Villaroche.

-11-69   The British state-owned company, Beagle Ltd, is placed in the hands of a receiver.

11-12-69   The first flight of the Hawker Siddeley Trident 3B airliner is made from Hatfield, Hertfordshire.

1970

31-1-70   Dr. Mikhail Mil, the greatest of all Soviet helicopter designers, dies in Moscow after a long illness.

27-2-70   The Abu Dhabi Defence Force takes delivery of the first of twelve Hawker Hunter ground-attack and fighter reconnaissance aircraft.

-7-70   The U.S. Air Force, having decided to adopt the U.S. Navy's Vought A-7D Corsair II shipboard attack fighter, takes delivery of the first aircraft destined for the 57th Fighter Weapons Wing at Nellis A.F.B. for development to Air Force Requirements.

-8-70   The pioneer British aircraft manufacturing company, Handley Page Ltd, having been placed in the hands of a receiver some months previously, is wound up. The work in hand is re-contracted with Hawker Siddeley and Scottish Aviation.

-10-70   The first Indian-manufactured Mikoyan MiG-21 supersonic fighter is handed over to the Indian Air Force.

19-12-70   A new world speed record for helicopters is set up by the American Sikorsky S-67 Blackhawk flown by Kurt Cannon over a 15/25-km course at 220·885 m.p.h. (355·485 kph).

21-12-70   The first prototype of the Grumman F-14A Tomcat carrier-based multi-mission aircraft for the U.S. Navy makes its first flight. On 30th December, during its second flight, the aircraft crashes, but both occupants escape unhurt.

1971

14-1-71   The first McDonnell Douglas F-4EJ Phantom built for Japan in the U.S.A. makes its first flight; 13 such pattern aircraft are to be delivered prior to manufacture of about 180 by Mitsubishi at Nagoya, Japan.

20-1-71   The *Luftwaffe* receives its first McDonnell Douglas RF-4E Phantom reconnaissance fighters. These are scheduled to equip

Aufklarungsgeschwader 51 "Immelmann" and *Aufkl. G.52.*

21-3-71   The first Westland WG.13 Lynx helicopter, scheduled for service with the British Army, makes its first flight.

-5-71   By this month the U.S. Navy has activated 27 squadrons equipped with the Vought Corsair II shipboard attack fighter.

8-5-71   The first prototype Dassault Mirage G.8 variable-geometry aircraft makes its first flight at Istres, France, flown by Jean-Marie Saget. Within four days it flies at Mach 2.03.

-7-71   The U.S. Air Force retires its last North American F-100 Super Sabres from combat service, the last unit so equipped being the 35th Tactical Fighter Wing based at Phan Rang in Vietnam.

-7-71   By this month purchase options for the BAC/Aérospatiale Concorde supersonic airliner had all been extended by the manufacturers for between 6 and 12 months. Options for 74 aircraft are held by 16 world airlines, but as yet none has placed a firm order. Development costs, originally estimated at £300m., have to date reached £650m., and a further rise to £850m. is forecast. Unit purchase price is estimated as being £18m. per aircraft.

14-7-71   The first flight by the VFW-Fokker 614G-1 is made at Bremen, Germany.

20-7-71   The Japanese Mitsubishi XT-2 two-seat supersonic trainer makes its first flight.

-8-71   The McDonnell Douglas DC-10 (Series 10) enters passenger service for the first time with United Airlines and American Airlines.

2-11-71   The first production Anglo-French Jaguar (in this instance a two-seat E-type) is flown by Bernard Witt at Toulouse-Blagnac, France.

-11-71   The first General Dynamics F-111D swing-wing multi-mission tactical aircraft are delivered to the 27th Tactical Fighter Wing, Cannon Air Force Base, New Mexico.

3-12-71
17-12-71   The Indo-Pakistan War. In this disastrous conflict the Indian Air Force is constantly on the offensive both against East and West Pakistan. According to reports current after the cease-fire, the Indian Air Force lose 45 aircraft in the air and a further 27 on the ground. The Pakistan Air Force lose 62 aircraft in the air and 32 on the ground.

17-12-71   The first flight of the first pre-production BAC-Aérospatiale Concorde *"01"* is made from Filton, England.

1972

21-1-72   The first prototype Lockheed S-3A Viking anti-submarine aircraft makes its first flight at Palmdale, California.

1-4-72   No. 41 (Fighter) Sqdn., R.A.F., having been disbanded in 1962, is re-formed in No. 38 Group, Air Support Command, R.A.F., with McDonnell Douglas Phantom FGR.2s, being based at Coningsby, Lincolnshire.

26-4-72   The first revenue services are flown by the Lockheed L.1011 TriStar three-jet airliner with Eastern Airlines on the Miami-Atlanta and Miami-New York routes in the U.S.A.

4-5-72   The first production SEPECAT Jaguar fighter is delivered for final acceptance trials by the *Armée de l' Air*. A three-month labour strike in the British Aviation Corporation's Warton factory puts the British production well behind that of France, and considerably delays deliveries to the R.A.F.

10-5-72   The first flight of the prototype Fairchild A-10A close-support aircraft is made.

30-5-72   The first flight of the prototype Northrop A-9A close-support aircraft is made at Edwards Air Force Base, California.

-6-72   B.O.A.C. places the first orders for the BAC/Aérospatiale Concorde supersonic airliner. Deliveries are scheduled for early 1975.

6-6-72   With the disbanding of No. 16 Sqdn., R.A.F., the English Electric Canberra is retired from the R.A.F. after 21 years' operational service. American derivatives, as well as Canberras in several other world air forces, continue at operational status.

18-6-72   A British European Airways Hawker Siddeley Trident IC (*G-ARPI*) crashes at Staines, Berkshire, England, killing all on board. This is **the worst disaster in British aviation history.**

21-6-72   The intercontinental version of the McDonnell Douglas DC-10 (the Series 30) is first flown.

29-8-72   The first Vought YA-7H Corsair II two-seat trainer is flown by John Konrad at Dallas Naval Air Station, Texas.

-12-72   As delays in peace negotiations to bring to an end American involvement in the Vietnam War continue, a substantial increase in the American bombing by B-52Hs of towns in the North is ordered. During the last half of the month these large aircraft fly upwards of 800 sorties, some prominence being given to the losses suffered. In fact a total of 17 of the 8-jet bombers were lost in 16 days.

CHAPTER 2

The World's Air Forces

The Lockheed F-104A Starfighter which, between 1955 and 1972, equipped more than a dozen world air forces

The pages which follow present a brief and necessarily undetailed survey of the growth and present levels of air power in 113 nations of the world. In each case the compilers have attempted to give the date and nature of the first appearance of the national air arm, and an indication of its original equipment; high points in the history of the service since that time; current estimates of manpower and aircraft strengths; and a list of the major military airfields.

The basis of the information quoted is, not unnaturally, an up-dating of material previously published elsewhere, in the several works which have been devoted entirely to analyses of this type in recent years. With certain obvious exceptions – such as Communist bloc forces – the responsible military authorities have been given the opportunity to comment on the accuracy of these estimates. In several cases they have declined to do so, on security grounds; others have been extremely helpful, and their adjustments have been carefully incorporated.

The compilers make no apology for the frequent use of the word "approximately" in the air force equipment lists which follow. As already stated, many air forces are less than anxious to advertise their orders of battle, and the manufacturers who supply them are subject to the same constraints. Again, it would be a confident man who felt able to quote exact numbers of training aircraft in service in any air force in the knowledge that it would be six months at least before his estimate was published. The compilers believe that a generally accurate picture of national air strengths emerges from this Chapter, and are more concerned to convey the essential nature of a force than to present minutely accurate statistics. They believe that the reader will find it of more value to know that the

Ruritanian Air Corps took delivery of North American F-86F Sabres in 1965, following a change of government in a neighbouring state, than that there are currently 55 rather than 67 Sabres operational. Aircraft are rarely purchased in a vacuum; the reasons for a particular acquisition often lie over the nearest international frontier, and it is for this reason that the countries of the world are here divided into five major groups, by geographical area.

The composition of an air force can speak volumes about the country which pays for it. From the size of the force may be deduced the financial position of the country, the proportion of funds available for defence, and useful pointers to the nature of the country's relations with her neighbours and the degree of sophistication achieved by her industries. The origin of her military aircraft is an indication of her stance in international relations, but a subtle one. India operates MiG-21s and Sukhoi Su-7Bs, but is by no means a member of the Eastern bloc. What common creed binds the operators of the ubiquitous Dassault Mirage III? A small and unsophisticated air force may argue stagnation, and a token gesture for reasons of domestic prestige, as in some of the remoter Central American and African states, where half a dozen Mustangs or MiG-15s rust peacefully beneath their flamboyant markings. Yet a score of North American T-28D piston-engined trainers, fitted out for light strike missions, may point the way to a vigorous counter-insurgency campaign being waged with unobtrusive Western support against dissidents financed from the East.

Again, an air force which seems large and sophisticated to a degree out of all proportion to the size and prominence of the country in question can draw the observer's attention to a number of special factors. Israel is the most obvious example – a tiny nation whose uniquely hostile neighbours, and unique human resources, have combined to produce the most skilled airmen in the world, flying a selection of enormously powerful aircraft. Libya boasts more than 100 Dassault Mirage fighters; but in fact only some 40 have been delivered, further deliveries are shrouded in uncertainty, and it will be a generation before there are 100 Libyan pilots trained to a standard which would pose a threat to any modern power. There is Saudi Arabia – a high, desolate, ambiguous country which in many ways still follows the paths of an earlier age of the world. Oil revenues have provided great riches, and a picturesque but extremely well-informed and vigorous monarchy has invested in a ready-made air defence system. Though Saudi Arabia is in many ways more isolated from the centres of world affairs than Libya, her purchases show a realism which rightly impresses her restless neighbours. Supersonic interceptors, a radar chain, missile batteries and integrating headquarters are operated by "contract" personnel from overseas while local replacements are being trained – and a useful back-up force of perfectly adequate ground attack types shows that the deadly toys of the 20th century have not blinded the Saudis to the less glamorous requirements of everyday life in the Middle East.

It is interesting to reflect on the ways in which various countries have faced the problems of the enormously increased cost of military aircraft. In the 1930s and 1940s an entire squadron of fighters or reconnaissance-bombers, to the latest international standards of performance, could be acquired for less than the cost of a single example of one of today's ultra-sophisticated machines. After the post-War surplus glut had become a golden memory for war-shattered European nations and ambitious *generalissimos*, the problem of replacements loomed. With the jet age came an increasing sophistication, and soaring costs. Each new combat type carried more of its controlling organisation into the air with it; the requirements of interception, low-level strike, all-weather navigation, radio countermeasures, automatic reconnaissance cameras, fire control computers – all increased the size, weight, power, complexity, and therefore the cost of the combat aircraft. Soon only the super-powers could afford an advanced air force at all; the less wealthy had to put up with cheap job lots of obsolescent types from the super-powers' constantly-changing inventory, with all the political implications of that situation. Now the manufacturers have realised that there are few nations in the world for whom F-111s or MiG-23s are a realistic, cost-effective buy. The smaller, simpler, cheaper and infinitely more practical Northrop F-5A or Tiger II, the Douglas Skyhawk, or even the venerable Hawker Hunter offer a much more useful air force for the majority of nations. The probability is

overwhelming that most of today's wars will require numbers of relatively unsophisticated, versatile ground-attack aircraft rather than ultra-modern air superiority designs. The war of the 1960s and 1970s is the war of the mined bridge and the ambushed jungle trail, the raided armoury and the stealthy bazooka-squad – Mao's "war of the flea".

If technology has increasingly placed the most up-to-date aircraft out of reach of all but the richest air forces, it has at least come up with a valuable consolation prize for the less generously funded. The great advances in self-contained weapons systems – "bolt-on goodies" in the shape of rocket pods and gun-packs – have brought effective counter-insurgency forces back within the reach of those most likely to need them, and least able to pay fancy prices for their equipment. The continued use of the ancient Douglas Skyraider in South-East Asia was the first significant step along this road. Now it is conventional wisdom that a T-28 or a SAAB-MFI 15, with a minimum of pilot and fuel-tank protection and a deadly load of underwing stores, can be the answer to a hard-pressed government's prayer. Trainers, with their low stalling speeds and generally good low-speed handling, make excellent counter-insurgency aircraft; and purpose-built developments, the "armed trainers" which appear frequently in the following lists, have begun to appear in numbers.

As long ago as 1957 a government minister of a major European power was able to command a respectful audience for a policy document which looked forward to the imminent disappearance of the manned combat aircraft in favour of the missile. Now, sixteen years later, aviation has changed out of all recognition. While technology continues to surpass itself in the production of such dream machines as the Concorde and SR-71, the MiG-23 and the Tupolev "Backfire", at the other end of the scale war-planes are being designed to a standard of cheapness and simplicity which recalls a previous generation; and there is no sign as yet that either avenue of development will reach a natural halt in the foreseeable future. The helicopter has made its debut as a combat weapon already, a step which few could have envisaged in 1957; it may be that this line of development soon reaches a dead end, due to the vulnerability of the rotary-winged craft, but it is more than likely that the Hawker Siddeley Harrier and its vertical take-off progeny will come to fill basically the same battle-field requirement. The manned air force is with us for another generation at the very least. There is as yet no substitute for a skilled pilot flying a fast and manoeuvrable aircraft armed with reliable guns. There may well be more than short-term significance in the fact that American pilots over "Thud Ridge", and Israeli pilots over the Suez Canal, have learnt how to physically dodge ground-to-air and air-to-air missiles, the relentless mechanical bloodhounds that stalked the pages of high-level forecasts only a few years ago.

1. EUROPE

ALBANIA

All attempts to establish an Albanian national air arm proved abortive until 1947 when the U.S.S.R. presented the new Albanian People's Army Air Force with twelve Yakovlev Yak-3 fighters and a handful of Po-2 biplane basic trainers. Soviet aid, including Mikoyan MiG-15 jet fighters, continued to flow during the 1950s, but of late the violently pro-Chinese line taken by Tirana has led to a change of military quartermasters.

Current strength is thought to be about 2,500 men. Types operated include the Shenyang F-6, the Chinese-built version of the Mikoyan MiG-19 fighter (10 aircraft), the Shenyang F-4 or MiG-17 (approximately 30 aircraft), and residual MiG-15s from the Russian batch, totalling perhaps 20 aircraft. Transport types include the Antonov An-2 and Ilyushin Il-14 (three of each), and there are some 10 Mil Mi-1 and Mi-4 helicopters. Yakovlev Yak-18s and MiG-15UTIs make up the training force.

Main air bases are situated at Tirana, Durazzo/Shijak, Valona and Berat/Kucove.

AUSTRIA

At the end of the First World War the *Deutschösterreichische Fliegertruppe* was formed in an attempt to retain wartime pilots and aircraft in the service of the new Austrian Republic which was founded amid the ashes of the old Austro–Hungarian Empire. After brief service in the Carinthian campaign it was disbanded. Between 1936 and 1938 there was a rapid acquisition of modern equipment for the new Austrian air force, and by the time it was amalgamated with the *Luftwaffe* in the latter year some ten squadrons were operational.

When Austria became a sovereign state once more in 1955, the *Österreichische Luftstreitkräfte* was formed with small numbers of Russian-built trainers. The first jets were three de Havilland Vampire trainers acquired in 1957. Currently the force has a personnel strength of about 4,000, and two combat squadrons each operating 20 SAAB 105E strike aircraft. Transports include the DHC-2 Beaver (six aircraft) and the Short Skyvan (two aircraft); and 59 helicopters are operated, of several French and American models. There is an assortment of training machines, including Vampires, Potez Magisters and North American T-6G Texans.

Main airfields are at Vienna/Schwechat, Tulln, Linz, Galzendoort, Graz/Thalerhof, Klagenfurt, Salzburg and Innsbruck.

BELGIUM

Military aviation in Belgium dates back to an army balloon unit in the first decade of the century. Aircraft were acquired in 1911. The *Compagnie des Aviateurs,* of four squadrons, was formed in 1913, and in the early days of the First World War Belgian airmen flew their handful of Farmans on reconnaissance missions. The force was reorganised on much more effective lines, as the *Aviation Militaire,* in 1915; several British, French and Italian combat types were acquired and flown in action with great distinction by the small air arm in the remaining years of the War. Some 65 Belgian airmen lost their lives. There was the inevitable cut-back in strength during the inter-War years.

When Germany attacked on 10th May 1940, the *Aeronautique Militaire* (renamed in 1925) mustered some 3,000 personnel and about 180 first-line aircraft, many of them biplanes of obsolescent design, but including a small number of Gloster Gladiators and Hawker Hurricanes. Most Belgian aircraft were destroyed on the ground, and the remainder in a series of gallant but

The MiG-17 fighter. The Russian second-generation jet aircraft which was built in large numbers during the nineteen-fifties and widely exported to Communist-bloc air forces; it is still in service in several countries, and is shown here in the markings of the Egyptian Air Force

hopeless dogfights. A number of Belgian personnel subsequently reached the U.K. and flew with the R.A.F.; in all, some 1,200 Belgians served as air- and ground-crew in the R.A.F., and two Belgian squadrons were formed within that Service. Others, based in the Congo in 1940, reached South Africa and served with the S.A.A.F. in North Africa. In 1946 the Belgian elements in the R.A.F. were disbanded and the *Force Aérienne Belge* was established.

Current strength is around 20,500 men. The two main combat types operated are the Lockheed F-104G Starfighter (some 100 aircraft equip four squadrons) and the Dassault Mirage 5BR and 5BA. There are 27 Mirage 5BAs, 63 Mirage 5BRs, and 16 Mirage 5BD trainers on the inventory. The transports in service include the C-119G Packet (approximately 33 aircraft in two squadrons); Douglas C-47, Douglas C-54, Douglas DC-6B and Hunting Pembroke types (totalling 23 aircraft) will be partially replaced during 1973 by twelve Lockheed C-130H Hercules due for delivery in March 1973. There are ten helicopters in service, and apart from the Mirage 5BDs mentioned above training is carried out on the Savoia-Marchetti SF.260 (36 aircraft), the Potez Magister (40 aircraft) and residual Lockheed T-33A aircraft.

Main airfields are at Beauvechain, Florennes, Bierset, Kleine Brogel, Melsbroek, Goetsenhoven, Brustem and Coxyde.

BULGARIA

The Bulgarian Army Aviation Corps operated Blériot and Bristol aircraft against the Turks as early as 1912–13, and during the First World War it served as a satellite force of the Central Powers. Between 1918 and 1937, in accordance with the Treaty of Neuilly, no military air arm was maintained. In 1937 the treaty was renounced and some eighty Polish aircraft were acquired. Bulgaria joined the Axis in 1941 and received considerable military aid including nearly 200 Messerschmitt Bf 109 fighters and 100 captured French Dewoitine D.520s. In 1944 Russia invaded the country, and thereafter it passed into the Soviet sphere of influence.

Today the Bulgarian Air Force has some 12,000 men and about 250 combat machines. Types in service include the Mikoyan MiG-21 (approximately 24 aircraft in two squadrons), the MiG-19 (approximately 72 aircraft in six squadrons), the MiG-17 ground-attack fighter (approximately 130 aircraft in eleven squadrons) and the MiG-17C reconnaissance fighter (approximately 24 aircraft in two squadrons). There is a single squadron of some dozen Ilyushin Il-28 jet reconnaissance-bombers. A transport fleet of about 30 machines includes Ilyushin Il-14, Ilyushin Il-12 and Lisunov Li-2 aircraft. There are some 30 helicopters in service, of Mil Mi-4 type, and numbers of MiG-15UTI, L-29 Delfin, Yak-11 and Yak-18 trainers.

There are major airfields at Sofia/Vrajdebna and Bozhurishte, and others at Telish, Tolbukhin, Balchik, Burgas, Yambol, Stara Zagora, Plovdiv, Graf Ignatiev and Karlovo.

CZECHOSLOVAKIA

The Czechoslovak Army Air Force was formed immediately after nationhood was achieved in 1918, based on wartime Czech Legion personnel from France and Russia, and with assistance from the French Government. By 1928 the force had 400 aircraft in 25 squadrons, with many nationally-designed and produced aircraft among them. Ten years later the Munich Agreement sold the country's future to Hitler, and in 1939 German troops split the republic in two at gunpoint. Czech refugee airmen had a distinguished record with the French air force in 1940 and thereafter with the R.A.F. (A Czech pilot was the top-scoring fighter pilot in the R.A.F. during the Battle of Britain.) A puppet Slovak Air Force operated alongside the *Luftwaffe* in Russia, with neither enthusiasm nor distinction.

For the brief period of national independence after the Second World War, the reborn Czech Air Force operated a mixture of captured *Luftwaffe* and surplus R.A.F. and Red Air Force equipment. In 1948 the Communist take-over was quickly followed by a ruthless purge of Western influence, and Russian equipment and organisation took over.

Currently the *Csekoslovenske Letectvo* musters about 18,000 men and some 600 combat aircraft, including the Mikoyan MiG-21 (approximately 150 aircraft), the MiG-19 (approximately 100 aircraft), the MiG-17 (approximately 80 aircraft), the MiG-15 (approximately 80), the Sukhoi Su-7B (approximately 150) and the Ilyushin Il-28 (approximately 60). A transport fleet of about 60 aircraft includes Antonov An-2 and An-12, Ilyushin Il-14 and Lisunov Li-2 types, and some 100 helicopters of Mil Mi-1, Mi-4, Mi-6 and Mi-8 models are operated. Apart from Yak, MiG and Ilyushin types, trainers include the indigenous L-29 Delfin (approximately 150 aircraft) and similar numbers of Zlin 226 and 326 models.

Among major airfields in the country are Prešov, Sliak, Barca, Poprad, Spišská Nová Ves, Ivanka, Lučenec, Bratislava, Pieřtány, Kunovice, Otrokovice, Brno, Přerov, Mosnov, Ceské Budějovice, Čáslav, Bechyně, Dobřany, Pilsen, Chocen, Pardubice, Milovice, Mimon, Žatec, Muchovo, Klecany, Gakovice, Letnany, Kbely, Ruzyne and Cheb.

The operational readiness of the force, and the freedom which it is allowed in day-to-day flying duties, must remain doubtful; anti-Soviet feeling in the armed forces following the invasion of 1968 and the replacement of the Dubcek regime is thought to be a continuing factor.

DENMARK

In 1912 the Danish army and navy each received their first aeroplanes – a Danish B & S monoplane for the

Soviet MiG-21Fs of the Finnish Air Force. Codenamed "Fishbed" by NATO, this Mach 2 fighter serves in the U.S.S.R., Poland, Czechoslovakia, Hungary, Egypt, Romania, Afghanistan, Cuba, Indonesia, East Germany, Iraq, Syria and Yugoslavia

former, and an Henri Farman for the latter. Neutral during the First World War, the country acquired some ex-German types and a number of Avro 504s after the Armistice, together with a few Potez machines. A Naval Flying Corps and Army Flying Corps were established in 1923. A reorganisation in 1932 gave the renamed Army Aviation Troops (*Haerens Flyvertropper*) an establishment of five squadrons. In 1940 four were in existence, one equipped with Gloster Gauntlets and three with Fokker C.V reconnaissance biplanes. After Denmark's occupation a few airmen made their way to Britain and flew with the R.A.F.

The two air arms were reformed after the War but worked towards amalgamation – which took place in 1950 with the establishment of the Royal Danish Air Force (*Flyvevaabnet*). The initial establishment was five squadrons, two of which flew Gloster Meteor jets.

Current strength is around 11,000 men, with seven combat squadrons. The types operated are the Lockheed F-104G Starfighter (32 aircraft), the North American F-100D Super Sabre (32 aircraft), the SAAB F-35 and RF-35 Draken (32 aircraft), the Hawker Hunter (16 aircraft), the Douglas C-47 (six aircraft), the Douglas C-54 (eight aircraft) and the Sikorsky S-61A helicopter (12 aircraft). The Air Force also operates for the Army a force of 12 Hughes 500M helicopters and some KZ.VII observer/liaison aircraft, and for the Navy eight Sud Alouette III helicopters.

Main airfields are situated at Aalborg, Karup, Aarhus/Tirstrup, Værløse, Kastrup, Bornholm, Odense/Beldringe, Skrydstrup and Vandel, with headquarters at Vedbæk.

EIRE

The Irish Army Air Corps was formed in 1922, and equipment acquired during the early years included eight Bristol F.2B Fighters and four Martinsyde Buzzards, six D.H.9 bombers and six Avro 504K trainers. New equipment was ordered in 1929, at which time the personnel strength was 27 officers and 126 other ranks. An establishment of three weak squadrons was maintained during the Second World War, equipped with a few Gloster Gladiators, Avro Ansons and Supermarine Walrus amphibians; despite Eire's neutrality and denial of facilities to Britain during the War, deliveries of Hawker Hurricanes were carried out in 1943.

The armed forces have received a generally low priority in Irish affairs since the War. The only jet aircraft acquired were a few de Havilland Vampire T.55 trainers. Three of these remain in service, together with eight DHC Chipmunks, four Provosts, two D.H. Doves, three Sud Alouette III helicopters and eight Cessna FR-172H patrol aircraft. The establishment provides for about 800 personnel.

The only military airfields are Baldonnel and Gormanston.

FINLAND

A small air arm was established during the war of independence from Russia in 1917, equipped with an assortment of German and French types mainly flown by Swedish volunteers. Following the recognition of nationhood in 1920 the Air Force (*Ilmavoimat*) was formed as a separate service, initially with mainly French equipment, although several British types were purchased in the 1920s and 1930s. The air force greatly distinguished itself – for its size – in the Winter War of 1939-40 with Russia, flying an assortment of combat types including Gloster Gladiators and Hawker Hurricanes, Brewster Buffalos and Curtiss Hawk 75s, Westland Lysanders and Bristol Blenheims. From 1941 to 1944 Finland fought against the U.S.S.R. alongside Germany, and received much German equipment including Messerschmitt Bf 109G fighters, Junkers Ju 88A and Dornier Do 17 bombers; foreign aircraft such as the Fiat G.50, Morane M.S. 406 and Fokker D.XXI were also operated. After the War Finland was restricted to an air force of 60 combat machines and 3,000 men by the Treaty of Paris. Initial post-War equipment was the Messerschmitt Bf 109G; the first jets were six D.H. Vampire FB.52s, acquired in 1955.

Current strength is 3,000. Types operated include the Mikoyan MiG-21F (20 aircraft), the Folland Gnat (nine aircraft), the Potez Magister light strike/jet trainer (16 aircraft), the Douglas C-47 (ten aircraft), the Hunting Pembroke C.53 (two aircraft) and small numbers of DHC-2 Beavers. Helicopters in service include Mil Mi-4, Sud Alouette and AB. 204B models. There are about 90 assorted trainers, including some 55 unarmed Potez Magisters and some 30 SAAB-91C Safirs. Twelve SAAB J-35 B.5 Drakens will replace the Gnats during 1973.

There are airfields at Jyväskylä, Pori, Utti, Kuopio, Tampere, and a number of other satellite sites.

FRANCE

The French *Aviation Militaire* received its first machines – a Blériot, two Farmans and two Wrights – in 1910. Expansion, and experiment with techniques and organisation, was lively. By 1914 the *Aviation Militaire* had 21 squadrons at home and four in the colonies; when aerial combat began in earnest in 1915, the first fighting squadrons were equipped with Morane-Saulnier monoplanes. The famous Roland Garros is credited with

introducing the machine-gun firing through the propeller arc; and throughout the War France's contribution of men and machines to the Allied war effort was to be enormous. Many of the great names of the first generation of air aces were French – Nungesser, Guynemer, Fonck – and French SPAD and Nieuport scouts equipped squadrons in all the main Allied air arms. By 1918 France had some 3,500 aircraft in 255 squadrons – this despite an overall figure of 60% casualties during the War.

Peacetime establishment was 180 squadrons in France and the Empire, and the inter-War years brought participation in several colonial campaigns. The *Armée de l'Air* was born as a separate service in the 1930s. The equipment situation in the years immediately prior to the Second World War was poor, owing to urgent modernisation of a force too long neglected, the nationalisation of the aircraft industry and the political instability of the republic. Foreign types were ordered as stop-gaps until new French designs currently under development could be delivered to the squadrons. In the event Germany's attack caught the French air force "between two stools" as far as procurement was concerned. The two air forces were of relatively similar numerical strength, but much French equipment was obsolescent; there were heroic episodes, but in common with other forces of the republic, the performance of the *Armée de l'Air* must be described as patchy. After numerous defections to the U.K., the Vichy regime disbanded the force in North Africa in 1942.

It was promptly reviewed by Free French elements, and by the close of the War the reborn service mustered 16 fighter squadrons, two reconnaissance squadrons, 12 bomber squadrons, and numerous transport and general duties units. Types flown included Spitfire, Thunderbolt, Mustang and Lightning fighters, Martin B-26 and Mitchell B-25 medium bombers, and Halifax heavy bombers. An expeditionary group on the Russian Front flew Yak fighters with great success. In the post-War years the re-establishment of a national aircraft industry

The Marcel Dassault Mirage III, France's most successful and widely-used close-support aircraft of the nineteen-sixties

was achieved, but in the meantime a vast assortment of British, American, German, Russian, Belgian and even Japanese aircraft were operated perforce. The air force saw extensive ground support action in Indo-China in the 1950s and in Algeria a few years later.

The current strength is around 101,000 men, organised in four main commands: Tactical Air Force (FATAC), Strategic Air Command (FAS), Air Defence Command (CAFDA), and Air Transport Command (COTAM). The total number of combat aircraft is around 550, with more than 100 transports and numerous liaison and training machines. FATAC consists of eight squadrons of Dassault Mirage IIIE, one of Mirage IIIB, three of Mirage IIIR/RD, two of North American F-100D Super Sabre, two of Dassault Mystère IVA, and two of Vautour II light strike aircraft. (Average squadron strength is about 15 machines.) FAS has Mirage IVA bombers of the nuclear *force de frappe* (58 aircraft) and Boeing KC-135F tankers (12 aircraft). CAFDA has five squadrons of Mirage IIIC, two of Vautour II, and three of Super Mystère B2. COTAM has seven tactical transport squadrons equipped with the Transall C.160 and Nord 2501; one heavy transport squadron with Bréguet 765s and Douglas DC-6Bs; two mixed light transport and liaison squadrons; and four helicopter squadrons with Sikorsky H-34s and Sud Alouette IIs and IIIs. Trainers include the Potez Magister, the M.S. 760 Paris, the M.S. 733, the Dassault Flamant, and various conversion types. Until 1971 at least, six B.A.C. Canberras were employed on special duties; and two squadrons of Douglas A-1D Skyraiders were maintained overseas.

Naval Aviation

As stated above, the naval *Service Aéronautique* dates from 1910. Maximum wartime strength was 1,260 aircraft – mainly seaplanes and reconnaissance types. In 1925 the renamed *Aéronautique Maritime* was divided up among various coastal areas and seaplane tenders. In the same year the first carrier, *Béarn*, joined the fleet, and subsequently naval aircraft supported ground troops in Morocco. In 1933 shore-based aircraft, amount to six squadrons, were handed over to the *Armée de l'Air*. During the Second World War *Béarn's* aircraft were landed and she was used for ferrying new machines from the U.S.A. Two other carriers, *Joffre* and *Painlevé*, were under construction (but never completed). After the fall of France, naval air elements which defected from Vichy to the Allies were attached to the *Armée de l'Air*. After the War France acquired two British carriers, renamed *Dixmude* and *Arromanches*; operating American types such as the Vought Corsair, Grumman Hellcat and Avenger, Douglas Dauntless and Curtiss Helldiver, they supported French ground forces in Indo-China in the late 1940s and early 1950s. Later two more carriers (*La Fayette* and *Bois-Belleau*) entered service; the first jets operated were French-built D.H. Sea Venoms.

Currently two fixed-wing carriers and two helicopter carriers are operated: *Clemenceau* and *Foch, Arromanches* and *Jeanne d'Arc*. Current aircraft strength of the *Aéronavale* amounts to about 430 aircraft, of which 129 are in first-line service; there are 28 Étendard IVM, eight Étendard IVP, 20 LTV F-8 Crusaders, 31 Bréguet Alizé, 28 Sikorsky S-58, nine Super Frelon (all in first-line service), and 61 patrol aircraft, comprising Bréguet Atlantic and Lockheed P-2 Neptunes (of which 27 and 20 respectively are in first-line service). In addition there are 164 fixed- and rotary-wing trainers, support aircraft, etc., of which 127 are in first-line service.

Army Aviation

The *Aviation Légère de l'Armée de Terre* operates about 600 helicopters (Sud Alouette II and III, SA.330 Puma, SA.341 Gazelle, Vertol H-21, Super Frelon, Bell 47 Sioux) and some 400 light fixed-wing communications and observer aircraft (Max Holste 1521M Broussards, and some Piper and Cessna types). About 40 aircraft are attached to each army division.

French military airfields include the following – though it should be noted that this is not a comprehensive list:

Nice, Mandelieu, Le Luc, Hyères, Istres, Orange, Montélimar, Montpellier, Carcassone, Toulouse/Blagnac, Tarbes, Bordeaux/Merignac, Cazaux, Cognac, Clermont, Ferrand, Lyon, Ambérieu, Rochefort, Vichy, St. Yan, Le Blanc, Avord, Dijon, Chareauoux, Nantes, Tours, Rennes, Lorient, Brest, Lannion, Carpiquet, Etampes, Chateaudun, Orléans, Evreux, Dreux, Villacoublay, Melun, Chaumont, Luxeuil, Belfort, Toul, Nancy, Strasbourg, Luneville, Chambley, Juvincourt, Châlons, Rosières, Cambrai, Valenciennes, Merville, Abbeville, St. Valéry and Bastia.

Naval air facilities include Toulon, Marignane, Hourtiquets, Lanvéoc, Les Mureaux and Ajaccio.

FEDERAL GERMAN REPUBLIC

Germany acquired her first aeroplanes – a dozen assorted Farmans, Wrights and Antoinettes – in 1910; Zeppelin dirigibles had already been in service for three years. The Naval Air Service was formed in 1911, and the army air section became the Military Aviation Service in October 1912. By 1914 the service had some 250 aircraft in 41 *Flieger-Abteilungen*, and over 1,000 personnel; the navy had 36 floatplanes. During the First World War Germany enjoyed an advantage in technical innovation or organisational excellence on several distinct occasions; the early introduction of the Fokker monoplane scout with a synchronised forward-firing machine-gun, the assembly of large units of pure fighter aircraft committed solely to aerial combat rather than reconnaissance, the bombing of London by dirigibles and huge long-range aeroplanes – all had a profound effect on aviation thinking. By 1918 the *Luftstreitkräfte* had some 80,000 officers and men, and 4,000 aeroplanes;

another 15,000 were under construction, and industrial output was nearly 20,000 machines per year.

The Treaty of Versailles saw the dispersal of existing forces and a ban on future military aviation. Aircraft were designed nevertheless, disguised as civil types, and men trained through civil flying clubs and secret foreign agreements. The *Luftwaffe* was established as a separate Service in 1935, and in the late 1930s many aircrew and aircraft were blooded in the Spanish Civil War; Germany provided Franco's Nationalist forces with an integrated expeditionary force, the *Legion Cóndor*, through which men and machines were rotated at regular intervals.

In September 1939 Germany invaded Poland, and the *Luftwaffe* displayed the vital part it could play in the new concept of "Lightning War" – involving pre-emptive strikes on enemy airfields, disruption of enemy communications and reinforcements, paratroop drops, massive ground support at the point of contact, and the maintenance of air superiority above the battlefield. Strength at that time was around 1,300 Messerschmitt Bf 109 fighters, a similar number of Dornier Do 17 and Heinkel He 111 bombers, and some 350 Junkers Ju 87 dive-bombers, backed by about 1,000 of other types; personnel stood at some 500,000. Successful in Poland, Norway and Denmark, Holland, Belgium and France by June 1940, the *Luftwaffe* suffered its first major reverse with the defeat of its daylight bombing offensive over Britain in July-September 1940. The bulk of the force moved East, and in June 1941 opened the invasion of the U.S.S.R. with a series of dazzling successes reminiscent of 1939-40. Technically superior in all respects to the Russian air arm, the Germans destroyed huge numbers of enemy aircraft in the first months. In 1942 the balance of air power in the Mediterranean swung to the Allies, and by 1943 Germany was on the defensive. A steady build-up of Russian strength from factories far out of enemy range; the intervention in Europe of the American forces, with their vast resources of men and aircraft; the loss of air superiority over the approaches to Germany in the West – all these factors combined to put the *Luftwaffe* on the defensive. With the invasion of Europe in 1944 and the almost simultaneous advance of the Red Army in the East, the *Luftwaffe* entered its last year of life. Loss of fuel sources and shortage of trained manpower crippled the Service; despite round-the-clock bombing by Allied air forces, the German industry had continued to meet high fighter production targets, and technical innovations such as the introduction of the world's first jet fighter to service (the Messerschmitt Me 262) were testimony to the continuing excellence of national design talents.

The *Luftwaffe* was resurrected in 1955, and committed to NATO. Current personnel strength is around 104,000 men. Main types operated include the Lockheed F-104G (495 aircraft), the McDonnell-Douglas RF-4E Phantom II (88 aircraft), the Fiat G.91R and T (300 aircraft), the C.160 Transall transport (82 aircraft), and the Dornier/

Bell UH-1D helicopter (134 aircraft). A variety of other transport and training aeroplanes are also in service. Some 210 McDonnell-Douglas F-4 Phantom IIs are on order for 1973.

Naval Aviation

The *Marineflieger*, established in 1957 for shore-based operations over the Baltic and North Sea, have a current strength of about 150 aircraft. The main types are the Lockheed F-104G (88 aircraft) and the Bréguet 1150 Atlantic (20 aircraft), while deliveries of 22 Westland Sea King helicopters are currently underway. Sikorsky CH-34 helicopters, Grumman HU-16 amphibians and various training and communications types are also in service.

The German airfields used mainly by the *Luftwaffe* rather than by other Allied nations include Fassburg, Celle, Wunsdorf, Geilenkirchen, Wahn, Buschel, Landsberg, Memmingen, Erding, Fürsten-Feldbruck, Manching, Neuburg, Lechfeld, Leipheim and Bad Tölz.

GERMAN DEMOCRATIC REPUBLIC

In 1955 a national air arm, the *Luftstreitkräfte und Luftverteidigung*, was formed on the basis of the air section of the *Volkspolizei*. Equipment and training were provided by Soviet and Czechoslovak sources.

Current strength is thought to be about 21,000 personnel. Types operated include the Mikoyan MiG-21 (approximately 110 aircraft), the MiG-19 (approximately 30 aircraft) and the Sukhoi Su-7B (approximately 40 aircraft). Transports include the Antonov An-2, Ilyushin Il-14M and Tupolev Tu-104. There are Mil Mi-1 and Mi-4 helicopters, and various Yakovlev, Zlin, MiG and Delfin trainers.

Airfields in East Germany are, of course, ultimately under Soviet control. It is not known which are reserved for *LSK* use under normal circumstances, but Cottbus, Drewitz, Kamenz, Bautzen, Marxwalde, Tutow, Jocksdorf and Klotsche are known to be among them.

GREECE

The Royal Hellenic Army acquired a handful of Farmans in 1912 and these saw service in the Balkan War of 1912-13. A naval air service was established in 1914 with British assistance. In 1916 the two sections were amalgamated in the Hellenic Air Service – a short-lived force which undertook some operations in the Allied cause. The two services separated, prefixing their titles with the word "Royal" and then removing it, only to restore it – according to the stormy domestic political situation. Generally the naval service "bought British" and the army "bought French" between the Wars. In 1931 a unified and separate Air Force was established at last.

Equipped with an assortment of French, Polish and British aircraft, the RHAF fought off Italian invasion in 1940, but fell to the German forces which intervened

Although originally designed as a shipboard fighter, the Mach 2 + McDonnell Douglas Phantom has entered service with the U.S.A.F., U.S. Navy, U.S. Marine Corps, the R.A.F., the Fleet Air Arm, and the air forces of Australia, Germany (as shown here), Greece, Iran, Israel, Japan and Korea. By the end of 1972 more than 4,500 had been built

in 1941. Squadrons of Free Greek personnel were formed in the Middle East by the R.A.F., and this basis for a revived RHAF was used on internal security duties during the civil war which followed liberation. It was not until Greece joined NATO in 1952 that the foundation for a realistic modern force was laid.

Today the Hellenic Air Force (see comments above) has about 23,000 personnel. Its strength is largely committed to Sixth Allied T.A.F., and main types operated include the Northrop F-5A Freedom Fighter (approximatcly 80 aircraft), the Lockheed F-104G (approximately 36 aircraft), the Convair F-102 Delta Dagger (approximately 18 aircraft), the Republic F-84F and RF-84F (approximately 80 aircraft); and transports including some 30 Douglas C-47s and smaller numbers of Nord Noratlas and Fairchild C-119G types. There are a few Grumman HU-16 amphibians, and helicopters including the Sikorsky H-19 (12 aircraft), Agusta-Bell 205 (six aircraft) and Bell 47G Sioux (ten aircraft). Training types include the Cessna T-37B and T-41, and the Lockheed T-33A.

There are airfields at Eleusis, Tatoi, Larissa, Souda, Sedes, Araxos, Thiva and Peloponessus, at Iraklion and Maleme on Crete, and at Maritsa on Rhodes.

HUNGARY

Hungary achieved nationhood in 1918 but had no air arm until 1936, when Fiat C.R.32 fighters and some Italian and German reconnaissance machines were acquired. Further Italian and German types were operated during the War when the Hungarian Army Air Force fought with the Axis in Russia; fairly extensive licence-building of German aircraft took place. Since 1949 the Communist regime has revived the air force and it has been equipped and organised under Soviet supervision.

The 1956 rising led to a lengthy period of stand-down, but in recent years the Service has taken its place once more with the other Warsaw Pact forces.

Current strength is believed to be around 20,000. There are about twelve fighter and ground-attack squadrons equipped with a total of some 150 MiG-21s, MiG-19s and Sukhoi Su-7Bs, and a single bomber squadron with Ilyushin Il-28s. Transports, helicopters and trainers include the usual mix of Ilyushin, Antonov, Mil, Yakovlev and Delfin types.

There are airfields at Miskolc, Debrecen, Matyasfold, Ferihegy, Kecskemét, Pécs, Tapolcza and Veszprém; and at Györ, Pápa, Szombathely, Szkszard, Dobovar and Tokol, although these may still be occupied by Soviet units, either wholly or partially.

ITALY

Army aviation units were established in 1911, and by 1914 the *Corpo Aeronautico Militare* had some 70 Blériot, Nieuport, Farman and Caproni machines. This figure increased to 1,800 aircraft during the First World War when Italy made a significant contribution to the Allied cause. With the appearance of Mussolini in 1923 the two Services merged their air components into the *Regia Aeronautica*, and a vigorous expansion led Italian aviation out of the post-War doldrums. By 1933 the Service had some 1,200 aircraft in 37 fighter, 34 bomber, 37 reconnaissance and several transport and maritime squadrons. The *Regia Aeronautica* sent expeditionary forces to Ethiopia and Spain in the late 1930s. When Italy entered the War on Germany's side in 1940 she had about 3,000 aircraft, of which 400 were obsolete and many others were on the borderline of obsolescence. During the period 1940–43 the *Regia Aeronautica* was mainly committed to the Mediterranean theatre, although token forces fought – and fared badly – on the Channel coast and in Russia. Once the Allies built up reasonable numbers of aircraft in the Mediterranean, the general obsolescence of Italian combat types became apparent. The most effective units were the S.M.79-equipped torpedo-bomber squadrons. Excellent airframe designs, such as the Fiat G.55 and Macchi C.202, suffered from lack of power.

After the Armistice of 1943 small air arms fought for both the Allies and the Axis, and were equipped with Italian and, respectively, American and German designs. After the War ended the *Aeronautica Militare Italiano* was formed, and in 1949 Italy joined NATO.

Current strength is about 73,000 men with about 330 combat aircraft. Types in service include the Lockheed F-104G (about 125 aircraft in six squadrons), the Fiat G.91R and G.91Y (about 100 aircraft in seven squadrons), the Republic F-84F and RF-84F (approximately 50 aircraft in four squadrons) and residual Canadair F-86K Sabres. Transports include the Fairchild C-119G, Douglas C-47, Douglas DC-6 and Convair 440, and Fiat G.222. There are about 170 helicopters – mainly Agusta-Bell 47 Sioux, Agusta-Bell 204B and Agusta A101G models. Trainers include the Aermacchi MB.326 and Savoia-Marchetti SF.260.

Airfields include Turin, Ghedi, Linate, Malpensa, Genoa, Villanova, Bergamo, Bolzano, Udine, Treviso, Padua, Venic, Bologna, Florence, Pisa, Fano, Ancona, Ciampino, Guidonia, Capodichino, Bari, Brindisi, Reggio, Catania, Comiso, Trapani, Palermo and Cagliari.

MALTA

The Royal Malta Artillery and Malta Police recently acquired four Bell 47G Sioux helicopters from Federal Germany, where personnel were trained in their use. They operate from Safi on coastal patrols.

NETHERLANDS

The Royal Netherlands Army and Indies Army acquired their first aircraft in 1911 and 1914 respectively. Neutral during the First World War, the country slowly built up its equipment from both Allied and Central Power sources, and secured numbers of ex-German machines in 1918. *Aviation Division* equipment was neglected in the 1920s and 1930s due to a neutralist stance, and a belief in the inevitability of defeat if that neutrality was violated. A last-minute attempt to provide a credible air defence led to orders at home and abroad in 1938; but by the German invasion of 1940 only some 30 Fokker D.XXI fighters and 20 Fokker G.1s, 16 Fokker T.V and 11 Douglas DB-8A bombers, and 40 or so reconnaissance machines were available for operations. These were largely destroyed after a heroic defence lasting five days. Escaped Dutch airmen formed squadrons of the R.A.F. and flew British and American fighters and bombers. In the East Indies

the Japanese attacks of 1941-42 found the Dutch with some 200 assorted aircraft – largely obsolescent; many were lost in action, but some units withdrew successfully to Australia and continued the fight. The Indies Army Air Service operated North American F-51D Mustang and Curtiss P-40N fighters and B-25 Mitchell bombers against Indonesian insurgents in the late 1940s.

The revived Army Aviation Service at home received its first jets – Gloster Meteor F.4s and F.8s – in 1948. The Netherlands joined NATO in 1952, and the following year a separate air force – *Koninklijke Luchtmacht* – was formed. Currently the Service has about 21,000 men. Equipment includes the Lockheed F-104G (90 aircraft), the TF-104G trainer (17 aircraft), and the RF-104G reconnaissance model (20 aircraft). The Northrop NF-5A and NF-5B (74 and 29 aircraft respectively) have replaced the last of the Hawker Hunters operated for many years. Transports include the Fokker F-27 Troopship (12 aircraft) and DHC-2 Beaver (nine aircraft); there are 77 Sud Alouette III helicopters and 60 Piper L-21 liaison and observation aircraft.

Naval Aviation

The story of the *Marine Luchtvaartdienst* before 1944 closely parallels that of the Army Air and Indies Army Air services. After the liberation in 1944 an aircraft carrier was acquired from Britain on loan until the light carrier *Karel Doorman* (previously H.M.S. *Venerable*) was commissioned in Dutch service on 28th May 1948. Initial carrier equipment included Fairey Firefly ground attack aircraft, Grumman Avengers, and later Hawker Sea Furies and Hawker Sea Hawk jets. The carrier was sold in 1969 and since then the only embarked aircraft have been Westland Wasp helicopters (nine aircraft) operating from *Von Speijk*-class guided missile frigates. Current equipment, apart from these helicopters, comprises the Bréguet 1150 Atlantic (nine aircraft), the Grumman S-2N Tracker (14 aircraft), the Lockheed SP-2H Neptune (17 aircraft), the Agusta-Bell UH-1 helicopter (seven aircraft) and the Beechcraft TC-45J (five aircraft).

There are military airfields at Leeuwarden, Eelde, Twenthe, Deelen, Soesterburg, Ypenburg, Zestienhoven, Volkel, Venray, Eindhoven, Zuid Limburg, Gilze-Rijen and Woensdrecht; naval air stations are located at De Kooy and Valkenburg.

NORWAY

The army and navy both acquired aeroplanes in 1912, and three years later the *Haerens Flyvapen* and *Marinens Flyvevaesen* were formed. Farman, Hansa-Brandenburg and Bristol F.2B designs were all built at Norwegian factories. Various British, American, German, Dutch and indigenous designs entered service with both forces between the Wars, but when Germany attacked in 1940 only a handful of Gloster Gladiators were available to mount a glorious but hopeless defence.

(Some 20 Curtiss Hawk 75A-4 monoplane fighters had been delivered but were still in their crates.) Escaped airmen formed two squadrons in the R.A.F. during the period 1940–44, and naval aircrews trained in Canada on aircraft which they eventually operated as part of R.A.F Coastal Command. In 1944 the *Kongelige Norske Luftforsvaret* was formed by amalgamation of the two services. Various British and American types were operated in the late 1940s, and D.H. Vampire jets were acquired in 1949. U.S. military aid was forthcoming following membership of NATO.

Current *KNL* strength is around 9,000 men. Types in service include the Lockheed F-104G (20 aircraft), the Northrop F-5A and RF-5A Freedom Fighter (80 aircraft), and the Lockheed P-3B Orion (six aircraft). Twenty-two CF-104 Starfighters are on order. Transports include the Lockheed C-130 Hercules (six aircraft), the Douglas C-47 (four aircraft) and the DHC-6 Twin Otter (four aircraft). A variety of trainers and liaison types are operated, and there are about 50 helicopters – largely Bell UH-1H Iroquois (32 aircraft) and Bell 47 Sioux models, with ten Sea Kings.

The *KNL* has for many years enjoyed an outstanding record of air safety. It operates from airfields at Gardermoen, Sola, Rygge, Bodø, Vaernes, Fornebu, Jarlsberg, Kjevik, Flesland, Bardufoss, Torp, Ørlandet, Andoya and Banak.

POLAND

Poland achieved nationhood in the confusion at the end of the First World War, and Poles who had been serving in the armed forces of several countries, Allied and Central Powers, came together bringing their equipment with them. There was confused aerial fighting in the brief war for independence, and an army air corps of seven squadrons, flying mainly French equipment, was established in 1919 and rapidly expanded. It showed to advantage in the war with Russia in 1919–20. A national aircraft industry was founded, and this provided most of the types which operated under Polish colours in the late 1920s and 1930s. Some designs were technically impressive for their day, but there were serious errors in the procurement policy, which left Poland fatally weak in 1939. Organisation of a separate Air Force, and expansion plans, came too late in 1938. When Germany invaded there were some 7,650 personnel and 678 operational machines available to the *Polskie Lotnictwo Wojskowe*, plus 760 second-line aircraft. The most effective were about 200 P.Z.L. P-11 high-wing monoplane fighters. After a spirited defence most of the air force was destroyed, the bulk of it in aerial combat and not on the ground, as German propaganda later claimed. The *PLW* inflicted substantial losses on the technically and numerically superior *Luftwaffe*, despite the mistaken policy of dispersing its strength between field armies.

Polish airmen fought in the air forces of France, Britain and the U.S.S.R., and made a significant contribution to the Allied victory. Those who had flown in the West were purged on their return to Communist Poland, and the post-War air force is completely Soviet-dominated. Current strength is about 25,000. There are thought to be 45 fighter squadrons with MiG-21, MiG-19 and MiG-17 aircraft; twelve squadrons of Sukhoi Su-7B ground-attack aircraft; three squadrons of MiG-17 reconnaissance models, and six Ilyushin Il-28 bomber squadrons. Squadron strength is believed to be 12, giving a total of about 800 combat aircraft. In addition some 50 transports of the usual Soviet types, about 50 Mil helicopters of various models, and some 300 trainers are in service.

Among the known airfields of the *PLW* are Słupsk, Gdansk, Elblag, Olsztyn, Rastemburg, Grudziadz, Stettin, Bydgószcz, Torun, Inowroclaw, Poznán, Šroda, Kutno, Warsaw, Siedlce, Brest, the Deblin complex, Świdnica, Lublin, Mielec, Krosno, Rzeszów, Cracow, Radom, Breslau, Lignica and Jelenia Góra.

PORTUGAL

Army and Navy aviation divisions were established in 1917, at which time Portugal was contributing two divisions to the Allied armies in France. Initial equipment included SPAD scouts, Bréguet bombers and Fairey flying boats. Progress in acquiring new aircraft and in organisation proceded steadily during the 1920s and 1930s. British, French and Italian types were purchased and licence-built; in 1937–38 Gloster Gladiator fighters and Hawker Hind bombers were ordered from Britain, Breda Ba.65 attack aircraft from Italy, and Junkers Ju 86 bombers from Germany. Portugal also placed the first overseas order for the Spitfire. Neutral during the Second World War but friendly to the Allies, Portugal received further British and American equipment including Hurricane, Airacobra and Curtiss Hawk 75A fighters, Bristol Blenheim and B-24 Liberator bombers, Sunderland flying boats and various second-line types. In 1957, badly in need of re-equipment, the Army and Navy air arms amalgamated to form the *Forca Aérea Portuguesa*; F-84G Thunderjets were acquired the following year. The *FAP* has experienced some difficulty in buying replacement aircraft of late, due to the opposition of some members of the international community to Portugal's colonial position. The *FAP* is operational in support of ground troops in Angola and Mozambique.

Current strength is about 17,500 men. Types operated include the Republic F-84G Thunderjet (about 25 aircraft), the North American F-86F Sabre (about 50 aircraft), the Fiat G.91R-4 (about 36 aircraft), the Douglas B-26 Invader (about 12 aircraft), the Lockheed PV-2 Harpoon (about 12 aircraft) and the Lockheed P-2E Neptune (about 12 aircraft). There are about 85 transports, including some 20 Nord Noratlas and some 40 Douglas C-47s. Also operated are some 100 helicopters – mainly Sud Alouette models, but with some SA.330

Pumas and Sikorsky UH-19A Chickasaws. Trainers include the North American T-6 Texan, Lockheed T-33A, Cessna T-37C and the D.H. Vampire T.55.

Main airfields include Oporto, Sintra, Ota, Montijo, Alverca and Aveiro in Portugal, and Lages in the Azores.

ROMANIA

The army formed a flying corps in 1910, and acquired a few Blériot, Farman, Bristol, Morane and, later, Nieuport types; these were quickly submerged by the Central Powers in 1914. In 1918 a Directorate of Army Aviation was established; strength was set at three groups each of three squadrons each of eight aircraft, and initial equipment included SPAD S.VII scouts, D.H.9 and Bréguet bombers. Procurement during the 1920s was mainly from France, but nationally-designed types, Polish P.Z.L. P-11 fighters, and British Hawker Hurricanes and Bristol Blenheims were acquired in the 1930s. Siding with the Axis during the Second World War, Romania received German and Italian aircraft – the Messerschmitt Bf 109, Heinkel He 111, Junkers Ju 87 and Savoia-Marchetti S.M. 79 among others – as well as operating the indigenous I.A.R. 80 fighters.

Since the Red Army drove the Germans out in 1944 Romania has been within the Soviet sphere of influence and draws equipment from the U.S.S.R., although of late there have been signs of a more assertively nationalist stance. Current strength of the air force is some 8,000 men, with about 250 combat aircraft. There are thought to be about 18 squadrons each with some 12 aircraft in the interceptor and ground-attack rôles, operating MiG-21, MiG-19 and MiG-17 types. Additionally there are two Ilyushin Il-28 bomber squadrons, two transport units with Ilyushin Il-12 and Il-14 aircraft, a small number of Mil helicopters and a variety of the usual Communist-bloc training types such as the Yak-11, MiG-15UTI and L-29 Delfin.

There are airfields at Satu Mare, Iaşi, Bacău, Cluj, Arad, Medias, Tecuci, Galati, Zilistea, Buza, Orasul, Turnisor, Targsorulnov, the Bucharest complex, Mamaia, Constanta, Călăraşi and Craiova.

SPAIN

The Aeronáutica Militar Española was established in 1911 with a dozen Farman, Bristol and Nieuport aircraft. Expansion was slow until 1918 when the AME and newly-formed Aeronáutica Navale acquired large numbers of war surplus machines of British, Italian and French design. The service saw extensive action in the Riff Wars of the 1920s. From a peak strength of about 700 machines, Spanish air power declined in the 1930s, and on the outbreak of civil war in 1936 the Republican government had some 200, the Nationalists about 60 aircraft. Apart from "volunteer" units from the U.S.S.R., the government acquired in its own right various Dewoitine, Lioré-Nieuport, Potez and Bloch designs during the War. Franco's victory brought about the merger of the two previous services as the new Ejercito del Aire in 1939, with about 1,000 aircraft, mainly German and Italian types. Some further deliveries were made during the Second World War, but most Spanish equipment was licence-built. A Spanish air group fought in Russia with the Luftwaffe. The post-War years saw the Service soldiering on with developed versions of such venerable designs as the Messerschmitt Bf 109 and Heinkel He 111, but in 1953 the leasing of bases to the

The Swedish Saab AJ 37 Viggen single-seat attack aircraft, shown here with two Rb 04 air-to-surface missiles. First flown on 8th February 1967, the Viggen is arguably Europe's most advanced multi-mission supersonic aircraft; a two-seat training version has also been developed, and to date 175 aircraft of both versions have been ordered for the Flygvapnet. First unit to be equipped with the AJ 37 was F7 Wing at Såtenäs

U.S.A. brought the first American equipment; the first jets operated were some 200 F-86 Sabres.

Current *EdA* strength is around 32,000 personnel. The main types flown are the Lockheed F-104G (20 aircraft), the McDonnell-Douglas F-4C(S) Phantom II (36 aircraft), the Dassault Mirage IIIE (30 aircraft), the Northrop SF-5A Freedom Fighter (70 aircraft) and about 60 North American F-86F Sabres, with 15 Dassault Mirage F1s on order. Small numbers of Lockheed P-3 Orion and Grumman HU-16 Albatross are operated on maritime duties; there are about 80 Douglas C-47 and smaller numbers of Lockheed C-130 Hercules, C-54 Skymaster, DHC-4 Caribou and CASA 207 Azor transports. Trainers include the armed HA-220, the Beech T-34 Mentor, the HA-200, the North American T-6G Texan, the Lockheed T-33A, and various conversion trainers. There are some 40 Sikorsky, Bell and Hiller helicopters, although this figure may rise sharply in the near future; interest has been expressed in acquiring up to 500 additional helicopters over the next five to ten years.

Military airfields include Vigo, Santiago, Lugo, Oviedo, Santander, Bilbao, Vitoria, Logroño, Burgos, León, Valladolid, Salamanca, Reus, Zaragoza, Muntadas, Barajas, Alcalá, Torrejon, Getafe, Mahón, Valencia, Albacete, Alicante, Murcia, Granada, Badajoz, Seville, Jerez and Malaga.

SWEDEN

The Swedish navy and army were presented with their first aircraft in 1911 and 1912. The strength of the two Services had grown to about 25 and 50 aircraft respectively by 1918. In the inter-War years the domestic industry built foreign designs under licence and also indigenous types; and in 1926 the *Flygvapnet* was formed by a merger of the two air services. Equipment was neglected until the late 1930s, but thereafter some 60 Gloster Gladiators, 40 Junkers Ju 86K and 100 Douglas DB-8A bombers, and numbers of training aircraft were built under licence. In 1940 72 Fiat C.R.42 and some Reggiane Re.2000 fighters were bought from Italy; during the war years indigenous SAAB-21 and SAAB-22 fighters, and SAAB-17 and SAAB-18 bombers were brought into service. Although Swedish volunteer units fought for Finland in 1939-40, Sweden remained neutral during the Second World War. The first jets acquired were 70 D.H. Vampires in 1946; later orders brought the total number operated to over 200. The indigenous SAAB-21R jet fighter followed in 1949. Recently the *Flygvapnet* has operated mainly Swedish designs – of considerable sophistication.

Currently the *Flygvapnet* has about 16,000 personnel and nearly 600 combat aircraft. The main type is the SAAB-35 Draken; about 400 of these are in the process of being partially replaced by the SAAB-37A Viggen, of which there will be initially some 175 in service. There

are at least 150 SAAB-32 Lansen fighters still in service, and a few D.H. Vampires and SAAB-29s on second-line duties. Transports flown include the Douglas C-47 and the Lockheed C-130 Hercules. There are about 20 helicopters, mainly Boeing-Vertol 107s; and a total of about 250 SAAB trainers of various models, from primary to advanced conversion. The Royal Swedish Navy operates at least 30 Boeing-Vertol, Agusta-Bell and Sud Alouette II machines. The Army also operates helicopters and light aircraft – about 70 of the former and 20 of the latter – and may have received numbers of Scottish Aviation Bulldog light strike/trainers by mid-1973.

Major military air bases include Hässlö, Hägernäs, Malmslätt, Froson, Ljungbyhed, Karlsborg, Såtenäs, Barkaby, Säve, Barkakra, Skavsta, Kalmar, Norrköping, Halmstad, Söderhamn, Uppsala, Kallinge, Tullinge and Kallax/Luleå.

SWITZERLAND

The Swiss *Fliegertruppe* was formed in 1914 with French and German equipment; some Swiss pilots flew in action with the French forces during the First World War, and they and foreign pilots who became Swiss citizens formed the basis of the post-War Service. By 1919 the renamed *Militär-Flugwesens* had about 100 machines. During the inter-War years the Service, reorganised several times, acquired foreign types such as the Fokker D.VII and Potez and Dewoitine designs, and home-produced machines such as the Haefeli M.7 and M.8. In 1936 a further reorganisation as a separate Service in all respects (the *Schweizerische Flugwaffe*) was followed by the acquisition of large numbers of modern combat aircraft, including some 90 Messerschmitt Bf 109Es. Switzerland maintained her neutrality during the War, and defended it so vigorously that certain other Allied and Axis military aircraft entered Swiss service by rather undignified channels.

Since the War Switzerland has kept up a progressive replacement of obsolescent equipment; and her aircrew, who undergo intensive initial training and a period of squadron service followed by annual refresher courses after they revert to the Reserve, meet a standard higher than that achieved in many "full-time" services. The permanent establishment of the *Kommando Flieger und Fliegerabwehrtruppen* is about 8,000, and some 40,000 reservists can be mobilised at short notice. Types operated include the Dassault Mirage IIIS and IIISR (57 aircraft), the Hawker Hunter F.58 (currently 120 aircraft, soon to be raised by a further 30), and the D.H. Venom FB.50 (currently 13 squadrons, soon to be partially replaced by Hunters). There are a variety of trainers, transports and communications aircraft, and some 140 helicopters, mainly Sud Alouettes.

Main airfields include Dubendorf, Emmen, Payerne, Magadine and Sitten.

UNITED KINGDOM

The Royal Flying Corps was formed in 1912, a descendant of the Air Battalion, Royal Engineers, and of the balloon columns which had been used in action in Africa as early as 1884. The Royal Navy's three-year-old Air Branch was briefly merged in the R.F.C., but split off in 1913 as the Royal Naval Air Service. By the outbreak of the First World War the R.F.C. had about 180 aircraft; the force which accompanied the Army to France in 1914 numbered 860 men and 73 machines. These latter were almost universally unarmed, and quite unsuitable for aerial combat, which was not seriously envisaged anyway; their function was pure reconnaissance. The Germans were quicker to grasp the essentials of air combat than the British, and it was only after a period of crisis in 1915-16 that the R.F.C. began to gear itself for the new sort of warfare. That bewilderment soon turned to mastery was demonstrated in 1918. When the R.F.C. and R.N.A.S. merged in April 1918 as the Royal Air Force, the combined Service had 30,000 officers and 330,000 men, and 22,650 aircraft in 200 squadrons. Fighters like the S.E.5A, Sopwith Snipe and Bristol F.2B had taken on and defeated Germany's best; the Handley Page 0/400s of the Independent Force had ushered in the age of strategic bombing of enemy industrial targets; and names like Ball, McCudden, Bishop and Mannock had passed into aviation history.

A swingeing reduction of strength in the immediate post-War years very nearly extinguished the R.A.F. completely; but the Service soldiered on in the rôle of colonial peace-keeper, slowly acquiring a variety of aircraft, and building its strength once more to a figure of 74 squadrons by 1933. The best-known of the many aircraft of the 1920s and 1930s were the Bristol Bulldog and Hawker Fury fighters and the Hawker Hart light bomber. At last, late in the 1930s, a belated decision to re-arm gave the R.A.F. its first monoplanes – the Vickers Wellington bomber, the Hawker Hurricane and Supermarine Spitfire fighters. But the threat from the east had been passively ignored too long, and by 1939 Germany's air force outnumbered the R.A.F. seven-to-two in aircraft and eight-to-one in men. At the outbreak of war Britain had 55 bomber squadrons, of which 22 had obsolete equipment; 35 fighter squadrons, of which 13 still flew biplanes; and 19 coastal squadrons. Twenty-seven squadrons were sent to France, and another 27 were based in the Middle East.

Driven from the continent in 1940, the R.A.F. fought and won the decisive Battle of Britain over the Channel coast and southern England. The forces in the Middle East did well against Italian pressure, but were badly mauled after German intervention. After the bulk of the *Luftwaffe* moved to Russia in 1941, R.A.F. intruders gradually built up British air supremacy over the coastal areas of occupied Europe, and the slackening of pressure on the home front allowed sufficient reinforcement of the Mediterranean and Far Eastern theatres to turn defeat into air supremacy there also. The night bombing offensive against German cities and industrial targets built up from the pin-pricks of 1940 to the 1,000-bomber holocausts of 1942-43; the twin-engined Wellingtons, Hampdens and Whitleys of the early years were replaced by the four-engined "heavies" – the Stirling, Halifax and Lancaster. In concert with the U.S.A.A.F. fighters based in Britain, the Spitfires, Typhoons and Tempests of Fighter Command massacred the *Luftwaffe* in 1944-45 to such an extent that by the end of the War in North-West Europe no German vehicle could move by daylight without extreme risk. The first squadron of Gloster Meteor jets became operational weeks before the end of the War. In 1945 the strength of the R.A.F. was 1,079,800 men, and 9,200 aircraft in 487 squadrons; 100 of these squadrons were composed of Commonwealth or Free European personnel. R.A.F. casualties had included 70,253 airmen lost on operations.

In the 1950s and 1960s the R.A.F. operated in many parts of the world in support of the Army and Royal Navy, who were supervising the dismantling of the British Empire under circumstances of varying cordiality. A founder-member of NATO, Britain has turned from world-wide commitment to concentration on continental Europe, while maintaining high-mobility forces to respond to the violation of remaining defence pacts. Aircraft in service since the War have included such world-beating designs as the English Electric Canberra, the Hawker Hunter and the BAC Lightning; but in recent years the R.A.F. has suffered severely from political manoeuvring in the area of aircraft procurement. Despite the introduction of the world's first operational vertical take-off fighter, the Hawker Siddeley Harrier, the undeniable weakness of the Service by international standards has led to the purchase of foreign equipment to fill the gap until advanced designs now under development by Britain and her allies can be brought into squadron service.

Current manpower strength is about 110,300 of all ranks. The main types operated include the McDonnell-Douglas Phantom FGR.Mk.2 (approximately 140 aircraft), the BAC Lightning (approximately 100 aircraft), the Hawker Siddeley Harrier (approximately 100 aircraft), the Hawker Siddeley Vulcan B.Mk.2 (approximately 50 aircraft), the Hawker Siddeley Buccaneer S.Mk.2 (approximately 50 aircraft), the Hawker Siddeley Hunter (approximately 60 aircraft), the BAC Canberra (approximately 60 aircraft) and the Hawker Siddeley Nimrod (approximately 40 aircraft). There are some 40 Handley Page Victor tankers, and transports include the Short Belfast (about 10 aircraft), the BAC VC-10 (14 aircraft), the Lockheed C-130K Hercules (66 aircraft), the Hawker Siddeley Andover (30 aircraft), the Bristol Britannia (approximately 20 aircraft) and the Hawker Siddeley Comet (six aircraft). There are about 130 helicopters – mainly Westland Wessex and SA.330 Puma, with some Westland WG.13 Lynx currently coming into service. Additionally there are numerous

ROYAL AIR FORCE AND
FLEET AIR ARM BASES
IN GREAT BRITAIN

Note: Many of the bases shown are not
currently operational, and are shown for
historical and reference purposes.
  Others are also currently operated by
the United States Air Force.

light general duties types and communications aircraft; and training is on B.A.C. 145 Provost, Folland (Hawker Siddeley) Gnat, Handley Page Hastings and Hawker Siddeley HS.125 Domine types, apart from conversion trainer versions of all major operational types.

Naval Aviation

There was active interest in flying by the Royal Navy before the First World War; the first take-off from a Royal Navy ship was officially recorded in 1912. During the War the R.N.A.S. took an active part in operations in several theatres, including the provision of conventional fighter squadrons for the war in France, and several daring early bombing raids on German targets. The R.N.A.S. disappeared into the R.A.F. in 1918, to re-emerge as the Fleet Air Arm in 1924, at which time five carriers were operated. A considerable expansion programme in the 1930s gave the Fleet H.M.S. *Ark Royal* before the outbreak of the Second World War, and shortly thereafter the Royal Navy had eight carriers at sea. Aircraft were initially of obsolescent types, but an offensive posture was adopted from the start; H.M.S. *Courageous* and *Glorious* were both sunk by mid-1940, and within two years H.M.S. *Hermes* – the first vessel in the world to be laid down as an aircraft carrier – had been sunk by Japanese carrier aircraft off Ceylon. *Ark Royal* at last lost her prolonged game of hide and seek with the U-Boats. But there were considerable successes to offset these losses, and by 1945 there were no less than 52 carriers of all classes, and 1,350 aircraft, in service with the Royal Navy. Among the F.A.A.'s most notable battle-honours were operations in the Mediterranean and the Battle of the Atlantic, and service against the Japanese in the final year of the War.

Despite the swingeing post-War reduction in strength, the Royal Navy maintained a leading position in the development of carrier techniques. Aircraft from H.M.S. *Triumph*, *Theseus*, *Glory* and *Ocean* supported U.N. ground forces in Korea. The first naval jets were D.H. Vampires, followed by D.H. Sea Venoms, Hawker Sea Hawks, Supermarine Scimitars and D.H. Sea Vixens. The most recent combat types embarked have been the Hawker Siddeley Buccaneer and the McDonnell-Douglas Phantom. In recent years there has been a shift in emphasis from carriers to missile-armed nuclear submarines, and it is current policy for the Royal Navy's fixed-wing rôle to disappear when H.M.S. *Ark Royal*, the last remaining carrier, is de-commissioned towards the end of the 1970s. Speculation is rife that a new class of "through-deck" cruisers will embark groups of eight vertical/short take-off jets, to enter service as *Ark Royal* is retired, but at the time of writing no positive order has been placed.

H.M.S. *Bulwark*, *Albion* and *Hermes* are now operated as commando carriers; each can accommodate a full Royal Marine Commando with its heavy weapons and transport, and embarks a strong force of troop-carrying and anti-submarine helicopters.

Current F.A.A. strength is about 124 combat aeroplanes, comprising the McDonnell-Douglas F-4K Phantom II (24 aircraft), the Hawker Siddeley Buccaneer S.2 (approximately 64 aircraft), and residual Hawker Siddeley Sea Vixen (not more than 36 aircraft). The Phantoms and Buccaneers are due to be handed over to the R.A.F. when *Ark Royal* is retired. In addition there are several flights of Fairey Gannet airborne early warning aircraft and Scimitar tankers; and communications aircraft including D.H. Sea Devon and Sea Heron, and Percival Sea Prince types. Some 300 helicopters are flown – mainly Westland Wessex (about 150 aircraft), Westland Wasp (about 90 aircraft), and Westland Sea King (about 60 aircraft), with some Westland-Bell 47G Sioux. The Westland WG.13 is due to replace the Wasp models within the next two years.

Army Aviation

The line between R.A.F. personnel temporarily attached to army formations, and army aircrew *per se*, became blurred during the closing stages of the Second World War with the appearance of such expedients as the Glider Pilot Regiment. In 1957 the Army Air Corps was established; this is not a permanent force, and most personnel are on secondment from other corps. Duties include observation and reconnaissance, communications and liaison, and a certain amount of light fire support. Squadrons are attached to army brigades. Equipment currently includes the Westland Scout helicopter (about 150 machines, due for early replacement by 250 Westland WG.13 Lynx), the Westland-Bell 47G Sioux helicopter (approximately 175 machines, due for early replacement by 300 Westland-Sud SA.340 Gazelles), and the DHC-2 Beaver light transport (about 40 aircraft).

UNION OF SOVIET SOCIALIST REPUBLICS

The establishment of the Tzarist army's Central Flying School at Gatchina in 1910 marked the beginning of real involvement in military aviation, although the possibilities of balloons had been under investigation for some years. The initial equipment of the Imperial Russian Flying Corps, a branch of the army, was mainly French but with some British machines; in all the Corps had about 250 aircraft and 300 pilots at the outbreak of the First World War, and the navy had another 100 machines. Igor Sikorsky's indigenous designs started to enter service in 1915, but most of the combat aircraft used in the War were French and British; it was a campaign relying far more upon bombing and reconnaissance and far less upon fighter combat than was the case in the West.

The air elements which came under revolutionary control in 1917 were organised the following year into the Red Air Fleet, renamed Soviet Military Aviation Forces (or *VVS*) in 1924. The end of the civil wars found the

Codenamed "Blinder" by NATO, the Tupolev Tu-22 has been flying since 1960, and is probably capable of a speed of Mach 1·5 at about 40,000 feet. Its bomb-load normally comprises a large air-to-surface missile (codenamed "Kitchen") and several hundred are known to be in squadron service both as bombers and electronic countermeasures aircraft. An aircraft is illustrated running up its two afterburning turbojets (of about 26,000 lb.s.t.) prior to take-off

VVS with about 300 machines, which were rapidly augmented by foreign purchase and licence production; Fokker and Ansaldo types were acquired in large numbers. The great names of Russian design, such as Polikarpov and Tupolev, began to emerge in the late 1920s. By 1930 there were some 1,000 aircraft in service. Russia produced the world's first enclosed cockpit, retracting undercarriage monoplane fighter – the Polikarpov I-16 – and attracted attention in the 1930s by her huge heavy bomber designs. Some 1,400 aircraft were sent to Spain during the Civil War of 1936–39, and thousands of personnel gained combat experience; others were blooded in China, in support of the Communist faction, and in the clashes with Japan in Mongolia in the late 1930s. During this period total strength was about 6,000 machines, of a wide variety of types, but Russia's technical isolation was a handicap. Some 2,000 aircraft were committed to the war against Finland, of which more than a quarter became casualties. By the time of the German invasion in 1941, *VVS* strength was around 15,000 first-line aircraft; some 10,000 of these were based in the western regions, standing in the path of the 2,770 *Luftwaffe* aircraft committed to the campaign.

Initial German successes were so sweeping, and the technical superiority of the outnumbered German aircraft was so marked, that the *VVS* (and its sister service, the *PVOS*, a positional defence organisation) lost some 8,500 machines in 1941. Shipments of British and American types, which were to reach a total of 15,000 aircraft, enabled the *VVS* to remain in existence while improved designs, such as the Yakovlev Yak-3 and Yak-9, the Ilyushin Il-2, the Tupolev Tu-2 and Lavochkin La-5, La-7 and La-9, could be brought into service in significant numbers. The *VVS* was at all times subordinated

to the demands of the ground armies, and its main strength lay in low-level ground support operations. The rigid standardisation, simple design, and great robustness which characterised all Soviet military equipment in the middle and late War years enabled the *VVS* to operate much more effectively than the technically more sophisticated *Luftwaffe* – under the primitive conditions of the front. At the end of the War the *VVS* had about 20,000 first-line aircraft; the industry which developed and built them had never been within range of German bombers.

Vigorous exploitation of captured German material in the field of jet aircraft led to the fairly early appearance of the Yak-15 and Yak-17 and Mikoyan MiG-9 designs; but the famous MiG-15, the most widely built and exported Communist jet, did not emerge until Russia had acquired and copied British Rolls-Royce jet engines. The MiG-15 clashed with the North American F-86 Sabre in Korea in the early 1950s, and the exposure of its shortcomings led to the MiG-17 of 1952, and the supersonic MiG-19 of 1955. The Tupolev Tu-16 long-range turboprop bomber, and the Ilyushin Il-28 jet bomber and Il-12 and Il-14 transports, were other widely-built post-war Russian designs. The current standard combat types of the entire Soviet bloc, the MiG-21 interceptor and Sukhoi Su-7 ground-attack aircraft, first appeared in 1958. One recent major type to enter service is the remarkable MiG-25 interceptor, a high-altitude Mach 3 aircraft whose performance appears to be markedly superior to that of any Western aircraft in service. In limited squadron service since 1971 is the variable-geometry single-seat MiG-23 fighter code-named "Flogger", but numbers are not thought to be significant; exactly the same applies to the variable-geometry development of the Sukhoi Su-7B, code-named "Fitter-B". A Tupolev variable-geometry bomber code-named "Backfire", with an estimated performance in the Mach 2·25–2·5 class and supersonic capability at low altitude, is believed to be undergoing pre-production evaluation programmes; twelve aircraft are thought to exist.

Current *VVS* manpower is believed to total about 500,000; an additional 500,000 (of whom some 300,000 are probably anti-aircraft personnel) serve with the *PVOS*, the air defence organisation which is distinct from the rest of the air forces. Obviously no detailed aircraft strength figures are available, but it has been estimated that the combined strength of *VVS* and *PVOS* is around 20,000 first-line machines, of which the *PVOS* operates about 3,500. Types in service include the MiG-25 and MiG-21 interceptors, with residual MiG-19 and MiG-17 types deployed alongside the Sukhoi Su-7 and Yakovlev Yak-28 in the tactical rôle. The Sukhoi Su-9 and Su-11 interceptors are also in service in some numbers, mainly with the *PVOS*. The *VVS* has approximately 1,000 bombers in service, including the Tupolev Tu-16 (about 600 aircraft), the Tu-20 (about 100 aircraft), the Tu-22 (about 200 aircraft) and the Myasishchev Mya-4 (about 100 aircraft). There are about 2,000 transports of various Tupolev, Ilyushin and Antonov models, and about 600 Mil and Yak helicopters of various versions.

Naval Aviation

The Independent Naval Air Fleet or *AVMF* has lost influence in recent years following the handover of all fighters and their personnel to the *PVOS* in 1960. Current strength of the *AVMF* is about 75,000 men. Long-range maritime reconnaissance is performed by some 400 Tupolev Tu-16, Tu-20 and Tu-22 bombers. There are probably another 200 fixed-wing aircraft, including 120 Beriev Be-6 flying-boats and Be-12 amphibians and various transport and communications types; and some hundreds of helicopters of Mil-4 and Kamov Ka-25A models. Twenty of the latter can be embarked on each of the navy's two 18,000-ton helicopter cruisers.

The compilers can publish no reliable information on Soviet air bases.

YUGOSLAVIA

Yugoslavia achieved nationhood in 1918, and former personnel of the Serbian Military Air Service, trained in France in 1912, provided a nucleus for the Yugoslav Army Aviation Department in 1923. Initial equipment included SPAD fighters and Bréguet reconnaissance bombers. By 1935 about 440 aircraft were in army service, and there were some 7,300 personnel. A thriving industry was producing licence-built combat types, and orders were placed for modern foreign equipment including Hawker Hurricane and Messerschmitt Bf 109E fighters, and Bristol Blenheim, Savoia-Marchetti S.M.79 and Dornier Do 17 bombers. Most

of these were destroyed during the brief but bloody campaign in which Germany occupied the country in 1941. Yugoslav patriots escaped to the U.K. in small numbers, and there were Yugoslav squadrons within the R.A.F. An Axis puppet Croatian Air Force flew German and Italian equipment, and drafts fought in Russia. The Jugoslav Air Force, or *JRV*, was established in 1945 when the country became a republic – influenced but emphatically not dominated by the Soviet Union; and much Western equipment was acquired.

Current *JRV* strength is around 20,000 men. Major types operated include the Mikoyan MiG-21F interceptor (about 60 aircraft), the Canadair Sabre Mk. 2 and Mk. 4 (about 100 aircraft), the Republic F-84G Thunderjet (not more than 90 aircraft), the Lockheed RT-33A (about 30 aircraft), and the indigenous Soko Jastreb and Kraguj armed strike developments of the Soko Galeb trainer (about 150 aircraft currently being introduced as Thunderjet replacements). There are another 150 or so Soko Galebs in the training rôle, alongside some 70 Lockheed T-33As and various primary and conversion types. Transports include about 15 Douglas C-47, four Douglas DC-6B and six Ilyushin Il-14 models; and there are some 40 helicopters – mainly Westland Whirlwinds and Mil Mi-4s.

There are airfields at Pola, Ljubljana, Cerklje, Lucko, Pleso, Zemonico, Zalusani, Tuzla, Butmir, Mostar, Nikšić, Titograd, Batajnica, Novi Sad, Vršac, Zemun, Niš, Petrovac and Skoplje.

2. NORTH, SOUTH AND CENTRAL AMERICA

ARGENTINA

The *Escuela de Aviación Militar* was established at El Palomar, Buenos Aires, in September 1912. Initial equipment comprised aircraft of Farman, Blériot and Morane manufacture. Both Argentine pilots and candidates from neighbouring states were trained at the school; and in the half-century since, Argentina has led the field in South American military aviation on several occasions. She was the first state in the area to recognise the vital importance of aviation in view of the vast distances between major cities; the first to establish a domestic aircraft industry; and the first to operate jet fighters.

The *Fuerza Aérea Argentina* has a current strength of around 17,000 officers and men. Most of the aircraft operated are of American origin, but the long tradition of French influence in Argentine procurement has not entirely disappeared. Equipment includes about 170 combat aircraft, about 130 transport and liaison aircraft, about 30 helicopters and about 130 trainers. The main types operated include the Dassault Mirage III fighter-bomber (12 aircraft), the Douglas A-4B and A-4F Skyhawk fighter-bomber (25 and 16 aircraft respectively), the North American F-86F Sabre fighter-bomber (about 25 aircraft), the BAC Canberra B.2 bomber (12 aircraft), and the locally-built Dinfia Pucana twin-turboprop counter-insurgency aircraft (80 aircraft). Transports include the Douglas C-47, the Lockheed C-130 Hercules, the Fokker F-27 Troopship and various Hawker Siddeley and de Havilland Canada types. French and American trainers, and American helicopters of various models, are also flown.

The *Comando de Aviación Naval* was formed in 1919 with the assistance of an Italian military mission. With about 250 pilots the Service currently operates some 45 combat aircraft, about 15 maritime reconnaissance aircraft, and various helicopters, transports and trainers. Main combat equipment comprises the Douglas A-4Q Skyhawk (16 aircraft delivered 1972), the Aermacchi MB.326K light strike/jet trainer (about 24 aircraft), some North American T-28 Fennec light strike/trainers, and Grumman Trackers and Lockheed Neptune patrol aircraft; four Sikorsky S-61D-4s are operated.

Major airfields used wholly or in part by the military include a complex of facilities near Buenos Aires, and fields at La Quiaca, Jujuy, Salta, Orán, Resistencia, San Juan, Córdoba, Monte Caseros, Mendoza, San Rafael, Santa Rosa, Mar del Plata and Bahía Blanca.

BOLIVIA

The Bolivian *Cuerpo de Aviación* was founded in 1924, and initially operated mainly French types.

The *Fuerza Aérea Boliviana* has been equipped in recent years with small numbers of aircraft of United States origin, under military aid programmes, but has no more than a very limited light strike or counter-insurgency capability. About 15 combat aircraft, 25 transport and liaison types, and 15 helicopters are operated. In addition, about 20 trainers could be given a light strike capability in an emergency. The aircraft in current service include the North American F-51D Mustang fighter-bomber (about a dozen aircraft), the North American AT-6 light strike/trainer, the North American T-6 Texan and T-28 trainers, the Douglas C-47 transport, Cessna liaison aircraft, and helicopters of Hughes and Hiller manufacture.

Airfields partly or wholly used by the military include Alto-La Paz, Charaña, Santa Cruz, Cochabamba and Puerto Suarez.

BRAZIL

Military aviation in Brazil began in 1913, with the establishment of a seaplane school at Rio de Janeiro. Army pilots began training shortly afterwards, and the Army Air Service was established with the assistance of a French mission at the close of the First World War. A key member of the Organisation of American States, Brazil has a large and efficient air force.

The *Fôrça Aérea Brasileira* numbers about 30,000 men, and operates some 100 or so combat aircraft, some 40 maritime reconnaissance and anti-submarine patrol aircraft, about 100 transports, about 40 helicopters, and approximately 170 trainers of various types. Main combat types in service include the Dassault Mirage III fighter-bomber (16 aircraft) and the Douglas A-4F Skyhawk fighter-bomber (15 aircraft), the Lockheed TF-33 light strike/jet trainer (54 aircraft), and the Douglas B-26K Invader bomber (18 aircraft). The various trainers in service are in the process of replacement by Brazilian-built Aermacchi MB.326 jet trainers, which have a light strike capability; the total order is reported to be for 112 machines. The maritime reconnaissance aircraft include the Lockheed PV-2 Neptune (14 aircraft) and the Grumman S-2A Tracker (13 aircraft); the transports cover a wide range of types from the Douglas C-47 to the Lockheed C-130E Hercules.

The Brazilian *Forca Aeronavale* operates a total of about 46 helicopters of various British and American models. After prolonged dispute, all fixed-wing military aircraft are operated by the Air Force, including those embarked on the aircraft carrier *Minas Gerais*.

Brazilian airfields include the Rio de Janeiro complex, Tefé, Santarém, Belém, Natal, Joao Pessóa, Recife, Maceió, Ipitanga, Vitória, Florianópolis, Pôrto Alegre, Uruguayana, São Paulo, Pennapolis, Campo Grande, Corumbá, Pampulha, Goyania, Carolina and Anapolis.

CANADA

After a false start in 1914, Canada's first realistic national air arm was formed in 1918 with the appearance of the Royal Canadian Naval Air Service. Two years later the Canadian Air Force was formed, and received the prefix "Royal" in 1923. In its early years the force carried out duties of a largely civil nature, and in fact it was not until 1938 that the R.C.A.F. was wholly separated from Army control and became a Service in its own right. At the outbreak of war it only had about 40 modern combat aeroplanes – Hawker Hurricanes, Fairey Battles and Bristol Blenheims – and a motley collection of obsolescent types. By 1941 sixteen R.C.A.F. squadrons were flying from the United Kingdom on operations against the Axis, flying a cross-section of the latest British combat aircraft. In all some 17,000 R.C.A.F. personnel gave their lives in action during the War, and no less than 8,000 were decorated by the British and Allied governments. Peak wartime strength was 90 squadrons.

In 1967 Canada's three armed services were amalgamated into a unified defence force under the title Canadian Armed Forces; the current strength of this organisation is around 90,000 men, of which total some 40,000 are engaged in aviation duties. Major aviation commands are Air Defence Command and Air Transport Command, and aircraft are also included in Mobile

Command and C.A.F. Germany.

The air combat strength of the C.A.F. currently stands at about 160 aircraft. Main types flown include the McDonnell-Douglas F-101 Voodoo interceptors of Air Defence Command (66 aircraft), the Canadair CF-5A fighter-bombers of Mobile Command (about 52 aircraft), and three squadrons of Lockheed CF-104 Starfighters with C.A.F. Germany (about 66 aircraft). Large numbers of transports are in service, ranging from the Lockheed C-130E Hercules and the Boeing 707-320C, to the venerable Douglas C-47; several models of DHC transport aircraft – the Beaver, Otter, Twin Otter, Caribou and Buffalo – are operated in quantity. Some 125 Bell UH-1N Iroquois and OH-58A Kiowa helicopters are currently in service, and a squadron of Sikorsky Sea King helicopters operate singly from Maritime destroyers. Grumman S2F-3 Tracker and Canadair CL-28 Argus aircraft carry out maritime reconnaissance and anti-submarine patrols.

Airfields partly or wholly at the disposal of the military include the following: Dawson and Whitehorse (in Yukon territory); Norman Wells, Yellowknife, Coral Harbour and Frobisher (in North-West Territories); Fort Nelson, Fort St. John, Prince George, Comox and Sea Island (in British Columbia); Grande Prairie, Cold Lake, Namao, Penhold, Calgary, Claresholm (in Alberta); Saskatoon and Moose Jaw (in Saskatchewan); Fort Churchill, Gimli, Winnipeg, Macdonald and Portage La Prairie (in Manitoba); North Bay, Ottawa, Clinton, Camp Borden, Centralia, Aylmer, London, Trenton, Downsview and Malton (in Ontario); Fort Chimo, Knob Lake, Bagotville, Quebec, Cartierville, St. Hubert, Dorval and Mount Joli (in Quebec); Chatham and Moncton (in New Brunswick); Dartmouth, Halifax, Yarmouth and Sydney (in Nova Scotia); Summerside (on Prince Edward Island); Stephenville, Gander and St. John's (in Newfoundland); and Goose Bay (in Labrador).

CHILE

The foundation of a flying school at Lo Espejo in February 1913 heralded the beginning of military aviation in Chile; the Military Aviation Service's first equipment consisted of three Blériots, but by 1915 ten machines were being operated by two squadrons. A Naval Aviation Service followed in 1919. In 1930 the two Services were combined as the *Fuerza Aérea de Chile*.

Current personnel strength stands at about 8,000 officers and men. The main types operated are the Hawker Hunter FGA. Mk. 9 and Mk. 71 fighter-bomber (27 aircraft), the Lockheed F-80C (ten aircraft), and residual Douglas B-26 Invader light bombers. Transports include one Lockheed C-130 Hercules, six Douglas DC-6Bs, about two dozen Douglas C-47s, and seven DHC Twin Otters. Jet trainers include eight Lockheed T-33s, five de Havilland Vampires, and four two-seat

Hunters. There are some 70 miscellaneous trainers and communications types, including some 45 Beech T-34s. Some 30 helicopters are operated, including the Bell 47 (eleven aircraft) and Hiller VH-12 (ten aircraft).

Military air bases include Los Condores (Iquique), Cerro Moreno (Antofagasta), Quintero, El Bosque, Los Cerrillos, Maquelme (Temuco), Tejual (Puerto Montt), and Chabunco (Punta Arenas).

COLOMBIA

Colombia's first flying school and military aviation Service dates from 1922. The military and naval elements were amalgamated into the *Fuerza Aérea Colombiana* in 1943, and a complete reorganisation was carried out with the assistance of a United States mission. Military aid followed from 1948 onwards.

The Service has a current strength of about 6,000 men, with between 20 and 30 combat aircraft, plus a number of trainers with a light strike capability, eight amphibians, some 50 transport aircraft of many types, and some 50 helicopters. Main types flown include Dassault Mirage III and Mirage 5 (18 aircraft), North American F-86F Sabre fighters (about six aircraft), Douglas B-26 Invader bombers (eight aircraft), Convair PBY-5A amphibians (eight aircraft), Douglas C-47 and C-54, and DHC-3 Otter transports, DHC-2 Beaver transports (12 aircraft), two Lockheed C-130 Hercules transports and 20 Bell 47 Sioux helicopters. Training aircraft include Beech T-34, Lockheed T-33A, Cessna T-41D and T-37C.

Airfields wholly or partly at the disposal of the military include Bogotá, Cali, Medellin, Bucaramanga, Cúcuta, Cartagena and Baranquilla.

CUBA

The Cuban Army's *Cuerpo de Aviacion* was formed in 1917 with United States assistance; initial equipment comprised six Curtiss JN-4D trainers.

At the time of the Castro revolution in the late 1950s the *Fuerza Aérea Ejercito de Cuba* numbered only about 2,000 personnel and operated four squadrons of obsolescent aircraft; prominent among these were the North American F-51D Mustang, the North American B-25J Mitchell, and the Douglas C-47. Jets, in the form of four Lockheed T-33A trainers, were acquired in 1955, and two Westland Whirlwind helicopters in 1958.

Today the *Fuerza Aérea Revolucionaria* is thought to have a strength of around 12,000 men. Current combat equipment is Soviet-supplied, comprising about 185 fighters and ground-attack types, some 50 transports, about 55 helicopters and 30 trainers. Main types flown are the Mikoyan MiG-21 interceptor (approximately 80 aircraft), the MiG-17 fighter (approximately 75 aircraft), the MiG-19 fighter (about 40 aircraft) and the MiG-15 fighter-bomber (about 20 aircraft). Transports include Antonov An-24 and Ilyushin Il-14 aircraft, and Mil Mi-4 and Mi-1 helicopters are also operated.

Major Cuban airfields include the Havana complex, San Julián, Kawama and Camagüey.

DOMINICAN REPUBLIC

Military aviation in the Dominican Republic dates only from the Second World War, when an aviation company was formed within the army, and various American trainers were acquired.

The *Aviación Militar Dominicana* currently numbers about 3,500 officers and men. There are about 45 combat aircraft, some 45 transports, about 14 helicopters and various trainers. The armed aircraft comprise about 20 D.H. Vampire F.1s (converted into fighter-bombers), a similar number of North American F-51D Mustangs, and about seven Douglas B-26 Invader bombers. There are two Convair PBY-5A amphibians, six Douglas C-47, six Curtiss C-46s, three DHC-2 Beavers and three Cessna 170s. The helicopters are of several different types.

There are military airfields at Azua, Barahona, Dajabón, Descubierta, La Romana, La Vega, Montechristi, Pedernales, Puerto Plata, Neiba, Santiago and San Juan.

ECUADOR

The *Cuerpo de Aviadores Militares* was established in 1920 with the assistance of an Italian mission; initial equipment included Italian and American types. In 1935 the Service was re-titled *Fuerza Aérea Ecuatoriana*, and a few American aircraft were acquired. Following the formation of the O.A.S. in 1948, American defence aid began to flow.

The Service has a current strength of about 3,500 personnel. Equipment comprises the Lockheed F-80C Shooting Star interceptor (ten aircraft), the Gloster Meteor FR.9 (eight aircraft), the BAC Canberra B.6 bomber (five aircraft) and a pair of Convair PBY-5A amphibians. Transport types include Douglas C-47 and DC-6B aircraft, and Beech C-45s. Three Bell 47 Sioux and one Hiller FH-1100 helicopters are operated, and there is a variety of trainers ranging from the Lockheed T-33A to the North American T-6 and T-28. Delivery of 8 BAC Strikemasters commences in 1973.

There are airfields at Quito, Manta, Guayaquil, Salinas, Loja, Latacunga, Cuenca and Riobamba.

EL SALVADOR

In 1923 a Military Aviation Service was established at Ilopango/San Salvador, with five Aviatik trainers. (This airfield remains the principal military air base today.) In 1948 membership of the O.A.S. brought a certain amount of American aid.

The *Fuerza Aérea Salvadurena* is about 1,000 strong, and operates about a dozen obsolete combat aircraft, a small number of transports and a collection of trainers. Types in service include the Vought F4U Corsair (about six aircraft), the North American F-51D Mustang (about six aircraft), the Douglas C-47, the North American T-6 and the Beech T-34 Mentor.

Airfields used by the military include Ilopango, San Miguel, Ahuachapán, Sonsonate, San Vicente, Chalatanango, Usultan and Zacatecoluca.

GUATEMALA

A French mission established the first aviation unit within the Guatemalan army in 1919-20; the first aircraft acquired were Avro 504s. (The *Fuerza Aérea de Guatemala* is still under army administration.) The first operational aircraft were a number of Boeing P-26As acquired in the late 1930s. Internal unrest at inopportune moments has prevented large-scale military aid from the U.S.A., and current strength is probably marginally lower than that in 1945.

With some 1,000 personnel, the Service operates about eleven North American F-51D Mustang fighter-bombers, five Douglas B-26 Invaders, six Douglas C-47 transports, a Hiller UH-12B helicopter, and a handful of trainers including North American T-6 Texans and Lockheed T-33A jets.

There are airfields at La Aurora/Guatemala City, Los Cipresales/Guatemala City, San José, Puerto Barrios and Flores.

HAITI

Haitian military aviation was organised by the U.S.A. in 1943, as the easiest way of providing a mail service. War-surplus trainer, transport and – ultimately – fighter aircraft were acquired in the late 1940s and early 1950s. With a current strength of about 250 men, the *Corps d'Aviation* is based at Duvalier Field, Port-au-Prince; there are airstrips at Les Cayes, Port de Paix, Cap Haïtien and Gonaïves. It is not known how many aircraft are in fact operational; the establishment comprises six North American F-51D Mustangs, two Beech C-45 and three Douglas C-47 transports, two North American T-6 and two T-28A trainers.

HONDURAS

The Honduran army established an aviation section in the early 1920s, its initial equipment consisting of a pair of Bristol F.2Bs. The proximity of Honduras to the Panama Canal Zone prompted U.S. aid from the early 1940s onward.

Current strength of the *Fuerza Aérea Hondurena* is perhaps 1,000 men. Main types operated are the Vought F4U Corsair fighter-bomber (about a dozen aircraft), the Douglas C-47 transport (four aircraft), and three Sikorsky H-19 helicopters. There are also a Douglas C-54 transport, some Cessna light communications types and a small number of North American T-6, Beech AT-11 and Lockheed T-33A trainers.

The main airfields are located at Tegucigalpa and Toncontin; about twenty smaller airstrips are distributed around the country, including Trujillo, Utila, Puerto Cortés, San Pedro, Gracias, La Paz and San Lorenzo.

JAMAICA

The Jamaica Defence Force has operated an Air Wing since 1963; current equipment comprises a DHC-6 Twin Otter transport, a Cessna 185 communications aircraft, and a pair of Bell 47G Sioux helicopters.

MEXICO

Although aircraft were used in the frequent revolutionary episodes which characterised Mexican history early in the century, it was not until 1924 that the *Fuerza Aérea Mexicana* was officially established, with D.H.4B aircraft. Mexico declared for the Allies in 1942 and placed bases at the disposal of the U.S.A., receiving in return a number of aircraft. A squadron equipped with Republic F-47D Thunderbolts narrowly missed seeing action in the Pacific theatre in 1945.

The Service currently numbers about 6,000 officers and men, and operates about 30 jet fighter-bombers, some 75 light strike/trainer aircraft, about 20 transports, 27 helicopters and about 35 pure trainers. Main types in service include the D.H. Vampire F.3 and Lockheed T-33A jets (about 15 of each type), the North American T-6G and T-28A light strike/trainer aircraft (about 45 and 30 aircraft respectively), Douglas C-47 and C-54 transports (six and five aircraft respectively), Bell 47G Sioux helicopters (18 aircraft), and Beech T-11 and T-34 Mentor trainers.

The main air base is Balbuena/Mexico City, and other military airfields include Guadalajara, Mazatlán, Mérida, Veracruz, Tehuantepec, Monterey, Oaxaca, Culiacan, Cananea, Tapachula, Campeche and San Luis Potosí.

The *Armada da Mexico*, the naval air arm, currently operates five Catalina amphibians and nine helicopters on search-and-rescue patrols.

NICARAGUA

Although a handful of Curtiss JN-4s and D.H.4s, had been flown by Nicaragua in the early 1920s, the *Fuerza Aérea de la Guardia Nacional* was not officially established until 1938. Modest U.S. military aid since 1948 has equipped the force, which is largely devoted to transport and communications.

Personnel currently number some 1,500, and about a dozen combat aircraft are operated, along with some seven transports, ten light communications aircraft, five helicopters and a small number of trainers some of which could, in an emergency, be given a light strike capability. Main types in service are the Lockheed T-33A light strike/jet trainer and the Douglas B-26 Invader bomber (about six of each type), the Douglas C-47 and Beech C-45 transports (three and four aircraft respectively), the Cessna 180 light communications aircraft, and the North American T-6G and T-28 trainers.

There are many airstrips scattered throughout the country, the main fields being Puerto Cabezas and Managua.

PARAGUAY

The Paraguayan army included an aviation section during the Gran Chaco War with Bolivia in the 1930s; this was established with the help of an Italian mission, largely equipped with Italian aircraft, and manned almost entirely by mercenaries. The air service, now the *Fuerza Aérea del Paraguay*, has not acquired any true combat aircraft since 1938, and concentrates on the more productive aspects of transport and communications.

The transport fleet, based on Campo Grande/Asunción, consists of about ten Douglas C-47s, two Douglas C-54s, a Convair 240 and a DHC-6 Twin Otter. There are North American T-6G and Fairchild M-62 trainers – six of the former reportedly armed – a Grumman Goose amphibian and 13 helicopters, mainly Bell 47G Sioux models.

PERU

Peru showed an interest in military aviation as early as 1912, and in 1920 acquired a dozen Avro 504s, four Morane-Saulnier Parasols and a Curtiss "Jenny" as the equipment of her first air arm. A vigorous programme of progressive re-equipment seems to have been followed from the earliest days, and today the *Fuerza Aérea Peruana* has the most technically sophisticated equipment on the continent.

With about 9,000 officers and men, the Service operates no fewer than 90 jet combat aircraft. Pride of place goes to the Dassault Mirage 5 (14 aircraft); other types flown include 16 Hawker Hunter F.52s, ten Lockheed F-80C Shooting Stars, 20 North American F-86F Sabres, and 22 BAC Canberra jet bombers of various versions. There are also eight Lockheed T-33A armed trainers, eight Douglas B-26 Invader bombers and six Lockheed PV-2 Harpoons. Five Grumman Albatross amphibians are in service. The transport element includes the DHC-2 Beaver (nine aircraft), the DHC-6 Twin Otter (three aircraft), and the DHC-5 Buffalo (sixteen aircraft). There are six Lockheed C-130 Hercules transports and 18 Beech Queen Airs. There are 23 helicopters of various models, and some 70 trainers including Dassault Mirage and Hawker Hunter two-seaters, and Cessna T-37B and T-41A models (26 and 25 aircraft respectively). Small numbers of Republic F-47D Thunderbolts remain in service.

Military airfields are located at Lima, Iquitos, Talara, Chiclayo, Trujillo, Pisco and Arequipa, and numerous other fields capable of handling jet aircraft.

UNITED STATES OF AMERICA

Balloons were used by the U.S. Army in both Civil and Spanish-American Wars, but the birth of air power may be dated more realistically in 1907, when the Aeronautical Division of the U.S. Signal Corps was formed – one N.C.O. and one soldier, under Capt. C. F.

Chandler. In 1908 one Wright "Flyer" biplane and one dirigible were acquired. At the outbreak of the First World War there were 92 officers and men, and eight machines; there had been more than twice this last figure, but "pusher" types had been grounded after heavy casualties in training (25% fatalities in the first 48 pilots). When the U.S.A. finally entered the War in 1917 she had no combat-worthy aircraft, and some 5,500 were acquired from Allied nations – mainly French and British types. The return of U.S. pilots who had been gaining experience with French and British air arms helped the rapid expansion of the Service, renamed U.S. Army Aviation Section since 1916.

Despite an establishment set at 2,500 aircraft in 1920, post-War apathy, inter-Service rivalry and lack of funds prevented anything like this strength being built up for years. The U.S. Army Air Service (1920) became the U.S. Army Air Corps (1926) and later the U.S. Army Air Force (1941), but it was not until well into the 1930s that equipment of realistic international standard became available, with the acquisition of the first monoplane fighters (Boeing P-26A) and bombers (Martin B-10). Rapid expansion followed recognition of America's plight in 1938 and 1939: about 800 combat aircraft, 700 of them obsolete, and 26,000 personnel including only some 2,000 pilots. (German strength in September 1939 stood at about 3,750 first-line aircraft, 500,000 men, and some 60,000–70,000 aircrew.) When Pearl Harbor brought America into the War two years later, the U.S.A.A.F. had about 2,800 first-line machines, of which 1,100 were combat-worthy, and 354,000 men. Standard fighter was the Curtiss P-40, while several hundred Bell P-39, Lockheed P-38 and older models were also in service. There was a variety of good medium bombers, and some 300 of the new B-17 and B-24 "heavies".

Loss of nearly all pre-War bases and aircraft in the Pacific in 1942 was followed by a steady build-up in Australia, and by December 1942 nearly 900 machines, mainly B-17s and C-47 transports, were in Britain. Unescorted daylight bombing was costly in losses, but improved range of fighters such as the P-38 and North American P-51 Mustang sent the pendulum in the other direction in 1943–44, until a crushing air superiority was established. The U.S.A.A.F. was heavily committed in all theatres of war, and backed by an unprecedented industrial effort. On VJ-Day first-line strength totalled 31,200 aircraft; 155 Groups, with 15,100 aircraft, were serving overseas. Personnel totalled about 2,250,000 men.

Post-War reduction was rapid, and strength reached low point in mid-1950, at the outbreak of the Korean War, with 48 Wings totalling some 20,000 aircraft of all types. By the end of that conflict the figure was 106 Wings, and in the last 20 years a steady expansion and progressive re-equipment with the most sophisticated types has kept the U.S.A.F. (a separate Service since 1947) the most powerful air force in the world. Current total

strengths are hard to calculate, but with some 810,000 personnel the U.S.A.F. probably operates about 20,000 aircraft. The main types in service are as follows:

Interceptors, fighters, fighter-bombers, reconnaissance fighters: Convair F-106A Delta Dart (about 200 aircraft); Convair F-102A Delta Dagger, McDonnell-Douglas F-101B Voodoo (about 60 aircraft); McDonnell-Douglas F-4 Phantom II (about 2,000 aircraft); McDonnell-Douglas RF-4C Phantom II (about 200 aircraft); Republic F-105 Thunderchief, North American F-100D Super Sabre, Northrop F-5A Freedom Fighter, LTV A-7D Corsair II (about 600 aircraft); General Dynamics F-111A (about 200 aircraft).

Bombers: Boeing B-52G and B-52H Stratofortress (about 400 aircraft); General Dynamics FB-111 (about 70 aircraft).

Light strike/trainers, specialist attack aircraft: Cessna A-37, Douglas AC-47, Fairchild AC-119 and AC-123, Lockheed AC-130.

Transport and tanker aircraft: Lockheed C-130 Hercules (about 300 aircraft); Lockheed C-141A StarLifter (about 300 aircraft); Lockheed C-5A Galaxy (about 100 aircraft); Boeing C-135 and KC-135 (several hundred aircraft); numerous light transport and communications types.

Airborne early warning aircraft: Lockheed EC-121.

Trainers: Beech T-34 Mentor, North American T-28 Trojan, Cessna T-41, Cessna T-27 and Northrop T-38A (in addition to training versions of many combat types)

Specialised reconnaissance aircraft: Lockheed SR-71C, Lockheed U-2, Martin B-57, McDonnell-Douglas EB-66 (countermeasures aircraft).

Helicopters: Kaman HH-43B Huskie, Sikorsky S-61 and HH-53.

U.S. Army

During the Second World War the U.S. Army operated some 4,500 light communications and observation aircraft, and acquired the first generation helicopters, then appearing, in the immediate post-War years. By the mid-1950s the Army had some 1,800 fixed-wing and a similar number of rotary-wing machines in service. The very sharply increasing use of helicopters in specialist rôles – including ground attack – over the past ten years has led the U.S. Army into the position as the world's foremost operator of these aircraft. Current equipment includes perhaps 10,000 helicopters, of the following models: Bell OH-13 Sioux (about 2,000 aircraft), Bell OH-58A Jetranger (about 2,200 aircraft), Bell UH-1 Iroquois (about 4,000 aircraft), Bell AH-1G Hueycobra (about 750 aircraft), Hughes OH-6A (about 1,300 aircraft), Boeing-Vertol CH-47A (about 600 aircraft), Sikorsky CH-37B (about 90 aircraft), and CH-54A (about 60 aircraft).

Fixed wing aircraft in service include the DHC-2 Beaver (about 800 aircraft), DHC-3 Otter (about 200 aircraft), Cessna L-19 Bird Dog (about 1,000 aircraft),

Grumman OV-1 Mohawk (about 300 aircraft); Beech C-45, Douglas C-47, Lockheed VC-140 Jetstar, Cessna T-41B (about 250 aircraft) and Beech T-42A (about 60 aircraft). In addition to the helicopters in operational service, some 1,200 helicopter trainers are in use.

U.S. Navy and U.S. Marine Corps

U.S. Navy interest in aviation dates back to the early years of the century, and the first funds for aircraft purchase were voted in 1911. There were about 20 machines in service when America entered the First World War, and more than 1,250 aircraft were operated by the Navy and Marine Corps by the end of the War. The first carrier, U.S.S. *Langley*, was converted from a collier in 1922. A steady programme of expansion gave the Navy eight carriers by 1941 (*Langley, Saratoga, Lexington, Ranger, Yorktown, Enterprise, Wasp* and *Hornet*), and eleven more were under construction. Naval and Marine air power played a decisive part in all the major actions of the Pacific War; by VJ-Day no less than 92 Navy and six Marine attack and escort carriers were operational. The main aircraft types operated included the Grumman F4F Wildcat and F6F Hellcat fighters, the Grumman TBF Avenger torpedo-bombers, the Douglas TBD Devastator torpedo-bombers and SBD Dauntless dive-bombers, the Curtiss-Wright SB2C Helldiver dive-bombers, and the Vought F4U Corsair fighters. Post-War cuts reduced aircraft strength from about 40,000 to around 10,000.

The first generation of carrier-borne jets arrived in time for the Korean War, including the Grumman F9F Panther and McDonnell F2H Banshee. Together with developed versions of wartime and post-war piston-engined attack aircraft, they carried out ground-support duties during that conflict. Currently there are 22 carriers on strength, of which 16 are operational at the time of writing. There are some 8,000 U.S. Navy aircraft in service. Main types flown include:

Interceptor fighters, fighter-bombers, reconnaissance fighters: McDonnell-Douglas F-4 Phantom II, LTV F-8 Crusader, McDonnell-Douglas A-4 Skyhawk, Grumman A-6A Intruder, LTV A-7E Corsair II, North American RA-5C Vigilante and LTV RF-8G Crusader.

Airborne early warning aircraft, maritime reconnaissance aircraft: Grumman E-2A Hawkeye, Grumman S-2E Tracker, and Lockheed P-3 Orion.

Helicopters: Sikorsky SH-3 Sea King, Sikorsky SH-34G, Kaman UH-2 Seasprite and Boeing-Vertol UH-46A.

U.S.M.C. aircraft strength currently stands at about 1,200. Among the main types flown are the McDonnell-Douglas F-4 Phantom II in various marks (17 squadrons), Grumman A-6 Intruder (12 squadrons), and the Lockheed KC-130F Hercules (three squadrons), while about one hundred Hawker Siddeley A-8A (Harrier) vertical/short take-off strike aircraft are expected to join the U.S.M.C. fixed-wing aircraft inventory during 1973.

Helicopters in service include Sikorsky UH-34D and Boeing-Vertol CH-46A models in 14 squadrons, more than 100 Sikorsky CH-53A Sea Stallion, about 24 Bell UH-1E and about 38 Bell AH-1G Iroquois. North American OV-10A Bronco armed reconnaissance aircraft (about 124 aircraft) are also flown.

The position of air bases in the United States is indicated on the accompanying map.

URUGUAY

Uruguay established a Department of Military Aviation in 1916, with a school – consisting of two or three Morane-Saulniers – at San Fernando. During the inter-War years numbers of French, Italian, British and American aircraft were operated by the *Aeronáutica Militar*. In the post-War years Uruguay's wartime gesture of making available to the U.S.A. brought her considerable military aid and a fairly wide variety of military aircraft.

Since 1952 the service has been designated *Fuerza Aérea Uruguaya*; current manpower is around 1,600. The combat element comprises ten Lockheed F-80C Shooting Star fighter-bombers, and six Lockheed T-33A light strike/jet trainers. There are 13 Douglas C-47s, five Curtiss C-46 Commandos, two Beech Queen Airs, two Fokker F-27M Troopships, two Fairchild-Hiller FH-227Bs, and a DHC-2 Beaver in the transport fleet. Three helicopters are flown, and there are 20 North American T-6G Texan and ten Beech T-11 trainers. Like the T-33As mentioned above, the Texans could be given a light strike capability.

Military airfields are situated at Melilla and Carrasco outside Montevideo, and at Melo, Colonia and Paysandú.

The *Aviacion Naval*, which has a main base at Laguna del Sauce and two other bases on the River Plate estuary, dates from as early as 1920. Current equipment includes five Grumman F6F-5 Hellcat fighters, three S-2A Trackers, two Martin Mariner flying-boats, six helicopters, and a number of trainer and liaison types.

VENEZUELA

First established with the aid of a French mission in 1920, the Military Air Service initially operated Caudron and Farman aircraft. The title changed to Military Aviation Regiment in 1936; the present style – *Fuerzas Aéreas Venezolanas* – appeared in the immediate post-War years, when the army and naval air arms were merged. The offer of bases to the U.S.A. during the War brought its usual reward, and today Venezuela has one of the largest and most efficient of South American air arms.

Personnel strength stands at around 9,000 men; the equipment operated includes some 75 combat aircraft, about 40 transports, about 32 helicopters, about 50 trainers and some light communications types. The bulk of the combat force is made up of 18 North American

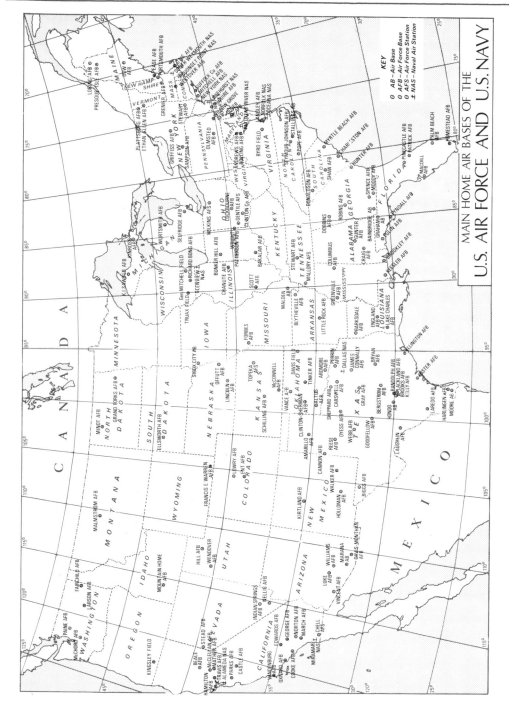

MAIN HOME AIR BASES OF THE
U.S. AIR FORCE AND U.S. NAVY

KEY

AB – Air Base
AFB – Air Force Base
AFS – Air Force Station
NAS – Naval Air Station

Note: Some municipal, State and commercial airports – not shown on the above map – are or have been also used by the military air forces and by the U.S. National Air Guard. Not all the bases and stations shown are currently active, but are included for historical and reference purposes. (Compiled from information provided by courtesy of the U.S. Air Force, U.S. Navy and the N.G.S.)

F-86F and 40 F-86K Sabre jet fighters, with a small residual force of D.H. Vampire and Venom fighter-bombers, and 15 BAC Canberra B.2 and P.R.3 aircraft. There are about 20 Douglas C-47 and C-54 transports, 18 Fairchild C-123Bs, and a Hawker Siddeley 748; four Lockheed C-130H Hercules were ordered in 1971. Twenty of the helicopters are Sud Alouette IIIs, the remainder Bell and Sikorsky designs. The trainers include the BAC Jet Provost T.52 (15 aircraft), the ubiquitous North American T-6G Texan, and various Beech aircraft. Delivery of 16 OV-10E Broncos commenced recently.

There are military airfields situated at Maracaibo, Coro, Caracas, Barcelona and Maturín.

3. THE MIDDLE EAST

ABU DHABI

One of several small local forces set up with British assistance in anticipation of the withdrawal of British regular forces from the Persian Gulf area, the Air Wing of the Abu Dhabi Defence Forces is largely manned by British and Commonwealth "contract" personnel, but Pakistani influence increases. Maintenance is carried out by a British civilian contractor. Equipment includes approximately a dozen Hawker Siddeley Hunter jet fighter/ground-attack aircraft, half a dozen transports (DHC-4 Caribous and Britten-Norman BN-2s) and a small number of Agusta-Bell 206 helicopters. 14 Dassault Mirage 5s are on order.

EGYPT

The Egyptian Air Force was created under British supervision in 1932. In 1939 Egypt was a sovereign monarchy, and the renamed Royal Egyptian Air Force operated small numbers of Avro Ansons, Gloster Gladiators and Bristol Blenheims. The service played no part in the Second World War, but received numbers of Hawker Hurricanes and Curtiss Tomahawk fighters. Supermarine Spitfires and a handful of heavy bombers were acquired in the post-War years, and some Douglas C-47s were fitted for bombing. Losses were heavy during the Israeli War of Independence in 1948, and serviceability was low. Hawker Furies and Gloster Meteor jets were acquired in the early 1950s, but Soviet influence became marked by 1956; in that year the air force, numbering about 3,500 with some 400 aircrew, received large numbers of Mikoyan MiG-15s and Ilyushin Il-28s, and Russian training facilities were offered. Egyptian personnel had not fully mastered this new equipment by the outbreak of the Sinai Campaign, and their showing in air combat was poor. The vast majority of the air force was destroyed on the ground by Anglo-French strikes.

By June 1967 the force had been built up to a total of some 330 first-line combat aircraft, with considerable reserves. Three air regiments, each of three squadrons, flew about 100 MiG-21F and MiG-21PF fighters; one regiment was equipped with some 30 MiG-17Fs and one with MiG-19s; five independent squadrons flew MiG-15bis and MiG-17s under army control; and there was a regiment of about 35 Il-28 bombers. A strategic bomber regiment had some 30 Tupolev Tu-16s fitted with Soviet *Kennel* missiles. Early morning strikes on 5th June 1967 destroyed the bulk of this force on the ground; small numbers got into the air but were generally outclassed by the Israelis. Total losses on the first two days of the Six-Day War reached 317 combat aircraft and helicopters, including 12 out of 17 brand-new Sukhoi Su-7Bs which were still with a conversion squadron. Israeli losses in the same period were 26, of which 23 were due to ground fire. The few surviving Egyptian units, mainly MiG-15 and MiG-17 ground-attack elements, fought with considerable courage over Sinai, but were soon wiped out.

Since 1967 the Egyptian Air Force has been built up once more, to greater strength, by the USSR, and Soviet aircrew have flown from Egyptian bases on reconnaissance duties. Most Soviet personnel have now been withdrawn, but the continued presence of a squadron of MiG-25 *Foxbats* is possible; prior to the recent deterioration in Russo-Egyptian relations they were based at Cairo West, and it was reported that Egyptian pilots received instruction on the type.

Current strength is about 20,000 men. Main types in service include the MiG-21 in various models (approximately 300 aircraft; an additional 150 MiG-21MFs, manned by Soviet personnel, were withdrawn in mid-1972), the MiG-17 and MiG-15 (approximately 150 aircraft), the Sukhoi Su-7B (more than 100 aircraft), the Ilyushin Il-28 (approximately 28 aircraft) and the Tupolev Tu-16 (approximately 15 aircraft). There are some 60 Antonov and Ilyushin transports and about the same number of Mil helicopters, and some 150 trainers of standard Soviet and Czech types.

Main airbases in Egypt include Cairo West, El Mansura, Inchas, Abu Sueir, Fayid, Kabrit, the Helouan complex, Beni Souef, El Minya, Hurghada, Luxor, Ras Banas and Deversoir – although the latter's proximity to the Suez Canal calls its serviceability into question. Military units are sometimes based at Cairo International.

IRAQ

The Royal Iraqi Air Force was established in 1931 with British assistance, and initial equipment comprised de Havilland Gipsy Moths and Puss Moths. Several other British biplane types were acquired in the 1930s, and immediately prior to the Second World War Gloster Gladiators and Avro Ansons operated alongside SM.79s and Breda Ba.65s ordered from Italy. Losses were heavy during the Raschid Ali rising against the British in 1941. Re-equipment with Hawker Fury fighter-bombers in 1946 was followed by the acquisition of the first jets, 12 de Havilland Vampires, in 1953. A dozen Hawker Hunter F.6 fighters were purchased shortly before the

The Fairchild C-119F Packet; developed from the C-82 which first flew in September 1944, the C-119 entered service with numerous air forces during the nineteen-fifties and is shown here in the insignia of Air Transport Command, Royal Canadian Air Force

1958 revolution which led to a severing of ties with Britain and the increase of Soviet influence. Soviet aid ceased in the mid-1960s after Israeli defectors presented Israel with several MiG-21s, but re-commenced after the Six-Day War. Iraq's part in that conflict was, as usual, largely verbal. A lone Tupolev Tu-16 was shot down after bombing the Israeli town of Netanya, and an Israeli reprisal raid destroyed nine MiG-21s and five Hunters on Iraqi airfields.

Current strength is around 7,500 men. There are thought to be some 220 combat aircraft including the MiG-21 (approximately 60 aircraft), the MiG-19 and MiG-17 (about 50 aircraft), the Sukhoi Su-7B (about 50 aircraft), and the Hawker Siddeley Hunter (about 36 aircraft). There are some ten Ilyushin Il-28 and eight Tu-16 bombers; about 45 Antonov and Ilyushin transports; and about 35 Mil and Westland Wessex helicopters. Trainers are of mixed British and Soviet types.

Main airfields are Habbaniyah, Baghdad/Raschid, Basra, Shaiba, Kirkuk and Mosul, and a base code-named *Hotel Three* on the pipe-line some 40 miles from the Iraqi-Jordanian frontier.

ISRAEL

The Israel Defence Force/Air Force, *Chel Ha'avir*, has its origins in clandestine light aircraft operated by the Hagganah during the British Mandate. The first official air arm, *Sherut Avir*, was established in 1948 and fought the War of Independence with great success despite severe supply problems. Initial combat aircraft comprised a small batch of Czech Avia C.210s (Czech-built

Junkers Jumo-engined Messerschmitt Bf 109Gs) and a captured Egyptian Spitfire; more Spitfires from Czecho-slovakia, a handful of Beaufighters and B-17 Fortresses, and some modified C-46 and C-47 transports also saw service, North American F-51D Mustangs, de Havilland Mosquitos, and in 1953/54, Gloster Meteors, were acquired before the Sinai Campaign of 1956. Dassault Ouragans and Mystères also fought in this campaign.

By 1967, with France as the main supplier, a force of about 250 combat aircraft had been built up. There were some 70 Dassault Mirage IIICJ interceptor/strike aircraft, some 40 Mystère IVAs and a similar number of Ouragans, about 60 Potez (Fouga) Magister armed trainers fitted for ground-attack, 18 Super Mystère B.2s, and 24 twin-engined Sud Vautours. The heavier types were committed to pre-emptive strikes on the first day of the Six-Day War, virtually destroying the Arab air forces on the ground; the Magisters were used in direct support of ground troops. Total losses in the War were 50 aircraft lost or scrapped.

In recent years France's altered political stance has forced Israel to look to the USA for aircraft. Currently the IDF/AF musters about 14,000 regulars and 6,000 quick-response reservists. There are about 60 McDonnell-Douglas F-4E Phantom IIs in service; some 75 McDonnell-Douglas A-4E and A-4M Skyhawks; and large numbers of Mirage IIICJs. About 30 each of the older Mystères and Ouragans are thought to be on strength, with about a dozen Super Mystère B.2s, and about 85 Magisters. The indigenous aircraft industry, which already supplies all ordnance and many spares, is reported to have delivered some 24 Mirage-derived heavy strike fighters codenamed *Barak* (Lightning). Second-line units operate squadrons of Nord Noratlas and Douglas C-47 transports, and nine helicopter squadrons are equipped with some 80 Agusta-Bell 205s, Sud Alouette IIIs, Super Frelons, Sikorsky Sea Stallions, and H-34 Choctaws.

The location of airbases is classified, but former R.A.F. facilities such as Ramat David, Hatzerim and Eknon are known to be in use. The main operational bases are in the remote Negev area.

It should be mentioned that man for man, the IDF/AF is generally conceded to be the most highly trained, highly motivated, highly skilled and highly experienced air force in the world today.

JORDAN

The Royal Jordanian Air Force traces its birth to a single D.H. Dragon Rapide operated by the "Arab Legion Air Force" in 1949. Under R.A.F. supervision a small air force was established in the early 1950s, and British methods and equipment have characterised the force at most stages of its existence. (Despite political freezes on several occasions, British influence remains noticeable.)

The first combat equipment comprised nine D.H. Vampires acquired in 1955, and the following year the new title was adopted. By June 1967 some 24 Hawker Hunters and 16 Vampires were in service, with small numbers of helicopters and light transports. This force was wiped out in the Six-Day War, the skill and fearless spirit of the Jordanian pilots drawing unstinted praise from Israeli observers.

Current strength is some 2,000 men and about 70 aircraft. The combat equipment comprises the Lockheed F-104A Starfighter (about 35 aircraft) and the Hawker Siddeley Hunter FGA. Mk. 9 (about 18 aircraft). There are Hawker Siddeley Dove and C-47 transports, and about eight helicopters of Sud Alouette and Westland Whirlwind type.

The jets operate from Mafraq and Amman, and there are smaller fields at Ma'an, Aqaba, and in the eastern desert.

KUWAIT

Another force formed with British assistance in the period before British withdrawal from the Gulf, the Kuwait Air Force dates from 1960. British seconded servicemen and "contract" officers run the force while local personnel are being trained. This small but sophisticated air arm has some 14 BAC Lightning F. Mk. 53 and T. Mk. 55 supersonic interceptors (with a strike capability); six BAC 167 Strikemaster light attack aircraft; six Hawker Siddeley Hunters; small numbers of DHC-4 Caribou transports; and about eight helicopters.

LEBANON

In 1943 the French Mandate ended, and the *Force Aérienne Libanaise* was established in 1949 with mainly British equipment. The first combat aircraft were small numbers of D.H. Vampires acquired in 1955. Thus far Lebanon has avoided major clashes with Israel, although a venturesome Lebanese Hunter was shot down over Israel during the Six-Day War. Current strength is about 1,000 and 1,200 men. The combat equipment comprises 6 Dassault Mirage IIIEL fighters, and ten Hawker Hunters. There are two Hunter and four Potez Magister trainers which could be equipped for attack if necessary. There are small numbers of transports of various types, and eight Sud Alouette helicopters.

Main airfields are believed to be Rayack, Khalde and Kleyate.

MUSCAT AND OMAN

The Sultan of Oman's Air Force, dating from 1959, is still largely manned by British and "contract" personnel and maintained by British civilian contractors. Current equipment comprises the BAC 167 Strikemaster (about 12 aircraft), the BAC Provost T.52 armed trainer (about five aircraft), and DHC-2 Beaver and ten Short Skyvan transports. Main bases are Beit-al-Falaj in the north, and Salalah in the south; the latter is the operational base for strikes against the insurgents now active in Dhofar Province.

SAUDI ARABIA

The present nation dates from 1926, but a few ex-R.A.F. D.H.9 bombers were operated during the tribal wars which preceded that date. By the outbreak of the Second World War a force of some 160 men and nine machines had been assembled, initially under British supervision but later manned by mercenaries of various nationalities; there were bases at Dhahran and Jeddah. Little further expansion took place until the early 1950s, when oil revenues and American airfield rent allowed a rebuilding of Saudi air power with Western assistance.

Currently the Royal Saudi Air Force has some 5,000 personnel, and additional aircrew and technical personnel serving under secondment or "contract" from the R.A.F. and other Western nations. Equipment comprises a sophisticated interceptor and missile force integrated with a radar chain. Combat types comprise the BAC Lightning F. Mk. 53 and T. Mk. 55 (about 35 aircraft), the BAC 167 Strikemaster (about 24 aircraft), and the North American F-86F Sabre (about 16 aircraft). There are some 25 transports of various American models including nine Lockheed C-130E Hercules, with four more on order; and about 38 helicopters – mainly Agusta-Bell types.

The main military airfields are Jeddah, Dhahran and Riyadh, with lesser facilities at Yanbu, Medina, Taif, Jubail, Ras Tanura and Dukhan.

SYRIA

Syria gained nationhood in 1943 with the ending of the French Mandate, and an air force was established in 1946. Initial equipment, in the form of Fiat trainers and various transports, did not arrive until 1949. Some 30 D.H. Vampires were acquired in 1952–53 by rather devious means, and later passed to Egypt. Syria purchased about 25 Gloster Meteors in the early 1950s, and some 40 late-model Spitfires; and from 1955 Soviet aid and instructors became available. The initial deliveries of MiG-15s were destroyed on the ground during the Arab-Israeli war of 1956.

By 1967 a force of about 40 MiG-21s, 60 MiG-17s, and small numbers of Soviet transports and helicopters had been assembled. The Six-Day War saw the destruction of probably 75% of this force, including virtually all the MiG-21s and about half the older combat types. Vigorous Soviet re-equipment followed immediately.

Current strength is about 12,000 men. There are thought to be approximately 120 MiG-21s in service, with some 50 Sukhoi Su-7Bs, and about 80 MiG-17s and MiG-15s. Small numbers of the usual Soviet trainers and helicopters are operated, and there is a mixture of Douglas C-47 and Ilyushin transports.

Main airbases are at Saigal, Damascus, Dumeyr, Marj Rhiyal, and *Tango Four* – a site on the pipe-line near Palmyra.

SOUTH YEMEN PEOPLE'S REPUBLIC

The former British protectorate of Aden ordered four BAC 167 Strikemasters in 1971; four Jet Provost T. Mk. 5 armed trainers were already in service, with six helicopters and small numbers of Douglas C-47 and DHC-2 Beaver transports. Links with the revolutionary regime have been severed, and it is not thought that, given the lack of spares and trained personnel, this force can be operational. Future equipment will no doubt come from Communist sources, but financial considerations make this unlikely in the immediate future; current friction with the United Arab Republic will not ease the position.

YEMEN

The Yemen Republican Air Force is the successor to the Yemen Air Force of the previous royalist regime, which operated a mixed collection of transports and communications types in the 1950s. In 1957 aid, in the form of the first dozen of a total of 36 Ilyushin Il-10 attack aircraft, was delivered by Czechoslovakia, together with a few Mil helicopters from Russia and Egyptian instructors. Large numbers of Egyptian, and some Soviet aircrew served in the Yemen during the long-drawn-out civil war between the royalist and republican factions in the 1960s, when a sizeable part of the Egyptian armed forces occupied the country. Yemenis have proved to have a remarkably low aptitude for flying,

and even now it is likely that the Republican Air Force is in fact manned by Egyptians.

Current equipment consists of a dozen MiG-17s, and about the same number of Il-28s, with small numbers of Ilyushin Il-14 and Douglas C-47 transports, Yakovlev Yak-11 trainers and Mil helicopters. There are airfields at San's, Taiz and Hodeida.

4. ASIA AND AUSTRALASIA

AFGHANISTAN

As long ago as 1924 the forces of King Amanullah were supported by an air arm, comprising initially a pair of Bristol F.2Bs and a small number of Russian R-2 reconnaissance machines. This force was destroyed during a civil war in 1929. The Royal Afghan Air Force was established in 1937 and acquired numbers of Hawker Harts and some Italian types; Italian and British assistance was given in training personnel. Small batches of Hawker Hinds and Avro Ansons, supplied just before and after the Second World War, were still in service in the mid-1950s when Soviet influence in the area increased. Russia and the USA have both given aid of various kinds, but the air force remains predominantly Russian-equipped.

Current strength is uncertain. There are seven fighter squadrons, some of which have Mikoyan MiG-21s but three of which are probably still equipped with the MiG-17. There are three squadrons of Ilyushin Il-28 bombers (approximately 45 aircraft), about 30 Ilyushin transports of various models, about two dozen Mil helicopters and various training types.

Major airfields are situated at Kabul/Sherpur, Mazar-i-Sharif, Jalalabad and Kandahar.

AUSTRALIA

The Australian Flying Corps was formed in 1913, and a total of four squadrons fought alongside the R.F.C. in the Middle East and on the Western Front; nevertheless the A.F.C. was disbanded in 1919. Reformed in 1920, it became the Australian Air Force in 1921, later being granted the prefix "Royal". Britain presented the embryo force with more than 100 war-surplus machines including S.E.5a, Sopwith, D.H.9, Avro 504K and Fairey IIID types. Between 1921 and 1937 only small numbers of additional aircraft were acquired, including Bristol Bulldogs, Westland Wapitis, Hawker Demons and Avro Ansons. An expansion programme gave the R.A.A.F. a strength of 3,500 men and 164 operational machines in 12 squadrons by the outbreak of war in 1939. Australia made a major contribution to the training of Allied aircrew, and Australians distinguished themselves on all fronts during the War, particularly in the Mediterranean and Pacific theatres. Australian squadrons flew most of the major American and British combat types of the period, as well as their own "home-grown" Commonwealth Boomerang ground-attack fighter. On VJ-Day R.A.A.F. strength in the Pacific area stood at around 132,000 personnel with 3,200 first-line aircraft in 52 squadrons; another 13,000 were serving in Europe, 2,000 of them in 16 R.A.A.F. squadrons and the remainder in R.A.F. units. Losses throughout the War totalled more than 10,000 killed and missing.

Peacetime establishment was set at around 15,000 personnel. In the early post-War years Australian squadrons fought alongside the USAF in Korea and the R.A.F. in Malaya. The first jet aircraft acquired were some 80 D.H. Vampires built under licence from 1949 onwards. In the mid-1950s licence-built Sabres and Canberras came into service.

Current strength is about 22,500 personnel. The main aircraft in service include the Dassault Mirage IIIOA (90 aircraft), the McDonnell-Douglas F-4E Phantom II (23 aircraft on lease pending decision on purchase of GD F-111C), the licence-built Aermacchi MB.326H (79 aircraft), the Lockheed P-3B Orion and P-2H Neptune maritime reconnaissance types (ten and 12 aircraft respectively), and numbers of Sabres and Canberras (32 and 23 respectively). The transport fleet comprises the DHC-4 Caribou (23 aircraft), the Lockheed C-130A and C-130E Hercules (12 of each aircraft), the Douglas C-47 (22 aircraft) and the Hawker Siddeley HS.748 (ten aircraft). Some 47 Bell UH-1 Iroquois helicopters are operated; some helicopter units saw action in support of Australian ground troops in Vietnam.

Naval Aviation

While amphibious machines had been operated from R.A.N. ships for years previously, the establishment of a Fleet Air Arm did not take place until 1948. Small numbers of Hawker Sea Furies and Fairey Fireflies were operated from H.M.S. *Sydney* over Korea in 1952–53. H.M.S. *Vengeance* was loaned by the Royal Navy in 1953 due to delays in the completion of H.M.A.S. *Melbourne*, which finally entered service in 1956. Jets, in the form of de Havilland Vampire trainers and Sea Venom fighters, were acquired in the mid-1960s.

Types currently in R.A.N./F.A.A. service are the McDonnell-Douglas A-4G Skyhawk (16 aircraft) and TA-4G (four aircraft), the Grumman S-2E Tracker (14 aircraft) and the Aermacchi MB.326H armed trainer (nine aircraft). There are 20 Westland Wessex and six Bell UH-1B Iroquois helicopters; orders were recently reported for ten Westland Sea King and about six WG.13 Lynx helicopters.

Army Aviation

The Australian Army Aviation Corps operates about 75 helicopters, mainly Bell 47G Sioux, but also with some Sud Alouette and Boeing-Vertol CH-47 Chinook types.

There are military airfields at Butterworth in Malaysia, and at (Victoria) Avalon, Ballarat, Point Cook, Laverton, Mangalore, Benalla, Essendon, Moorabbin, Fisherman's Bend; (New South Wales), at Wagga, Fairbairn, Kingsford Smith, Richmond, Bankstown, Williamtown, Rathmines, Dubbo, Parkes, Broken Hill, Bourke and (Fleet Air Arm) Nowra and Schofield; (Queensland), at Amberley, Eagle Farm, Charleville, Blackall, Longreach, Winton, Cloncurry, Charter Towers, Townsville, Garbutt, Normanton, Cairns, Camooweal and Iron Range; (Northern Territory), at Alice Springs, Daly Waters, Katherine, and (Fleet Air Arm) Darwin; (South Australia), at Oodnadatta, Woomera, Mallala and Parafield; (Western Australia), at Forrest, Cunderdin, Albany, Perth, Kalgoorlie, Geraldton, Carnarvan, Learmouth, Onslow, Port Hedland, Broome, Halls Creek, Derby and Wyndham; at Cambridge/Tasmania; and at Port Moresby, Lae and Finshhafen in New Guinea.

A BAC Canberra B.8 of the Indian Air Force. Introduced into R.A.F. service in 1951 as its first jet bomber, the Canberra has probably been more widely exported than any other twin-jet bomber during the past twenty years, serving with the air forces of the U.S.A., Argentine, Australia, Ecuador, India, New Zealand, Pakistan, Peru, Rhodesia, South Africa and Venezuela

BURMA

The Union of Burma Air Force dates from 1955. The U.K. played a large part in establishing the force and providing initial equipment and instructors. Types in service have included Supermarine Spitfires, D.H. Mosquitos and Hawker Sea Furies.

Current strength is about 6,000 men. Types operated include the North American F-86F Sabre (about 12 aircraft), Lockheed T-33A (ten aircraft), D.H. Vampire T.55 (six aircraft), DHC-3 Otter (six aircraft), Douglas C-47 (six aircraft), Beech C-45 (four aircraft) and BAC Provost T. Mk. 53 armed trainer (about 30 aircraft). There are some 25 helicopters of various Kaman, Sud, Bell and Mil models.

The main airfields are Mingaladon and Meiktila, with lesser facilities at Myitkyina, Bhamo, Lashio, Mandalay, Kentung, Namsan, Heho, Magwe, Akyab, Marsin, Toungoo, Moulmein, Tavoy and Mergui.

CAMBODIA

Cambodia did not gain full independence from France until 1955. The original title of the air arm was Royal Khmer Aviation; initial equipment, which arrived in 1954–55, comprised small numbers of Japanese-built Fletcher FD.25A light strike aircraft and Morane-Saulnier MS.733 Alcyon armed trainers. A neutralist foreign policy was followed, and several types of French, American and Russian aircraft were acquired. A *coup*, and subsequent widespread operations in Cambodia by American, South Vietnamese and North Vietnamese forces during the period 1970–72, have completely altered the picture.

A pro-American regime is currently in control and the re-named Cambodian Air Force has some 2,500 personnel augmented by numerous American advisors. Exact strengths are not known. There are certainly some 20 Douglas A-1 Skyraiders in service, and at least the same number of North American T-28D Trojan light strike aircraft – possibly considerably more. The motley transport fleet comprises about a dozen C-47s, six Dassault Flamants, and small numbers of DHC-2 Beavers, Antonov An-2s and Ilyushin Il-14s. There are at least 15 helicopters, and at least 40 trainers ranging from North American T-6G Texans to Potez Magister jets.

The main base is at Pochentong outside the capital, Phnom-Penh; additional bases have no doubt been built by American teams.

CHINA, PEOPLE'S REPUBLIC

In the period before the First World War various regional warlords included aircraft of different types in their forces, but their effectiveness was dubious, as was that of the official national army and naval air arms after the foundation of the republic in 1911. In 1919 British and American missions helped establish the Chinese Aviation Service, and in the early 1920s at least 100 aircraft were operated; the first types acquired were Avro 504 trainers, Handley Page 0/400 bombers and Vickers Vimy transports. Morane-Saulnier, Bréguet and Ansaldo types were also purchased, and saw much confused action in the chaotic internal disorders which afflicted China between the Wars. Japanese invasion brought a measure of unified action under the Central Government of Chiang Kai-shek; an American mission helped organise an effective air force. Types operated during the 1930s included Curtiss Hawk, Fiat CR.32, and various Russian and British fighters, and many different U.S., Italian, German and Russian bomber and transport types. At least two of the "regional air forces" survived for a few years into the Sino-Japanese War. Soviet and American types were supplied to the Central Government, along with volunteer pilots; and in the areas they occupied the Japanese set up various puppet air arms flying Japanese equipment. The most numerous Central Government Air Force combat type was the Curtiss P-40, of which nearly 400 were supplied; 150 North American B-25 Mitchell bombers were also provided.

After the War the Chinese Air Force was established with various American types and some ex-Canadian D.H. Mosquitos. In 1949 the victorious advance of the Communist faction forced the withdrawal of the Nationalist Government to the off-shore island of Taiwan, and Soviet influence replaced American in the Chinese armed forces. Many different types of Soviet combat and support aircraft were supplied, up to and including the MiG-21, before relations between China and the U.S.S.R. finally broke down. In the early 1960s, shortly after the rift, there is evidence that the sudden shortage of spares and fuel had serious consequences for the operational readiness of the People's Air Force. A growing national aircraft industry has to some extent recouped the position; however, exact current strengths are not known. It is likely that while large, the People's Air Force is not generally at the highest level of operational efficiency, by international standards. This is mainly due to the isolationist stance of recent years, and current trends toward increased international contact may change the situation.

The Air Force of the Chinese People's Liberation Army has some 180,000 personnel, and perhaps 3,000 aircraft. It has been speculated that this total comprises about 50 or 60 Air Regiments, each of about 30 aircraft, equipped with fighter and fighter-bomber types; perhaps 20 Regiments of bombers; and the remainder transports, trainers, helicopters and communications types. The main fighter type is the Shenyang F-6 – a licence-built MiG-19. Numbers of Shenyang F-4 (MiG-17) fighter-bombers remain in service in the ground-support rôle; and there are residual F-2s (MiG-15s) in the training units. It is reported that without Soviet sanction a simplified version of the MiG-21, re-designated F-9, is in production as an interceptor. The Ilyushin Il-28 is the most numerous bomber in service, with some Tupolev Tu-4 and Tu-16 types; it is reported that a Chinese-built modification of the latter is also being produced at Shenyang. Transports and helicopters, trainers and light aircraft cover the full spectrum of Soviet types. No information can be given about Chinese airbases.

Naval Aviation

At the present time China has no aircraft carriers and no warships capable of embarking anything larger than a helicopter or a slung amphibian. Nevertheless, the navy is believed to have about 1,000 land-based aircraft, including some 350 jet fighters and fighter-bombers in the MiG/Shenyang series, and perhaps 80 Ilyushin Il-28s, as well as transports, reconnaissance and liaison helicopters, and seaplanes.

CHINA, TAIWAN

American equipment was supplied to Chiang Kai-shek's Nationalist Air Force to replace the 160-odd aging Second World War types with which it escaped from the mainland. The first jets were Republic F-84G Thunderjets, followed by North American F-86 Sabres, F-100 Super Sabres, and, in the early 1960s, Lockheed F-104A and F-104G Starfighters.

The Chinese Nationalist Air Force has a strength of some 65,000 men, and nearly 300 first-line combat aircraft. Main types in service include the Lockheed F-104 Starfighter (approximately 60 aircraft), Lockheed RF-104G (about 25 aircraft), McDonnell-Douglas RF-101 (about 25 aircraft), North American F-100A Super Sabre (about 90 aircraft), and Northrop F-5A Freedom Fighter (about 80 aircraft). There are some 130 transports of various Douglas, Curtiss, Fairchild and Beech models; numbers of Grumman amphibians; and some 15 helicopters. Much larger numbers of Bell UH-1H Iroquois helicopters, and licence-built AIDC-Bell models, are in service with the Chinese Nationalist Army.

There are military airfields at Tainan and Taihoku.

HONG KONG

Half-a-dozen Auster spotter aircraft and Sud Alouette III helicopters are operated under R.A.F. supervision by local auxiliary personnel from Kai Tak airfield.

INDIA

The Indian Air Force was established in 1933 under R.A.F. supervision, with an initial strength of one flight of Westland Wapiti general purpose biplanes. In 1940 a full squadron of Wapitis was formed for army co-operation duties; strength on the outbreak of war was about 285 officers and men. Expansion was much speeded by Japanese entry into the War; from early operations designed to take over some of the R.A.F.'s load on the North-West Frontier, the new force quickly graduated to full-scale combat status. Seven Hurricane and two dive-bomber squadrons were operational by 1943, and Indian units distinguished themselves in the Imphal and Arakan campaigns. By mid-1944 strength

was up to 30,000 men and ten squadrons; and in 1945 the prefix "Royal" was granted.

On partition in 1947, the new Indian Air Force consisted of seven fighter squadrons mainly equipped with the Spitfire, but with some Hawker Tempests, and one transport squadron. More Tempests were delivered shortly thereafter, and a few B-24 Liberator bombers were repaired and put into service. The first jets were a batch of D.H. Vampires acquired in the late 1940s. The national aircraft industry, based on Hindustan Aircraft Ltd. at Bangalore, made early strides.

Equipment throughout the 1950s and 1960s has been partly of British origin, with the exception of Dassault Mystère IVAs and Ouragans, and MiG-21 and Sukhoi Su-7B types acquired from Russia on favourable terms after the border clashes with Communist China in the mid-1960s. The brief campaign against Pakistan in the same period exposed certain weaknesses which the Indian Air Force has since remedied; while no detailed account of losses in the Indo-Pakistan war of December 1971 has been released by either side, India seems to have achieved air superiority over the battlefield, and her losses are not thought to have been very great.

Before the outbreak of the war the Indian Air Force had a strength of about 90,000 men. Main types in service are the MiG-21 (approximately 200 aircraft), Hawker Siddeley Hunter (approximately 150 aircraft), Hindustan HF-24 Marut (about 50 aircraft), BAC Canberra B.8 and PR.57 (about 75 aircraft) and D.H. Vampire (about 40 aircraft). (It is thought that losses during the 1971 war fell mainly among the Hunters, Gnats and Canberras, and the strength in MiG-21s is unlikely to have been reduced significantly.) The transport fleet numbers about 275 aircraft, including the Fairchild C-119 Packet and Douglas C-47 (approximately 60 of each type), the Antonov An-12 (about 30 aircraft), DHC-3 Otter (about 30 aircraft), Ilyushin Il-14 (about 24 aircraft), Hawker Siddeley HS.748 (about 25 aircraft) and DHC-4 Caribou (about 15 aircraft). There are about 100 Mil Mi-4 and 120 Sud Alouette helicopters, with residual Sikorsky and Bell types.

Naval Aviation

India acquired her single carrier, I.N.S. *Vikrant*, in 1961. The 16,000-ton former H.M.S. *Hercules* embarks an air group of 16 Hawker Sea Hawk jet attack aircraft, four Bréguet Alizé anti-submarine aircraft, and two Sud Alouette III torpedo-helicopters. Total numbers on strength with the Indian Navy are approximately 35 Sea Hawks, 12 Bréguet Alizés, ten Sud Alouette IIIs, six Westland Sea King helicopters, and numbers of Hindustan HT-2 and D.H. Vampire T.55 trainers. Six more Alouette IIIs and three more Sea Kings are on order.

Among India's military airfields are Trivandrum, Madura, Cochin, Tanjore, Kolar, Tiruchirappalli, Tambaram, Bangalore, Madras, Arkonam, Belgaum, Raichur, Vijayawada, Alir, Hyderabad, Rajahmundry,

Visakhapatnam, Bidar, Warangal, Poona, Santa Cruz, Adilabad, Aurangabad, Akola, Raipur, Bhubaneshwar, Nagpur, Jharsuguda, Kalaikunda, Dum Dum, Barrack-pore, Chakulia, Bilaspur, Baroda, Jamnagar, Bhuj, Ahmedabad, Bhopal, Jubbulpore, Ranchi, Asansol, Agartala, Satna, Gaya, Lalitpur, Rampurhat, Imphal, Kumbhirgram, Allahabad, Benares, Gwalior, Pali, Jodhpur, Kanpur, Gorakpur, Manipur Road, Bhawi, Jaipur, Agra, Lucknow, Texpur, Gurgaon, Mohanbari, Bikaner, Palam, Saharanpur, Ambala, Ferozepore, Amritsar, and Jammu – this last was fought over in the 1971 war, however, and is probably too near the cease-fire line for use, whatever its present condition.

INDONESIA

The *Angkatan Udara Republik Indonesia* was estab-lished in 1950 upon independence from the Nether-lands; a Dutch mission assisted with the organisation of the force, which was presented with ex-Netherlands North American F-51D Mustang and B-25 Mitchell types. At various times British, American, Indian, Dutch and Egyptian assistance was given in training personnel, and numbers of aircraft were acquired from both Western and Communist sources. The volatile foreign policy pursued by the Soekarno and Suharto regimes has led to a very low rate of serviceability through lack of spares and technical aid, as various former suppliers severed ties of co-operation with Indonesia. Current aircraft strengths should not be considered as operational strengths.

The *A.U.R.I.* currently numbers some 50,000 men (in-cluding airborne forces), and has some 180 combat air-craft. Types operated include about 15 MiG-21s, about 35 MiG-19s, about 40 MiG-17s, about 20 MiG-15s, about 30 Ilyushin Il-28s, about 25 Tupolev Tu-16, about a dozen North American B-25 Mitchells and residual F-51D Mustangs. There are about 60 transports includ-ing Lockheed C-130 Hercules, Fokker F-27 Troopship, DHC-3 Otter, Short Skyvan, Douglas C-47, Antonov An-12 and Ilyushin Il-14 models. There are some 40 assorted French, American and Soviet helicopters, and various training and liaison types including some half-dozen Scottish Aviation Twin Pioneers recently pre-sented by Malaysia.

Military airfields include Kotaradja, Sabang, Medan, Padang, Djambi, Palembang, Djakarta, Pangkalbinang, Bandung, Kalidjati, Tanjungpandang, Djokjakarta, Semarang, Surabaia and Den Pasar (in Sumatra); Kupang, Ocussi, Dilli and Baucau (in Timor); Pon-tianak, Bandjermasin, Tarakan and Balikpapan (in Borneo); Mesado, Gorontalo and Makassar (in Cele-bes); Morotai and Ambon (in the Moluccas).

IRAN

Persian interest in military aviation dates from 1922, and the army acquired its first aircraft, a Junkers-F 13, in that year. The Iranian Air Force was established as a branch of the army in 1924 with a motley collection of Russian, French and German types, flown from Teheran/Galeh-Morghi by an equally motley collection of Russian, French and German pilots. In 1932 the re-named Imperial Iranian Air Force began a programme of expansion, and Hawker Fury and Hart aircraft were purchased during the 1930s. Occupied by Britain and Russia during the Second World War, Iran took no significant steps to expand her air power until the late 1940s; in the post-War years Hawker Hurricanes, Republic Thunderbolts and other wartime types were acquired. The first jets were Lockheed T-33A trainers delivered in 1956, followed by a batch of Republic F-84G Thunderjets.

Current strength is about 17,000 men. The main com-bat types operated are about 32 McDonnell-Douglas F-4D Phantom IIs, and about 80 Northrop F-5A Free-dom Fighters. There are between 30 and 40 transports, including ten Lockheed C-130 Hercules and ten Douglas C-47s; and some 220 helicopters of various models, mainly Agusta-Bell 205s and 206As. Four Lockheed P-3C Orion maritime patrol aircraft are on order.

There are military airfields at Tabrız, Mehrabad, Meshed, Kermanshah, Isfahan, Ahwaz, Bushire, Jask, Zahedan and Kerman.

JAPAN

The birth of Japanese military aviation may be traced to the setting up of a joint army/navy research com-mittee in 1909, to develop interest in aeronautics and lay the foundations for an aircraft industry. The Army and Navy Air Forces were established in 1911; initial equip-ment comprised a handful of Farman, Blériot and Wright machines. In the early years the Navy Air Force lagged behind the Army Air Force in the development of avia-tion and acquisition of aircraft, due to funding difficul-ties. Japan was nominally a combatant on the side of the Allies in the First World War, but her aerial involvement was necessarily confined to the occupation of Tsingtao, the secondment of a few pilots to the French and Italian forces, and operations in Siberia during the Russian civil war. Both services were expanded vigorously during the inter-War years, the J.A.A.F. largely with French assistance, the J.N.A.F. with British.

The Army and Navy were both equipped with aircraft of indigenous design during the late 1920s and early 1930s; the industry had built up its experience and plant by various licence-building programmes. Three carriers – *Hosho*, *Akagi* and *Kaga* – were in service with the navy by 1930, and carrier production was pursued as vigorously as aircraft design. Both services fought in China and Manchuria during the 1930s, and in Mongolia the army squadrons involved in the clash with Russia showed considerable prowess. It was in China that the first of Japan's wartime generation of aircraft was blooded successfully, yet surprisingly little international attention was paid to the revolutionary Mitsubishi A6M2

Currently entering service with the Japanese Maritime Self-Defence Force is the four-turboprop Shin Meiwa PX-S anti-submarine maritime reconnaissance flying-boat

Reisen, or "Zero" fighter. By the end of 1941 China was virtually defeated, and the Japanese Navy had six carriers in service and more building.

Japan's initial successes in the Second World War were based on the J.N.A.F., which quickly won air supremacy over most of the Pacific theatre; army squadrons followed as rapidly as airfields could be captured and prepared. However, the loss of four carriers and the bulk of the experienced aircrews at Midway in 1942 was a blow from which the Navy Air Force never fully recovered. Japan was unable to hold the vastly dispersed empire she had captured so swiftly, and the steady build-up of American naval and air strength in the Pacific soon forced the J.A.A.F. and J.N.A.F. on to the defensive. Although many sound designs were produced – the later models of the *Reisen*, the Nakajima Ki-44, Ki-84 and Ki-61 fighters, the Mitsubishi Ki-67 bomber, and the Kawasaki Ki-45 among them – the Japanese industry was unable to maintain the volume of production the situation demanded, harassed as it was by the deteriorating supply of raw materials and the Allied bombing offensive. By 1945 suicide tactics were adopted.

The Japanese Air Self-Defence Force was established in 1954 under U.S. sponsorship with numbers of training aircraft. By the end of 1955 the first combat unit, a squadron of North American F-86F Sabre jet fighters, was operational. Within three years strength had risen to some 650 machines, of which more than 300 were combat types. The Japanese industry has been rebuilt, and the first indigenous designs of jet trainers have been in service for more than 12 years now, although to date combat equipment has been exclusively acquired from

the U.S.A. A large-scale re-equipment programme has recently been announced, which will involve the production of some hundreds of Japanese-designed aircraft including Mitsubishi F-1 close-support fighters.

Currently the Air Self-Defence Force has some 40,000 personnel and about 500 combat aircraft. Main types in service are about 175 Lockheed F-104J Starfighters, and about 220 North American F-86F and RF-86F Sabres. There are Curtiss C-46 and Japanese-designed NAMC YS-11 transports; Sikorsky and Vertol helicopters; and assorted American and Japanese trainers. Deliveries of about 50 NAMC C-1 jet transports are taking place, and about 75 Mitsubishi T-2 supersonic trainers are on order. Some 104 F-4EJ Phantom IIs are currently being built under licence, and the first two squadrons will be operational in 1973.

Naval Aviation

The Japanese Maritime Self-Defence Force was also established in 1954, largely as an anti-submarine force, and one of the first types operated was the Grumman TBM Avenger – one of the aircraft which had played such havoc with the Japanese Navy ten years before. Current equipment includes the Japanese-built turboprop version of the Lockheed Neptune, the Kawasaki P-2J maritime reconnaissance aircraft (approximately 45 aircraft), the Grumman S-2A Tracker (about 55 aircraft) and the Shin Meiwa PS-1 turbo-prop flying boat (of which about 35 will be delivered). Helicopters include the Sikorsky SH-34J (about 14 aircraft), the Mitsubishi-built Sikorsky SH-3A Sea King (about 55 aircraft), the Mitsubishi-Sikorsky S-62A (about eight aircraft), and the Kawasaki-Vertol 107 (about 14 air-craft). There are also assorted jet and piston-engined trainers of American and Japanese design; and residual Grumman HU-16 amphibians.

Army Aviation

The Japanese Ground Self-Defence Force operates some 400 helicopters, and recently-announced plans include funding for the acquisition of over 200 more. Main types in service are about 82 Kawasaki-Bell H-13 Sioux, about 79 Fuji-Bell UH-1B Iroquois, about 42 Kawasaki-Vertol 107, about 60 Kawasaki-Hughes OH-6A, about 12 Sikorsky H-19 Chickasaw and about 14 Mitsubishi-Sikorsky S-62. Fixed-wing types include small numbers of Mitsubishi MU-2C light transports and Cessna O-1 spotters.

Japanese airbases include Chitose, Misawa, Matsu-shima, Niigata, Komatsu, Yokota, Atsugi, Tachikawa, Nagoya, Yokosuka, Kisarazu, Hamamatsu, Itami, Miho, Bofu, Iwakuni, Kushimoto, Ashiya, Itazuke, Tsuiki and Kanoya.

KOREA (DEMOCRATIC PEOPLE'S REPUBLIC)

The Korean People's Armed Forces Air Force dates from 1955; the previous designation was K.P.A.F.A. Corps. This service was established in 1948 around the nucleus of a small army aviation division, sponsored by the Soviet Union after the end of the Second World War. When the North Korean forces invaded South Korea in June 1950 the Corps had some 150 first-line aircraft of obsolescent Soviet design, mainly Yakovlev Yak-9P fighters and Ilyushin Il-10 attack aircraft; within weeks this force had been virtually destroyed and the survivors were pulled back into Manchuria. At the Antung com-plex north of the Yalu River they were trained by Russian and Chinese instructors on the MiG-15 jet fighter, which first flew into action in November 1950; but throughout the War very few North Korean na-tionals flew on operations, the brunt being borne by Soviet and Chinese "volunteers". A rapid expansion of the force followed the 1953 Armistice, and Ilyushin Il-28 bombers and MiG-17 fighters were soon supplied.

It is believed that the current strength of the Air Force is around 30,000 men. The main types in service include about 90 MiG-21s, about 340 MiG-17s, about 60 MiG-15s, about 20 MiG-19s and about 60 Il-28s; a pro-portion of the fighters are the Chinese-built Shenyang versions. There are about 50 transports of various Soviet types, and perhaps the same number of Mil heli-copters. The usual Soviet trainers are also flown.

Among major airfields in North Korea are Uiju, Sinuiju, Taechon, Namsi, Saamchan, Yonpo, Pyong-ni, Sunan, Wonsan, Pyongyang and Oksan-ni.

KOREA (REPUBLIC)

The Republic of Korea was established in 1948, and the R.O.K.A.F. in 1949; although under American sponsorship the service was initially manned by Koreans who had flown with the Japanese in the Second World War. Only trainers and light aircraft had been supplied by the time the Communists crossed the 38th Parallel in 1950, and the establishment was less than 200 men. By late 1952 a Wing of North American F-51D Mustangs was operational and flying ground-support missions, and the service had some 140 aircraft at the time of the Armistice in 1953. In 1955 the training of Korean pilots on F-86 Sabres was under way, and the first squadron of these jets was operational the following year.

Current strength is around 23,000 personnel and 190 combat aircraft. Types in service include about 20 McDonnell-Douglas F-4D Phantom II, about 40 North-rop F-5A Freedom Fighters, and about 130 North American F-86D, F-86F and RF-86F Sabres. Transports include the Douglas C-47, Curtiss C-46 and Aero Com-mander 500; and there are small numbers of Sikorsky H-19 Chickasaw and Bell UH-1D Iroquois helicopters.

Major airfields include Chunchon, Kangnang, Seoul, Kimpo, Inchon, Suwon, Hoeng Song, Chungju, Osan, Taijon, Pyongtaik, Kunsan, Pohang, Taigu, Pusan, Chinhai and Sachon.

LAOS

The Laotian Army Aviation Service was established under American sponsorship in 1954 for ground-support operations in the long-drawn-out guerilla war which has dogged the country since 1953. Initial equip-ment was limited to spotters and transports; armed versions of the T-6G Texan and T-28 trainers were later acquired. In 1960 the service was re-named Royal Lao Air Force.

Current equipment is believed to comprise the North American T-28D Trojan (about 80 aircraft), some 14 AC-47 and UC-47 ground support aircraft, 17 transports (mainly C-46 and C-47 types), 38 Cessna and Beaver liaison and spotter types, and 28 Sikorsky UH-34 heli-copters.

The main airfields are believed to be Savannakhet and Pakse, although American teams have certainly built new facilities in recent years.

MALAYSIA

Malaysia achieved nationhood in 1963, and the Royal Malaysian Air Force dates back to a British-sponsored Malayan Air Force formed in 1958. (A tradi-tion of voluntary and auxiliary air activity in the former colony may be traced back to 1936.) Training was carried out within the framework of the auxiliary service during the 1950s, and at one stage small numbers of Super-marine Spitfires were acquired. In the interim between Malayan independence and the formation of the Federa-tion of Malaysia, the M.A.F. operated trainers and light transports. Royal Malaysian Air Force personnel saw action against Indonesia during the "confrontation" of the 1960s.

Current strength of the R.M.A.F. is about 4,500 men. The types operated comprise ten Commonwealth CA-27 Avon-Sabre fighter-bombers, 20 Canadair CL-41G Tebuan armed trainers, and – possibly by the time this is read – ten Dassault Mirage 5 ground-attack fighters. There are some 45 transports, including ten Handley Page Heralds, 12 DHC-4 Caribous and 14 Scottish Aviation Pioneers and Twin Pioneers; and about 30 Sud Alouette and Sikorsky helicopters. Some 33 BAC Provost and Scottish Aviation Bulldog trainers are operated.

Among mainland airfields in Malaysia are Alor Star, Kota Bharu, Gong Kedah, Kuala Trengganu, Ipoh, Kuantan, Butterworth, Kuala Lumpur and Kluang.

MONGOLIAN PEOPLE'S REPUBLIC

Military aviation, sponsored by Soviet Russia, dates back to the mid-1920s. Although there were said to be some 450 combat aircraft in Mongolian service in 1938, at a time of great tension between Russia and Japan, it is certain that the pilots as well as the machines were in fact largely Russian. The current force of some 700 men is largely occupied with internal communications and transport duties; completely dominated by the central Soviet authorities, it has some Mongolian aircrew, but it is not known how many.

Current equipment includes some dozen MiG-15 fighters, and unknown numbers of Antonov An-2 and An-12, Ilyushin Il-12 and Il-14 transports. Mil Mi-4 helicopters and Yakovlev Yak-11 and Yak-18 trainers are operated. The location of military airfields is not known, but the main civil facilities are situated at the capital, Ulan-Bator, and at Sain-Shand. It is likely that these are also used by the military.

NEPAL

The Royal Nepalese Army recently took delivery of a Short Skyvan transport, while one Sud Alouette helicopter and a VIP-transport version of the Skyvan are operated by the royal household.

NEW ZEALAND

The New Zealand Permanent Air Force was formed in 1923 with war-surplus R.A.F. aircraft including ten Bristol F.2Bs, ten D.H.4s and nine D.H.9s; personnel were drawn from among those New Zealanders who had fought throughout the War in the British air services. The force, which was much restricted by funding difficulties between the Wars, remained under Army control until 1937, although the style Royal New Zealand Air Force was adopted three years earlier. The Dominion's first contribution to the Allied war effort was to hand over, and provide crews for 30 Vickers Wellington bombers ordered just before the outbreak of the Second World War. Thereafter the R.N.Z.A.F. made a major contribution to the aircrew training programme, and provided a total of 27 squadrons in the field, mainly in the Far East –

but also to some extent in Europe and the Mediterranean. Twelve fighter units flew Curtiss P-40s and later Vought Corsairs; six bomber squadrons operated Lockheed Hudsons and Venturas; and there were single squadrons of both Douglas Dauntless dive-bombers and Grumman Avenger torpedo-bombers.

Post-War reductions led to an establishment of five regular squadrons backed by four reserve units. Aircraft operated by the regular units in the 1950s included D.H. Vampires, D.H. Mosquitos, BAC Canberras and Short Sunderland flying boats. The reserve organisation was stood down in 1957.

Current personnel strength of the R.N.Z.A.F. is around 4,500. There is one squadron with ten McDonnell-Douglas A-4K Skyhawk jet fighter-bombers, one with 12 D.H. Vampire FB.9s, one with six BAC Canberra jet bombers, and one with five Lockheed P-3B Orion maritime reconnaissance aircraft. At the time of writing ten BAC 167 Strikemasters are in the process of delivery to replace the Vampires. Transports include five Lockheed C-130H Hercules, 15 D.H. Devons, and nine Bristol Freighters. There are about 30 Bell UH-1H Iroquois and 47G Sioux helicopters.

The Royal New Zealand Navy operates small numbers of Westland Wasp helicopters.

PAKISTAN

The Royal Pakistan Air Force came into being with the partition of India in 1947. Initial equipment included one squadron (and later three squadrons) of Hawker Tempest fighters, Douglas C-47 transports, and North American T-6 Harvard trainers. Hawker Fury fighters and Handley Page Halifax IX bombers entered service in small numbers over the next few years, with miscellaneous second-line types. In 1954 – by which time the first jets were in service, 36 Vickers Attacker FB.2s – Pakistan became a member of SEATO and began to receive assistance from America. In 1956 the country became a republic and the "Royal" prefix was dropped from the service's title; in the same year an initial batch of North American F-86 Sabres was delivered. American aid was suspended due to clashes between Pakistan and India in the mid-1960s, and Pakistan turned to Communist China as an arms supplier, receiving Shenyang F-6 (MiG-19) fighters and Ilyushin Il-28 bombers in the years that followed.

Strength of the Pakistan Air Force *prior to the war with India in December 1971* stood at around 15,000 men. Combat types in service comprised some 112 F-86F Sabres; about 80 Shenyang F-6s; about 32 BAC Canberra and 16 Il-28 light jet bombers; ten Lockheed F-104A Starfighters and 18 Dassault Mirage III fighter-bombers. There were small numbers of Lockheed T-33A reconnaissance aircraft, Lockheed C-130 Hercules and Douglas C-47 transports, and about 30 helicopters of various French, Soviet and American types.

It may be concluded, tentatively, that the December

1971 war cost Pakistan about half her Sabres, and significant numbers of Canberras and Il-28s; several transports were certainly destroyed on the ground. It is not likely that the F-104A, Shenyang F-6 or Mirage III strength has been very significantly altered, although the loss of facilities and personnel in East Pakistan may have been seriously detrimental to operational readiness states in the remaining force. Some 28 Mirage 5s are thought to have been delivered since the War.

Military airfields are located at Jimwani, Mauripur, Karachi, Drigh Road, Hyderabad, Nawabshah, Jacobabad, Quetta, Lahore, Sargodha, Miran Shah, Kohat, Chaklala, Peshawar, Risalpur, Chilas and Gilgit.

PHILIPPINES

Small numbers of light aircraft were operated on internal security duties by the Philippine Constabulary in the 1930s; this force was the nucleus for a Philippine Army Air Force which the U.S.A. began to establish in 1940 with the gift of 12 Boeing P-26 fighters. Most of these were destroyed on the ground by Japanese air attack, and for the remainder of the War Philippine personnel were administered by American forces. In 1946 the Philippine Republic was established, and in 1947 a separate Air Force was set up; initial equipment was the North American F-51D Mustang and the Douglas C-47 transport. United States aid has continued ever since; the first jets, F-86F Sabres, replaced the Mustangs from 1957 onwards.

The present strength of the Philippine Air Force is about 9,000 men. Types in service include the Northrop F-5A Freedom Fighter (about 20 aircraft), the North American F-86F Sabre (about 30 aircraft), ten Douglas C-47s, the NAMC YS-11, the Fokker F-27 Troopship and the Aero Commander 500. There are a few Grumman HU-16 Albatross amphibians, about 20 helicopters of various American types, and an assortment of orthodox trainers.

Philippine military airfields include Laong, San Fernando, Baguio, Clark Field, Florida Blanca, Manila, Cavite City, Lipa, San José, Legaspi, Guiuan, Iloilo, Cebu, Tacloban, Sibulan, Cagayan, Cotabato and Zamboanga.

SINGAPORE

Singapore withdrew from the Federation of Malaysia in 1965 and set up her own forces, although strong defence links are maintained with the Federation. The Singapore Air Defence Command currently has some 300 personnel, and operates 16 BAC 167 Strikemasters, 30 Hawker Siddeley Hunter FGA.74s, FR.74As and T.75s, and eight Sud Alouette III helicopters, as well as small numbers of liaison aircraft. Orders for small numbers of the Dassault Mirage F.1 multi-mission fighter may have been placed by the time of publication, and six Short Skyvan transports are currently on order.

The main airfield on Singapore island is the former R.A.F. base at Tengah; there are other facilities at Changi, Seletar and Singapore International Airport.

SRI LANKA

The Royal Ceylon Air Force was established with R.A.F. assistance in 1950, and during the next eight years small numbers of trainers and light transports were acquired from Britain. Twelve BAC Jet Provost armed trainers were delivered in 1958. In recent years the renamed Republic of Sri Lanka has suffered internal disorders and the present regime has pursued a more volatile policy towards international relations than was previously the case.

An appeal for aid against insurgents brought the extended loan of six MiG-17 fighters and a small Soviet advisory mission early in 1971. Current equipment comprises these MiGs, nine BAC Jet Provosts, nine D.H. Dove and Heron light transports, nine DHC-1 Chipmunk primary trainers and 15 assorted helicopters. The air force is based at Katunayake and China Bay.

THAILAND

The Royal Siamese Flying Corps was formed, with four Nieuport and four Blériot machines, in 1914; three Siamese engineer officers returned from training in France in 1913. More than 100 Siamese personnel received training in France during the First World War, in which Siam declared for the Allies. A small Siamese air expeditionary corps served with the Allied occupation forces in the Rhineland in 1918; the following year they returned home with numbers of SPAD, Nieuport-Delage and Bréguet aircraft, and the service was re-named Royal Siamese Aeronautical Service. During the inter-War years pilots were sent for training in a number of different countries. Curtiss Hawk II and III fighters were purchased and licence-built during the 1930s, and Martin 139 bombers and Hawk 75N fighters were acquired shortly before the Second World War. After a period of confused relations between Thailand (re-named in 1939), Japan and the Vichy French authorities in Indo-China, Thailand was occupied by the Japanese; small numbers of Japanese aircraft were operated by a puppet air component. With the liberation, R.A.F. personnel were seconded to assist rebuild the service with British types such as the Spitfire and Fairey Firefly. American aid was forthcoming during the 1950s, and continues to the present day; Grumman Bearcat fighters and various second-line types were supplied, and in 1957 the first jets – 30 Republic F-84G Thunderjets. F-86F Sabres followed in 1962.

Currently the R.T.A.F. has a personnel strength of about 25,000. Types operated include about 25 Northrop F-5A Freedom Fighters, about 60 North American F-86C and F-86F Sabres, about 20 T-6G Texans, 40 T-28D Trojan armed trainers, and small numbers of Lockheed RT-33As. There are some 30 transports of various American types including about 20 Douglas C-47s, and just over 100 helicopters including some 50 Bell UH-1H Iroquois, 22 Sikorsky CH-34C and 16 Kawasaki KH-4. There are some Grumman HU-16 Albatross amphibians in service, and the usual assortment of American types. Small numbers of Albatrosses and Grumman S-2F Trackers are operated by Royal Thai Navy personnel. The para-military Royal Thai Border Police also operate about 30 helicopters of various American types.

There is a considerable American presence in Thailand, both as advisory personnel and as orthodox combat elements operating over South-East Asia from leased Thai bases. The following selection of known Thai airfields is therefore likely to be somewhat incomplete: Chieng Mai, Lampang, Mae Sot, Loei, Meng Phitsanulok, Ta Khli, Korat, Koke Kathiem, Bankok, Chantaburi and Don Muang.

TURKEY

In 1912 Turkey acquired a mixed force of British and French aircraft, flown by foreign pilots; and in 1914 the Turkish Flying Corps was established with German assistance. In fact both aircraft and personnel were almost exclusively German throughout the First World War, although a few Turkish air observers took part in missions against British targets. The main types operated were A.E.G.C.IV. Rumpler and Albatros reconnaissance aircraft, with some Halberstadt D.II fighters. The terms of the Treaty of Versailles, forbidding military aviation in the former Central Powers, seem to have been applied very half-heartedly in the case of Turkey; France actively encouraged Turkish aviation, and after the establishment of the Turkish Republic in 1923 this attitude appears to have become widespread. Britain also trained Turkish personnel and supplied aircraft, and by 1935 the air force had some 160 machines. By the outbreak of the Second World War there were about 8,500 officers and men, including about 450 pilots, and some 370 aircraft including Heinkel He 111D bombers, Bristol Blenheims and P.Z.L. P-24 fighters. Both Allies and Axis wooed Turkey unsuccessfully during the War, and the types supplied included Hawker Hurricanes, Fairey Battles, Curtiss P-40s, Supermarine Spitfires, Consolidated B-24 Liberators, Bristol Beauforts and Focke-Wulf Fw 190As. Britain and America supplied quantities of surplus wartime types after 1945; and with Turkish membership of NATO in 1952 a full-scale American aid and assistance programme got under way. The first jets – Republic F-84G Thunderjets – were acquired in 1952; a total of 300 of this type was eventually supplied.

Current strength of the *Türk Hava Kuvvetleri* is around 50,000 men, and nearly 550 combat aircraft. Types operated include about 36 Lockheed F-104G Starfighters, about 25 Convair F-102A Delta Daggers, about 140 Northrop F-5A Freedom Fighters, about 200 North American F-100C Super Sabres, about 125 North American F-86 Sabres and about 25 Republic RF-84F Thunderflashes. Some 40 McDonnell-Douglas F-4E Phantom IIs are also on order. Rather small transport and helicopter forces operate the usual range of American types, including ten Lockheed C-130E Hercules, and there are orthodox trainer types ranging from Harvards to Starfighter conversion models. The Turkish Army also operates a number of Agusta-Bell helicopters.

Military airfields include Yeşilkoy, Bandirma, Balikesir, Bursa, İzmir, Akhisar, Eskişehir, Afyon, Euvercinlik, Etimesut, Mersifon, Sivas, Kayseri, Erzurum, Van, Diyarbakir, Malatya, Adana and Konya.

PEOPLE'S REPUBLIC OF VIETNAM

The Vietnamese People's Air Force was born in the late 1950s, with Communist Chinese assistance. China and the Soviet Union have competed in the provision of aid – and in the consequent achievement of influence – but while most of the equipment seems to have been provided by the U.S.S.R., it is thought that China has most influence over personnel. Strength is calculated at about 4,500 men. Current equipment levels are believed to include perhaps 80 MiG-21PF fighters, 60 MiG-17s, 40 MiG-15s, a small number of Ilyushin Il-28s, and about 60 transports of the conventional Communist models. U.S. sources claim 174 MiGs destroyed in combat since 1965. There are thought to be about 50 Mil helicopters. The compilers have little reliable information regarding airfields.

REPUBLIC OF VIETNAM

The present Vietnamese Air Force traces its origins back to 1951 when the French began to train local personnel on light communications and transport aircraft. After the French withdrawal and the partition of Indo-China in 1954–55, numbers of Grumman F8F Bearcat fighter-bombers, Douglas C-47 transports and North American T-6G Texan trainers were acquired. The force has been expanded and re-equipped under American sponsorship in recent years.

Current strength is about 25,000 personnel and about 1,800 aircraft – but many of the recently-delivered aircraft are in storage. Types including 164 Cessna A-37Bs, 65 Douglas A-1 Skyraiders, 35 Northrop F-5 Freedom Fighters, about 630 Bell UH-1H Iroquois helicopters and 50 CH-47 Chinook helicopters were in service at the beginning of October 1972. With the sudden expansion required by the Vietnamese "cease-fire" and withdrawal of U.S. troops, large additional deliveries were made, not all of them permanent; various leasing arrangements were entered to "tide over" the VNAF. These recent deliveries include an additional 126 Northrop F-5s, between 75 and 100 more A-37Bs, 20 Skyraiders and 32 C-130 Hercules transports. The transport fleet already operated some 45 Douglas C-47s, and numbers of Fairchild C-119Gs, DHC-4 Caribous and DHC-2 Beavers.

Main airfields are Bien Hoa, Saigon/Tan Son Nhut,

The Japanese NAMC YS-11A twin-turboprop short-medium range airliner which first flew on 30th August 1962. Similar in many respects to the Hawker Siddeley HS.748, this Rolls-Royce Dart-powered aircraft has achieved considerable sales success and is in service with airlines in Canada as well as Japan and throughout the Pacific and the Far East. 32-, 48- and 60-seat versions have been produced, together with cargo and military versions. More than 200 had been delivered by the end of 1972

Da Nang, Nhatrang, Dalat, Ban Me Thout, Tourane and Hue – although the latter is probably in very poor repair.

5. AFRICA

ALGERIA

Shortly after Algeria won her independence in 1962 the foundations of the *Force Aérienne Algérienne* were laid by a gift of five MiG-15 fighter-bombers from Egypt, who also supplied the pilots. Of the current strength of about 170 combat aircraft of Soviet origin, it cannot be said with any certainty how many are actually operational. Personnel strength is reported to be about 2,000; the majority of the aircrew and technical personnel are almost certainly foreign "advisers". The reported personnel strength is remarkably low to operate some 140 Mikoyan MiG-21F, MiG-17 and MiG-15 fighters and fighter-bombers, about 30 Ilyushin Il-28 bombers, eight Antonov An-12 and four Ilyushin Il-18 transports, about 30 Mil Mi-4 and 20 Sud SA.330 Puma helicopters, 28 Potez Magister armed jet trainers, various basic trainers and light communications aircraft.

Ex-French military airfields are situated at Tafaroui, Oran/La Senia, Maison Blanche, Blida, Boufarik, Sétif, Batna, Telerema, Philippeville, Bône, Biskra, Ouargla, Ghadames, Fort Flatters, Ghat, Tamanrasset, In Salah, Bidon, Aoulef, El Goléa and Colomb Béchar.

CENTRAL AFRICAN REPUBLIC

On achieving independence from France in 1960 the Republic was granted limited military aid, including five aircraft for the fledgling *Force Aérienne Centafricaine*. These comprise three Max Holste 1521M Broussard light transport and communications machines, a Douglas C-47 transport and a Sud Alouette II helicopter. It is not thought likely that they are flown or maintained by C.A.R. nationals.

There are airstrips at Bangui, Bambari, Bossangoa and Bouar, although the operational condition of all but the first must remain a matter for conjecture.

CHAD

The *Escadrille Tchadienne* was established, with exactly the same equipment as that handed over to the Central African Republic, in 1960. In 1969–70 at least one of France's two remaining squadron's of Douglas A-1 Skyraider light strike aircraft operated in Chad in support of ground forces campaigning against insurgent tribes, but it is extremely unlikely that any of these aircraft were handed over to the Republic. There is an airfield at Fort Lamy, and possibly others at Fort Archambault, Mondou and Abéché.

DEMOCRATIC REPUBLIC OF THE CONGO (KINSHASA)

A variety of aircraft operated in the Congo during the civil war and subsequent rebellion by the Communist-inspired Simba movement in the early 1960s, largely flown by mercenaries from white southern Africa. At one stage 15 North American T-28A armed trainers and six Douglas B-26 Invader bombers operated in support of government mercenary columns; they were provided by the U.S.A. through a "charter" organisation designated WIGMO, and flown by free-lance Hungarian and Cuban pilots.

Currently the *Force Aérienne Congolaise* has some 1,000 personnel, and has been organised by an Italian military mission. Equipment includes the Aermacchi MB.326GB light strike/jet trainer (approximately 17 aircraft), the North American T-6 and T-28A Trojan light strike/trainers (approximately 15 aircraft in all), and a number of transport types including the Douglas C-47 and DC-4, the DHC-4 Caribou, and D.H. Dove and Beech 18 light transports. There are about six Alouette III and seven Sud SA.330 Puma helicopters, and a handful of trainers including Piaggio 148s.

Major airfield facilities are located at the former Ndolo/Leopoldville, and at Kamina – main military airfield during the civil war and rebellion. Other airstrips are scattered round the country, notably at Stanleyville, Elizabethville, Luluabourg and Jadotville.

CONGO (BRAZZAVILLE)

On independence in 1960 the republic received from France three Max Holste Broussards, one Douglas C-47 and one Sud Alouette II helicopter. Airfields are available at Brazzaville and Pointe-Noire.

DAHOMEY

On independence in 1960 Dahomey received the same aircraft as the C.A.R., Chad and Congo/Brazzaville (see above) and has since acquired an Aero Commander 500B passenger transport. It is assumed that they are based on the capital, Porto Novo, or the main port of Cotonou.

ETHIOPIA

As early as 1924 the Ethiopian empire was negotiating the purchase of military aircraft. By the time the Emperor Haile Selassie came to the throne in 1930 the Imperial Ethiopian Aviation mustered six Potez 25 bombers, a Morane trainer, a de Havilland Gipsy Moth and a Breda trainer. These were operated on reconnaissance and ambulance missions during the Italian invasion of 1935; one of the pilots involved was Count Carl Gustav von Rosen – a name which came to prominence once more during the Nigerian civil war of the late 1960s.

In 1946 Count von Rosen led a group of advisers who established the Imperial Ethiopian Air Force. Swedish influence has remained strong. The mainstay of the Force's operational units was for many years the SAAB-17A bomber, of which 66 were purchased; eight Fairey Firefly fighter-bombers were also acquired in 1952. During the 1960s American aid commenced.

The present strength of the Imperial Ethiopian Air Force is about 3,000. Main types in service include eight Northrop F-5A Freedom Fighters, 12 North American F-86F Sabres, six BAC Canberra B.2s, eight SAAB-17As, six North American T-28 Trojan light strike/trainers, and a few Lockheed T-33A light strike/jet trainers. Transports include 12 C-119s, six Douglas C-47s, two Douglas C-54s, three D.H. Doves and one Ilyushin Il-14. There are small numbers of Sud Alouette and Agusta-Bell helicopters, and unarmed SAAB 91 Safir, North American T-28 and Lockheed T-33A trainers.

Major military airfield facilities are located at Bishoftu and Djidjigga. Smaller strips are at Dalle, Auasc, Dire Dawa, Debra Marcos, Dessie, Bahrdar and Gondar.

GABON

On independence in 1960 Gabon acquired two Max Holste 1521M Broussard light transport aircraft from France. It is not thought that any other aircraft have been acquired since. There is an airfield at Libreville.

GHANA

The Ghana Air Force was established in 1959 with the aid of Israeli and Indian military instructors. A year later some R.A.F. personnel were seconded as instructors. DHC Chipmunk trainers, and various DHC transport types, were supplied. Small numbers of Russian helicopters and transports acquired by the Nkrumah regime were returned by the new government after the former president was deposed and exiled.

Current strength is around 1,000 men. Main types operated include the DHC-2 Beaver (12 aircraft), the DHC-3 Otter (11 aircraft), the DHC-4 Caribou (eight aircraft), the Aermacchi MB.326F jet trainer (five aircraft), and some DHC Chipmunk and Hindustan HT-2 basic trainers. A helicopter squadron operates the Westland Whirlwind and Wessex (six and three aircraft respectively) and the Hughes 269 (four aircraft).

There are airfields at Accra and Takoradi, and several smaller airstrips throughout the country.

GUINEA REPUBLIC

The current regime in the Guinea Republic is pursuing an unpredictable foreign policy, and information is not forthcoming. At least one helicopter – a Bell 47G Sioux – is in service. Whether there are any other aircraft actually operational in the republic is not known. The Soviet Union made an offer of small numbers of Mikoyan MiG-17 fighters (and presumably promised training facilities, if not in the U.S.S.R. then through one of her "client" governments in Africa), but it seems unlikely that delivery has actually taken place.

IVORY COAST

One of the French colonies which gained independence in 1960, the Ivory Coast has a rather larger air element than her neighbours. The *Force Aérienne de Côte d'Ivoire* operates five Max Holste 1521M Broussard, three Douglas C-47 and one Fokker F-27 Troopship transports. Also in service are an Aero Commander 500 passenger aircraft, a Beech 18, a Dassault Mystère 20 and seven Sud Aviation helicopters (including two Pumas). Three Cessna 337s are operated.

It is presumed that most of this fleet is based on airfields at the major towns of Abidjan, Bouaké, Gagnoa and Grand Bassam.

KENYA

R.A.F. assistance in building up the Kenya Air Force has been given since independence in 1963. The first combat aircraft entered service in 1971 – six BAC 167 Strikemaster light strike/jet trainers. Other aircraft operated include the DHC-2 Beaver and DHC-4 Caribou transports (seven and four aircraft respectively), six DHC Chipmunk and five Scottish Aviation Bulldog trainers. There is also an Aero Commander 500 passenger aircraft.

LIBYA

When the present regime assumed power in 1970, Libya had an air force with a strength of two Auster observation aircraft, two Lockheed T-33A jet trainers and a Douglas C-47 transport; the first batch of seven Northrop F-5A fighter-bombers supplied under an agreement between the previous monarchy, and the United States, in consideration of base facilities, had also been delivered. Current combat strength is thought to be nine Northrop F-5As, and between 30 and 40 Dassault Mirage IIIE fighter-bombers of a total order for 60 Mirage IIIEs and 50 Mirage 5s. French Government embargos on delivery of war material to nations involved in the Middle East crisis cast the delivery of the remainder of the order into doubt, however; the present rate is about 15 aircraft per year, and without French co-operation Libya is unlikely to be able to bring what forces she has to a realistic state of combat readiness. Second-line aircraft in service include six Lockheed C-130 Hercules, nine Douglas C-47 transports, ten Sud Alouette II and Super Frelon helicopters, small numbers of MiG-15UTI and Lockheed T-33A jet trainers, and a Dassault Falcon transport.

MALAGASY REPUBLIC

With French assistance the former colony of Madagascar has established the small *Armée de l'Air Malgache*; types in service include the Douglas C-47 transport (three aircraft), the Max Holste 1521M Broussard light transport (six aircraft), the Dassault 315 Flamant light transport (two aircraft) and one Bell 47G Sioux and one Sud Alouette III helicopters. They are thought to be based at Tananarive and Diego Suarez.

MALI

On independence the *Force Aérienne du Mali* was brought into being with the usual Douglas C-47, and a pair of Broussards. Two more C-47s have since been acquired from the U.S.A.; conflicting reports suggest the possibility that the U.S.S.R. has supplied Mali with a handful of obsolete MiG-15s, but even if this is so they are unlikely to be operational – by international standards.

MAURITANIA

The *Force Aérienne de la Republique Islamique de Mauritanie* consists of a Douglas C-47 and two Broussard light transports.

MOROCCO

Al Quwwat Alijawwiya Almalakiya Marakishaya – The Royal Maroc Air Force – dates from independence in 1956. French and Spanish aid played a large part in the early days of the Force. During the 1960s, however, both American and Soviet equipment has been delivered.

With about 4,000 officers and men, the Force has the following aircraft in service: about 17 Northrop F-5A Freedom Fighters, two Northrop RF-5A, about 24 Potez Magister light strike/trainers, about 25 North American T-28A trainers, ten Douglas C-47 and six Fairchild C-119G transports, about 45 North American T-6G Texan trainers and eight Potez Magister jet trainers. There are some 25 helicopters of various models, and probably a few residual aircraft of small batches of Mikoyan MiG-17, Ilyushin Il-28 and MiG-15UTI types supplied in 1961. There are various light transport and communications types, such as the Broussard and the Beech Twin Bonanza.

The main air base is at Kenitra, where an American military mission is located. Other major airfields in the country include Fez, Meknès, Tetuan, Tangier, Rabat, Casablanca, Sidi Slimane, Port Lyautey, Nouasseur, Boulhaut, Agadir, Marrakesh and Ben Guérir.

NIGER

The *Force Aérienne de Niger* operates a Douglas C-47 and three Max Holste Broussard transports, presumably based at Niamey.

NIGERIA

The Federal Nigerian Air Force, established in 1964 with the aid of Indian and West German missions, was a fairly sizeable force of transports, trainers and liaison aircraft from its beginnings. With the civil war of the late 1960s came an urgent requirement for combat aircraft, which were supplied by the Soviet Union and flown by a mixture of Egyptian and white mercenary pilots.

Current equipment includes the Mikoyan MiG-17C fighter (ten aircraft) and a few MiG-15s; three Ilyushin Il-28 bombers; small numbers of the L-29 Delfin, MiG-15UTI and BAC Jet Provost trainers – all of which have a light strike capability with minor modifications; three Douglas C-47 transports, 20 Dornier Do 27 liaison aircraft and 14 Piaggio P.149D trainers. There are also three Westland Whirlwind and seven Sud Alouette II helicopters.

RHODESIA

An Air Section of the Permanent Staff Corps was set up in Southern Rhodesia in 1936, and during the Second World War the government of the dominion manned and maintained three combat squadrons in the R.A.F. British personnel were trained in Rhodesia, whose excellent weather conditions were one reason for the continuation of the scheme after the War. The Southern Rhodesia Air Force was formed in the late 1940s, and the first operational aircraft – eleven Spitfires – were acquired in 1951; they were replaced by D.H. Vampires two years later.

Rhodesia's international isolation since UDI in 1965 has prevented her from replacing obsolescent aircraft. Current strength is about 1,200 men, and equipment consists of one squadron of about 12 BAC Canberra B.2 jet bombers, one squadron of about 12 Hawker Hunter FGA.9 ground-attack fighters, one squadron of about 12 D.H. Vampire FB.9 fighter-bombers, a squadron of Aermacchi-Lockheed AL.60C5 Trojan light strike aircraft, about four Douglas C-47 transports and eight Sud Alouette III helicopters. There are small numbers of two-seat Hunters and Vampire trainers, and lightly-armed BAC Provost T.53s.

The main airfields in Rhodesia are at Salisbury (Belvedere and Cranborne), Thornhill, Moffat, Kumalo and Francistown.

SOMALI

The basis for the *Cuerpo Aeronautica del Somalia* was an Italian-sponsored air corps established before independence of the British and Italian-administered halves of the present republic in the early 1960s. Soviet aid has been received over the past ten years. Current strength totals about 2,000 men, and equipment is believed to include about a dozen Mikoyan MiG-15 and about six MiG-17 fighters, about six Beech C-45 transports, a Douglas C-47 and an Antonov An-24. Trainers include about ten Piaggio P.148s, about 20 Yakovlev Yak-11s and about six MiG-15UTIs.

SOUTH AFRICA

The South African Aviation Corps was formed in 1915 with ex-Royal Naval Air Service equipment, and saw action against German forces in East Africa, before disbandment in 1918. Two years later the South African Air Force was established with a gift of 100 ex-R.A.F. combat and training aircraft. There was a major expansion and re-equipment programme in the late 1930s, and at the outbreak of the Second World War there were some 100 aircraft in service, including Hawker Hurricanes and Bristol Blenheims. There were about 1,500 officers and men.

S.A.A.F. units fought alongside the R.A.F. with great distinction in North and East Africa and Southern Europe in the Second World War, as well as providing extensive maritime patrols from South Africa; at peak strength the S.A.A.F. in the Mediterranean theatre had

27 squadrons, and total manpower totalled 45,000 men and women. In the post-War period the regular force was much reduced, and organised to be capable of rapid reinforcement and mobilisation in time of emergency, from Reserve and Active Citizen Force personnel.

Current strength of the *Suid Afrikaanse Lugmag* is about 8,000, and equipment includes some 300 combat aircraft as well as about 60 transports, and some 100 helicopters. Main types operated include about 40 French Dassault Mirage IIICZ, IIIRZ and IIIEZ fighter aircraft, about 30 Canadair CL-13 Sabre 6s (of which half are in reserve), about 32 Hawker Siddeley Buccaneer low-level jet strike aircraft, and eight Hawker Siddeley Nimrod maritime reconnaissance aircraft. In reserve are about 30 D.H. Vampire FB.9s, about nine BAC Canberra B.2s and a similar number of Avro Shackleton bombers – as well as the Sabres mentioned above. The Active Citizen Force operates approximately 170 armed Aermacchi MB.326 light strike aircraft. Combat strength is increasing with licence production of the Dassault Mirage III within South Africa. The transport fleet musters about 40 Douglas C-47s, nine Transall, seven Lockheed C-130 Hercules, and about four Douglas C-54 Skymasters. Liaison aircraft in service include the Piaggio P.166 and the Cessna 185. There are some 56 Sud Alouette II and III helicopters, 20 Sud SA.330 Pumas, and about 16 Super Frelons, in addition to eight Westland Wasps for embarked service aboard South African warships. Among training aircraft flown are about 80 unarmed versions of the MB.326; in an emergency they could no doubt be converted to the light strike rôle without difficulty.

Main airfields in South Africa include Pietersburg, Pretoria/Waterkloof and Zwartkop, Johannesburg/Jan Smuts, Germiston, Dunnottar, Durban, Bloemspruit, Bloemfontein, Mafeking, Kimberley, Beaufort West, King Williamstown, East London, Port Elizabeth, Oudtshoorn, Brooklyn, Wingfield, Langebaanweg and – in South-West Africa – Windhoek, Alexander Bay and Keetmanshoop.

SUDAN

The Sudanese Air Force was established in 1959, shortly after independence. The emphasis was upon internal security operations and domestic transport. The long civil war between north and south regions of the country, recently brought to a close by diplomacy, saw the introduction of combat types to the inventory. Current strength is around 400 men, with about two dozen combat aircraft. Main types in service include the Mikoyan MiG-21 fighter-bomber (about 16 aircraft), about eight BAC Jet Provost T.52 light strike/jet trainers, three BAC Pembroke transports, three Fokker F-27 Troopships and five Antonov An-24s. Training types include the BAC Provost T.51 and the BAC 145 T.5 (about three and five aircraft respectively). The main air base is at Khartoum.

TANZANIA

The Tanzanian People's Defence Force Air Wing has no combat aircraft, although the recent confrontation with Uganda, involving sporadic air operations by the latter, will probably hasten the delivery of the handful of MiG-17s which have reportedly been on order for about two years. The Air Wing was originally set up with the aid of a *Luftwaffe* mission, and has a strength of about 300 men. Current equipment comprises the DHC-3 Otter and DHC-4 Caribou transports (five and four aircraft respectively), and Antonov An-2 and approximately seven Piaggio P.149 trainers. This fleet is believed to be based at Dar-es-Salaam. Should combat types be acquired, however, it is possible that base facilities would be set up nearer the country's international frontiers, perhaps at one of the major towns in the north or west such as Mwanza or Tabora.

TOGO

The *Force Aérienne Togolaise* operates a Douglas C-47 transport and two Max Holste 1521M Broussards, presumably based at Lomé.

TUNISIA

It was four years after independence, in 1960, that Tunisia acquired her first aircraft – SAAB trainers – although a Swedish mission had been working since 1957 to establish an air arm. The force has a current strength of some 600 men and about 20 combat aircraft. These comprise about a dozen North American F-86F Sabres and about eight Aermacchi MB.326B light strike/jet trainers. In addition there are three Dassault Flamant transports, eight Sud Alouette II helicopters, about 12 North American T-6G Texan and 14 SAAB-91D trainers.

These aircraft are thought to be based at Tunis/El Aouina and Bizerte.

UGANDA

The Uganda Army Air Force/Police Air Wing was set up in 1964, and has a current strength of about 450 personnel. Serviceability is not known, but the following aircraft are known to have been delivered: Mikoyan MiG-15 (seven aircraft), Potez Magister light strike/jet trainer (12 aircraft), six Douglas C-47 and one DHC-4 Caribou transports, five L-29 Delfin and four Piaggio P.149 trainers, two Westland Scout helicopters and ten light communications types including Piper and Cessna models. These aircraft are presumably based on Entebbe. It must be noted that General Amin announced, at the time of writing, the expulsion of the four British pilots and four mechanics who are thought to be the only trained personnel in Uganda; and that during recent border clashes with Tanzania the only aircraft known to have flown operationally were light communications types and perhaps a single MiG. Libyan aid missions are currently in Uganda, and the situation is fluid.

ZAMBIA

The Zambia Air Force was formed on independence in 1964 with R.A.F. aid, and a handful of transport types. In recent years Italian influence has taken over. With a strength of about 450 men, the Force operates about 40 aircraft. There are four Soko Jastreb light strike/jet trainers, and two Soko Galeb unarmed models. Transports include two Douglas C-47s, four DHC-4 Caribou and six DHC-2 Beavers. There are five Agusta-Bell 205 helicopters, and about 20 trainers including Savoia-Marchetti SF.260, Scottish Aviation Bulldog and DHC Chipmunk types.

~ CHAPTER 3 ~
The World's Airlines

The Fokker F.27 Friendship, a highly successful and widely used short/medium range airliner built by Fokker-VFW in the Netherlands and by Fairchild Hiller in Maryland, U.S.A. About 600 had been delivered by the beginning of 1973

One of the anachronisms of aviation was the long period which elapsed before air transport by aeroplane became accepted as realistic and economic. The early pioneers of this century's first decade had almost universally pursued flying for sport with few industrial or scientific institutions established for the technical advancement of their craft. After some degree of reliability had been wrung from the early designs, it was the military authorities who sought to exploit the potentials thus promised, while the onset of the First World War brought about a diversion away from what would presumably have been a natural course for aviation – that of providing carriage of fare-paying passengers.

It was not until the early 1920s that any real steps were taken to provide international air travel, and this was almost universally undertaken in adaptations of wartime aircraft, so utterly destitute were the major nations after the First World War.

Such has been the extraordinary process of technical evolution attained by mankind's efforts during the past fifty years that today about 150 of the world's nations operate some 750 airlines, flying about 15,100 aircraft over 9,670,000 miles of world air routes and carrying an estimated 236,750,000 passengers per year.

The following is a necessarily brief summary of today's commercial aviation industry throughout the world, presented in the same five main regions as in the previous Chapter on military aviation.

1. EUROPE
AUSTRIA

The principal Austrian airline is *Österreichische Luftverkehrs-Aktiengesellschaft* (Austrian Airlines), which commenced flying operations in 1958. Today it operates international and domestic flights with about a dozen aircraft including five Sud Caravelle VIRs, three BAC Viscount 837s and two Hawker Siddeley HS.748s.

The other principal operator is *Österreichische Flugbetriebs Gesellschaft MbH* (Austrian Airtransport) which operates freight and charter flights with leased Caravelles and Viscounts.

Main commercial airports are located at Vienna (Aspern Airport), Innsbruck and Salzburg.

BELGIUM

Commercial aviation of international character started in Belgium with the foundation of SABENA in the early 1920s. Today SABENA (*Société Anonyme Belge d'Exploitation de la Navigation Aérienne*) carries about 1¼ million passengers annually on routes in Europe, Asia, Africa and America. It owns about 40 airliners including 12 Boeing 707s, ten Caravelles, five Boeing 727s and two Boeing 747s.

The other principal company is Belgian International Air Services SA (BIAS), a charter and tour operator based at Antwerp which mainly operates a dozen aircraft of the feederliner type.

Other Belgian operators are Brussels Airways SA (for charter and air taxi), Delta Air Transport (feederline), and *Société Belge de Transports par Air SA* (Sobelair, a charter and cargo carrier).

International airports are located at Charleroi-Gossellies, Liége-Bierset and Ostend – which together handle about 380,000 passengers annually.

BULGARIA

State carrier in Bulgaria is *Bulgarski Vzduszni Linii* (Bulgarian Airlines Balkan, TABSO) which, based at Sofia, operates a fleet believed to number about 50 Russian aircraft including Tupolev Tu-134, Ilyushin Il-24, Antonov An-24 and several other types, over routes in Europe, Asia and Africa.

A charter and tour operator is Bulair which is also based on Sofia with Antonov An-12 and Ilyushin Il-18 aircraft.

CZECHOSLOVAKIA

The principal international airport of Czechoslovakia is at Prague and this alone handles more than 1½ million passengers annually, and some 50,000 aircraft movements.

The only Czech airline is *Ceskoslovenské Státní Aerolinie* (CSA), which was formed in the early 1920s. It is based at Prague and its current fleet of 40 airliners carry about 1·3 million passengers annually on routes in Europe, to the Middle East, to the Far East and to Cuba, as well as on domestic flights. This fleet includes about 20 Ilyushin Il-14s, six Il-18s, five Tupolev Tu-104s and four Il-62s.

DENMARK

Main national carrier in Denmark is Sterling Airways A/S, which carries about a million passengers annually in a fleet of ten Douglas DC-6Bs and about a dozen Sud Caravelle and Super Caravelle airliners over worldwide routes.

Cimber Air operates two Nord 262s and two Hawker Siddeley Herons on internal scheduled flights and external charter work. A/S Consolidated Aircraft Corporation (CONAIR) owns four Douglas DC-7s, and Scanair operates three Douglas DC-8-33s between Scandinavia and the Mediterranean on tour charter work.

The main civil airports are situated at Copenhagen/Kastrup, Sønderborg and Rönne. The first named airport possesses three runways, of which one is over 11,000 feet long; the airport handles over five million passengers, 40,000 tons of freight and 140,000 aircraft movements annually.

EIRE

The Republic of Ireland's national airline is *Aer Lingus* whose headquarters are located at Dublin airport. The airline carries over a million passengers annually on European routes in a twenty-strong fleet of B.A.C. One-Elevens, BAC Viscounts and eight Boeing 737s.

The trans-Atlantic airline is *Aerlinte Eirann*, also based at Dublin, which flies four Boeing 707-348s, two 720-048s, two 747s, and a 707-320C.

Air charter and tour operations are undertaken by *Air Turas Teoranta* with four Douglas DC-7Fs and two DC-4s.

The international airports are at Dublin and Shannon which together handle more than two million passengers and over 110,000 aircraft movements.

FINLAND

National airline of Finland is *Finnair Oy* (FINNAIR), which operates on routes throughout Europe and to the U.S.A. with about 30 aircraft, including a pair of Douglas DC-8-62s, eight Super Caravelles and seven Convair Metropolitans, as well as some obsolescent aircraft on lease. The airline carries about 430,000 passengers annually.

Operating half-dozen piston-engined American aircraft, the charter company *Kar-Air Oy*, undertakes cargo work throughout the world.

The main international airport is located 12 miles north of the capital, Helsinki, and handles about 950,000 passengers annually. A smaller airport at Malmi, seven miles north-east of Helsinki, nevertheless handles almost twice as many aircraft movements (about 80,000 per year).

FRANCE

Although aviation made substantial strides towards maturity in France before the First World War, and although there were several instances of "passenger"-flights in those early days, little was accomplished to bring commercial transportation to the point of economic viability. It was not until after the Armistice that international passenger-carrying was undertaken commercially, and it was not until 30th August 1933 that *Air France*, the national airline, was established. Since the Second World War, nationalisation of the French aircraft industry has provided stimulus to the growth and prosperity of this airline, which today operates over one hundred aircraft – ranging from five Boeing 747 and 34 Boeing 707 inter-continental jets to 44 Sud Caravelles. It also expects to receive eight Concorde supersonic airliners in the next three years. Its routes are worldwide and it carries just over five million passengers annually.

Second largest French airline is *Air Inter*, a domestic feederline which carries about two million passengers annually in a fleet of ten Caravelles, a dozen BAC Viscounts and ten Fokker Friendships.

There are numerous other smaller companies, including the following: *Air Alpes* (operating about eight light aircraft on flights in the French Alps and Riviera, Corsica and Sardinia); *Compagnie Air Fret* (flying four Lockheed Super Constellations and five Douglas DC-4 freighters in Europe, Africa and Asia); *Compagnie Air Transport* (flying vehicle ferry flights on peripheral routes to neighbouring countries and islands); *Escadrille Mercure* (operating taxi and charter services out of Le Bourget, Nice, Marseilles and Algiers with five Broussards, four Beech 18s, three SFERMA Marquis and a number of American twin-engined aircraft); *Union de Transports Aériens* (an international carrier flying ten Douglas DC-8s of various types and carrying about 300,000 passengers annually).

The principal French commercial airports are at Brest-Guipavas, Bordeaux-Merignac, Calais-Marck, Chartres-Champhol, Cherbourg, Maupertus, Cholet le Pontreau, Deauville, Lyon, Marseilles, Pau-Uzeine, Perpignan, Saint Brieuc, Saint Denis, Saint Etienne, Tarbes and Toulouse-Blagnac.

GERMANY

Possessed of a number of airships prior to the first World War, Germany was almost alone in achieving a form of commercial air travel before 1914. However, owing to the demands of the post-War restrictions it was to be the mid-1920s before Germany was permitted to undertake conventional commercial aviation. In spite of the pervading limitations both upon aviation and aircraft manufacture, Germany managed to establish and maintain a national airline, *Deutsche Lufthansa,* second to none. Interrelated with this airline was the growth of the *Luftwaffe,* for which pilots were surreptitiously trained and eventually employed in wartime bomber capacities.

Since the War, *Deutsche Lufthansa Aktiegesellschaft* has grown in step with Germany's recovery to a position of considerable efficiency and capacity. Today it carries five million passengers to ninety world destinations annually in a fleet of over one hundred aircraft (excluding chartered airliners). Mainstays on the European routes are the Boeing 727 and 737, of which *Lufthansa* fly 21 and 25 respectively. Intercontinental routes are flown by 21 Boeing 707s and five 747s. Three Concordes are also on order.

Second in size is *Condor Flugdienst GmbH* (*CFG*), an international carrier flying Boeing 707s, 727s and 737s. Taxi, feederline and charter companies include *Air Lloyd,* Atlantis Airways, *General Air GmbH,* Germanair, *Luft-Lloyd GmbH* and *Lufttransport Unternehman GmbH.*

Principal domestic and international airports are situated at Bremen, Dusseldorf, Frankfurt, Hamburg, Munich, Nuremburg, Stuttgart and Berlin (Tegel and Templehof). These nine airports handle over twenty million passengers annually, and their rate of traffic expansion in greater than that of any other country in the world. The brand-new terminal facilities at Frankfurt are impressive in the extreme.

GERMANY (EAST)

National carrier is *Interflug* (*Gesellschaft fur Internationalen Flugverkehr mbH*), based on Berlin and equipped wholly with Russian aircraft – including about 15 Ilyushin Il-18, six Antonov An-24B, a Tupolev Tu-124, three Tu-134 and two Tu-154 airliners. These aircraft fly routes in Eastern Europe and the Middle East and carry about a million passengers annually.

GIBRALTAR

The local airline, Gibraltar Airways Ltd., operates a Hawker Siddeley Trident between "the Rock", Portugal and Morocco, and also to the United Kingdom in conjunction with British European Airways.

GREECE

Operating throughout Europe and the Middle East, and to the U.S.A., Olympic Airways has a fleet of five Boeing 707s, three Hawker Siddeley Comet 4Bs, and five Boeing 727-284s. There are also six Douglas DC-6Bs and five DC-3s, as well as some French helicopters operating taxi services. The international airport, at which Olympic's main facilities are based, is at Thessalonika.

HUNGARY

Like most East European airlines, the Hungarian state airline, *Magyar Legikozlekedesi Vallalat* (*Malev*) is wholly Russian equipped, and operates domestic, European and Middle Eastern routes. Its fleet comprises seven Ilyushin Il-14s, seven Il-18s and two Tupolev Tu-134s.

ICELAND

Iceland's national carrier is Icelandair (*Flugfelag Islands HF*), flying domestic routes and routes to London, Glasgow, Bergen, Oslo, Copenhagen and the Faroes. Its fleet comprises three Fokker Friendships, two Douglas DC-6Bs, two DC-3s, a BAC Viscount and a Boeing 727. The transatlantic carrier is *Loftleidir* (*Loftleidir Icelandic Airlines*) which flies five Canadair CL-44s and four Douglas DC-6Bs between Scandinavia and New York *via* Luxembourg, London and Iceland, and handles about 200,000 passengers annually.

Domestic carriers are *Flugthjonustan, Flugsyn HF* and *Nordurflug* (the latter also providing fish-spotting services and freight operations). Almost all the aircraft flown by these companies are American – mainly Beechcraft, Cessna and Piper designs.

ITALY

Italy operates nine sizeable companies, of which Alitalia is the largest and is growing fastest. Its routes are worldwide (including flights to Australia) and the fleet is predominantly Douglas-built, with 22 DC-8s and 40 DC-9s. There are also seven Boeing 747s and 18 Sud Caravelle VINs. These aircraft carry over four million passengers annually.

Next in size – flying a dozen Fokker Friendships and six DC-9s – is *Aero Trasporti Italiani* (*ATI*), carrying half-a-million passengers in internal routes. Central European routes are flown by the five DC-6Bs and four Caravelles of *Societa Aerea Mediterranea.* Domestic and taxi services are provided by *Aerolinee Italia SpA* (with two Fokker Fellowships and five Handley Page Heralds), and *Aertirrena SpA* (with half-a-dozen Britten-Norman Islanders, a Handley Page Jetstream and a handful of American aircraft).

There are also two helicopter carriers (*Compagnia Italiana Elicotteri* and *Societa Italiana Esercizio Elicotteri*), between them flying some twenty aircraft.

Italy's main international airport is Leonardi da Vinci Airport at Rome/Fiumicino, handling 120,000 aircraft movements and nearly five million passengers annually.

LUXEMBOURG

Based on Luxembourg airport is the airline LUXAIR (*Société Anonyme Luxembourgeoise de Navigation Aérienne*) flying three Fokker Friendships and a BAC

Viscount on European routes. These aircraft carry about 130,000 passengers annually, while the airport handles 25,000 aircraft movements and 350,000 passengers.

NETHERLANDS

Oldest airline in the world today is KLM (*Konninklijke Luchtvaart Maatschappij N.V.*, Royal Dutch Airlines), founded on 7th October 1919 and based on Schiphol Airport, Amsterdam. It was also the first European airline to operate the classic Douglas DC-3 in 1936. With the exception of five Boeing 747s and a single Fokker Friendship, the airline is today Douglas-equipped, flying 24 DC-8s (of various sub-variants) and 23 DC-9s throughout the world.

Another Schiphol-based airline is Martinair Holland (*Martins Luchtvervoer Maatschappij NV*) which operates two DC-8s, three DC-9s, two Convair 640s, a DC-6A and a Fokker Fellowship on worldwide charter and executive flights, and aerial photography. Third of the Dutch airlines is *Luchtvaartmaatschappij Transavia Holland NV*, flying six DC-6s, a Boeing 707-320C, and two Caravelle IIIs on worldwide services.

Holland's main commercial airports, apart from Schiphol, are located at Rotterdam and Eelde (five miles south of Groningen). Schiphol has about 130,000 aircraft movements and handles about 2,700,000 passengers annually.

NORWAY

Like other Scandinavian countries, Norway is served principally by S.A.S. (see Sweden), although there are four indigenous airlines. Largest of these is Braathens South American and Far East Air Transport A/S (*Braathens SAFE*); flying about 2,200 miles of unduplicated routes, the airline operates two Boeing 737s, six Fokker Friendships, five Fokker Fellowships and five Douglas DC-6Bs. It carries nearly a million passengers a year.

Fjellfly A/S provides charter and scheduled domestic services using about a dozen Piper and Cessna light aircraft, as well as two Scottish Aviation Twin Pioneers and three aged Norduyn Norsemen.

Fred Olsens Flyselskap A/S, a long-established carrier, flies three DC-6s and one or two older aircraft, principally on cargo flights; and *Wideroes Flyveselskap A/S* does charter, air survey and ambulance work (mainly in North Norway) with five DHC Otters, a Twin Otter, a Norduyn Norseman and three Cessna light aircraft.

Norway's three principal civil airports are Oslo/Fornebu, Bergen and Kristiansand. Oslo handles nearly 100,000 aircraft movements each year, as well as about 1,700,000 passengers.

POLAND

National carrier is LOT-Polish Airlines (*Polskie Linie Lotnicze*), with a route mileage of 22,557 throughout Europe, the Middle East and Russia. As is to be expected, its equipment is today wholly of Russian origin (as it

has been ever since the Second World War), comprising six Tupolev Tu-134s, eight Ilyushin Il-18s, ten Il-24s and 12 Antonov An-24s. Its headquarters are at Warsaw and it carries over three-quarters of a million passengers annually.

PORTUGAL

Transatlantic airline is *Transportes Aéreos Portugueses SARL* (TAP) which operates seven Boeing 707s, five Boeing 727s and three Caravelles, the latter types flying routes in Europe and Africa. The airline carries about 700,000 passengers annually.

Routes to the Azores are flown by the two Douglas DC-3s and Hawker Siddeley Doves of *Sociedade Acoriana de Transportes Aéreos Lda* (*SATA*).

The international airport at Lisbon has about 36,000 aircraft movements annually and handles 1,600,000 passengers.

ROMANIA

Romania's state airline, *Transporturile Aeriene Romane* (TAROM) is unusual among East European carriers in being partly equipped with Western aircraft – for its fleet includes six BAC One-Elevens. Also operated are 11 Ilyushin Il-18s, three Antonov An-24Bs, and some Il-14s and Li-2s. The routes extend throughout Europe and the Middle East.

SPAIN

The Spanish national airline, *Iberia, Lineas Aereas de Espagna, SA*, is a large carrier, flying more than 80 aircraft over about 120,000 route miles throughout Europe, America and Africa. The fleet includes three Boeing 747s, a dozen Douglas DC-8s, 18 DC-9s, 19 Caravelles, 15 Convair 440s, eight Fokker Friendships and some DC-3s, DC-4s and Carvairs. The airline carries 3·4 million passengers annually.

Next in size, carrying a million passengers, is *Spantex SA Transportes Aereos* which flies five Convair 990s, five DC-7s, two DC-6s, five DC-4s, seven DC-3s and four Fokker Friendships as well as some light feederline types.

Air Spain SA operates three BAC Britannias on charter work; *Aviacion y Comercio SA* flies six Convair 440s in the Iberian peninsula and North Africa; *Trabajos Aereos y Enlaces SA* (TAE) operates three DC-7Cs and a BAC One-Eleven on charter; and *Trans Europa Compania de Aviacion SA* (TECA) has four DC-7s and four DC-4s. All these airlines maintain their principal base facilities at Madrid international airport.

SWEDEN

The major Scandinavian airline, Scandinavian Airlines System (S.A.S.), was formed on 13th August 1946 by means of an international amalgamation between Swedish Inter-continental Airlines (SILA), Swedish *Aktiebolaget Aerotransport* (ABA), Norwegian Airlines (DNL) and Danish Airlines (DDL). Today S.A.S. is

A McDonnell Douglas DC-9-20 of Scandinavian Air Services

based at Brömma Airport, Stockholm, and has a fleet of 15 Douglas DC-8s (Models 55, 55F, 62, 62F and 63), 26 DC-9s (Models 21 and 40), two Boeing 747Bs and a dozen Sud Caravelle IIIs. Flying worldwide routes amounting to 128,000 miles, this airline carries over four million passengers annually.

Largest all-Europe Swedish carrier is Transair Sweden AB which operates passenger and freight services with three Boeing 727s and ten DC-7Bs. Charter operations are also flown by Fairline AB using until recently a pair of Curtiss C-46s, and Falconair Charter Ltd., using two Lockheed L-188Cs and three BAC Viscount 784Ds.

The largest wholly-domestic carrier is *Linjeflyg Aktiebolaget* which carries annually over half-a-million passengers on 3,230 miles of domestic routes in 14 Convair 330s and 440s, and two Nord 262s.

Non-scheduled and feederline services are provided by *AB Lapplandsflyg Linjeflyg*, based at Umeå, with a dozen light American aeroplanes and helicopters.

Principal international airports are Brömma/Stockholm, Bulltofta/Malmö and Torslanda/Göteborg.

SWITZERLAND

Formed between the Wars as the result of amalgamation of *Ad Astra-Aéro* and *Balair*, Swissair (*Swissair-Schweizerische Luftverkehr-Aktiengesellschaft*) continued flights in Europe during the Second World War between Zurich, Stuttgart and Berlin, but these services were discontinued on 17th August 1944 following the destruction of a Swiss DC-2 during an American air raid on Stuttgart.

Today Swissair flies world routes totalling 113,000 miles, carrying over three million passengers in nine DC-8s, 17 DC-9s, six Convair 990As, two Boeing 747Bs, five Caravelle IIIs and three Fokker Friendships. *Balair Ltd.* today operates charter and scheduled services with two Convair 990As, a DC-9, three DC-6Bs, two DC-4s and three Fokker Friendships.

Local charter, feederline and taxi services are provided

extensively in Switzerland by four companies: *Air Glaciers SA, Aerodrome Regional de Montreux SA, Alpar Flug-und-Flugplatzgesellschaft AG*, and *Alpine Luft transport AG*, using modern light American and Swiss aeroplanes and French helicopters.

Main intercontinental airport is Kloten/Zürich which handles 3·5 million passengers and 120,000 aircraft movements annually. The other intercontinental airport is Cointrin/Geneva, handling two million passengers and 95,000 aircraft movements on a single 12,792-foot runway. Basle-Mulhouse Airport also handles international traffic.

U.S.S.R.

Largest single airline in the world is the Russian state carrier, *Aeroflot*. As this vast organisation not only undertakes orthodox air commerce (passenger and freight carriage), but also regular ambulance, agricultural and air survey work as well as many other services, it is almost impossible to impart any reliable, detailed breakdown of aircraft flown, route mileages and airports.

First active domestic carrier in Russia was *Dobrolet*, formed in 1923, and later the same year followed the Ukrainian carrier *Ukrvozdukhput*. A third airline was *Zakavia*. Equipment was largely provided by German manufacturers which had been obliged to move away from Germany so as to avoid contravention of the Versailles Treaty.

Aeroflot was formed in 1932 and soon after acquired the state monopoly for domestic air commerce. Although it continued to provide air services throughout the Second World War, most of these were closely associated with support of the armed forces. After the War almost all the equipment was of military origin, although the Russians had been quick to adopt and adapt the American Douglas DC-3; this classic transport entered service as the Lisunov Li-2 and remained in service for many years, as did Russia's first post-War indigenous airliner, the Ilyushin Il-12 – which entered service in 1947.

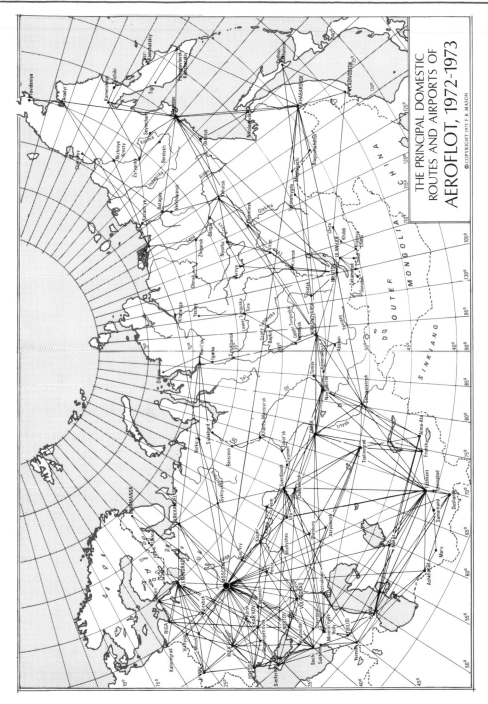

THE PRINCIPAL DOMESTIC ROUTES AND AIRPORTS OF **AEROFLOT, 1972-1973**

© COPYRIGHT 1973 F. K. MASON

Today no other airline (state or otherwise) approaches the size or capacity of *Aeroflot*. With a fleet of nearly 4,000 aircraft, of which almost 1,000 are airliners available to operate scheduled services, *Aeroflot* serves well over 3,500 cities, towns and rural settlements throughout the vast area of the U.S.S.R., operating a route mileage which is believed to have reached at least 350,000 miles of unduplicated routes between Europe and the Pacific, and from well inside the Arctic Circle to the tropics. To this should be added the huge workload associated with agriculture, forestry, fire-control, fishery administration and ambulance duties – tasks which are undertaken by the Antonov An-2, of which more than 2,000 are used by *Aeroflot*.

It would be too superficial a view to express that Soviet airline equipment is "copied" from leading Western designs, any more than the designers of one Western nation may follow the trends of another – although this was unquestionably the case in post-War equipment. Perhaps it would be more realistic to comment merely upon the similarity of design concepts between East and West, and remark that the Russian designs tend to enter service some two years after their Western "counterparts". Examples of these parallels may be seen in the An-24/Fokker Friendship, Il-62/VC-10, Tu-154/Trident-Boeing 727, and Tu-144/Concorde.

No reliable figures can be quoted for in-service numbers, but the following types are in or entering operation (in addition to the Tu-144, whose future is by no means assured at the time of writing): Antonov An-2, An-10/12, An-14, An-22, An-24, Beriev Be-30, Ilyushin Il-12/14, Il-18, Il-62, Lisunov Li-2, Tupolev Tu-104, Tu-114, Tu-124, Tu-134, Tu-154, Yakovlev Yak-12 and Yak-40. Helicopters are widely used and include the Kamov Ka-15, Ka-18, Ka-26, Mil Mi-1, Mi-2, Mi-4, Mi-6, Mi-8 and the very big Mi-10.

Principal routes and commercial airports (or airports with substantial commercial facilities) are shown in the accompanying map.

UNITED KINGDOM

Although the first British airline company (Aircraft and Travel Ltd.) was registered in October 1916, the first scheduled airline flight by a British aeroplane was not flown until 25th August 1919 (see page 22). Thereafter for several years the British flag was carried by a number of companies including Daimler Airways, Handley Page Transport and Instone Air Lines.

The first British national airline, Imperial Airways, was formed on 1st August 1924 by the amalgamation of the above companies and the British Marine Air Navigation Company. Imperial Airways became one of the world's greatest airlines between the Wars and opened up the famous Empire routes to South Africa and the Far East – gaining an enviable reputation with the Short C-Class flying-boats in the late nineteen-thirties.

Imperial and British Airways were amalgamated to form British Overseas Airways Corporation on 4th August 1939, but the Second World War brought about an almost complete curtailment of passenger services by BOAC.

After the War there were three main British national carriers, BOAC, British European Airways and British

Unquestionably the most widely used general purpose civil aircraft in the world is the Antonov An-2, shown here equipped for agricultural duties. More than 2,000 of these aircraft are believed to be in service with Aeroflot, many of them operating third-level services between isolated settlements in the U.S.S.R.

South American Airways – although the latter was short-lived. Today BOAC and BEA operate extensive services throughout Europe and the World, and have been joined by numerous other carriers, so that Britain occupies third position (after America and Russia) among world nations in commercial aviation.

The following is a list of the leading British carriers in January 1973; the fleets and brief details are those notified at the end of 1972, but re-equipment is constant and fleets may have undergone slight changes during the following months.

Aurigny Air Services Ltd.

8 Britten-Norman Islander	Flies services between the Channel Islands and Northern France. Carries about 50,000 passengers annually; over 80,000 revenue ton miles.

Bristow Helicopters Ltd.

Approx. 100 helicopters	Flies international helicopter charter services.

Britannia Airways Ltd.

6 Boeing 737-204 2 Boeing 737-204C 4 BAC Britannia 102	Tour flights between U.K. and Mediterranean. Operates a route mileage of 35,000, carries over half a million passengers and returns more than 50 million revenue ton miles annually.

British Air Ferries Ltd.

6 Aviation Traders ATL-98 Carvair 2 Canadair CL-44	Flies freight charter worldwide and scheduled services within Europe. Operates a route mileage of 3,254, carries about 30,000 passengers and returns almost 7 million revenue ton miles annually.

British Caledonian Airways Ltd.

8 Boeing 707-320C 3 BAC VC-10 13 BAC One-Eleven-500 7 BAC One-Eleven-200	Operates worldwide services. Since take-over of British United Airways Ltd., in November 1970, annual returns of route mileage and passengers carried have not given a realistic idea of Company's operations.

British European Airways

26 H.S. Trident 3 15 H.S. Trident 2 20 H.S. Trident 1 9 H.S. Comet 4B 8 BAC Vanguard 9 BAC Merchantman 18 BAC One-Eleven-510 20 BAC Viscount	Operates extensive high-density routes throughout Europe, North Africa and the Eastern Mediterranean. Route mileage 60,500. Carries 7,800,000 passengers and returns over 340 million revenue ton miles annually.

2 H.S. Heron 7 Boeing 707 8 Helicopters 6 Lockheed TriStar (on order)	It is announced that late in 1973 BEA will merge with British Overseas Airways Corporation.

British Island Airways Ltd.

6 Handley Page Herald 4 Douglas DC-3	Operates in North-West Europe on a route mileage of 2,900, carrying over 500,000 passengers annually.

British Midland Airways Ltd.

7 BAC Viscount 3 BAC One-Eleven-523 2 Douglas DC-4	Operates U.K. and European services, including charter and air survey work.

British Overseas Airways Corporation

16 Boeing 707-436 2 Boeing 707-336B 7 Boeing 707-336C 2 Boeing 707-336QC 11 BAC VC-10 16 BAC Super VC-10 13 Boeing 747-136 5 BAC-*Aérospatiale* Concorde (on order)	Britain's state intercontinental carrier with a route mileage of 320,700. Carried 2,141,000 passengers and returned 1,111 million revenue ton miles in 1971–72. Merger with British European Airways announced for late 1973.

Channel Airways Ltd.

2 BAC One-Eleven-208 4 H.S. 748 9 BAC Viscount 812 2 H.S. Heron	Operates domestic routes and charter services with Northern Europe, as well as freighting.

Court Line Ltd.

11 BAC One-Eleven-500 1 BAC One-Eleven-400 2 H.S. 748 Series 2A 2 Lockheed TriStar	Flights throughout Europe. More than half a million passengers carried annually; approximately 20 million annual revenue ton miles.

C.S.E. Aviation (Carlisle) Ltd.

14 Cessna 150 6 Beagle Pup 2 Beagle 206	Charter and other services in Western Europe. Carries approximately 3,000 passengers annually.

Dan-Air Services Ltd.

16 H.S. Comet 4 7 H.S. 748 5 BAC One-Eleven-400 3 Boeing 727 2 Boeing 707	Operates worldwide services, carrying about 400,000 passengers and returning over 20 million revenue ton miles annually.

Thurston Aviation Ltd. (*HARTEX*)

3 Britten-Norman Islander 4 Piper PA-23 Apache 1 Piper PA-28-160 Cherokee 1 Piper PA-31 Navajo	Operates miscellaneous services in the U.K. and Europe, carrying more than 2,500 passengers and returning over 60,000 revenue ton miles annually.

A Hawker Siddeley 748 Series 2A in the livery of Polynesian Air Lines. First flown in June 1960 as the Avro 748, this short/medium range airliner has enjoyed substantial world sales, nearly 300 having been built by 1973 – including a number of military versions for the R.A.F. and other air forces

Humber Airways Ltd. (HAL)

2 Britten-Norman Islander
1 Piper PA-23 Aztec

Operates in the U.K. and Northern Europe, carrying about 1,500 passengers annually.

Laker Airways Ltd.

5 BAC One-Eleven-320L
2 Douglas DC-10
2 Boeing 707-138B

Worldwide routes and charter services. Carries over a quarter million passengers and returns about 20 million revenue ton miles annually.

Loganair Ltd.

3 Britten-Norman Islander
4 other light aircraft

Operates services in the U.K. and Western Europe.

McAlpine Aviation Ltd.

3 Piper PA-31 Navajo
3 Piper PA-23-250 Aztec
2 Piaggio P-166B Portofino
2 Piper PA-30 Twin Comanche
1 H.S. Dove Mk. 8

Operates charter services throughout the U.K., Europe and North Africa, carrying more than 4,000 passengers annually.

Monarch Airlines Ltd.

4 BAC Britannia 300
3 Boeing 707-720B

Provides worldwide charter services, carrying about 200,000 passengers and returning more than 10 million revenue ton miles annually.

Northeast Airlines Ltd.

4 BAC One-Eleven-416
3 H.S. Trident 1E
3 H.S. 748 Series 1 and 2
16 BAC Viscount

Now includes Cambrian and BKS companies. Flies scheduled routes throughout U.K. and in Western Europe. Carries over 1½ million passengers annually and returns 2·7 million revenue ton miles.

Skyways Coach Air Ltd.

7 H.S. 748 Series 1 and 2
1 H.S. Comet 4
5 H.S. Comet 4B
1 H.S. Comet 4C
2 BAC One-Eleven-300
2 BAC One-Eleven-400
1 BAC One-Eleven-414
2 Boeing 707
2 Boeing 727

Flies scheduled, charter and tour services between the U.K. and Northern Europe. Route mileage is 1,130, over a quarter-million passengers carried annually, and over 5 million revenue ton miles.

The principal international airports in the British Isles, with annual number of passengers handled (1968 figures) are: London Heathrow (13·2 million), Gatwick (2·07 million), Manchester (1·55 million), Jersey (1·1 million), Glasgow (1·4 million), Belfast (977,000), Luton (707,800), Edinburgh (628,000), Liverpool (545,000), Prestwick (518,000) and Southend (504,000).

2. NORTH, SOUTH AND CENTRAL AMERICA

ARGENTINA

A country where aviation's origins date from the years before the First World War, Argentina has a number of sizeable carriers, of which *Aerolineas Argentinas* is the state intercontinental carrier, based at Buenos Aires with a fleet of six Boeing 707-387Bs, two H.S. Comet 4Cs, four Sud Caravelle VIRs, six NAMC YS-11As and eleven Hawker Siddeley 748s. Its longest stage route is between Buenos Aires and Madrid, Spain.

There are two other international airlines: *Aerotransportes Litoral Argentino SA* flies four BAC One-Eleven-400s, three One-Eleven-500s, and two NAMC YS-11-300s between Argentina, Bolivia, Chile and Paraguay. *AUSTRAL (Compania Argentina de Transportes Aereos)* operates four BAC One-Eleven-420s, three BAC One-Eleven-521s and two NAMC YS-11-300s between Argentina, Uruguay and Chile. Between them these two airlines carry about half a million passengers annually over nearly 30,000 miles of unduplicated routes.

Major commercial air transport facilities are located at Buenos Aires, Tucumán, Córdoba, Mendoza and Gallegos.

BAHAMAS

The principal air traffic of the Bahamas is operated by Bahamas Airways Ltd., linking the islands with Jamaica, the Turks and Caicos and the U.S.A. It flies about ten aircraft including three BAC One-Eleven-517s and four Hawker Siddeley 748 Series 2s, over 5,170 route miles, carrying more than half a million passengers annually.

A Boeing 707-355C is flown by International Air Bahama on a service between Nassau and Luxembourg. Nassau is the principal international airport.

BOLIVIA

Bolivia's main international carrier is *Lloyd Aero Boliviano (LAB)*, operating scheduled services between the home country and Peru, Brazil, Argentina and Chile, carrying about 300,000 passengers annually. Although currently undergoing re-equipment, the 1972 fleet included two Fairchild F.27 Friendships and a Boeing 727-100, and some of the older Douglas piston-engined airliners may also have survived.

Another airline, *TABSA Bolivian Airways*, is also being re-equipped and provides freight services throughout Central and South America.

BRAZIL

There are three main airlines in Brazil, of which the intercontinental carrier is Varig Brazilian Airlines *(SA Empressa de Viacao Aerea Rio Grandense)* whose routes extend throughout Latin America, Europe, the U.S.A. and to Japan. Its route mileage is about 106,000 and about 1½ million passengers are carried annually. The large fleet of about eighty aircraft includes eight Boeing 707s (of various types), two Convair 990As, and ten Hawker Siddeley 748 Series 2s.

The main domestic operator is *Viacao Aerea Sao Paulo (VASP)* which flies five Boeing 737-200s, two BAC One-Eleven-422s, twelve BAC Viscounts, six NAMC YS-11A-200s and about thirty piston-engined American transport aircraft.

Third carrier, with routes throughout South America, is *Servicos Aereos Cruzeiro do Sul SA*. This carries about three-quarters of a million passengers annually over 23,500 route miles in a fleet of about twenty aged Douglas DC-3s, seven Sud Caravelle VIRs and eight NAMC YS-11A-200S.

Principal international transport facilities are located at the Viracopos Campinas Airport at Sao Paulo.

CANADA

As would be expected in a vast nation whose relatively remote areas are only readily accessible by air, Canada has numerous fairly large domestic carriers in addition to the three major international transport airlines.

Air Canada operates a route mileage of 78,000, extending to Central America, and through Europe to Moscow, and carries 6½ million passengers annually. Its fleet of over a hundred airliners include 38 Douglas DC-8s, three Boeing 747-133s, ten Lockheed TriStars, 49 Douglas DC-9s, fifteen Vickers Vanguards and 25 Viscounts. At the time of writing Air Canada was still keeping open its options for the purchase of four BAC-*Aérospatiale* Concorde supersonic airliners.

Canadian Pacific Air flies a route mileage of 58,450, and carries over a million passengers throughout Europe, America and the Orient. It operates eleven Douglas DC-8s (of which four are the long-range 63-Series), fourteen Boeing 737-217s, and two Boeing 727-100s.

Pacific Western Airlines flies a variety of scheduled and charter services throughout Western and North-West Canada, an air bus service between Edmonton and Calgary, and world-wide charter operations. Its fleet includes four Lockheed Hercules, two Boeing 707-138Bs, and four Boeing 737-200 and -200QC airliners. There are also some older piston-engined transports.

Scheduled domestic airlines include TransAir-Midwest Ltd. (whose fleet includes two Boeing 737s and two NAMC YS-11A-330s), QuebecAir (with five Fairchild F.27 Friendships and two BAC One-Eleven-304s), and Eastern Provincial Airways (with three DHC-2 Turbo Beavers, five DHC-2 Beavers, six DHC-3 Otters and one DHC-6 Twin Otter as well as a number of older Douglas aircraft and five Consolidated PBY-5As for water-bombing).

Canada's main airports (with 1968–69 passenger-handling totals) are Gander, Newfoundland (254,000), Ottawa, Ontario (870,000), Quebec (405,000), Toronto

International (5·2 million) and Vancouver International (2·05 million).

CHILE

Chile's international operator is *Linea Aerea Nacionale Chile* (*LAN*) which, based at Santiago, carries half a million passengers throughout South America, the U.S.A. and the South Pacific in four Boeing 727-100s, a Boeing 707-330B, three Sud Caravelle VIRs, nine Hawker Siddeley 748s, eight Douglas DC-6s and half a dozen DC-3s.

COLOMBIA

In addition to six minor scheduled airlines, Colombia has one sizeable carrier, *Avianca* (*Aerovias Nacionales de Colombia*). With a fleet of about forty airliners (including two Boeing 707-320Bs, three Boeing 707-720Bs, four Boeing 727s, two Boeing 737-159s, and two Hawker Siddeley 748s) this airline carries about two million passengers over a route mileage of 41,000 throughout North and South America and Western Europe.

COSTA RICA

Apart from two charter and taxi operators, the main carrier is *Lineas Aereas Costarricenses SA* (*LACSA*), which flies about 63,000 passengers annually on routes totalling 3,000 miles in Central America. It flies two BAC One-Eleven-409 and one One-Eleven-531 in addition to half-a-dozen obsolescent piston-engined transports.

CUBA

The state airline *Cubana* (*Empresa Consolidada Cubana de Aviacion*), operates both domestic and international services to Prague, Madrid and Central America. As might be expected, its equipment is mainly of Russian origin and includes ten Ilyushin Il-14s, two Il-18s and about six Antonov An-24Bs. Four BAC Britannia 318s and some six American piston-engined transports were in use three years ago and some of these may still be operating.

ECUADOR

The only carrier of any note in Ecuador is *Aerovias Ecuatorianas* (*AREA*) which operates a Hawker Siddeley Comet 4 and three Douglas piston-engined airliners.

EL SALVADOR

With a route mileage of 4,900 throughout Central America and the southern states of the U.S.A., the main carrier is TACA International Airlines SA with two BAC One-Eleven-407s, two BAC Viscount 700s and a Douglas DC-4.

GUATEMALA

The one airline, *AVIATECA* (*Empresa Guatemalteca de Aviacion SA*), operates routes totalling 5,500 miles in Central America, Mexico and the southern states of the U.S.A. with one BAC One-Eleven-516 and four Douglas DC-6/6Bs.

JAMAICA

Of the two airlines based at Kingston, Air Jamaica is the largest, operating through the Caribbean to North America with a long-range Douglas DC-8-61 and two DC-9-32s. It also has on order two Lockheed TriStars.

The other carrier is Jamaica Air Services, a local operator which flies a Hawker Siddeley H.S. 748 and three Hawker Siddeley Herons on feederline services.

MEXICO

Mexico has two principal international airlines, of which Aeromexico is the larger, flying four Douglas DC-8-50s, nine DC-9-10s and two DC-10-30s throughout North America and to Europe. It also operates domestic services.

The other carrier is *Mexicana* (*Compania Mexicana de Aviacion SA*) which flies three Hawker Siddeley Comet 4Cs, four Boeing 727-64s and seven Douglas DC-6s throughout the Caribbean and to the U.S.A.

There are also about a dozen scheduled domestic and feederline operators and air charter and taxi companies whose equipment is also exclusively American.

NICARAGUA

With a route mileage of 4,100, Nicaragua's one airline, *LANICA* (*Lineas Aereas de Nicaragua SA*), flies a BAC One-Eleven-412, a Douglas DC-6 and two DC-4s.

PERU

Peru's intercontinental airline is *APSA* (*Aerolineas Peruanas SA*) with routes totalling 18,000 miles and serving South, Central and North American destinations, as well as Madrid, Paris and London. Its fleet consists of six Convair 990As and a Douglas DC-8-52.

The main domestic carrier is *Faucett SA* (*Compania de Aviacion Faucett SA*), an old-established airline founded by an American, Elmer J. Faucett. For many years it was unique in that it designed and built its own transport aircraft, as well as owning two of the nation's largest airports, at Lima and Trujillo.

Today it operates a fleet which includes two BAC One-Eleven-476s, a Boeing 727-100, six Douglas DC-6Bs, four DC-4s and half a dozen DC-3s.

PUERTO RICO

With routes totalling 5,000 miles, Caribbean Atlantic Airlines Inc. (CaribAir), based at San Juan International Airport, operates four Douglas DC-9-30s and five Convair CV-640s between almost all the West Indian islands and Miami, Florida.

A small scheduled feederline is operated by Puerto

Rico International Airlines Inc. (Prinair), using about a dozen Hawker Siddeley Herons.

TRINIDAD

One of the largest West Indies-based airlines is British West Indian Airways (BWIA) which, with three Boeing 727-100s, a Boeing 707-138 and four BAC Viscounts, has routes throughout the Caribbean, touching the northern parts of South America and extending to the U.S.A. It carries more than 300,000 passengers annually over the 7,000 miles of routes flown.

UNITED STATES OF AMERICA

Such is the nature of air travel's integral part of American life that the U.S. airline industry is the largest in the world, although obviously no single airline approaches in size that of the giant Russian state organisation, *Aeroflot*. Nevertheless, the all-powerful "top twelve" airlines, namely Allegheny, American Airlines, Braniff, Continental, Delta, Eastern, National, Northeast Orient, Pan American, TWA, United and Western Airlines, operate the world's densest traffic routes, and between them carry a total of no fewer than 126·7 million passengers annually (1971 figures). The following is a summary of these airlines, together with other major carriers in the U.S.A.

Airline	Fleet (*Notified July–December 1972, as being current March 1973*)	Route Mileage	Passengers Carried	Revenue Ton Miles (*Average 1969–72*)	Operations
Allegheny Airlines Inc. (merged with Mohawk Airlines Inc.)	33 Douglas DC-9-31 30 BAC One-Eleven-200 27 Convair 580 32 Fairchild FH-27 Friendship 12 *Aérospatiale Frégate* 5 Boeing 727-287	8,000 (Approx.)	6·8 million	170 million	Domestic U.S.A. and into Canada.
American Airlines Inc.	46 Boeing 707-323 70 Boeing 707-720 41 Boeing 727-223 57 Boeing 727-23 28 BAC One-Eleven-401 16 Boeing 747-123 24 Douglas DC-10	16,280	19·4 million	2,167 million	Throughout the North American continent.
Braniff International Inc.	8 Boeing 707-320C 4 Boeing 707-227 5 Boeing 707-720-027 6 Douglas DC-8-62 33 Boeing 727 12 BAC One-Eleven-200 1 Boeing 747-127	28,830	6·7 million	751 million	Domestic and international throughout North, Central and South America.

A Boeing 727-90QC of Alaska Airlines Inc. No fewer than 1,035 Boeing 727s have been ordered by the world airlines

Airline	Fleet (*Notified July–December 1972, as being current March 1973*)	Route Mileage	Passengers Carried	Revenue Ton Miles	Operations
			(*Average 1969–72*)		
Continental Air Lines Inc.	28 Boeing 727-224 19 Douglas DC-9-10F 11 Boeing 707-324C 2 Boeing 707-321C 7 Boeing 707-720-24B 4 Boeing 747-124 8 Douglas DC-10-10	–	–	–	Domestic scheduled services, charter and freight throughout U.S.A.
Delta Air Lines Inc.	67 Douglas DC-9 (various) 14 Boeing 727 (various) 18 Lockheed TriStar 5 Boeing 747-132	14,690	11·6 million	890 million	Coast-to-coast domestic routes and services to Central America and Caribbean.
Eastern Air Lines Inc.	15 Boeing 707-720 50 Boeing 727 (various) 24 Boeing 727-25QC 18 Boeing 727-225 17 Douglas DC-8 17 Douglas DC-8-61 6 Douglas DC-8-63 86 Douglas DC-9 (various) 4 Boeing 747-125 37 Lockheed TriStar	30,500	2·9 million	1,500 million	Operates between about 100 airports in the U.S.A., Central America and the Caribbean.
National Airlines Inc.	12 Boeing 727-35 25 Boeing 727-235 13 Douglas DC-8 (various) 2 Douglas DC-8-61 2 Boeing 747-135	6,210	5·41 million	480 million	Operates principally on the coastal routes of the U.S.A.
Northwest Orient Airlines Inc.	35 Boeing 707-351B and C 15 Boeing 707-720-51B 30 Boeing 727-51/51C 25 Boeing 727-251 10 Boeing 747-151 5 Boeing 747-251B 14 Douglas DC-10-20	–	–	–	Domestic services in the U.S.A., and international routes to the Far East.
Pan American World Airways Inc.	25 Boeing 707-321 56 Boeing 707-321B 30 Boeing 707-321C 5 Boeing 707-121B 8 Boeing 707-720B 20 Boeing 727-21 4 Boeing 727-21QC 4 Douglas DC-8 33 Boeing 747-121	82,500	10·1 million	3·3 million	Round-the-world services, and routes between the U.S.A., Europe, Africa, the Middle East, Australia, New Zealand, the South and Central Pacific, the Caribbean and South America.
Trans World Airlines Inc. (TWA)	58 Boeing 707-131 and -131B 54 Boeing 707-331 and -331 B/C 22 Convair 880 33 Lockheed TriStar 35 Boeing 727 and 727QC 32 Boeing 727-231 19 Douglas DC-9 15 Boeing 747-131	50,600	14·5 million	17,100 million	Operates services throughout the U.S.A., and to Europe, the Middle East, North and East Africa, and the Far East.

Airline	Fleet (Notified July–December 1972, as being current March 1973)	Route Mileage	Passengers Carried	Revenue Ton Miles (Average 1969–72)	Operations
United Airlines Inc.	152 Boeing 727 (various) 75 Boeing 737-222 18 Boeing 747-122 26 Boeing 707-720 80 Douglas DC-8 (various)	18,000	27·7 million	3,100 million	Operates extensive services throughout the U.S.A. and Canada, and the North Pacific.
Western Airlines Inc.	5 Boeing 707-347C 5 Boeing 707-320C 30 Boeing 707-720 and -720B 10 Boeing 727-247 30 Boeing 737-247 3 Boeing 747	24,500	5·8 million	422 million	Operates mainline services throughout the northern and western states of the U.S.A., also Mexico, Canada, Alaska and the North Pacific to the Far East.
Air California Inc.	10 Boeing 737-200 2 Douglas DC-9-10	2,400	650,000	–	Scheduled services in California.
Airlift International Inc.	4 Boeing 727-172C 5 Douglas DC-8F and -63F 1 Boeing 707-300 10 Other aircraft	9,800	570,000	3·9 million	Worldwide commercial and military charter services.
Air West Inc.	33 Fairchild F.27 Friendship 9 Douglas DC-9-10 16 Douglas DC-9-30 4 Boeing 727-100 and -200	9,900	3·1 million	3·6 million	Operates scheduled services throughout the western states, western Mexico and Alberta, Canada.
Alaska Airlines Inc.	3 Boeing 727-90QC 1 Convair 990A 28 Other aircraft	–	–	–	Domestic services in Alaska, and to Seattle, Washington.
Flying Tiger Line Inc.	17 Douglas DC-8-63F 2 Canadair CL-44	14,000	194,000	460 million	Operates transcontinental and worldwide freight charter services.
Hawaiian Airlines Inc.	7 Douglas DC-9 8 Convair 640	400	1·5 million	20·1 million	Operates throughout the Hawaiian Islands.
Los Angeles Airways Inc.	5 Sikorsky S-61L helicopters 4 DHC-6-600 Twin Otter	300	320,000	1·1 million	Operates scheduled and express services within California.
North Central Airlines Inc.	15 Douglas DC-9-30 34 Convair 580	7,500	3·1 million	7·4 million	Operates services in the Mid-West and central states of the U.S.A., and to Canada.
Ozark Air Lines Inc.	21 Fairchild FH-227 6 Douglas DC-9-10 6 Douglas DC-9-30	6,100	2·3 million	52 million	Operates services throughout the twelve mid-west and western states of the U.S.A.
Pacific Southwest Airlines Inc.	8 Boeing 727-14 19 Boeing 727-214 11 Boeing 737-214 2 Douglas DC-9-30 2 Lockheed TriStar	–	4·2 million	–	Operates high-density services through the western states of the U.S.A.
Piedmont Airlines	12 Boeing 737-201 21 NAMC YS-11A-200 10 Fairchild FH-227 18 Martin 404	6,300	2·2 million	59 million	Operates high-density services throughout the eastern states of the U.S.A.

Airline	Fleet (Notified July–December 1972, as being current March 1973)	Route Mileage	Passengers Carried	Revenue Ton Miles (Average 1969–72)	Operations
Saturn Airways Inc.	2 Douglas DC-8-61F 2 Douglas DC-8-50 10 Douglas DC-6A	–	92,000	136 million	Worldwide air charter and freight services.
Seaboard World Airlines Inc.	1 Boeing 707CF 4 Douglas DC-8-55CF 12 Douglas DC-8-63CF	10,000	149,000	420 million	Operates charter and freight services between the U.S.A. and Europe.
Southern Airways Inc.	20 Martin 404 10 Douglas DC-9	6,500	1·3 million	32 million	Operates scheduled services in the eastern states.
Trans Caribbean Airways Inc.	6 Douglas DC-8F and -61 5 Boeing 727-100 and -200 2 Boeing 747	16,000	800,000	· 184 · million	Operates services between New York, Washington, D.C., and the Caribbean.
Trans International Airlines Inc.	7 Douglas DC-8 (various) 5 Douglas DC-8-63CF/C 2 Boeing 727-171C 3 Douglas DC-10	–	–	–	Operates services throughout the U.S.A.
Universal Airlines Inc.	3 Douglas DC-8-61F 4 Douglas DC-9-33F 40 Other aircraft	–	–	–	Charter, contract and freight services operated throughout the U.S.A.
World Airways Inc.	8 Boeing 707 6 Boeing 727 6 Boeing 747C 4 Other aircraft	–	600,000	94 million	Operates worldwide services.

To illustrate the ascendancy gained by the American commercial aircraft manufacturing industry, the following is a list of the principal airliners delivered by, or on order at February 1973:

Boeing 707 (all versions)	876 (production running down)
Boeing 727 (all versions)	1,035
Boeing 737 (all versions)	341
Boeing 747 (all versions)	224
Douglas DC-8 (all versions)	556 (production complete)
Douglas DC-9 (all versions)	736
Douglas DC-10 (all versions)	203
Lockheed TriStar (all versions)	122 + 46 sales options

There are more than 200 state, municipal and international airports in the U.S.A., of which the following are the busiest (1969–72 average passengers handled in brackets): Atlanta, Georgia (14·5 million); John F. Kennedy Airport, New York (20·5 million); O'Hare International Airport, Chicago, Illinois (figures incomplete, but believed to be over 20 million); Los Angeles, California (figures incomplete, but believed to exceed 30 million); Newark, New Jersey (7·3 million); San Francisco Airport, California (14·8 million).

VENEZUELA

The two main airlines of Venezuela are both based at Caracas. *Aerovias Venezolanas SA (AVENSA)*, with a Sud Caravelle, a Douglas DC-9-30, five Convair 580s and half a dozen older aircraft, operates domestic and limited international services, while *Linea Aeropostal Venezolana (LAV)* flies domestic routes and services to Curacao, Trinidad and Guyana with six Hawker Siddeley 748 Series 2As, a Douglas DC-9-10 and a fleet of about a dozen DC-3s.

3. THE MIDDLE EAST

BAHRAIN

Operating a scheduled service between the Trucial States and Muscat-Oman, Gulf Aviation Company Ltd. flies two BAC One-Eleven-432s, two Fokker F.27 Friendships, a Hawker Siddeley Trident and four Douglas DC-3s, carrying about 200,000 passengers annually.

CYPRUS

Cyprus Airways Ltd. flies routes totalling 2,500 miles between Nicosia and Athens, Rhodes, Tel Aviv, Cairo, Istanbul and Ankara, flying about 70,000 passengers in a fleet which includes five Hawker Siddeley Trident 1Es and two BAC Viscount 806s.

IRAN

The national carrier is Iran National Airlines Corporation (Iran Air), which flies two Boeing 707-386s and four Boeing 727-86s as well as about a dozen older

The classic Douglas DC-3 had already been recognised as an advanced and efficient transport before the Second World War. Heavy production during the War ensured a prolific supply to hundreds of commercial carriers in the past thirty years and is still widely used the world over

Douglas piston-engined aircraft. It operates services through the Middle East to London, Paris, Frankfurt, Geneva and Moscow, and to India.

IRAQ

Flying three Hawker Siddeley Trident 1Es and three BAC Viscount 735s over 10,000 route miles throughout the Middle East and Europe, Iraqi Airways Ltd. is based at Basrah, the country's principal international airport.

ISRAEL

Largest and certainly the most prestigious airline in the Middle East is El Al Israel Airlines which, in the face of constant political opposition and even physical hazard from other countries, has pursued an operating policy to link the Middle East with Europe, North and South America. After disposing of its first generation equipment (comprising Bristol Britannia turboprop airliners), El Al has acquired a fleet of eight Boeing 707-320s, two Boeing 707-720Bs and three Boeing 747-258Bs. Its routes extend to 28,480 miles, and it carries well over half a million passengers yearly and returns over 160 million revenue ton miles.

The principal international airport is Lod Airport at Tel Aviv, whose four runways handle 14,000 aircraft movements annually. Over a million passengers pass through this airport each year.

JORDAN

Jordan's national airline is Alia, Royal Jordanian Airlines, which with two Boeing 707-320Cs. three Sud Caravelle 10Rs and a Fokker F.27 Friendship, flies

services throughout the Middle East, to Athens, Paris, Rome, London and Benghazi.

KUWAIT

Third behind Israel's El Al and Lebanon's Middle East Airlines, Kuwait Airways Corporation operates over 20,000 route miles throughout the Middle East to Europe and to Karachi and Bombay. It carries a quarter of a million passengers annually.

The Kuwait International Airport handles 14,000 aircraft movements and half a million passengers each year.

LEBANON

Although it does not operate as far as America, as does El Al Israel Airlines, Middle East Airlines (Airliban) flies routes totalling over 40,000 miles in the Middle East, East and West Africa, Western Europe and India and Pakistan, carrying half a million passengers in a fleet which includes three Boeing 707-320Cs, and a number of jet airliners leased from European companies.

At the time of writing, Middle East Airlines was also keeping open purchase options on two BAC-*Aérospatiale* Concorde supersonic airliners.

UNITED ARAB REPUBLIC

As political front-runner of the U.A.R., Egypt is the parent nation of the United Arab Airlines, which operates extensive routes throughout Europe, Asia, Africa and the Far East, totalling more than 40,000 miles, and carries about 400,000 passengers annually. Its fleet comprises three Boeing 707-320Cs, seven Antonov An-24Bs and two Ilyushin Il-18s. It is believed that there may also be about four Hawker Siddeley Comet 4Cs in service.

Egypt's principal commercial airport is Cairo International Airport.

4. ASIA AND AUSTRALASIA

AFGHANISTAN

The main airline is Ariana Afghan Airlines which operates limited international services between Afghanistan and Europe, through the Middle East, with a Boeing 727C and two Douglas DC-6s. The routes cover 21,000 miles and about 40,000 passengers are carried each year.

AUSTRALIA

As would be expected, with large distances to be covered between towns and cities, commercial aviation has long been established in Australia, and in 1945 all transport companies were nationalised.

The largest intercontinental airline is Qantas Airways Ltd., with a worldwide route mileage of over 150,000 to the United Kingdom, North Africa and South Africa, as well as Hong Kong and islands in the South Pacific. Its fleet includes 21 Boeing 707-338Cs and five Boeing 747-238Bs, as well as a small number of older piston-engined transports. At the time of writing Qantas retained purchase options on four BAC-Aérospatiale Concorde supersonic airliners.

Operating domestic services within Australia and to New Guinea is Ansett Airlines of Australia. Although its routes extend to only 20,000 miles, Ansett carries an annual total of well over two million passengers – four times the number carried by Qantas. Its fleet of more than fifty aircraft includes 16 Douglas DC-9s, 12 Fokker F.27 Friendships, six Boeing 727s, six BAC Viscounts and four Fokker F.28 Fellowships.

Of roughly the same size as Ansett, but with a route mileage of more than 50,000, Trans-Australia Airlines (Air Australia) flies five Boeing 727s, six Douglas DC-9s, 14 Fokker F.27 Friendships, three BAC Viscount 800s and eight DHC-6 Twin Otters. It carries an annual total of 2·4 million passengers.

Major commercial airports in Australia (with passengers handled annually shown in brackets) are Adelaide (870,000), Brisbane (990,000), Canberra (380,000), Darwin (76,000), Essenden (2·1 million), Hobart (200,000), Launceston (180,000), Perth (380,000), and Sydney Kingsford Smith Airport (3·4 million).

BURMA

Undergoing modernisation is Union of Burma Airways (UBA), a small airline based on Rangoon which operates domestic routes between 31 airports and strips with half a dozen Douglas DC-3s. Its international routes extend to Phnom-Penh in Cambodia, Calcutta and Chittagong, using seven Fokker F.27 Friendships and three BAC Viscount 761s. These aircraft carry more than 300,000 passengers annually.

CAMBODIA

Royal Air Cambodge operates limited international services through South-East Asia with a Sud Caravelle, two Douglas DC-6s and a DC-3, carrying about 70,000 passengers each year.

CEYLON

Ceylon's airline, Air Ceylon Ltd., operates a weekly service to the United Kingdom through the Middle East and Europe with a Hawker Siddeley Trident 1E, and more frequent services to India and Singapore with two Douglas DC-3s and a Hawker Siddeley 748. Domestic routes are flown by an *Aérospatiale Frégate*.

CHINA

At present undergoing reorientation as regards equipment, the Civil Aviation Administration of China (CAAC) operates a very large domestic network (of about 19,000 miles), as well as routes to Burma, Vietnam, Korea and the U.S.S.R. Hitherto its passenger fleet has been of principally Russian origin with about 50 Ilyushin Il-14s, 11 Ilyushin Il-12s and nine Ilyushin Il-18s. About ten years ago six BAC Viscount 843s were purchased in Britain, and more recently six Hawker Siddeley Trident 2Es and two NAMC YS-11A-200s have joined the fleet.

In addition to its scheduled passenger work, CAAC also conducts extensive forestry, agricultural and freight services with a fleet of nearly 300 Antonov An-2s and about a dozen Alouette helicopters.

It is generally considered that unless trade relations between China and the U.S.S.R. improve markedly in the near future, many of the Russian aeroplanes will have to be replaced by British, Japanese and American equipment, and it is significant that much interest has been shown recently in increasing the purchase of Hawker Siddeley Tridents. CAAC has also sought purchase options on three BAC-Aérospatiale Concorde supersonic airliners.

FIJI

With a small fleet of three Hawker Siddeley 748 Series 2As and four Hawker Siddeley Herons, Fiji Airways Ltd. operates a 6,000-mile scheduled network service between the Fiji Islands, the New Hebrides, British Solomons, Port Moresby, Tonga and the Gilbert islands. About 100,000 passengers travel on these services annually.

GUAM

Flying scheduled inter-island services, Air Micronesia Inc., based at Saipan, operates several leased aircraft in addition to a Boeing 727-24C and two Douglas DC-6As.

HONG KONG

Hong Kong's Cathay Pacific Airways Ltd. provides an extensive network service amounting to nearly

22,000 miles, extending as far as India, Singapore, Bangkok, Okinawa and Tokyo. Its seven Convair 880-22Ms carry about half a million passengers each year.

INDIA

With commercial aviation originating firmly in the British *Raj* of the nineteen-twenties and early 'thirties, India today is served by one sizeable intercontinental airline and an international and domestic carrier – as well as half a dozen smaller charter and freight operators.

Air India operates intercontinental routes totalling nearly 40,000 miles between Bombay, New York, Moscow, London, Tokyo, Singapore, Jakarta, Sydney, Perth, Mauritius, Kuwait, Nairobi and Entebbe. Its fleet comprises five Boeing 707-437s, three Boeing 707-337s, two Boeing 707-337Cs and four Boeing 747-237Bs. It also holds purchase options on two BAC-*Aérospatiale* Concordes.

Operating a somewhat smaller route mileage (of about 22,000 miles) throughout India, Nepal, Burma, Ceylon and Afghanistan, Indian Airlines Corporation has a sizeable fleet of some fifteen Fokker F.27 Friendships, 24 Hindustan-built Hawker Siddeley 748s, twelve BAC Viscounts, six Sud Caravelles, seven Boeing 737-2A8s, and about half a dozen Douglas DC-3s. These airliners carry over three million passengers each year.

INDONESIA

Operating intercontinental services which extend throughout the Far East, through the Middle East to Europe (Rome and Amsterdam), Garuda Indonesian Airways is based at Jakarta with an airliner fleet which includes twelve Fokker F.27-600 Friendships, six Fokker F.28 Fellowships, two Douglas DC-9-30s, three DC-8-54s, two Lockheed Electras, about half a dozen DC-3s and some obsolescent types such as Convair 340s and 440s.

Domestic services are provided by *PN Merpati Nusantari* with three Pilatus Porters, three Dornier Do 28s, two Scottish Aviation Twin Pioneers and two DHC-2 Beavers.

JAPAN

Japan's commercial air transport industry is largely a product of the last twenty-five years owing to the prohibition of civil aviation activities which was enforced under the surrender terms at the end of the Second World War.

The national intercontinental carrier is *Nihon Koku Kabushiki Kaisha* (Japan Air Lines) which operates an extensive world network, as well as domestic services. Latest information available indicates a fleet of about 90 aircraft including 35 Douglas DC-8s (of which about half are the long-range -60 series), 18 Boeing 727s, six

Convair 880Ms, nine Boeing 747-246Bs and seven Boeing 747-146s. At the time of writing, the airline also holds options on three BAC-*Aérospatiale* Concordes, and is regarded as a key potential operator whose options, if confirmed, would be highly influential among other intercontinental carriers in South-East Asia and the Pacific area.

All Nippon Airways Co. Ltd. is the principal domestic operator, giving high density route services among 34 cities with a fleet comprising sixteen Boeing 737-281s, nine NAMC YS-11-110s and twenty-three -200s, eight Boeing 727-81s, 24 Fokker F.27 Friendships and about five BAC Viscount 828s. There are also about a dozen helicopters and ten older types in service.

Toa Airways Co. Ltd., based at Hiroshima, operates an inter-island network with eighteen NAMC YS-11-100s, ten YS-11A-200s, and two YS-11A-300s as well as a dozen piston-engined aircraft.

Operating an 8,000-mile internal network and carrying about three-quarters of a million passengers annually, Japan Domestic Airlines Co. Ltd. flies three Boeing 727s and fifteen NAMC YS-11s of various types.

The Tokyo International Airport handles about 70,000 aircraft movements and 7·5 million passengers annually.

KOREA

Fast growing commercial air transport in the Far East is reflected in the fleet size of Korean Air Lines, a carrier which operates services between Seoul and Saigon, Tokyo and Hong Kong with a Boeing 747F, a Boeing 707-365C, four NAMC YS-11-100s, four YS-11A 300s, a Douglas DC-9-30 and five Fokker/Fairchild Friendships.

MONGOLIA

Wholly integrated with Soviet air transport services in Eastern Siberia, Mongolia nevertheless operates a domestic carrier, Mongolian Airlines (*Mongolflot*) with a small fleet of Ilyushin Il-14s. Services to Peking and Irkutsk are flown by about four Antonov An-24s. Like *Aeroflot*, *Mongolflot* undertakes other civil operations, such as forestry and agricultural work, using Antonov An-2s.

NEPAL

Reflecting conflict of different political influences in the country, Royal Nepal Airlines flies services to Dacca, Calcutta and New Delhi with a small number of Russian aircraft as well as two Hawker Siddeley 748s, half a dozen Douglas DC-3s and a Fokker F.27-200 Friendship.

NEW GUINEA

Carrying over 100,000 passengers annually, Ansett Airlines of Papua New Guinea operates an internal service with two Fokker F.27 Friendships, four Piaggio P-166s and about six Douglas DC-3s.

NEW ZEALAND

There are about eight carriers in New Zealand, of which Air New Zealand and New Zealand National Airways Corporation are the largest.

Air New Zealand, based at Auckland, operates four Douglas DC-8-52s, two Lockheed Electras and three Douglas DC-10-30s (as yet still on order) to Australia and throughout the South Pacific to Los Angeles, California (via Honolulu and Tahiti). Its route mileage is almost 50,000 and it carries nearly 300,000 passengers annually.

New Zealand National Airways, based at Wellington, operates high-frequency domestic services with a dozen Fokker F.27-100 Friendships, four Boeing 737-219s and four BAC Viscount 807s, over a route mileage of 3,500.

PAKISTAN

Although to some extent altered as a result of the recent conflict with India and by the establishment of Bangladesh, Pakistan International Airlines with a fleet which, in mid-1972, included 14 Fokker F.27 Friendships, four Boeing 707-340Cs, three Boeing 707-720Bs and four Hawker Siddeley Trident 1Es, still operates an intercontinental air service. At that time the airline had almost 50,000 miles of routes throughout the Far East, Middle East, Africa and extending to Europe, and was carrying about 1·3 million passengers annually.

PHILIPPINES

Three carriers operate in the Philippines, of which Philippine Air Lines are the largest. With a fleet of three Douglas DC-8-53s, two long-range DC-8-63s, twelve Hawker Siddeley 748s, twelve Fokker F.27-100 Friendships, four BAC One-Eleven-402 and three One-Eleven-527s, this airline flies domestic services as well as routes to Australia, Japan and the U.S.A.

Air Manila Inc. operates six Fairchild Friendships and two Handley Page Dart Heralds on domestic services carrying about 200,000 passengers annually. Also on domestic routes is the airline, Filipinas Orient Airways Inc. with four NAMC YS-11-100s, three Aérospatiale Frégates, a Douglas DC-6 and six DC-3s.

SINGAPORE

A sizeable operator is Malaysia-Singapore Airlines Ltd., which serves routes over 28,000 miles from Singapore to Australia, Indonesia, Thailand, the Philippines, Hong Kong and Japan. Its fleet includes three Boeing 707s, five Boeing 737-112s, two Boeing 747s, four Hawker Siddeley Comet 4s, eight Fokker F.27 Friendships and three Britten-Norman Islanders. It carries just over one million passengers each year.

TAIWAN

Largest of the Formosa-based carriers is China Airlines Ltd., which flies routes to Japan, Korea, Malaysia, Saigon, Hong Kong, Bangkok and Okinawa, carrying over 200,000 passengers annually in two Boeing 707-320s, two Boeing 727s, six Douglas DC-4s and about half a dozen older aircraft.

Operator of fairly widespread charter services is Air Asia Co. Ltd., with two Boeing 727-92Cs, a Douglas DC-6B and a dozen ex-military transport types.

VIETNAM

Obviously reflecting the American military presence in the country, Air Vietnam grew to sizeable proportions during the late nineteen-sixties, and in 1972 was operating throughout the Far East with two Boeing 727-21QCs, three Douglas DC-6Bs, one DC-6, nine DC-4s, sixteen DC-3s and six Curtis C-46s. It was operating routes of over 21,000 miles and carrying 1·5 million passengers annually.

5. AFRICA

ALGERIA

The sole international carrier is Air Algerie which serves a network throughout North Africa, the Middle East and parts of Europe with five Sud Caravelles, three Convair 640s, two Boeing 727-200s, a Boeing 737-2D6 and a small number of Douglas DC-3s. It carries about half a million passengers annually.

ANGOLA

Flying four Fokker F.27 Friendships and about three Douglas DC-3s on routes totalling nearly 7,000 miles in South-West Africa, the state operator Direccao de Exploracao dos Transportes Aereos carries about 150,000 passengers annually.

BOTSWANA

Botswana National Airways operates a BAC Viscount 700-series and some piston-engined Douglas aircraft over 1,430 miles on scheduled services to Johannesburg, Livingstone and Lusaka, in addition to limited charter work.

CONGO

The main national carrier is Air Congo which carries almost 250,000 passengers annually in a fleet comprising two Douglas DC-8-33s, eight Fokker Friendships, two Sud Caravelles, six Douglas DC-4s and about four DC-3s. Its services link the Congo with Zambia, Tanzania, Kenya, Uganda, Nigeria, Belgium, Italy and France.

ETHIOPIA

With international routes centred on Haile Selassie International Airport, Addis Ababa, extending for 27,000 miles throughout Africa, the Middle East, Europe, India and Pakistan, Ethiopian Airlines operates a fleet which includes two Boeing 707-320s, two Boeing 707-720Bs, three Douglas DC-6Bs and six DC-3s.

GHANA

Ghana Airways operates a single BAC VC-10 on services to London *via* Rome and Zurich, and two BAC Viscounts and two Hawker Siddeley 748 Series 2As on regional domestic routes.

IVORY COAST

Carrying over 300,000 passengers each year, the airline *Air Afrique* operates services to France, Italy, Switzerland and New York, U.S.A., with a fleet comprising five Douglas DC-8-63s, two Sud Caravelles and three Douglas DC-4s. It also has ordered three Douglas DC-10-30s.

KENYA

The intercontinental airline, East African Airways Corporation, is based principally at Nairobi with a route mileage which extends over nearly 40,000 miles throughout East Africa, the Middle East to Europe, India and Pakistan. It operates three BAC VC-10s, two Super VC-10s, three Hawker Siddeley Comet 4s, four Fokker F.27-200 Friendships, four Douglas DC-3s and four DHC-6 Twin Otters.

MADAGASCAR

Although Air Madagascar (*Société Nationale Malgache de Transports Aériens*) operates domestic services with a variety of light American aircraft, it also flies routes to neighbouring islands, to Johannesburg and to Paris *via* Djibouti and Marseilles using a Boeing 707-328B, a Boeing 737-200, four Douglas DC-4s and three Douglas DC-3s.

MALAWI

Carrying almost 40,000 passengers annually, Air Malawi Ltd. is currently modernising its equipment with a Hawker Siddeley 748 Series 2 and a BAC One-Eleven-475. It still operates four BAC Viscounts and three Douglas DC-3s on routes throughout Central and Southern Africa.

MALI

Evidence of recent Soviet influence in the country is provided by the equipment of Air Mali (*Société Nationale Air Mali*) which flies routes, totalling nearly 15,000 miles, to France and in North Africa, with two Ilyushin Il-18s, an Il-14 and two Antonov An-24s.

MOROCCO

Royal Air Maroc (*Compagnie Nationale de Transports Aériens*) operates routes totalling over 15,000 miles along the North African coast and through Spain to Western Europe with five Sud Caravelle 3s and a Boeing 727-200.

NIGERIA

Largest of Nigeria's carriers is Nigeria Airways (WAAC (Nigeria) Ltd.), based at Lagos, operating domestic and regional services and a service to Frankfurt, London, Madrid and Rome over routes totalling nearly 7,000 miles with seven Fokker F.27 Friendships and five Douglas DC-3s.

RHODESIA

Operating air services with neighbouring African states over 6,000 route miles, Air Rhodesia Corporation carries over quarter of a million passengers annually in four BAC Viscount 700s and three Douglas DC-3s. Modernisation is obviously much overdue but has clearly been delayed by sanctions exercised against Rhodesia since 1966.

SOUTH AFRICA

South Africa operates a number of carriers ranging from South Africa Airways, a substantial intercontinental airline, to half a dozen charter and air taxi companies.

South African Airways is based at Johannesburg and, with a route mileage of over 55,000 covering services throughout Africa, to Europe, Australia, and North and South America, carries nearly 1½ million passengers annually in nine Boeing 707s, seven Boeing 727s, six Boeing 737-244s, five Boeing 747-244Bs, seven BAC Viscount 813s, two Hawker Siddeley 748s and some Douglas DC-3s.

Trek Airways Pty. Ltd., also centred at Johannesburg, flies a Boeing 707 and two Lockheed L-1649A Starliners to Europe and the Far East. Regional scheduled and charter services are provided by Africair Ltd. (with Douglas DC-3s and DC-4s), by Comair (with Douglas DC-3s), and Swazi Air Ltd. (with Douglas DC-3s and a number of American twin engined light aircraft).

SUDAN

Limited international services and a domestic network is undertaken by Sudan Airways, based at Khartoum, with a fleet which includes two Hawker Siddeley Comet 4Cs, four Fokker F.27 Friendships, three DHC-6 Twin Otters and two Douglas DC-3s.

TUNISIA

Tunisia's growing tourist industry is served by the airline Tunis Air (*Société Tunisienne de l'Air*) which flies international services to Europe and throughout the Mediterranean area with four Sud Caravelles, an *Aérospatiale Frégate*, a Boeing 727-200 and a small number of Douglas DC-3s and DC-4s.

～ CHAPTER 4 ～
The Classic Aircraft

The Boeing F4B-4 shipboard fighter of the U.S. Navy

The story of aviation is a continuing narrative of mankind's personal courage, skill and determination to master an element into which he first launched himself just seventy years ago, in a machine which would thereafter – he hoped – continue to support him in that element. This chapter describes briefly the progress of that machine during those seventy years. At the same time, it goes without saying that man's whole outlook has changed towards his flying vehicle, from the plaything of an adventurous few to the harbinger of mass destruction or the world-ranging airliner of the peaceful traveller. But the skill of the designer has never outstripped the skill of the pilot.

The Wright *Flyer* remained the only practical flying machine for almost four years, to some extent protected from legitimate development (or even plagiarism) by others through strict patenting. Its success in achieving flight did much to blind other would-be designers of the potentialities of the monoplane, and aircraft design became firmly established on the path of biplane configuration for almost thirty years before the monoplane was universally accepted as the most efficient. This is perhaps all the more strange when one realises that two outstanding European designs of the late 1900s were monoplanes.

First of these was the French *Antoinette*, produced by Levavasseur towards the end of 1908 – encouraged but scarcely influenced by the Wright biplane which was demonstrated by Wilbur Wright for the first time in France in August that year. Both the first successful *Antoinette* monoplanes used flap-type ailerons for lateral control, but shortly afterwards they reverted to wing-warping – a practice widely used at that time.

The other great monoplane line was the series designed by Louis Blériot, commencing late in 1908. His *Type VIII* was an extraordinarily prophetic design, featuring front-mounted tractor engine, enclosed fore-fuselage, twin mainwheel and tailwheel undercarriage, ailerons, elevator and rudder control surfaces. Blériot himself achieved an 8½-mile cross-country flight in this before the end of 1908. Although Blériot reverted (unsuccessfully) to a biplane in his *Type X*, his classic *Type XI* gained everlasting fame for its flight (with *le Patron* at the controls) across the English Channel on 25th July 1909. Production aircraft were powered by 25-h.p. Anzani, 30-h.p. Darracq, 45-h.p. J.A.P. and 50-h.p. Gnome engines and remained in production until 1914. Many pioneering flights in distant parts of the world were made in Blériot *Type XIs*.

Despite this apparent excursion into monoplane design, the mainstream development lay along the biplane's path. Certainly in America the Wrights dominated the scene, and were joined by Glenn Curtiss in 1908 who produced four aeroplanes in that year, including the famous *June Bug*. Just how dominating a position was that held by the Wrights may be judged from the fact that after U.S. Army trials of the Wright biplane at Fort Myer in September 1908 the first military aircraft specification was issued based on those trials. Drawn up by Lieutenant George C. Sweet of the U.S. Navy Department, this specification called for a two-seater capable of flying 200 miles, and capable of alighting on land or water. Within two months of the issue of that specification, the Wright biplane had achieved a flight of 77 miles and had carried a passenger in addition to the pilot on other flights.

Notwithstanding the success of the Wrights, parallel work was during 1909-11 being done by countless other constructors. The Short brothers had formed their own company in England to develop the Wright, Henry and Maurice Farman had commenced design and construction of their famous biplanes, as had the Voisin brothers, John A. Douglas McCurdy had built and flown his *Silver Dart* in Canada, and at Rheims on 29th August 1909 thirty-eight aeroplanes congregated at the first international flying meeting.

Some of the early enthusiasts tried to exploit the infant aviation for commercial ends; the first mail was carried by air by a Blériot monoplane in Britain on 9th September 1911, and in the U.S.A. a fortnight later (also by a Blériot). A token freight flight was made in Britain in July that year by a *Valkyrie* monoplane.

It was to be the military authorities throughout the world that were to sponsor – or at any rate encourage – the greatest acceleration in aircraft design. Apart from the U.S. Army trials in 1908, many nations realised the use to which the aeroplane could or would be put in times of war, and not only did their governments send selected pilots to Europe for training, but also conducted trials to decide on possible aircraft equipment for their armies and navies. It fell to Britain, which had assumed a leading position with France in aviation matters, to conduct the world's first competitive military aircraft trials, on Salisbury Plain during August 1912. These trials attracted numerous British and foreign biplanes and monoplanes, and a number of significant performances were returned. Alas for the ineptitude of human judgement the trial was won by the least realistic design of all – Cody's irrelevant *Cathedral*. Whereas this clumsy old biplane was clearly at the end of its development, aircraft like the *Avro* cabin biplane, the *Hanriot* monoplane and Geoffrey de Havilland's brilliant *B.E.2* were almost ignored; yet these were the very designs which realistically foreshadowed the trends in aviation.

Thus were the first faltering steps taken in the realm of military aviation in Britain. Progress, if such it could be termed, was being matched in France and Germany. 1912 had also seen the formation of the Royal Flying Corps in five separate sections: the Central Flying School, the Military Wing, the Naval Wing, the Royal Aircraft Factory at Farnborough, and the Reserve. It was two accidents suffered by aircraft being flown by R.F.C. pilots in 1912 that were to influence military aircraft design in Britain in a manner quite out of proportion to their real significance. On 5th July a *Nieuport* monoplane, flown by Capt. E. B. Loraine of the R.F.C., crashed killing the pilot and his passenger; and on 10th September a *Bristol* monoplane crashed near Oxford, also killing the two occupants. Without any enquiry of substance the Secretary of State for War issued an order banning the use of monoplanes by the Military. Such were the rewards offered by the War Office to the manufacturers of military aircraft that this order virtually killed the development of monoplanes for twenty years thereafter.

AEROPLANES FOR WAR

So much has been written about the events of the First World War that an interesting prelude to that terrible conflict has been almost completely overshadowed, for by the time the R.F.C. was formed in April 1912, air warfare as such was already more than six months old.

Army manoeuvres, in which aircraft participated, had taken place in Italy in August 1911, and when war between Italian and Turkish forces broke out the following month in Libya an Air Flotilla was sent to Tripoli – consisting of nine aircraft, five "combat" pilots, six reserve pilots and 29 mechanics. The aircraft were two *Blériot XIs*, two *Farman Longhorns*, three *Nieuport* monoplanes and two *Etrich Taubes*. First war flight ever undertaken was that by the Flotilla Commander, Captain Carlos Piazza – a reconnaissance flight in a *Blériot XI* on 23rd October. After reconnaissance there followed artillery spotting, and the first combat damage to an aeroplane was suffered by the *Nieuport* flown by Captain Riccardo Moizo when it was hit in the wings by rifle fire from the ground on 25th October. The first bombs (2-kg Cipelli grenades) were dropped by 2nd Lieutenant Giulio Gavotti on 1st November, and in February the following year Piazza's *Blériot XI* was equipped with a camera for aerial photography. Other aerial duties performed during this prophetic campaign included leaflet-dropping, and night bombing and reconnaissance.

Thus had French and Austrian aeroplanes received their baptism of fire. None of the aircraft had been designed for war duties in mind, and all were improvisations of current sporting types. That wartime application of the aeroplane was by 1914 being seriously considered however may be seen in the fact that by the outbreak of the First World War numerous military personnel had been trained as pilots.

Yet when the Great War erupted there were still scarcely any aeroplanes which could really be considered to have been designed with combat requirements in mind. No aeroplane included any gun armament, and certainly nothing that could be considered as protection for the occupant. Air-to-air combat had not been seriously considered, and the first military flights on the Western Front were almost entirely devoted to tactical reconnaissance; the greatest hazards, apart from those resulting from bad weather and recalcitrant engines, were expected to be from small-arms fire from the ground.

The first true fighting aircraft flown by the R.F.C. was the *Vickers Fighting Biplane No. 5*, better known as the *"Gun Bus"*. Powered by a 100-h.p. Gnôme Monosoupape which bestowed a top speed of 70 m.p.h. (112 kph), this two-seater "pusher" was armed with a single Lewis gun in the front of the nacelle. It was with these aircraft that the first homogeneous fighter squadron of the R.F.C. went to France in July 1915, and it was a member of this Squadron, 2nd Lieutenant G. S. M. Insall, who won the first Victoria Cross for an action involving the destruction of an aeroplane. On 7th November 1915 he forced down a German Aviatik two-seater and completed its destruction by dropping an incendiary bomb on it. Returning over the lines, Insall's *Gun Bus* was hit by ground fire and a forced landing was made just inside the French lines where it was promptly shelled. Fortunately the aircraft was not hit and was repaired during the night; at dawn Insall flew back to his Squadron.

The *Gun Bus* represented the first generation of fighting aeroplanes. Although tractor biplanes had been flying for some years, their whirling propellers prevented the fixed mounting of a forward-firing gun, and the "pusher" layout was the obvious expedient – despite the considerable drag offered by the maze of tail struts and booms. The relatively low speed of the *Gun Bus* made it a lengthy business to engage the more conventional tractor biplanes used by German reconnaissance units – whose aircraft were in any case usually armed with a flexible machine gun firing aft at any pursuer. As shown in Chapter 1, it was the development of the synchronised forward-firing gun armament which revolutionised air warfare – and had not the ridiculous ban on British monoplanes prevented development of the Fokker monoplane configuration, it is quite likely that air combat between monoplane scouts would have been commonplace by 1916.

As it was the pusher biplane soldiered on for many months – despite fast mounting losses among both French and British aircraft. The *D.H.2* and *F.E.2b* survived in front-line service until 1917, and were contemporaneous with the French *Caudron G.III* – which, although widely used as a trainer, was also flown on anti-airship patrols. The Germans, on the other hand, never used "pushers" in service (the *Schutte-Lanz C I* and *Euler C I* were type-tested in 1915 and 1916 respectively but discarded).

The *Aviatik C I* represented the classic German design of the early War months, entering service with the Military Aviation Service in mid-1915. Powered by a 160-h.p. Mercedes D III engine, this reconnaissance two-seater had a top speed of 88 m.p.h. (141 kph). It featured a curious seating arrangement in that the pilot occupied the rear cockpit, while the observer/gunner sat in front with his Parabellum gun clipped to a rail on either side of his cockpit. It was an *Aviatik C I* that featured in Insall's fight of 7th November 1915.

Perhaps one of the greatest recognisable contributions by pre-War biplane design to the classic Wartime designs was that by the little Sopwith Tabloid which had made its debut at Hendon on 29th November 1913. Official tests had shown the aircraft capable of a speed of 92 m.p.h. (148 kph), a performance which had prompted its manufacturers to develop a float-equipped version for participation in the 1914 Schneider Trophy – a contest which it duly won, flown by Howard Pixton, at 86·7

m.p.h. (139 kph). About twenty *Tabloids* were ordered before the War and thirty-six were delivered to the R.F.C. and R.N.A.S. between October 1914 and June 1915. It was a *Tabloid* flown by Flight Lieutenant R. L. G. Marix of Commander Samson's Eastchurch Squadron of the R.N.A.S. based at Antwerp that bombed the airship shed at Düsseldorf on 8th October 1914, destroying the brand-new *Zeppelin Z.IX*. *Tabloids* served both as seaplanes and landplanes, and did not carry a standard fixed armament, although one or two were fitted with a Lewis gun above the top wing.

The *Tabloid* disappeared from service during the summer of 1915, but already the Sopwith company had developed a new floatplane from the Schneider Trophy winner. Dubbed the *Sopwith Schneider*, this small floatplane was powered by a 100-h.p. Gnôme Monosoupape, or 110 h.p. Clerget, and had a top speed of about 90 m.p.h. 136 *Schneiders* were built, and were followed by the *Sopwith Baby*, of which 286 were built, and this classic little floatplane scout continued in service with the R.N.A.S. until the end of the War. Later on, some *Babies* were fitted with a single synchronised Lewis gun, and were frequently used on anti-airship patrols over the North Sea. With their squat fuselages, compact single-bay wings and great manoeuvrability, the *Sopwith Schneider* and *Baby* were certainly indicative of the form the high performance scout would follow from 1915 onwards.

THE CLASSIC GERMAN SCOUTS

This then was the pattern of warplane design in 1915. The British and French striving to adapt the best of their peacetime designs to the requirements of combat; the Germans content to pursue a passively efficient, though orthodox biplane tractor design. The appearance of the *Fokker monoplanes*, though hurriedly introduced into service, changed all that. The *Fokker E I*, which appeared in service in June-July 1915, was powered by an 80-h.p. Oberursel and armed with a single synchronised machine gun. The next operational version was the *E III*, powered by a 100-h.p. Oberursel U I, and this entered service in August that year and, with a top speed of about 85 m.p.h. (141 kph), this was regarded as the standard service version.

For all its tactical superiority, the real attributes of the *Fokker monoplanes* should be judged in their real perspective. Certainly they achieved a definite degree of air superiority during the late summer and autumn of 1915. They represented the vehicle of the first tactical breakthrough in air warfare in that they enabled the fighter pilot to fly along the line of his gunsight, thereby aiming his gun along his line of flight. The first true "fighter pilots" came into being – Leutnant Oswald Boelcke and Fähnrich Max Immelmann. But the monoplanes were still relatively slow and the 100-h.p. Oberursel was unreliable. Yet despite these, as well as troubles with guns and ammunition during the winter of 1915-16,

BLERIOT XI. Although of a slightly later design than that in which Louis Blériot made his famous cross-Channel flight in July 1909, the Blériot XI epitomises the superiority of early French monoplane designs at a time when European designers were concentrating upon adaptations of and developments from the Wright biplane. Used by numerous sporting pilots in the early days of flying, the Blériot XI came to be used in the early months of the First World War. (*Photo: By courtesy of the Shuttleworth Collection*)

CAUDRON G.III. The aircraft shown here (*No. 2531, Sergeant Millot*) is one of about three G.III trainers to have survived from the First World War, and is preserved at *La Musée de l'Air,* Paris. Another example (No. *3066*) has been painted to represent a machine used at the R.N.A.S. Flying School at Vendôme, France, in 1917 and is preserved at the R.A.F. Museum, Hendon. Although possessed of no fixed armament, these aircraft were sometimes flown against Zeppelins – their pilots using rifles, grenades and pistols. (*Photo: By courtesy of La Musée de l'Air*)

the *E IIIs* did considerable execution among Allied aircraft at the time.

But the synchronised machine-gun – which after all was in limited use by the French – was not the be-all and end-all of air fighting in those days, and the appearance of "pusher" scouts with forward-firing guns and a speed equal to or superior to that of the *Fokker* did much to eliminate the "scourge" early in 1916. By the end of the winter there were numerous *D.H.2s* and *F.E.2bs* in service, and the French squadrons were by then equipped with the *Nieuport 11*. All these aircraft – if not more technically advanced than the *Fokker E III* – were capable of holding their own, or at least able to show a clean pair of heels. And it was not long before gun synchronising gear appeared in British aircraft, both Vickers and Scarff-Dibovski designs appearing in 1916.

Before passing on to the next distinct generation of fighting scouts, mention should be made here of the strangely-named *Sopwith 1¼-Strutter*, which served in huge numbers both as single-seat bombers and two-seat "fighters". With a top speed at sea level of 106 m.p.h. (170 kph), the fighter version was armed with a forward-firing synchronised Vickers gun and a rear-mounted Lewis gun, while the bomber could carry four 56-lb. (24 kg) bombs. Over 1,500 were built in Britain for the R.F.C. and R.N.A.S., and reports suggest that as many as 4,500 were built in France. They were used all over the world right up to the end of the War.

The loss of air superiority by the Germans to the *D.H.2s* and *Nieuports* in the spring of 1916 prompted the introduction of a new generation of fighting scouts in a successful bid to restore the situation. Among the first of these was the *Albatros D I* biplane which began to reach the *Jagdstaffeln* in the autumn of the year. Powered by a 150- or 160- h.p. Mercedes D III engine, it was the most powerful German scout yet introduced and had a top speed of 109 m.p.h. (175 kph). It also featured what was then considered to be a devastating forward-firing armament of twin synchronised Spandau machine guns. Followed almost immediately by the *Albatros D II*, the new scouts became operational in September when a patrol was made on the 17th by *Jasta 2* led by Oswald Boelcke. On the same day Manfred von Richthofen, also flying a *D II* of *Jasta 2* scored his first victory. On 23rd November this great German pilot scored his eleventh victory in his *D II* when he shot down Major Lanoe G. Hawker, V.C.

The ascendancy gained by the *D Is* and *IIs* was not seriously threatened during the winter of 1916–17, and was further confirmed with the appearance of the *Albatros D III* in the spring, which, although slightly slower than the *D II* was somewhat more manoeuvrable, and it was in a scarlet *D III* that von Richthofen quickly added to his score. "Bloody April", so long remembered by the R.F.C. as a terrible month for casualties, was the heyday of the German *Albatros* scouts, the principal victims being the poorly armed B.E.2c reconnaissance machines.

Reaction to "Bloody April" was swift, and it was the introduction of the *S.E.5* and *SPADs* that in turn brought about the introduction of the *Albatros D V* and *D Va*, and *Fokker Dr. I*. Again, there was little improvement in the speed performance of the *Albatros*, the main aerodynamic and structural improvements being adopted to increase manoeuvrability.The little *Fokker Dr. I* triplane was however a new design departure – although of course triplanes were almost as old as flying itself. The success of the *Sopwith Triplane* (of which more anon) during the spring of 1917 had prompted the manufacturers of the Central Powers to consider the benefits of this layout, and the *Dr. I* entered front-line service in August that year. Powered by a 110-h.p. Oberursel UR II which bestowed a top speed of 103 m.p.h. (165 kph), the triplane was extremely agile and its principal exponents were undoubtedly Manfred von Richthofen and Werner Voss. The latter pilot received his *Dr. I* on 28th August 1917 but was shot down and killed by Lieutenant A. Rhys-Davids in an *S.E.5* of No. 56 Squadron on 23rd September – by which date the German pilot had amassed a score of 48 victories.

With the introduction of vastly improved fighting scouts by the Allies during 1917, the German grasp on air superiority over the Western Front was being harshly contested, and it is necessary to return to the summer of 1916 to briefly examine the Allies' mid-War combat equipment. The *Nieuport 17* and *Sopwith Pup* squadrons had done their best to match the *Albatros* scouts, and although representing a marked improvement over previous Allied aircraft and achieving some individual successes, they could do little to change the overall picture.

Perhaps most famous of all the Nieuports, the *Nieuport 17* joined front-line squadrons in May 1916, and in the hands of such pilots as Nungesser and Ball quickly made its presence felt. Normally armed with a single synchronised Vickers gun and a Lewis gun mounted on the top wing, the *Nieuport 17* was powered by a 110-h.p. or 130-h.p. Clerget and had a top speed of 107 m.p.h. (172 kph). It is interesting to record that the Lewis gun mounting – which consisted of a sliding rail which enabled the gun to be pulled back and down to fire upwards at an enemy aircraft overhead – was devised by a Sergeant Foster of No. 11 Squadron, R.F.C.; it was adopted by the *S.E.5* and became the favourite weapon of several leading fighter pilots in later months.

The *Sopwith Pup* was perhaps best remembered among all First World War aeroplanes for its delightful flying characteristics. It is possible that the *Pup* was initiated as an answer to the *Fokker E III* monoplane, yet the latter had virtually disappeared from service by the time the British scout appeared in squadron service in September 1916. Powered by a variety of 80- and 100-h.p. engines and armed with a single synchronised machine gun, it had a top speed of 111·5 m.p.h. (180

AVRO 504K. One of the classic trainers of all time, the Avro 504 (of which about a dozen survive today) first flew in 1913; the "J" variant became the R.F.C.'s standard trainer, and the "K" version, powered by a 100 h.p. Monosoupape, 110 h.p. Le Rhône or 130 h.p. Clerget, was introduced in 1918. A total of 8,340 Avro 504s was built during the War and were widely used at home and abroad. The example shown here was built by Canadian Aeroplanes Ltd., Toronto.
(Photo: By courtesy of the Canadian National Aeronautical Collection, Ottawa)

L.V.G. C VI. Although not as well known as the classic Fokker and Pfalz scouts, the German L.V.G. reconnaissance two-seaters were highly efficient designs, several thousand of the C V version being manufactured from 1917 onwards. Like the C V, the C VI, of which about 1,000 were built in 1918, was powered by a 200 h.p. Benz Bz IV six-cylinder engine, and was also used for mail and other commercial purposes after the Armistice. It had a top speed of 106 m.p.h. (170 kph).
(Photo: By courtesy of Michael Vines, Air Portraits)

kph). *Pups* first joined No. 1 Naval Wing and by the end of 1916 the aircraft of No. 8 (Naval) Squadron had destroyed 20 enemy aircraft. Although never able to more than hold its own against contemporary German scouts (principally owing to its inferior armament installation), R.F.C. *Pups* fought hard in the 1917 Battles of Arras, Messines, Cambrai and Ypres, and continued in action until the end of the year.

THE LAST WARTIME SCOUTS

The last eighteen months of the War were indeed rich in aircraft design, and this climacteric phase on the Western Front was heralded by the appearance of the *S.E.5*, with a patrol flown by No. 56 Squadron on 22nd April 1917 appropriately led by Captain Albert Ball. This pilot scored his first victory in an *S.E.5* on the following day when he shot down an *Albatros* over Cambrai. But Ball did not like the *S.E.5,* preferring the more nimble *Nieuport*. Powered by a 150-h.p. Hispano-Suiza, it was a somewhat ponderous machine though capable of a speed of about 125 m.p.h. (201 kph) at sea level (a speed which was further improved by about 8 m.p.h. (13 kph) by increasing the engine's compression ratio).

On the same day that 56 Squadron flew its first patrol with *S.E.5s*, No. 1 (Naval) Squadron was in action with the *Sopwith Triplane* for the first time, shooting down three two-seaters in an action of 16,000 feet over the Western Front. Rather superior to the *Fokker Dr. I* in performance, the *Triplane* only served with squadrons of the Royal Naval Air Service, but it came to be admired by friend and foe alike. With a 130-h.p. Clerget engine it had a top speed of 117 m.p.h. (188 kph), but most aircraft were armed with but one synchronised Vickers gun. Undoubtedly the finest exponent of the *Triplane's* fighting qualities was Raymond Collishaw, commander of "Black Flight" – "B" Flight of No. 10 (Naval) Squadron – all of whose pilots were Canadians. Between May and July 1917 this Flight destroyed 87 enemy aircraft, and in 27 days during June Collishaw alone shot down sixteen German aircraft, of which all but three were enemy single-seat scouts.

We now turn to what was probably the best-known of all British scouts of the War – the *Sopwith Camel* – the first British scout to mount the classic weapon installation of twin synchronised Vickers guns. The *Camel* was a somewhat tricky aircraft to master, the tendency to drop its nose in a right-hand turn being bestowed by the considerable torque effect of the short-nose-mounted rotary engine; to correct it required coarse use of rudder, and if a turn was tightened when full rudder had been applied the *Camel* would quickly spin out. The finest pilots quickly learned to benefit from these idiosyncrasies in combat and in time it became a much-feared adversary among any but the best German airmen. No fewer than 5,490 *Camels* were built, and it is not therefore surprising that many of the most interesting feats of arms were

achieved in this aircraft. It was a Canadian pilot, Captain A. R. Brown, of No. 209 Squadron who, in a *Camel*, finally shot down Baron Manfred von Richthofen, the greatest ace of the First World War. And it was Captain J. L. Trollope of No. 43 Squadron who, on 24th March 1918, first shot down six enemy aircraft in a single day – a feat repeated less than a month later by Captain H. W. Woollett of the same squadron. With a 110-h.p. Le Rhône, the *Camel* had a sea level maximum speed of 122 m.p.h. (196 kph).

A direct development of and a replacement for the *Camel* was the *Sopwith Snipe*, but this superb scout did not reach squadrons in France until September 1918. It was however the aircraft in which Major W. G. Barker earned his award of the Victoria Cross on 27th October that year for his famous fight in which, though badly wounded in arm and thigh, he destroyed four enemy aircraft and damaged at least two others; despite constant attacks by numerous *Fokker D VIIs*, he managed to return to his side of the lines where he survived a crash landing.

While British equipment centred on the *Pup*, *S.E.5* (and the later *S.E.5a*), *Sopwith Triplane, Camel* and *Snipe,* the French aircraft industry was building two classic scouts, the *Nieuport N.28* and *SPAD XIII*. The *Nieuport N.28C-1*, powered by a 165-h.p. Gnôme 9-N rotary engine, gained immortal fame as equipment of the First Pursuit Group of the American Expeditionary Force in 1918, joining the 27th, 94th, 95th and 147th Aero Squadrons in France during the spring and summer of that year. The brilliant *SPAD XIII* was a magnificent fighter, and certainly matched the *Snipe* although it entered service some four months earlier than the British aircraft. It was powered by a 235-h.p. Hispano-Suiza 8BEc and possessed the astonishing top speed of 138 m.p.h. (221 kph) at sea level, armed with two synchronised Vickers guns. It replaced almost all previous scouts with French squadrons, and equipped at least seven squadrons of the American Expeditionary Force, as well as No. 19 Squadron of the R.F.C. (for a short time). Almost every French ace who survived to fight in the bitterest warfare of 1918 flew the *SPAD XIII*, their ranks including such names as Guynemer, Fonck, Nungesser, Madon, Boyeau, Coiffard, Pinsard and Deullin. Ace pilots of the American squadrons included Rickenbacker, Lufbery and Luke.

The greatest of all German scouts facing this galaxy of Allied stars was unquestionably the *Fokker D VII*, another product of the brilliant designer Reinhold Platz. The success of this aircraft lay in its extreme simplicity to fly. It was very manoeuvrable, twin-gun-armed and capable of a speed of about 115 m.p.h. (184 kph). By the autumn of 1918, as German pressure against the Western Front reached its peak before the final collapse, no fewer than 41 *Jastas* had been fully equipped with this aircraft. Perhaps no better tribute can be paid to it than to remark that in drawing up the terms of Armistice the Allied

THE SOPWITH BABY. Believed to be unique is this Sopwith Baby floatplane, developed from the Sopwith Tabloid (winner of the 1914 Schneider Trophy) by way of the Schneider seaplane, and preserved by the Fleet Air Arm at Lee-on-Solent. Armed with a single Lewis gun, the Baby was widely used by the R.N.A.S. in Britain and the Mediterranean, and aboard warships of the Royal Navy. They could carry two 65-lb. (30 kg) bombs and were sometimes used on anti-airship patrols, armed with Ranken darts or Le Prieur rockets. (*Photo, dated June 1970: By courtesy of Leslie Hunt, Esq.*)

THE SOPWITH SNIPE. Almost certainly the best single-seat scout produced by the Allies during the First World War, the classic Snipe reached the Western Front in September 1918. It survived until the mid-1920s as the R.A.F.'s standard fighter and, with No. 25 Squadron, was Britain's only home defence fighter between April 1920 and September 1922. Armed with two synchronised machine guns, it had a top speed of 119 m.p.h. (191 kph). (*Photo: By courtesy of the Canadian National Aeronautical Collection, Ottawa, via Leslie Hunt, Esq.*)

Powers specifically required all *Fokker D VII* first-line aircraft to be handed over by Germany.

One other family of scouts should be mentioned here. These were the Italian *S.V.A.* (Savoia-Verduzio-Ansaldo) aircraft, of which the *S.V.A.5* was probably the best known. Powered by a 220-h.p. S.P.A.6A engine, this version was capable of a sea level speed of 143 m.p.h. Some quite extraordinary long-range wartime flights were undertaken on the Austrian front with these aircraft and there is no doubt that the Austrians had a healthy regard for them.

THE BIG WARPLANES

The dramatic escapades by German *Gothas* and British *Handley Pages* in the West during the last eighteen months of the War seem to have overshadowed the interesting events on the Eastern Front at the beginning of the War. As early as 15th February 1915 the giant Russian *Sikorsky Ilya-Mourametz V* four-engined bomber dropped 600-lb. (270 kg) of bombs over Germany's Eastern Front, this great aircraft being developed from the world's first four-engined aircraft, the *Sikorsky Grand* of 1913.

Germany herself initiated the design of large bombing aircraft in 1914 with the G-Type (*Grosskampfflugzeug*) aircraft – the "big warplanes" or battleplanes. Numerous designs appeared, usually powered by two engines, but undoubtedly the best known were the *Gotha G IV* and *G V*, large biplanes with two 260 h.p. Mercedes D IVa engines and a three-man crew. These aircraft first appeared towards the end of 1916, coinciding with German realisation of the airship's bombing limitations. Capable of carrying about 1,000 pounds (450 kg) of bombs – usually made up of 110 lb. (50 kg) bombs – the *Gothas* joined No. 3 Heavy Bomber Squadron, based in Belgium, and commenced their famous raids against London and South-East England. Though the direct effects of these raids were much exaggerated for some years, they caused an outcry at the shortcomings of the Metropolitan air defences, and in due course brought about the formation of the Royal Air Force with the integration of air defence within a single Air Ministry.

Extending the battleplane formula, the Germans adopted a still larger class of bomber, the R-Type (*Riesenflugzeug*). These were huge aircraft and were therefore built in rather smaller numbers than the G-Types, and were all individual designs from several manufacturers. The best known was the *Zeppelin Staaken R VI*, a four-engined biplane with a span of 138 ft. 5 in. (42·2 m), a crew of seven, and capable of carrying up to about 4,500 pounds (2000 kg) of bombs. Used for raiding in the East and West during 1917 and 1918, an *R VI* of *Riesenflugzeugabteilung 501* dropped the first one-ton (1000 kg) bomb on Britain on 16th/17th February 1918, hitting the Royal Chelsea Hospital.

By comparison British heavy bombers were to some extent similar in concept although reaching squadron service about six months later than their German counterparts. The first truly operational British heavy bomber was the *Handley Page 0/100*, of which 46 were built and reached the R.N.A.S. 5th Wing in France in November 1916. Unfortunately one of the first aircraft accidentally landed intact behind the German lines during its delivery flight – later lending credence to the allegation that the *Gotha* bombers were "copies" of the *0/100*; in fact the German aircraft pre-dated the *0/100* by six months and were rather different in design concept. From the *0/100* was developed the *0/400*, of which about 400 were built in Britain and a further 107 in America. Powered by two 360-h.p. Rolls-Royce Eagle VIII engines, the standard *0/400* had a crew of three, could carry sixteen 112-lb. (50 kg) bombs, and had a maximum sea level speed of 97·5 m.p.h. (157 kph). It was widely used in 1918, providing the main strategic bombing strength of the R.A.F.'s Independent Force.

Much larger than the 100-ft.-span *0/400* was the *Handley Page V/1500*. Capable of carrying a half-ton bomb-load from Britain to Berlin, the *V/1500* was motivated by the German raids on London in 1917. Only three of these aircraft had been completed by the end of the War and none was ever flown against Germany.

MAKING-SHIFT FOR PEACE

The return to peace brought a determination to exploit aviation for peaceful purposes. The enormous expense of war had however exhausted the major nations and financial resources were strictly limited both in national and commercial exchequers – despite the considerable advances made in aircraft technology and manufacture during the War years. Three other obstacles stood in the way of commercial air travel, namely the almost total lack of knowledge of the problems of long distance commercial route operation, the absence of route-staging facilities and airports, and the lack of suitable passenger-carrying aircraft. All these difficulties might only be overcome with the expenditure of huge sums of money – or by the make-shift efforts by enthusiastic private individuals.

It was thus scarcely surprising that the first post-War commercial aircraft were not more than thinly-disguised wartime bombers. In Britain the famous *de Havilland D.H.4A* and *D.H.9A* aircraft were pressed into service on the short-haul European routes, carrying no more than two or three passengers in acute discomfort; only marginally better conditions were available in the larger *Handley Page* aircraft.

France was more fortunate in that she possessed in 1918 a bomber which was more readily adaptable for passenger work – the *Farman Goliath*. In its way, this was an outstanding aircraft; a large all-wooden biplane, powered by two 260-h.p. Salmson CM.9 engines and capable of carrying up to twelve passengers at a cruising speed of about 90 m.p.h. (144 kph), the *Goliath* served routes between Paris, London and Brussels. About 60

THE FAIREY SWORDFISH. Immortalised by its magnificent record during the Second World War (with notable achievements in the Battle of the Atlantic, the Battles of Taranto and Cape Matapan, and against the *Bismarck*), the torpedo-carrying "Stringbag" was an anachronism, having originated in a specification issued as early as 1932. It survived throughout the War, serving on almost every British aircraft carrier in every theatre of operations. (*Photo: By courtesy of the Fleet Air Arm, Lee-on-Solent, via Leslie Hunt, Esq.*)

THE GLOSTER GLADIATOR. Last R.A.F. biplane fighter, the Gladiator entered service in January 1937. Had the Munich Crisis brought about world war in September 1938, it would have been Britain's standard interceptor. As it was, it served in combat in France, Norway, Belgium, Finland, Greece and the Middle East, and despite its obsolescence was able to achieve numerous successes against much more modern enemy aircraft. With an armament of four guns, it had a top speed of 253 m.p.h. (407 kph). (*Photo: By courtesy of Michael Vines, Esq., Air Portraits*)

were built and continued route flying until the mid-1920s.

The first truly classic British civil airliner was the *Vickers Vimy Commercial*, which was a substantially-modified version of the *Vimy* bomber. It was in the *Vimy* bomber that some of the truly great long distance pioneering flights were made – of which the non-stop crossing of the Atlantic by Alcock and Brown, and the Ross brothers' England-to-Australia flight (both in 1919) stand out on the pages of History. The *Vimy Commercial* first flew in 1919 and featured a much enlarged fuselage with accommodation for ten passengers. Though not built in large numbers for commercial operators, it nevertheless was the forerunner of a long line of similar Vickers passenger carriers which continued to give faithful service for almost fifteen years.

The oldest airline to retain its original name is KLM Royal Dutch Airlines, and this famous carrier operated some of the earliest passenger-carrying aircraft *designed as such*. Even before the end of the War, the Fokker company had produced a four-passenger high-wing monoplane, the *F II*, and the prototype was flown to the Netherlands in 1920. Subsequently this single-engined aircraft was produced in Amsterdam and served KLM, *Deutsche Luft-Reederei, Deutscher Aero Lloyd, Lufthansa* and *Sabena* – continuing in service until well into the 1930s.

One of the loopholes of the Treaty of Versailles lay in the allowance made for German manufacture of commercial aircraft after the War – a freedom eagerly exploited by such manufacturers as Junkers, who forthwith produced the small *J 13* (later re-designated the *F 13*) – the first all-metal commercial transport monoplane used by airlines. This classic little four-seat aircraft was fitted with a 185-h.p. BMW IIIa engine and remained in production until 1930, by which time more than 300 had been built. It appeared in numerous versions, fitted with wheel, float and ski undercarriages, and led to the development of the famous three-engined Junkers family of the nineteen-thirties.

In the military sphere of aviation it was perhaps to be expected that the aftermath of the "war to end wars" would be characterised by a dearth in new military aircraft designs. The enormous building programmes planned in 1918 had gained such momentum by the time of the Armistice that the coming of peace left huge stocks and, with the inevitable cut-back in personnel, few airmen to fly them. In the R.A.F. the *Sopwith Snipe*, the *Bristol F.2B Fighter* and the *D.H.9* existed in substantial numbers and, in the strictures imposed by an ingratiating Government poised nervously on a social knife-edge, these aeroplanes had to provide the main strength of the R.A.F. for half-a-dozen years after 1918. Such was the withdrawal from a belligerent posture that for almost two years the whole defence of Britain at home rested on a single squadron (No. 25) equipped with *Snipes*.

But, just as the crises of 1916 had engendered a barrage of squabbling between the generals and admirals, each greedy to take what they could from an infant aircraft industry, the austerity of post-War years threatened the continued existence of the R.A.F.; neither the Navy nor Army saw any reason for the peacetime continuation of an Air Force as a separate Service. It was this pressure which, far from breaking the will of men like Trenchard and the Salmond brothers, lent stimulus for an *esprit* within the tiny Royal Air Force, with the result that when given the chance to prove its worth in successive brittle situations in the Middle East during the early nineteen-twenties, it was not found wanting. Despite an aircraft inventory almost entirely composed of war-surplus aeroplanes, the mere presence of the R.A.F. at Chanak averted an almost inevitable clash of armies in Turkey, while the successful policing by a tiny R.A.F. contingent of Iraq (which country had long frustrated a large and costly force of British soldiers) demonstrated the relatively inexpensive manner in which a flexible "go-anywhere, do-anything" air force might be used. This type of overseas deployment of the Royal Air Force continued for another fifty years – though shrinking overseas commitments during the nineteen-sixties brought about a different policy, that of long-range reinforcement from a home-based striking force.

Thus it was that development of military aeroplanes all but stagnated in Britain in the early 'twenties, and herein lay the first great lesson to be learned in the establishment of a national aviation policy: that once a nation adopts a philosophy of withdrawal from technological front-running, the regaining of a position among the world leaders will occupy many years, great will to succeed and vast sums of money. Britain, France, Russia and America have all overlooked this lesson – to their cost both in lives and economics. The post-War years found no better situation in France, and in Germany, of course, the banning of all work on military aeroplanes prompted German aircraft industrialists to seek suitable locations abroad for the continuation of their activities. It was to be expected perhaps that the smaller manufacturers, which may have profited commercially in time of war, would opt out of aircraft work in peacetime, but when the great Sopwith company went into voluntary liquidation in 1920 it must have seemed that Britain had little chance of ever recovering the lead in technology she had built by 1918.

America, on the other hand, with scarcely a modern warplane of her own in production in 1918, to some extent built her post-War technology on the *D.H.4* and the *D.H.9*, and the famous Liberty engine she was producing for them.

However, America identified one area of aircraft development which other nations, in their poverty, were obliged largely to ignore, at least for the time being. This was in metal construction, and throughout the inter-War period American all-metal aircraft were

THE HAWKER HART. Designed by the late Sir Sydney Camm, the Hart day bomber first entered service early in 1930; it was powered by the famous Rolls-Royce Kestrel V-12 engine and possessed a top speed of 184 m.p.h. at a time when European interceptor fighters were capable of no more than 170 m.p.h. Developed from the Hart was a whole family of fighters, bombers, army co-operation and naval aircraft – the Demon, Audax, Osprey, Hind, Hardy and Hector. The aircraft shown here has been flying constantly since 1930 and has been preserved by its manufacturers.

THE DE HAVILLAND D.H.88 COMET. Flown by C. W. A. Scott and Tom Campbell Black, this famous aeroplane *Grosvenor House* won the great MacRobertson Race from Mildenhall, England, to Melbourne, Australia, in October 1934. Of wooden stressed-skin construction and powered by D.H. Gipsy Six R engines, the Comet provided considerable experience in the design of the classic Mosquito high-speed bomber of the Second World War. G-ACSS is today preserved in the Shuttleworth Collection at Old Warden Aerodrome, Bedfordshire. (*Photo: By courtesy of E. A. Chris Wren, Esq.*)

prominent.

In contrast, the first generation of British post-War interceptors to be favoured with support from scanty funds, the *Gloster Grebe* and *Hawker Woodcock* fighters, were, in reality, little more than limited extensions of the wartime *Snipe* formula: bulky radial engines driving wooden propellers, synchronised twin-Vickers guns located just in front of the pilot's face, and, above all, fabric-covered wooden construction. Manoeuvrable they might be, but for some years this generation of biplanes suffered all manner of problems – not least of which that of wing and tail flutter.

Engine development, an expensive technology at the best of times, was also excruciatingly slow, and British aircraft were to a great extent dependent on three main types, the Rolls-Royce Eagle, the Bristol Jupiter and the recalcitrant and heavy Armstrong Siddeley Jaguar.

It was the advances in America that motivated a determination in Britain in the mid-'twenties to break from the stultifying wartime formulae. First, the American victory in the 1923 Schneider Trophy had focused attention on the beautiful *Curtiss CR-3* racing seaplanes, with their clean lines and low-profile engine cowling. This was followed by a series of negotiations by Richard Fairey to secure the Curtiss D-12 engine and rights to incorporate other advanced design features in his own aeroplanes, the result being the outstanding *Fairey Fox* light bomber. Unfortunately this classic design never attracted more than an impulsive and sadly shortlived reaction from an otherwise impassive Air Ministry, and the life of the *Fox* was very limited.

It was Rolls-Royce that secured the vital breakthrough in in-line engine design with its evolution of cylinder banks cast in one block in place of the weighty individual cylinders, and the Eagle gave place to the Falcon and – in 1927 – the Kestrel. With a strikingly increased power-weight ratio and low frontal area, the Kestrel paved the way for the design of fighters and light bombers that could certainly match the appearance and performance of the *Fox*.

But to a degree still limited by minimal expenditure on research and development, the age-old prejudice against the monoplane (that had continued in Britain since 1912), and the conservative retention of the wood-working trades in the Service establishments, the great majority of British military aircraft were, until the early 'thirties, still fabric-covered wooden biplanes. And of course the biplane in Europe still reigned supreme. In the R.A.F., the *Gloster Gamecock* and the *Bristol Bulldog* (both with radial, air-cooled engines) were chosen to supplant the *Woodcock, Snipe* and *Grebe*.

Moving up the scale among military aeroplanes, the *Hawker Horsley* was adopted by the R.A.F. as a light bomber, an uninspired design whose specification was compromised by Air Staff vacillation, an inability to pursue a rational policy in the development of bombs; the result was dependence upon the "250-lb" bomb,

which was impossible to aim efficiently (owing to its extraordinary shape), and the 112-lb bomb, which did precious little damage even if it was dropped accurately. The *Horsley*, however, gave yeoman service as a torpedo bomber for a number of years with the coastal squadrons.

The heavy night bomber – Trenchard's focal point of his defence policies – continued along the path pioneered in the R.A.F. by the *Handley Page 0/400* and *Vickers Vimy*, with the *Handley Page Hyderabad* and *Hinaidi*, steadfast workhorses, yet unimaginative with their puny bombloads and agonisingly low performance. Yet the move from *Hyderabad* to *Hinaidi* was an important transition in that the latter aircraft, with its metal primary structure, introduced new skilled metal-working maintenance trades to the R.A.F. bomber stations.

Mainstay of the British heavy bomber squadrons from 1925 to 1933 was the *Vickers Virginia*, a direct descendant of the *Vimy*. Capable of carrying up to 3,000 pounds of bombs, the *Virginia* underwent continuous development during which wooden construction was replaced by metal. Nevertheless, long before the venerable bomber was retired from the R.A.F. it had become an anachronism among the world's heavy bombers.

SHEDDING THE UPPER WING

If the gradual change from wood to metal represented one break with tradition during the period 1926-30, the recognition of the monoplane's superiority came to be accepted in the same period – apparently with reluctance by the British Air Staff. Perhaps the most dramatic demonstration of this superiority was provided by the Schneider Trophy races, yet despite the success of Mitchell's Supermarine S.5 in the 1927 race, and the obvious advance represented by the truly beautiful lines of this seaplane, Britain's military aviation administration steadfastly set its face against such a radical, and presumably costly influence in its own requirements. Only one British service monoplane originated at this time – the *Fairey Hendon* – and although this big bomber was the outcome of a 1927 requirement it didn't reach R.A.F. squadrons until 1936. Preference, within the terms of this requirement, was given to the *Handley Page Heyford* – yet another twin-engined biplane bomber which, joining the R.A.F. in 1933, soldiered on almost until the Second World War.

The most outstanding military aircraft of the early 1930s were perhaps the American *Boeing B-9* and *Martin B-10* bombers; the latter was an extraordinarily prophetic aeroplane, developed privately by the Glenn L. Martin company as a means of getting back into the bomber business. Both were mid-wing monoplanes with retractable undercarriages. The *B-9* was flown in 1931, a year before the *B-10*, and featured open cockpits and gun positions; with a top speed of 188 m.p.h., it could carry up to 2,620 pounds of bombs. The *B-10B* featured enclosed cockpit and gun positions, and lifted the same bombload, but its top speed of 213 m.p.h. was far in

THE DE HAVILLAND DRAGON RAPIDE. Representing the means by which short-haul air transport came to maturity in the immediate pre-War years, the classic Dragon Rapide wore the hallmark of safety and reliability made famous by de Havilland's Moth series. Such were the numbers built that it was widely used as a radio and navigation trainer by the R.A.F. (as the Domine) during the War, and in the immediate post-War years survived as a light feeder-liner and executive transport. (*Photo: By courtesy of Leslie Hunt, Esq.*)

THE DOUGLAS DC-3. Unquestionably the greatest air transport of all time, the DC-3 first flew in 1935, introduced new standards of reliability and luxury to medium-range air routes throughout the world before the War, and has never been fully replaced. Built in huge numbers during the War as the Dakota, Skytrain and Skytrooper, it became the Allies' standard troop transport, the backbone of the Berlin airlift in 1949 and countless post-War air fleets. Armed versions have seen action in Vietnam. (*Photo: By courtesy of McDonnell-Douglas, via Leslie Hunt, Esq.*)

excess of the standard interceptors in service in Europe – epitomised by the *Bristol Bulldog*.

In the R.A.F.'s fighter situation in 1930 lay all the results of the parsimonious attitudes of government and treasury alike. In the absence of a military threat from Germany, the nearest potential enemy was France, and for half a dozen years the deployment and equipment of the R.A.F. was planned accordingly. The majority of interceptor squadrons were based well inland, it being intended that an enemy bombing force could only be effectively dealt with after it had crossed the coast. This duty was deemed capable of being carried out by such fighters as the *Bristol Bulldog*, a radial-engined biplane with a top speed of 174 m.p.h. which remained in R.A.F. service until 1936. A token interceptor force of three squadrons, equipped with the *Hawker Fury*, was based on the Channel Coast at Tangmere and Hawkinge. Although regarded as no more than a refinement of the old two-gun biplane formula, the *Fury* was perhaps one of the most beautiful aeroplanes of the old generation ever built, made possible principally by use of the Rolls-Royce Kestrel engine, but also by Sydney Camm's fastidious attention to detail. It had a top speed of 204 m.p.h., but only limited production was deemed necessary until 1936 – by which time it was obsolete.

The *Hawker Fury* may have appeared as a blind alley, but its true value lay in another direction, which will be evident in due course. Camm's other design, which emerged with the *Fury* in 1929-30, was the *Hawker Hart* light bomber. This was recognised as an outstanding design at the time, the criterion being its creditable performance, including a top speed of 184 m.p.h.

In fact the *Hart* was outstanding during only the first two years of its Service life, after which it was nothing short of mediocre, yet it was perhaps one of the most important aeroplanes ever produced by Britain in peacetime.

The world depression of 1929-31 left the British aircraft industry in a parlous state, while the British Government clutched at any straw that would justify further delays in rearmament. The *Hawker Hart* was a relatively inexpensive general purpose aeroplane, which was developed to perform all manner of duties with the R.A.F. – army co-operation progressively by the *Audax*, *Hardy* and the *Hector*, coastal and shipboard duties by the *Osprey*, day bombing by the *Hind* and interception by the *Demon* fighter. Worthwhile orders were received from Sweden, Latvia, Estonia, Persia, India, South Africa, Afghanistan, Portugal, Spain and Jugoslavia, and the growing dependence by the R.A.F. on these variants resulted in unprecedented orders being received by Hawkers, whose small factories at Kingston and Brooklands were quite inadequate to accommodate such production demands. Other members of the British aircraft industry were less fortunate and would have fallen on hard times had not the Hawker management embarked on a profitable and far-reaching policy of sub-

contracting. The Gloster Aircraft Company was bought up, and production contracts let to Avro, Vickers, Boulton Paul, Westland, Bristol and Armstrong Whitworth – all built Hawker aircraft, and all survived. Herein lay the seeds of the great Hawker Siddeley Group. It is not too much to say that the *Hart*, more than any other aircraft, saved the British aircraft industry by keeping 24,000 aircraft workers employed between 1933 and 1936.

But world events in the early 'thirties had brought on a quickening of nations' pulses. Germany and Japan made moves that could not be ignored by countries becoming painfully aware of their own military weaknesses. In terms of air defence, the aeroplane had reached a crossroads. America by 1934 had already taken the road of the monoplane and had introduced the classic *Boeing P-26A* monoplane fighter; Germany, in great secrecy, had started work on the *Messerschmitt Bf 109*; the Russian Nikolai Polikarpov's *I-16 Ishak* ("Little Donkey") had flown as early as 1933, while in Britain two great fighter designers, Camm and Mitchell, were each at work on aircraft that were to become the *Hawker Hurricane* and the *Supermarine Spitfire*.

Of these, the first generation of monoplane interceptors, the British and German aircraft were the most successful and longest-lived. Camm's *Hurricane* was the logical development of the *Hawker Fury* biplane, using a wholly related form of fabricated structure, whereas the most graceful *Spitfire* was a more complex evolution of metal stressed-skin construction, allied with aerodynamic profiles evolved from the successful Schneider Trophy winners of 1927-31. As such, the *Hurricane* was in effect half a generation before the *Spitfire*. Yet both were evolved with one vital concept in mind – that of carrying into combat a battery of no fewer than eight free-firing machine guns. When one recalls that the *Hawker Fury* entered R.A.F. service as a "super-fighter" in 1931 with an armament of two synchronised Vickers guns and a top speed of just over 200 m.p.h., the advance of the *Hurricane* and *Spitfire*, joining the R.A.F. in 1937-38 with eight free-firing guns and a speed of well over 300 m.p.h., may be well appreciated in its true perspective.

Willi Messerschmitt's classic *Bf 109* was a contemporary of the *Hurricane*, though by experience gained in Spain (during the Spanish Civil War) and the support lent by a totalitarian and aggressive authority, the German fighter soon overtook the Hawker fighter and came to match the *Spitfire*. It was to become a feature of the war in the air that successive developments of these two great aircraft kept almost perfect step.

But before turning to other areas of monoplane acceptance it is necessary just to pause to look at the last chapter of biplane development. There was a period of twilight while the new monoplanes were being designed and developed; this was the heyday of the last biplane fighters – the *Gloster Gauntlet* and *Gladiator* in Britain, the *Heinkel He 51* and *Arado Ar 68* of Germany (which fought with the *Legion Cóndor* in Spain), and the *Fiat CR.32* and *CR.42* in Italy. But whereas the German biplanes were firmly discarded in 1938–39, the British and Italian biplanes remained to soldier on for some years into the Second World War. Indeed, had war followed immediately after the Munich Crisis in September 1938, the British air defence would have rested almost entirely upon the *Gauntlet* and *Gladiator* for, at that time, only three *Hurricane* squadrons existed, and no *Spitfires* had reached a fully operational status.

One other biplane was to pursue an agonisingly long career in the same skies as the nimble monoplane fighters. This was the *Fairey Swordfish*, a naval torpedo-bomber which had originated long ago in 1932. Impeded with all manner of supposedly essential accoutrements deemed necessary for shipboard operations, the venerable "Stringbag" fought its way into the Second World War and, in countless actions both great and small, suffered almost complete extinction in combat. Furthermore its successor, the *Fairey Albacore* biplane, was also a disgraceful anachronism supposedly engendered by a belief that biplanes were still necessary to lift a torpedo off the deck of an aircraft carrier.

It is often cited that one of the values of the warplane is that it fosters accelerated development of the commercial airliner. While this is probably true in numerous areas of detailed equipment and in aero-engine development, it was certainly not true in the case of the monoplane. Three of the world's greatest advocates of the monoplane, Anthony Fokker, Dr. Hugo Junkers and the Ford company of America had been producing commercial monoplanes since the nineteen-twenties – as had Armstrong Whitworth in Britain since 1932 with the *Atalanta*. The *Fokker F.VII*, the *Junkers-G 24s* and *31s*, and *Ford Tri-Motors* gave many years' service with nothing to suggest evidence to support the Military's suspicions of the monoplane's lack of integrity.

It was probably the *Junkers Ju 52* and *52/3m* that finally set the seal on commercial acceptance of the monoplane, the former first flying in 1930, and the famous three-engined version in 1932. Designed by Dipl. Ing. Ernst Zindel, the *Ju 52/3m* provided the backbone of *Lufthansa's* European services between 1933 and 1938, and later became Germany's principal military transport during the Second World War. In due course these aircraft served the airlines of Argentina, Australia, Austria, Belgium, Bolivia, Brazil, Czechoslovakia, Denmark, Ecuador, France, Great Britain, Greece, Hungary, Italy, Mozambique, Norway, Peru, Poland, Romania, South Africa, Spain, Sweden and Uruguay, in addition to Germany.

But if the *Junkers Ju 52/3m* set a seal on the monoplane's approbation, it was the American *Douglas DC-3* that reaped the full reward. Developed from the *DC-2* (winner of the handicap section of the famous Mac-Robertson Race from Britain to Australia in 1934), the *DC-3* is unquestionably the greatest commercial aeroplane ever designed, in terms of life-span – which is, after all, a measure of an aircraft's value to its sponsors and operators. The *DC-3* (alias the *Dakota*, *Skytrain* and *Skytrooper*, as it was named when it entered military service during the War), first flew on 17th December 1935 – the thirty-second anniversary of the Wright brothers' first flight. It entered service with countless airlines in America and elsewhere during the latter half of the nineteen-thirties and forthwith set about netting worthwhile commercial profits for airlines which had hitherto struggled with marginal reserves. It brought comfort and reliability undreamed of only half-a-dozen years before. It carried literally millions of men about the war theatres between 1939 and 1945, taking them into battle and evacuating them when they were wounded. What is more it continued to serve more than one hundred nations during the next twenty-five years, even being introduced into combat as a "gun-ship" during the recent Vietnam War. No other single design has so influenced the progress of air transport as the truly classic "*Dak*".

A similar success story might have attended the British *Short Empire* (C-Class) flying-boats had not the Second World War interfered with its introduction to commercial operation and sidetracked long-range travel away from water-based airliners. The graceful *Empire* flying-boats, offering great luxury, were leading the world inter-continental travel just before the War, with their safe and leisurely voyages down the old British Empire air routes through Africa, the Middle East, Asia and the Far East. They were also just opening up the North Atlantic route when war came and effectively put an end to their economic exploitation. They found a substantial application in wartime as the *Short Sunderland* maritime patrol aircraft, which served R.A.F. Coastal Command and other air forces right up to the nineteen-sixties, by which time their traditional duties had been assumed by land-based aircraft.

THE GREATEST WAR

Contrary to popular expectations when war erupted in Europe in 1939, there were to be no immediate "secret weapons" – save that of Germany's use of air power itself. The world had become aware through clever propaganda of the *Messerschmitt Bf 109*, the *Dornier Do 17* (the so-called "Flying Pencil"), the *Heinkel He 111* and the *Junkers Ju 87* – the hated Stuka dive-bomber. What burst upon an unprepared world was the weapon of *Blitzkrieg*, the unrestrained and wholly-integrated use of man and machines on the ground with men and machines in the air, moving as one and blasting everything in their path. Given the essential element of tactical surprise, nothing could stand in the way. In those early weeks that witnessed the defeat of Poland, the superiority of the *Ju 87*, the *Bf 109* and *Bf 110* seemed to be confirmed. Little was said of

THE HAWKER HURRICANE. Sydney Camm's masterpiece, the 8-gun Hurricane was the R.A.F.'s first monoplane fighter, entering service in 1937 – almost a year before the Spitfire. It was the victor of the Battle of Britain, equipping more than 30 squadrons, and fought in every campaign against Germany, Italy and Japan before 1943. More than 14,000 were built, and 3,000 were supplied to Russia. Though inferior to the contemporary Bf 109E, it was immensely rugged and was also used as a fighter-bomber, recce and anti-tank fighter. (*Photo: By courtesy of Leslie Hunt, Esq.*)

THE BRISTOL BLENHEIM IV. Introduced into service in 1937, the Blenheim I was the R.A.F.'s first fast light monoplane bomber, and was also the world's first radar-equipped night fighter. The Mark IV bomber served in every war theatre prior to 1942, and the example shown above served with the Finnish Air Force against Russia in the Winter War of 1939-40. Though sadly under-armed, the Blenheim served in large numbers until more up-to-date bombers were delivered in 1941-42. (*Photo: F. K. Mason collection*)

the gallant fight offered by the Polish Air Force in its outdated *P.Z.L. P-11* fighters – which were simply overwhelmed by enormous numbers of German aircraft in the air, and hopelessly undermined by ruined bases on the ground.

In its class the *Junkers Ju 87* was an imaginative weapon. Characterised by its grotesque cranked wing, it seemed to personify ruthlessness, and there is no doubt that in the skies over a nation unprepared for war it was a terrible weapon capable of delivering its bombs with uncanny accuracy. With this weapon Hitler blasted his way, first through Poland and then through Norway, Holland, Belgium and France, and much later into Russia and along the coast of North Africa. With sirens and bombs screaming, this was the harbinger of total war.

It was in the Battle of Britain that the *Stuka* was first checked. Not that the people of Britain were any less prone to the terrors of dive-bombing, not that there were less suitable targets; the *Ju 87* simply flown into the same sky as a determined and highly developed force of nimble and hard-hitting interceptor fighters. Between the 8th and 18th August 1940, over a hundred-mile stretch of British coastline, the once-vaunted *Stukageswader* of the *Luftwaffe* were hacked to shreds,

Another component of Göring's arsenal to suffer in the early months of the War was the so-called *Zerstörer* or "destroyer", the *Messerschmitt Bf 110*. This was a new concept in fighter design – in effect a very heavily armed escort fighter – capable of accompanying the bomber force and, supposedly, destroying any interceptor that might molest the raiders. Again, as long as the opposing fighters were not too modern, this theory held good – again until the Battle of Britain, when the *Bf 110s* were pitted against interceptors which carried a gunpower even more devastating than their own. The *Zerstörergeschwader* suffered heavily and if one examines their defeat more closely one can detect one of the root causes of the *Luftwaffe's* defeat in the daylight Battle of Britain, for it was the *Bf 110's* very inability to protect Göring's bomber formations that led to the deployment of the excellent *Messerschmitt Bf 109E* single-seat fighters (nicknamed "Emils") as escort for the more ponderous bomber formations. Indeed, the *Zerstörer* formations themselves were so vulnerable that they required escorting! So long as the dangerous "Emils" could be tied to the bomber formations, the *Hurricanes* and *Spitfires* would not be prey to the ravages of "free-chasing" combat groups sweeping the airfields of Kent and Sussex awaiting the return of British fighters, low on fuel and out of ammunition. Göring's pride, the *Bf 110*, seldom saw the same service again as an escort fighter; rather, it moved into the night where, equipped with the strange paraphernalia which was radar, it did great execution among British bombers over Germany later in the War.

Among the bombers with which Britain went to war,

"ruggedness" would probably best describe their common feature. There was the extraordinary *Armstrong Whitworth Whitley* heavy bomber, a severely rectangular aeroplane which always gave the impression of an impending crash – its marked nose-down attitude resulting from the high angle of incidence at which its wings were set on the fuselage. This was the bomber that, loaded with huge quantities of propaganda leaflets, did more than any other to create a litter problem in North-West Germany for the first six months of the War. It shared one important feature with another British bomber, the *Vickers Wellington*, in that it carried a heavy tail-armament of four machine guns in a power-operated turret.

Like the *Whitley*, the *Wellington* was an immensely robust aeroplane, capable of withstanding great battle damage – and this it certainly had to do, as the result of a mistaken British policy of daylight operations by unescorted heavy bombers which involved the early *Wellington* squadrons in disastrous casualties. Too much store had been set by the nose and tail guns of these bombers and, pitted against the "Emils" of Northern Germany they suffered no less than Göring's *Kampfgeschwader* in the summer skies of 1940. The *Wellington* required no alterations to suit it to night bombing, and from mid-1940 for two years there was seldom a night that some squadron or other did not set out to bomb targets in enemy-occupied Europe. It was a Wellington that dropped the first 4,000-pound "blockbuster" bomb – in a raid on Emden in 1941.

Third of the British bomber trio at the beginning of the War was the *Handley Page Hampden*, less of a heavy bomber than the other two, although it dropped the R.A.F.'s first 2,000-pound bomb – in an attack on the *Scharnhorst* at Kiel in July 1940. More manoeuvrable than the *Whitley* and *Wellington*, the *Hampden* was probably nearer to the German medium-bomber concept in that it grouped its crew forward, without locating a gunner in the extreme tail.

Two early Victoria Crosses were awarded to *Hampden* crew members in 1940. One was to Flt. Lt. R. A. B. Learoyd, who flew his bomber at very low level in intense *Flak* to bomb the Dortmund-Ems Canal on 12th August, returning home safely in a shattered aircraft. The other was awarded to the 18-year-old wireless-operator, Sgt. J. Hannah, whose *Hampden* was set on fire over Antwerp on 15th September; two crew members baled out, but Hannah attacked the fire with extinguishers and his log book, enabling his pilot to bring the charred hulk back to base.

The R.A.F.'s other important aeroplane at the beginning of the War was the *Bristol Blenheim* which, mediocre though it was in terms of performance, was used in large numbers and provided the means by which numerous operational techniques were evolved. Developed from the "*Britain First*" monoplane of pre-War years – a private venture sponsored by Lord Rothermere

THE HAWKER TYPHOON IB. Initiated by Sydney Camm in 1937 as a Hurricane replacement, the Sabre-powered Typhoon entered R.A.F. service in 1941 but was for many months dogged by engine and structural problems. Never an outstanding interceptor fighter, this powerful single-seater found immortality as a rocket-equipped ground-strafer in 1944 as the decimator of German armies and armoured columns striving to disengage from the invading Allied armies in Northern Europe. (*Photo: By courtesy of the R.A.F. Museum, Hendon, via Leslie Hunt, Esq.*)

THE DE HAVILLAND MOSQUITO B.35. An all-time classic, the wooden, Rolls-Royce Merlin-powered Mosquito served as a day and night fighter, medium and fighter-bomber, recce aircraft, trainer and transport, entering service with the R.A.F. in 1941. The bomber versions were unarmed, relying on their great speed to evade enemy interceptors, and the Mark XVI carried a 4,000-lb. (1816 kg) bomb to Berlin. The B.35 version equipped several post-War R.A.F. Bomber Command squadrons, until replaced by the Canberra. (*Photo: By courtesy of Leslie Hunt, Esq.*)

The Rolls-Royce Merlin engine was a milestone of technical excellence as well as being the most widely used engine by the Allies during the Second World War, being used in the Hurricane, Spitfire, Battle, Henley, Lancaster, Mosquito, Fulmer, Halifax, York, Mustang, and many other lesser aircraft

in 1934–35 – the "short-nosed" *Blenheim* was built in large numbers as a medium bomber and delivered to the R.A.F. at home and overseas. A fighter version was used during the Battle of Britain with singularly little success, suffering more casualties to friendly guns than to those of the enemy owing to its similarity to the *Junkers Ju 88*. Nevertheless the *Blenheim* was the world's first radar-equipped night fighter, a small number of No. 25 Squadron aircraft being fitted with rudimentary sets in 1940; and a similar aircraft, flown by Fg. Off. G. Ashfield of the Fighter Interception Unit, destroyed a *Dornier Do 17* on 22nd/23rd July 1940, thereby becoming the first ever to shoot down an enemy aircraft in an interception using airborne radar. The *Blenheim* was flown by several foreign air forces, the "long-nosed" Mark IV continuing in service with R.A.F. bomber squadrons until 1942.

Unlike the *Blenheim*, the German *Junkers Ju 88* was only entering service at the outbreak of war, and remained in service, in one shape or another, until the end. Although frequently mis-employed, the *Ju 88* was an efficient bomber with a good turn of speed. It was conceived as a dive-bomber but came to be used more for level bombing at medium altitude, and also as a heavily-armed *Zerstörer* during and after the Battle of Britain. Like the *Bf 110* it became a highly effective night fighter, second only to the *Mosquito*.

It is not often realised that while Britain was fighting for survival in the Battle of Britain, she was already producing the weapons with which to take the War back to Germany. While her *Wellingtons, Whitleys* and *Hampdens* were making raids – whose lack of effect only

became evident later – she was also re-equipping with the *Short Stirling* four-engine heavy bomber. These big aeroplanes first went into action early in 1941 and were soon joined by the *Avro Manchester* two-engine "heavy" and the *Handley Page Halifax*. The *Stirling* and *Halifax* were great weightlifters for their day and certainly showed the Germans the R.A.F.'s determination in 1941 to repay in full the retribution for Göring's night *Blitz* of the previous winter. The *Stirling* was something of a disappointment as it had a poor performance when carrying a worthwhile bombload, while the *Manchester* suffered constant failures of its Rolls-Royce Vulture engines. When it was decided to abandon these engines, the *Manchester* was withdrawn from service.

Avro's had however already been experimenting with a development of the *Manchester*, and by installing four Rolls-Royce Merlin engines – whose integrity was undoubted – they produced the *Lancaster*, one of the greatest bombers of all time. It would be impossible in the space available here to do justice to the exploits of this great aircraft. A total of 7,366 were built (over 400 of them in Canada), itself a prodigious feat, and in due course they came to provide the backbone of "Bomber" Harris' night bomber offensive against Germany in 1942–45. Among their famous raids were the daylight attack on Augsburg on 17th April 1942 (which earned its leader, Sqdn. Ldr. J. D. Nettleton, the Victoria Cross),

THE LOCKHEED P-38J LIGHTNING. First flown on 11th February 1939, the Lightning was probably the fastest fighter in production when the Second World War broke out in September that year, with a speed of about 390 m.p.h. The "J" variant, shown here, became one of the great escort fighters of the U.S. Eighth Air Force, and it was with this version that Capt. Richard I. Bong became the U.S.A.A.F.'s top-scoring pilot with 40 confirmed victories. The preserved example, shown here, was photographed at Van Nuys on 3rd October 1965. (*Photo: By courtesy of Roger Baker, Esq.*)

THE NORTH AMERICAN P-51D MUSTANG. The Mustang is generally regarded as having been the finest long-range escort fighter of the Second World War. With a top speed of 437 m.p.h., the P-51D (later redesignated F-51D) fought in all theatres in that War, and went on to equip numerous post-War air forces – and to fight with distinction in Korea. More recently they have become favourites as racing aircraft, taking part with outstanding success in numerous events during the nineteen-sixties. The F-51 shown here was photographed at Reno in September 1968. (*Photo: Via, and by courtesy of Leslie Hunt, Esq.*)

and the famous raid against the Mohne, Eder and Sorpe dams (the immortal Guy Gibson winning another Victoria Cross). Nine Victoria Crosses were awarded to *Lancaster* crew members during the War. *Lancasters* dropped the first 8,000-pound bombs (on Essen on 10th/11th April 1942), the first 12,000-pound deep-penetration "Tallboy" bomb (on the Saumur tunnel on 8th June 1944), and the 22,000-pound "Grand Slam" bomb (on the Bielefeld Viaduct on 14th March 1945). A total of 59 squadrons of R.A.F. Bomber Command were equipped with *Lancasters* during the War.

The switch to night bombing by the *Luftwaffe* towards the end of the Battle of Britain highlighted a painful deficiency in night fighters in the R.A.F., despite the early efforts by the *Blenheims*. This was to some extent remedied by the introduction of the *Bristol Beaufighter* which was being delivered to the night fighter squadrons from September 1940 onwards. (In fact the first such aircraft fell into German hands before the Battle was over.) This was a powerful and heavily-armed twin-engined aircraft with a gun armament of no less than four 20-mm cannon and six machine-guns, and a top speed of about 330-m.p.h. Although flown by such famous night fighter pilots as Sqdn. Ldr. John Cunningham, the *Beaufighter* was handicapped initially by inadequate radar, but as its operators gained experience in its use they gradually obtained better results and by 1941 were downing significant numbers of Göring's night raiders.

While the *Beaufighter* remained in service for many months, eventually performing all manner of duties, including daylight rocket and torpedo attacks on enemy shipping, its successor, the *de Havilland Mosquito*, appeared and quickly earned a reputation second to none. Originally conceived as a high-speed unarmed bomber, capable of outdistancing any interceptor, the immortal "Mossie" came to be used as a night fighter and photo-reconnaissance aircraft as well. By use of a wooden construction (of course infinitely more sophisticated with its sandwich-balsa technique than the fabricated structures of old), the *Mosquito* was produced quickly and in large numbers, a total of 7,781 being built (including many in Canada and Australia). As a night fighter and intruder, armed with four 20-mm. cannon and equipped with improved radar, it became the R.A.F.'s standard equipment, while other versions were capable of carrying 4,000-pound "blockbuster" bombs as far as Berlin – such raids being frequent in 1944 and 1945. Fighter-bomber versions carried out a number of spectacular "set-piece" attacks, perhaps the most famous being the raid on the Gestapo H.Q. in Oslo in September 1942, the attack on Amiens prison on 18th February 1944, the attack on the Kleizkamp Art Galleries in The Hague on 11th April 1944, and the raid on a building in Copenhagen containing Gestapo records of Danish patriots on 21st March 1945.

Two other important fighters were introduced to ser-vice in 1941, the R.A.F.'s *Hawker Typhoon* and the *Luftwaffe's Focke-Wulf Fw 190*. Conceived back in 1937 as a successor to the *Hurricane*, the *Typhoon* was certainly an impressive aeroplane with an armament of either twelve machine-guns (soon abandoned in service) or four 20-mm. cannon, and a top speed of about 410 m.p.h. But it soon ran into trouble both with engine and airframe – the big Napier Sabre 24-cylinder engine suffering constant failure as a result of accelerated development, and the rear fuselage being inadequately stressed for combat manoeuvres. At low altitude the *Typhoon* was however effective in dealing with "sneak" raiders over Southern England in 1942–43, but its real value emerged much later when, after the Allied landings in Normandy in 1944, it was flown with deadly effect as a ground-attack fighter against enemy forces, discharging salvoes of bombs and rockets on the masses of German vehicles seeking to escape through the Falaise "gap".

Kurt Tank's *Focke-Wulf Fw 190* was a true classic among fighters for, unlike the *Typhoon*, it possessed a fairly thin wing which bestowed better manoeuvrability at greater altitudes. Yet from the outset this aeroplane was envisaged both as a fighter and a fighter-bomber, and was more than a match for the *Spitfire V* and *Hurricane II* which equipped R.A.F. fighter squadrons in 1941. Powered by a 1,700-h.p. B.M.W. 801Dg radial, air-cooled engine, the *Fw 190A-3* had a top speed of 391 m.p.h. Successive developments of the *Fw 190*, culminating in the superb *Focke-Wulf Ta 152*, provided the main fighter equipment of the *Luftwaffe* right up to the end of the War.

AMERICA GOES TO WAR

The devastating attack on Pearl Harbor on 7th December 1941 brought the United States and Japan into the War, and with them all manner of aircraft, good and bad. America, which had produced so many promising and advanced warplanes during the nineteen-thirties, had nevertheless pursued an isolationist policy preferring to introduce new equipment into her services slowly, while at the same time supplying aircraft in large numbers to France and Britain in 1940.

The two main aircraft supplied to Britain at the beginning of the War had been the *Lockheed Hudson* twin-engined maritime patrol aircraft and the *North American Harvard*. The former was a much-needed replacement for the *Avro Anson* with R.A.F. Coastal Command and was a sound and reliable aeroplane which continued in service with coastal squadrons until 1943, a total of 2,071 being delivered (of which 800 were purchased by Britain before the introduction of "Lend-Lease").

It was a *Hudson* of No. 224 Squadron which shot down the first German aircraft to be destroyed by the R.A.F. in the Second World War, shooting down a *Dornier Do 18* flying-boat over Jutland on 8th October 1939.

The *Harvard* was the most widely-used advanced

THE HAWKER SEA FURY. Last piston-engined fighter used operationally by British air forces, the Sea Fury was a Bristol Centaurus-powered development of the Tempest fighter which saw combat at the end of the Second World War. Joining the Fleet Air Arm in 1947, the 460-m.p.h. (738 kph) Sea Fury was heavily engaged in combat over Korea in 1951–53, occasionally meeting and defeating Communist MiG-15 jet fighters. The example shown here was one of a batch of Mark 20 target tugs supplied to *Deutsche Luftfahrt Beratungsdienst* in 1960. (*Photo: F. K. Mason collection*)

THE AVRO LINCOLN. Developed from the wartime classic Lancaster heavy bomber, the Lincoln was R.A.F. Bomber Command's last piston-engined heavy bomber. Intended for Far Eastern service, it was too late to see wartime service, but remained with bomber squadrons until 1955 when it was replaced by Canberra and Valiant jet bombers. Powered by four Rolls-Royce Merlin 85s, it had a top speed of 319 m.p.h. (512 kph), a maximum bomb-load of 14,000 lb. (6356 kg) and a crew of seven. (*Photo: By courtesy of Leslie Hunt, Esq.*)

trainer during the Second World War and, of a total of 16,855 built, just over 5,000 were supplied to British and Commonwealth air forces. Long remembered for its harsh crackling sound, created by the propeller tips turning at supersonic speed, it was a superb training aircraft, docile yet capable of introducing young pilots to many of the vagaries of modern fighters. Long after the Second World War the *Harvard* (or *Texan* as it was known in American service) was still giving sterling service, even being used relatively recently as a "counter-insurgency" armed attack aircraft.

America's main fighter equipment at the time of her entry into the War was the *Curtiss P-40 Warhawk*. Deliveries of the early versions (known as *Tomahawks*) had been made to the R.A.F. at home and in Africa in 1940, but despite a maximum speed of 350 m.p.h., their light armament caused them to be relegated to army co-operation duties in Northern Europe. These and the U.S.A.A.C.'s *P-40B* were essentially no more than contemporaries of the *Spitfire I* and *Hurricane I*, but as with the British fighters they were quickly improved with more powerful engines and, as the *P-40N* and *Kittyhawk* (in the R.A.F.), emerged as excellent fighter-bombers with an armament of six half-inch machine guns and capable of carrying 500 pounds of bombs.

Without doubt the best American fighters of the War were the *Lockheed P-38 Lightning*, the *Republic P-47 Thunderbolt* and the *North American P-51 Mustang*, of which only the *Lightning* had started being delivered to the U.S. Army Air Corps before Pearl Harbor. Although it was the fastest fighter in production anywhere at the outbreak of the War in 1939 (the early aircraft had a top speed of around 390 m.p.h.), and was ordered for the R.A.F. in March 1940, deliveries only started towards the end of 1941, and when evaluated by the British was rejected by the R.A.F.

Nevertheless later substitution of Allison engines giving increased power and armament standardisation with a single 20-mm. Hispano cannon and four 0·5-inch machine guns resulted in the *P-38J* which, with drop tanks, was one of America's best long-range fighters, also capable of carrying two 1,600-pound bombs. It was extensively used in the Pacific theatre, and was flown by Major Richard I. Bong, America's top-scoring fighter ace. It was also used in the European and Mediterranean theatres in 1942–45 as an escort and ground-attack fighter, though to less effect than the *P-47* and *P-51*. The *P-38* was the first aircraft to drop napalm "bombs" – these weapons being first used on 17th July 1944 over France.

The *Republic P-47 Thunderbolt* may have seemed to some extent a similar concept as that of the *Hawker Typhoon*, in that they both appeared as heavyweights among single-engined fighters. This was not the case for, when the *XP-47* appeared in 1940, it was an attempt to produce a *lightweight* fighter with only two machine-guns. The *XP-47* never flew because the war in Europe had demonstrated the uselessness of such an aircraft. Under the leadership of Alexander Kartvelli a new design was evolved using the big 2,000-h.p. Pratt & Whitney R-2800 radial engine. This, the *XP-47B*, was first flown on 6th May 1941 and was the *Thunderbolt's* true prototype. Deliveries of the "mighty Jug" started in 1942 to the three squadrons of the 56th Fighter Group and this unit was soon on its way to England, where the big fighter was held to some ridicule by R.A.F. pilots who predicted trouble for the Americans when faced by the agile *Messerschmitt Bf 109s* and *Focke-Wulf Fw 190s*. Certainly there were some early difficulties, but within six months the Americans were demonstrating the strength and manoeuvrability of the *Thunderbolt* and, with its heavy armament of eight 0·5-inch machine-guns, were accumulating substantial victory scores. The most widely-used version in Europe, the *P-47D*, had a top speed of about 430-m.p.h. and a range of 500 miles – the latter being doubled by the use of drop tanks. Both of America's top-scoring fighter pilots in Europe (Lt.-Col. Francis Gabreski with 31 victories, and Lt.-Col. Robert S. Johnson with 28) flew the *Thunderbolt*.

Last of the trio was the superb *North American P-51 Mustang* which, in its early days – powered by an Allison V-1710 engine of unspectacular character – had been no more than mediocre. It owed its origin to a British requirement in 1940 and was largely ignored by the U.S. Army Air Corps until, immediately after Pearl Harbor, aircraft awaiting delivery to the R.A.F. were requisitioned for American defence. It has been said that only direct intervention by General "Hap" Arnold secured the P-51 as standard equipment for the U.S.A.A.F. The *Mustang I* was, like the *P-40*, not rated highly by the R.A.F. who relegated the aircraft to secondary duties with army co-operation squadrons, but also recommended substitution of the Allison by the Rolls-Royce Merlin. This transformed the *Mustang* to such an extent that Packards undertook licence-production of the Merlin and the fighter re-appeared as the *P-51B* and *D* with Packard-built V-1650 engines. With a top speed of about 440 m.p.h., an armament of six 0·5-inch machine guns and able to carry two 1,000-pound bombs, the *P-51D* (of which 7,956 were built) was the best American fighter of the War. Its long range (2,080 miles) enabled it to accompany American bombers to Berlin and back, flying from Britain. Just before the end of the War a final production version started to appear, the *P-51H* which, powered by a 2,220-h.p. V-1650-9 engine, had a top speed of 487 m.p.h. Only a few of the 555 built reached the U.S.A.A.F. in the Far East before Japan surrendered.

The *F-51* (as the *Mustang* was re-designated after the War) started being phased out of operational service in 1949, but when the Korean War broke out in 1950 three Fighter-Bomber Groups of the U.S.A.F., equipped with *F-51Ds* and *F-51Hs*, were rushed to Korea where they continued to fight, until finally replaced by much later aircraft. Apart from the R.A.F. (who equipped 24 squadrons with *Mustang IIIs* and *IVs*), numerous other

THE BAC STRIKEMASTER. Although scarcely endowed with classic characteristics, the Strikemaster is nevertheless wholly representative of the unsophisticated warplane to which numerous smaller air forces – unsupported by lavish resources – turned during the troubled 1960s. Just as so many classic light training aircraft were adapted to provide a dual capability, so the Provost and Jet Provost trainers were strengthened to incorporate weapon carriage and ground attack strength factors. (*Photo: By courtesy of the British Aircraft Corporation*)

THE BAC-AEROSPATIALE CONCORDE. Whatever the future holds for the Concorde supersonic airliner, it is assured of a prominent place in aviation history. Opposed by self-styled "environmentalists" and supported by powerful industrial, technical and political factions, the Concorde's general design originated in British drawing offices in the late 1950s before demonstrating the feasibility of Anglo-French collaboration in manufacture. Requiring £1,000 million for development, the Concorde will cruise at Mach 2·2 with accommodation for up to 144 passengers. It is expected to halve transatlantic flight times. (*Photo: By courtesy of the British Aircraft Corporation*)

world air forces equipped with the *P-51* and this classic aeroplane continued to serve operationally well into the 1960s, and became a favourite racing aircraft among sporting pilots in several countries.

Moving on to the larger aircraft, the *North American B-25 Mitchell* and the *Martin B-26 Marauder* twin-engined medium bombers were used by the U.S.A.A.F. in all theatres, and by the R.A.F. The *Mitchell*, appropriately named after General "Billy" Mitchell who had campaigned so ardently in support of American air power in the 1920s, leapt into world headlines with the astonishingly courageous attack on Japanese home targets on 18th April 1942, only four months after the Japanese attack at Pearl Harbor. Undertaken as a much-needed boost for American morale among all the appalling defeats being suffered almost daily at that time, sixteen *Mitchells*, led by that indomitable firebrand, Lt.-Col. Jimmy Doolittle, took off from the deck of the carrier, U.S.S. *Hornet* (itself an outstanding feat), steaming 800 miles from the Japanese mainland, and carried out a daring attack on targets in and around the capital, all but one of the bombers crashing in China or Chinese waters. Most of the crews survived and Doolittle was promptly awarded the Medal of Honor and promoted Brigadier General for his part in this display of American defiance.

The *Mitchell* was much developed and improved during the War years and a total of 9,792 was built before the Japanese surrender in 1945. Production continued until 1954, by which year a further 894 had been built. It was not withdrawn from the U.S.A.F. until 1959.

The *Martin B-26 Marauder* was of much the same concept as the *Mitchell*, although slightly faster, heavier and eventually capable of carrying a heavier bombload. It did however possess a much higher wing-loading and this led to some unpopularity for it was undoubtedly a tricky aeroplane to land. It was a very robust aircraft and, although originally classed as a light bomber, it eventually carried bombloads of up to 4,000 pounds – almost half that of the *B-24 Liberator* heavy bomber. It also equipped five squadrons of the R.A.F. and five in the South African Air Force.

We come now to the most famous of all American war-planes, that most famous duet that was the *Boeing B-17 Flying Fortress* and the *Consolidated B-24 Liberator* heavy bombers. The story of the *B-17* dates from 1934 when, without any Government backing, the Boeing Airplane Company initiated the design of a four-engined, heavily-armed heavy bomber, designated the Model 299. With a registered trade name of *Flying Fortress*, the prototype flew in July 1935 (before even the *Hurricane, Spitfire* and *Bf 109*) and, with Air Corps support forthcoming in 1936, entered production and was first delivered to the Air Corp's 2nd Bombardment Group in 1937. It thus was unquestionably the world's foremost heavy bomber long before the Second World War, yet fewer than 150 *Y1B-17s, B-17Bs, Cs* and *Ds* had been

delivered by the time of the Japanese attack of December 1941. The R.A.F. had, in an attempt to increase the weight of its bombing strength, ordered twenty *B-17Cs* and these equipped No. 90 Squadron, making 22 raids over Northern Europe from high altitude. Because of incorrect bombing techniques, the Squadron suffered heavy casualties, and these, together with difficulties with the Norden bomb-sight and numerous engine failures, led to withdrawal of the *Fortress* from R.A.F. Bomber Command.

Entry of America into the War led to a quickening development of the *B-17E* which reached U.S.A.A.F. bomber squadrons early in 1942. Powered by four 1,200-h.p. Wright Cyclone GR-1820-65 turbo-supercharged radial engines, armed with twelve 0·5-inch machine-guns and crewed by twelve men, the *B-17E* could carry up to 17,600 pounds of bombs over short ranges, or 4,000 pounds over 2,000 miles, and had a top speed of 317 m.p.h. at 25,000 feet. Twelve such aircraft of the 97th Bombardment Group made the U.S.A.A.F.'s first raid in Europe on 17th August 1942 with an attack on Rouen, France.

Increasing experience in combat led progressively to the *B-17F* and *B-17G* (with increased armour, armament and other alterations), and by the end of the War no fewer than 12,731 *Flying Fortresses* had been built. To those who saw them, the spectacles provided by massed formations of "Forts" flying out on raids over Europe will never be forgotten; nor will the tremendous air battles with massed German fighters ever be forgotten by the thousands of American airmen who fought their big bombers through the upper skies to reach their targets deep inside enemy territory in 1943-45.

Although never quite capable of firing the public's imagination as did the *B-17*, the *Consolidated B-24 Liberator* was built in greater numbers than any other American aircraft during the Second World War, the extraordinary total of 18,279 being built at a cost of $4,320,000,000, at five vast factories in California, Texas, Michigan and Oklahoma. Development of the *Liberator* was much more spectacular than that of the *B-17*, for the *XB-24* prototype flew on 29th December 1939, less than one year after the initial design had been started. Production aircraft were on the point of entering service when Japan attacked, and delivery rates were rapidly increased in 1942, Bombardment Groups in the Pacific theatre, India, the Middle East and Britain being deployed during that year. They performed many more daylight raiding sorties than those by the *B-17*, perhaps their most famous attack being that at low level on the Ploesti oil complex on 1st August 1943. In this raid by 177 *Liberators* of the 98th and 376th Bombardment Groups, involving a round-trip of 2,700 miles from Benghazi, Libya, resulted in the loss of 57 aircraft and the award of no fewer than five Congressional Medals of Honor.

At about the same time that the prototype *Liberator*

THE HAWKER SIDDELEY HARRIER. Stemming from widespread efforts during the 1950s to achieve vertical take-off by fixed-wing aircraft, the Harrier originated in the private venture P.1127 which first lifted-off in 1960. Numerous significant "firsts" were achieved by the P.1127 (and the service evaluation Kestrel version), and the Harrier entered R.A.F. service as the world's first operational vertical take-off fighter in April 1969. The aircraft shown above is the AV-8A supplied to the U.S. Marine Corps. (*Photo: By courtesy of Hawker Siddeley Aviation Ltd.*)

THE GRUMMAN F-14 TOMCAT. Although marred by the loss of the first prototype in an accident in December 1970, the Tomcat swing-wing naval fighter is scheduled to join U.S. Navy squadrons in 1973. Spurred by the apparent superiority of Russian in-service fighters – such as the MiG-25 – the two-seat Tomcat has a Mach 2+ capability, powered by two TF-30 turbofans, and will perform numerous alternative mission duties with mixed gun and missile armament, or reconnaissance equipment. (*Photo: By courtesy of the Grumman Aerospace Corporation*)

was passing through its final assembly stages, General "Hap" Arnold, Chief of the U.S. Army Air Corps, recommended that work should be started in America on a new super-bomber with a 2,000-mile radius of action. This was sanctioned on 2nd December 1939 and ultimately led to the development of the *Boeing B-29 Superfortress*. Only America, with her vast industrial resources committed to war production, could have undertaken such a project. The first *XB-29* was flown by Edward Allen on 21st September 1942 and the first true production aircraft were delivered just a year later. None were flown against European targets, and the entire combat strength of *Superfortresses* was pitted against the Japanese. A total of 3,987 was built.

By current standards they were indeed super-bombers, with a range of 4,200 miles, able to lift 20,000 pounds over lesser ranges and possessing a top speed of about 360 m.p.h. From 5th June 1944, when they first went into action against the Japanese, until VJ-Day, the *B-29s* of the 20th and 21st Bomber Commands set about an offensive which, in terms of destruction, has only ever been matched by that of R.A.F. Bomber Command. The tremendous fire raids on Tokyo and other Japanese cities culminated when two *Superfortresses*, christened *"Enola Gay"* and *"Bock's Car"* dropped the two atomic bombs, "Little Boy" and "Fat Boy" on Hiroshima and Nagasaki, thereby demonstrating the horror of nuclear war – but bringing to an end a World War that had already cost the lives of more than fifty million people.

PEACE AND THE JET ERA

The Second World War had been fought in the air almost entirely by aeroplanes powered by piston engines, yet four days before Germany marched into Poland she achieved the world's first flight with an aeroplane powered by a jet engine. On 27th August 1939, in conditions of the utmost secrecy, Flugkapitän Erich Warsitz first flew the *Heinkel He 178V1*, powered by a single Heinkel HeS 3B turbojet, from Marienehe in Germany.

Unbeknown to their enemies, both Britain and Germany had for some years been working on gas turbines for aircraft; in Britain, Frank Whittle had reached the bench-running stage of his first engine, and a development of this first flew in the little *Gloster E.28/39* research aircraft on 15th May 1941, but the lead achieved by Germany had become almost unassailable and a twin-engine jet fighter prototype, the *Heinkel He 280V1*, had already flown on 2nd April that year. The *He 280* did not however achieve success, and it was the *Messerschmitt Me 262* (first flown under jet power on 18th July 1942) that narrowly achieved combat status first. The first operational combat unit equipped with the *Me 262* was *Erprobungskommando 262,* although this unit was also charged with service evaluation of the new aircraft. It was activated early in the summer of 1944, but in September

it was re-designated as a conventional combat unit as *Kommando Nowotny* – so named after its leader, Major Walter Nowotny, a young Austrian fighter ace who had already won the Knight's Cross with Oakleaves, Swords and Diamonds. The *Me 262*, although a tricky – some said dangerous – aircraft to fly, was so far ahead of other fighter designs (with a top speed of about 540 m.p.h. and an armament of four 30-mm. cannon) that there were occasions when its depredations among American daylight bomber formations undoubtedly lessened their operations and, had not Hitler personally intervened to insist that they be diverted to other duties, an all-out defence effort by *Me 262*-equipped squadrons might well have brought the daylight raids to a halt.

The R.A.F. had, however, managed to introduce their first jet fighter, the *Gloster Meteor*, into squadron service, the first aircraft going into action against the flying bombs with No. 616 Squadron on 27th July 1944. Powered by two 1,700-pound static thrust Rolls-Royce Welland turbojets, the *Meteor I* had a top speed of about 480 m.p.h. at 30,000 feet and 420 m.p.h. at sea level, and was armed with four 20-mm. Hispano cannons. The *Meteor III* soon followed with a substantially improved performance, and small numbers of these fighters went to the Continent with Nos. 504 and 616 Squadrons just before the end of the War in Europe where they carried out a number of sweeps. Alas for the analysts, there was never recorded a confrontation between British and German jet fighters.

The *Meteor* was to become an important aircraft in the R.A.F., for later versions remained in front-line service until 1957. Perhaps its greatest peacetime claim to fame was the setting up of two world speed records in 1945 and 1946 at 606 m.p.h. and 616 m.p.h. respectively. It was also the world's first aeroplane to fly with propjets – turbojets geared to drive propellers – with the first flight by an experimental version on 20th September 1945 powered by two Rolls-Royce Trent engines. The *Meteor* was also developed into a two-seat trainer and night fighter, and was widely exported during the nine years following the Second World War.

America was slow off the mark with jet aircraft, and her first such aircraft, the *Bell XP-59A*, did not fly until 2nd October 1942. This aircraft, though conceived as a fighter, was disappointing and was relegated to training duties for the pilots of the *Lockheed P-80A Shooting Star*, whose first prototype flew on 9th January 1944.

Continuation of the *Meteor's* service so long after the Second World War reflected the British Government's parsimonious attitude towards its armed forces, so much so that when United Nations forces were called to resist aggression by North Korea the Royal Air Force was unable to contribute any up-to-date aircraft, such pilots who served in that War being seconded to fly with the U.S. Air Force. Between 1946 and 1950 quite inadequate support was given in Britain to research and development, just as it had been lacking during the years after the First World War, and Britain's technological lead over the rest of the world simply evaporated – despite strong denials to the contrary at the time. Engine development continued (albeit almost entirely at private expense), so that British engines at least were in some demand overseas.

While the *Meteor* and *Vampire* struggled on in service (and, it must be said, enjoyed considerable export success among the world's smaller air forces), the *Lockheed Shooting Star* continued to serve in the U.S.A.F. and fought in the Korean War which broke out in 1950. But, benefiting from the aerodynamic advances made by the wartime *Messerschmitt Me 262* – whose detailed technical analyses were made available in America – a brilliant design team at North America under A. F. Weissenberger and Art Patch evolved the *F-86 Sabre*. The prototype was flown by George Welch on 1st October 1947 and within seven months this aircraft was dived at supersonic speed. The *Sabre* entered service with the 94th Fighter Squadron (the famous "Hat in the Ring" squadron) in February 1949 and within two years other squadrons were being deployed throughout the world.

There had been no immediate intention to send *Sabres* to Korea when war broke out, but the appearance of the Russian *MiG-15* which, in the early months, demonstrated a clear superiority over all other U.N. aircraft including the *F-80 Shooting Star*, required that the balance be restored, and by the end of 1950 the first *F-86* Wing had been deployed in the war theatre.

The surprise presence of the *MiG-15* in Korea was the outcome of work, almost exactly in step with that in America, carried out in Russia with the assistance of German engineers. There is no doubt that the ill-advised export of Rolls-Royce jet engines to Russia in 1947 had done much to accelerate jet engine development in that country, with the result that the *MiG-15* was generally similar in performance to the *Sabre*. These, therefore, were the two classic fighters of the early 1950s. They represented the second generation of jet fighters of the early "transonic era", but were still wholly dependant upon a gun armament. Just as the *Sabre* came to be used by numerous overseas air forces – not least those of N.A.T.O. – so the *MiG-15* was widely exported among Communist-bloc nations, and both are still to be seen in their respective skies some twenty years later.

Britain's entries in this generation of fighters were to some extent reminiscent of the old *Hurricane* and *Spitfire* in that they came from the same parent companies, but there were two significant differences. This time, without the spur of national re-armament, instead of being front-runners of the generation, her aircraft were about six years in arrears when compared with those of America and Russia. And, although of no more than academic significance, it was to be the Hawker design that was to outlast that of Supermarine. The *Supermarine Swift* ran into serious problems at about the time it joined the R.A.F., and although these were to some extent over-

come fairly quickly the service life of the aircraft was short, and after relegation to tactical reconnaissance it had all but disappeared within four years.

Sydney Camm's *Hawker Hunter* was more fortunate for, although it also suffered early troubles (in that gun firing at high altitude caused engine surging and flame-out) and had a marginally lower performance than the *Swift*, it quickly won substantial British and N.A.T.O. support and remained in front-line service for more than fifteen years. Apart from being a particularly attractive design and a "pilot's aircraft", it possessed a transonic performance and a heavy gun armament of four 30-mm. Aden cannon – an armament only hitherto matched in service by the wartime *Messerschmitt Me 262*. The *Hunter*, with its long-run production (about 2,000 were built), attracted numerous customers and it eventually served with the air forces of Abu Dhabi, Belgium, Chile, Denmark, Holland, India, Iraq, Jordan, Kuwait, Lebanon, Peru, Qatar, Rhodesia, Saudi Arabia, Singapore, Sweden and Switzerland, as well as the Royal Air Force and Fleet Air Arm.

For all its undoubted commercial success – which may indeed continue for some years yet to come – the *Hunter* was an anachronism soon after it appeared as an interceptor. With direct involvement in Korea to lend urgency to continuous development of military aircraft, America embarked on her "Century-series" interceptors, a generation which was scarcely equalled for ten years between 1953 and 1963.

The series started with the *North American F-100 Super Sabre*, a fully-supersonic development of the *F-86* and which first reached the 479th Fighter Day Wing of the U.S.A.F. in November 1953. Armed with four Pontiac 20-mm. cannon, this imposing fighter established the world's first supersonic speed record on 20th August 1955, and, with continuous development, remained in combat service with the U.S.A.F. until July 1971.

The *McDonnell F-101 Voodoo* was characterised by very long range capability (2,800 miles) and, with other excellent interceptor designs in being, it was assigned to tactical reconnaissance. With a maximum speed of 1,220 m.p.h. it was for ten years the fastest such aircraft in the world.

The *Convair F-102 Delta Dart* and its development, the *F-106 Delta Dagger*, were advanced weapon systems – the term applied to describe a wholly-integrated system of locating, intercepting and destroying an enemy, the aircraft being only a vehicle within that system. Whereas the *F-102* was capable of marginally supersonic flight, the *F-106* was a true Mach 2 aircraft, and both have been deployed for fifteen years as the principal manned-fighter defence force in the U.S.A., armed with sophisticated air-to-air guided missiles.

The *Lockheed F-104 Starfighter* was the most spectacular of all the "Century-series" aircraft. Dubbed the "manned missile", this Mach 2 interceptor was designed as a compact, gun- and missile-armed aircraft which

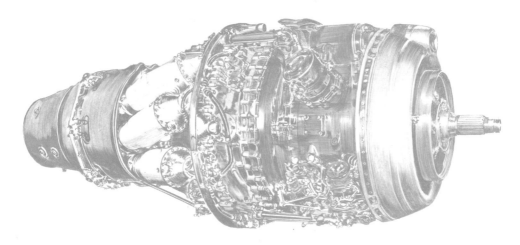

Although design of the classic Rolls-Royce Dart turbo-prop engine began in 1945 and first entered service in the Vickers Viscount in 1953, this engine has been progresively developed ever since and latest versions give over 3,000 e.h.p. Darts have been used in the Fokker Friendship, Hawker Siddeley Argosy, Handley Page Herald, Grumman Gulfstream, NAMC YS-11 and many other aircraft. Over 6,000 have been built

was destined for deployment with home-based and N.A.T.O. units of the U.S.A.F. It was Germany, however, anxious to reconstitute a powerful national defence air force, who negotiated licence rights to acquire the *F-104G Super Starfighter*, and this version was adopted as standard equipment for the N.A.T.O. components provided by Germany, Holland, Belgium, Italy and Greece, as well as being licence-built in Japan and Canada. The *Luftwaffe's F-104Gs* gained a certain notoriety in the mid-1960s due to a high accident rate in service; seen in retrospect, this was not so much a reflection upon the aircraft – rather that with something like a vacuum in her industry and air force, imposed for about seventeen years after the War, the nation possessed none of the sophisticated knowledge and training continuity so essential in the operation of an advanced aircraft such as the *Super Starfighter*.

Last of the "Century-series" aircraft to reach operational status was the *Republic F-105 Thunderchief*, a Mach 2 fighter-bomber; this impressive aeroplane joined the U.S.A.F. in May 1958 and later saw much service in the Vietnam War. Capable of lifting external bombloads of up to seven tons, the *F-105* was certainly an outstanding design; yet, suffering fairly heavy casualties in that unfortunate conflict, it proved in the face of stiff ground defences the vulnerability of single-engined tactical support aircraft – a lesson that may have lent weight to the U.S.A.F.'s determination to adopt the *McDonnell Douglas F-4 Phantom II* twin-engined shipboard tactical strike aircraft as standard land-based equipment.

Equipment of the U.S. Navy had been no more than equal to that of other naval air forces after the War until the mid-1950s, although the introduction of the *North American FJ-4B Fury* (a development of the *F-86 Sabre*) brought a limited nuclear-strike capability to the tactical units of the U.S. Navy's carrier-based forces. This advance was substantiated with the appearance of the *McDonnell F-4H Phantom II* in 1958. Of singularly unusual appearance, with its outboard wing dihedral, sharply anhedralled tailplane and drooping nose, the *Phantom* is a truly impressive aeroplane with a maximum speed well in excess of Mach 2, a phenomenal climb performance and a maximum bombload capacity of up to seven tons. Designated the *F-110*, the big fighter was ordered by the U.S.A.F. in 1962–63 and joined the *Thunderchief* on support operations in Vietnam. During the latter half of the 1960s several other air forces have decided to adopt the *Phantom* – it being clearly the most advanced in-service interceptor/tactical support fighter available in the West; among these air forces have been the British Fleet Air Arm, the Royal Air Force, the German *Luftwaffe*, and the air forces of Holland, Canada, Japan and several other nations.

While America has enjoyed superiority in fighter aircraft among Western nations during the past fifteen years, the aircraft industries of other nations have struggled to keep pace, although with only limited production requirements the resulting aircraft have tended to lag or otherwise to represent only limited answers to current tactical demands. The French *Dassault Mirage III* and the *British Aircraft Corporation Lightning* have enjoyed long careers in service both with the *Armée de l'Air* and the Royal Air Force. The *Mirage* has been introduced into a number of foreign services, including those of

Australia, Israel, South Africa and Switzerland.

American bombers have also dominated the post-War years, although the R.A.F. V-force, small though it was, flew aircraft that for ten years were undoubtedly advanced designs. After the War, R.A.F. Bomber Command equipped its heavy squadrons with a number of *Boeing B-29s* – named *Washingtons* – to supplement its *Avro Lincolns*, which were developed from the classic *Lancaster*. However it had been intended to re-equip all bomber squadrons with jet aircraft as early as possible, to replace the remaining *Mosquitos* and *Lincolns*, and the outcome of a 1945 Specification was the twin-jet *English Electric Canberra* which first flew on 13th May 1949. It entered R.A.F. squadron service in May 1951 and subsequent versions continued in service until the late 1960s – a period of service artificially lengthened by the government decision taken to abandon the controversial *British Aircraft Corporation TSR-2*.

The V-bombers, the *Vickers Valiant*, the *Avro Vulcan* and the *Handley Page Victor*, were, for their period, advanced designs – all strictly subsonic, but capable of development and great weightlifters. They were dogged by changing politics and strategic commitments – for instance, the abandoning of the *Skybolt* missile programme was a major setback, while the winding up of Handley Page undoubtedly shortened the life of the *Victor*. The *Vulcan* alone has survived in service for sixteen years and, equipped with the *Blue Steel* stand-off bomb, provided a minor component of the West's deterrent force.

The American bombers, though to some extent dogged by similar problems (the outcome of enormous costs), have certainly represented a formidable array of striking power. After the uncertainties of the late 1940s, the U.S. Air Force was charged with a policy of deterrence – the maintenance of a massive striking force of strategic bombers, widely based throughout the world, and later maintaining a proportion of these bombers in the air at all times by means of constant flight-refuelling.

The first such aircraft to constitute the inventory of the U.S. Strategic Air Command was the mammoth *Convair B-36* which was conceived long ago in 1941 and first flown on 8th September 1945. Deliveries of early aircraft, powered by six piston engines, commenced to S.A.C. in 1947 and were followed by the *B-36D*, powered by an additional four General Electric J47 turbojets mounted under the outer wings. Bombload of these huge aircraft was two 42,000-pound bombs and speed 439 m.p.h. A total of 375 was built before production ended on 14th August 1954, and S.A.C. retired its last *B-36* on 12th February 1959, thereafter becoming an all-jet force.

The first pure-jet strategic bomber of the U.S.A.F. was the six-jet *Boeing B-47 Stratojet* (although the four-jet *North American B-45 Tornado* was used by the Air Force as a strategic reconnaissance bomber in relatively small numbers). The *B-47* was an advanced design when it first flew in July 1948, employing a thin, swept wing, with six General Electric J47 turbojets mounted in pods.

With a crew of three it was capable of carrying up to 20,000 pounds of bombs over short distances – which could be extended by flight refuelling. A total of 2,041 *Stratojets* was built – the peak in-service strength of about 1,800 aircraft being achieved in 1957.

Finally among the great bombers there was the most impressive project of all – in terms of effort and aircraft striking power – the *Boeing B-52 Stratofortress*. In effect this was a scaled-up *B-47*, though of course a totally new design, the H-variant being powered by eight TF-33 turbofans each delivering 17,000 pounds thrust. At a gross take-off weight of 488,000 pounds, it was Strategic Air Command's principal weapon for fifteen years between 1957 and 1972; capable of lifting off the ground up to 80,000 pounds of conventional bombs over unlimited ranges (using flight refuelling), the *B-52H* was also the worldwide-based deterrent, armed with nuclear weapons. A total of 744 *Stratofortresses* was built between 1954 and 1962, and a force of about 150 participated in the Vietnam War culminating in the controversial attacks on targets in and around Hanoi in December 1972 – when at least 17 of these big aeroplanes were lost to Communist defences.

THE JET AIRLINERS

The introduction of the jet airliner to service in the early 1950s can, in retrospect, be seen as the peaceful emancipation of the aeroplane. For while piston-engined airliners had been in service for more than 25 years, their technology had generally been dictated by efforts in the military field – efforts that became total in the Second World War. After the War the aircraft and aero-engine designer was able to apply more attention to the commercial exploitation of their achievements, achievements that could perhaps be more imaginative than the interim generation of bomber developments such as the *Stratocruiser* and *Tudor* airliners which stemmed from the *Boeing B-29* and *Avro Lancaster/Lincoln* heavy bombers.

The *de Havilland Comet* four-jet airliner was the first attempt to produce a wholly new concept for air travel – fast, smooth and efficient. That it was at least five years ahead of its time no one could deny. But such was the great expanse of technology that there were areas which had not been adequately mastered when the first *Comet 1s* entered service in 1952 with B.O.A.C. It was a bold venture and had it succeeded there is little doubt that British commercial aviation might have held its lead for many years – such was the importance pinned on the *Comet*. Alas, structural fatigue and an inadequate knowledge of piloting techniques cost the loss of several *Comet 1s*. All the early aircraft were withdrawn from commercial service and a re-design undertaken; this delayed the eventual re-introduction to service for so long that, by the time the definitive *Comet 4* appeared, Boeings had introduced the classic *Model 707*.

Although B.O.A.C.'s *Comet 4* 60/81-seaters marginally

"won the race" to inaugurate a fast jet trans-Atlantic passenger service in October 1958, the *Boeing 707* 124/150-seat airliners were not far behind. Moreover, with almost 200 aircraft on the order books (including some for B.O.A.C.) scheduled for delivery by the end of 1960, it was clear that the American aircraft and air passenger industries had by then achieved an unassailable lead. During the past fifteen years the *Boeing 707* has emerged as the "DC-3 of the intercontinental routes", with more than 700 built and delivered to almost fifty world airlines.

The *Boeing 707* was soon joined by other large four-jet airliners, notably the *Douglas DC-8, Convair 880* and *990*, and the *British Aircraft Corporation VC-10* and *Super VC-10*. The American designs all achieved substantial support from world airlines, meeting a fairly broad spectrum of individual demands by permutations of range and accommodation adaptations, a design feature that has been particularly noticeable among American commercial projects, and much less so among British and other designs. An attempt to remedy this shortcoming was made in the excellent *VC-10* with the much "stretched" *Super VC-10*. This airliner, with its rear-mounted engines, has been a highly efficient vehicle, the most popular among passengers on the Atlantic routes, and there is no doubt that B.O.A.C. has profited considerably from its operation. But the *VC-10*, being introduced on these routes in 1954, was half a generation late, and by the time it could be offered to world airlines most of them were already committed to heavy expenditure elsewhere.

While the air travel industry has been growing enormously all over the world in the past fifteen years, there has been much speculation behind the scenes as how best to exploit the most profitable means of serving the travelling population. America, once again, was the first to identify the immediate answer, the introduction of a very high capacity jet airliner – the Jumbo Jet which would not involve a disruption of air traffic patterns, in that they would not be significantly faster than the existing *707s, DC-8s, 880s, 990s* and *VC-10s*. Runways need not be lengthened or strengthened, while passenger-handling facilities at airports would have to be increased in any case simply to cope with the heavier passenger traffic that was already foreshadowed. In other words, the *Boeing 747* has tended to fit into a pattern of world airline operation which – at great expense already involved – existed and was socially and economically acceptable.

The *Boeing 747* is a remarkable aircraft both in concept and achievement. It was, after all, only first announced on 13th April 1966, and was immediately supported by an order, worth \$525 million, for twenty-five aircraft for Pan American. The first of these was delivered late in 1969, and by the end of 1972 no fewer than 250 of these huge aeroplanes had been delivered or were on order. With accommodation for up to 500 passengers (and plans to increase this much further), the *747* now dominates the Atlantic routes, and there is no competitor in this field in sight for many years. Moreover, with an expenditure of billions of dollars committed to the purchase of these airliners – which seem capable of accommodating the likely passenger traffic for many years to come – it is difficult to see where another airliner could compete economically.

One therefore arrives at the one possible area in which competition may be offered. It can be argued that mankind has always looked for greater speed in transportation and, subject to an absence of annoyance to the community at large, there is no reason to believe that this quest has suddenly ended. Thus it was in the early 1960s that design teams of Britain and France, with government support, entered collaboration to produce a supersonic airliner – which was to emerge as the *British Aircraft Corporation/Aérospatiale Concorde*, designed to carry up to 144 passengers across the Atlantic and capable of a maximum speed of about Mach 2·3. (A very similar and parallel airliner concept is the Russian *Tupolev Tu-144*, which has continued an almost identical flight trial programme to that of the *Concorde*.) At one time sales options for 74 of these £20 million airliners were held by about 16 world airlines, although very recently (February 1973) a number of these options lapsed, and the economically-viable future of *Concorde* seems precarious. Nevertheless, it was not part of *Concorde's* operating concept to capture the bulk of intercontinental passenger traffic, it being intended purely to provide a very rapid service for a specific proportion of that traffic. There seems little doubt that, if and when B.O.A.C. and Air France (the only firm customers at the time of writing) introduce their prestigious service between America and Europe, perhaps in 1975, sufficient inroads can be made into the revenues of other airlines, those airlines (whose profits may have swelled by operation of the *Boeing 747*) may feel it necessary to opt once more for the *Concorde*. The danger lies, once again, in the delays of exploiting an excellent aeroplane. That the *Concorde* is a superb design surely cannot be denied, but too often in the past an excellent design has been offered at a time when the market does not want it, or cannot afford it. It remains only for the *Concorde* to prove that the biggest airlines cannot afford to be without it.

～ CHAPTER 5 ～
The World's Aircraft

The pages which follow present a chronological listing of some 300 important civil and military aircraft types, of all periods and nationalities. Each type is described in the briefest terms, and its major characteristics are indicated in a form of specification, to place it in its correct perspective in the history of aviation.

The criteria by which the compilers selected these aircraft were necessarily less than rigid. Some aircraft are unavoidable choices by reason of the great technical breakthroughs which they represented. Others had no particular claim to technical originality, but appeared so exactly at the right time, in the right class, at the right price that they sold in their thousands, and have become household words by their sheer ubiquity. The major combat types flown by the great powers during the World Wars must obviously be included; those two brief periods of global carnage saw swifter technical advance in the field of aviation than has occurred at any other time. Through the post-War explosion in civil aviation, there are other types which have become familiar sights to everyone in the civilised world, and which must be included if the list is to have any meaning. Again, the Cold War has tended to divide the world into camps, within which the Superpowers distribute military equipment from their own factories – and certain types have been scattered so widely that they have come to represent the ideologies of their respective blocs, rather than any narrow national identity. All in all, to use an imprecise but appropriate expression, these 300 aircraft are simply the types of which most people have heard. The purpose of this Chapter is to enable the reader to fit his perhaps patchy knowledge into a firm framework of time and place; and, by comparison of the performance of this aircraft with that, to trace the story of international competition in aircraft design down the years.

In each case the variant of the aircraft series selected

for specification in these pages is a major production variant. In a few cases, where an unusually adaptable design has been developed continuously over a number of years – to the extent that early and late models have little in common – then two separate specifications are included.

Each type is described in general terms – "Single-seat fighter", "Medium bomber" – and normally, but not invariably, in the terms in use at the time of its appearance. That a heavy bomber of 1918 was a good deal lighter than a strike-fighter of 1972 is no reason not to refer to it by its correct contemporary classification! The nationality of the type is indicated in a self-explanatory manner, but note should be taken that in the case of some aircraft which have been built under licence in a country other than that of the original design, the nationality of the constructor rather than the original designer is quoted. The date which follows each nationality is the date of *the introduction into service of the production machine*, not the date of the first prototype. Note also that this date refers to *the exact variant quoted* in the title, not the series as a whole.

The shortened specification gives dimensions in Imperial and metric units, rounded off to the nearest quarter-inch in the former case. If "biplane" or "triplane" is not specifically indicated, then the aircraft is a monoplane design. In the case of multi-wing designs, the wing span quoted is that of the upper wing. Armament calibres are quoted in the unit of the design nationality – in millimetres where indicated thus (two 7·92 mm MG) or in parts of the inch (four 0·303 MG). The suffix (MG) indicates a machine-gun firing solid or incendiary bullets; lack of suffix indicates a cannon, generally or capable of firing explosive ammunition.

The question of external war-load is complex and open to much misinterpretation. The much-abused description "fighter-bomber" has been used here with caution, and is only applied to machines designed from the outset to fulfill an important ground attack rôle. Experience has shown that virtually *any* aircraft can have bombs attached to its belly and wings in an emergency! The distinction between an interceptor-fighter and a fighter-bomber has become blurred almost to invisibility in these days of multi-mission strike aircraft. Again, the strong-points under an aircraft can be used to accommodate such a vast range of bomb-loads, rockets, rocket-pods, gun-packs, fuel and napalm tanks, and guided missiles that it would be quite impossible to quote here the various possible combinations, together with all the limiting factors. The compilers have restricted themselves to the barest indication of the total external load carried, without trying to qualify the figure. The heading "Maximum load" in the specifications refer to the internal maximum of a bomber; the sum of internal and external, of an aircraft which carries both; or the maximum external load of an aircraft limited to external stores. In some cases, where the aircraft's primary rôle was the achievement of air superiority although a small bomb-load could be carried at need, we have ignored the latter as unimportant.

The question of range is also vexed. The range of an aircraft is subject to so many limiting factors and qualifications – variables of bomb-load, internal and external fuel load, in-flight refuelling, altitude, speed maintained, statutory reserves at destination, and even weather – that the compilers have omitted this figure altogether; brief notes on range may be found in some of the entries, at the end of the rest of the specification.

Finally a brief summing-up of the aircraft's importance, success, reputation, degree of use, and so forth, is quoted. This may refer either to the actual variant named in the heading to the entry, or to the series as a whole.

The specifications include data under the following headings:
S: Wing span.
L: Overall fuselage length.
RD: Rotor diameter (on helicopters).
P: Powerplant, i.e. number, rating and type of engines. Jet power ratings are quoted in pounds of static thrust at sea level, "dry" – that is, without afterburning.
A: Armament, i.e. number and calibre of fixed guns and flexibly-mounted guns, with sometimes an indication of external war-load.
W: Normal loaded or maximum loaded take-off weight.
MS: Maximum level speed.
CS: Cruising speed.
OC: Operational ceiling.
ML: Maximum load (see remarks above).
C: Normal crew.

Wright Flyer I One-man experimental biplane, USA, 1903. *S*: 40 ft 4 in (12·34 m); *P*: 12 hp Wright; *W*: Approx. 820 lb (370 kg); *MS*: Approx. 30 mph (48 kph). *The first historic aeroplane in which Orville Wright made*

man's first powered, sustained and controlled flight on Thursday 17th December 1903 at Kill Devil Hills, near Kitty Hawk, North Carolina.

Maurice Farman M.F.7 Longhorn General duty biplane, Fr., 1913. *S*: 51ft 0 in (15·61 m); *L*: 37 ft 2¾ in (9·87 m); *P*: One 70 hp Renault; *W*: 1,885 lb (856 kg); *MS*: 59 mph (95 kph); *OC*: 12,000 ft (3600 m). *Although reflecting outdated design ideas, the Longhorn was typical of Allied aircraft during the first six months of the War; it was used by the RFC but quickly relegated to training duties.*

B.E.2a Two-seat general purpose military biplane, U.K., 1913. *S*: 38 ft 7½ in (11·77 m); *L*: 29 ft 6½ in (9·00 m); *P*: One 70 hp Renault; *W*: 1,600 lb (726 kg); *MS*: 70 mph. (113 kph); *OC*: 10,000 ft (3048 m). *The aircraft in which the RFC flew to France in 1914, and carried out reconnaissance sorties armed with pistols, rifles, hand-grenades and grappling-hooks.*

Avro 504K Two-seat biplane trainer, UK, 1914. *S*: 36 ft 0 in (11·02 m); *L*: 29 ft 5 in (9·06 m); *P*: One 100 hp Gnôme Monosoupape; *W*: 1,800 lb (817 kg); *MS*: 83 mph (133 kph); *OC*: 13,000 ft (3980 m). *A total of 8,340 of this classic trainer was built in Britain during the War; some were used operationally in the early War months for bombing by the RFC and RNAS. In post-War years they became popular sporting lightplanes.*

Fokker E.I Single-seat monoplane scout, Ger., 1915. *S*: 29 ft 3 in (8·91 m); *L*: 22 ft 1¾ in (6·75 m); *P*: One 80 hp Oberursel; *A*: One 7·92 mm MG; *W*: 1,239 lb (562 kg); *MS*: 81 mph (130 kph). *The E.I, E.II and E.III developments of Fokker's original M.5 prototype were the first true fighting scouts in the world; armed with synchronised forward-firing machine-gun and flown by pilots such as Oswald Boelcke and Max Immelmann, they all but swept the Allies from the skies of France between autumn and spring 1916.*

de Havilland D.H.2 Single-seat biplane scout, U.K., 1915. *S*: 28ft 3 in (8·61 m); *L*: 25 ft 2½ in (7·68 m); *P*: One 100 hp Gnôme Monosoupape; *A*: One 0·303 MG; *W*: 1,440 lb (653 kg); *MS*: 93 mph (150 kph); *OC*: 14,000 ft (4267 m). *Powered by a "pusher" engine, the D.H.2 contributed greatly to the defeat of the "Fokker Scourge" in 1915–16. It appeared in autumn 1915, but a year later was being hopelessly outfought by the new Albatros D.I and D.II.*

Martinsyde G.100 Elephant Single-seat biplane scout, U.K., 1916. *S*: 38 ft (11·58 m); *L*: 26 ft 6½ in (8·08 m); *P*: One 120 hp Beardmore; *A*: Two 0·303 MG; *W*: 2,424 lb (1100 kg); *MS*: 95 mph (153 kph); *OC*: 14,000 ft (4267 m). *Not a true "fighter", the Elephant could carry up to 336 lb (152 kg) of bombs, and was used as an attack and general purpose type rather than a scout proper. It was a robust but rather undistinguished type, and only one RFC squadron was entirely equipped with Elephants.*

Sopwith Pup Single-seat biplane scout, U.K., 1916. *S*: 26 ft 6 in (8·07 m); *L*: 19 ft 3¾ in (5·88 m); *P*: One 80 hp

Le Rhône; A: One 0·303 MG; W: 1,225 lb (555 kg); MS: 111 mph (178 kph); OC: 17,500 ft (5334 m). *The first realistic tractor-engined single-seat fighting scout in RFC and RNAS service; known for its delightful handling qualities.*

Roland C.II Two-seat biplane reconnaissance aircraft, Ger., 1916. S: 33 ft 10¾ in (10·33 m); L: 24 ft 8¼ in (7·52 m); P: One 160 hp Mercedes D.III; A: Two 7·92 mm MG; W: 2,886 lb (1309 kg); MS: 102 mph (165 kph). *Speed and climb characteristics of the magnificently streamlined C.II were comparable with the Allied single-seat scouts sent up against them. A weakness, both in action and normal flying, was very restricted downward visibility.*

Sopwith 1½-Strutter Two-seat biplane scout, U.K., 1916. S: 33 ft 6 in (10·21 m); L: 25 ft 3 in (7·69 m); P: One 110 hp Le Rhône 9J; A: Two 0·303 MG; W: 2,205 lb (1000 kg); MS: 103 mph (166 kph); OC: 16,000 ft (4877 m). *Widely developed and exported aircraft, saw RFC and RNAS service as single-seater, two-seater, fighter, and bomber, and was licence-built in several countries after the War.*

Nieuport 17 Single-seat biplane scout, Fr., 1916. S: 26 ft (7·92 m); L: 19 ft 7 in (5·96 m); P: One 113 hp Le Rhône; A: One 0·303 MG; W: 1,232 lb (558 kg); MS: 107 mph (172 kph); OC: 17,500 ft (5334 m). *When introduced early in 1916 the N.17 was the fastest and deadliest scout at the Front. It did much to reverse the German success gained by the Fokkers in 1915-16, was used by many Allied aces, and saw service with all Allied air arms.*

SPAD S.VII Single-seat biplane scout, Fr., 1916. S: 25 ft 7 in (7·79 m); L: 20 ft 4 in (6·19 m); P: One 180 hp Hispano-Suiza 8Ab; A: One 7·65 mm *or* 0·303 MG, *or* two 0·303 MG, W: 1,553 lb (704 kg); MS: 132 mph (212 kph); OC: 21,500 ft (6553 m). *Major French scout type, widely used by Allied air forces, later developed into SPAD S.XIII with even greater success.*

R.E.8 Two-seat biplane reconnaissance bomber, U.K., 1917. S: 42 ft 7 in (12·97 m); L: 27 ft 10½ in (8·49 m); P: One 140 hp RAF 4a; A: Two 0·303 MG; W: 2,870 lb (1302 kg); MS: 102 mph (164 kph); OC: 13,500 ft (4115 m); ML: 225 lb (102 kg). *The most numerous and important British two-seat reconnaissance type of the War, serving from the beginning of 1917 until the Armistice.*

Albatros D.III Single-seat biplane scout, Ger., 1917. S: 29 ft 8¼ in (9·05 m); L: 24 ft ½ in (7·33 m); P: One 160 hp Mercedes D.III; A: Two 7·92 mm MG; W: 1,949 lb (886 kg); MS: 103 mph (165 kph); OC: 16,400 ft (5000 m). *One of the major German fighter types, entered service with Jagdstaffeln early spring 1917, and largely responsible for heavy Allied losses of "Bloody April". Flown with success by all major German aces of the day.*

Pfalz D.III Single-seat biplane scout, Ger., 1917. S: 30 ft 10 in (9·40 m); L: 27 ft 9¾ in (6·95 m); P: One 160 hp Mercedes D.III; A: Two 7·92 mm MG; W: 1,903 lb (865 kg); MS: 103 mph (165 kph). *Contemporary of the*

Albatros D.III and D.V *with the Jagdstaffeln in 1917; not as widely used as those designs, and apart from excellent dive characteristics, not as successful.*

Sopwith Triplane Single-seat triplane scout, U.K., 1917. S: 26 ft 6 in (8·07 m); L: 18 ft 10 in (5·74 m); P: One 110 hp Clerget 9Z; A: One 0·303 MG; W: 1,450 lb (658 kg); MS: 116 mph (187 kph). *Despite its brief career – serving with RNAS units only, in the spring and early summer of 1917 – the Sopwith Triplane made a great impression and directly inspired the design of the Fokker Dr. I. Fast-climbing and manoeuvrable, it easily outflew the Albatros D.V.*

Bréguet 14B2 Two-seat biplane reconnaissance bomber, Fr., 1917. S: 47 ft 1¼ in (14·36 m); L: 29 ft 1¼ in (8·87 m); P: One 300 hp Renault 12F; A: Three or four 0·303 MG; W: 3,892 lb (1765 kg); MS: 110 mph (177 kph); OC: 19,000 ft (5791 m); ML: 555 lb (256 kg). *Classic general purpose type, served with more than 90 French squadrons and with Belgian, American, Czech, Polish and civilian operators in post-War years.*

Hanriot HD-1 Single-seat biplane scout, Fr., 1917. S: 28 ft 6½ in (8·69 m); L: 19 ft 1¾ in (5·83 m); P: One 110 hp Le Rhône 9J; A: One 0·303 MG; W: 1,360 lb (617 kg); MS: c. 110 mph (177 kph); OC: 20,500 ft (6248 m). *Almost ignored in France, the HD-1 was widely used by Italian and Belgian squadrons; it was popular and reliable, and its performance was comparable to that of the Nieuport 17.*

Sopwith Camel F.1 Single-seat biplane scout, U.K., 1917. S: 28 ft (8·53 m); L: 18 ft 9 in (5·72 m); P: One 130 hp Clerget 9B; A: Two 0·303 MG; W: 1,453 lb (659 kg); MS: 113 mph (181 kph); OC: 19,000 ft (5791 m). *Standard RFC and RAF fighter from mid-1917 to Armistice, the very manoeuvrable Camel was a match for any enemy at medium altitudes. It was also used extensively for ground-attack missions.*

de Havilland D.H.4 Two-seat biplane reconnaissance bomber, U.K., 1917. S: 42 ft 4½ in (12·91 m); L: 30 ft 8 in (9·34 m); P: One 230 hp Siddeley Puma; A: Two 0·303 MG; W: 3,610 lb (1637 kg); MS: 106 mph (170 kph); OC: 13,500 ft (3978 m); ML: 448 lb (203 kg). *Reliable and widely used general purpose two-seater.*

Ansaldo S.V.A.5 Single-seat biplane scout, It., 1917. S: 29 ft 10¼ in (9·09 m); L: 26 ft 7 in (8·10 m); P: One 205 hp SPA 6A; A: Two 0·303 MG; W: 1,995 lb (905 kg); MS: 143 mph (230 kph). *Faster and with longer range than any other aircraft on the Italian Front in 1917, the S.V.A. series were widely used as reconnaissance fighters, and, post-War, as mail aircraft.*

Ö. Aviatik (Berg) D.I Single-seat biplane scout, Aust. Hung., 1917. S: 26 ft 3 in (8·00 m); L: 22 ft 9½ in (6·95 m); P: One 200 hp Austro-Daimler; A: Two 8 mm MG; W: 1,878 lb (852 kg); MS: 115 mph (185 kph); OC: 20,170 ft (6148 m). *Though plagued by overheating and gun troubles, the first indigenous Austro-Hungarian fighter was a sound design which handled well; it was popular with*

The Sopwith Triplane, as used by the Royal Naval Air Service in France during 1917

pilots, and saw widespread action on the Italian Front.

Fokker Dr. I Single-seat triplane scout, Ger., 1917. *S*: 23 ft 7 in (7·19 m); *L*: 18 ft 11 in (5·77 m); *P*: One 110 hp Le Rhône; *A*: Two 7·92 mm MG; *W*: 1,290 lb (585 kg); *MS*: 102 mph (164 kph); *OC*: 20,000 ft (6096 m). *Manoeuvrable and fast-climbing, the Dr. I was used with great success in 1917 but was outdated by 1918. Its most famous exponent was Manfred von Richthofen.*

S.E.5a Single-seat biplane scout, U.K., 1917. *S*: 26 ft 7½ in (8·11 m); *L*: 20 ft 11 in (6·36 m); *P*: One 200 hp Hispano-Suiza or Wolseley; *A*: Two 0·303 MG; *W*: 1,940 lb (880 kg); *MS*: 120 mph (193 kph); *OC*: 19,500 ft (5943 m). *Efficient and reliable fighter widely used by RFC in 1917-18, and a match for contemporary German equipment.*

Bristol Fighter F.2B Two-seat biplane fighter, U.K., 1917. *S*: 39 ft 3 in (11·96 m); *L*: 25 ft 10 in (7·87 m); *P*: One 275 hp Rolls-Royce Falcon III; *A*: Two 0·303 MG; *W*: 2,780 lb (1261 kg); *MS*: 119 mph (191 kph); *OC*: 20,000 ft (6096 m). *Very successful design widely used by RFC, RAF and Commonwealth air forces during and after War; able to dog-fight with single-seat contemporaries on realistic terms.*

Gotha G.IV Biplane heavy bomber, Ger., 1917. *S*: 77 ft 9 in (23·70 m); *L*: 40 ft 0 in (12·2 m); *P*: Two 260 hp Mercedes D.IVa; *A*: Three 7·92 mm MG; *W*: 8,042 lb (3648 kg); *C*: Three; *MS*: 84 mph (135 kph); *OC*: 16,400 ft (5000 m); *ML*: 660 lb (300 kg). *With the Staaken "Giants", the aircraft used for the first systematic bomber aeroplane raids on Britain in 1917-18.*

Curtiss JN-4D Two-seat biplane trainer and general duties aircraft, USA, 1917. *S*: 43 ft 7¼ in (13·29 m); *L*: 27 ft 4 in (8·33 m); *P*: One 90 hp Curtiss OX-5; *W*: 2,130 lb (966 kg); *MS*: 75 mph (120 kph); *OC*: 11,000 ft (3352 m). *The "Jenny" was used in great numbers during and after the War as a trainer, and hundreds of surplus machines were sold cheaply to clubs, air circuses, etc.*

Phönix D.II Single-seat biplane scout, Aust. Hung., 1918. *S*: 32 ft 2 in (9·8 m); *L*: 21 ft 7½ in (6·618 m); *P*: One 200 hp Hiero; *A*: Two 7·92 mm MG; *W*: 1,775 lb (805 kg); *MS*: 112 mph (185 kph); *OC*: 19,685 ft (6000 m). *Fast-climbing Austro-Hungarian scout which was notably successful on the Italian Front in the last months of the War, although only built in very short production runs.*

Fokker D.VII Single-seat biplane scout, Ger., 1918. *S*: 29 ft 3½ in (8·9 m); *L*: 22 ft 11½ in (6·95 m); *P*: One 160 hp Mercedes D.III; *A*: Two 7·92 mm MG; *W*: 2,112 lb (960 kg); *MS*: 118 mph (189 kph); *OC*: 22,000 ft (6706 m). *Magnificent fighter, particularly successful at high altitude, and the most formidable equipment generally available to the Jagdstaffeln before the Armistice of 1918.*

Sopwith 7F 1 Snipe Single-seat biplane scout, UK, 1918. *S*: 30 ft 0 in (9·14 m); *L*: 19 ft 10 in (6·04 m); *P*: One 230 hp Bentley B.R.2; *A*: Two 0·303 MG; *W*: 2,020 lb (916 kg); *MS*: 119 mph (191 kph); *OC*: 20,000 ft (6096 m). *Small numbers served at the Front in the last months of the War; with electrical heating, oxygen, pilot armour, etc., they demonstrated how far design had progressed since 1914. Many served on after 1918, and as late as 1926 Snipes were on active service in the Middle East.*

Nieuport N.28C-1 Single-seat biplane scout, Fr., 1918. *S*: 26 ft 3 in (8·00 m); *L*: 20 ft 4 in (6·19 m); *P*: One 165 hp Gnôme 9N; *A*: Two 0·303 MG; *W*: 1,625 lb (737 kg); *MS*: 122 mph (196 kph); *OC*: 17,000 (5182 m). *Not the most impressive of the Nieuport fighters, the N.28 is chiefly remembered as the type with which the American Expeditionary Force squadrons made their combat debut in 1918 – for lack of sufficient SPAD S.XIIIs.*

Handley Page 0/400 Heavy bomber, UK, 1918. *S*: 100 ft (30·48 m); *L*: 62 ft 10¼ in (19·16 m); *P*: Two 360 hp Rolls-Royce Eagle VIII; *A*: Five 0·303 MG; *W*: 13,360 lb (6060 kg); *C*: Three; *MS*: 97·5 mph (157 kph); *OC*: 8,500 ft (2591 m); *ML*: 1,792 lb (813 kg). *First generation RAF strategic bomber, pioneer of mass raids on German industrial targets.*

Sopwith Dolphin I Single-seat biplane scout, UK, 1918. *S*: 32 ft 6 in (9·91 m); *L*: 22 ft 3 in (6·78 m); *P*: One 200 hp Hispano-Suiza; *A*: Three or four 0·303 MG; *W*: 2,008 lb (911 kg); *MS*: 115 mph (185 kph); *OC*: 18,500 ft (5639 m). *Manoeuvrable and heavily-armed type, with good high altitude performance, flown by four RFC squadrons in 1918; chiefly recognizable by negative-stagger wings.*

de Havilland D.H.9 Two-seat reconnaissance bomber, UK, 1918. *S*: 42 ft 4½ in (12·91 m); *L*: 30 ft 6 in (9·29 m); *P*: One 230 hp Siddeley Puma; *A*: Two 0·303 MG; *W*: 3,669 lb (1664 kg); *MS*: 111 mph (187·6 kph); *OC*: 16,000 ft (4877 m); *ML*: 460 lb (209 kg). *Although handicapped by poor performance at operating altitudes and indifferent pilot visibility for reconnaissance, the D.H.9 had widespread surplus sales and was used by civilian and military operators all over the world in the 1920s.*

Siemens-Schuckert D.III Single-seat biplane scout, Ger., 1918. *S*: 27 ft 8 in (8·43 m); *L*: 18 ft 8½ in (5·7 m); *P*: One 160 hp Siemens Halske Sh III; *A*: Two 7·92 mm MG; *W*: 1,595 lb (725 kg); *MS*: 112·5 mph (180 kph); *OC*: 26,250 ft (8000 m). *Small numbers of the S.S. D.III and D.IV reached a few squadrons before the Armistice; they were superior in high-altitude characteristics to all contemporaries, and capable of remarkable climbing performances – the standard D.III reached 13,000 ft in 9 minutes.*

de Havilland D.H.10 Three-seat biplane bomber, UK, 1918. *S*: 65 ft 6 in (19·96 m); *L*: 39 ft 7½ in (12·07 m); *P*: Two 395 hp Liberty 12; *A*: Two-four 0·303 MG; *W*: 9,000 lb (4082 kg); *MS*: 113·5 mph (183 kph); *OC*: 15,000 ft (4572 m); *ML*: 1,380 lb (626 kg). *Engine delays caused the D.H.10 to miss the War; it was used in India and the Middle East on a variety of duties in the early 1920s.*

Vickers Vimy Biplane heavy bomber, UK, 1918. *S*: 68 ft 0 in (20·72 m); *L*: 43 ft 6½ in (13·25 m); *P*: Two 360 hp Rolls-Royce Eagle VIII; *A*: Four 0·303 MG; *W*: 12,500 lb (5669 kg); *C*: Three; *MS*: 103 mph (165 kph); *OC*: 7,000 ft (2133 m); *ML*: 4,000 lb (1814 kg). *Too late for war service, the Vimy was used for several pioneer long-distance flights, and much experimental work by the RAF.*

Junkers-F13 Six-seat light passenger aircraft/mailplane, Ger., 1920. *S*: 58 ft 2¾ in (17·75 m); *L*: 31 ft 6 in (9·60 m); *P*: One 185 hp BMW IIIa; *W*: 3,814 lb (1730 kg); *CS*: 87 mph (140 kph); *OC*: 13,120 ft (4000 m). *Civil status saved the F 13 from being axed by Armistice controls and the all-metal monoplane was an important milestone in aircraft design. Over 300 were built between 1919 and 1932, serving throughout the world.*

Farman Goliath 14/16-passenger biplane airliner, Fr., 1920. *S*: 86 ft 10 in (26·50 m); *L*: 47 ft 0 in (14·33 m); *P*: Two 300 hp Salmson CM.9; *W*: 10,515 lb (2500 kg); *CS*: 74·5 mph (120 kph); *OC*: 13,120 ft (4000 m). *France's first important post-war airliner which inaugurated several north European inter-capital routes. It flew with French, Czech and Belgian air lines.*

Fairey Flycatcher Single-seat carrier fighter, UK, 1923. *S*: 29 ft 0 in (8·83 m); *L*: 23 ft 0 in (7·01 m); *P*: One 400 hp Armstrong Siddeley Jaguar; *A*: Two 0·303 MG; *W*: 2,979 lb (1351 kg); *MS*: 133 mph (214 kph); *OC*: 19,000 ft (5791 m). *First fighter specifically designed for Fleet Air Arm carriers; reliable and popular, it served from 1923 until the early 1930s.*

Fokker C.VD Two-seat biplane reconnaissance aircraft, Hol., 1925. *S*: 41 ft 1 in (12·5 m); *L*: 31 ft 3 in (9·53 m); *P*: One 520 hp Hispano-Suiza; *A*: Two-four 7·92 mm MG; *W*: 4,222 lb (1915 kg); 140 mph (225 kph); *OC*: 22,966 ft (7,000 m). *The capacity to take several interchangeable powerplants and sets of wings gave the C.V great flexibility of rôle and performance. Fighter, recce and bomber versions were exported to many countries between the Wars, and licence production was widespread. C.Vs saw action early in the Second World War in Dutch, Norwegian and Hungarian colours.*

Junkers G24 9-seat passenger airliner, Ger., 1925. *S*: 98 ft 1 in (29·9 m); *L*: 51 ft 6 in (15·7 m); *P*: Three 280/310 hp Junkers L5; *W*: 14,330 lb (6500 kg); *CS*: 113 mph (182 kph); *OC*: 15,420 ft (4700 m). *First widely-used member of the famous Junkers trimotor family, the G 24 flew with numerous air lines in Europe. About 60 were built.*

Fairey IIIF Biplane reconnaissance bomber/general duties aircraft, UK, 1926. *S*: 45 ft 9 in (13·94 m); *L*: 34 ft 4 in (10·46 m); *P*: One 570 hp Napier Lion XIA; *A*: Two 0·303 MG; *W*: 6,300 lb (2857 kg); *C*: Two or three; *MS*: 120 mph (193 kph). *Built in greater numbers than any other British military aircraft between 1918 and 1936, except the Hawker Hart variants, and used by both RAF and Fleet Air Arm for a wide range of duties.*

Supermarine S.5 Single-seat racing floatplane, UK, 1927. *S*: 26 ft 9 in (8·15 m); *L*: 24 ft 3½ in (7·40 m); *P*: One 875 hp Napier Lion; *W*: 3,242 lb (1470 kg); *MS*: 319 mph (513 kph). *Reginald Mitchell's 1927 Schneider Trophy winner, design forerunner of subsequent winner and ancestor of the Spitfire fighter.*

Fokker F.VIIb-3m 9/10-passenger trimotor airliner, Hol.,

1928. *S*: 71 ft 2¾ in (21·71 m); *L*: 47 ft 7 in (14·5 m); *P*: Three 300 hp Wright Whirlwind J6; *W*: 11,684 lb (5300 kg); *MS*: 130 mph (210 kph); *OC*: 14,435 ft (4400 m). *Classic high-wing trimotor airliner which first served KNILM in the Netherland East Indies and KLM, and was later exported to a dozen countries in the early 1930s.*

Bristol Bulldog IIA Single-seat biplane fighter, UK, 1929. *S*: 33 ft 10 in (10·85 m); *L*: 25 ft 2 in (7·67 m); *P*: One 490 hp Bristol Jupiter VIIF; *A*: Two 0·303 MG; *W*: 3,530 lb (1600 kg); *MS*: 178 mph (286 kph); *OC*: 29,300 ft (8930 m). *Major RAF interceptor in the early-to-mid-1930s.*

Ford 5AT-E 14-seat trimotor airliner, USA, 1929. *S*: 74 ft 0 in (24·05 m); *L*: 49 ft 10 in (16·38 m); *P*: Three 330 hp Wright Whirlwind; *W*: 10,130 lb (4599 kg); *MS*: 132 mph (212 kph); *OC*: 18,600 ft (6045 m). *Originating after Henry Ford acquired control of the Stout Metal Airplane Company, the famous family of all-metal Ford trimotors quickly gained an enviable reputation for ruggedness and reliability. Of similar design philosophy as Fokker and Junkers trimotors.*

Hawker Hart Two-seat biplane light bomber, UK, 1930. *S*: 37 ft 3 in (11·35 m), *L*: 29 ft 4 in (8·94 m); *P*: One 525 hp Rolls-Royce Kestrel; *A*: Two 0·303 MG; *W*: 4,554 lb (2065 kg); *MS*: 184 mph (296 kph); *OC*: 22,800 ft (6949 m); *ML*: 520 lb (235 kg). *Classic inter-War design, which on its introduction outperformed all contemporary fighters. It was widely exported both in its original form and in developed forms such as the Audax, Demon and Hind.*

Hawker Fury Single-seat biplane fighter, UK, 1930. *S*: 30 ft 0 in (9·14 m); *L*: 26 ft 8 in (8·12 m); *P*: One 525 hp Rolls-Royce Kestrel; *A*: Two 0·303 MG; *W*: 3,490 lb (1583 kg); *MS*: 207 mph (333 kph); *OC*: 26,000 ft (7925 m). *Not acquired in large numbers by the RAF, the Fury is chiefly remembered as the RAF's first 200-mph fighter and for the classic purity of its lines; it was widely exported.*

Curtiss P-6E Hawk Single-seat biplane fighter, USA, 1931. *S*: 31 ft 6 in (9·60 m); *L*: 23 ft 2 in (7·06 m); *P*: One 700 hp Curtiss V-1570; *A*: Two 0·303 MG; *W*: 2,760 lb (1251 kg); *MS*: 198 mph (318 kph); *OC*: 24,700 ft (7528 m). *Major USAAC pursuit aircraft series, whose variants were in production for more than 10 years.*

Handley Page H.P. 42 24/38-passenger biplane airliner, U.K. 1931. *S*: 130 ft 0 in (42·25 m); *L*: 89 ft 9 in (29·16 m); *P*: Four 550 hp Bristol Jupiter X or XI; *W*: 29,500 lb (13400 kg); *CS*: 100 mph (160 kph). *Majestic and economic airliners of Imperial Airways during the 1930s, the "Hannibal"-Class set new standards in comfort, quietness and cuisine in air travel – albeit at a stately speed of 100 mph.*

Boeing P-12E Single-seat fighter biplane, USA, 1931. *S*: 30 ft 0 in (9·14 m); *L*: 20 ft 3 in (6·16 m); *P*: One 500 hp Pratt & Whitney R-1340; *A*: Two 0·30 MG; *W*: 2,690 lb (1219 kg); *MS*: 190 mph (305 kph); *OC*: 26,300 ft (8616 m). *Definitive model of final major series of biplanes to serve with U.S. Army Pursuit units.*

Boeing F4B-4 Single-seat naval biplane fighter, USA, 1932. *S*: 30 ft 0 in (9·14 m); *L*: 20 ft 4¾ in (6·21 m); *P*: One 500 hp Pratt & Whitney R-1340; *A*: Two 0·30 MG or one 0·30 and one 0·50 MG; *W*: 3,087 lb (1400 kg); *MS*: 184 mph (296 kph); *OC*: 24,800 ft (7620 m). *US Navy version of Army's P-12 design, and major carrier fighter equipment until 1937.*

Fiat CR.32 Single-seat biplane fighter, It., 1933. *S*: 31 ft 1¼ in (9·48 m); *L*: 24 ft 3¾ in (7·41 m); *P*: One 600 Fiat A.30; *A*: Two 12·7 mm MG; *W*: 4,220 lb (1914 kg); *MS*: 220 mph (354 kph); *OC*: 25,250 ft (7620 m). *Well-designed fighter which saw action in Spain and China, and was quite widely exported, but was largely withdrawn from front-line units by the outbreak of the Second World War.*

A Ford 5AT-E, known affectionately as the Tin Goose, of Maddux Air Lines

The Boeing P-26A of the United States Army Air Corps, shown here in the markings of the 19th Pursuit Squadron, based at Wheeler Field, Hawaii, in 1934–35

Handley Page Heyford I Biplane heavy bomber, UK, 1933. *S*: 75 ft 0 in (22·86 m); *L*: 58 ft 0 in (17·67 m); *P*: Two 575 hp Rolls-Royce Kestrel IIIS; *A*: Three 0·303 MG; *W*: 16,750 lb (7598 kg); *C*: Four; *MS*: 142 mph (229 kph); *OC*: 21,000 ft (6401 m); *ML*: 3,150 lb (1429 kg). *Last RAF biplane bomber, which was still in second-line service as a trainer in 1940. Reliable, simple to fly and service, and highly manoeuvrable, the huge and stork-like Heyford was long remembered by air display crowds who saw it looped!*

Boeing P-26A Single-seat fighter, USA, 1934. *S*: 27 ft 11½ in (8·52 m); *L*: 23 ft 10 in (7·26 m); *P*: One 500 hp Pratt & Whitney R-1340; *A*: Two 0·30 MG *or* one 0·30 and one 0·50 MG; *W*: 2,955 lb (1340 kg); *MS*: 234 mph (376 kph); *OC*: 27,400 ft (8351 m). *Open cockpit, fixed undercarriage, braced monoplane – first all-metal and first monoplane fighter in US service. Later saw action against Japanese in Chinese and Philippine hands.*

Gloster Gauntlet I Single-seat biplane fighter, UK, 1935. *S*: 32 ft 9½ in (9·99 m); *L*: 26 ft 2 in (7·97 m); *P*: One 640 hp Bristol Mercury VI; *A*: Two 0·303 MG; *W*: 3,970 lb (1801 kg); *MS*: 230 mph (370 kph); *OC*: 33,500 ft (10211 m). *Popular and manoeuvrable fighter in old tradition, widely used by RAF from 1935–39, the Gauntlet would have been main British fighter had war broken out over Munich Crisis, 1938.*

P.Z.L. P-11c Single-seat fighter, Pol., 1935. *S*: 30 ft 2½ in (10·72 m); *L*: 25 ft 2 in (7·55 m); *P*: One 645 hp Bristol Mercury VI; *A*: Four 7·7 mm MG; *W*: 3,500 lb (1590 kg); *MS*: 242 mph (390 kph); *OC*: 24,400 ft (8000 m). *Advanced in its day, this open-cockpit, fixed-undercarriage fighter was completely outclassed by 1939; but its pilots flew it with remarkable results during Poland's hopeless defence.*

Short S.23 Empire Flying-boats 16/24-seat flying-boat airliner, UK, 1936. *S*: 114 ft 0 in (37·05 m); *L*: 88 ft 0 in (28·60 m); *P*: Four 920 hp Bristol Pegasus XC; *W*: 43,500 lb (19750 kg); *CS*: 165 mph (265 kph); *OC*: 20,000 ft (6500 m). *Ordered from the drawing board, the famous "C"-Class flying-boats flew extensive passenger and mail services between 1936 and 1939 over the old Commonwealth air routes. From them was developed the Sunderland maritime reconnaissance flying-boat of the Second World War.*

Savoia-Marchetti SM.81 Medium bomber-transport, It., 1935. *S*: 78 ft 9 in (24·0 m); *L*: 60 ft 3 in (18·36 m); *P*: Three 670 hp Piaggio P.X RC. 35; *A*: Five 7·7 mm MG; 22,167 lb (10055 kg); *C*: Five; *MS*: 200 mph (322 kph); *ML*: 4,400 lb (1996 kg). *Officially dubbed "Pipistrello" (Bat) and unofficially "Lumaco" (Slug), the SM.81 saw action in Spain, Ethiopia, Greece and throughout the Mediterranean theatre, as a faithful "workhorse"; some flew as far afield as Russia.*

Fairey Swordfish Three-seat torpedo-bomber biplane, UK, 1935. *S*: 45 ft 6 in (13·87 m); *L*: 35 ft 8 in (10·9 m); *P*: One 750 hp Bristol Pegasus 30 ;*W*: 7,510 lb (3410 kg); *MS*: 138 mph (221 kph). *Last British combat biplane (with the Fairey Albacore), the famous "Stringbag" scored memorable torpedo successes in the battles of Taranto and Matapan, and against the Bismarck in the Atlantic.*

Avia B-534 Single-seat biplane fighter, Cz., 1935. *S*: 30 ft 10 in (9·4 m); *L*: 26 ft 7 in (8·1 m); *P*: One 650 hp licence-built Hispano-Suiza 12Ybrs; *A*: Two 7·7 mm MG; *W*: 4,736 lb (1985 kg); *MS*: 225 mph (363 kph); *OC*: 36,100 ft (11,000 m). *Standard Czech fighter in pre-War years, and used in Russia by German-puppet Slovak Air Force.*

de Havilland D.H.89 Dragon Rapide 6/8-seat light biplane transport, UK, 1935. *S*: 48 ft 0 in (15·60 m); *L*: 34 ft 6 in (11·21 m); *P*: Two 200 hp D.H. Gipsy Six; *W*: 5,500 lb (2497 kg); *MS*: 157 mph (252 kph); *OC*: 19,500 ft (6340 m). *Originally produced as a light passenger aircraft, the Rapide served numerous small carriers and came to be used for communications and training by the RAF during the Second World War; 737 were built between 1935 and 1945.*

Grumman F3F-1 Single-seat biplane carrier fighter, USA, 1936. *S*: 32 ft 0 in (9·75 m); *L*: 23 ft 3½ in (7·09 m); *P*: One 700 hp Pratt & Whitney Twin Wasp Jr.; *A*: One 0·30 and one 0·50 MG; *W*: 4,116 lb (1867 kg); *MS*: 231 mph (372 kph); *OC*: 29,500 ft (8992 m). *Last US Navy and Marines biplane fighter; served with all units active between 1936 and 1941; last combat squadron re-equipped with Wildcats only in October 1941.*

Douglas DC-3 21-seat medium-range airliner, USA, 1935. *S*: 95 ft 0 in (30·88 m); *L*: 64 ft 6 in (21·96 m); *P*: Two 900 hp Wright Cyclone GR-1820-G102A; *W*: 24,000 lb (10900 kg); *MS*: 230 mph (369 kph); *CS*: 185 mph (296 kph); *OC*: 23,200 ft (7540 m). *All-time classic airliner developed from the DC-2, and has seen service throughout the world; was the most widely-used troop transport (as the Dakota) in the War, and has been used in every conceivable rôle for 37 years. No single design has taken its place.*

Polikarpov I-16 Type 4 Single-seat fighter, USSR, 1936. *S*: 29 ft 6½ in (9·00 m); *L*: 20 ft 1¼ in (6·13 m); *P*: One 700 hp M-25; *A*: Two 7·62 mm MG; *W*: 3,135 lb (1422 kg); *MS*: 283 mph (456 kph); *OC*: 30,440 ft (9278 m). *First closed-cockpit, retractable-undercarriage monoplane fighter in service anywhere in the world, the I-16 fought in Spain and Mongolia, but was completely outclassed by the Bf 109E in 1941.*

Avro Anson General purpose aircraft, UK, 1936. *S*: 56 ft 6 in (17·29 m); *L*: 42 ft 3 in (12·93 m); *P*: Two 350 hp Armstrong Siddeley Cheetah IX; *W*: 8,000 lb (3632 kg); *A*: Two 0·303 MG; *C*: Three; *MS*: 188 mph (301 kph); *OC*: 16,000 ft (4900 m); *ML*: 360 lb (163 kg). *Originally a coastal reconnaissance aircraft, the Anson was the RAF's first monoplane with retractable undercarriage. In the War it was relegated to training duties and production continued until May 1952 by which time 10,020 had been built (2,882 in Canada).*

Fiat BR.20 Medium bomber, It., 1936. *S*: 70 ft 8 in (21·53 m); *L*: 52 ft 9 in (16·07 m); *P*: Two 1,000 hp Fiat A.80 RC.41; *A*: Four 7·7 mm MG; *W*: 22,266 lb (10100 kg); *C*: Four; *MS*: 267 mph (430 kph); *OC*: 24,935 ft (7600 m); *ML*: 2,204 lb (1000 kg). *Sturdy design, exported to Japan during Sino-Japanese War, and used in Spanish Civil War. Operated by Regia Aeronautica in Mediterranean theatre and – briefly – on Channel Coast, the BR.20 was generally outclassed by 1943.*

Gloster Gladiator I Single-seat biplane fighter, UK, 1937. *S*: 32 ft 3 in (9·82 m); *L*: 27 ft 5 in (8·35 m); *P*: One 830 hp Bristol Mercury IX; *A*: Four 0·303 MG; *W*: 4,592 lb

(2083 kg); *MS*: 253 mph (407 kph); *OC*: 32,800 ft (9997 m). *Last RAF biplane fighter; still in service in 1940-41, the Gladiator equipped squadrons involved in some of the epic defences and defeats of the early War years, in France, Norway, Malta, Greece and the desert.*

Mitsubishi G3M1 Naval bomber, Jap., 1937. *S*: 82 ft 0¾ in (25·0 m); *L*: 53 ft 11½ in (16·45 m); *P*: Two 910 hp Kinsei 3; *A*: Three 7·7 mm MG; *W*: 16,848 lb (7642 kg); *C*: Five; *MS*: 216 mph (348 kph); *OC*: 24,540 ft (7480 m); *ML*: 1,764 lb (800 kg). *Although obsolescent by the outbreak of War, developed versions of the "Nell" served until 1943 in first-line land-based naval bomber squadrons. The warships "Repulse" and "Prince of Wales" were sunk by G3Ms.*

Bristol Blenheim I Medium bomber, UK, 1937. *S*: 56 ft 4 in (17·17 m); *L*: 39 ft 9 in (12·11 m); *P*: Two 840 hp Bristol Mercury VIII; *A*: Two 0·303 MG; *W*: 12,500 lb (5670 kg); *C*: Three; *MS*: 285 mph (459 kph); *OC*: 27,280 ft (8315 m); *ML*: 1,000 lb (454 kg). *Advanced in its day, and marking a new standard of speed and up-to-date monoplane design for the RAF, the Blenheim I was quite widely exported. Feeble armament and load led to considerable development, and later models served until 1944.*

Nakajima B5N-1 Three seat carrier attack aircraft. Jap., 1937. *S*: 50 ft 11 in (15·51 m); *L*: 33 ft 10 in (10·31 m); *P*: One 770 hp Hikari 3; *A*: One 7·7 mm MG; *W*: 8,850 lb (4014 kg); *MS*: 229 mph (369 kph); *OC*: 24,300 ft (7407 m). *The standard carrier-borne torpedo-bomber from Pearl Harbor to mid-1944, the "Kate" could carry conventional bomb-loads of 800 kg (1764 lb).*

Savoia-Marchetti SM.79-I Medium bomber, It., 1937. *S*: 69 ft 6 in (21·18 m); *L*: 53 ft 2 in (16·20 m); *P*: Three 750 hp Alfa Romeo 126RC34; *A*: Three 12·7 mm MG and one 7·7 mm MG; *W*: 23,643 lb (10724 kg); *C*: Five; *MS*: 267 mph (430 kph); *OC*: 21,325 ft (6500 m); *ML*: 2,200 lb (1000 kg). *The Sparviero is best remembered for its service with the highly skilled Italian torpedo-bomber squadrons in the Mediterranean theatre.*

Dornier Do 17E-1 Reconnaissance bomber, Ger., 1937. *S*: 59 ft 0¾ in (18·00 m); *L*: 53 ft 3¾ in (16·25 m); *P*: Two 750 hp BMW VI 7·3; *A*: Three 7·92 mm MG; *W*: 15,000 lb (6804 kg); *C*: Four; *MS*: 236 mph (380 kph); *OC*: 18,050 ft (5502 m); *ML*: 2,200 lb (998 kg). *Used with success over Spain and Poland, and in the West in 1940 in its developed Do 17Z version; obsolescent by mid-War years.*

de Havilland D.H.82A Tiger Moth Light sporting 2-seat biplane, UK, 1937. *S*: 29 ft 4 in (8·97 m); *L*: 23 ft 11 in (7·31 m); *P*: One 130 hp D.H. Gipsy Major; *W*: 1,825 lb (828 kg); *MS*: 109·5 mph (175 kph); *OC*: 17,000 ft (5200 m). *Developed from the famous D.H. Moth of the late 1920s, the Tiger Moth appeared in 1931 and became the most popular British club lightplane. Thousands survived the War having been used as the RAF's standard ab initio trainer.*

Hawker Hurricane I Single-seat fighter, UK, 1937. *S*: 40 ft 0 in (12·19 m); *L*: 31 ft 4 in (9·55 m); *P*: One 1,030 hp Rolls-Royce Merlin II; *A*: Eight 0·303 MG; *W*: 6,218 lb (2,820 lb); *MS*: 322 mph (518 kph); *OC*: 33,400 ft (10180 m). *Classic fighter aircraft, winner of Battle of Britain, 1940. The RAF's first closed-cockpit, retractable-undercarriage monoplane fighter, the Hurricane made up in ruggedness and reliability for what it lacked in speed compared with the Bf 109. Much developed, later versions saw wide service as fighter and ground-strafers on all fronts.*

Fokker D.XXI Single-seat fighter, Hol., 1937. *S*: 36 ft 0 in (10·97 m); *L*: 26 ft 11 in (8·20 m); *P*: One 760 hp Bristol Mercury VIII; *A*: Four 7·92 mm MG; *W*: 4,510 lb (2050 kg); *MS*: 270 mph (435 kph); *OC*: 31,160 ft (9500 m). *Although outclassed by 1940, the sturdy fixed-undercarriage D.XXI saw action with the Dutch and Finnish forces, and distinguished itself with the latter, in prolonged defiance of Soviet forces.*

Curtiss Hawk 75 Single-seat fighter, USA, 1937. *S*: 37 ft 4 in (11·37 m); *L*: 28 ft 7 in (8·71 m); *P*: One 875 hp Wright Cyclone; *A*: One 0·30 MG and one 0·50 MG; *W*: 5,305 lb (2406 kg); *MS*: 280 mph (451 kph); *OC*: 31,800 ft (9693 m). *First US Army fighter with closed cockpit, retractable undercarriage. In service with several countries in its export version, including France, Netherlands East Indies and Finland.*

Fairey Battle Light bomber, UK, 1937. *S*: 54 ft 0 in (16·46 m); *L*: 52 ft 1¾ in (15·89 m); *P*: One 1,440 hp Rolls-Royce Merlin III; *A*: Two 0·303 MG; *W*: 10,792 lb (4895 kg); *C*: Three; *MS*: 257 mph (413 kph); *OC*: 25,000 ft (7620 m); *ML*: 1,500 lb (680 kg). *Obsolete in every way by the outbreak of War, the Battles of the Advanced Air Striking Force, RAF, were massacred in France in 1940, in a series of heroic but sacrificial actions. Surviving aircraft used in many training rôles later in the War.*

Mitsubishi Ki-21-Ia Medium bomber, Jap., 1938. *S*: 73 ft 9¾ in (22·50 m); *L*: 52 ft 6 in (16·00 m); *P*: Two 950 hp Nakajima Ha-5 Kai; *A*: Three 7·7 mm MG; *W*: 16,520 lb (7916 kg); *C*: Four; *MS*: 268 mph (432 kph); *OC*: 28,215 ft (8600 m); *ML*: 2,205 lb (1000 kg). *Popular and reliable with its Army crews, the Ki-21 was blooded over China in 1938. It remained in use in developed versions until 1945, but by 1943 was outclassed by Allied fighters.*

Consolidated PBY-4 Catalina Patrol flying-boat, USA, 1938. *S*: 104 ft 0 in (31·69 m); *L*: 65 ft 2 in (19·86 m); *P*: Two 1,050 hp Pratt & Whitney R-1830-72; *A*: Two 0·30 MG and two 0·50 MG; *W*: 22,295 lb (10113 kg); *MS*: 198 mph (319 kph); *OC*: 25,400 ft (7742 m). *The Catalina, later developed into an amphibian, was one of the most successful general purpose aircraft of all time – in its development, its popularity and widespread use, it can be classed as a "floating DC-3".*

Handley Page Hampden Medium bomber, UK, 1938. *S*: 69 ft 2 in (21·08 m); *L*: 53 ft 7 in (16·33 m); *P*: Two 980 hp Bristol Pegasus; *A*: Four 0·303 MG; *W*: 18,750 lb (8505 kg); *C*: Four; *MS*: 265 mph (426 kph); *OC*: 22,700 ft (6918 m); *ML*: 4,000 lb (1814 kg). *An advanced design at the time of its introduction, the "Flying Suitcase" was inadequately armed by the standards of 1940–41. Nevertheless, with the Whitley and Wellington, it bore the brunt of bomber operations in the first half of the War.*

Lioré et Olivier LeO 45 Medium bomber, Fr., 1938. *S*: 73 ft 10½ in (22·52 m); *L*: 56 ft 2½ in (17·17 m); *P*: Two 920 hp Gnome-Rhône 14N; *A*: One 20 mm, and two 7·5 mm MG; *W*: 25,128 lb (11398 kg); *C*: Four; *MS*: 298 mph (480 kph); *ML*: 3,086 lb (1400 kg). *One of the more effective French aircraft in service in 1940, the LeO 45 was not available in large enough numbers to affect the outcome of the Battle of France.*

Junkers Ju 87B-1 Two-seat dive-bomber, Ger., 1938. *S*: 45 ft 3¼ in (13·79 m); *L*: 36 ft 1 in (10·99 m); *P*: One 900 hp Junkers Jumo 211; *A*: Three 7·92 mm MG; *W*: 9,336 lb (4235 kg); *MS*: 217 mph (349 kph); *OC*: 26,250 ft (8000 m). *The immortal Stuka – an extremely effective pinpoint attack aircraft which played a large part in German victory in 1940 but was vulnerable to realistic fighter defence.*

Short Sunderland I Patrol flying-boat, UK, 1938. *S*: 112 ft 8 in (34·33 m); *L*: 85 ft 8 in (26·10 m); *P*: Four, 1,010 hp Bristol Pegasus XXII; *A*: Seven 0·303 MG; *W*: 44,600 lb (20231 kg); *C*: Eight; *MS*: 210 mph (338 kph); *OC*: 17,000 ft (5182 m). *The Sunderland served with RAF Coastal Command, in successive versions, until 1958 – eloquent testimony to its reliability and ruggedness. The wartime models carried 2,000 lb (908 kg) of bombs or depth-charges for anti-submarine attack, and proved capable of defending themselves against fighters far out over the Atlantic.*

Potez 631 Three-seat heavy fighter, Fr., 1938. *S*: 52 ft 6 in (16·00 m); *L*: 36 ft 4 in (11·07 m); *P*: Two 700 hp Gnome-Rhône 14 M4/M5; *A*: Two 20 mm, five 7·5 mm MG; *W*: 8,289 lb (3760 kg); *MS*: 275 mph (442 kph). *Produced in four different versions as a day and night fighter, reconnaissance aircraft, light bomber and army co-operation type, the P.63 series were the most numerous French aircraft in service in 1940. Manoeuvrable, but very under-powered.*

Messerschmitt Bf 109E-3 Single-seat fighter, Ger., 1939. *S*: 32 ft 4¼ in (9·85 m); *L*: 28 ft 3¾ in (8·63 m); *P*: One 1,150 hp Daimler-Benz DB 601A; *A*: Two 7·92 mm MG and three 20 mm; *W*: 5,523 lb (2505 kg); *MS*: 354 mph (570 kph); *OC*: 36,090 ft (11000 m). *The Bf 109 was Germany's major single-engined fighter from 1938–45, and the E-3 variant was the type in service during the blitzkrieg victories in the West, and the Battle of Britain. So much development work was carried out throughout the War that late Bf 109G and K variants still equipped about half the fighter force in 1945.*

Armstrong Whitworth Ensign I 27-seat medium-range airliner, UK, 1939. *S*: 123 ft 0 in (39·97 m); *L*: 114 ft 0 in (37·05 m); *P*: Four 850 hp Armstrong Siddeley Tiger IX;

The longest-lived and most widely used of all trainers, the North American T-6A Texan

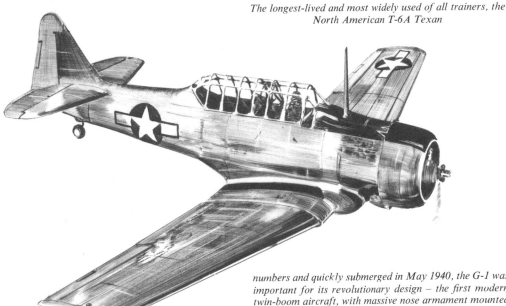

W: 49,000 lb (22250 kg); *MS*: 205 mph (329 kph); *OC*: 18,000 ft (5850 m). *Remarkably handsome shoulder-wing airliner ordered by Imperial Airways in 1935, the Ensign was prevented from flying normal services by the War. Re-engined as the Mk. II, they operated arduous wartime flights until retired in 1945.*

Fiat CR.42 Single-seat biplane fighter, It., 1939. *S*: 31 ft 9 in (9·67 m); *L*: 27 ft 0¼ in (8·23 m); *P*: One 840 hp Fiat A.74R; *A*: Two 12·7 mm MG *or* one 7·7 mm and one 12·7 mm MG; *W*: 5,060 lb (2295 kg); *MS*: 274 mph (440 kph); *OC*: 33,500 ft (10211 m). *Well-designed but in-evitably obsolescent biplane which bore brunt of Mediter-ranean theatre fighting until monoplane types reached Italian squadrons in quantity late in 1941. Also saw action with expeditionary force in Russia.*

Armstrong Whitworth Whitley V Heavy night bomber, UK, 1939. *S*: 84 ft 0 in (25·60 m); *L*: 72 ft 6 in (22·10 m); *P*: Two 1,075 hp Rolls-Royce Merlin X; *A*: Five 0·303 MG; *W*: 28,200 lb (12791 kg); *C*: Five; *MS*: 230 mph (370 kph); *OC*: 26,000 ft (7955 m); *ML*: 7,000 lb (3175 kg). *Whitleys saw considerable RAF Bomber Command service in 1939–42, and then soldiered on in a variety of second-line rôles.*

Fokker G-1A Heavy fighter, Hol., 1939. *S*: 56 ft 4 in (17·15 m); *L*: 37 ft 10¾ in (11·50 m); *P*: Two 830 hp Bristol Mercury; *A*: Nine 7·92 mm MG; *W*: 10,582 lb (4800 kg); *C*: Two-three; *MS*: 295 mph (475 kph); *OC*: 30,500 ft (9300 m). *Only available to the Luchtvaartafdeling in small*

numbers and quickly submerged in May 1940, the G-1 was important for its revolutionary design – the first modern twin-boom aircraft, with massive nose armament mounted in a central fuselage nacelle. There was also provision for a small bomb-load when operating in the attack rôle.

North American T-6A Two-seat trainer, USA, 1940. *S*: 42 ft 0 in (12·80 m); *L*: 29 ft 0 in (8·84 m); *P*: One 600 hp Pratt & Whitney R-1340; *A*: Two 0·30 MG; *W*: 5,155 lb (2338 kg); *MS*: 210 mph (338 kph); *OC*: 24,300 ft (7407 m). *One of the world's classic trainers, the Texan has seen service in almost every nation which has an air force for the past 30 years; it is still in widespread use, indeed in combat: several countries have fitted it with gun-packs and rocket-pods for operation as a COIN ground-attack type.*

Messerschmitt Bf 110C-4 Two-seat heavy fighter, Ger., 1939. *S*: 53 ft 5 in (16·28 m); *L*: 41 ft 6¼ in (12·65 m); *P*: Two 1,100 hp DB 601A; *A*: Five 7·92 mm MG and two 20 mm; *W*: 15,300 lb (6940 kg); *MS*: 349 mph (561 kph); *OC*: 32,000 ft (9753 m). *A failure as a heavy escort fighter, the Bf 110 was much developed and saw widespread and successful service as a night-fighter, heavy ground-attack fighter, reconnaissance fighter, etc.*

Fiat G.50 Single-seat fighter, It., 1939. *S*: 36 ft 0½ in (10·98 m); *L*: 25 ft 6 in (7·77 m); *P*: One 840 hp Fiat A.74 RC 38; *A*: Two 12·7 mm MG; *W*: 5,296 lb (2402 kg); *MS*: 293 mph (472 kph); *OC*: 35,270 ft (10750 m). *An old-fashioned-looking humped-back low-wing monoplane with an open cockpit, the G.50 embodied the weaknesses of Italian fighters in the days of the Hurricane and Bf 109: inadequate power, inadequate armament and poor develop-ment potential. Like most Italian types, its handling characteristics were however excellent.*

Heinkel He 111H-6 Medium bomber, Ger., 1939. *S*: 74 ft 1½ in (22·59 m); *L*: 54 ft 5½ in (16·59 m); *P*: Two 1,340* hp Junkers Jumo 211; *A*: Six 7·92 mm MG and one 20 mm; *W*: 25,000 lb (11340 kg); *C*: Five; *MS*: 258 mph (415 kph); *OC*: 25,500ft (7772 m); *ML*: 5,510 lb (2499 kg). *Major variant of much developed He 111 series, Germany's main bomber from mid-1930s to 1942; delays in appearance of more modern types forced continued service long after overtaken by Allied designs.*

Focke-Wulf Fw 200C Condor Heavy bomber/transport, Ger., 1939. *S*: 107 ft 9½ in (32·85 m); *L*: 76 ft 11½ in (23·45 m); *P*: Four 1,200 hp Bramo 323; *A*: Two 7·92 mm MG, three 13 mm MG and one 20 mm; *W*: 50,045 lb (22700 kg); *C*: Six; *MS*: 224 mph (361 kph); *OC*: 19,000 ft (5791 m); *ML*: 4,620 lb (2095 kg). *An airliner pressed into service in 1939 through absence of a Luftwaffe long-range bomber, the Condor did useful maritime patrol work but never had the structural strength of a true heavy bomber – thus the unimpressive bomb-load.*

Morane Saulnier MS.406 Single-seat fighter, Fr., 1939. *S*: 34 ft 10 in (10·61 m); *L*: 26 ft 10 in (8·17 m); *P*: One 860 hp Hispano-Suiza HS 12Y; *A*: Two 7·5 mm MG and one 20 mm; *W*: 5,610 lb (2540 kg); *MS*: 304 mph (490 kph); *OC*: 32,800 ft (10000 m). *The remarkably ungraceful MS.406 was the least effective French fighter of 1940. Half the fighter pilots killed in the Battle of France flew MS.406s, but claims were much lower than by the D.520 and Curtiss Hawk units, despite the great gallantry of French, Czech and Polish pilots. This first "modern" French fighter was also flown by Turkey, Switzerland and Finland.*

Mitsubishi A6M2 Reisen ("Zero") Single-seat naval fighter, Jap., 1940. *S*: 39 ft 4½ in (12·0 m); *L*: 29 ft 8¾ in (9·06 m); *P*: One 940 hp Sakae 12; *A*: Two 7·7 mm MG and two 20 mm; *W*: 5,313 lb (2410 kg); *MS*: 331·5 mph (534 kph); *OC*: 32,800 ft (10000 m). *Fine original design, which completely out-fought British and US contemporaries in the first year of the Pacific war. As modern Allied types appeared in 1943 and 1944, however, developed versions of the "Zero" were unable to maintain their technical lead.*

Junkers Ju 52/3mg7e Military transport, Ger., 1940. *S*: 95 ft 10 in (29·21 m); *L*: 62 ft 0 in (18·89 m); *P*: Three 830 hp BMW 132T; *A*: One 13 mm MG and two 7·92 mm MG; *W*: 24,320 lb (11032 kg); *MS*: 189 mph (304 kph); *OC*: 18,000 ft (5486 m). *18-passenger version of the much developed and widely-used bomber-transport tri-motor, which saw service from the Spanish Civil War until the 1960s. Float-plane version also built in small numbers. Germany's standard transport and paratroop aircraft throughout War.*

Aichi D3A1 Two-seat naval dive-bomber, Jap., 1940. *S*: 47 ft 2 in (14·36 m); *L*: 33 ft 5¼ in (10·19 m); *P*: One 1,000 hp Mitsubishi Kinsei-43; *A*: Three 7·7 mm MG; *W*: 8,047 lb (3650 kg); *MS*: 240 mph (386 kph); *OC*: 30,050 ft (9300 m); *ML*: 815 lb (370 kg). *Standard carrier-borne dive-bomber from Pearl Harbor until 1943–44, the "Val" was the third of the famous I.J.N.A.F. carrier air group trinity of the early War years – "Zero", "Kate" and "Val".*

Vickers Wellington IC Medium bomber, UK, 1940. *S*: 86 ft 2 in (26·26 m); *L*: 64 ft 7 in (19·68 m); *P*: Two 1,000 hp Bristol Pegasus XVIII; *A*: Six 0·303 MG; *W*: 30,000 lb (13608 kg); *C*: Five; *MS*: 243 mph (391 kph); *OC*: 21,000 ft (6401 m); *ML*: 4,500 lb (2041 kg). *The most modern bomber in RAF service at the outbreak of War; the geodetic construction gave the "Wimpey" enormous strength, and it remained in service in second-line rôles well into the 1950s. Wellingtons bore the brunt of the early bombing campaign while the true "heavies" were being developed.*

Curtiss P-40B Tomahawk Single-seat fighter, USA, 1940. *S*: 37 ft 4 in (11·37 m); *L*: 31 ft 8¾ in (9·67 m); *P*: One 1,040 hp Allison V-1710; *A*: Four 0·303 MG; *W*: 7,326 lb (3323 kg); *MS*: 352 mph (566 kph); *OC*: 32,400 ft (9875 m). *Standard USAAF fighter at outbreak of War; saw action in China, Pacific and Mediterranean with US, British and Commonwealth air forces until more modern fighters became available.*

Bloch MB.152 C1 Single-seat fighter, Fr., 1940. *S*: 34 ft 7 in (10·54 m); *L*: 29 ft 10¼ in (9·10 m); *P*: One 1,100 hp Gnome-Rhône 14N25; *A*: Two 7·5 mm MG and two 20 mm; *W*: 5,937 lb (2693 kg); *MS*: 300 mph (482 kph). *A robust machine which saw considerable action in the last weeks of the Battle of France, the MB.152 was handicapped by poor manoeuvrability and unreliable armament.*

Dewoitine D.520 Single-seat fighter, Fr., 1940. *S*: 33 ft 5½ in (10·19 m); *L*: 28 ft 8½ in (8·74 m); *P*: One 930 hp Hispano-Suiza 12Y45; *A*: Four 7·5 mm MG and one 20 mm; *W*: 6,144 lb (2787 kg); *MS*: 332 mph (535 kph); *OC*: 33,620 ft (10247 m). *The best French fighter of the War, coming into service in inadequate numbers in 1940, the D.520's excellent handling made it a realistic match for the faster Bf 109. In the short Battle of France D.520s accounted for 108 enemy aircraft for 85 losses.*

Bristol Beaufighter I Two-seat heavy fighter, UK, 1940. *S*: 57 ft 10 in (17·62 m); *L*: 41 ft 4 in (12·59 m); *P*: Two 1,400 hp Bristol Hercules XI; *A*: Six 0·303 MG and four 20 mm; *W*: 21,000 lb (9526 kg); *MS*: 321 mph (517 kph); *OC*: 26,500 ft (8077 m). *With its massive armament and early A.I. radar, the Beaufighter was the RAF's first really successful night fighter. Later versions also served as attack aircraft, with rocket and torpedo armament, and earned a formidable reputation as "ship-busters", in both European and Pacific theatres.*

Short Stirling B.I Heavy bomber, UK, 1940. *S*: 99 ft 1 in (30·19 m); *L*: 87 ft 3 in (26·52 m); *P*: Four 1,590 hp Bristol Hercules XI; *A*: Eight 0·303 MG; *W*: 70,000 lb (31752 kg); *C*: Eight; *MS*: 260 mph (419 kph); *OC*: 20,500 ft (6248 m); *ML*: 14,000 lb (6350 kg). *First RAF four-engined "heavy", bore brunt of long-range night raids during 1941–42, largely replaced by Halifax and Lancaster during 1943.*

Boulton Paul Defiant I Two-seat turret fighter, UK, 1940. *S*: 39 ft 4 in (11·99 m); *L*: 35 ft 4 in (10·77 m); *P*: One 1,030 hp Rolls-Royce Merlin III; *A*: Four 0·303 MG;

W: 8,350 lb (3788 kg); *MS*: 304 mph (489 kph); *OC*: 30,350 ft (9251 m). *Delays in production led to Defiants, with indifferent performance and no forward guns, being massacred by Bf 109s in 1940. They were quite effective against bombers, and saw considerable service as stop-gap night-fighters in 1941, while specialised aircraft were being developed.*

Junkers Ju 88A-1 Medium bomber, Ger., 1940. *S*: 65 ft 10½ in (20·07 m); *L*: 47 ft 1½ in (14·36 m); *P*: Two 1,200 hp Junkers Jumo 211; *A*: Two 13 mm MG and four 7·92 mm MG; *W*: 26,700 lb (12111 kg); *C*: Four; *MS*: 292 mph (469 kph); *OC*: 27,880 ft (8534 m); *ML*: 5,510 lb (2499 kg). *Uniquely versatile aircraft series which included dive, level and torpedo bombers, day and night fighters, and a wide range of specialised versions.*

Supermarine Spitfire IIA Single-seat fighter, UK, 1940. *S*: 36 ft 10 in (11·22 m); *L*: 29 ft 11 in (9·11 m); *P*: One 1,175 hp Rolls-Royce Merlin III; *A*: Eight 0·303 MG; *W*: 6,275 lb (2846 kg); *MS*: 370 mph (595 kph); *OC*: 32,800 ft (9997 m). *Although the Battle of Britain was over before Spitfires were delivered in numbers sufficient to eclipse the importance of the Hurricane, the series was in service from September 1938 until well into the 1950s. It served in every theatre of war, proved highly suitable for development, and was exported in considerable numbers. It remains the classic British aircraft of the War, and has been called the most beautiful aircraft ever built.*

Grumman F4F-3 Wildcat Single-seat carrier fighter, USA, 1940. *S*: 38 ft 0 in (11·58 m); *L*: 28 ft 9 in (8·76 m); *P*: One 1,200 hp Pratt & Whitney Twin Wasp; *A*: Four 0·50 MG; *W*: 7,065 lb (3204 kg); *MS*: 330 mph (531 kph); *OC*: 37,000 ft (11277 m). *Standard US Navy and Marine fighter at outbreak of War, which bore brunt of early defensive fighting in the Pacific. Also exported to Britain.*

Douglas Boston III Light bomber, USA, 1941. *S*: 61 ft 4 in (18·69 m); *L*: 47 ft 6 in (14·47 m); *P*: Two 1,600 hp Wright Cyclone R-2600 A5B; *A*: Seven 0·303 MG; *W*: 20,230 lb (9176 kg); *C*: Four; *MS*: 338 mph (544 kph); *OC*: 27,600 ft (8412 m); *ML*: 2,000 lb (907 kg). *RAF bomber version of the very versatile and much-developed A-20 series, which saw widespread Allied service in a variety of rôles.*

Macchi C.202 Single-seat fighter, It., 1941. *S*: 34 ft 8½ in (10·57 m); *L*: 29 ft 0½ in (8·85 m); *P*: One 1,075 Alfa Romeo RA-1000; *A*: Two 7·7 mm MG and two 12·7 MG; *W*: 6,460 lb (2930 kg); *MS*: 370 mph (595 kph); *OC*: 37,750 ft (11582 m). *Development of earlier, under-powered MC.200, with licence-built Daimler-Benz engine; fast and very manoeuvrable, the MC.202 Folgore was superior to all Allied fighters in the Mediterranean theatre except the Spitfire.*

Douglas SBD-2 Dauntless Naval dive-bomber, USA, 1941. *S*: 41 ft 6 in (12·64 m); *L*: 32 ft 2 in (9·80 m); *P*: One 1,000 hp Wright R-1830-32; *A*: Three 0·30 MG; *W*: 10,360 lb (4699 kg); *C*: Two; *MS*: 252 mph (406 kph); *OC*: 26,000 ft (7925 m); *ML*: 1,200 lb (544 kg). *Main strike weapon of US carriers in the critical battles of 1942, the SBD was not only an excellent dive-bomber but also a considerable "dogfighter", and accounted for many Japanese aircraft in air-to-air combat.*

Bell P-39D Airacobra Single-seat fighter, USA, 1941. *S*: 34 ft 0 in (10·36 m); *L*: 29 ft 9 in (9·07 m); *P*: One 1,150 hp Allison V-1710-35; *A*: One 37 mm, two 0·50 MG, and four 0·30 MG; *W*: 8,200 lb (3720 kg); *MS*: 360 mph (580 kph); *OC*: 32,100 ft (9784 m). *Heavy, clumsy and very inadequate above 15,000 ft, the P-39 nevertheless had a successful career as a ground-strafer, particularly with the Soviet Air Force; in that rôle its heavy armament paid dividends.*

The famous Douglas SDB Dauntless dive bomber of the U.S. Navy and Marines which participated in the great battles of the Coral Sea, Midway and the Eastern Solomons

Hawker Typhoon IB Single-seat fighter-bomber, UK, 1941. *S*: 41 ft 7 in (12·67 m); *L*: 31 ft 10 in (9·70 m); *P*: One 2,180 hp Napier Sabre IIA; *A*: Four 20 mm; *W*: 11,700 lb (5307 kg); *MS*: 404 mph (650 kph). *Initially plagued by technical problems, the Typhoon was rushed into service too quickly, to counter the Fw 190A. Weak at altitude, it was adequate at around 10,000 ft, and for- midable at low level. Best remembered as the rocket-armed fighter which played a major part in ground-strafing over Europe in 1944.*

North American B-25C Mitchell Medium bomber, USA, 1941. *S*: 67 ft 6¾ in (20·59 m); *L*: 52 ft 10¾ in (16·12 m); *P*: Two 1,700 hp Wright R-2600-13; *A*: Two 0·30 MG and two 0·50 MG; *W*: 33,500 lb (15195 kg); *C*: Five; *MS*: 284 mph (457 kph); *OC*: 21,200 ft (6462 m); *ML*: 5,200 lb (2359 kg). *A much-developed design widely used for a variety of attack rôles by many Allied air forces in all theatres of war. Late models carried a 75 mm gun in the nose. Best remembered as the equipment of Col. Doo- little's carrier-borne Tokyo raiders in April 1942, the B-25 is still in service with some of the world's remoter air arms.*

Nakajima Ki-43-IIa Hayabusa Single-seat fighter, Jap., 1942. *S*: 35 ft 6¾ in (10·88 m); *L*: 29 ft 3¼ in (8·92 m); *P*: One 1,150 hp Nakajima Ha-115; *A*: Two 12·7 mm MG; *W*: 5,710 lb (2590 kg); *MS*: 329 mph (529 kph); *OC*: 36,750 ft (11201 m). *IJAAF contemporary of the Navy's A6M "Zero", and standard equipment of Army fighter units in 1942. Like many Japanese fighters, it was supremely manoeuvrable but weak and under-gunned.*

Martin B-26B Marauder Medium bomber, USA, 1942. *S*: 71 ft 0 in (21·64 m); *L*: 58 ft 3 in (17·75 m); *P*: Two 1,920 hp Pratt & Whitney R-2800-43; *A*: Four 0·50 MG

and three 0·30 MG; *W*: 37,000 lb (16783 kg); *C*: Five; *MS*: 282 mph (454 kph); *OC*: 21,700 ft (6614 m); *ML*: 4,800 lb (2177 kg). *Most important USAAF medium bomber in the European theatre, the B-26 was a beautiful and advanced design which gained a reputation as a demanding machine to fly. Later models mounted up to eleven 0·50-cal. guns.*

Ilyushin Il-2m3 Two-seat attack aircraft, USSR, 1942. *S*: 48 ft 0½ in (14·6 m); *L*: 38 ft 0½ in (11·6 m); *P*: One 1,770 hp AM38F; *A*: Two 7·62 mm MG, one 12·7 mm MG and two 23 mm; *W*: 12,135 lb (5,510 kg); *MS*: 251 mph (404 kph); *OC*: 19,500 ft (6000 m); *ML*: 1,320 lb (600 kg). *The very strong and hard-hitting Il-2m3 Shtur- movik was one of the best specialised designs to emerge from the War – a most effective ground-attack machine used in great numbers by the Soviet air forces, which in its developed Il-10 form saw many years post-War service in the Eastern bloc.*

Boeing B-17F Flying Fortress Heavy bomber, USA, 1942. *S*: 103 ft 9½ in (31·63 m); *L*: 74 ft 9 in (22·78 m); *P*: Four 1,200 hp Wright R-1820-97; *A*: Nine 0·50 MG and one 0·30 MG, *or up to* ten 0·50 MG and two 0·30 MG; *W*: 40,260 lb (18262 kg); *C*: Ten; *MS*: 325 mph (523 kph); *OC*: 35,000 ft (10668 m); *ML*: 8,000 lb (3629 kg). *Despite its unimpressive bombload, the B-17 earned a place in history as the backbone of the USAF daylight bombing campaign over Europe, 1942–45. Large numbers made up for individual weakness; and just as important a contribu- tion were the casualties inflicted on the German fighter units drawn into the air by the daylight formations.*

The Martin B-26F **Marauder** *light/medium bomber of the U.S.A.A.F. Despite a high wing loading which resulted in some unpopularity among pilots, the Marauder was a very efficient design and gave magnificent service with the Ninth Air Force in Europe in support of the Allied invasion of 1944*

de Havilland Mosquito B.IV Fast medium bomber, day and night fighter, UK, 1942. *S*: 54 ft 2 in (16·51 m); *L*: 40 ft 4 in (12·29 m); *P*: Two 1,460 hp Rolls-Royce Merlin 21; *W*: 21,462 lb (9735 kg); *C*: Two; *MS*: 380 mph (611 kph); *OC*: 34,000 ft (10363 m); *ML*: 4,000 lb (1814 kg). *The "Wooden Wonder", an extremely successful and adaptable design which served the RAF until the 1950s. Fighter versions had heavy cannon armament in the nose; bomber versions were unarmed and relied on their remarkable performance.*

Commonwealth CA-12 Boomerang Single-seat fighter, Australian, 1942. *S*: 36 ft 0 in (10·97 m); *L*: 26 ft 9 in (8·15 m); *P*: One 1,200 hp licence-built Pratt & Whitney R-1830 S3C4G Twin Wasp; *A*: Two 20 mm and four 0·303 MG; *W*: 7,699 lb (3492 kg); *MS*: 305 mph (491 kph); *OC*: 34,000 ft (10363 m). *Indigenous Australian fighter, mainly used by army co-operation units as low-level ground support fighter.*

Chance Vought F4U-1 Corsair Single-seat fighter-bomber, USA, 1942. *S*: 40 ft 11¾ in (12·49 m); *L*: 33 ft 4½ in (10·17 m); *P*: One 2,000 hp Pratt & Whitney Twin Wasp; *A*: Six 0·50 MG; *W*: 11,090 lb (5030 kg); *MS*: 415 mph (667 kph); *OC*: 37,000 ft (11277 m); *ML*: 2,000 lb (907 kg). *Standard Marine and Navy carrier fighter of 1943–45, which remained in limited service during Korean War; one of the great naval aircraft of all time.*

Kawasaki Ki-45-KAIa Two-seat heavy fighter, Jap., 1942. *S*: 49 ft 3¼ in (15·01 m); *L*: 34 ft 1½ in (10·40 m); *P*: Two 1,000 hp Nakajima Ha-25; *A*: Two 12·7 mm MG, one 7·92 mm MG and one 20 mm; *W*: 11,632 lb (5276 kg); *MS*: 335 mph (539 kph); *OC*: 30,000 ft (9144 m). *Useful design, widely developed and used as ground- and ship-strafer, bomber interceptor and night fighter.*

Henschel Hs 129B-1 Single-seat ground attack aircraft, Ger., 1942. *S*: 46 ft 7 in (14·19 m); *L*: 31 ft 11¾ in (9·74 m); *P*: Two 740 hp Gnome et Rhône 14M; *A*: Two 7·92 mm MG, two 20 mm and one 30 mm; *W*: 11,266 lb (5110·25 kg); *MS*: 253 mph (407·15 kph); *OC*: 29,530 ft (9000 m). *Specialised attack aircraft used for tank-busting in Africa and Russia, with a variety of weapon systems, some highly sophisticated.*

Avro Lancaster B. Mk. I Heavy bomber, UK, 1942. *S*: 102 ft 0 in (31·08 m); *L*: 69 ft 6 in (21·18 m); *P*: Four 1,280 hp Rolls-Royce Merlin XXII; *A*: Eight 0·303 MG; 65,000 lb (29484 kg); *C*: Seven; *MS*: 275 mph loaded (442 kph); *OC*: 21,500 ft (6560 m); *ML*: 18,000 lb (8165 kg). *The classic heavy bomber of the War – able to carry enormous loads to distant targets, reliable, robust and adaptable. More than 7,000 were built, and derivatives of the series served for years after the War.*

Douglas DC-4 42-seat medium-range airliner, USA, 1942. *S*: 117 ft 6 in (35·95 m); *L*: 93 ft 11 in (28·73 m); *P*: Four 1,540 hp Pratt & Whitney Twin Wasp R-2000; *W*: 73,800 lb (33505 kg); *MS*: 280 mph (449 kph); *OC*: 22,500 ft (6885 m). *Designed in 1939 as a 4-engined replacement for the DC-3, the DC-4 was taken over by the USAAF when America entered the War. A total of 1,163 was built and hundreds flew with post-War air lines. It was the first large aircraft to be fitted with tricycle undercarriage.*

Grumman TBM Avenger Torpedo-bomber, USA, 1942. *S*: 54 ft 2 in (16·51 m); *L*: 40 ft 11½ in (12·48 m); *P*: One 1,900 hp Wright R-2600-20; *A*: Three 0·50 MG and one 0·30 MG; *W*: 17,895 lb (8117 kg); *C*: Three; *MS*: 276 mph (444 kph); *OC*: 30,100 ft (9175 m). *With the Douglas Dauntless dive-bomber, the classic USN carrier attack type of the Pacific War. Exported in some numbers, the Avenger was still in service with one or two of the remoter air forces until recent years.*

Messerschmitt Me 210A-1 General purpose heavy fighter, Ger., 1942. *S*: 53 ft 7¼ in (16·34 m); *L*: 36 ft 8¼ in (11·18 m); *P*: Two 1,395 hp DB 601F; *A*: Two 7·92 mm MG, two 13 mm MG, and two 20 mm; *W*: 17,857 lb (8100 kg); *C*: Two; *MS*: 385 mph (620 kph); *OC*: 22,965 ft (7000 m). *Although later developed models in the 210/410 series were used with moderate success in a number of rôles, the early Me 210A was very unstable, leading to scandals which tarnished Willy Messerschmitt's reputation.*

Mitsubishi G4M2a Type 1 Medium bomber, Jap., 1943. *S*: 81 ft 8 in (24·89 m); *L*: 64 ft 4¾ in (19·63 m); *P*: Two 1,850 hp Mitsubishi Kasei 25; *A*: Four 20 mm and one 7·7 mm MG; *W*: 27,557 lb (12500 kg); *C*: Seven; *MS*: 272 mph (438 kph); *OC*: 29,360 ft (8949 m); *ML*: 2,200 lb (998 kg). *Naval land-based bomber, code-named "Betty" by the Allies, encountered throughout the Pacific War in various versions; finally used as mother-plane for Oka suicide aircraft. Notoriously prone to catch fire.*

Focke-Wulf Fw 190A-8 Single-seat fighter, Ger., 1943. *S*: 34 ft 5½ in (10·50 m); *L*: 29 ft 4 in (8·84 m); *P*: One 1,700 hp BMW 801; *A*: Two 13 mm MG and four 20 mm; *W*: 9,424 lb (4274 kg); *MS*: 405 mph (652 kph); *OC*: 37,400 ft (11398 m). *Major variant of series which won back German air superiority over Channel, 1941–42; remained in widespread service until 1945.*

Kawasaki Ki-61-I Hien Single-seat fighter, Jap., 1943. *S*: 39 ft 4½ in (12·0 m); *L*: 28 ft 8½ in (8·75 m); *P*: One 1,100 hp Army Type 2; *A*: Four 12·7 mm MG; *W*: 6,504 lb (2950 kg); *MS*: 368 mph (592 kph); *OC*: 37,730 ft (11600 m). *IJAAF fighter of sound design, nearer to international standards of armament, protection and strength than the aging Ki-43 Hayabusa it replaced in some squadrons; the engine was licence-built DB 601A, and later models had cannon armament.*

Lockheed P-38L Lightning Single-seat heavy fighter, USA, 1943. *S*: 52 ft 0 in (15·84 m); *L*: 37 ft 10 in (11·53 m); *P*: Two 1,475 hp Allison V-1710; *A*: Four 0·50 MG, one 20 mm; *W*: 14,100 lb (6396 kg); *MS*: 414 mph (667 kph); *OC*: 44,000 ft (13411 m). *Classic twin-boom design with long range and useful ground-attack capability, used widely in all theatres in a variety of rôles, but more in the Pacific where range was most valuable. Best-known exponent was Maj. Richard Bong, top-scoring US fighter* *ace of War, all of whose 40 confirmed victories were gained while flying P-38s.*

Consolidated B-24J Liberator Heavy bomber, USA, 1943. *S*: 110 ft 0 in (33·52 m); *L*: 67 ft 2 in (20·47); *P*: Four 1,200 hp Pratt & Whitney R-1830; *A*: Ten 0·50 MG; *W*: 56,000 lb (25401 kg); *C*: Ten; *MS*: 300 mph (482 kph); *OC*: 28,000 ft (8534 m); *ML*: 5,000 lb (2268 kg). *Definitive model of heavy bomber, second to B-17 in public acclaim, but in fact built and used in much greater numbers in many theatres of war.*

Mitsubishi Ki-46-III Reconnaissance aircraft, Jap., 1943. *S*: 48 ft 2¾ in (14·70 m); *L*: 36 ft 1¼ in (11·00 m); *P*: Two 1,350 hp Mitsubishi Ha-112-II; *W*: 12,620 lb (5724 kg); *C*: Two; *MS*: 391 mph (630 kph); *OC*: 34,450 ft (10500 m). *Its performance gave the Ki-46 relative immunity from interception until the last year of the War; but unarmed and unarmoured, it was easy prey once intercepted. A heavily armed B-29-interceptor version appeared in late 1944.*

Handley Page Halifax III Heavy bomber, UK, 1943. *S*: 99 ft 0 in (30·17 m); *L*: 71 ft 7 in (21·81 m); *P*: Four 1,615 hp Bristol Hercules XVI; *A*: Nine 0·303 MG; *W*: 65,000 lb (29484 kg); *C*: Seven; *MS*: 282 mph (453 kph); *OC*: 24,000 ft (7315 m); *ML*: 10,000 lb (4536 kg). *Major variant of RAF's most important heavy bomber after the Lancaster; more than 6,000 Halifaxes were built, flying more than 82,000 operational sorties and drooping nearly 250,000 tons of bombs.*

Republic P-47D Thunderbolt Single-seat fighter-bomber, USA, 1943. *S*: 40 ft 9 in (12·42 m); *L*: 36 ft 1 in (11·0 m); *P*: One 2,300 hp Pratt & Whitney R-2800; *A*: Eight 0·50 *MG*; *W*: 17,500 lb (7938 kg); *MS*: 433 mph (696 kph); *OC*: 42,000 ft (12802 m). *One of two main USAAF fighter types in service, the Thunderbolt played a major part in winning air supremacy over Europe and earned a formidable reputation as a ground-attack fighter.*

Yakovlev Yak-9M Single-seat fighter, USSR, 1943. *S*: 32 ft 9¾ in (10·00 m); *L*: 27 ft 11½ in (8·55 m); *P*: One 1,210 hp M-105PF; *A*: Two 12·7 mm MG and one 20 mm; *W*: 6,746 lb (3060 kg); *MS*: 360 mph (580 kph); *OC*: 36,090 ft (11000 m). *The Yak series fighters, built in greater numbers than any other Soviet aircraft, were crude by Western standards, but rugged and, at low levels, very effective. Some saw action early in the Korean War.*

Lavochkin La 5FN Single-seat fighter, USSR, 1943. *S*: 32 ft 5¾ in (9·8 m); *L*: 27 ft 10¾ in (8·5 m); *P*: One 1,650 hp M-82FN; *A*: Four 20 mm; *W*: 7,408 lb (3360 kg); *MS*: 402 mph (647 kph); *OC*: 32,800 ft (10000 m). *Like the Yak fighters, the radial-engined Lavochkins could outfight any German type below 15,000 ft. The La 5FN was the most widely used variant of the series.*

Dornier Do 217M-1 Medium bomber, Ger., 1943. *S*: 62 ft 4 in (19·00 m); *L*: 55 ft 9¼ in (17·00 m); *P*: Two 1,750 hp DB 603A; *A*: Four to six 7·92 mm MG, two 13 mm MG and one 20 mm; *W*: 36,817 lb (16700 kg); *C*: Four; *MS*: 348 mph (560 kph); *OC*: 24,000 ft (7315 m); *ML*: 8,820 lb (4000 kg). *Late version of bomber series begun by Do 17; used for anti-shipping strikes with various guided bombs.*

Heinkel He 177A-5/R-2 Heavy bomber, Ger., 1943. *S*: 103 ft 1¾ in (31·44 m); *L*: 66 ft 11 in (20·39 m); *P*: Two 2,950 hp DB 610A-1/B-1; *A*: Three 7·9 mm MG, three 13 mm MG, and two 20 mm; *W*: 59,966 lb (27200 kg); *C*: Six; MS: 303 mph (488 kph); *OC*: 26,250 ft (8000 m); *ML*: 13,200 lb (5988 kg). *Plagued by development problems, the He 177, Germany's only truly original heavy bomber to emerge from the War, saw only limited service – but was the aircraft used for the few genuinely "strategic" bombing raids mounted by the Luftwaffe in 1944.*

Heinkel He 219A-7/R-1 Two-seat night fighter, Ger., 1944. *S*: 60 ft 8¼ in (18·50 m); *L*: 50 ft 11¾ in (15·54 m); *P*: Two 1,900 hp DB 603G; *A*: Six 30 mm and two 20 mm; *W*: 33,730 lb (15300 kg); *MS*: 416 mph (670 kph); *OC*: 40,000 ft (12192 m). *With remarkable performance and ultra-heavy armament, pre-production He 219s scored great successes when tested in combat in 1943, but there were production problems and the type was cancelled after very few deliveries.*

Junkers Ju 88 G-7b Heavy night fighter, Ger., 1944. *S*: 65 ft 10½ in (20·07 m); *L*: 51 ft 1½ in (15·58 m); *P*: Two 1,880 hp Junkers Jumo 213E; *A*: One 13 mm MG and six 20 mm; *W*: 28,900 lb (13109 kg); *C*: Two; *MS*: 389 mph (626 kph); *OC*: 32,800 ft (9997 m). *Highly sophisticated and very successful night-fighter development of the basic bomber, fitted with FuG 218 Neptun search radar.*

North American P-51D Mustang Single-seat fighter-bomber, USA, 1944. *S*: 37 ft 0¼ in (11·28 m); *L*: 32 ft 3¼ in (9·83 m); *P*: One 1,650 hp Rolls-Royce Merlin V-1650; *A*: Six 0·50 MG; *W*: 10,000 lb (4836 kg); *MS*: 437 mph (703 kph); *OC*: 41,000 ft (12497 m). *Second major USAAF fighter, used in all theatres of war; major contribution to victory was success as long-range escort for heavy daylight bombers over Europe.*

Hawker Tempest V Single-seat fighter, UK, 1944. *S*: 41 ft 0 in (12.49 m); *L*: 33 ft 8 in (10·25 m); *P*: One 2,180 hp Napier Sabre IIA; *A*: Four 20 mm; *W*: 11,500 lb (5216 kg); *MS*: 436 mph (702 kph); *OC*: 36,500 ft (11125 m). *Most powerful piston-engined British fighter of the War, more than a match for any piston-engined contemporary over North-West except the rare Ta 152, and credited with several Me 262 jets. Also used as ground-attack aircraft with two 1,000 lb bombs or eight 60 lb rockets.*

Boeing B-29 Superfortress Heavy bomber, USA, 1944. *S*: 141 ft 3 in (43·05 m); *L*: 99 ft 0 in (30·17 m); *P*: Four 2,200 hp Wright Cyclone R-3350-23; *A*: Twleve 0·50 MG and one 20 mm; *W*: 120,000 lb (54432 kg); *C*: Eight; *MS*: 357 mph (575 kph); *OC*: 33,600 ft (10241 m); *ML*: 20,000 lb (9072 kg). *The ultimate heavy bomber of the War – the aircraft which bombed Japan into defeat, dropped the A-bomb, and went on to fight in the Korean War. Notable features were remote-controlled armament barbettes,* *pressurised crew accommodation. Many raids were flown without guns or gunners, to increase the bombload.*

Nakajima Ki-84-Ia Hayate Single-seat fighter, Jap., 1944. *S*: 37 ft 1 in (11·30 m); *L*: 32 ft 6 in (9·90 m); *P*: One 1,800 hp Nakajima Ha-45-II; *A*: Two 12·7 mm MG and two 20 mm; *W*: 8,576 lb (3890 kg); *MS*: 388 mph (624 kph); *OC*: 36,100 ft (11003 m). *IJAAF fighter squadrons re-equipped with the Ki-84 in the last year of the War. It had the traditional Japanese strengths and weaknesses – fast, extremely manoeuvrable, light controls, but poor pilot protection. By 1944 Japanese industry was unable to supply enough to tilt the balance.*

Mitsubishi J2M5 Raiden Single-seat fighter, Jap., 1944. *S*: 35 ft 5¼ in (10·8 m); *L*: 32 ft 7½ in (9·94 m); *P*: One 1,820 hp Mitsubishi Kasei-26a; *A*: Four 20 mm; *W*: 7,676 lb (3482 kg); *MS*: 382 mph (615 kph); *OC*: 36,910 ft (11250 m). *Plagued by engine development delays, and indecision over its production status, the "Jack" appeared with land-based IJNAF interceptor squadrons too late to affect Japan's fortunes; nevertheless, it was an effective bomber-destroyer of good high-altitude performance, preferred by most pilots as a "B-29-killer".*

Vickers Supermarine Spitfire XIV Single-seat fighter, UK, 1944. *S*: 36 ft 10 in (11·23 m); *L*: 32 ft 8 in (9·95 m); *P*: One 2,050 hp Rolls-Royce Griffon 65; *A*: Two 20 mm and four 0·303 MG; *W*: 8,500 lb (3856 kg); *MS*: 448 mph (721 kph); *OC*: 44,500 ft (13564 m). *Developed version of original pre-War design. Later models served into the 1950s with British auxiliary units and several foreign air forces.*

Mitsubishi Ki-67-Ib Hiryu Army heavy bomber, Jap., 1944. *S*: 73 ft 9¾ in (22·50 m); *L*: 61 ft 4¼ in (18·70 m); *P*: Two 2,000 hp Mitsubishi Ha.104; *A*: Four 12·7 mm MG and one 20 mm; *W*: 30,346 lb (13765 kg); *C*: Six; *MS*: 334 mph (538 kph); *OC*: 31,070 ft (9470 m); *ML*: 3,520 lb (1597 kg). *Faster, more manoeuvrable and better armed than its Japanese contemporaries, the Ki-67 was pressed into service in a variety of rôles including torpedo-bombing, flying bomb mother-ship, suicide attacks, etc.*

Messerschmitt Me 163B-1 Single-seat rocket interceptor, Ger., 1944. *S*: 30 ft 7 in (9·32 m); *L*: 18 ft 8 in (5·70 m); *P*: One 3,750 lb.s.t. Walter HWK 109-509A-2 liquid-fuel rocket motor; *A*: Two 30 mm; *W*: 9,500 lb (4309 kg); *MS*: 596 mph (960 kph); *OC*: 39,500 ft (12040 m). *World's only rocket aircraft in squadron service; highly volatile fuel and engine rendered the Komet as dangerous to its crews as to the enemy. Single unit operational as positional defence interceptors, 1944–45, and about a dozen victories were recorded. Performance included climb to 39,500 ft in 3·35 minutes.*

Messerschmitt Bf 109K-4 Single-seat fighter, Ger., 1944. *S*: 32 ft 6½ in (9·92 m); *L*: 29 ft 7 in (9·02 m); *P*: One 1,550 hp Daimler Benz DB605; *A*: Two 13 mm and one 30 mm; *W*: 7,438 lb (3370 kg); *MS*: 452 mph (728 kph); *OC*: 41,000 ft (12500 m). *This interceptor had a pres-*

surised cockpit; water-methanol injection gave power of around 2,000 hp for short bursts.

Messerschmitt Me 262A-1a Single-seat fighter, Ger., 1944. *S*: 40 ft 11½ in (12·48 m); *L*: 34 ft 9½ in (10·60 m); *P*: Two 1,980 lb.s.t. Junkers Jumo 109-004 turbojets; *A*: Four 30 mm; *W*: 14,101 lb (6396 kg); *MS*: 542 mph (873 kph); *OC*: 36,090 ft (11000 m). *World's first operational jet fighter, whose performance and armament were clearly in a different class from any contemporary. Had interceptor service not been delayed by high-level insistence on use as a fighter-bomber, Allied losses could have been catastrophic.*

Focke-Wulf Ta 152H-1 Single-seat fighter, Ger., 1945. *S*: 47 ft 6¾ in (14·49 m); *L*: 35 ft 5½ in (10·80 m); *P*: One 1,880 hp Junkers Jumo 213; *A*: Two 20 mm and one 30 mm; *W*: 11,025 lb (5000 kg); *MS*: 472 mph (760 kph); *OC*: 48,560 ft (14801 m). *Remarkable high-altitude fighter designed by Kurt Tank; a handful reached squadrons in last weeks of War. Water-methanol injection gave high top speeds for short bursts.*

Heinkel He 162A-2 Single-seat interceptor fighter, Ger., 1945. *S*: 23 ft 7¼ in (7·20 m); *L*: 29 ft 8½ in (9·05 m); *P*: One 1,760 lb.s.t. BMW 003E-1 turbojet; *A*: Two 20 mm; *W*: 5,480 lb (2486 kg); *MS*: 522 mph (840 kph); *OC*: 36,000 ft (10973 m). *"Last ditch" jet fighter, developed from first sketches to flying prototype in three months; never saw combat although one unit became operational in April 1945. Light wood-metal construction, hastily designed and dangerously unreliable.*

Grumman F8F-1 Bearcat Single-seat carrier fighter, USA, 1945. *S*: 35 ft 6 in (10·82 m); *L*: 27 ft 6 in (8·38 m); *P*: One 2,400 hp Pratt & Whitney R-2800-34W; *A*: Four 0·50 MG; *W*: 9,334 lb (4234 kg); *MS*: 434 mph (699 kph); *OC*: 38,900 ft (11857 m). *High-performance interceptor which all but missed Second World War; saw action with French forces in Indo-China, using its capacity for 3,000 lb underwing bombload.*

Lockheed 049 Constellation 43-seat long-range airliner, USA, 1946. *S*: 123 ft 0 in (39·97 m); *L*: 95 ft 1 in (30·91 m); *P*: Four 2,200 hp Wright Duplex Cyclone R-3350-C18-BA1; *W*: 90,000 lb (40860 kg); *MS*: 340 mph (545 kph); *OC*: 24,600 ft (8000 m). *One of the important post-War airliner families, the Constellation was developed from the USAAF's C-69 which was cancelled at the end of the War. It was ordered by numerous airlines – by BOAC after failure of the Avro Tudor.*

de Havilland Hornet F.I Single-seat heavy fighter, UK, 1946. *S*: 45 ft 0 in (13·72 m); *L*: 36 ft 8 in (11·17 m); *P*: Two 2,070 hp Rolls-Royce Merlin; *A*: Four 20 mm; *W*: 16,100 lb (7303 kg); *MS*: 472 mph (760 kph); *OC*: 37,500 ft (11430 m). *The ultimate development of the twin-piston-engined fighter, the Hornet served with the RAF, and with the FAA as a carrier aircraft, into the 1950s. Later marks had a useful ground-attack capability, and saw action during the Malayan Emergency.*

Yakovlev Yak-18A Two-seat trainer, USSR, 1947. *S*: 34 ft 9¼ in (10·60 m); *L*: 27 ft 11¾ in (8·55 m); *P*: One 260 hp Ivchenko A1-14R; *W*: 2,901 lb (1316 kg); *MS*: 162 mph (260 kph); *OC*: 16,600 ft (5060 m). *Produced in great numbers as the standard basic trainer for Soviet civilian and military pilots, the Yak-18 is still in use all over the world.*

Latécoère 631 46-seat flying-boat airliner, Fr., 1947. *S*: 188 ft 5 in (57·43 m); *L*: 142 ft 7 in (43·46 m); *P*: Six 1,600 hp Wright Cyclone GR-2600-A5B; *W*: 157,300 lb (71350 kg); *MS*: 245 mph (395 kph). *Envisaged in 1938, the Laté 631's development was interrupted by the War, and only eight were built. They provided considerable luxury but they only served Air France for about one year.*

Hawker Sea Fury Mk. X Single-seat naval fighter, UK, 1947. *S*: 38 ft 4¾ in (11·70 m); *L*: 34 ft 3 in (10·44 m); *P*: One 2,480 hp Bristol Centaurus; *A*: Four 20 mm; *W*: 10,660 lb (4835 kg); *MS*: 465 mph (749 kph); *OC*: 36,180 ft (11028 m). *Britain's last piston-engined fighter, the Sea Fury fought over Korea with the Fleet Air Arm, and has been widely exported as a general-purpose fighter-bomber.*

Antonov An-2P General purpose biplane light transport, USSR, 1948. *S*: 59 ft 8½ in (18·18 m); *L*: 41 ft 10 in (12·75 m); *P*: One 1,000 hp Shvetsov ASh-62IR; *W*: 12,125 lb (5500 kg); *MS*: 157 mph (253 kph); *OC*: 14,275 ft (4350 m). *An apparent anachronism, the An-2 is an enormously successful "hack" built in large numbers and in service all over the world. The passenger version accommodates up to 14, including crew.*

de Havilland Vampire 5 Single-seat fighter, UK, 1948. *S*: 38 ft 0 in (11·58 m); *L*: 30 ft 9 in (9·37 m); *P*: One 3,100 lb.s.t. D.H. Goblin; *A*: Four 20 mm; *W*: 12,360 lb (5606 kg); *MS*: 535 mph (860 kph); *OC*: 40,000 ft (12192 m). *Classic first generation jet fighter which formed, with the Meteor, the backbone of RAF fighter strength in late 1940s and early 1950s. Widely exported, and still in service with several air forces.*

Ilyushin Il-12 27/30-seat medium-range airliner, USSR, 1948. *S*: 104 ft 0 in (31·07 m); *L*: 69 ft 11 in (21·31 m); *P*: Two 1,700 hp ASh-82FN; *W*: 38,030 lb (17250 kg); *CS*: 217 mph (350 kph); *OC*: 21,500 ft (6600 m). *First Russian post-War airliner of wholly original design, the Il-12 was built in huge numbers (some estimates suggest more than 3,000) and served with almost every Eastern bloc air line.*

Gloster Meteor 8 Single-seat fighter, UK, 1949. *S*: 37 ft 2 in (11·32 m); *L*: 44 ft 7 in (13·58 m); *P*: Two 3,500 lb.s.t. Rolls-Royce Derwent V; *A*: Four 20 mm; *W*: 15,700 lb (7122 kg); *MS*: 592 mph (952 kph); *OC*: 45,000 ft (13716 m). *Major variant of first RAF jet fighter which had been in limited action during the War; this version saw action in Korea with RAAF.*

Lockheed T-33A Two-seat trainer, USA, 1949. *S*: 38 ft. 10½ in (11·85 m); *L*: 37 ft 9 in (11·51 m); *P*: One 5,400 lb.s.t. Allison J33-A-35; *A*: Various external combinations or none; *W*: 11,965 lb (5428 kg); *MS*: 600 mph (966 kph); *OC*: 47,500 ft (14480 m). *Trainer version of* F-80C, *first US jet fighter in squadron service; more than 6,000 built, used by more than 30 nations, and still in widespread service.*

North American F-86A Sabre Single-seat fighter, USA, 1949. *S*: 37 ft 1¼ in (11·30 m); *L*: 37 ft 6 in (11·43 m); *P*: One 5,200 lb.s.t. General Electric J-47; *A*: Six 0·50 MG; *W*: 15,876 lb (7201 kg); *MS*: 679 mph (1092 kph); *OC*: 48,000 ft (14630 m). *The fighter responsible for winning back United Nations' air superiority over Korea from Chinese MiG-15s in 1951. Developments of the Sabre have been exported in vast numbers to Europe, Asia, Africa, the Middle East and South America, and there has been considerable licence production. One of the classic jet designs of the post-War years.*

Beechcraft Bonanza 4-seat light aircraft, USA. 1949. *S*: 32 ft 10 in (10·0 m); *L*: 25 ft 2 in (7·67 m); *P*: One 250 hp Continental IO-470-C; *W*: 2,900 lb (1315 kg); *MS*: 210 mph (338 kph); *OC*: 21,300 ft (6490 m). *Over 5,400 Bonanza light cabin aircraft were produced for the civilian market between 1948 and 1957, during which period a further 723 were built (as the T-34A and B) for the USAF and USN.*

Mikoyan-Gurevitch MiG-15 Single-seat fighter, USSR, 1949. *S*: 33 ft 1½ in (10·10 m); *L*: 36 ft 4 in (11·10 m); *P*: One 5,450 lb.s.t. RD-45; *A*: Two 23 mm and one 37 mm; *W*: 14,240 lb (6465 kg); *MS*: 670 mph (1072 kph); *OC*: 51,000 ft (15550 m). *First Soviet combat jet to see extensive service, and chiefly remembered as the main enemy type in the later stages of the Korean War. Widely exported, and still in service with some of the smaller air arms.*

Douglas AD-5 Skyraider General purpose attack aircraft, USA, 1950. *S*: 50 ft 0 in (15·24 m); *L*: 40 ft 0 in (12·19 m); *P*: One 2,700 hp Wright Cyclone; *A*: Four 20 mm; *W*: 17,000 lb (7711 kg); *C*: One to three; *MS*: 270 mph (434·5 kph); *OC*: 26,000 ft (7925 m). *Probably the most "developable" military aircraft ever built, the Skyraider was designed in 1944 and produced from 1945-1957, yet is still in combat service with US and other air forces. The series includes everything from a single-seat attack aircraft capable of carrying 7,000 lb of stores, to a three-seat airborne early warning aircraft.*

Ilyushin Il-28 Medium bomber, USSR, 1950. *S*: 68 ft 0 in (20·75 m); *L*: 62 ft 0 in (18·9 m); *P*: Two 5,955 lb.s.t. VK-1; *A*: Four 23 mm; *W*: c. 44,000 lb (19960 kg); *C*: Four; *MS*: 580 mph (935 kph); *OC*: 44,000 ft (13411 m). *Code-named "Beagle", this basic Soviet tactical bomber was very widely exported in the 1950s and early 1960s. It still serves with several "third world" air arms.*

Boeing B-47A Stratojet Strategic bomber, USA, 1950. *S*: 116 ft 0 in (35·36 m); *L*: 109 ft 10 in (33·38 m); *P*: Six 6,000 lb.s.t. General Electric J47-GE-25; *A*: Two 20 mm; *W*: 206,700 lb (93760 kg); *C*: Three; *MS*: 606 mph (976 kph); *OC*: 40,500 ft (12344 m); *ML*: 20,000 lb (9072 kg). *Important design, pioneering swept wings on* aircraft larger than fighters, and "suspended" engine nacelles.

English Electric Canberra B. Mk. 2 Medium bomber, UK, 1951. *S*: 63 ft 11½ in (19·49 m); *L*: 65 ft 6 in (19·96 m); *P*: Two 6,500 lb.s.t. Rolls-Royce Avon; *W*: 46,000 lb (20865 kg); *C*: Two; *MS*: 570 mph (917 kph); *OC*: 48,000 ft (14630 m); *ML*: 8,000 lb (3629 kg). *First British jet bomber, widely developed both in the UK and abroad, and still in service with several air forces including the RAF and USAF.*

Sikorsky S-55 General purpose helicopter, USA, 1951. *RD*: 49 ft 0 in (14·94 m); *L*: 42 ft 2 in (12·85 m); *P*: One 600 hp Pratt & Whitney R-1340-57; *W*: 6,835 lb (3102 kg); *MS*: 105 mph (169 kph); *OC*: 12,900 ft (3932 m). *More than 1,700 examples of this best-known of all helicopter series have been built, and it has been sold to nearly 30 nations. It is still in widespread service all over the world, in various forms, the basic military transport version accommodating 10 men.*

Avro Shackleton Mk. 1 Maritime reconnaissance bomber, UK, 1951. *S*: 120 ft 0 in (36·58 m); *L*: 77 ft 6 in (23·62 m); *P*: Four 2,450 hp Rolls-Royce Griffon 57; *A*: Two 20 mm and two 0·50 MG; *W*: 86,000 lb (39010 kg); *C*: Ten; *MS*: 298 mph (480 kph); *OC*: 19,200 ft (5852 m); *ML*: 20,000 lb (9072 kg). *Design successor to the famous Lancaster and Lincoln, the Shackleton served, in its later versions, until replaced by Nimrods in the late 1960s and early 1970s.*

de Havilland Comet 1 36-seat medium-range jet airliner, UK, 1952. *S*: 115 ft 0 in (37·37 m); *L*: 93 ft 0 in (30·22 m); *P*: Four 4,450 lb.s.t. D.H. Ghost 50 Mk. I; *W*: 105,000 lb (47670 kg); *CS*: 490 mph (785 kph); *OC*: 35,000 ft (11375 m). *The true achievement of this, the world's first jet airliner, was sadly overshadowed by a series of disastrous accidents in service. After redevelopment to the much-stretched Mk. 3/4, it had been overtaken by American technology – but did in fact achieve the first scheduled jet passenger service across the North Atlantic.*

Dassault MD.450 Ouragan Single-seat fighter, Fr., 1952. *S*: 40 ft 3¾ in (12·29 m); *L*: 35 ft 2¾ in (10·74 m); *P*: One 5,000 lb.s.t. Rolls-Royce Nene 104B; *A*: Four 20 mm plus 2,000 lb (907 kg) underwing stores; *W*: 17,416 lb (7900 kg); *MS*: 584 mph (940 kph); *OC*: 42,650 ft (13000 m). *France's first indigenous jet in service; exported to Israel and India, it has seen combat, and is still in second-line service.*

Airspeed Ambassador 47-passenger medium-range airliner, UK, 1952. *S*: 115 ft 0 in (37·3 m); *L*: 82 ft 0 in (26·75 m); *P*: Two 2,625 hp Bristol Centaurus 661; *CS*: 260 mph (435 kph). *Elegant "Elizabethan"-Class airliner in BEA service, the Ambassador continued to fly passengers for 6½ years; during that time it carried almost 2½ million passengers and flew 1,000 million air route miles.*

Bell 47G Sioux Three-seat light helicopter, USA, 1953. *RD*: 35 ft 1½ in (10·71 m); *L*: 31 ft 7 in (9·62 m); *P*: One 200 hp Franklin 6V4-200-C32; *W*: 2,350 lb (1066 kg);

MS: 100 mph (161 kph); *OC*: 10,900 ft (3322 m). *Most widely built series of helicopters in world – from more than 5,000 produced since earliest version in 1945. Specialised versions for every military and civil rôle are in use all over the world.*

Republic F-84F Thunderstreak Single-seat fighter-bomber, USA, 1953. *S*: 33 ft 7¼ in (10·24 m); *L*: 43 ft 4¾ in (13·22 m); *P*: One 7,220 lb.s.t. Curtiss-Wright J-65; *A*: Six 0·50 MG; *W*: 25,226 lb (11443 kg); *MS*: 658 mph (1059 kph); *OC*: 36,150 ft (11019 m); *ML*: 6,000 lb (2722 kg). *Standard NATO fighter-bomber from the mid-1950s, the Thunderstreak is still in service with a number of overseas air forces; it saw action with the French air force at Suez in 1956.*

Beech T-34 Mentor Two-seat trainer, USA, 1953. *S*: 32 ft 10 in (10·00 m); *L*: 25 ft 11¼ in (7·9 m); *P*: One 225 hp Continental 0-470-13; *W*: 2,950 lb (1338 kg); *MS*: 189 mph (304 kph); *OC*: 20,000 ft (6100 m). *More than 1,200 T-34s have been built, in the USA and under licence abroad. No longer in use by the USAF and USN, it is still in widespread service with many other air forces.*

Mil Mi-4 General purpose helicopter, USSR, 1953. *RD*: 68 ft 11 in (21·00 m); *L*: 55 ft 1 in (16·80 m); *P*: One 1,700 hp Shvetsov ASh-82V; *W*: 17,196 lb (7800 kg); *MS*: 130 mph (210 kph); *OC*: 18,045 ft (5500 m). *Most widely built and exported of Soviet helicopters, the Mi-4 has superficial resemblance to Sikorsky S-55 and Westland Whirlwind, but much higher performance. Rear clam-shell doors give great payload versatility up to total of 3,527 lb (1600 kg).*

Nord 2501 Noratlas Medium transport, Fr., 1954. *S*: 106 ft 7½ in (32·50 m); *L*: 72 ft 0½ in (21·96 m); *P*: Two 2,040 hp SNECMA-Bristol Hercules 758; *W*: 45,415 lb (20600 kg); *CS*: 208 mph (335 kph); *OC*: 24,600 ft (7500 m). *Standard French and German transport of the 1950s and early 1960s, with capacity of about 7½ tons of freight, 45 troops or 36 paratroops. Exported to Portugal, Israel and Niger.*

Grumman S-2A Tracker Anti-submarine aircraft, USA, 1954. *S*: 69 ft 8 in (21·23 m); *L*: 42 ft 3 in (12·88 m); *P*: Two 1,525 hp Wright R-1820-82WA; *W*: 26,300 lb (11930 kg); *C*: Four; *MS*: 287 mph (462 kph); *OC*: 23,000 ft (7000 m). *With provision for internal and external stores including torpedoes and rockets, and combining for the first time the rôles of sub-hunter and sub-killer, the Tracker has been widely exported.*

North American F-100A Super Sabre Single-seat fighter, USA, 1954. *S*: 38 ft 9¼ in (11·81 m); *L*: 47 ft 1¼ in (14·35 m); *P*: One 9,700 lb.s.t. Pratt & Whitney J-57; *A*: Four 20 mm; *W*: 25,000 lb (11340 kg); *MS*: 852 mph (1371 kph); OC: 44,900 ft (13716 m). *First truly supersonic fighter in the West; widely exported and still in use by many air forces.*

Hawker Sea Hawk F.B. Mk. 3 Single-seat carrier fighter-bomber, UK, 1954. *S*: 39 ft 0 in (11·88 m); *L*: 39 ft 10½ in (12·15 m); *P*: One 5,000 lb.s.t. Rolls-Royce Nene 101;

A: Four 20 mm; *W*: 13,220 lb (5997 kg); *MS*: 560 mph (902 kph); *OC*: 43,200 ft (13167 m). *Standard British carrier jet of the mid-1950s, saw action at Suez; exported to India, Holland and Germany.*

Fouga CM.170 Magister Two-seat armed trainer, Fr., 1954. *S*: 39 ft 10¼ in (12·15 m); *L*: 33 ft 0 in (10·06 m); *P*: Two 880 lb.s.t. Turboméca Marboré IIA; *A*: Two 7·62 mm MG; *W*: 6,834 lb (3100 kg); *MS*: 444 mph (715 kph); *OC*: 36,000 ft (11000 m). *Extremely successful jet trainer with light gun armament and wide range of under-wing weapons; exported to many countries and still in service all over the world.*

Vickers Valiant B. Mk. I Heavy bomber, UK, 1955. *S*: 114 ft 4 in (34·84 m); *L*: 108 ft 3 in (32·99 m); *P*: Four 10,000 lb.s.t. Rolls-Royce Avon; *W*: 138,000 lb (62597 kg); *C*: Five; *MS*: 560 mph (901 kph); *OC*: 54,000 ft (16460 m); *ML*: 21,000 lb (9526 kg). *Britain's first V-bomber, designed to deliver nuclear or conventional weapons. Saw action at Suez, 1956; dropped first British A-bomb, 1956.*

Lockheed P2V-7 Neptune Maritime patrol aircraft, USA, 1956. *S*: 103 ft 10 in (31·64 m); *L*: 91 ft 8 in (27·93 m); *P*: Two 3,500 hp Wright R-3350-32W turboprops and two 3,400 lb.s.t. Westinghouse J34-WE-36 turbojets; *W*: 80,000 lb (36288 kg); *C*: Nine; *MS*: 364 mph (586 kph); *OC*: 33,000 ft (10058 m). *Late model of extremely versatile patrol/ASW aircraft; first prototype flew in 1945, and large numbers are still serving with half-a-dozen air forces.*

Myasishchev Mya-4 Heavy bomber, USSR, 1956. *S*: 170 ft 7 in (52·00 m); *L*: 162 ft 5 in (49·50 m); *P*: Four 19,180 lb.s.t. Mikulin AM-3D; *A*: Six-eleven 23 mm; *W*: 352,750 lb (160000 kg); *C*: Eight; *MS*: 559 mph (900 kph); *OC*: 39,375 ft (12000 m); *ML*: c. 9,920 lb. (4500 kg). *Estimated data on "Bison", still in service with naval aviation long-range reconnaissance units, where range of 3,100 miles (5000 km) is useful despite low ceiling.*

Vickers Viscount 800 Series 52/70-seat medium-range airliner, UK, 1956. *S*: 93 ft 8½ in (28·56 m); *L*: 85 ft 8 in (26·11 m); *P*: Four 1,990 hp Rolls-Royce Dart 525 turboprops; *W*: 72,500 lb (32886 kg); *CS*: 357 mph (575 kph); *OC*: 25,000 ft (7620 m). *Stretched version of the world's first successful turboprop airliner, the Viscount 700 Series, which started scheduled services in April 1953 with BEA. A total of 444 Viscounts was built before production ended in March 1964.*

Dornier Do 27A-4 Light general purpose type, Ger., 1956. *S*: 39 ft 4½ in (12·00 m); *L*: 31 ft 6 in (9·60 m); *P*: One 270 hp Lycoming GO-480-B; *W*: 4,070 lb (1850 kg); *MS*: 141 mph (227 kph); *OC*: 10,825 ft (3300 m). *With a capacity of 6–8 people, the versatile Do 27 can be used for training, reconnaissance, liaison, casualty evacuation and light transport. It is in use in Germany, Spain, Switzerland, Portugal, Belgium, Sweden, Turkey and several African countries.*

Hawker Hunter F. Mk. 6 Single-seat fighter-bomber, UK,

1956. *S*: 33 ft 8 in (10·25 m); *L*: 45 ft 10½ in (13·96 m); *P*: One 10,000 lb.s.t. Rolls-Royce Avon 200 series; *A*: Four 30 mm; *W*: 17,750 lb (8051 kg); *MS*: 725 mph (1166 kph); *OC*: 51,500 ft (15696 m). *Major variant of fighter series which formed backbone of RAF strength 1954–1965, still in service; exported to many overseas air forces. About 2,000 built.*

Piper Tri-Pacer 4-seat light aircraft, USA, 1956. *S*: 29 ft 3½ in (8·9 m); *L*: 20 ft 8¾ in (6·32 m); *P*: One 150 hp Lycoming 0-320; *W*: 2,000 lb (908 kg); *MS*: 139 mph (222 kph); *OC*: 15,000 ft (4575 m). *Very popular sporting and club training light aircraft of the late 1950s and early 1960s, the Tri-Pacer was widely exported.*

MiG-17F Single-seat fighter, USSR, c. 1956. *S*: 31 ft 6 in (9·60 m); *L*: 38 ft 4½ in (11·70 m); *P*: One 5,950 lb.s.t. Klimov VK-1A; *A*: Three 23 mm plus external stores; *W*: 11,795 lb (5350 kg); *MS*: 711 mph (1145 kph); *OC*: 49,200 ft (15000 m). *Very widely built and exported development of the MiG-15 – still serving with many air forces in various versions.*

Aero Commander 680 Super 5/7-seat light passenger aircraft, USA, 1956. *S*: 44 ft 0¾ in (13·42 m); *L*: 35 ft 5 in (10·8 m); *P*: Two 340 hp Lycoming GSO-480-G1A-6; *W*: 7000 lb (3175 kg); *MS*: 260 mph (418 kph); *OC*: 26,567 ft (7800 m). *Representative of a class of executive twin popular in the USA was the Aero Commander series, an elegant high-wing aircraft of which more than 650 were built, including some for the USAF and US Army.*

Tupolev Tu-16 "Badger-B" Medium range reconnaissance bomber, USSR, c. 1956. *S*: 110 ft 0 in (33·50 m); *L*: 120 ft 0 in (36·50 m); *P*: Two 20,950 lb.s.t. Mikulin AM-3M; *A*: Seven 23 mm; *W*: c. 150,000 lb (68000 kg); *C*: Seven; *MS*: 587 mph (945 kph); *OC*: 42,650 ft (13000 m); *ML*: c. 19,840 lb (9000 kg). *The B-version usually carries large anti-shipping missiles underwing instead of internal warload. Still in Soviet service in later versions, the Tu-16 has been exported to Arab nations and to Indonesia.*

Douglas A-3B Skywarrior Naval attack aircraft, USA, 1957. *S*: 72 ft 6 in (22·10 m); *L*: 76 ft 4 in (23·27 m); *P*: Two 12,400 lb.s.t. Pratt & Whitney J57-P-10; *A*: Two 20 mm; *W*: 73,000 lb (33112 kg); *C*: Three; *MS*: 610 mph (982 kph); *OC*: 41,000 ft (12500 m). *Much developed "workhorse", used in many rôles by USN, and by USAF as the B-66 Destroyer. Electronic reconnaissance and counter-measures versions carry as many as four extra crew, with equipment, in the weapons bay. Small numbers of specialised models still in service.*

Dassault Super Mystère B.2 Single-seat fighter, Fr., 1957. *S*: 34 ft 5¾ in (10·51 m); *L*: 46 ft 1¼ in (14·05 m); *P*: One 7,495 lb.s.t. SNECMA Atar 101G; *A*: Two 30 mm plus external stores; *W*: 22,046 lb (10000 kg); *MS*: 743 mph (1195 kph); *OC*: 55,775 ft (17000 m). *Europe's first production aircraft with supersonic performance in level flight, the Super Mystère served with the French and*

Israeli forces. In the latter service it saw action in the Six Day War, and is still operational.

Lockheed U-2B Single-seat reconnaissance aircraft, USA, 1957. *S*: 80 ft 0 in (24·38 m); *L*: 49 ft 7 in (15·11 m); *P*: One 17,000 lb.s.t. Pratt & Whitney J75; *W*: 15,850 lb (6842 kg); *OC*: "65,000 ft plus" (19810 plus). *The notorious spy-plane in which Major Powers was shot down over the USSR on 1st May 1960, now obsolescent in the days of spy satellites and SR-71s!*

Gloster Javelin F.A.W. Mk. 9 Two-seat all-weather fighter, UK, 1958. *S*: 52 ft 0 in (15·85 m); *L*: 56 ft 9 in (17·30 m); *P*: Two 10,630 lb.s.t. Bristol Siddeley Sapphire 203/204; *A*: Two 30 mm plus four Firestreak missiles; *W*: 42,930 lb (19473 kg); *MS*: 684 mph (1101 kph); *OC*: 49,500 ft (15087 m). *Delta-wing fighter, in service with RAF from 1956 to 1967.*

Hawker Siddeley Gnat F. Mk. 1 Single-seat fighter, UK, 1958. *S*: 22 ft 2 in (6·75 m); *L*: 29 ft 9 in (9·06 m); *P*: One 4,520 lb.s.t. Bristol Orpheus 701; *A*: Two 30 mm plus external stores up to 1,000 lb (454 kg); *W*: 6,650 lb (3010 kg); *MS*: 695 mph (1118 kph); *OC*: 50,000 ft (15000 m). *The tiny, very manoeuvrable Gnat was not purchased for the RAF except in its two-seat trainer version, but was bought by Finland, and in large numbers by India. It saw action in both recent clashes between India and Pakistan.*

Bristol Britannia Series 300 212/222-passenger airliner, UK, 1958. *S*: 142 ft 3 in (43·6 m); *L*: 124 ft 3 in (37·6 m);

P: Four 4,450 ehp Bristol Proteus turboprops; *W*: 185,000 lb (84990 kg); *CS*: 357 mph (575 kph). *Classic first-generation long-range turboprop airliner, the Britannia served with BOAC, Aeronaves de Mexico, El Al and other airlines for more than six years.*

MiG-19SF Single-seat interceptor, USSR, 1958. *S*: 29 ft 6¼ in (9·00 m); *L*: 41 ft 1¾ in (12·54 m); *P*: Two 5,732 lb.s.t. Klimov RD-9B; *A*: Three 30 mm plus missiles; *W*: 19,180 lb (8700 kg); *MS*: 902 mph (1452 kph); *OC*: 58,725 ft (17900 m). *Russia's first supersonic fighter in squadron service, the MiG-19 has been exported to many foreign air forces and has been built abroad, both with and without licence agreement.*

Fairey Gannet AEW Mk. 3 Airborne early warning aircraft, U.K., 1959. *S*: 54 ft 7 in (16·64 m); *L*: 43 ft 11 in (13·39 m); *P*: One 3,875 ehp Bristol Siddeley Double Mamba 102; *W*: c. 24,000 lb (c. 10890 kg); *C*: Three; *MS*: 250 mph (402 kph); *OC*: 25,000 ft (7620 m). *Anti-submarine warfare versions of the Gannet served on Royal Navy carriers from 1955 onwards; Germany, Australia and Indonesia also operated aircraft of this series.*

Bréguet 1050 Alizé ASW aircraft, Fr., 1959. *S*: 51 ft 2¼ in (15·60 m); *L*: 45 ft 6 in (13·87 m); *P*: One 2,100 eshp Rolls-Royce Dart RDa.21 turboprop; *A*: Various internal and external combinations of homing torpedoes, depth-charges and rockets; *W*: 18,100 lb (8210 kg); *C*: Three; *MS*: 282 mph (454 kph). *French and Indian carriers still carry Alizé flights for ASW patrol; they have a range of approximately 1,325 miles.*

The Gloster Javelin F.A.W.7, shown here in the colours of No. 23 (Fighter) Squadron, R.A.F. This large, missile-armed delta-wing aircraft was the last British fighter designed specifically as a night fighter and remained in service until 1972

Ilyushin Il-18 75/100-seat airliner, USSR, 1959. *S*: 122 ft 8½ in (37·40 m); *L*: 117 ft 9½ in (35·90 m); *P*: Four 4,250 ehp AI-20 turboprops; *W*: 134,920 lb (61200 kg); *CS*: 388 mph (625 kph); *OC*: 32,800 ft (10000 m). *An elegant airliner in roughly the same category as the Vanguard/Electra, the Il-18 has been built in large numbers (nearly 300 serving with Aeroflot) and is in service with numerous USSR "client" nations.*

Convair F-106A Delta Dart Single-seat interceptor, USA, 1959. *S*: 38 ft 3½ in (11·67 m); *L*: 70 ft 8¾ in (21·56 m); *P*: One 17,200 lb.s.t. Pratt & Whitney J75-P-17; *A*: Four Hughes Falcon air-to-air and two Douglas Genie nuclear missiles; *W*: 35,500 lb (16103 kg); *MS*: 1525 mph (2455 kph); *OC*: 57,000 ft (17375 m). *Despite its age, the performance of the F-106A, and its advanced electronic guidance and fire control equipment, have ensured it a continuing place in the USAF Air Defense Command until the present day.*

Douglas DC-8 Series 10 105-seat airliner, USA, 1959. *S*: 142 ft 5 in (43·41 m); *L*: 150 ft 6 in (45·87 m); *P*: Four 13,500 lb.s.t. Pratt & Whitney JT3C-6; *W*: 273,000 lb (12383 kg); *CS*: 542 mph (873 kph); *OC*: 41,000 ft (12500 m). *Second of the first-generation trio of American big-jet airliners, the DC-8 has been extensively developed, 556 being operated by more than 30 world airlines. The much-stretched DC-8 Super 61 has accommodation for up to 259 passengers.*

McDonnell F-101B Voodoo Two-seat interceptor fighter, USA, 1959. *S*: 39 ft 8 in (12·09 m); *L*: 67 ft 4¾ in (20·54 m); *P*: Two 11,990 lb.s.t. Pratt & Whitney J-57-P-55; *A*: Three Hughes Falcon air-to-air and two Douglas Genie nuclear missiles; *W*: 39,900 lb (18098 kg); *MS*: 1,120 mph (1802 kph); *OC*: 52,000 ft (15850 m). *Interceptor development of USAF Tactical Air Command fighter, still in service with Canadian and Nationalist Chinese forces.*

Boeing 707-120 179/189-seat long-range airliner, USA, 1959. *S*: 130 ft 10 in (39·87 m); *L*: 144 ft 6 in (44·04 m); *P*: Four 13,500 lb.s.t. Pratt & Whitney JT3C-6; *W*: 257,000 lb (116575 kg); *MS*: 623 mph (1002 kph); *OC*: 31,500 ft (9600 m). *Most widely-used big-jet airliner (840 ordered), the 707 was built in numerous variations according to customer requirements, and entered service with the USAF for transport, tanker and other duties. Later versions were turbofan-powered.*

Boeing B-52G Stratofortress Heavy bomber, USA, 1959. *S*: 185 ft 0 in (56·39 m); *L*: 157 ft 7 in (48·03 m); *P*: Eight 13,750 lb.s.t. Pratt & Whitney J57-P-43W; *A*: One 20 mm rotary; *W*: 480,000 lb (217720 kg); *MS*: 630 mph (1014 kph); *OC*: 55,000 ft (16750 m); *ML*: 65,000 lb (29484 kg). *US Strategic Air Command's super-heavy conventional or nuclear bomber, stressed for high- or low-level attack, with a range of at least 8,000 miles. Some 450 remain in service.*

Kaman HH-43B Huskie General purpose helicopter, USA, 1960. *RD*: 47 ft 0 in (14·33 m); *L*: 25 ft 2 in (7·67 m); *P*: One 860 shp Lycoming T53-L-1B shaft turbine; *W*: 5,969 lb (2708 kg); *MS*: 120 mph (193 kph); *OC*: 25,000 ft (7620 m). *Eight-man rescue version of box-like helicopter with contra-rotating rotors. Various models in the series exported to Iran, Colombia, Pakistan, Morocco, Burma and Thailand.*

Sud-Aviation Caravelle III 80-seat medium range airliner, Fr., 1960. *S*: 112 ft 6¼ in (34·30 m); *L*: 105 ft 0 in (32·01 m); *P*: Two 11,400 lb.s.t. Rolls-Royce Avon 527; *W*: 101,413 lb (46000 kg); *CS*: 484 mph (779 kph); *OC*: 32,800 ft (10000 m). *One of the finest airliners produced in Europe, the Caravelle was France's first in-service jet transport, joining Air France in 1959. The Mk. III and later versions have flown with more than 30 world air lines.*

Fokker F.27 Mk. 400M Troopship Medium military transport, Hol., 1960. *S*: 95 ft 2 in (29·00 m); *L*: 77 ft 3½ in (23·56 m); *P*: Two 2,050 shp plus 525 lb.s.t. Rolls-Royce Dart RDa.7 turboprops; *W*: 43,500 lb (19730 kg); *C*: Three; *CS*: 302 mph (486 kph); *OC*: 29,500 ft (9000 m). *Military version of most successful short/medium range airliner in Europe; with military payload of around 12,900 lb (5850 kg), this model has been sold to half-a-dozen air forces.*

General Dynamics/Convair 880 Model 22 94/110-seat medium range airliner, USA, 1960. *S*: 120 ft 0 in (36·58 m); *L*: 129 ft 4 in (39·42 m); *P*: Four 11,200 lb.s.t. General Electric CJ-805-3; *W*: 184,500 lb (83690 kg); *CS*: 615 mph (990 kph); *OC*: 41,000 ft (12500 m). *The Convair 880 was the third of the American big-jet trio, first entering service with Delta Air Lines in May 1960. 64 aircraft were flown by nine air lines. The developed Convair 990A entered service in 1962.*

Sukhoi Su-7B Single-seat ground-attack fighter, USSR, 1960. *S*: 29 ft 3½ in (8·93 m); *L*: 57 ft 0 in (17·37 m); *P*: One 15,430 lb.s.t. Tumansky R-31; *A*: Two 30 mm plus external weapons; *W*: 31,965 lb (14500 kg); *MS*: 1085 mph (1750 kph); *OC*: 49,700 ft (15150 m). *Still in Soviet service, and exported to Cuba, Czechoslovakia, East Germany, Egypt, Hungary, India, Poland, North Vietnam, etc. For its designed rôle its usual underwing stores – a pair of 500 kg bombs or a pair of rocket pods – are unimpressive.*

de Havilland Canada DHC-4 Caribou Transport, Can., 1960. *S*: 95 ft 7½ in (29·15 m); *L*: 72 ft 7 in (22·13 m); *P*: Two 1,450 h.p. Pratt & Whitney R-2000-7M2; *W*: 28,500 lb (12928 kg); *MS*: 182 mph (293 kph); *OC*: 24,800 ft (7560 m); *ML*: 8,740 lb (3965 kg). *Rugged medium-range general purpose transport, with good short-runway and rough-field performance; in service with over a dozen nations as freighter, troop or paratroop transport, ambulance, etc.*

Avro Vulcan B. Mk. 2 Strategic bomber, UK, 1960. *S*: 111 ft 0 in (33·83 m); *L*: 99 ft 11 in (30·45 m); *P*: Four 20,000 lb.s.t. Rolls-Royce-Bristol Olympus 301; *W*: c. 190,000 lb (86180 kg); *C*: Five; *MS*: c. 620 mph (998 kph); *OC*: 65,000 ft (19800 m); *ML*: 21,000 lb (9525 kg). *At the* *time of introduction in the 1950s the huge delta-wing Vulcan was invulnerable to contemporary fighters, and a major part of the Western strategic deterrent. Still in service in a low-level intruder rôle.*

Republic F-105D Thunderchief Heavy single-seat strike fighter, USA, 1960. *S*: 34 ft 11¼ in (10·65 m); *L*: 67 ft 0¼ in (20·43 m); *P*: One 17,200 lb.s.t. Pratt & Whitney J75-P-19W; *A*: One 20 mm plus external stores totalling 12,000 lb (5444 kg); *W*: 52,546 lb (23832 kg); *MS*: 1,388 mph (2235 kph). *With its enormous warload, including air-to-air missiles for its own defence, and high performance, the F-105 series was a mainstay of the US bombing campaign over North Vietnam. Losses were quite heavy, and as production ceased in 1964 it is not known how many remain in front-line service with the USAF.*

Tupolev Tu-114 Rossiya 170/220-seat airliner, USSR, 1961. *S*: 165 ft 8 in (51·10 m); *L*: 177 ft 6 in (54·10 m); *P*: Four 14,795 eshp Kuznetsov NK-12MV turboprops; *W*: 376,990 lb (171000 kg); *MS*: 540 mph (870 kph); *OC*: 39,370 ft (12000 m). *Produced in parallel with the Tu-95 ("Bear") bomber, the Tu-114 was a large intercontinental airliner which served on long-distance Aeroflot routes throughout the 1960s; it had no Western counterpart.*

Mil Mi-10 "Flying crane" helicopter, USSR, 1961. *RD*: 114 ft 10 in (35·00 m); *L*: 107 ft 9¾ in (32·86 m); *P*: Two 5,500 shp Soloviev D-25V shaft turbines; *W*: 95,791 lb (43450 kg); *MS*: 124 mph (200 kph); *OC*: 9,850 ft (3000 m). *Enormous machine standing more than 30 ft high, which "squats" on such loads as a bus or prefab building, and lifts them – and 28 passengers – over ranges up to 150 miles.*

North American T-28D Trojan Two-seat light attack aircraft, USA, 1962. *S*: 40 ft 7 in (12·37 m); *L*: 32 ft 10 in (10·00 m); *P*: One 1,300 hp Wright R-1820-56S; *A*: Various external store loads totalling 4,000 lb (1814 kg); *W*: 8,495 lb (3853 kg); *MS*: 352 mph (567 kph). *Attack version of T-28A trainer of the late 1950s, widely used as an effective, simple COIN aircraft; equips several Asian air forces, and in its French modified form – "Fennec" – saw action in Algeria. Many serve in Vietnam.*

Tupolev Tu-124 22/44-seat airliner, USSR, 1962. *S*: 83 ft 9½ in (25·55 m); *L*: 100 ft 4 in (30·58 m); *P*: Two 11,905 lb.s.t. Soloviev D-20P turbofans; *W*: 83,775 lb (38000 kg); *MS*: 603 mph (970 kph). *The first Soviet transport with turbofan engines, the Tu-124 was a civil development of the Tu-104 bomber. Some were exported to East Germany, Czechoslovakia, India and Iraq.*

Dassault Étendard IVM Single-seat naval fighter, Fr., 1962. *S*: 31 ft 6 in (9·60 m); *L*: 47 ft 3 in (14·40 m); *P*: One 9,700 lb.s.t. SNECMA Atar O8B; *A*: Two 30 mm plus external stores totalling 3,000 lb (1361 kg); *W*: 22,652 lb (10275 kg); *MS*: 674 mph (1085 kph); *OC*: 49,210 ft (15000 m). With a batch of F-8 Crusaders, the Étendards provide the strike force for France's aircraft carriers.*

Fiat G.91R-3 Single-seat tactical fighter, It., 1962. *S*: 28 ft 1 in (8·56 m); *L*: 33 ft 9 in (10·29 m); *P*: One 5,000

lb.s.t. Bristol Siddeley Orpheus; *A*: Two 30 mm; *W*: 11,800 lb (5352 kg); *MS*: 675 mph (1087 kph); *OC*: 43,000 ft (13106 m). *Light, simple ground-attack fighter designed for ease of operation from crude front-line airstrips. This version is licence-built in Germany in large numbers, and also operated by Portugal.*

Lockheed F-104G Super Starfighter Single-seat multi-mission fighter, USA, 1962. *S*: 21 ft 11 in (6·68 m); *L*: 54 ft 9 in (16·69 m); *P*: One 10,000 lb.s.t. General Electric J79-GE-11A; *A*: One 20 mm rotary plus external stores (nuclear or conventional) up to total of 4,000 lb (1814 kg); *W*: 19,841 lb (9000 kg); *MS*: 1,550 mph (2496 kph); *OC*: 55,000 ft (16764 m). *Notorious for its accident rate in Luftwaffe service, the F-104 is in fact technically reliable, and serves successfully with nearly a dozen Western air forces; it is widely licence-built in several versions.*

Douglas A-4E Skyhawk Single-seat naval attack aircraft, USA, 1962. *S*: 27 ft 6 in (8·38 m); *L*: 41 ft 4 in (12·59 m); *P*: One 8,500 lb.s.t. Pratt & Whitney J52; *A*: Two 20 mm; *W*: 24,500 lb (11113 kg); *MS*: 673 mph (1083 kph); *OC*: 47,900 ft (14600 m); *ML*: 8,200 lb (3720 kg). *Excellent light-weight, low-cost, simple-to-operate attack aircraft, still in production and service with US Navy and Marines, and as short-take-off land-based fighter-bomber with several air forces.*

Antonov An-24 44/50-seat medium-range airliner, USSR, 1962. *S*: 95 ft 9½ in (29·20 m); *L*: 77 ft 2¼ in (23·53 m); *P*: Two 2,550 ehp Ivchenko AI-24 turboprops; *W*: 46,297 lb (21000 kg); *CS*: 310 mph (500 kph); *OC*: 29,360 ft (8950 m). *Several hundred of this twin-turboprop shoulder-wing airliner have been built since it first joined Aeroflot in 1962, flying with European, Asian and Middle Eastern air lines. It approximates to the Fokker Friendship.*

Chance Vought F-8E Crusader Single-seat naval fighter, USA, 1962. *S*: 35 ft 2 in (10·71 m); *L*: 54 ft 6 in (16·61 m); *P*: One 10,000 lb.s.t. Pratt & Whitney J57-P-20; *A*: Four 20 mm; *W*: 28,000 lb (12701 kg); *MS*: 1,120 mph (1803 kph); *OC*: 59,000 ft (17983 m); *ML*: 5,000 lb (2268 kg). *First supersonic carrier aircraft, which solved problems of reconciling carrier deck requirements with high speed by hydraulically-operated variable incidence wing.*

Grumman OV-1B Mohawk Tactical reconnaissance aircraft, USA, 1962. *S*: 48 ft 0 in (14·63 m); *L*: 41 ft 0 in (12·50 m); *P*: Two 1,400 shp Lycoming T53-L-701 turboprops; *W*: 19,230 lb (8722 kg); *C*: Two; *MS*: 297 mph (478 kph); *OC*: 30,300 ft (9235 m). *With external store points to enable it to carry out ground-attack missions with up to 3,740 lb (1696 kg) loads, and excellent STOL and rough-field characteristics, the Mohawk is basically a sophisticated reconnaissance aircraft and "airborne radar station" for the US Army.*

Sud-Aviation Alouette III General purpose helicopter, Fr., 1962. *S*: 36 ft 1¼ in (11·00 m); *L*: 33 ft 4½ in (10·17 m); *P*: One 870 shp Turboméca Artouste IIIB shaft turbine; *A*: Various combinations depending on rôle; *W*: 4,630 lb (2100 kg); *MS*: 130 mph (210 kph); *OC*: 13,940 ft (4250 m). *Very successful type, in widespread service with some thirty air arms – apart from civilian use. Basically a five-man transport, the Alouette has appeared in shipboard, ambulance, flying crane, and close-support models – the latter mounting 7·62 mm MGs and 20 mm cannon, rocket pods and anti-tank missiles.*

Tupolev Tu-95 Strategic bomber, USSR, 1962. *S*: 167 ft 4 in (51·00 m); *L*: 162 ft 5 in (49·50 m); *P*: Four 14,795 ehp Kuznetsov NK-12M turboprops; *A*: Six 23 mm; *W*: 340,000 lb (154200 kg); *MS*: 530 mph (850 kph); *OC*: c. 50,000 ft (c. 15000 m); *ML*: 25,000 lb (11340 kg) plus. *Estimated data on "Bear-B", believed to have unrefuelled range of no less than 7,800 miles (12550 km). First model appeared in 1955, late models still in service in maritime reconnaissance rôle. Strong resemblance to Tu-114 airliner, and AWACS version code-named "Moss".*

Aero L-29 Delfin Two-seat trainer, Cz., 1963. *S*: 33 ft 9 in (10·29 m); *L*: 35 ft 5½ in (10·81 m); *P*: One 1,962 lb.s.t. Motorlet M-701; *W*: 7,230 lb (3280 kg); *MS*: 407 mph (655 kph); *OC*: 36,000 ft (11000 m). *Since selection as standard Warsaw Pact air force trainer, the robust L-29 has since seen widespread use. The USSR has taken more than 2,000, and several African and Arab countries have L-29s in service.*

Grumman A-6A Intruder Carrier-borne attack aircraft, USA, 1963. *S*: 53 ft 0 in (16·15 m); *L*: 54 ft 7 in (16·64 m); *P*: Two 9,300 lb.s.t. Pratt & Whitney J52-P-8A; *W*: 60,625 lb (27500 kg); *C*: Two; *MS*: 685 mph (1102 kph); *OC*: 41,660 ft (12700 m). *Yet another "Skyraider replacement", the Intruder can deliver up to 16,000 lb of offensive stores, and has seen considerable action over Vietnam.*

Tupolev Tu-28P Two-seat interceptor, USSR, 1963. *S*: 65 ft 6 in (20·00 m); *L*: 98 ft 6 in (30·00 m); *P*: Two 27,560 lb.s.t. turbojets of unknown type; *A*: Usual load, four "Ash" missiles; *W*: c. 99,000 lb (45000 kg); *MS*: 1,150 mph (1850 kph); *OC*: 64,000 ft (19500 m). *Estimated data of heavy and probably long-range interceptor; only one version of probable multi-purpose design.*

Bell UH-1D Iroquois General purpose helicopter, USA, 1963. *RD*: 48 ft 0 in (14·63 m); *L*: 41 ft 10¾ in (12·77 m); *P*: One 1,400 shp Lycoming T53-L-11 shaft turbine; *A*: Various loads depending on rôle; *W*: 9,500 lb (4309 kg); *CS*; 127 mph (204 kph); *OC*: 12,600 ft (3840 m). *The work-horse of the Vietnam War, with basic accommodation for approximately 12 troops. Many different versions, including "gunships", depending on local requirements. Extensive licence production in Germany, and of closely-related Agusta-Bell 204B version in Italy.*

Pilatus Porter STOL Utility aircraft, Swit., 1963. *S*: 49 ft 8 in (15·13 m); *L*: 33 ft 5½ in (10·20 m); *P*: One 340 hp Lycoming GSO-480-B1A6; *W*: 4,444 lb (2015 kg); *MS*: 167 mph (268 kph); *OC*: 17,400 ft (5300 m). *Highly adaptable utility high-wing aircraft – widely exported for rescue, ambulance and agricultural duties – the Porter has been produced in landplane, floatplane and skiplane versions, and in 1965–66 was joined by the turboprop version (the Turbo-Porter). Production figures near 300.*

Antonov An-12 Medium transport, USSR, 1963. *S*: 124 ft 8 in (38·00 m); *L*: 108 ft 3 in (33·00 m); *P*: Four 4,250 shp Ivchenko AI-20K turboprops; *A*: Occasionally two 20 mm; *W*: 119,050 lb (54000 kg); *C*: Five; *MS*: 373 mph (600 kph); *OC*: 33,500 ft (10200 m). *With maximum payload of 44,090 lb (20000 kg), the An-12 is the standard medium range (c. 2,000 miles) transport, freighter, para-*

The Northrop F-5A Freedom Fighter, shown here in Turkish Air Force markings, is a relatively inexpensive Mach 1·4 aircraft which has been adopted by numerous air forces

troop aircraft, etc., of the Soviet bloc, and is in wide use in "third world" nations.

Hawker Siddeley Sea Vixen F(AW) Mk. 2 Two-seat naval fighter, UK, 1964. *S*: 50 ft 0 in (15·24 m); *L*: 55 ft 7 in (16·94 m); *P*: Two 11,250 lb.s.t. Rolls-Royce Avon 208; *A*: Various external load combinations; *W*: 35,000 lb plus (15,875 kg plus); *MS*: c. 645 mph (1038 kph); *OC*: c. 48,000 ft (14630 m). *Standard Fleet Air Arm fighter, in Mk. 1 version since 1959 and Mk. 2 since 1964, the Sea Vixen was the first British fighter without gun armament; Firestreak, Bullpup or Red Top missiles, and pods of unguided air-to-air rockets, were carried instead.*

Handley Page Victor B. Mk. 2 Heavy bomber, UK, 1964. *S*: 120 ft 0 in (36·58 m); *L*: 114 ft 11 in (35·03 m); *P*: Four 20,600 lb.s.t. Rolls-Royce Conway 201 turbofans; *W*: c. 200,000 lb (90720 kg); *C*: Five; *MS*: c. 615 mph (990 kph); *OC*: "60,000 ft plus" (18300 m plus); *ML*: One Blue Steel stand-off bomb, or 35,000 lb (18150 kg) of conventional bombs. *RAF's third V-bomber; early versions entered service in 1958, last Bomber Command unit re-equipped 1969. Still in limited reconnaissance use, and serves as air-to-air refuelling tanker.*

North American RA-5C Vigilante Carrier reconnaissance/ strike aircraft, USA, 1964. *S*: 53 ft 0¼ in (16·16 m); *L*: 75 ft 10 in (23·11 m); *P*: Two 10,900 lb.s.t. General Electric J79-GE-8; *W*: c. 80,000 lb (c. 36300 kg); *C*: Two; *MS*: 1,385 mph (2230 kph); *OC*: 64,000 ft (19500 m). *Primarily a sophisticated naval reconnaissance type, the RA-5C has a considerable secondary strike capability, and can carry a wide range of nuclear and conventional weapons internally and externally.*

BAC VC-10 135/151-seat long-range airliner, UK, 1964. *S*: 146 ft 2 in (44·55 m); *L*: 158 ft 8 in (48·36 m); *P*: Four 21,000 lb.s.t. Rolls-Royce Conway RCo.42; *W*: 312,000 lb (14152 kg); *CS*: 568 mph (914 kph); *OC*: 42,000 ft (12800 m). *Popular for its cabin quietness, the VC-10 (and the 163/180-seat Super VC-10) fly BOAC's transatlantic and other long-haul routes. It was late in the race for big-jet orders however and has been overshadowed by the Boeing 707 and Douglas DC-8.*

Westland Wessex HU Mk. 5 General purpose helicopter, UK, 1964. *RD*: 56 ft 0 in (17·07 m); *L*: 48 ft 4½ in (14·74 m); *P*: Two 1,250 shp Rolls-Royce Gnome (one Mk. 112 and one Mk. 113) shaft turbines; *A*: Various loads depending on rôle; *W*: 13,500 lb (6124 kg); *MS*: 132 mph (212 kph); *OC*: 14,100 ft (4297 m). *Commando carrier transport version (10 troops) of multi-rôle series in service since 1960 with RAF and RN, and exported to four foreign operators. British development of Sikorsky S-58.*

Dassault Mirage IV-A Strategic bomber, Fr., 1964. *S*: 38 ft 10½ in (11·85 m); *L*: 77 ft 1¼ in (23·50 m); *P*: Two 10,362 lb.s.t. SNECMA Atar 09K-50; *W*: 69,665 lb (31600 kg); *C*: Two; *MS*: 1,454 mph (2340 kph); *OC*: 65,600 ft (20000 m); *ML*: One 50-kiloton nuclear bomb, or four Martel air-to-surface missiles, or sixteen 450 kg conventional bombs. *France's independent nuclear delivery system, in service with CFAS, is a twin-engined scale-up of the basic Mirage III design; with a range of about 2,500 miles, the Mirage IV-A normally operates with tanker aircraft.*

Tupolev Tu-22 Tactical strike/reconnaissance aircraft, USSR, 1964. *S*: 90 ft 10 in (27·70 m); *L*: 132 ft 11 in (40·53 m); *P*: Two 26,000 lb.s.t. turbojets of unknown type; *A*: One 23 mm; *W*: 184,970 lb (83900 kg); *C*: Three; *MS*: 920 mph (1480 kph); *OC*: 60,000 ft (18300 m). *Estimated data on rear-engined "Blinder-A", in widespread service with Soviet air force and naval aviation units.*

Hawker Siddeley HS.125 7/8-seat executive aircraft, UK, 1964. *S*: 47 ft 0 in (14·33 m); *L*: 47 ft 5 in (14·45 m); *P*: Two 3,750 lb.s.t. Rolls-Royce-Bristol Viper 601; *W*: 23,300 lb (10568 kg); *MS*: 508 mph (818 kph); *OC*: 41,000 ft (12500 m). *Successful British twin-jet executive aircraft (of which a trainer version is with the RAF as the Domine). Widely exported (approximately 220 out of 280 ordered); the latest 600 Series developed largely for the USA.*

BAC One-Eleven 89-seat short/medium-range airliner, UK, 1965. *S*: 88 ft 6 in (26·97 m); *L*: 93 ft 6 in (28·50 m); *P*: Two 10,330 lb.s.t. Rolls-Royce Spey-25 Mk. 506 turbofans; *W*: 79,000 lb (35833 kg); *MS*: 541 mph (871 kph); *OC*: 35,000 ft (10670 m). *Successful rear-engined airliner series of which the Series 200 is described here. More than 200 of this and later series in service or on order at time of writing.*

McDonnell Douglas DC-9 Series 30 105/115-seat medium-range airliner, USA, 1965. *S*: 93 ft 5 in (28·47 m); *L*: 119 ft 3½ in (36·37 m); *P*: Two 14,000 lb.s.t. Pratt & Whitney JT8D-7 turbofans; *W*: 98,000 lb (44450 kg); *CS*: 561 mph (903 kph). *Highly successful member of DC-9 series rear-twin-fan airliner, total orders for which at the time of writing amounted to 706 (including 26 for the military).*

BAC Lightning F. Mk. 6 Single-seat multi-mission fighter, UK, 1965. *S*: 34 ft 10 in (10·61 m); *L*: 55 ft 3 in (16·84 m); *P*: Two 12,690 lb.s.t. Rolls-Royce Avon 301; *A*: Various loads of gun packs, rocket pods, Firestreak missiles, etc., up to total of 6,000 lb (2722 kg); *W*: 48,000 lb (21770 kg); *MS*: 1,450 mph (2335 kph); *OC*: 60,000 ft (18300 m) plus. *Standard British interceptor at the time of writing, the Lightning in its late developed forms has considerable attack capability, including low-level delivery of "unconventional" weapons. Exported to several Arab nations.*

Northrop F-5A Freedom Fighter Single-seat tactical fighter, USA, 1965. *S*: 25 ft 3 in (7·70 m); *L*: 47 ft 2 in (14·38 m); *P*: Two 2,720 lb.s.t. General Electric J85-GE-13; *A*: Two 20 mm plus external store loads up to 6,200 lb (2812 kg); *W*: 20,576 lb (9333 kg); *MS*: 925 mph (1489 kph); *OC*: 50,000 ft (15250 m) plus. *Relatively cheap, simple multi-rôle fighter supplied to many countries* *under aid programmes since first deliveries to Iran in 1965.*

Hawker Siddeley Andover C. Mk. 1 Medium range tactical transport, UK, 1965. *S*: 98 ft 3 in (29·95 m); *L*: 78 ft 0 in (23·77 m); *P*: Two 3,245 eshp Rolls-Royce Dart 201 turboprops; *W*: 50,000 lb (22680 kg); *MS*: 265 mph (426 kph); *OC*: 24,000 ft (7300 m); *ML*: 13,500 lb (6125 kg). *Strengthened and modified version of HS.748 airliner, in service with RAF; unique feature is "kneeling" undercarriage to bring rear loading door close to ground.*

Lockheed P-3B Orion Maritime reconnaissance bomber, USA, 1965. *S*: 99 ft 8 in (30·37 m); *L*: 116 ft 10 in (35·61 m); *P*: Four 4,910 eshp Allison T56-A-14 turboprops; *W*: 135,000 lb (61235 kg); *C*: Ten; *MS*: 473 mph (761 kph); *OC*: 28,300 ft (8625 m). *With major structural components borrowed from the Lockheed Electra airliner, the Orion has an internal weapons bay of 7,250 lb (3290 kg) capacity, and extra underwing attachment points for torpedoes, rockets, depth charges, flares, tracking and marking devices, etc. Operational radius is approximately 1,500 miles.*

Lockheed C-141A Starlifter Heavy military transport, USA, 1965. *S*: 159 ft 11 in (48·74 m); *L*: 145 ft 0 in (44·20 m); *P*: Four 21,000 lb.s.t. Pratt & Whitney TF33-P-7 turbofans; *W*: 316,600 lb (143600 kg); *C*: Four; *CS*: 564 mph (908 kph); *OC*: 41,600 ft (12680 m). *First heavy jet to be designed from outset as a military transport, the Starlifter has a maximum payload of 92,000 lb (42638 kg); it has transported a 50,000 lb load over 7,500 miles in 18¼ flying hours.*

SAAB J35F Draken Single-seat multi-mission fighter, Swed., 1966. *S*: 30 ft 10 in (9·40 m); *L*: 50 ft 4 in (15·35 m); *P*: One 12,790 lb.s.t. Rolls-Royce/Volvo RM6C; *A*: One 30 mm plus four guided missiles; *W*: 33,070 lb (15000 kg); *MS*: 1,320 mph (2125 kph); *OC*: 49,200 ft (15000 m). *Initial version entered Swedish squadron service in 1959; later developed versions have achieved Mach 2 performance and a sophisticated range of optical mission capability. Sweden's standard interceptor, also exported to Denmark and on order by Finland.*

Aermacchi MB.326B Two-seat armed trainer, It., 1966. *S*: 34 ft 8 in (10·56 m); *L*: 34 ft 11¼ in (10·65 m); *P*: One 2,500 lb.s.t. Rolls-Royce-Bristol Viper 11; *A*: Two 7·7 mm MG plus combinations of underwing rocket-pods, guns, bombs and tanks; *W*: 8,300 lb (3765 kg); *MS*: 501 mph (806 kph); *OC*: 41,000 ft (12500 m). *Successful and adaptable jet trainer design, serving in several dual-purpose trainer/attack versions with the world's air forces; particularly large-scale licence production in South Africa and Brazil.*

Lockheed SR-71A Two-seat ultra-high-performance reconnaissance aircraft, USA, 1966. *S*: 55 ft 7 in (16·95 m); *L*: 107 ft 5 in (32·74 m); *P*: Two 32,500 lb.s.t. Pratt & Whitney J58; *W*: 170,000 lb (77110 kg); *MS*: c. 2,300 mph (3700 kph); *OC*: 80,000 ft (24400 m) plus. *Described as being "straight out of Dan Dare", and with an appearance*

as futuristic as its performance, the boron-fuelled SR-71A can cross the USA, coast-to-coast, in less than an hour. A missile-armed interceptor version designated YF-12A also exists in prototype form.

Bréguet 1150 Atlantic Maritime reconnaissance/ASW aircraft, Fr., 1966. *S*: 119 ft 1 in (36·30 m); *L*: 104 ft 2 in (31·75 m); *P*: Two 6,105 ehp SNECMA/Rolls-Royce Tyne 21 turboprops; *W*: 95,900 lb (43500 kg); *C*: Twelve; *MS*: 409 mph (658 kph); *OC*: 32,800 ft (10000 m.) *The large weapons bay (approx. 29 × 5 × 6 ft) accommodates a wide variety of bombs, torpedoes, mines, depth-charges, etc., and four nuclear or conventional missiles can be carried underwing. Maximum range is 5,590 miles (9000 km).*

Sud-Aviation Super Frelon General purpose helicopter, Fr., 1966. *RD*: 62 ft 0¼ in (18·90 m); *L*: 59 ft 3¾ in (18·08 m); *P*: Three 1,500 shp Turboméca Turmo IIIC3 shaft turbines; *A*: Various loads according to rôle; *W*: 26,455 lb (12000 kg); *MS*: 158 mph (255 kph); *OC*: 10,830 ft (3300 m). *In French, Israeli and South African service, the Super Frelon has appeared in civil and military transport, ASW, fire-fighting, mine-laying and various other configurations.*

Boeing-Vertol ACH-47A Chinook Ground-support helicopter, USA, 1966. *RD*: 59 ft 1¼ in (18·02 m); *L*: 51 ft 0 in (15·54 m); *P*: Two 2,650 shp Lycoming T55-L-7 shaft turbines; *A*: One 40 mm grenade-launcher, two 20 mm and seven 7·62 mm MG; *W*: 31,358 lb (14223 kg); *MS*: 127 mph (204 kph); *OC*: 9,200 ft (2804 m). *Armoured gunship version of 30–40 man transport in service since 1962, a large twin-rotor machine with a wide range of battlefield and second-line applications.*

General Dynamics F-111A Two-seat variable-geometry fighter, USA, 1967. *S*: Wings forward, 63 ft 0 in (19·20 m); wings swept, 31 ft 11½ in (9·74 m); *L*: 73 ft 6 in (22·40 m); *P*: Two 12,500 lb.s.t. Pratt & Whitney TF30-P-3 turbofans; *A*: Various external load combinations; *W*: c. 80,000 lb (36300 kg); *MS*: 1,650 mph (2655 kph); *OC*: 60,000 ft (18300 m) plus. *Dogged by mismanagement and technical problems, the introduction of the world's first "swing-wing" aircraft to service attracted much unfavourable comment – later, developed versions are much more reliable.*

Hindustan HF-24 Marut Mk. 1 Single-seat fighter, Ind., 1967. *S*: 29 ft 6¼ in (9·00 m); *L*: 52 ft 0¾ in (15·87 m); *P*: Two 4,850 lb.s.t. Rolls-Royce-Bristol Orpheus 703; *A*: Four 30 mm plus external loads up to 4,000 lb (1814 kg); *W*: 19,734 lb (8951 kg); *MS*: 674 mph (1085 kph); *OC*: 45,925 ft (14,000 m). *Potentially a Mach 2 fighter if a suitable engine can be secured, the Marut was designed by a team led by Kurt Tank, designer of the Fw 190. It has been plagued by engine problems throughout a long development life, and the Orpheus-powered Mk. 1 tactical fighter, with useful but unexciting performance, is merely a stopgap.*

Tupolev Tu-134 64/80-seat medium-range airliner, USSR,

1967. *S*: 95 ft 1¾ in (29·00 m); *L*: 112 ft 8¼ in (34·35 m); *P*: Two 14,990 lb.s.t. Soloviev D-30 turbofans; *W*: 98,105 lb (44500 kg); *CS*: 540 mph (870 kph); *OC*: 37,370 ft (12000 m). *A robust airliner which, with the later Tu-134A, is currently serving with Aeroflot, Malev, Balkan Bulgarian, Polish LOT, Yugoslav Aviogenex, Iraqi and EgyptAir air lines.*

Canadair CL-41G Tebuan Two-seat light attack aircraft, Can., 1967. *S*: 36 ft 6 in (11·13 m); *L*: 32 ft 0 in (9·75 m); *P*: One 2,950 lb.s.t. General Electric J85-J4; *A*: Various external loads up to 4,000 lb (1814 kg); *W*: c. 11,400 lb (5171 kg); *MS*: 486 mph (782 kph); *OC*: 43,000 ft (13105 m). *Malaysian export version of basic Canadair CL-41A Tutor trainer, in armed form.*

Vought A-7A Corsair II Single-seat tactical fighter, USA, 1967. *S*: 38 ft 8¾ in (11·80 m); *L*: 46 ft 1½ in (14·06 m); *P*: One 11,350 lb.s.t. Pratt & Whitney TF30-P-6 turbofan; *A*: Two 20 mm plus external loads up to 15,000 lb (6804 kg); *W*: 32,500 lb (14742 kg); *MS*: 578 mph (930 kph). *"A-4 Skyhawk replacement" whose success, with both USAF and USN in several versions, has not been affected by the continued service life of its forerunner.*

Lockheed C-130K Hercules Military transport, USA, 1967. *S*: 132 ft 7 in (40·41 m); *L*: 97 ft 9 in (29·78 m); *P*: Four 4,500 ehp Allison T56-A-15 turboprops; *W*: 155,000 lb (70310 kg); *C*: Four-five; *MS*: 384 mph (618 kph); *OC*: 33,000 ft (10060 m). *Extremely versatile and successful transport, with payload of up to 42,525 lb (20650 kg); more than 1,500 ordered, and in use in various forms with air forces of 23 nations, since C-130A appeared in 1955.*

The Lockheed C-130 Hercules medium/long range combat transport which is in service with the U.S.A.F., U.S. Navy, U.S. Marine Corps, U.S. Coast Guards, the R.A.F., and the air forces of Argentine, Australia, Brazil, Canada, Indonesia, Iran, New Zealand, Norway, Pakistan, Saudi Arabia, South Africa, Sweden and Turkey

Britten-Norman BN-2A Islander General purpose light transport aircraft, UK, 1967. *S*: 49 ft 0 in (14·94 m); *L*: 35 ft 7¾ in (10·86 m); *P*: Two 260 hp Lycoming 0-540-E4C5; *W*: 6,300 lb (2857 kg); *MS*: 170 mph (273 kph); *OC*: 14,600 ft (4450 m). *Versatile 10-seater with widespread military and civil application. "Defender" version, with wing strong-points and radar, can mount a maximum 2,300 lb (1043 kg) underwing load of weapons and fuel tanks, and has provision for beam-mounted machine-guns. Ten-hour flight endurance and 870-mile range are valuable features.*

Beriev Be-12 Tchaika Maritime patrol flying-boat, USSR, 1967. *S*: 97 ft 6 in (29·70 m); *L*: 99 ft 0 in (30·20 m); *P*: Two 4,000 shp Ivchenko AI-20 turboprops; *W*: 65,035 lb (29500 kg); *MS*: 379 mph (610 kph). *Estimated data on latest Soviet flying-boat, code-named "Mail"; there appears to be no internal weapons bay, but six external strong-points. Range is estimated at around 2,500 miles (4000 km).*

Antonov An-22 Heavy military transport, USSR, 1967. *S*: 211 ft 4 in (64·40 m); *L*: 189 ft 7 in (57·80 m); *P*: Four 15,000 shp Kuznetsov NK-12MA turboprops; *W*: 551,160 lb (250000 kg); *C*: Five-six; *MS*: 460 mph (740 kph). *This vast and extremely ugly aircraft does not fall far short of the Lockheed Galaxy in size and performance. Maximum payload is believed to be 176,350 lb (80000 kg), and range with that load, 3,100 miles. Range with 99,200 lb (45000 kg) is 6,800 miles.*

Ilyushin Il-62 115/198-seat airliner, USSR, 1967. *S*: 141 ft 9 in (43·20 m); *L*: 174 ft 3½ in (53·12 m); *P*: Four 23,150 lb.s.t. Kuznetsov NK-8-4 turbofans; *W*: 357,000 lb (162000 kg); *CS*: 560 mph (900 kph): *OC*: 39,400 ft (12000 m). *Intercontinental airliner in VC10/Super VC-10 category, the IL-62 is flying with Aeroflot, CSA Czech Airlines, East German Interflug, EgyptAir and Polish LOT air lines.*

Bell AH-1G HueyCobra Ground support helicopter, USA, 1967. *RD*: 44 ft 0 in (13·41 m); *L*: 44 ft 5¼ in (13·54 m); *P*: One 1,400 shp Lycoming T53-L-13 shaft turbine; *A*: One 7·62 mm rotary plus various external loads of weapons; *W*: 9,500 lb (4309 kg); *CS*: 196 mph (315 kph); *OC*: 11,500 ft (3500 m). *Fast, armoured tactical escort and attack machine which has had extensive combat in Vietnam.*

Dassault Mirage IIIS Single-seat multi-mission fighter, Fr., 1968. *S*: 27 ft 0 in (8·22 m); *L*: 49 ft 3½ in (15·03 m); *P*: One 9,430 lb.s.t. SNECMA Atar 09C; *A*: Two 30 mm plus external loads; *W*: 29,760 lb (13500 kg); *MS*: 1460 mph (2350 kph); *OC*: 55,775 ft (17000 m). *Produced in many versions, tailored to the requirements of various customers, the Mirage first appeared in service in 1961; since then more than 1,000 have been ordered, and it serves with a dozen air forces.*

BAC 167 Strikemaster Light attack aircraft, UK, 1968. *S*: 36 ft 11 in (11·25 m); *L*: 34 ft 0 in (10·36 m); *P*: One 3,410 lb.s.t. Rolls-Royce-Bristol Viper turbojet; *A*: Various external loads up to 3,000 lb (1360 kg); *W*: 11,500 lb (5216 kg); *MS*: 472 mph (760 kph); *OC*: 40,000 ft (12200 m). *Strike development of Jet Provost trainer*

of the 1950s, designed for export to generally undeveloped countries; nearly 100 currently on order or in service.

Cessna A-37B Two-seat light attack aircraft, USA, 1968. *S*: 35 ft 10½ in (10·93 m); *L*: 29 ft 3½ in (8·93 m); *P*: Two 2,850 lb.s.t. General Electric J85-GE-17A; *A*: Various external loads up to 5,400 lb (2450 kg); *W*: 12,000 lb (5443 kg); *MS*: 478 mph (769 kph); *OC*: 41,765 ft (12730 m). *Attack version of T-37 trainer, for use in South-East Asia.*

Sukhoi Su-11 Single-seat interceptor, USSR, 1968. *S*: 30 ft 0 in (9·15 m); *L*: 68 ft 0 in (20·5 m); *P*: Two 22,046 lb.s.t. turbojets of unknown type; *A*: Usual load, two "Anab" missiles; *W*: 35,275 lb (16000 kg); *MS*: 1650 mph (2655 kph). *Estimated data of latest serving development of earlier Su-9 interceptor; US sources suggest that some 600 are currently in service with Soviet defence units.*

McDonnell Douglas F-4K Phantom FG. Mk. 1 Two-seat multi-mission fighter, USA, 1968. *S*: 38 ft 5 in (11·70 m); *L*: 57 ft 11 in (17·65 m); *P*: Two 12,500 lb.s.t. Rolls-Royce Spey 201 turbofans; *A*: External load combinations up to 16,000 lb (7258 kg); *W*: 58,000 lb (26308 kg); *MS*: 1,386 mph (2230 kph); *OC*: c. 71,000 ft (21641 m). *Anglicised version of the mighty Phantom II, standard US fighter and strike aircraft; early models entered service in 1963, British deliveries commenced in 1968. In service with several Western nations, the Phantom has proved its ruggedness and versatility in sustained combat service over Vietnam, and in Israeli service.*

North American OV-10A Tactical support aircraft, USA, 1968. *S*: 40 ft 0 in (12·19 m); *L*: 41 ft 7 in (12·67 m); *P*: Two 715 shp AirResearch T76-G-10/12 turboprops; *A*: Four 0·30 MG plus external loads up to 3,600 lb (1632 kg); *W*: 9,908 lb (4494 kg); *C*: Two; *MS*: 281 mph (452 kph). *Multi-rôle COIN type; rear fuselage compartment*

The Hawker Siddeley Harrier, the world's first and only operational vertical take-off close support strike fighter

also accommodates freight totalling 3,200 lb (1452 kg), five paratroopers or two stretcher-cases and a medical attendant.

Transall C-160F Tactical/strategic transport, Ger./Fr., 1968. *S*: 131 ft 3 in (40·00 m); *L*: 106 ft 3½ in (32·40 m); *P*: Two 6,100 eshp Rolls-Royce Tyne 22 turboprops; *W*: 108,250 lb (49100 kg); *C*: Four; *MS*: 333 mph (536 kph); *OC*: 27,900 ft (8500 m). *With a maximum payload of 35,270 lb (16000 kg) and a range of about 2,800 miles (4500 km), this international design has excellent STOL performance. Turkey and South Africa have placed orders.*

Hawker Siddeley Harrier GR. Mk. 1 Single-seat vertical take-off tactical fighter, UK, 1969. *S*: 25 ft 3 in (7·7 m); *L*: 45 ft 6 in (13·87 m); *P*: One 19,000 lb.s.t. Rolls-Royce-Bristol Pegasus 101 vectored-thrust turbofan; *A*: Various external loads up to 5,000 lb (2270 kg); *W*: 25,000 lb (11340 kg) plus; *MS*: 737 mph (1186 kph) plus; *OC*: 50,000 ft (15240 m) plus. *World's first operational V/STOL combat aircraft; further versions with increased power and loads under development. In service with RAF and USMC.*

Hawker Siddeley Nimrod MR. Mk. 1 Maritime reconnaissance and ASW aircraft, UK, 1969. *S*: 114 ft 10 in (35·00 m); *L*: 126 ft 9 in (38·63 m); *P*: Four 11,500 lb.s.t. Rolls-Royce RB.168 Spey turbofans; *A*: Wide variety of weapons carried internally according to mission; *W*: 175,500 lb (79605 kg); *C*: Twelve; *MS*: 575 mph (926 kph). *Sophisticated reconnaissance/anti-submarine/counter-measures development of Comet airliner.*

Westland Sea King General purpose helicopter, UK, 1969. *RD*: 62 ft 0 in (18·90 m); *L*: 55 ft 9¾ in (17·01 m); *P*: Two 1,500 shp Rolls-Royce-Bristol Gnome H.1400 shaft turbines; *A*: Various loads according to rôle; *W*: 16,999 lb (7710 kg); *CS*: 131 mph (211 kph); *OC*: 10,000 ft (3050 m). *Already in RN service as submarine hunter/killer, this British development of the basic Sikorsky S-61 has many applications. In the transport rôle it accommodates 22 troops. Export orders placed by Germany, India and Norway.*

MiG-21F Single-seat multi-mission fighter, USSR, c. 1970. *S*: 23 ft 5½ in (7·15 m); *L*: 44 ft 2 in (13·46 m); *P*: One 11,240 lb.s.t. Tumansky RD-11-300; *A*: Two 23 mm plus external load combinations; *W*: 20,725 lb (9400 kg); *MS*: 1,385 mph (2230 kph); *OC*: 59,050 ft (18000 m). *Latest and most versatile version of Russia's standard interceptor since 1960; in various models the MiG-21 has been exported to all the USSR's "client" air forces, and has been built under licence in India.*

Boeing 747-100 382-seat long-range airliner, USA, 1970. *S*: 195 ft 8 in (59·64 m); *L*: 231 ft 4 in (70·51 m); *P*: Four 45,000 lb.s.t. Pratt & Whitney JT9D-3W turbofans; *W*: 710,000 lb (322050 kg); *MS*: 595 mph (958 kph); *OC*: 45,000 ft (13715 m). *First of the so-called jumbo-jets, the 747 is a truly monstrous airliner capable, in its high-density versions, of carrying up to 500 or more passengers. At the*

time of writing 209 aircraft are on order by 30 world air lines. Lufthansa has taken delivery of the 707-200F freighter capable of lifting a payload of 257,858 lb (116962 kg).

Hispano HA-200E Super Saeta Two-seat trainer, Sp., 1970. *S*: 35 ft 10¼ in (10·93 m); *L*: 29 ft 5¼ in (8·97 m); *P*: Two 1,058 lb.s.t. Turboméca Marboré VI; *A*: Two 7·7 mm MG plus various external loads; *W*: 7,937 lb (3600 kg); *MS*: 430 mph (690 kph); *OC*: 42,650 ft (13000 m). *Developed version of HA-200A Saeta, designed for Spanish Air Force by Willy Messerschmitt in mid-1950s. Ground-attack version, single-seat and with armour and increased wing strong-points, is currently under development – designated HA-200.*

Lockheed C-5A Galaxy Heavy military transport, USA, 1970. *S*: 222 ft 8½ in (67·88 m); *L*: 247 ft 10 in (75·54 m); *P*: Four 41,000 lb.s.t. General Electric TF39-GE-1 turbofans; *W*: 728,000 lb (330200 kg); *C*: Five; *CS*: 571 mph (919 kph); *OC*: 34,000 ft (10360 m). *The biggest military aircraft in the world, the C-5A can operate from an 8,000 ft (2440 m) runway and can lift 265,000 lb (120200 kg). Total hold volume is 42,825 cu. ft. (1213 m³), and typical loads include 345 troops; or an M-60 heavy tank, five M113 armoured personnel carriers, two Iroquois helicopters, one 2½-ton truck and one 15-cwt truck! Range is 3,510 miles (5650 km).*

Hawker Siddeley Buccaneer S. Mk. 2B Low-level strike aircraft, UK, 1970. *S*: 44 ft 0 in (13·41 m); *L*: 65 ft 5 in (19·33 m); *P*: Two 11,100 lb.s.t. Rolls-Royce RB.168-1A Spey turbofans; *W*: 56,000 lb (25400 kg); *C*: Two; *MS*: 645 mph (1038 kph); *OC*: 16,000 lb (7257 kg). *With a range of 2,300 miles and numerous load combinations, the S.2B is the definitive model of this originally-naval under-the-radar strike aircraft.*

Mikoyan MiG-25 Single-seat interceptor/reconnaissance aircraft, USSR, 1971. *S*: 40 ft 0 in (12·20 m); *L*: 69 ft 0 in (21·00 m); *P*: Two 24,250 lb.s.t. Tumansky (?); *A*: Four air-to-air missiles; *W*: Maximum take-off, 64,200 lb (29120 kg); *MS*: 2,200 mph (3542 kph); *OC*: 73,000 ft (22250 m). *Estimated data of very high performance aircraft "encountered" over Sinai by Israeli Phantoms in 1971 – they were unable to make contact. "Foxbat" has also been reported in Algeria. In the intercept rôle, with "snap-down" missiles, its efficiency against low-level intruders is thought to depend on guidance from accompanying control aircraft, of Tu-114 "Moss" type.*

SAAB AJ37 Viggen Single-seat multi-mission fighter, Swed., 1971. *S*: 34 ft 9¼ in (10·60 m); *L*: 53 ft 5¾ in (16·30 m); *P*: One 14,770 lb.s.t. Volvo RM8 turbofan; *A*: Various loads of rocket-pods, missiles, gun-packs, bombs, mines and camera packs on seven strong-points; primary weapon of the AJ37 model is the RB04 air-to-ground missile; *W*: c. 35,275 lb (16000 kg); *MS*: 1,320 mph (2125 kph). *The canard-plan Viggen is basically a very high performance attack aircraft with a secondary intercept capability.*

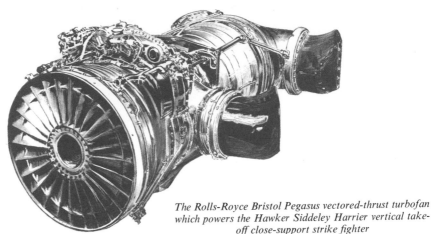

The Rolls-Royce Bristol Pegasus vectored-thrust turbofan which powers the Hawker Siddeley Harrier vertical take-off close-support strike fighter

Sud-Aviation SA.330 Puma General purpose helicopter, Fr., 1971. *RD*: 49 ft 2½ in (15·00 m); *L*: 46 ft 1½ in (14·06 m); *P*: Two 1,300 shp Turboméca Turmo IIC4 shaft turbines; *W*: 14,110 lb (6400 kg); *MS*: 174 mph (280 kph); *OC*: 17,220 ft (5250 m). *Basic tactical transport, with capacity for 20 troops, the SA.330 has many other applications such as search-and-rescue, executive transport (6 seats), ambulance (6 stretchers and 6 seats), and flying crane (5,510 lb/2500 kg external load).*

Tupolev Tu-154 128/164-seat medium/long-range airliner, USSR, 1972. *S*: 123 ft 2½ in (37·55 m); *L*: 157 ft 1¾ in (47·90 m); *P*: Three 20,950 lb.s.t. Kuznetsov NK-8-2 turbofans; *W*: 185,188 lb (84000 kg); *CS*: 605 mph (975 kph); *OC*: 39,350 ft (12000 m). *Intended to replace the Il-18 and other airliners, the Trident/Boeing 727-style Tu-154 is a sophisticated aft-trifan design flying Aeroflot domestic routes, and is due to join CSA Czech and EgyptAir air lines.*

Shin Meiwa PS-1 Patrol and ASW flying boat, Jap., 1972. *S*: 108 ft 8¾ in (33·14 m); *L*: 109 ft 11 in (33·50 m); *P*: Four 2.850 ehp licence-built General Electric T64-IKI-10 turboprops; *A*: Large and varied internal and external load of rockets, torpedoes, depth-charges, sonobuoys, etc. *W*: 94,800 lb (43000 kg); *C*: Ten; *MS*: 340 mph (547 kph); *OC*: 29,500 ft (9000 m). *Despite its size, the PS-1, which entered squadron service late in 1972, has excellent STOL characteristics. Patrol endurance is 15 hours. An air/sea rescue version is under development, with provision for five medical personnel and 18 stretcher cases.*

Lockheed TriStar 256/400-seat medium-range airliner, USA, 1972. *S*: 155 ft 4 in (47·34 m); *L*: 178 ft 8 in (54·35 m). *P*: Three 42,000 lb.s.t. Rolls-Royce RB.211-22B 3-shaft turbofans; *W*: 430,000 lb (195045 kg); *MS*: 575 mph (923 kph); *OC*: 35,000 ft (10670 m). *Rolls-Royce-powered competitor of the DC-10 for the big wide-bodied*

trifan market. Fragile politics threatened the existence of both engine and airframe makers but production plans survived and orders now exceed 100 plus a further 50 options.

Piper PA-28-180 Cherokee 4-seat private light aircraft, USA, 1972. *S*: 30 ft 0 in (9·14 m); *L*: 23 ft 6 in (7·16 m); *P*: One 180 hp Lycoming 0-360-A3A; *W*: 2,400 lb (1089 kg); *MS*: 152 mph (245 kph); *OC*: 13,000 ft (3975 m). *Since the first production Cherokee flew on 10th February 1961, over 19,500 aircraft in this popular series have been delivered. The above figures relate to the 1972 model.*

Aero Spacelines 377SGT Guppy-201 Heavy freighter, USA, 1972. *S*: 156 ft 3 in (47·62 m); *L*: 143 ft 10 in (43·84 m); *P*: Four 4,912 eshp Allison 501-D22C turboprops; *W*: 170,000 lb (77110 kg); *CS*: 288 mph (463 kph); *OC*: 25,000 ft (7620 m). *Surely one of the most grotesque yet obviously functional families of aircraft is the series of conversions applied to the venerable Stratocruiser airliner. Their huge cargo holds (sic) are designed to accommodate bulky items such as spacecraft boosters, airliner fuselage sections, etc.*

SEPECAT Jaguar Single-seat tactical fighter, UK/Fr., 1973. *S*: 27 ft 10¼ in (8·49 m); *L*: 50 ft 11 in (15·52 m); *P*: Two 4,620 lb.s.t. Rolls-Royce-Turboméca Adour turbofans; *A*: Two 30 mm plus external loads up to 8,000 lb (3629 kg); *W*: 29,762 lb (13,500 kg); *MS*: 1,056 mph (1700 kph). *Data refers to 6th prototype of British tactical version of this international, multi-mission aircraft. Both British and French single-seat tactical support fighters, a French carrier fighter, and both British and French two-seat trainers with operational strike capacity are under development; RAF deliveries will commence in 1973.*

Northrop F-5E Tiger II Single-seat multi-mission fighter, USA, 1973. *S*: 26 ft 8½ in (8·14 m); *L*: 48 ft 2½ in (14·69 m); *P*: Two 3,500 lb.s.t. General Electric J85-GE-21; *A*:

Two 20 mm plus external load combinations; *W*: 21,834 lb (9903 kg); *MS*: 1056 mph (1700 kph); *OC*: 53,500 ft (16305 m). *Air superiority development of F-5A concept, designed primarily as a relatively cheap and simple, high-performance "dog-fighter" for export, particularly to forces already operating F-5As in the attack rôle. Prototype flew late in 1972 and considerable Middle East orders are certain.*

Grumman F-14A Tomcat Two-seat variable-geometry naval fighter, USA, 1973–74. *S*: Wings swept, 33 ft 2½ in (10·12 m); wings forward, 64 ft 1½ in (19·54 m); *L*: 61 ft 10½ in (18·86 m); *P*: Two 20,600 lb.s.t. Pratt & Whitney TF30-P-413 turbofans; *A*: One 20 mm, four Sparrow or Phoenix missiles and four Sidewinder missiles; *W*: 57,300 lb (25990 kg); *MS*: "1,320 mph plus" (2125 kph plus). *Few details have been released, and the above data on the F-14A give little precise idea of its capabilities. Testing continues, and the first deliveries are scheduled for the USN late in 1973.*

BAC-Aérospatiale Concorde 128/144-seat supersonic airliner, UK/Fr., 1974–75. *S*: 84 ft 0 in (25·60 m); *L*: 203 ft 11½ in (62·17 m); *P*: Four 38,050 lb.s.t. Rolls-Royce-SNECMA Olympus 593 Mk. 602; *W*: 385,000 lb (174640 kg); *CS*: 1450 mph (2333 kph); *OC*: Approx. 60,000 ft (18290 m). *Unquestionably the most controversial aircraft in history, the Concorde is equally the greatest aeronautical achievement by any European aircraft industry. Developed*

at a cost of almost £1,000 million, this supersonic airliner will reduce the transatlantic flight time by almost 50%. Options for 27 aircraft from 9 air lines have been indicated but as yet only French and British national air lines have confirmed their options.

McDonnell Douglas F-15 Eagle Single-seat air superiority fighter, USA, 1974–75. *S*: 42 ft 9¾ in (13·05 m); *L*: 63 ft 9¾ in (19·45 m); *P*: Two 29,000 lb.s.t. Pratt & Whitney F100-PW-101 turbofans; *A*: One 20 mm, plus various external weapons loads; *W*: c. 40,000 lb (18145 kg); *MS*: "1,650 mph plus" (2655 kph plus). *Prototype flew in mid-1972; service deliveries are scheduled for 1974–75. Few details released yet of this high-performance design, in which manoeuvrability and acceleration have taken priority over tactical support considerations.*

Tupolev Tu-144 98/130-seat supersonic airliner, USSR, 1975 (?). *S*: 90 ft 8½ in (27·65 m); *L*: 190 ft 3½ in (58·00 m); *P*: Four 28,660 lb.s.t. (plus) Kuznetsov NK-144 turbofans; *W*: 395,000 lb (179,150 kg); *CS*: 1,550 mph (2500 kph); *OC*: 65,000 ft (20000 m). *The Soviet Union's competitor in the supersonic airliner market, the Tu-144 (code-named "Charger") has been flying since 31st December 1968. Just as with Anglo-French Concorde, some doubts as to future of this aircraft are voiced from time to time, and as yet no export orders have been announced.*

ᴄᴎ CHAPTER 6 ᴎᴄ
Aviation's Great Personalities

It may seem invidious to present only a limited selection of names from the rich harvest of aviation's great men and women, for by the very nature of the perils faced and supreme endeavour manifest it is a characteristic of the human race that there will always be those whose contribution to progress and achievement is exceptional. Scarcely a step forward in aviation since that day in 1903, when the Wright brothers achieved their prodigious feat, has been accomplished without its attendant hazards, without brilliant ingenuity or without unselfish sacrifice.

No two commentators on the history of aviation, if asked to select a couple of hundred great names, would produce even similar lists – so wide is the realm of endeavour. Indeed, every nation on earth has its own champions, just as one could perhaps even confine one's selection to outstanding pilots, or designers, or even tycoons.

So the following list must be a compromise to some extent, seeking to present some outstanding names from various branches of the "profession of aviation" – both those who have been airborne and chairborne. Genius is a quality of the academician, valour that of the combatant. These outstanding qualities intermingle throughout the following roll whether they be of the pioneer pilot, the designer, the commander or the inventor. Seventy years of unparalleled progress has been accomplished by the conjoined attributes of this great family

*　　　*　　　*

AARON, Acting Sergeant Arthur Louis, V.C., D.F.M.
c. 1920–1943. British bomber pilot. One of the most outstanding of all Victoria Cross awards to an airman was that made to Sergeant Aaron, pilot of a No. 219 Squadron Stirling bomber for his supreme act of self-sacrifice during a raid on Turin, Italy, on the night of 12th/13th August 1943. Having flown from Britain across the Alps his aircraft was running up to the target when it was attacked by a night fighter. Members of the crew were killed or wounded, one engine was put out of action and all the other three badly damaged, while Aaron was hit in the lung and right arm, his jaw was broken by a bullet and the lower part of his face torn away. Despite being carried aft by his crew he twice resumed control of the damaged bomber, eventually giving instructions for flight to North Africa. He managed to remain conscious long enough to instruct his bomb-aimer how to land the aircraft at Bone – a feat successfully accomplished despite a jammed undercarriage and 4,000 pounds of live bombs aboard which could not be jettisoned. Nine hours later he died, but the remaining crew members survived through the unsurpassed gallantry of this young pilot.

Captain Albert Ball, V.C., D.S.O. and 2 Bars, M.C., Chevalier de la Légion d'Honneur, R.F.C.

ARNOLD, General of the Air Force Henry H., U.S.A.F.
1886–1950. American air commander. Born at Gladwyne, Pennsylvania, "Hap" Arnold graduated from the U.S. Military Academy in 1907, entered the Aviation Section of the Signal Corps in 1911, being taught to fly by the Wright brothers. In the First World War he rose to temporary Colonel as Assistant Director of the Air Corps. In 1930 he became Chief of the Air Corps, rising to full General by May 1943. Never a man to suffer fools gladly, Arnold was responsible for American determination to pin its faith in heavily-armed day bombers, the B-17 and B-24 – a strategic policy that has persisted in the U.S.A.F. to this day. In June 1949 he was commissioned a permanent "five-star" General of the Air Force, the only such commission ever signed.

AURIOL, Jacqueline Born 1918. French woman pilot. "Jackie" Auriol, daughter-in-law of the late French President Vincent Auriol, learned to fly in 1947. Surviving serious injuries in a flying accident in 1949, she progressed to helicopters and eventually jet aircraft. She became a full-time test pilot at Brétigny in 1950 and in 1951 established a new women's 100-km. closed circuit speed record of 510·01 m.p.h. (818·18 kph) in a French-built Vampire, raising it the following year to 533·29 m.p.h. (855·92 kph). On 31st May 1955 she established a new straight-line world speed record for women with a speed of 715·19 m.p.h. (1151 kph) in a Mystère IV fighter.

BADER, Group Captain Douglas Robert Stewart, C.B.E., D.S.O. and Bar, D.F.C. and Bar, Légion d'Honneur, Croix de Guerre (France) Born 21st February 1910. British fighter pilot. Commissioned in the R.A.F. in 1930 at Cranwell, Douglas Bader suffered a serious accident in a Bristol Bulldog during 1931 in which he lost both legs; despite learning to fly again with artificial legs in 1932, he was invalided out of the Service in 1933. He rejoined the R.A.F. on the outbreak of War in 1939 and rose to command No. 242 Squadron during the Battle of Britain as a fully operational pilot despite his dependence upon artificial legs. He was credited with 22½ aerial victories before being shot down in 1941, after which he remained a P.O.W. until the end of the War.

BALL, Captain Albert, V.C., D.S.O. and two Bars, M.C., R.F.C. First British fighter pilot whose career received wide publicity; Britain did not subscribe to the "ace" system. Ball was credited with 44 confirmed victories, most gained by charging straight at the enemy with guns blazing rather than by sophisticated stalking; his favourite angle of attack was from underneath. He flew Nieuports and S.E.5s with Nos. 11, 60 and 56 Squadrons, R.F.C. He crashed fatally after diving into cloud on 6th May 1917; his body bore no wound, and his death is still unexplained. A posthumous Victoria Cross was awarded.

BARACCA, Major Francesco, Medaglia d'Oro al Valore Militare (with two palms), Silver Medal (with two palms) 1888–1918. Italy's leading ace of the First World War with 34 confirmed victories, Baracca was commissioned in the cavalry, and qualified as a pilot in 1912. Flying Nieuports with the *70a Squadriglia*, he gained five victories in 1916. In May 1917 he went on to SPAD S.VIIs, and led the *91a Squadriglia* from June that year. He was awarded the Gold Medal for Military Valour, his country's top honour, in March 1918. He fell on 19th June 1918, probably to ground fire. His *cavallino rampante* – "prancing horse" – insignia is still commemorated in the badge of an Italian Starfighter unit.

BEAMONT, Wing Commander Roland Prosper, C.B.E., D.S.O. and Bar, D.F.C. and Bar, D.F.C. (U.S.A.). Born 10th August 1920. One of the great names among British test pilots, "Roly" Beamont served with R.A.F. Fighter Command during the Second World War, commanding No. 609 (Typhoon) Squadron and the first Tempest Wing, destroying ten enemy aircraft and thirty-two flying bombs. He was also attached to Hawker Aircraft Ltd in 1941–42 as experimental test pilot, and joined Gloster Aircraft Company in 1945 as test pilot, flying Meteors. He moved to English Electric in 1947, remaining Chief Test Pilot until 1961. He first flew the Canberra bomber in May 1949 and the P.1 (Lightning prototype) on 4th August 1954, and was the pilot of the first British aircraft to exceed Mach 2. He became Deputy Chief Test Pilot of the British Aircraft Corporation in 1960 and was the pilot of Britain's first supersonic bomber (TSR-2) on 29th September 1964. He established a number of altitude and transatlantic speed records during the nineteen-fifties, and is today Manager of Flight Operations, Preston Division of the British Aircraft Corporation.

BEDFORD, Alfred William, O.B.E., A.F.C. Born 18th November 1920. British test pilot. Considered by many to be one of the greatest British post-War test pilots, Bill Bedford served as a fighter pilot from 1940 until 1945 with Nos. 605, 135 and 65 Squadrons, becoming a flying instructor thereafter until 1949. Joining Hawkers from Farnborough as test pilot in 1951 he was appointed Chief Test Pilot to the company after Neville Duke from 1956 to 1967. Responsible for much of the development flying of the Hunter, he gained several world point-to-point speed records, was awarded important Trophies and Society medals, and gained numerous world "firsts" with the vertical take-off P.1127 and Kestrel aircraft. Very popular among the flying fraternity, Bedford was also a keen and accomplished sailplane pilot.

BENNETT, Air Vice-Marshal Donald Clifford Tyndall, C.B., C.B.E., D.S.O. Born 14th September 1910. British commercial and bomber pilot, and airline executive. Don Bennett transferred to the R.A.F. from the Royal

Group Captain John Cunningham, C.B.E., D.S.O. and two Bars, D.F.C. and Bar, R.A.F.

Australian Air Force in 1931, and joined Imperial Airways in 1935. Pilot of the first commercial East-to-West Atlantic crossing in 1938 in Short Mercury/Mayo composite aircraft. Co-founder of the Atlantic Ferry Service in 1940. Re-commissioned in the R.A.F.V.R. in 1941, and led attack on the *Tirpitz* in Trondheim Fjord on which he was shot down, but escaped via Sweden. Founded the R.A.F. Pathfinder Force in 1943 and commanded it until May 1945. After the War he became a Director and General Manager of British South American Airways, piloting the "Starflight" Lancastrian on the first survey flight in 1946.

BIRKIGT, Dr. Marc, Grand Officer de la Légion d'Honneur 1878–1953. Swiss engineer. It was in 1904 that the great Genevese Marc Birkigt, assisted by the Spanish industrialist Damien Mateu, founded the Hispano Suiza Motor Company at Barcelona in Spain. Up to 1914 Birkigt was engaged in the design and development of motor cars and commercial vehicles, but during the First World War he produced a series of fine aero-engines for France, and licences for overseas production were granted to Britain and Italy, and, later, the U.S.A. Georges Guynemer's (*q.v.*) famous "Stork" squadron, equipped with Hispano Suiza-powered SPADs, adopted the company's badge (a stork) as that of the squadron. Long interested in weapon design, Birkigt produced the famous 20-mm. Hispano gun and in 1938 established a manufacturing company in Britain which later produced thousands of these guns for the R.A.F. during the Second World War. Frequently showered with high honours throughout his life, Marc Birkigt died in Switzerland on 15th March 1953 after a long illness.

The late Marc Birkigt (1878–1953), the Genevese engineer who founded the great Hispano Suiza company

BISHOP, Air Marshal William Avery, V.C., C.B., D.S.O. and Bar, M.C., D.F.C., E.D. 189?–1956. Second most successful British and Empire pilot of the First World War, with 72 confirmed victories, Bishop was a Canadian. Never a very brilliant pilot, and hospitalised more than once after clumsy landings, he was a natural air fighter who came into his element in combat. He flew Nieuport 17s with No. 60 Squadron R.F.C., and led No. 85 Squadron with S.E.5As in 1918. He was awarded the Victoria Cross for a lone sortie over the airfield of *Jasta 5* on 2nd June 1917, typical of his aggressive style; and ended his combat career by shooting down 25 aircraft in 36 flying hours over a period of twelve days. He died in retirement in 1956.

BLÉRIOT, Louis 1872–1936. French pioneer aviator and constructor who achieved lasting fame for his epoch-marking cross-Channel flight on 25th July 1909. From his car lamp and searchlight business he entered aeronautics and collaborated with the Voisin brothers around 1907 and thereafter remained a strong protagonist of the monoplane. By the outbreak of the First World War, his company had built over 800 aircraft of 40 different types. During the War he amalgamated with Deperdussin to form SPAD – manufacturers of the superb fighters of those years, and one of the companies nationalised by the French Government between the Wars.

BOELCKE, Hauptmann Oswald 1891–1916. German scout pilot. The world's first true fighter leader and tactician, Boelcke, a two-seater pilot, rose to fame when selected to fly one of the very few Fokker monoplanes available in 1915. Combat success was matched by technical and organisational ability, and a natural flair for leadership. He commanded *Jagdstaffel 2*, the first offensive unit of single-seat aircraft in the world, which swept the Western Front in their new Albatros scouts; many future aces were among his hand-picked and carefully coached pilots. He died after an aerial collision, with 40 confirmed victories, and his unique place in aviation history is still commemorated today by the honour-title of a *Luftwaffe* squadron.

BOLLING, Colonel Raynal Cawthorne 1877–1918. American air staff officer. Born at Hot Springs, Arkansas, Bolling was a graduate of Harvard Law School and was at the turn of the century on course for a political career. Always a disciple of national military preparedness, he joined the New York National Guard as a cavalryman and by the time President Wilson mobilised the National Guard in 1916 Bolling had learned to fly and forthwith joined the Air Service as a major. When America joined the War, Bolling was sent to Europe to investigate means by which its air participation – industrial production, training and combat participation – could best be integrated with that of the Allies. He continued to work in France, being largely responsible for the integration of the air elements of the American Expeditionary Force into the British sector of the Western Front. Never far from the front line, Bolling accidentally strayed into German-held territory on 26th March 1918 and was killed. He was awarded the Distinguished Service Medal posthumously.

BONG, Major Richard Ira, U.S.A.A.F. (Congressional Medal of Honor, two Silver Stars, seven D.F.C.s and fifteen Air Medals). Born at Superior, Wisconsin, on 24th September 1920; died in aircraft accident, 6th August 1945. Richard Bong received his first combat posting in 1942 having been trained to fly the Lockheed P-38 Lightning – the fighter on which his entire combat career was spent. He served in the Pacific theatre against the Japanese with the 9th Fighter Squadron of the 49th Fighter Group and 39th Fighter Squadron of the 35th Fighter Group. By April 1944 he had destroyed 28 enemy aircraft and then was appointed a gunnery officer with V Fighter Command; nevertheless he voluntarily flew a further 30 combat missions and increased his score by a further 12. His score of 40 victories placed Bong at the head of Allied fighter pilots during the Second World War. On being posted back to the States he became a test pilot for the Lockheed Aircraft Corporation, and it was while flying a jet P-80 Shooting Star that engine failure resulted in a crash in which he died.

BRABAZON OF TARA, 1st Baron of Sandwich, Lt.-Col. John Theodore Cuthbert Moore-Brabazon, P.C., G.B.E., M.C., Hon. F.R.Ae.S., Hon.LL.D. 1884–1964. British pioneer aviator, motorist and holder of R.Ae.C. Pilot's Certificate No. 1. A man of great influence throughout his long aeronautical career who first flew in 1909. He joined the R.F.C. in 1914, specialising in aerial photography – being partly responsible for the first practical aerial camera in 1915. He was Minister of Transport in 1940–41, and Minister of Aircraft Production, 1941–42. Chairman of the first Brabazon Committee, he was largely responsible for the formulation of Britain's post-War civil aircraft requirements. A big man, "Brab" was witty and popular, and was an outspoken critic of inflammable fuels in commercial aircraft.

BRAHAM, Wing Commander John Randall Daniel, D.S.O. and two Bars, D.F.C. and two Bars, A.F.C., Croix de Guerre Belge Born 6th April 1920. British intruder and night fighter pilot. With more gallantry decorations than any other British and Commonwealth soldier, sailor or airman, Bob Braham flew Blenheim night fighters with No. 29 Squadron throughout the Battle of Britain, but did not make his first kill until 24th August 1940, while his second did not fall until March 1941. Thereafter, with the start of night intruder operations over Europe, his score gradually mounted while flying Beaufighters with Nos. 29 and 141 Squadrons, and Mosquitos of No. 2 Group. His final score of 29 victories (of which 19 were gained at night) placed him seventh in the list of R.A.F. fighter pilots during the Second World War.

BRANCKER, Air Vice-Marshal Sir William Sefton,

K.C.B., A.F.C., F.R.Ae.S. 1877–1930. Serving with the Royal Artillery, "Branks" was wounded in the South African War, but learned to fly in 1913. He became Deputy Director of Military Aeronautics in 1914, and commanded the R.F.C. in the Middle East in 1917, being promoted to Major-General in the R.A.F. the following year. In 1919, with Holt Thomas, he organised the first regular London-Paris air service, and in May 1922 was appointed Director of Civil Aviation as an ardent supporter of air transport and flying for sport. His death in the R.101 airship tragedy on 5th October 1930 deeply shocked the aviation world.

BRAND, Air Vice-Marshal Sir Christopher Joseph Quentin, K.B.E., D.S.O., M.C., D.F.C. Born 1893. South African air commander. Born in Cape Colony, Quentin Brand joined the R.F.C. in 1916 from the Army. Between spells in France, he did much pioneer work on night fighting in 1917 in defence of London and was one of the first to destroy an enemy bomber in night air combat. With Sir Pierre Van Ryneveld, he made the pioneer flight from London to Cape Town in 1920 (for which he was knighted), and was seconded to the Egyptian Government as that country's Director-General of Aviation from 1932–36. He was placed in command of the important No. 10 Group, Fighter Command, during the Battle of Britain, and retired from the R.A.F. in 1943.

BRÉGUET, Louis 1880–1955. French engineer. Was designer of a helicopter in 1907 which succeeded in leaving the ground, but lacked control. Was an early advocate of all-metal construction, and his company produced the most widely-used French reconnaissance aeroplane in the First World War. After 1918 the Bréguet company concentrated on metal aircraft for the French Air Force.

BROADHURST, Air Chief Marshal Sir Harry, G.C.B., K.B.E., D.S.O. and Bar, D.F.C. and Bar, A.F.C., Legion of Merit (U.S.A.), Knight Grand Cross of the Order of Orange Nassau (Netherlands) Born 28th October 1905. Joining the R.A.F. in the mid-1920s, Harry Broadhurst served as a fighter pilot on Nos. 41 and 19 Squadrons during the 1930s. After numerous commands and staff appointments he commanded No. 83 Group of 2nd Tactical Air Force throughout the invasion campaign in Europe, 1944–45. He went on to command Bomber Command from 1956 to 1959, during which time he narrowly escaped from a crashing Vulcan bomber at London Airport. Thereafter he joined Hawker Siddeley Aviation Ltd., in 1965 becoming Deputy Managing Director.

BROWN, Charles Edward, F.I.B.P., F.R.P.S. Born 1896. British air photographer. Charles Brown is world renowned as one of the leading exponents of air-to-air photography, and was a war correspondent with 2nd Tactical Air Force, 1944–45. He had a brilliant capability of combining aerial studies of aircraft with the skyscape – often resulting in spectacular pictures, seemingly impossible to "pose". His colour photography during the War is almost unique among top class air-to-air studies, and many of his pictures hang in the R.A.F. Museum at Hendon.

BRUMOWSKI, Hauptmann Godwin 1889–1937. Leading First World War ace of the Austro-Hungarian Empire, Brumowski was killed in a crash at Schiphol, Holland, in 1937 – ironically, as a passenger. Originally an observer, he taught himself to fly to such good effect that he was given command of *Fliegerkompagnie 12*, a mixed two-seater/single-seater unit, in 1916; his first single-seater command, equipped with Brandenburg D.I scouts, was *Flik. 41*. His tireless efforts to reorganise his country's fighter units on more effective lines were hampered by high-level conservatives. Nevertheless, he achieved between 35 and 40 personal victories, and his flight of red, skull-bedecked Albatros D.IIIs had periods of great success over the Italian front in the winter of 1917–18.

BULMAN, Group Captain Paul Ward Spencer, C.B.E., M.C., A.F.C. and two Bars 1896–1963. One of the greatest test pilots of the inter-War years, "George" Bulman joined the R.F.C. from the artillery in 1915, remaining an R.A.F. test pilot at Farnborough from 1919 until 1925 when he joined the H. G. Hawker Engineering Company, remaining Chief Test Pilot until 1945. Immensely popular and much respected for his work, he tested such famous aircraft as the Woodcock, Horsley, Hart, Fury, Henley and Hurricane. Thereafter he retired to private business and when he died he had been all but forgotten for the important work he did to develop the profession of test pilot both in Europe and the U.S.A.

The late Group Captain Paul Ward Spencer Bulman, C.B.E., M.C., A.F.C.

CALDWELL, Group Captain Clive Robertson, D.S.O., D.F.C. and Bar, Polish Cross of Valour Australian fighter pilot. Born at Sydney, New South Wales, on 28th July 1910, "Killer" Caldwell was the top-scoring Australian fighter pilot of the Second World War. Sent to join No. 250 (Tomahawk) Squadron, forming at Aqir, Palestine, in 1941, he quickly became one of the top-scoring desert pilots, and in January 1942 took command of No. 112 Squadron (the "Sharks"). He was posted to command the Kenley Spitfire Wing in May that year, by which time he was credited with 20½ victories. Recalled to Australia in September 1942, Caldwell took command of No. 1 Fighter Wing, R.A.A.F., flying from Darwin, and before the end of the War added a further eight victories to his score.

CAMM, Sir Sydney, C.B.E., F.R.Ae.S. 1895–1966. Aircraft designer. Unquestionably one of the great geniuses of aircraft design, especially that of fighter aircraft. An aircraft model enthusiast as a young man, Camm was employed by Martinsyde during the First World War and joined Hawkers in 1923, becoming Chief Designer in 1925, and a Director in 1935. His great designs included the Hart (and many variants), the Fury biplane, Henley, Hurricane, Typhoon, Tempest, Sea Fury, Sea Hawk, Hunter and Harrier. Although a shy man, Camm commanded great loyalty and affection, and attributed the success of his designs to the continuity of his hand-picked design team. Knighted in 1953 for his services to aviation, he died while still in office.

CAMPBELL, Captain Douglas Born 1896. American military pilot. The first American-trained pilot, flying with an American unit, to score an aerial victory, and one of three pilots to fly the first American patrol over German lines (on March 19th 1918, with Lufbery and Rickenbacker, *qq.v.*). A pilot with the 94th Aero Squadron, Campbell's historic victory was gained on 14th April, near Toul, over an Albatros scout. On 31st May 1918 he scored his fifth kill, becoming the first ace to serve exclusively with the American forces. He scored one more victory before a bad wound on 6th June 1918 put him out of the War. He became a vice-president of Pan American Grace Airways in 1939.

CAREY, Group Captain Frank Reginald, C.B.E., D.F.C. and two Bars, A.F.C., D.F.M., Silver Star (U.S.A.). Born 1912. The modest pilot "who could never remember how many aircraft he'd shot down", Frank Carey was born at Brixton in London and joined the R.A.F. as an apprentice at the age of 15. He was for three years a mechanic on No. 43 Squadron – the squadron with which he flew as a flight commander during the Battle of Britain. He later flew Hurricanes with No. 245 Squadron, formed and commanded No. 135 Squadron in Burma, and ended the War with a final score officially estimated at 28 victories – although some authorities consider it likely to have been rather higher.

Group Captain Geoffrey Leonard Cheshire, V.C., D.S.O. and two Bars, D.F.C.

CAYLEY, Sir George, 6th Baronet 27.12.1773–15.12.1857 British scientist and "father" of the aeroplane. Inventor of the tension-spoke wheel, caterpillar tractor and hot-air engine, Cayley also made important contributions to lifeboats, railway equipment and artificial limbs. He was a great humanitarian, a happy family man who was greatly involved in unemployment relief. In the realm of aeronautics, his great achievements included the setting down of the mathematical principles of heavier-than-air flight, the first use of models for flying research (1804, a model monoplane with fixed wing amidships and a fuselage terminating in a tail with vertical and horizontal surfaces), the first to define the importance of streamlining, the first to suggest the lift benefits of biplanes and triplanes, the first to construct a man-carrying glider (1852–53), the first to demonstrate the benefits of a curved aerofoil, and the first to suggest the use of an internal combustion engine for aeroplanes. His man-carrying glider flew in either 1852 or 1853 at Brompton Hall, near Scarborough, Yorkshire.

CHANUTE, Octave 18.2.1832–23.11.1910 Paris-born American engineer. Emigrating to New York at the age of six, Chanute later became a railroad engineer, and in the 1860s specialised in iron bridge construction, gaining fame and fortune in the development of many of the great American railroads. Assisted by a solid background in engineering, he started collecting a mass of aeronautical data, and published his classic *Progress in Flying Machines* in 1894, the year in which he built his first model glider. Thereafter he constructed a number of man-carrying gliders on which more than a thousand accident-free flights were made before the turn of the century. Unlike the Wrights, Chanute never guarded his secrets,

but made his findings available to all – and there is no doubt that these greatly assisted the Wright brothers in the successful evolution of their immortal *Flyer*.

CHENNAULT, Lieutenant General Claire Lee *c.* 1895–1958. American air commander. Pursuing an extraordinary career in spite of severe handicaps, Chennault won fame for his leadership of the Air Volunteer Group fighting the Japanese in China. Refused the chance to fly during the First World War, he finally joined the famous 94th ("Hat in the Ring") Squadron and the 19th Squadron during the 1920s, later becoming a flying instructor. In 1936, suffering from chronic bronchitis, he was retired from the Air Corps but promptly went to China. In 1941 he recruited 100 Air Corps, Navy and Marine pilots and negotiated the shipment of a like number of P-40 fighters; under his command this force – the "Flying Tigers" – fought the Japanese with outstanding success. In 1942 the A.V.G. was absorbed into the 14th Air Force in China and Chennault placed in command. After the War Chennault founded an airline, Civil Air Transport, to supply much-needed stores to starving Chinese – and to the French in the Indo-Chinese War. After a long illness he finally died of cancer in 1958.

CHESHIRE, Group Captain Geoffrey Leonard, V.C., D.S.O. and two Bars, D.F.C. Born 7th September 1917. British bomber pilot and humanist extraordinary. Entering the R.A.F. in 1939 from the R.A.F.V.R., Leonard Cheshire served on Nos. 102 and 35 (Bomber) Squadrons before commanding No. 76 Squadron in 1942. Appointed to command No. 617, the "Dambusters" squadron after Guy Gibson's famous raid, he led a series of hazardous raids with outstanding results – often pinpointing the target at great personal risk. For constant gallantry was awarded the Victoria Cross on 9th September 1944, and subsequently was the British observer at the delivery of the atomic bomb on Nagasaki in 1945. Since the War, Leonard Cheshire has devoted his life to the relief of suffering, was Founder of the Cheshire Homes for disabled and homeless sick, and Co-founder of the Mission for the Relief of Suffering.

CHICHESTER, Sir Francis, K.B.E., F.I.N. 1901–1971. British air and sea navigator. Although Sir Francis gained his greatest fame as a result of his lone sea voyages which he made late in his life, he was active in the inter-War years making long-distance flights in light aircraft. Notable among these was the second solo flight from England to Australia in 1929, the first solo crossing of the Tasman Sea in 1931, and the first seaplane solo flight from New Zealand to Japan, also in 1931. He served in the R.A.F. during the Second World War and was appointed Senior Navigation Officer at the Empire Central Flying School, 1943–45.

CLOSTERMANN, Wing Commander Pierre H., D.S.O., D.F.C. and Bar, Grand Officier de la Légion d'Honneur, Croix de Guerre (France, with 25 palms), Croix de Guerre Belge. Born, *c.* 1922. French fighter pilot. Pierre Clostermann achieved combat status in the Second World War relatively late when, in January 1943, he joined No. 341 (Alsace) Squadron of the Biggin Hill Wing as a sergeant pilot flying Spitfires. Nevertheless in little over two years he had been commissioned, flown with Nos. 602 (Spitfire) and 274 (Tempest) Squadrons, commanded No. 3 (Tempest) Squadron, and eventually No. 122 Fighter Wing, and been credited with 33 victories – of which most were enemy fighters. He was thus France's top-scoring pilot of the Second World War, and third in the R.A.F. after Pattle and Johnson.

COBHAM, Sir Alan John, K.B.E., A.F.C. Born 1894. British pioneer survey pilot. One of the great survey pilots of the 1920s, Alan Cobham was an ex-R.F.C. pilot when he formed the Berkshire Aviation Company in 1919, giving joy-rides to 5,000 passengers; he was a de Havilland test pilot in 1921, and made a 5,000-mile flight round Europe that year; in 1922 he made a Belgrade-to-London flight in one day, made a 12,000-mile flight round Europe, North Africa and the Middle East in 1923, won the King's Cup Race in 1924, flew Sir Sefton Brancker to Rangoon and back in the winter of 1924–25, flew to South Africa and back in 1925–26, and to Australia and back in 1926. He piloted a Short Singapore flying boat on a 23,000-mile flight round Africa in 1927–28, and conducted the Air Ministry survey flight down the Nile to the Belgian Congo in 1931. He pioneered commercial flight refuelling in Britain in the 1930s, reconstituting Flight Refuelling Limited in 1948, of which he is today Life President.

COCHRAN, Jacqueline (Mrs. Floyd Odlum) American woman pilot. Probably America's best-known woman pilot of the last twenty-five years, Jacqueline Cochran set up a number of world speed records for women over straight-line and closed-circuit courses in 1952–53, eventually establishing a 100-km closed-circuit speed record at 652·5 m.p.h. (1047 kph) in a Canadair F-86E Sabre over the Mojave Desert, California, on 18th May 1953. Exactly eleven years later to the day she achieved the fastest-ever speed by an aeroplane piloted by a woman, at 1429·2 m.p.h. (2294 kph) in an F-104G Super Starfighter. Miss Cochran is perhaps better known however for her trans-atlantic record-breaking flight of 22nd April 1962 in a Lockheed Jetstar when she set up more than thirty point-to-point speed records – of which 26 still stand in 1973.

CODY, Samuel Franklin 1861–1913. American (later naturalised British) engineer and pioneer aviator. Of Irish stock, "Bill" Cody grew up as a Texan farmer whose horse-dealing brought him to England in 1896. His early interest in box kites developed during the early 1900s, and his man-carrying kites attracted the attention of the military. From kiting, Cody went on to design an aeroplane-like tail structure for the airship *Nulli Secundus,* and thereafter commenced rudimentary aeroplane design at Farnborough, Hampshire. He achieved the first

officially-recognised aeroplane flight in Great Britain at Farnborough on 16th October 1908 in his *British Army Aeroplane No. 1,* a flight of 1,390 ft (460 m). He was killed on 7th August 1913 when he and his passenger fell from their aircraft after structural failure over Farnborough.

COLLISHAW, Air Vice-Marshal Raymond, C.B., D.S.O. and Bar, O.B.E., D.S.C., D.F.C. 1893– . A Canadian sailor from Nanaimo, British Columbia, Collishaw became the leading First World War fighter pilot of the Royal Naval Air Service. He is best remembered for leading the "Black Flight" of Sopwith Triplanes of No. 10 Naval Squadron in the summer of 1917, and eventually recorded 60 aerial victories. He remained in the R,A.F., rising to senior rank; after the Armistice he commanded a squadron with the expeditionary forces in Russia. In the Second World War he commanded R.A.F. forces in Egypt at the time that Italy declared war in June 1940, and pursued a brilliant strategy in conditions of scant combat equipment against the numerically superior *Regia Aeronautica.*

COPPENS DE HOUTHULST, Chevalier Willy Born 1892. Leading ace of the tiny but excellent Belgian *Aviation Militaire* in the First World War, with 37 confirmed victories. Transferring from the 2nd Grenadiers to the air arm in September 1915, he had to take leave and borrow funds to cross to England and learn to fly at a civilian school at Hendon! After a period flying two-seaters he reached *1ere Escadrille* in July 1917, but flew his Hanriot HD.1 without success for many weeks. His first victory was scored on April 25th 1918; his remarkable total score, amassed by October 14th that year, included 26 balloons – he was second only to Michel Coiffard of France at destroying these difficult and heavily protected targets. Crash-landing after his last fight, he lost a leg to shrapnel wounds. He stayed in the Service until 1940, and retired to Switzerland.

CUNNINGHAM, Group Captain John, C.B.E., D.S.O. and two Bars, D.F.C. and Bar, Silver Star (U.S.), F.R.Ae.S. Born 1917. One of the wartime R.A.F.'s most famous night fighter pilots and well-known post-War test pilot, John Cunningham flew in the Battle of Britain with No. 604 Squadron in early Blenheim night fighters, later moving on to the Beaufighter and Mosquito with Nos. 604 and 85 Squadrons. By the end of the War he had scored 20 victories, of which 19 were at night. He re-joined de Havillands after the War (he had been apprenticed at their famous Technical School during the 1930s) and was appointed Chief Test Pilot, his being the responsibility for development flying of such aircraft as the Comet, D.H. 110 (Sea Vixen), Venom, Trident and many others.

CURTISS, Glenn Hammond 1860–1930. American engineer. From early motor engineering Curtiss joined Dr. Alexander Bell in 1908 assisting in the production of four biplanes – of which the *June Bug* was the most famous. In

Wing Commander Pierre H. Clostermann, Grand Officier de la Légion d'Honneur, Croix de Guerre with 25 palms, Croix de Guerre Belge, D.S.O., D.F.C. and Bar

this, Curtiss became the first American to fly after the Wright brothers when on 20th June 1908 he covered 1,266 ft (420 m). A fortnight later he made a flight of 5,090 ft (1700 m) to win the *Scientific American* trophy. In 1914 Curtiss was unsuccessful litigant in attempts to contest the world patent limitations posed by the Wright brothers. During the First World War Curtiss supplied flying boats to the R.N.A.S., and his company manufactured large numbers of the famous "Jenny" trainers for the R.F.C., U.S. Flying Services and other air forces. His N.C.4 flying boats achieved the first stage-by-stage crossing of the Atlantic in 1919.

DEERE, Group Captain Alan Christopher, D.S.O., O.B.E., D.F.C. and Bar, A.F.C., D.F.C.(U.S.A.), Croix de Guerre (France) Born 12th December 1917 in Auckland, New Zealand. British (New Zealander) fighter pilot. Al Deere joined the R.A.F. early in 1938 and served with No. 54 (Spitfire) Squadron in the Battle of Britain during which he had some spectacular crashes and escapes. In 1943 he was promoted to lead the famous Biggin Hill Wing and by the end of the War he was credited with 21½ enemy aircraft destroyed.

DE HAVILLAND, Captain Sir Geoffrey, O.M., C.B.E., A.F.C., R.D.I., F.R.Ae.S., F.I.Ae.S. 1882–1965. British aircraft designer and manufacturer. One of the greatest figures in British aviation for fifty years. Granted R.Ae.C. Aviator's Certificate No. 53 on 7th February 1911, "D.H." was employed as a designer at the Royal Aircraft Factory at Farnborough, and joined Holt Thomas in 1914 as Chief Designer of the Aircraft Manufacturing Co. His D.H.1 pusher biplane appeared in 1915, and this was followed by numerous other highly successful designs (notably the D.H.4 and 9) before he

registered his own de Havilland company in 1920. Outstanding success with the famous Moth biplanes was followed by development of the Mosquito and Vampire, and later the Comet airliner. Greatly saddened by the loss of two sons in flying accidents, D.H. was a much-loved and respected man, greatly interested in natural history.

DEMOZAY, Wing Commander Jean, D.S.O., D.F.C. and Bar, Légion d'Honneur, Ordre Libération, Croix de Guerre (France), D.F.C. (U.S.A.), Croix de Guerre Belge, Czech War Cross French fighter pilot. Born at Nantes, France, Jean Demozay joined the R.A.F. on the outbreak of war in 1939 but missed the Battle of Britain. Flying Hurricanes and Spitfires of Nos. 1 and 242 Squadrons, he destroyed 21 enemy aircraft in the air and five more on the ground by February 1943. Later he was sent on a mission to the U.S.S.R. and finished the War commanding a bomber group. After the War he was made deputy commandant of *Armée de l'Air* training schools, but was killed on 19th December 1945 when the aircraft in which he was travelling from London crashed at Le Duc.

DONALDSON, Air Commodore Edward Mortlock, C.B., C.B.E., D.S.O., A.F.C. and two Bars, Legion of Merit (U.S.A.) Born 22nd February 1912. Distinguished British fighter pilot who joined the R.A.F. in 1931 and won the Fighter Command Air Firing Trophy in two consecutive years. Commanded No. 151 (Hurricane) Squadron in the Battle of Britain. Commanded Colerne – the first permanent jet fighter base, 1945, and led the R.A.F. High Speed Flight, 1946, establishing World Speed Record of 616 m.p.h. (988 kph) in Gloster Meteor IV on 7th September. After numerous post-War commands, he retired from the R.A.F. in 1961 to become the respected air correspondent of *The Daily Telegraph*.

DOOLITTLE, Lieutenant-General James H., Congressional Medal of Honor, Hon.K.C.B. American pilot, air commander and company executive. Born 14th December 1896. Serving as a military pilot from 1917 to 1930, during which period he made a number of outstanding pioneering and proving flights (including the first coast-to-coast crossing of the U.S.A. in a single day on 4th September 1922), Jimmie Doolittle was appointed manager of Flight Operations in the Shell Oil Company from 1930–40. He gained immortal fame in his leadership of the famous B-25 raid on Tokyo on 18th April 1942, having flown off the carrier *Hornet*. Six months later he took command of the U.S. 12th Air Force, the following year commanding the U.S. Strategic Air Force in Italy, and then the famous 8th Air Force in Britain, 1944–45. He returned to the Shell Oil Company from 1946–58 as a Director and Vice-President.

DOUGLAS, Donald Wills Born 1892. Aircraft designer and manufacturing executive. Honorary chairman of the board of the McDonnell Douglas Corporation since 1967, Douglas started his career as chief engineer for the

Glenn L. Martin Co. in 1915-16. In the period 1916-17 he was chief civilian aeronautical engineer to the U.S. Signal Corps, returning to his post as chief engineer of Martin in 1917-20. In 1920 he formed the Douglas Co., as president, and retained the presidency of Douglas Aircraft (1928-57). From 1957-67 he was chairman of the board and chief executive officer.

DOUGLAS, 1st Baron of Kirtleside, Marshal of the Royal Air Force William Sholto Douglas, G.C.B., M.C., D.F.C. 1893-1970. British air commander and airline senior executive. Gaining an aviator's certificate in France in 1913, Sholto Douglas commanded Nos. 43 and 84 (Fighter) Squadrons of the R.F.C. in the First World War, was chief pilot of Handley Page Transport Ltd., in 1919, returned to the R.A.F. in 1920 and commanded the R.A.F., Sudan, 1929-32. He was appointed to command Fighter Command, 1940-42, during the turn to the offensive after the Battle of Britain; commanded Coastal Command, 1944-45, and became Military Governor of the British Zone in Germany after the War. After retirement from the R.A.F. he became a director of B.O.A.C. in 1948-49, thereafter Chairman of B.E.A.

DOWDING, 1st Baron of Bentley Priory, Air Chief Marshal Hugh Caswall Tremenheere, G.C.B., G.C.V.O., C.M.G. Born 1882, died 1971. Dowding was probably one of the greatest air commanders and certainly one to whom the Western world owes most, for he it was who commanded R.A.F. Fighter Command during the critical Battle of Britain, the winning of which brought about survival of the free nations in the face of Nazi Germany in 1940. He had joined the Army as far back as 1900, but was commissioned in the R.F.C. in 1914, and R.A.F. in 1918. Successive promotions brought him command of the Fighting Area, Air Defence of Great Britain during 1929-30, after which he was Air Member for Research and Development until 1936, when he assumed command of the newly-established Fighter Command. During the nineteen-thirties he was to a great extent responsible for the development and introduction of the Hurricane and Spitfire fighters and of radar, and radar-equipped night fighters. His commands resulted in the air defence system which forestalled the *Luftwaffe* in 1940 and became the prototype on which almost every other such system has been modelled since.

DUKE, Squadron Leader Neville Frederick, D.S.O., O.B.E., D.F.C. and two Bars, A.F.C. Born 11th January 1922. British fighter pilot and test pilot. One of the best known post-War test pilots, Neville Duke had had distinguished service as an R.A.F. fighter pilot during the War, only narrowly missing the Battle of Britain. His first posting was to No. 92 Squadron and he destroyed his first German aircraft over France on 25th June 1941. Sent to North Africa, he joined No. 112 Squadron (the "Sharks") flying Tomahawks. He remained fighting in the Mediterranean theatre and eventually became the second-highest scoring pilot in the Middle East Com-

Air Chief Marshal Lord Dowding of Bentley Priory, G.C.B., G.C.V.O., C.M.G., Commander-in-Chief, R.A.F. Fighter Command, 1936-1940

mand with 28 victories, flying with Nos. 112, 145 and 92 Squadrons. He returned home and eventually became a test pilot with Hawker Aircraft Ltd.; in 1951 he was appointed Chief Test Pilot and was thus responsible for seeing the Hunter through its early development. On 31st August 1953 he established a new world record in the prototype Hunter at 722 m.p.h. (1158 kph). This modest, extremely likeable man, who will long be remembered for his beautiful flying at Farnborough in the early 1950s, retired from test flying in 1956.

EAKER, General Ira C., U.S.A.F. Commissioned in the U.S. Army in 1917, Eaker transferred to the aviation branch immediately, and qualified as a pilot in 1918. He enjoyed rapid promotion between the Wars and commanded the 20th Pursuit Group in 1941. Promoted Brigadier-General in January 1942, he commanded the Flying Fortress and Liberator units of the 8th Bomber Command in England in 1942, and was appointed general commanding the 8th Air Force in 1943. He flew personally on the first Fortress mission, to Rouen marshalling yards on 17th August 1942, in *"Yankee Doodle"*, a B-17E of 97th Bombardment Group. He was C.-in-C., Mediterranean Allied Air Forces, 1944, and Chief of the U.S. Air Staff, 1945-47. Eaker became chairman of the advisory board of Hughes Aircraft in 1961.

EARHART, Miss Amelia (Mrs. Putnam) American woman pilot. A contemporary of Amy Johnson, Amelia Earhart performed a number of remarkable long distance flights in the years before the airlines opened up the transoceanic routes. Her memorable flights included the first solo crossing of the Atlantic by a woman, flying a Lockheed Vega from Newfoundland to Londonderry, Northern Ireland, on 20th-21st May 1932, the first non-stop air crossing of the United States by a woman, flying from Los Angeles to New York on 25th August 1932, and her solo flight from Honolulu to Oakland, California, on 11th-12th January 1935. She lost her life during an attempt to fly round the world with Captain Fred Noonan when their aircraft was lost in the Pacific between Howland Island and New Guinea on 2nd July 1937.

EDWARDS, Sir George Robert, C.B.E., F.R.S., B.Sc.(Eng.), Hon.D.Sc., Hon.F.R.Ae.S., Hon.F.A.I.A.A. Born 1908. Aircraft designer and company director. Chairman and Managing Director of the British Aircraft Corporation today, Sir George Edwards joined Vickers-Armstrongs Ltd., in 1935, becoming Experimental Works Manager in 1940 and Chief Designer in 1945. Numerous directorships followed in post-War years, and he was elected President of the Royal Aeronautical Society, 1957-58. In the past dozen years he has been widely represented as a strong advocate for the BAC-Aérospatiale Concorde supersonic airliner, for which his company is a principal manufacturing partner.

EDWARDS, Air Commodore Hughie Idwal, V.C., C.B., D.S.O., O.B.E., D.F.C. Born 1914. Australian bomber pilot and air commander. Joining the Royal Australian Air Force from the Australian Army in 1935, Hughie Edwards transferred to the R.A.F. in 1936. Flying Blenheims at the outbreak of the Second World War, he led a raid by Blenheims of No. 105 Squadron on Bremen on 4th July 1941 and despite severe wounds (which resulted in the loss of an arm) he returned to base – to be awarded the Victoria Cross. Despite the disability he remained in the R.A.F., being appointed to numerous commands at home and abroad, including R.A.F. Wattisham, 1953-56, R.A.F. Habbaniyah, 1956-58, and the Central Fighter Establishment, 1958-60. He retired from the R.A.F. in 1963 and returned to Australia.

EMBRY, Air Chief Marshal Sir Basil Edward, G.C.B., K.B.E., D.S.O. and three Bars, D.F.C., A.F.C., Commander of the First Degree Order of Dannebrog (Denmark), Grand Officer of the Order of Orange Nassau (Netherlands), Commandeur de la Légion d'Honneur, Croix de Guerre (France) Born 1902. British military pilot and air commander. Basil Embry has enjoyed one of the most eventful careers of any airman. Commissioned in the R.A.F. in 1921, served in Iraq, 1922-27;

was awarded the A.F.C. for operations in Kurdistan and Southern Desert; was A.1 flying instructor at the Central Flying School, 1929-32; attended the R.A.F. Staff College in 1933; served in India, 1934-39 (being mentioned in despatches during the Mohmand operations, 1935, and awarded the D.S.O. in Waziristan, 1938). In the Second World War, he served in Bomber and Fighter Commands, in operations over Germany, Norway, Britain, N.W. Europe and the Western Desert. He also accomplished one of the most spectacular escapes from enemy captivity in 1940 when he was shot down while leading a raid by No. 107 Squadron. Though wounded in the leg, he made his way through the length of France to Spain, and thence back to England. He retired in 1956 to live in Australia.

ESMONDE, Lieutenant-Commander Eugene, V.C., D.S.O. 1909-1942. British naval pilot. An ex-R.A.F. pilot who served aboard naval vessels between the Wars, Esmonde was also an Imperial Airways pilot during the mid-1930s. In 1939 he joined the Fleet Air Arm, and escaped from H.M.S. *Courageous* when she was torpedoed later that year. Flying Swordfishes he participated in the strike which crippled the *Bismarck* in May 1941, but it was on 12th February 1942 that Esmonde met his death when, again leading Swordfishes of No. 825 Squadron, he flew against the German warships, *Scharnhorst*, *Gneisenau* and *Prinz Eugen*, escaping up the Channel. In the face of an inferno of anti-aircraft fire the entire formation was destroyed and none of the crews were ever seen again. As leader of this attack, Esmonde was posthumously awarded the Victoria Cross – the first Fleet Air Arm member so honoured.

FAIREY, Sir Charles Richard, M.B.E., F.R.Ae.S., F.I.Ae.S., Commander l'Ordre de la Courone (Belgium), Medal of Freedom (U.S.A.) 1887-1956. British engineer and manufacturer. Prior to the formation of the Fairey Aviation Company at Hayes, Middlesex, in 1915, Richard Fairey had been Works Manager and Chief Engineer with Short Bros Ltd. Benefiting from experience gained from sub-contract work on Sopwith aircraft, Fairey established himself with the post-War Fairey III series of aircraft, and in 1925 by acquiring rights in the Curtiss D.12 engine, Reed propeller and other advanced aircraft features, introduced the advanced Fox light bomber. Bitterly critical of the Government which ordered the Hawker Hart rather than the Fox, Fairey nevertheless produced the immortal Swordfish torpedo-carrying biplane, and the ill-starred Battle bomber. Considered by many to be quick-tempered and intolerant, Fairey is however remembered for his generosity, prodigious memory and great courage during his long and ultimately-fatal illness.

FARMAN, Henry 1874-1958. British (later naturalised French) engineer and pioneer aviator and manufacturer. One of the great names among pioneer airmen in Europe, Henry Farman had already made his name as a motoring and motor-cycle racer when he ordered a Voisin biplane in 1907. Within a year he had made a 17-mile flight and was already designing his first aircraft. The early aircraft (dubbed Longhorns and Shorthorns) featured throughout Europe in the pre-War years, and were widely used for training early in the First World War. After the War, conversion of the Farman twin-engined bomber brought France's first airliner, the Goliath. Henry's brother Maurice, although concerned with many of the Farman products, never achieved the same measure of fame.

FEDDEN, Sir Alfred Hubert Roy, Kt., M.B.E., Hon.D.Sc., Hon.F.R.Ae.S., C.Eng., M.I.Mech.E., F.R.S.A., F.B.I.S. Born 1885. British aero-engine designer. Originally engaged in motor car design before the First World War, Roy Fedden founded the Engine Department of the Bristol Aeroplane Company in 1920, remaining its Chief Engineer until 1942 – responsible for the design and development of all engines produced in that period (among them the Jupiter, Mercury, Hercules, Taurus, Centaurus, etc.). After this he chaired numerous advisory committees, led missions overseas and attended frequent conferences dealing with the progress of aircraft powerplants. Always a staunch champion of British aviation and its industry, Roy Fedden was three times President of the Royal Aeronautical Society – in 1938, 1939 and 1945.

FOLLAND, Henry Phillip, O.B.E., F.R.Ae.S., F.I.Ae.S., F.R.S.A. 1889–1954. British aircraft designer. Employed as a design section leader at the Royal Aircraft Factory at Farnborough during the First World War, Folland was responsible for the B.S.1 development, and shortly after for the outstanding S.E.5. Following the Parliamentary agitation against the nationalised aircraft industry, Folland joined the British Nieuport and General Aircraft Company to continue the S.E.5 trend with the Nighthawk. Subsequently he joined the Gloucester Aircraft Company, where his line of successful biplane racers culminated in the Gauntlet and Gladiator biplane fighters. In 1937 he left Glosters to found his own company, but it was only after his death that its first successful aircraft, the Gnat, entered service with the R.A.F.

FONCK, Captaine René Paul, Croix d'Officier de la Légion d'Honneur, Belgian Croix de Guerre, French Croix de Guerre with 28 palms, M.C. and Bar, M.M. Born in the Vosges in 1894, René Fonck died peacefully in his sleep in Paris on 18th June 1953. From frustration in the trenches at the beginning of the First World War, he joined *Escadrille C.47* flying Caudron G.IVs in June 1915. In 1917 he transferred to the *Cigognes* group, gaining victory after victory – on at least two occasions destroying six enemy aircraft in a single day. He was a deadly marksman, a master of deflection shooting capable of extraordinary economy of ammunition, frequently destroying enemy aircraft with only five or

six rounds. He was officially credited with a total of 75 victories, a score which placed him at the top of the list of Allied pilots in the First World War.

FRANTISEK, Sergeant Josef, D.F.M., Czech War Cross, Virtuti Militari, Croix de Guerre (France) Czech fighter pilot. A regular pilot of the Czech Air Force, Jo Frantisek left his native country after the Nazi invasion in 1938, and in March 1939 joined the Polish Air Force. By the end of the Polish campaign, he had destroyed his first German aircraft and then moved to Romania, where he was interned. Escaping, he moved through the Balkans to Syria where he found a boat for France. In May 1940 he joined the *Armée de l'Air* and fought over France and Belgium before making his way to England the following month. By this time he had destroyed 11 enemy aircraft. Posted as a sergeant pilot to No. 303 (Polish) Squadron, Frantisek re-opened his account with the destruction of a Bf 109 on 2nd September 1940. Five weeks later he was killed – his score with the R.A.F. standing at 17, making him the top scoring Allied pilot in the Battle of Britain. With a total score of 28, he was the highest-scoring Czech pilot.

GABRESKI, Colonel Francis S., U.S.A.F. Born 1919. American fighter pilot. Had it not been for an unfortunate flying accident over enemy territory, which resulted in his being made prisoner, many consider that Gabreski would have emerged as America's top ace of the Second World War. As it was, as leader of the 61st Fighter Squadron, flying P-47 Thunderbolts from Eng-

Oberst (later Generalleutnant) Adolf Galland, Oakleaves, Swords and Diamonds of the Knight's Cross of the Iron Cross, Luftwaffe 1934–1945

land, his combat career in that War was cut short when his score was 31 aerial victories – top American score in Europe. But Gabreski went on to Korea where, flying F-86s as Deputy Commander of the 4th Fighter Interception Wing, he shot down a further 6½ MiG-15 jet fighters, becoming America's seventh "jet ace". A most attractive and likeable character, Gabreski must be considered as one of the all-time great fighter pilots.

GABRIELLI, Professor Dott. Ing. Guiseppe, F.A.I.A.A., M.A.S.M.E., M.S.A.W.E., M.S.A.E., F.R.Ae.S. Born 1903. Italian aircraft designer. Today a Staff Professor of Aircraft Design at the Turin Polytechnic, Gabrielli joined Fiat S.p.A. in 1931, bringing with him a new design mentality that was to place the company among the leaders of European aircraft industry. One of the first fighters in which he took a leading design responsibility was the Fiat G.50 monoplane (the "G" signifying Gabrielli's design), an aircraft which saw considerable wartime service; in later years it was followed by the G.55 fighter and a number of piston-engined trainers. The latest designs to stem from Gabrielli's design department have been the successful Fiat (now Aeritalia) G.91 series of tactical fighter ground/attack aircraft, the G.95 and G.222 transport.

GALLAND, Generalleutnant Adolf Born 1912. Most famous surviving *Luftwaffe* commander of 1939-45; holder of Knight's Cross with Diamonds, 104 confirmed victories. Flight commander in Spain, 1937-38; led fighter wing *JG 26 "Schlageter"* on Channel Front in 1940. Became General of Fighters on Mölders' death, and held the appointment with distinction until relieved for opposing Hitler's views in January 1944. Ended War leading élite jet fighter squadron, *JV 44*, in action. Entered commercial aviation in 1950s, became director of *Air Lloyd*. Germany's youngest general of modern times.

GIBSON, Wing Commander Guy Penrose, V.C., D.S.O., and Bar, D.F.C. and Bar 1918-1944. The award of the Victoria Cross to Guy Gibson was made for one of the most famous and spectacular exploits of the Second World War. Prior to the War Gibson had flown Hinds, Blenheims and Hampdens with No. 83 Squadron, and in 1940 joined a Beaufighter night fighter squadron for a short spell (destroying at least four enemy aircraft) before returning to bombers – commanding No. 106 (Lancaster) Squadron and taking part in many famous raids. In March 1943 No. 617 Squadron was formed for the expressed purpose of dropping Barnes Wallis' special mines on large dams in Germany, and Gibson was given command. In the early hours of 17th May that year the Squadron attacked the Mohne, Sorpe and Eder dams with spectacular results, but with the loss of eight out of nineteen Lancasters sent. As leader of the attack, Gibson was awarded the Victoria Cross, but little over a year later he was shot down and killed during a raid on Rheydt in the Rhineland.

GÖRING, Reichsmarschall Hermann 1893-1946. First World War pilot, commander of *Jasta 27* and later *Jagdgeschwader Richthofen,* 22 confirmed victories. Flew with Swedish air force in 1920s. Close political associate of Hitler in 1920s and 1930s, one of top three in Nazi hierarchy. Despite lack of any real expertise in aviation matters, Göring was appointed C.-in-C. of the reborn *Luftwaffe*, and German Air Minister; most professional decisions were taken initially by Erhard Milch (*q.v.*). A self-publicising *poseur*, Göring's personal ambition adversely affected his command qualities throughout the War; his subservience to Hitler, capricious and ill-informed decisions, and justifiable lack of confidence in his own expertise hampered his subordinates – many of them brilliant officers – at all levels. Convicted of war crimes, he committed suicide by poison in his comdemned cell in October 1946.

GRAHAME-WHITE, Claude 1879-1959. Pioneer British aviator. Grahame-White was probably the best-known of all pre-War British fliers and was a great crowd attraction at the early Hendon meetings. Awarded R.Ae.C. Aviator's Certificate No. 6 on 26th April 1910, "G.W." was undoubtedly the outstanding British pilot of that year, being winner of the Gordon Bennett Contest in New York. As such it was he more than any other who raised British prestige in the air above that of France and America. In the early days of the War, he was commissioned in the R.N.A.S. and initiated night patrols over London. Although his factory was awarded con-

The late Sir Frederick Handley Page, C.B.E.

tracts for military aircraft, he became critical of the Government over delays. After a bitter struggle to gain settlement of his claims after the War, he sold Hendon and later spent much of his time abroad. He died on his 80th birthday at Nice.

GRAY, Wing Commander Colin Falkland, D.S.O., D.F.C. and two Bars Born 1914. New Zealand fighter pilot. Born at Papanui, Christchurch, New Zealand, Colin Gray was christened on the day that news arrived of the naval victory at the Falkland Islands, and was one of a pair of twin brothers destined to fly with the R.A.F. in the Second World War. Colin joined the R.A.F. in 1939 and was posted to No. 54 (Spitfire) Squadron before the Battle of France. He fought in the Battle of Britain, destroying 14 enemy aircraft and sharing in the destruction of two others. Later he fought over Malta, Tunisia and Sicily, at one time commanding No. 81 Squadron. By the end of the War his score had risen to $27\frac{1}{2}$, placing him at the top of New Zealand fighter pilots, and 14th in the R.A.F. list. He remained in the R.A.F. after the War and in 1954–55 commanded the fighter station at Church Fenton. He retired in 1961 and returned to New Zealand.

GUYNEMER, Capitaine Georges Marie Ludovic Jules 1894–1917. First World War French "ace", second only to Fonck (*q.v.*), with 54 confirmed victories, he served with *Escadrille N.3* (later *SPA.3*) of the "Storks" group. A thin and delicate youth with romantic good looks, he was an unrivalled popular hero; France went into deep mourning when he finally failed to return from a mission on 11th September 1917. His health had been broken for some time, and he had already survived being shot down seven times. No trace of his body was ever found, and his fate remains a mystery.

HAFNER, Raoul, C.Eng., F.R.Ae.S. Born 1905. Austrian-born rotorcraft designer. For years the leading designer of rotorcraft in Britain, Raoul Hafner produced his first helicopter design in 1927. During the Second World War he did much research on rotorcraft for the Ministry of Aircraft Production – designing the Rotachute in 1940 and the Rotaplane in 1942. He was appointed Chief Designer (Helicopters) with the Bristol Aeroplane Company, designing the Type 171 (1945), Type 173 (1947) and Type 192 (1953). From 1960 until 1969 he was Technical Director (Research) with Westland Aircraft Ltd.

HANDLEY PAGE, Sir Frederick, C.B.E., F.R.Ae.S., F.C.G.I., F.I.Ae.S. British pioneer constructor and aircraft industrialist. Handley Page entered the aircraft industry in 1908 when he formed his company, originally to build aeroplanes of other people's design. Embarking on his own designs (the monoplane Types A, B, C, D, E and F) in 1912, he produced his first successful biplane, the Type G in 1913, but it was with the big 0/100 and 0/400 bombers that Handley Page first made his mark, following these with the huge V/1500. In the inter-War years many of the R.A.F.'s heavy bombers stemmed from his

London factory at Cricklewood, among them the Hinaidi, Heyford, Harrow and Hampden. His wartime Halifax was one of the mainstays of R.A.F. Bomber Command, and in post-War years was followed by the Hastings transport and Victor four-jet bomber. Always an individualist, Sir Frederick resisted Government pressure to amalgamate with one of the big manufacturing groups, but did not live to see the tragic winding-up of his company at the end of the 1960s.

HARRIS, Marshal of the Royal Air Force Sir Arthur Travers, Bt., G.C.B., O.B.E., A.F.C., LL.D. Born 1892. British air commander. By the time "Bomber" Harris took command of the British air offensive against Germany in 1942, he had already had a long and distinguished military career. Joining the R.F.C. in 1915, he was commissioned in the R.A.F. in 1918, commanded squadrons in India, 1920–21, in Iraq 1921–24 and in Britain 1925–29. He was Deputy-Director of Operations and Intelligence at the Air Ministry in 1934, commanded No. 4 Bomber Group in 1937–38, and No. 5 Bomber Group in 1939–40. He took command of R.A.F. Bomber Command from 1942 until the end of the War, and was responsible for mounting the great bombing offensive against the Third Reich. His numerous foreign decorations include the Legion of Merit and D.S.M. (U.S.A.), and Grand Officer of the Legion of Honour and Croix de Guerre.

HARTMANN, Major Erich ("Bubi") Born 1922. Most successful fighter pilot of all time, with 352 confirmed victories; holder of Knight's Cross with Diamonds.

Air Vice-Marshal James Edgar Johnson, C.B., C.B.E., D.S.O. and two Bars, D.F.C. and Bar, D.F.C. (U.S.A.), Legion of Merit, Air Medal, Légion d'Honneur Belge, Croix de Guerre Belge, Order of Leopold.

Oberst Hajo Herrmann, Oakleaves and Swords of the Knight's Cross of the Iron Cross, Luftwaffe c. 1938–1945

Hartmann flew with *JG 52* in Russia throughout his career, which lasted only 2½ years – from October 1942 until May 1945. In four weeks of the summer of 1944 he recorded 78 victories, including 19 in two days. Imprisoned for ten years by the Russians, he was released in 1955 and rejoined the *Luftwaffe,* rising to high rank in the 1960s.

HAWKER, Harry George 1891–1921. Australian pioneer pilot. A pioneer in every sense and instinct, Harry Hawker came to England in 1912 in search of work and excitement. One of the Sopwith School's star pupils, he was awarded Aviator's Certificate No. 297 on 17th September 1912, and within a month had won the Michelin Trophy and £500 for a duration flight of 8 hr. 23 min. By the end of 1913 he had become Britain's outstanding pilot and as such was instrumental in raising the prestige of Sopwith aircraft prior to the First World War. Throughout the War Hawker continued, despite failing health, to test almost all Sopwith's aircraft, and when the company went into voluntary liquidation in 1920, Hawker formed his own general engineering company to take over the business. After a gallant but abortive attempt to fly the Atlantic in 1919, Hawker was killed while practising for the 1921 Aerial Derby. His name lives on in the huge Hawker Siddeley Group, formed in the 1930s by take-over of ailing members of the British aircraft industry.

HAWKER, Major Lanoe George, V.C., D.S.O. c. 1890–1916. British military pilot. Having been awarded Aviator's Certificate No. 435 at Hendon in March 1913, Hawker transferred to the R.F.C. from the Royal Engineers at the outbreak of War, and served with the earliest squadrons to reach the front. He was awarded the Victoria Cross in 1915, and the following February led the first British all-fighter squadron – No. 24, R.F.C. – to France in an effort to counter the "Fokker Scourge". The de Havilland D.H.2 "pusher" fighter of Hawkers' squadron achieved considerable early success; he himself has been termed "the English Boelcke" for his vision and qualities of leadership. It was in a fight with No. 24 Squadron that Oswald Boelcke (*q.v.*) died on 26th October 1916. Hawker was shot down and killed by Manfred von Richthofen (*q.v.*) the following month.

HEINKEL, Ernst 1888–1958. Aircraft designer; chief designer for Albatros in 1913, he transferred to the same post with Hansa-Brandenburg the following year. During the First World War he designed a series of combat float-planes, of which the most successful were the W.12, W.19, W.29 monoplane and post-War W.33. He started his own company in 1922, and it was finally merged with the modern German industrial group VFW in the early 1960s. Best remembered designs are the ubiquitous He 111 medium bomber; and the He 280, the world's first turbojet fighter, built as a private venture and not supported by the German air ministry.

HERRMANN, Oberst Hajo Born 1913. German military pilot. Originally a bomber pilot, awarded the Knight's Cross for operations on Heinkels of *Kampfgeschwader 4* and Junkers Ju 88s of *KG 30*, Herrmann joined the *Luftwaffe* Operational Staff in 1942. The following year he conceived, formed and led the free-lance single-seat night fighters of the *"Wilde Sau"* ("Wild Boar") organisation. He commanded the 30th and the 1st *Jagddivision*, and became Inspector of Aerial Defence in December 1943. Late in 1944 he led the 9th *Fliegerdivision*, and formed the controversial *Rammkommando "Elbe"*, a last-ditch interception unit which must be classed as a near-suicide squadron. With 320 bomber missions, twelve ships sunk, and nine heavy bombers shot down to his record, and considering his staff activities, Herrmann must be granted to be one of the most energetic and imaginative middle-rank *Luftwaffe* commanders of the War.

HOEPPNER, Generalleutnant Ernst Wilhelm von Died 1922. German commander. Appointed Commanding General of the Imperial German Army Air Service (*Kogenluft*) in November 1916, after several high posts including Chief of the General Staff of the 2nd and 3rd Armies. An able commander, under whose leadership the service retained its morale and effectiveness right up to the Armistice, although hampered by shortages of aircraft and veteran personnel.

HUGHES, Howard R. Born 1905. American manufacturing tycoon and former pilot. Hughes, a man of legendary and wide-ranging business interest, retains his presidency of the Hughes Aircraft Company. In January 1937 he established a new transcontinental record of

7 hours 28 minutes; and in November 1947 he flew – on its only flight – the world's then-largest aircraft, his own Hughes H.2 *Hercules* flying boat. This aircraft, weighing 190 tons and powered by eight engines, was 219 feet long and had a span of 320 feet – the latter is still a world record.

HUGO, Group Captain Petrus Hendrik, D.S.O., D.F.C. and two Bars, Croix de Guerre (France), D.F.C. (U.S.A.) Born 20th December 1917 in Cape Province, South Africa. South African fighter pilot. Son of a French Huguenot sheep farmer, "Dutch" Hugo achieved a remarkable record during the Second World War: the destruction of 22 enemy aircraft and at least 55 enemy land vehicles, a hand in the sinking of about 20 enemy ships, and the accumulation of over 1,000 operational flying hours. A Group Captain at 24, he had flown Gladiators with No. 615 Squadron during the Battle of France and fought with the Squadron in Hurricanes in the Battle of Britain; badly wounded in the Battle, he later became a flight commander, was given command of No. 41 (Spitfire) Squadron in November 1941, in the following year commanded the Tangmere Fighter Wing, and in July 1942 led the Hornchurch Spitfire Wing. Shortly afterwards he was posted to North Africa where he remained almost until the end of the War.

ILYUSHIN, Engineer-General Sergei Vladimirovich, Hero of Socialist Labour (Hammer and Sickle Gold Medal), Order of Lenin Born, c. 1910. Soviet aircraft designer. During the 1930s Sergei Ilyushin headed a design team at the Soviet Central Design Bureau, and his first significant product was the CKB-55 two-seat ground-attack prototype which won a competition against Sukhoi's Su-6 in 1938–39. Developed from this was the CKB-57, in effect the prototype of the famous Il-2 *Shturmovik* – for which Ilyushin established a separate design bureau, and which remained the principal equipment of Soviet ground attack forces until the end of the War. As early as 1943 the Ilyushin designers were working on transport aircraft and ever since the War there has been a steady flow of excellent Ilyushin-designed jet bombers and commercial airliners.

IMMELMANN, Leutnant Max 1890–1916. Born at Dresden, Immelmann was Germany's first great individual "ace". One of the handful of pilots flying Fokker monoplane scouts with synchronised forward-firing machine-guns, Immelmann scored his first kill on 1st August 1915. He gained another 14 victories by the time of his death on 18th June 1916, but the psychological impact of the "Fokker scourge" on Allied aircrew was out of all proportion to actual losses. He became a figure of legendary proportions, at home and abroad; the "Immelmann turn" (a half-loop with a roll out at the top) still keeps his name alive.

JABARA, Major James, U.S.A.F. Born 10th October 1923. American fighter pilot. James Jabara, from Wichita, Kansas, was a veteran of the Second World

The Royal Saxon Reserve-Lieutenant Max Immelmann, Commander of the Order of St. Heinrich, Knight of the Ordre Pour le Mérite, Knight of the Iron Cross, 1st and 2nd Class, etc.

War (with 3½ enemy aircraft to his credit) before he was sent to Korea in 1950 with the 4th Fighter Interception Wing flying F-86A Sabres. He became America's first "jet ace" during this tour of operation, destroying six Communist MiG-15s (his fifth victim falling on 20th May 1951). His second tour commenced on 12th January 1953, this time flying F-86Fs, and in six months he destroyed a further nine MiG's, to become the War's second-highest scoring pilot, after Joseph McConnell (*q.v.*).

JESCHONNEK, Generaloberst Hans 1899–1943. German air commander. Flew with *Jasta 40* in the First World War. Moved from *Reichswehr* to *Luftwaffe*, 1933, as staff officer in Milch's team. Head of operations staff of General Staff, April 1937. Chief of the *Luftwaffe* General Staff from February 1939 until his suicide in 1943. Closely associated with the policy of concentrating all available offensive air power in support of ground forces, he was the scapegoat blamed by Hitler and Göring after the failure by the *Luftwaffe* to secure air superiority over the Kursk salient during the vital battles of July-August 1943.

JOHNSON, Miss Amy (Mrs. J. A. Mollison) British woman pilot. Amy Johnson was a courageous young pilot who participated in the much-publicised long distance pioneer flights in light aircraft between the Wars. Her great flights included the first solo flight from Britain to Australia by a woman in a D.H. Moth in May 1930, her solo flight from England to South Africa and back in a Puss Moth in November and December 1932, and her flight with her husband, Jim Mollison, from Wales to Connecticut, U.S.A., in a D.H. Dragon in July 1933. She was tragically killed in an unexplained accident while flying in the Air Transport Auxiliary on 5th January 1941 when her aircraft fell into the Thames Estuary.

JOHNSON, Air Vice-Marshal James Edgar, C.B.E., D.S.O. and two Bars, D.F.C. and Bar, D.F.C. (U.S.A.), Legion of Merit, Air Medal, Order of Leopold, Croix de Guerre Belge. Born 1915. British fighter pilot. Johnnie Johnson officially headed the list of British and Commonwealth fighter pilots of the Second World War with a score of 38. He joined No. 616 (Spitfire) Squadron before the end of the Battle of Britain but did not score his first victory until he shot down a Bf 109 in May 1941. His first D.F.C. was awarded in September 1941 after completing over fifty fighter sweeps, and a Bar followed a year later. In March 1943 Johnson was promoted to lead the Kenley Wing of Spitfires, charged with escorting American bomber formations. He continued to fly on operations almost continuously until the end of the War. Afterwards he decided to remain in the Service, was awarded his Belgian decorations in 1947, and in 1950 was sent to Korea to report on the lessons of air fighting, being awarded the American Air Medal in December that year, and the Legion of Merit in 1951.

JOHNSON, Lieutenant Colonel Robert S., D.S.C., D.F.C. (with 8 clusters), Silver Star, Air Medal (with 4 clusters) Born 1920. American fighter pilot. Second-highest scoring American pilot in Europe during the Second World War, Bob Johnson flew all his combat missions in the big P-47 Thunderbolt. An incorrigible flying enthusiast since his early youth, he was assigned to the 56th Fighter Group six months after Pearl Harbor, arriving in England on 13th January 1943. With the task of escorting American daylight bombers over Europe, the 56th Group quickly established a big reputation in combat, and in little over a year Johnson had taken over leadership of the 61st Squadron, and was credited with the destruction of 28 enemy aircraft. He was recalled to the U.S.A. in June 1944.

JONES, Captain Oscar Philip, C.V.O., O.B.E., F.R.G.S., F.R.Ae.S. Born 1898. British airline pilot. Widely regarded as the "grand old man" among British airline pilots, "O.P." served in the R.F.C. and R.A.F. in the First World War, joined Instone Air Line in 1922 and was an airline captain continuously until 1955 on European, Empire and Intercontinental routes; he was a founder pilot of Imperial Airways in 1924, and B.O.A.C.

in 1940, and made numerous pioneer long-distance commercial flights. He has flown over 21,600 hours on 128 different aircraft types, and carried 139,000 passengers – mostly during years when airliners seldom carried more than 30-40 passengers per flight. He was awarded the Britannia Trophy in 1951.

JUNKERS, Hugo 1859-1935. Multi-disciplined scientist and technologist. For most of his life a thermodynamicist, and founder of a gas heating company, he is mainly remembered for his research into diesel propulsion and in the field of all-metal cantilever monoplanes; his development of the thick-section cantilever wing and welded metal construction culminated in 1918 in operational types (J-9 and J-10) which saw limited action. Always of stoutly liberal beliefs, Junkers turned to civil designs in the 1920s; his eventual masterpiece was the almost literally immortal Ju 52/3m trimotor, incorporating his full-span trailing edge flaps. In 1934, shortly after the Nazi take-over, he was retired as politically unreliable, and died the next year. His *JFA* became, late in the Second World War, the biggest single aircraft company in the world, with 140,000 employees. His name lived on after his death in a way he would have deprecated – with the Ju 87 *"Stuka"* and Ju 88 bomber. A true pioneer, he was 56 when his first design flew.

KAZAKOV, Staff Captain Alexander Alexandrovich, Orders of St. George and St. Vladimir, D.S.O., M.C., D.F.C., Legion d'Honneur 1891-1919. Russian military pilot. Little is known of Kazakov, and his total number of aerial victories is obscure; but with at least 17, probably 32, and possibly 40 he was certainly Russia's leading

Staff Captain Alexander Alexandrovich Kazakov, Knight Grand Cross of the Order of St. Stanislas, the Sword of the Order of St. George, Knight Grand Cross of the Order of St. Vladimir with Swords, D.S.O., M.C., D.F.C., Chevalier de la Légion d'Honneur, Imperial Russian Air Service

First World War ace. His best known exploit was his first victory on 18th March 1915; flying an unarmed Morane monoplane, he brought down an Albatros two-seater with a grapnel trailed from his machine on a steel cable. He went on to command the 19th Corps Air Squadron from August 1915, and the three-squadron No. 1 Fighter Group from 1917. He flew with the R.A.F. Expeditionary Force in North Russia during the Civil War, and died in an inexplicable flying accident the day after learning of the withdrawal of the British force.

KESSELRING, Generalfeldmarschall Albert Born 1885. German artillery officer who took staff post in Air Ministry in 1933. Chief of *Luftwaffe* General Staff, 1936–37. A.O.C.-in-C., *Luftflotte 1*, 1939. A.O.C.-in-C., *Luftflotte 2*, from January 1940; with Sperrle (*q.v.*), commander of German forces in Battle of Britain. Retained command of *Luftflotte 2* in Russia (June-December 1941) and Mediterranean (1942–43); simultaneously C.-in-C., South, 1942–45. As commander of German forces in Italy he distinguished himself as a "ground general"; appointed C.-in-C., West, March 1945. Sentenced to death by British Military Court, 1947, for responsibility for atrocities committed by his troops in Italy; sentence commuted to imprisonment, released October 1952.

KINCHELOE, Captain Iven Carl, Jr. 1928–1958. American fighter pilot and test pilot. Born at Detroit, Iven Kincheloe gained an aeronautical engineering degree at Purdue University, Indiana, before learning to fly. Flying F-86A Sabres at the outbreak of the Korean War in 1950, he was sent to Edwards Air Force Base to check out the new F-86E before being assigned to combat duty with the 325th Fighter Interceptor Squadron in Korea. Transferring to the 25th Fighter Squadron at Suwon in 1952, flying F-86Es, he shot down ten Communist aircraft, of which five were MiG-15s, before being posted home. He was then sent to the Empire Test Pilots' School in England, after which he was assigned to the U.S.A.F. Flight Test Center at Edwards Air Force Base for advanced research flying and did much initial evaluation of such aircraft as the F-100, F-101, F-102, F-104 and F-105. On 25th May 1956 he first flew the Bell X-2 rocket aircraft and thereafter made a number of spectacular flights. On 7th September that year he was acclaimed "the first man in space" when he attained a height of 126,200 feet in the X-2. It was planned that he should fly the X-15 research aircraft in 1958, but was killed when the engine of his F-104 failed and his aircraft crashed on 26th July that year.

KINGABY, Group Captain Donald Ernest, D.S.O., A.F.C., D.F.M. and two Bars, D.F.C. (U.S.A.), Croix de Guerre Belge British fighter pilot. The only recipient of three Distinguished Flying Medals, Don Kingaby joined No. 92 Squadron towards the end of the Battle of Britain and had scored five kills before that great Battle had closed. Serving with, and later leading No. 122 (Spitfire)

Squadron, and as leader of the Hornchurch Spitfire Wing, Kingaby shot down 22½ enemy aircraft – most of them Bf 109s and Fw 190s. After the end of the War he elected to remain in the R.A.F. and was given command of No. 72 Squadron.

KOZHEDUB, Colonel-General Ivan Nikitaevich, Gold Star Medal of the Hero of the Soviet Union (thrice), Order of Lenin Born, c. 1919. Soviet fighter pilot. Highest-scoring Allied pilot of the Second World War, Ivan Kozhedub was also only one of three recipients of three Gold Stars of the Medal of the Hero of the Soviet Union (the others being Aviation Major-General Aleksandr Ivanovich Pokryshkin, *q.v.*, and Marshal Georgiy Konstantinovich Zhukov) during the War. Kozhedub flew throughout his combat career in Lavochkin fighters; his first operational sortie was flown on 26th March 1943, and thereafter flew principally in the Kharkov area in La 5s, La 5FNs and La 7s. His last sortie was flown on 19th April 1945, by which time he had flown 520 combat sorties and destroyed 62 German aircraft – comprising 22 Focke-Wulf Fw 190s, 19 Messerschmitt Bf 109s, 18 Junkers Ju 87s, two Heinkel He 111s and a Messerschmitt Me 262 jet fighter. Kozhedub was still included in the Soviet Air Force Active List six years ago.

LACEY, Squadron Leader James Harry, D.F.M. and Bar Born 1917. British fighter pilot. Highest-scoring British N.C.O. pilot in the Battle of Britain, the indomitable "Ginger" Lacey destroyed 15½ enemy aircraft in that great air campaign, flying Hurricanes with No. 501 Squadron. He was commissioned in 1941 and commanded Nos. 155 and 17 Squadrons in India, Ceylon, Burma, Malaya and Japan. When the War ended he had achieved 28 victories in air combat. He retired from the R.A.F. in 1967.

LANGLEY, Samuel Pierpont 22.8.1834–27.2.1906. American mathematician and solar radiation physicist. Langley began building powered model aeroplanes in the 1890s, launching them from a houseboat on the Potomac River. His unmanned 14-ft. span models achieved sustained, powered flights of up to 4,200 feet during 1896 (powered by a single steam engine mounted amidships). In 1901 his petrol-engined quarter-scale model was the first (unmanned) aeroplane to achieve sustained flight, and his first full-size manned aeroplane was ready for flight in 1903 when the Wright brothers achieved their success at Kitty Hawk. In both Langley's attempts at manned flight, the *Aerodrome* fouled its launcher and, in view of the Wrights' success, the American Government terminated its support of Langley.

LAVOCHKIN, Engineer Lieutenant-General Syemyon Alexander, Hero of Socialist Labour (Hammer and Sickle Gold Medal), Order of Lenin Born 1900, in Smolensk. Soviet aircraft designer. Educated at the Kursk Gymnasium, Lavochkin left school in 1918 to participate in the Civil War which followed the October Revolution. After three years combat service, he was accepted late in

1920 by the Moscow Aviation Institute, graduating brilliantly. In the Second World War he was assisted initially with the LaGG-1 and LaGG-3 fighters by Gorbunov and Gudov, but these aircraft were not widely produced. His La-5N and La-7 fighters were excellent aircraft, were built in very large numbers and remained in production up to the end of the War. However, though these fighters probably did more than any others to win and maintain Soviet air superiority over the Eastern Front late in 1944, Lavochkin's fame died with the return to peace, and although he continued working long after VE-Day, he died in 1965 – his brilliant wartime work almost forgotten.

LeMAY, General, Curtis Emerson, U.S.A.F. Born 1906. American air commander. Commissioned in 1930, LeMay rose quickly to senior rank. He commanded the 305th Bombardment Group, a European Theatre unit flying B-17 Fortresses, in 1943, and in that year was promoted to command the 3rd Bomb Division. In 1945 LeMay was given command of the 21st Bomber Command, flying B-29 Superfortresses from the Marianas, and later in the year he commanded the 20th Air Force on Guam. He became Deputy Chief of the Air Staff for Research and Development before the year was out, and moved to the post of Commanding General, U.S.A.F. Europe, in 1947. Chiefly remembered as the founder and architect of Strategic Air Command, LeMay had a highly individual and demanding style of leadership. Since retiring from the Service he has become chairman of the board of Networks Electronic Corp., and has involved himself in politics – on one occasion standing for the vice-presidency as the team-mate of Governor George Wallace of Alabama.

LILIENTHAL, Otto 1848–1896. German civil engineer and pioneer glider pilot. Lilienthal published his classic *Der Vogelflug als Grundlage der Fliegekunst* (The Flight of Birds as the Basis of Aviation) in 1889, and, despite his conviction that powered flight would be achieved by wing-flapping, he built five fixed-wing monoplane and two biplane gliders between 1891 and 1896. Piloting these himself, Lilienthal achieved sustained flights near Berlin and at the Rhinower Hills, near Stöllen, eventually travelling more than 750 ft. (250 m). Although he had been experimenting with a small carbonic acid gas engine, he was killed when one of his gliders crashed on 9th August 1896 before he could progress further with powered flight.

LINDBERGH, Brigadier General Charles Augustus, Congressional Medal of Honor, U.S.A.F. Reserve Born 1902. Pioneer long-distance pilot. "Slim" Lindbergh found immortal fame when, on 20th–21st May 1927 he made the first solo, nonstop transatlantic flight in the Ryan *"Spirit of St. Louis"* single-engine monoplane, flying from New York to Paris – a feat which earned him the Congressional Medal of Honor. After a number of long-distance flights, in company with his wife in 1933, fame

Major Gervais Raoul Lufbery, Chevalier de la Légion d'Honneur, Médaille Militaire, Croix de Guerre with 10 palms, M.C.

brought personal tragedy when his infant son was kidnapped and killed. During the Second World War he visited the Pacific Theatre as a civilian technical representative of the U.S. aircraft industry and, flying "unofficially", is known to have shot down at least one Japanese aircraft.

LITVAK, Junior Lieutenant Lydia, Gold Star of a Hero of the Soviet Union, Order of Lenin 1921–1943. Russian woman fighter pilot. Lydia Litvak was the highest-scoring Soviet woman fighter pilot of the Second World War (and thus presumably the most successful woman fighter pilot in the world) with 12 confirmed victories. One of thirty Russian women who received the Gold Star during the War, she served with the mixed-sex 73rd Guards Fighter Air Regiment, flying Yak fighters, but was killed in action on 1st August 1943.

LUFBERY, Major Gervais Raoul 1885–1918. An American citizen of French parentage, Lufbery was a leading member of the *Escadrille Lafayette*, the squadron of American volunteer pilots flying with the *Service Aéronautique*, 1916–18. A patient, mechanically-skilled pilot, he showed great leadership qualities, and gained many decorations and promotions. He was killed in action on 19th May 1918, as commander of the American 94th Aero Squadron. His final score of 17 confirmed victories is surpassed only by those of Rickenbacker and Luke (*qq.v.*) among American pilots.

LUKE, Lieutenant Frank, Jr. 1897–1918. America's second highest-scoring ace of the First War, Luke flew with the 27th Aero Squadron in July-September 1918, gaining 21 confirmed kills. He was undisciplined, self-assertive, unpopular and resentful of any authority, but a born combat pilot. His first victory – while breaking formation against orders – was gained on 16th August.

His last (three balloons shot down on the evening of his death, 28th September) were gained while AWOL and flying without authority. He survived a crash, but was killed after starting a gun-battle with German troops sent to capture him. He was awarded a posthumous Congressional Medal of Honor.

LUNDBERG, Bo Klas Oskar, F.R.Ae.S., Hon.F.A.I.A.A. Born 1907. Swedish aeronautical engineer. Bo Lundberg has attracted recent notoriety in international circles as an outspoken critic of the supersonic airliner, but his long and distinguished career is often overlooked. He was designer and test pilot for *AB Svenska Järnvägsverkstäderna Aeroplanavdelningen*, Linköping, from 1931–35; Chief Designer of the Royal Swedish Air Board (responsible for the J22 aircraft), 1940–44; Chief of the Structures Department, Aeronautical Research of Sweden. 1944–47.

MACMILLAN, Wing Commander Norman, O.B.E., M.C., A.F.C., D.L. Born 1892. British pilot and aviation writer. Before taking up writing during his retirement, Norman Macmillan had a long and active career in aviation. Transferring to the R.F.C. as a pilot from the infantry in 1916, he served in Belgium, France and Italy in the First World War, was appointed Chief Test Pilot to the Fairey Aviation Company during the period 1924–30. He was the first British pilot to cross the Andes, 1931.

MALAN, Group Captain Adolph Gysbert, D.S.O. and Bar, D.F.C. and Bar, Légion d'Honneur, Croix de Guerre (France), Czech War Cross, Croix de Guerre Belge 1910–1963. South African fighter pilot. A born leader and one of the most famous R.A.F. fighter pilots of the Second World War, "Sailor" Malan (so named from his pre-War merchant navy service) led the famous No. 74 (Spitfire) Squadron (the "Tigers") in the Battle of Britain, by the end of which he was credited with eighteen victories. In 1941 he was promoted to lead the Biggin Hill Wing, and the following year commanded the Biggin Hill fighter station. His final War score was officially stated as thirty-two victories, which placed him third in the list of R.A.F. fighter pilots. He returned to South Africa where he took up farming and in the 1950s became interested in politics. He died in September 1963.

MANNOCK, Major Edward, V.C., D.S.O. and two Bars, M.C. and Bar Died 1918. Highest scoring British and Empire pilot of the First World War, with 73 confirmed victories; contemporary sources believed this was a conservative figure. He was blind in one eye, and his acceptance for flying duties is a mystery. Interned in Turkey early in the War, he flew Nieuports and S.E.5As with Nos. 40, 74 and 85 Squadrons, R.F.C., commanding the latter for the last month of his life. A painstakingly careful leader with a knack for encouraging novices, he was a merciless fighter in a war generally notable for a degree of chivalry between enemies. He was shot down by ground fire on 26th July 1918, and never found. His

Group Captain Adolph Gysbert Malan, D.S.O. and Bar, D.F.C. and Bar, Légion d'Honneur, Croix de Guerre, Czech War Cross, Croix de Guerre Belge.

posthumous Victoria Cross award was made months later, and for years he was a relatively obscure figure.

MARSEILLE, Hauptmann Hans-Joachim 1919–1942. German fighter pilot. Credited with the highest number of aerial victories against the R.A.F. and Commonwealth forces, and awarded the Knight's Cross with Oakleaves, Swords and Diamonds. Marseille served first on the Channel Coast, showing no particular skill, and in April 1941 was posted to North Africa with *Jagdgeschwader 27*. By the time of his death in a baling-out accident on 30th September 1942 he had been credited with 158 victories in 382 missions; this total has often been challenged, and certain detailed claims seem hard to substantiate, but generally Marseille's record emerges intact – he was a remarkable marksman and a fine fighter pilot.

MARTIN, Glenn L. 1886–1955. One of America's foremost aviation pioneers, Martin began building gliders in 1907. The following year he designed and built a powered "pusher" aircraft, and taught himself to fly in it. In 1909 he established one of the first aircraft factories in the United States, and at various times in the period 1909–16 he established speed, altitude and endurance records. He obtained an F.A.I. Aviator's Certificate in 1911, and held Aero Club of America Expert Aviator's Certificate No. 2. He first incorporated the Glenn L. Martin Co. at Santa Ana in 1911, and received his first War Department order – for the TT trainer – in 1913. After a short-lived

Squadron Leader Archibald Ashmore McKellar, D.S.O., D.F.C. and Bar, A.A.F.

merger with the Wright Company in 1917 he re-established the Glenn L. Martin Company in Cleveland, and between the Wars built several notable types for the U.S. Army and Navy, the mail service and foreign governments. The best-known products of his bureau are probably the Martin B-10 bomber, the series of Clippers, the Maryland and Baltimore bombers for the R.A.F., and the Martin B-26 Marauder bomber.

MARTIN, Sir James, C.B.E., D.Sc., C.Eng., F.I.Mech.E., F.R.Ae.S. Born 1893. Aircraft designer and engineer. Among the design accomplishments of this brilliant engineer were the Martin balloon barrage cable cutter, the 12-gun nose for the Douglas Havoc night fighter, the Spitfire's jettisonable hood, the flat feed for the 20-mm. Hispano gun, the advanced Martin-Baker prototype fighters, aircraft ejector seats (for which he received numerous awards associated with work on air safety), and important components for guns, gun mountings, propellers, etc. He was awarded the Royal Aero Club's Gold Medal in 1964, and remains today Managing Director of Martin-Baker Aircraft Co. Ltd.

McCONNELL, Captain Joseph, Jr., U.S.A.F. Born 1922. American fighter pilot. Joseph McConnell, whose home town was Dover, New Hampshire, was the highest-scoring fighter pilot in the Korean War. Flying with the 51st Fighter Wing relatively late in the War did not win his fifth victory until 16th February 1953; he was shot

down on 12th April but baled out over the Yellow Sea and was rescued by helicopter. His tenth victory over Communist Mig-15s was gained on 24th April; three more victims fell to his guns early in May, and on 18th May he destroyed three in a single day, to finish with a score of 16. Posted home at the end of the War, he was assigned to Edwards Air Force Base, but was tragically killed when operationally testing an early F-86H Sabre on 26th August 1954.

McCUDDEN, Major James Thomas Byford, V.C., D.S.O. and Bar, M.C. and Bar, M.M. Died 1918. British fighter pilot of the First World War, credited with 57 victories, McCudden rose through the ranks in January 1917 after nearly a year at the front as a two-seater, and later a D.H.2 pilot. Most of his victories were scored while a flight commander with No. 56 Squadron, flying S.E.5As. He was awarded the Victoria Cross in April 1918, with 57 victories; he never flew in action again, but was killed in an accident in September while flying to take command of No. 60 Squadron. His brilliance was firmly based on his past as a mechanic; he had a thorough technical grasp of aircraft and machine-guns, and employed his expertise in careful "stalking" of enemies and in picking his own conditions for a fight.

McGUIRE, Major Thomas Buchanan, Jr., Congressional Medal of Honor, U.S.A.A.F. 1920–1944. American fighter pilot. Born at Ridgewood, New Jersey, on 1st August 1920, McGuire joined the U.S. Army Air Corps in 1941 and, like Major Richard I. Bong (*q.v.*), trained on the Lockheed P-38 Lightning. Credited with the destruction of 38 Japanese aircraft while flying with the 9th Fighter Squadron, 49th Fighter Group, and 431st Fighter Squadron of the 475th Fighter Group. On Christmas Day 1944 McGuire was leading fifteen P-38s as escort for a raid on Mabalacat aerodrome in the Philippines when his guns jammed in combat with "Zero" fighters. Instead of abandoning the fight, he went to the assistance of another pilot, attempting to draw the fire of an enemy fighter. Unfortunately he was too low and crashed to his death. He was nevertheless America's second highest scoring pilot of the Second World War.

McKELLAR, Squadron Leader Archibald Ashmore, D.S.O., D.F.C. and Bar Born 1912. British fighter pilot. "Archie" McKellar's claims to fame were varied; as a peacetime member of the Auxiliary Air Force flying Spitfires, he shot down the first German aircraft to fall on British soil after the outbreak of the Second World War – a Heinkel He 111 which fell near Dalkeith in October 1939. Posted to No. 605 (Hurricane) Squadron, he was a flight commander throughout the Battle of Britain. During one month this dynamic little pilot (he was only five-feet-three-inches high) was credited with seventeen victories and in the same period was awarded the D.S.O. and two D.F.C.s. He was killed in an unexplained crash on 1st November, the day after the Battle of Britain ended – at that time the highest-scoring, most decorated pilot of the Auxiliary Air Force. His final official score was 21 enemy aircraft destroyed, 3 probably destroyed and 3 damaged.

MESSERSCHMITT, Willy Born 1898. Aircraft designer; first worked, as teenage enthusiast, with glider pioneer Friedrich Harth in 1910–14. His embryo company, formed while he was still a student, merged with *Bayerische Flugzeugwerke* in 1927, with Messerschmitt as chief designer. Several promising light types and transports emerged from the bureau, helped by powerful friends (including Rudolf Hess) and hampered by powerful enemies (including Erhard Milch, *q.v.*) and by years of economic uncertainty. Eventually the Bf 109 fighter brought commercial success, and immortality. Messerschmitt's record was always uneven, however; the Bf 109 and Me 262 balanced failures such as the Bf 110 day fighter and the Me 210. Post-War, Messerschmitt joined Hispano Aviacion in Spain, designing the successful HA-200 *Saeta* and, for Egypt, the abortive HA-300.

MIKOYAN, Engineer Colonel-General Artem, Hero of Socialist Labour (Hammer and Sickle Gold Medal), Order of Lenin 1905–1970. Soviet aircraft designer. One of the best-known of Soviet fighter designers, Artem Mikoyan established his design bureau just before the Second World War, working with the mathematician Mikhail Gurevich. Their first successful fighter, produced early in the Second World War was the MiG-3. Undoubtedly their prestige has been enhanced over the past twenty years by the successful MiG-15, MiG-17, MiG-19 and MiG-21 family of fighters which has been the mainstay of Communist bloc air forces, while the MiG-25 must be regarded as one of the most advanced in-service all-weather combat aircraft in the world. Artem Mikoyan died on 9th December 1970 at the age of 65.

MIL, Engineer General Mikhail Leontyevich, Hero of Socialist Labour (Hammer and Sickle Gold Medal), Order of Lenin Born 1909. Soviet rotorcraft designer. His early work on Soviet helicopters and gyroplanes dates from around 1930 when employed in the Central Design Bureau, Mil designed the first helicopter (the Mi-1) to enter squadron service in the Soviet Union, in 1951. This was followed by the Mi-2, 3 and 4 designs, for which he was awarded the Order of Lenin in 1969. Very large helicopters have been produced by the Mil bureau during the 1960s, culminating in the huge Mi-12 – the largest such aircraft in the world. Mikhail Mil died on 31st January 1970 after a long illness.

MILCH, Generalfeldmarschall Erhard 1892–1971. German airman of the First World War, Director of *Deutsche Lufthansa* from 1926, Secretary of State for Air from 1933, Inspector-General of *Luftwaffe* from 1939, Director-General of Equipment from 1941. Brilliant organiser whose sound long-term plans for air force development clashed with Göring's consistently optimistic claims; Göring made every effort to ease Milch out

of favour. One of the principal architects of growth of *Luftwaffe* technical and personnel strength in pre-War years.

MILES, Frederick George, F.R.Ae.S., M.S.A.E. Born 1903. British aircraft designer. Elder of two famous brothers, Fred Miles had engaged in all manner of aircraft work during the 1920s before he was appointed a Director and Chief Designer of Phillips and Powis Aircraft in 1932, and afterwards formed Miles Aircraft Ltd. Among his well-known designs were the Miles Hawk, Magister, Master and Monarch.

MILES, George Herbert, F.R.Ae.S., C.Eng., M.S.A.E. Born 1911. British aircraft designer. Younger brother of F. G. Miles (*q.v.*), George Miles joined Phillips and Powis Aircraft in 1936, and later became Technical Director and Chief Designer of Miles Aircraft Ltd., remaining with this company until 1948. His designs for the company included the Messenger, Monitor, Aerovan, Gemini and Marathon. Since then he has been Chief Designer at Airspeed Ltd (responsible for the design development of the Ambassador), and more recently with Beagle Aircraft Ltd., with which company he was responsible for the design of the B.206 aircraft.

Brigadier General William Mitchell, Medal of Honor, D.S.C., D.S.M., Commandeur de la Légion d'Honneur, U.S.A.A.C.

MITCHELL, Reginald Joseph, C.B.E., A.M.I.C.E., F.R.Ae.S. 1895–1937. British aircraft designer. Although he died from tuberculosis at the early age of 42, R. J. Mitchell was unquestionably one of the most famous aircraft designers of all time. A quiet, unassuming man, he joined the design section of the Supermarine works in 1916. After the War he took over the re-design of the Sea Lion as the Mark II, which won the 1922 Schneider Trophy for Britain. Deeply impressed by the superiority of the American seaplane winners of the 1923 Trophy, he embarked on his brilliant seaplane series which culminated in the wins in the famous Trophy race by the S.5 in 1927, the S.6 in 1929 and the outright win by the S.6B in 1931. By way of a number of unsuccessful fighter designs, Mitchell evolved the classic Spitfire, the greatest achievement for which he could have wished, but he only lived to see the prototype fly, and he died on 11th June 1937.

MITCHELL, Brigadier General William, D.S.C., D.S.M. (U.S.), Commandeur de la Légion d'Honneur (France) *c.* 1880–1936. American air commander and strategist. Though effectively opposed by Navy and Army traditionalists during his lifetime, "Billy" Mitchell may be regarded as one of the principal architects of American air power. Enlisting as a private in the 1st Wisconsin Infantry in 1898, being commissioned and serving in the Signal Corps, he transferred to the Aviation Section in 1916. In August 1918 he commanded, as a colonel, all American air units on the Western Front. The bombing operations carried out under his command made a deep impression on him and soon after returning home he conducted his famous bombing trials against warships to demonstrate the potentialities of air power. His outspoken criticism of the staff traditionalists brought sharp conflict with authority and was suspended from duty for five years by court-martial. He preferred to resign his commission to continue his campaign to strengthen his country's air force. He died in New York on 19th February, and only after his death was the strength of his advocacy of air power fully recognised in America.

MÖLDERS, Oberst Werner ("Vati") 1913–1941. Germany's most influential fighter leader of 1938–41, Mölders was first to reach each new record of victories and each decoration. Brilliantly successful with *Legion Cóndor* in Spain (14 victories), he led *III/JG 53* "*Pik As*" in Battle of France, then *JG 51* (named after him, posthumously) during the Battle of Britain. His appointment as Inspector of Fighters in summer of 1941 was short-lived; he died in a transport aircraft crash when going to Udet's funeral in November 1941, before his promotion to general's rank could be promulgated. Holder of Knight's Cross with Diamonds, 115 confirmed victories.

NAVARRE, Sous-Lieutenant Jean M. D. 1895–1919. French scout pilot. A flamboyant extrovert who wore a lady's silk stocking over his head instead of a helmet, Navarre was one of France's earliest aces of the First

Oberst Werner Mölders, Oakleaves, Swords and Diamonds of the Knight's Cross of the Iron Cross, Luftwaffe 1936–1941

World War. As a corporal flying Morane two-seat monoplanes, he participated in France's third aerial victory of the War on 1st April 1915, when his observer Robert brought down an Aviatik with three rounds of rifle fire. Navarre graduated to single-seaters, earning promotion, decorations and considerable fame as he amassed a total of twelve victories; many were gained while flying a brightly-painted Nieuport *Bébé* over the Verdun sector in the spring of 1916. He was badly injured in June 1916, and did not see active service for another two years. He died as a Morane-Saulnier test pilot, practising for a victory fly-past over Paris. He is remembered as one of the founders of the high-spirited and colourful traditions of the early fighter pilots.

NICOLSON, Wing Commander James Brindley, V.C., D.F.C. 1917–1945. British fighter pilot. The only member of R.A.F. Fighter Command to be awarded the Victoria Cross, Nicolson was a regular officer who, as Flight Commander on No. 249 (Hurricane) Squadron during the Battle of Britain in 1940, was attacked by enemy fighters near Southampton on 16th August. His aircraft was fatally crippled but, despite severe burns, he remained at the controls long enough to attack the enemy and may have destroyed one of the Messerschmitts before baling out. He recovered in hospital, only to lose his life in a Liberator crash in the Bay of Bengal shortly before the end of the War.

Major Walter Nowotny, Oakleaves, Swords and Diamonds of the Knight's Cross of the Iron Cross, Luftwaffe 1940–1944

NORTHROP, John Knudson Born 1895. American aircraft designer. Served with the U.S. Signal Corps in 1918. A designer for Lockheed Aircraft Co. of Santa Barbara, 1919–20, Northrop joined Douglas Aircraft as a project engineer in 1923 and worked for the company for three years. He was co-founder of Lockheed Aircraft in 1927, and the company's chief designer, 1927–28, during which time he designed the Lockheed Vega. From 1929 onwards he was involved in his own companies, as vice-president and chief engineer of the Northrop Aircraft Co. (1929–31) and the Northrop Corporation (1932–37). He was co-founder and president of Northrop Aircraft Incorporated from 1939, and remained an engineering consultant to the company after giving up full-time participation in 1953. He was the co-designer of several aircraft, notably the A-17 of 1935, the P-61 of 1941, and the F-89 Scorpion of 1948.

NOWOTNY, Major Walter 1920–1944. Leading Austrian ace of 1939–45 and commander of the world's first operational jet fighter unit – the evaluation squadron named after him when testing Me 262s, July-December 1944. His earlier career included very distinguished service as squadron officer in Russia, culminating in command of I/JG 54 "Grünherz" and first achievement of 250 victories, including 10 in one day. Crashed and died landing after jet mission against bombers, November 1944; holder of Knight's Cross with Diamonds. 258 confirmed victories.

NUNGESSER, Lieutenant Charles Eugène Jules Marie 1892–1927. Third-ranking French "ace" of the First World War, with 45 confirmed victories, Nungesser was a larger-than-life figure. Ex-racing driver, distinguished ex-Hussar officer, and former teenage runaway to South America, he was first posted to a bomber unit, but persisted in flying his Voisin like a fighter. His combat career was punctuated by many crashes and wounds, and he was in constant pain from his injuries; towards the end of the War he had to be carried to and from his aircraft – like the German "ace" Rudolf Berthold. To escape the boredom of a glittering social life after the Armistice he went "barnstorming" in the U.S.A., and finally disappeared during an attempt to fly the Atlantic East-West in May 1927.

PARK, Air Chief Marshal Sir Keith Rodney, G.C.B., K.B.E., M.C., D.F.C. Born 1892. British (New Zealander) air commander. Joining the R.F.C. in 1917 from the Army, Keith Park remained in the R.A.F. after the First World War and commanded No. 25 Squadron in 1920 at a time when it constituted the only fighter defence force in Britain, and also No. 111 Squadron in 1927-28. Various staff appointments followed during the 1930s, but in 1940 he was the much-respected commander of the vital No. 11 Group, Fighter Command, còvering South-East England during the Battle of Britain. Later he became Air Officer Commanding, Egypt and Malta, and Commander-in-Chief, Middle East in 1944. His final appointment was Allied Air Commander-in-Chief, South-East Asia, in 1945–46.

PASHLEY, Flight Lieutenant Cecil Lawrence, M.B.E., A.F.C., Hon.C.R.Ae.S. British pioneer and veteran flying instructor. 1891–1969. Pashley started glider flying at Hockley in 1908, learnt to fly on a Blériot XI and was awarded Aviator's Certificate on 18th July 1911. In that year he founded a flying school at Shoreham, and designed and built his own aircraft for competition flying. During the 1914–1918 War he served as an Admiralty-approved test pilot and instructor – among his pupils were Mick Mannock and John Alcock. Was Chief Flying Instructor with South Coast Flying School between the Wars, and as an R.A.F. flying instructor in the U.K. and Southern Rhodesia in the Second World War. In 1961 he received the Award of Merit for 50 years of flying, and only gave up active flying a year or so before his death.

PATTLE, Squadron Leader Marmaduke Thomas St. John, D.F.C. and Bar 1913–1941. South African fighter pilot. Officially credited with 28 victories, "Pat" Pattle almost certainly gained many more and is widely believed to have topped the Allied list of fighter scores in the Second World War. What is particularly significant is that his combats took place in relatively remote theatres of war, and in the short space of nine months, between June 1940 and April 1941, in North Africa and Greece. Most of his actions were fought in Gladiators with No. 80 Squadron, but in the last days of his life he flew Hurricanes as leader of No. 33 Squadron in Greece. He was eventually shot down and killed in a combat against enormous odds over Eleusis Bay on 20th April 1941. Quiet, unassuming and very popular among his fellow pilots, Pattle never attracted publicity and is now referred to as the "forgotten ace" of the R.A.F.

PENROSE, Harald James, O.B.E., C.Eng., F.R.Ae.S. Born 1904. British test pilot. Harald Penrose turned to historical writing on retirement from a long and active flying career in 1963. He joined Westlands in 1925, flying as Chief Test Pilot from 1931 until 1953, during that period undertaking much of the development flying of such aircraft as the Wallace, Wapiti, Lysander, Whirlwind and Welkin.

PILCHER, Percy Sinclair 1866–1899. Naval architect and pioneer British glider pilot. Joining the Royal Navy at the age of 13 and retiring at 19, Percy Pilcher was later appointed Assistant Lecturer in Naval Architecture at Glasgow University where he built the *Bat* glider. In 1896 he built his *Gull* and *Hawk* gliders, and the following year achieved a flight of 250 yards, thereafter applying his efforts to the design of an engine. He was however fatally injured in 1899 in an accident to *Hawk*.

POKRYSHKIN, Aviation Major-General Aleksandr Ivanovich, Gold Star Medal of the Hero of the Soviet Union (thrice), Order of Lenin (twice), Order of the Red Banner (thrice) Born, *c.* 1922. Soviet fighter pilot. Second-highest scoring Russian and Allied fighter pilot of the Second World War, after Kozhedub (*q.v.*), Pokryshkin destroyed 59 German aircraft before the end of the War. Most of his victories were scored while commanding a Guards Regiment flying Yak-9Us late in 1944.

PORTAL OF HUNGERFORD, 1st VISCOUNT, Marshal of the Royal Air Force Charles Frederick Algernon, K.G.. G.C.B., O.M., D.S.O. and Bar, M.C., D.C.L., LL.D. Born 1893. The great leader of the R.A.F. during the Second World War, Portal transferred to the R.F.C. from the Army in 1915 to fly as an observer. He graduated from the Central Flying School as a pilot in 1916, remaining in the R.A.F. as a squadron leader after the War. Numerous staff appointments followed and he became A.O.C.-in-C., Bomber Command, in 1940. The same year he was appointed Chief of the Air Staff, a position he retained until 1946.

QUILL, Jeffrey Kindersley, O.B.E., A.F.C. Born 1913. British test pilot. Jeffrey Quill joined the R.A.F. on a short service commission in 1931 before being appointed assistant test pilot to Vickers Aviation Ltd., and Vickers (Supermarine) Ltd., in 1936–38. Much of the early Spitfire development flying was carried out by him, more so when he became Senior Test Pilot at the Supermarine Works in 1938. In 1940 he served with R.A.F. Fighter Command during the Battle of Britain to gain first-hand experience with the Spitfire in operational use. He is today Sales Manager (Military Aircraft) of the British Aircraft Corporation.

RAYNHAM, Frederick P. 1892–1954. British pioneer pilot and test pilot. One of the colourful sporting pilots at Hendon and Brooklands before the First World War, Fred Raynham undertook test flying for A. V. Roe and others during the War, and afterwards did considerable flying for Sopwith and the Hawker Company until 1925. He later went to India where he undertook extensive survey flying.

RICHTHOFEN, Generalfeldmarschall Wolfram Freiherr von 1895–1945. German commander. Cousin of Manfred and served under him in *Jagdgeschwader 1* in 1917–18. Held *Luftwaffe* staff post, 1933; served in Spain, 1936–38, and became commander of *Legion Cóndor,* November 1938. Foremost exponent of close-support operations, this "Stuka General" commanded the dive-bombers of *Fliegerkorps VIII* in Poland, France, Balkans and Russia with great success. In July 1942, A.O.C.-in-C., *Luftflotte 4*, and A.O.C.-in-C., South-East. In June 1943, A.O.C.-in-C., *Luftflotte 2* (Mediterranean). Placed on reserve list because of illness, November 1944, and died of brain tumour, July 1945.

RICHTHOFEN, Rittmeister Manfred, Freiherr von 1882–1918. "The Red Baron" – the most famous fighter pilot of all time, and most successful German pilot of his

Marshal of the Royal Air Force The Viscount Portal of Hungerford, K.G., G.C.B., O.M., D.S.O. and Bar, M.C.

war, with 80 confirmed victories. His career has attracted much ill-informed and sensational publicity. A protégé of Boelcke (*q.v.*), he commanded *Jasta 2* in 1917, and subsequently *Jagdgeschwader 1*, comprising four *Jastas*; bright identifying colour schemes led to the nickname "Richthofen's Flying Circus". Although he flew many aircraft, he is popularly associated with a bright red Fokker Dr. I triplane. A cold, calculating hunter, he took no avoidable personal risk; he was shot down and killed under ambiguous circumstances on 21st April 1918.

RICKENBACKER, Captain Edward V. Born 1890. American racing driver from Columbus, Ohio, who became America's leading First World War fighter ace, with 26 confirmed victories. After service in various non-combatant capacities, he finally succeeded in transferring to the 94th Aero Squadron in March 1918; by the end of September he led it. Active in the automobile and airline industries between the Wars, he undertook several roving commissions for his government in the Second World War, and survived 21 days on a life-raft in the Pacific after a forced ditching. He became Chairman of Eastern Airlines in 1953. His many decorations include the Congressional Medal of Honor.

ROCKWELL, Sous-Lieutenant Kiffin Yates 1892–1916. First American pilot to shoot down an enemy aircraft, 18th May 1916, while serving with the *Escadrille Lafayette*. Rockwell and his brother Paul enlisted in the French Foreign Legion in 1914 and fought in the trenches for many months; both were wounded, and Kiffin Rockwell transferred to the air service in the spring of 1915. A founder-member of the *Escadrille Lafayette* – the famous squadron of American volunteers – he was shot down and killed on 23rd September 1916.

ROE, Sir Alliott Verdon, O.B.E., F.R.Ae.S. 1877–1958. Pioneer British aviator, constructor and industrialist. Despite hardships bordering on poverty, "A.V." persevered with the development of early triplanes at Brooklands in 1908 – and even achieved short hops in 1909. In 1912 the Government ordered the Type E biplane – later designated the Type 500. But it was the 504 that was to bring fortune to A. V. Roe, for no fewer than 8,340 were built during the War years. Numerous prototypes followed the War, but in 1928 he sold his interests in the old company and purchased an interest in S. E. Saunders Ltd., of Cowes, thereby forming Saunders-Roe. Thereafter he pursued his favourite venture of constructing flying-boats.

ROLLS, The Hon. Charles Stewart 1877–1910. Pioneer British motorist and aviator. Trained as an engineer, Charlie Rolls was the younger partner of Rolls-Royce Ltd., and before becoming an accomplished pilot he had already achieved considerable fame as a balloonist and motor racing driver in the early 1900s. On 2nd June 1910, flying a Short-built Wright biplane, he flew from Dover to the French coast and back, thereby becoming the first

Englishman to fly an aeroplane across the Channel, the first to make a double crossing, and the first cross-Channel pilot to land at a predetermined spot without damage to his aircraft. His Aviator's Certificate was No. 2 (awarded on 8th March 1910) but he became the first British aeroplane pilot to lose his life while flying when his French-built Wright biplane suffered a structural failure at Bournemouth on 12th July 1910.

ROYCE, Sir Frederick Henry 1863–1933. British engineer. Trained in locomotive engineering, Royce designed his first car in 1903 and this attracted the attention of the Hon. C. S. Rolls, resulting in the formation of Rolls-Royce Ltd. in 1906. Superb car design and manufacture continued but it was not until the First World War (after the death of Rolls) that the company started manufacture of aero-engines – commencing with the Falcon which powered the famous Bristol F.2B Fighter. Semi-invalid by the early 1920s, Royce wintered at Le Canadel each year where a small team of engineers developed his ideas. The great Rolls-Royce Merlin engine stemmed from the Kestrel which was introduced before Royce's death in 1933.

RUDEL, Oberst Hans-Ulrich Born *c.* 1915. German dive-bomber pilot. The only man ever awarded the Golden Oakleaves to the Knight's Cross, on 1st January 1945; the decoration was created for him. The *Luftwaffe's* greatest *Stuka* pilot of the War, and probably the greatest ground-attack pilot of all time, he flew 2,530 combat missions and is credited with destroying 519 Soviet armoured vehicles as well as numerous other targets. He was captured by U.S. forces in May 1945, as commander of *Schlacht Geschwader 2 "Immelmann"*.

SAMSON, Air Commodore Charles Rumney, C.M.G., D.S.O. and Bar, A.F.C., Chevalier Légion d'Honneur, French Croix de Guerre 1883–1931. Pioneer of naval aviation, and larger-than-life figure; even brief notes of his career would fill more space than is available. Selected highlights included R.N. seagoing service in 1898; becoming the first British pilot to take-off from a ship in an aeroplane in 1911; commanding the Naval Wing, R.F.C., in 1912; leading R.N.A.S. squadrons in Belgium in 1914, and Dardanelles in 1916, during the latter of which campaigns he personally bombed Atatürk's staff car; commanded first "carrier task force" in history (three seaplane carriers operated against Turks in Middle East); and commanded Brigade of French troops at Battle of Orchies, 1916. He transferred to the R.A.F. in 1918.

SANTOS-DUMONT, Alberto 1873–1932. Brazilian inventor, balloonist and pioneer aviator. Son of a Brazilian coffee planter, Santos-Dumont was probably the best-known aeroplane pilot between 1906 and 1908. He made his first balloon ascent in 1897, and thereafter a number of airships; he also made a helicopter in 1905 but this was unsuccessful. On 12th November 1906 he established the world's first officially-ratified flying record with a flight of 722 ft (220 m) in his own *14-bis* aeroplane. In 1908 he flew the world's first ultra-light aeroplane (weight, 260 lb), but thereafter ill-health diverted him from practical aviation, and when he died in 1932 from disseminated sclerosis in Brazil he had become almost forgotten throughout the world.

SASSOON, Air Commodore the Rt. Hon. Sir Philip Albert Gustave David, 3rd Baronet, P.C., C.B.E., C.M.G., M.P. British politician and member of wealthy banking family. In later years Philip Sassoon was a great influence in his support of British aviation – both sporting and commercial. He had been Private Secretary to Sir Douglas Haig during the First World War, and was Under-Secretary of State for Air during the years 1924–29 and 1931–33. He was Air Commodore in the Auxiliary Air Force, and his influence was to a great extent responsible for the growth and prestige of that Service before the Second World War.

SAUNDBY, Air Marshal Sir Robert Henry Magnus Spencer, K.C.B., K.B.E., M.C., D.F.C., Officier de la Légion d'Honneur (France), Croix de Guerre Belge (with palm), Grand Officer of the Order of Leopold (Belgium), Commander of the Order of Merit (U.S.A.) Born 1896. British air commander. Joined the R.F.C. from the Army in 1915. Service in France, 1916–17 (wounded and mentioned in despatches); served on No. 45 Squadron in Iraq, 1922–25, and No. 58 (Night Bomber) Squadron, 1926–27. In the Second World War he was appointed S.A.S.O., Bomber Command, 1941–42 (thrice mentioned in despatches), and Deputy A.O.C.-in-C., Bomber Command, 1943–45, under "Bomber" Harris (*q.v.*).

SCHNAUFER, Major Heinz-Wolfgang 1922–1950. Leading German night-fighter ace of 1939–45, survived the War with 121 night victories and Knight's Cross with Diamonds. Flew mainly as flight commander and later squadron leader with *NJG 1*, and led *NJG 4* from November 1944. Once shot down seven R.A.F. bombers in 17 minutes, and two more within the same 24 hours. Died after car crash in France, July 1950.

SCOTT, Sheila, O.B.E. British competitive pilot. Perhaps best known among post-War British women pilots, Sheila Scott started flying in 1959 and has since achieved 77 world class air records, and won over 50 trophies. She achieved fame for her "Round the World Record Flight" in 1966 and was awarded the Britannia Trophy in 1968. She currently holds British and American commercial licences.

SEEKT, General Hans von German commander. Chief of the Army Command at the residual Defence Ministry (*Reichswehr Ministerium*) allowed to Germany by the Versailles treaty, and the man principally responsible for the steady progress in the 1920s towards the re-birth of military air power. He surrounded himself with picked officers who later rose to high *Luftwaffe* command; nurtured civil aviation with a clear appreciation of its

Major Heinz-Wolfgang Schnaufer, Oakleaves, Swords and Diamonds of the Knight's Cross of the Iron Cross

value in the long run; and concluded secret foreign training agreements.

SHORT, Eustace 1875–1932. British aeronautical engineer. Second-oldest of three famous brothers, Eustace was the actual founder of the company of Short Bros. Ltd. After the First World War he designed a huge balloon, intending to attack the world altitude record. In 1926 he learned to fly, and thereafter did a considerable amount of flying. He died from a heart attack shortly after landing from a flight at Rochester on 8th April 1932.

SHORT, Hugh Oswald, F.R.Ae.S., F.Z.S., F.R.A.S. 1883–1970. British balloonist, aircraft constructor and industrialist. Youngest of the Short brothers, Oswald made his first balloon ascent in 1898, and designed his first balloon envelope two years later. Before and during the First World War he concentrated on the design and manufacture of seaplanes. In 1916 he pioneered experiments using duralumin for aircraft construction, and in 1919 produced the first stressed-skin all-metal aeroplane. In 1924 he initiated the design of the first all-metal stressed-skin flying-boat hull, thereafter directing the design of the Sarafand, Singapore, Calcutta and Empire flying boats. His company was taken over by the Government during the Second World War and he retired, to some extent aggrieved by a sense of the injustice.

SHORT, Horace Leonard 1872–1917. British engineer. Oldest of the three Short brothers, Horace was trained in engineering at Stanton Ironworks, Nottingham. His extraordinary inventiveness introduced the folding wing for naval aircraft – which made possible the Short 184 and 320 biplanes of the First World War. In fact the development of the British seaplane owes more to Horace Short than is generally credited. Awe-inspiring in appearance and intimidating to many, Horace Short was however widely admired and regarded by his subordinates with lasting loyalty.

SIEGERT, Oberstleutnant Wilhelm 1872-1929. German infantry officer who had taught himself to fly in 1910, and was influential in the early years of German military aviation. Played a prominent part in the formation of the first bombing units. Second in command to Major Thomsen, the first *Feldflugchef*, in 1915, Siegert was appointed *Inspekteur der Fliegertruppen* in July 1916, and made many contributions to operational efficiency.

SIGRIST, Frederick, M.B.E. 1880-1957. British engineer. Accompanied Sopwith into aviation in 1910 and became his right-hand man; was appointed Works Manager of the Sopwith Company in 1914, responsible for the enormous output of Sopwith aircraft during the First World War. He became joint managing director of the H. G. Hawker Engineering Company and later of Hawker Aircraft Ltd. Having been paid a bonus for every Sopwith aeroplane produced, he retired a very wealthy man, but suffering from ill-health.

SIKORSKY, Igor Alexis, F.R.Ae.S., F.I.Ae.A. 1891-1972. Russian-born (later naturalised American) engineer. As a young man, Sikorsky was the first successful Russian aircraft designer, being responsible for some of the world's largest multi-engined aircraft. After the First World War he escaped to France where he designed for Amiot and Caudron. In 1930 he went to the U.S.A. where he founded Sikorsky Aircraft Corporation, which became a division of United Aircraft Corporation. He had long been interested in rotary-wing aircraft and he produced his first successful helicopter in 1939, from which have been developed a long line of designs famous throughout the world.

SKALSKI, Wing Commander Stanislaw, D.S.O., D.F.C. and two Bars, Virtuti Militari, Polish Cross of Valour, Polish Gold, Silver and Bronze Crosses of Merit Born 27th November 1915. Russian-born Polish fighter pilot. Highest-scoring and most decorated Polish pilot in the R.A.F. Flying obsolete P.Z.L. P-11 fighters in the Polish campaign of 1939, Skalski destroyed five German aircraft before managing to reach London to join the R.A.F. Flying with No. 501 (Hurricane) Squadron and later No. 303 (Polish) Squadron in the Battle of Britain, he shot down a further eight enemy aircraft. Fighting over Northern Europe and the Western Desert, he led Nos. 317 (Polish) and 601 Squadrons of the R.A.F., and later No. 2 (Polish) Fighter Wing flying P-51 Mustangs. His final score was 22½ enemy aircraft destroyed while with the R.A.F., plus the five shot down in 1939. He returned to Poland after the War, only to be imprisoned by the

Russians; released later, he started work on his autobiography *Black Crosses over Poland*.

SOPWITH, Sir Thomas Octave Murdoch, C.B.E., F.R.Ae.S. Born 1888. British engineer, pioneer pilot, manufacturer and industrialist. Son of a wealthy engineer, Tom Sopwith came to Brooklands in 1910 and gained Aviator's Certificate No. 31 on 22nd November that year. For little more than one year he continued flying – becoming one of the best half-dozen British pilots in 1911 before concentrating upon the manufacture of his own aircraft. With men like Hawker and Sigrist around him, his company became the largest aircraft manufacturer in the private sector of the industry during the First World War, producing such aircraft as the Tabloid, 1½-Strutter, Pup, Camel and Snipe. Faced with heavy post-War claims, the Sopwith company went into voluntary liquidation, its business being carried on by Hawkers, of which Sopwith became Chairman. With a continuous line of successful aircraft the new company moved to a position of such strength by the mid-1930s that Sopwith commenced construction of the vast Hawker Siddeley Group by take-over of and merging with other companies. He is today regarded by many as the "grand old man" of British aviation.

SPERRLE, Generalfeldmarschall Hugo Born 1885. German airman of the First World War, served in the *Reichswehr* 1919-1935, and commanded *Legion Cóndor* in Spain, 1936-37. A.O.C. *Luftflotte 3* and A.O.C. West from February 1939; with Kesselring (*q.v.*), commander of German forces in Battle of Britain, 1940. Retained

Oberst Johannes Steinhoff, Oakleaves and Swords of the Knight's Cross of the Iron Cross, Luftwaffe c. 1936–1945

Luftflotte 3 command until transferred to reserve in August 1944.

STEINHOFF, General Johannes ("Mäcki") Born 1913. Flight commander in *JG 26* in September 1939, Steinhoff rose steadily, commanding *II/JG 52* in February 1942, and *JG 77* in March 1943. After much service in Russia and the Mediterranean theatre, he led the Me 262 jet fighter unit *JG 7* in December 1944, and flew with *JV 44* the following month; seriously burned in Me 262 take-off crash, April 1945. Joined the re-born *Luftwaffe* in the 1950s, and currently holds senior command.

STUDENT, Generaloberst Kurt Born 1890. German pilot who served in the Imperial Flying Service throughout the First World War, commanding *Jasta 9* and *Jagdgruppe 3*. Active in organising clandestine flying training in the 1920s, and commanded Rechlin experimental station in the 1930s. Most prominent commander of German airborne troops. Commanded *Fliegerdivision 7* and Inspector of Paratroops, 1938. Commanded airborne formations in the West, 1940, and Crete, 1941. Appointed C.-in-C., Army Group "H" in the West, November 1944, and G.O.C. Parachute Troops in January 1945.

SUKHOI, Aviation Engineer Major-General Pavel Osipovich, Hero of Socialist Labour (Hammer and Sickle Gold Medal, twice), Order of Lenin (thrice), Order of the Red Banner of Labour (twice), Order of the Red Star Born 1895. Soviet aircraft designer. Little is known of the early academic career of Pavel Sukhoi, except that during the early 1930s he attended the *TsAGI* (Central Aero- and Hydrodynamics Institute) as a student of A. N. Tupolev (*q.v.*), whom he later assisted in a junior capacity with the design of the Ant-25 aircraft. It was under Sukhoi's leadership that the I-14 was produced in competition with Nicolai Polikarpov's I-15, but it was the latter aircraft that was chosen for production. Sukhoi evidently established his own bureau before the War, and its best-known product was the Su-2 attack bomber. Much more recently the Sukhoi bureau has produced very efficient jet aircraft, the Su-7 swept-wing fighter-bomber, Su-9 delta-wing fighter and Su-11 delta-wing tactical fighter. Variable-geometry versions of the Su-7 and a STOL version of the Su-11 have also appeared in recent years.

TEDDER, 1st Baron of Glenguin, Marshal of the Royal Air Force Arthur William Tedder, G.C.B., Médaille Militaire (Italy) Born 1890. British air commander. Seconded to the R.F.C. from the Dorsetshire Regiment in the First World War, Arthur Tedder remained in the R.A.F. and commanded No. 207 Squadron at Constantinople, 1922–23. After numerous staff appointments between the Wars, he eventually became Air Officer Commanding-in-Chief, Middle East, in 1941–43, and Deputy Supreme Commander, Allied Expeditionary Force under Eisenhower in Northern Europe, 1944–45. Probably the greatest British air commander of the Second World War.

Squadron Leader Marmaduke Thomas St. John Pattle, D.F.C. and Bar, R.A.F.

TRENCHARD, Marshal of the Royal Air Force, The Lord, G.C.B., D.S.O., D.C.L., LL.D. 1873–1956. British air commander. Having entered the army in 1893, Trenchard was seriously wounded in the South African War, but was granted Aviator's Certificate No. 270 in 1912 and became an instructor at the Central Flying School. He was appointed to command the R.F.C. in 1915. In and out of political favour towards the end of the War he was Chief of the Air Staff from 1918–1929. Tall, with an austere personality, Trenchard was the uncompromising architect of the R.A.F. during a period of inter-Service jealousy, although his outspoken belief in the invincibility of the bomber left the R.A.F. critically weak in its interceptor forces. When he died he was buried with high honour in Westminster Abbey.

TUCK, Wing Commander Robert Roland Stanford, D.S.O., D.F.C. and two Bars, D.F.C. (U.S.A.) Born 1st July 1916. British fighter pilot. Destined to become popularly regarded as the dashing epitome of the classic fighter pilot, Bob Tuck joined the R.A.F. in 1935 and was posted to No. 65 (East India) Squadron in 1936. He was a Flight Commander with No. 92 (Spitfire) Squadron when he first went into action in May 1940. He remained with 92 Squadron almost throughout the Battle of Britain (shooting down 10½ enemy aircraft) before taking command of 257 (Hurricane) Squadron, and by the end of 1940 had accumulated 18 victories. In 1941 he was promoted to lead the Duxford Wing until October when he was taken off operations and sent to America to lecture on air combat. In December he returned to lead the Biggin Hill Spitfire Wing, but was shot down and made prisoner on 28th January 1942, his final score standing at 29 victories. He escaped from his prison camp in January 1945, made his way to the advancing Russian armies and was later repatriated to Britain.

TUPOLEV, Engineer Lieutenant-General Andrei Nikolaevich, Hero of Socialist Labour (Hammer and Sickle Gold Medal, twice), Order of Lenin (twice) Born 1888. Soviet aircraft designer. For many years respected as the "senior" member among Soviet design bureaux, Tupolev was long associated with the *TsAGI* (the Central Aero- and Hydrodymanics Institute), and such designers as Petlyakov and Sukhoi (*q.v.*) were among his pupils, and later collaborators. The first successful aircraft wholly assigned to the Tupolev bureau was the Tu-2, a twin-engined bomber of the mid-War years. It was also responsible for the TB-4 four-engined bomber. Post-War jet aircraft designs included the Tu-14 twin-jet bomber of 1948 (for which Tupolev and thirteen co-workers were awarded a Stalin Prize of 150,000 roubles in 1952), the Tu-16 bomber, the Tu-104, the Tu-114, and so on. Latest creation produced under the leadership of this venerable engineer's son, Dr. Alexei A. Tupolev, is the Tu-144 supersonic airliner.

TWISS, Peter, O.B.E., D.S.C. and Bar Born 1921. British test pilot. Peter Twiss joined the Fleet Air Arm in 1939, serving aboard catapult-equipped ships in 1941 and later as a night fighter pilot on intruder operations. He was the first pilot in the world to establish a speed record of more than 1,000 m.p.h. when on 10th March 1956 he set up a World Speed Record of 1,132 m.p.h. in the Fairey FD.2 delta research aircraft. He was appointed Chief Test Pilot to Fairey Aviation Ltd., 1957–60.

UDET, Generaloberst Ernst 1896–1941. Second-highest scoring German ace of the First World War with 62 confirmed victories; commanded *Jastas 37, 11* and *4*. Between 1918 and 1935 became well known as test pilot, air racer, stunt flyer and sportsman. Joined *Luftwaffe* in 1935; Inspector of Fighters and Dive-bombers, February 1936. Director of Technical Department of *RLM* (Air Ministry), June 1936. February 1939, post redesignated Director General of Directorate General of Air Force Equipment. A brilliant pilot, whose rise was due to his popularity and his long friendship with highly-placed Germans rather than to any deep political convictions, he became increasingly disenchanted with his position and the progress of the War, and killed himself in November 1941.

VANCE, Lieutenant Colonel Leon Robert, Medal of Honor, U.S.A.A.F. 1916–1944. American bomber pilot. Born at Enid, Oklahoma, Vance was a West Point

graduate of 1939, being commissioned in the U.S. Army. Transferring to the Air Corps as a pilot in June 1940, he commanded a squadron in Texas in 1941 and eventually became Deputy Group Commander of the 489th Bombardment Group, flying Liberators. On 5th June 1944 Vance was flying as mission commander on a raid over France when his Liberator was badly damaged by ground fire; his pilot was killed, several crew members wounded and he himself severely wounded in the foot. Despite losing three engines and in considerable pain, Vance took control and continued over the target and re-crossed the English Channel. With great courage he held the aircraft level so his wounded crew could bale out. He himself ditched the big aircraft and was miraculously rescued; he was rushed to hospital and was awarded the Medal of Honor. But on his evacuation back to America, the aircraft in which he was travelling was lost without trace together with all its occupants.

VOISIN, Gabriel Born 1886. French pioneer aircraft constructor. With his younger brother Charles (1888–1912), Gabriel Voisin found fascination in kiting during the early 1900s and, anticipating the development of the powered aircraft, founded Aéroplanes Voisin in 1905. Their early designs were flown by numerous pioneers, often making the first aeroplane flights in European countries. Successful designs were produced during the First World War, although Gabriel's temperament prompted him to leave his company to produce high quality cars. Though almost forgotten during his life in retirement, Gabriel Voisin was unquestionably one of the foremost pioneers of European aviation.

VOSS, Leutnant Werner 1897–1917. Fourth German "ace" of the First World War; a cavalryman with an Iron Cross 1st Class won on the ground, he transferred and became a pilot in 1916. After two-seater service he went to *Jasta Boelcke*, then *Jastas 5, 14* and *10*, commanding the latter. Killed in September 1917 in an epic last fight against seven British fighters led by McCudden, Voss was a front-line fighter pilot just a year, in which time he gained 48 victories, and the *Pour le Mérite*. He was an early and successful exponent of the Fokker Dr. I triplane.

WADE, Wing Commander Lance C., D.S.O., D.F.C. and two Bars 1915–1944. American fighter pilot with the R.A.F. Born in Tucson, Arizona, Lance Wade was the son of a pilot who had flown in the *Escadrille Lafayette* in the First World War; he became the top-scoring American pilot in the R.A.F. and was the most decorated American to hold a British rank in the British forces. He flew Hurricanes with No. 33 Squadron, shooting down fifteen Italian and German aircraft over the Western Desert by the end of 1942, when he was posted to command No. 145 (Spitfire) Squadron. In July 1943 he took command of a Spitfire Wing over Sicily and Italy, but was killed on 12th January 1944 when his Auster light-plane crashed well behind the Allied lines in Italy. His award of the D.S.O. was made posthumously, and his final score was 25 victories.

WALLIS, Sir Barnes Neville, Kt., C.B.E., D.Sc., Sc.D., F.R.S., R.D.I., F.C.I.E., F.I.P.I., Hon.F.I.Mech.E., Hon.F.R.Ae.S., F.S.E., F.S.I.A.D. British engineer and aircraft designer. Born 26th September 1887. Barnes Wallis started a long and distinguished career by training as a marine engineer with J. S. White & Co. Ltd., from 1905 until 1913; he was Assistant Chief Designer with Vickers, 1913–1915; served with the Army and R.N.A.S., 1915; was Chief Designer of the Airship Department of Vickers Ltd., 1916–1921; Chief Designer (Structures) with Vickers Aviation Ltd., 1930–37 (responsible for the design and construction of the airship *R-100*, also for the design of the Wellesley and Wellington bombers with geodetic structure); Assistant Chief Designer, Vickers-Armstrongs Ltd., 1937–1945 (was responsible, *inter alia*, for bomb design, including the special mines used against the Mohne, Sorpe and Eder dams in 1943). After the War he was the originator of the swing-wing concept, as well as several other advanced aeronautical design concepts.

WHITTLE, Air Commodore Sir Frank, K.B.E., C.B., M.A., F.R.S., Hon.M.I.Mech.E., Hon.F.R.Ae.S. British engineer. Born 1st June 1907. Frank Whittle joined the R.A.F. in 1923 and it was while he was at the R.A.F. College at Cranwell that he wrote his famous thesis on gas turbines. After normal flying service as a pilot with No. 111 (Fighter) Squadron, an instructor at C.F.S., and a floatplane test pilot at Felixstowe, he attended Cambridge University, 1934–1937, and was placed on the Special Duty List to work on gas turbine development which culminated in the design and production of the first successful Whittle jet engine – the first such engine to fly (in the Gloster E.28/39 aircraft) outside Germany.

WICK, Major Helmut 1915–1940. After Mölders and Galland (*q.v.*), the most successful German fighter pilot of the first year of the War. Wick gained 56 victories between 22nd November 1939 and his death in action over the Channel on 28th November 1940. He rose to flight commander in July 1940, squadron commander in September, and wing commander (*Kommodore* of *Jagdgeschwader 2 "Richthofen"*) in October, and was awarded the Knight's Cross with Oakleaves.

WRIGHT, Orville 1871–1948. Younger brother of Wilbur, Orville Wright won the toss to take the *Flyer* aloft for the first time at 10.35 a.m. on Thursday 17th December 1903. Five years later, while Wilbur was in Europe giving his famous demonstration flights, Orville suffered a bad accident at Fort Myer, Virginia, in which Lieutenant Thomas Etholen Selfridge lost his life –

thereby becoming the first aeroplane fatality. Orville was badly injured. Never really adept in business, he sold his interest in the Wright company in 1915, preferring to apply his efforts to aerodynamic research. Often criticised during his early career for his reluctance to divulge details of his pioneer design work, Orville was later much admired for the advice and assistance he gave to others.

WRIGHT, Wilbur 1867–1912. American engineer and pioneer aviator. Elder of the two famous Ohio brothers, Wilbur was perhaps best known in Europe for his scintillating display of flying near Le Mans, France, in August 1908. Although the brothers had been progressing with their *Flyer* in America for five years, there was some scepticism in Europe, whose constructors and pilots had only just managed to cover relatively short distances in the air. On the last day of 1908, Wilbur achieved a flight of 77 miles in 2 hr. 20 min. 23 sec.

WYKEHAM, Air Marshal Sir Peter Guy, K.C.B., D.S.O. and Bar, O.B.E., D.F.C. and Bar, A.F.C., Order of Dannebrog (Denmark), Air Medal (U.S.A.), F.R.Ae.S. Born 1915. British fighter pilot and air commander. Commissioned in the R.A.F. in 1937, Peter Wykeham-Barnes (as he was then) flew with No. 80 (Gladiator) Squadron and No. 274 Squadron early in the Second World War, and later commanded Nos. 73, 257 and 23 Squadrons, the Kenley Fighter Sector, No. 140 Wing, and the R.A.F. fighter stations at North Weald and Wattisham. He served with the U.S.A.F. during the Korean War, and became Air Officer Commanding, No. 38 Group in 1960–62. His final appointment in the R.A.F. was Deputy Chief of the Air Staff at the Ministry of Defence, 1967–68, before retiring in 1969 to become export consultant to various companies.

YAKOVLEV, Aviation-General Alexander Sergyeyevitch, Hero of Socialist Labour (Hammer and Sickle Gold Medal, twice), Order of Lenin (twice) Born, Moscow, 1906. Soviet aircraft designer. Yakovlev gained his first experience in aircraft construction when he helped to build a glider in 1923. Later in the 1920s, assisted by Government members K. Voroshylov and A. Mikoyan, he established an aircraft plant in Moscow – on a site later occupied by the vast Yakovlev factory, one of the three largest in Western Russia. His first successful military aircraft, the Yak-1 fighter, entered service in 1940, but his most successful wartime fighter was the Yak-9 of the 1943–45 period. In 1942 the Yak organisation was evacuated eastwards and occupied State Aircraft Factory No. 153, which built more fighter aircraft than any other – with the likely exception of the Messerschmitt Bf 109.

APPENDIX

THE HIGHEST AWARDS FOR GALLANTRY MADE TO MILITARY AIRMEN

GREAT BRITAIN AND THE BRITISH COMMONWEALTH

The First World War

Captain A. Ball, V.C., D.S.O.**, M.C., *Chevalier de la Légion d'Honneur,* R.F.C.

Major W. G. Barker, V.C., D.S.O., M.C.**, *Chevalier de la Légion d'Honneur, Croix de Guerre, Virtuti Militari,* R.F.C.

Captain A. W. Beauchamp-Proctor, V.C., D.S.O., M.C.*, D.F.C., R.A.F.

Lieutenant-Colonel W. A. Bishop, V.C., D.S.O.*, M.C., D.F.C., *Chevalier de la Légion d'Honneur, Croix de Guerre,* R.F.C.

Lieutenant R. B. Davies, V.C., D.S.O., A.F.C., R.N.A.S.

Major L. G. Hawker, V.C., D.S.O., R.F.C.

Lieutenant G. S. M. Insall, V.C., M.C., R.F.C.

Lieutenant A. Jerrard, V.C., R.A.F.

Captain A. J. Liddell, V.C., M.C., R.F.C.

Major E. Mannock, V.C., D.S.O.**, M.C.*, R.A.F.

Major J. T. B. McCudden, V.C., D.S.O.*, M.C.*, M.M., *Croix de Guerre,* R.A.F.

Lieutenant A. A. McLeod, V.C., R.A.F.

Sergeant T. Mottershead, V.C., D.C.M., R.F.C.

Major L. W. B. Rees, V.C., O.B.E., M.C., A.F.C., R.F.C.

Lieutenant W. B. Rhodes-Moorhouse, V.C., R.F.C.

Captain W. Leefe Robinson, V.C., R.F.C.

Flight Sub-Lieutenant R. A. J. Warneford, V.C., R.N.A.S.

Captain F. M. F. West, V.C., M.C., R.A.F.

The Second World War

Acting Flight Sergeant A. L. Aaron, V.C., D.F.M., R.A.F.

Pilot Officer C. Barton, V.C., R.A.F.V.R.

Acting Squadron Leader I. W. Bazalgette, V.C., D.F.C., R.A.F.V.R.

Flying Officer K. Campbell, V.C., R.A.F.V.R.

Group Captain G. L. Cheshire, V.C., D.S.O.**, D.F.C., R.A.F.

Flying Officer J. A. Cruikshank, V.C., R.A.F.V.R.

Air Commodore H. I. Edwards, V.C., C.B., D.S.O., O.B.E., D.F.C., R.A.F.

Lieutenant-Commander E. Esmonde, V.C., D.S.O., R.N.

Flying Officer D. E. Garland, V C., R.A.F.

Wing Commander G. P. Gibson, V.C., D.S.O.*, D.F.C.*, R.A.F.

Lieutenant R. H. Gray, V.C., D.S.C., R.C.N.V.R.

Sergeant T. Gray, V.C., R.A.F.

Sergeant J. Hannah, V.C., R.A.F.

Flight Lieutenant D. E. Hornell, V.C., R.C.A.F.

Warrant Officer N. Jackson, V.C., R.A.F.

Acting Flight Lieutenant R. A. B. Learoyd, V.C., R.A.F.

Flying Officer D. S. A. Lord, V.C., D.F.C., R.A.F.

Wing Commander H. G. Malcolm, V.C., R.A.F.

Flying Officer L. T. Manser, V.C., R.A.F.V.R.

Flight Sergeant R. H. Middleton, V.C., R.A.A.F.

Pilot Officer A. C. Mynarski, V.C., R.C.A.F.

Acting Squadron Leader J. D. Nettleton, V.C., S.A.A.F.

Flight Lieutenant W. E. Newton, V.C., R.A.A.F.

Flight Lieutenant J. B. Nicolson, V.C., D.F.C., R.A.F.

Acting Squadron Leader R. A. M. Palmer, V.C., D.F.C., R.A.F.V.R.

Acting Flight Lieutenant W. Reid, V.C., R.A.F.V.R.

Squadron Leader S. K. Scarf, V.C., R.A.F.

Captain E. Swales, V.C., D.F.C., S.A.A.F.

Flight Sergeant G. Thompson, V.C., R.A.F.V.R.

Squadron Leader L. H. Trent, V.C., D.F.C., R.N.Z.A.F.

Flying Officer L. A. Trigg, V.C., D.F.C., R.N.Z.A.F.

Sergeant J. A. Ward, V.C., R.N.Z.A.F.

THE UNITED STATES OF AMERICA

The First World War

2nd Lieutenant Erwin R. Bleckley, Medal of Honor, U.S.A.S.

1st Lieutenant Harold E. Goettler, Medal of Honor, U.S.A.S.

2nd Lieutenant Frank Luke, Jr., Medal of Honor, U.S.A.S.

1st Lieutenant Edward V. Rickenbacker, Medal of Honor, U.S.A.S.

Between the Wars

Captain Charles A. Lindbergh, Congressional Medal of Honor

The Second World War

Lieutenant-Colonel Addison E. Baker, Medal of Honor, U.S.A.A.F.

Major Richard I. Bong, Medal of Honor, U.S.A.A.F.

Major Horace S. Carswell, Jr., Medal of Honor, U.S.A.A.F.

Brigadier General Frederick W. Castle, Medal of Honor, U.S.A.F.

Major Ralph Cheli, Medal of Honor, U.S.A.F.

Colonel Demas T. Craw, Medal of Honor, U.S.A.F.

Lieutenant-Colonel James H. Doolittle, Medal of Honor, U.S.A.A.F.

Staff Sergeant Henry E. Erwin, Medal of Honor, U.S.A.A.F.

2nd Lieutenant Robert E. Femoyer, Medal of Honor, U.S.A.A.F.

1st Lieutenant Donald J. Gott, Medal of Honor, U.S.A.A.F.

Major Pierpont M. Hamilton, Medal of Honor, U.S.A.A.F.

Lieutenant-Colonel James H. Howard, Medal of Honor, U.S.A.A.F.

2nd Lieutenant Lloyd H. Hughes, Medal of Honor, U.S.A.A.F.

Major John L. Jerstad, Medal of Honor, U.S.A.A.F.

Colonel Leon W. Johnson, Medal of Honor, U.S.A.A.F.

Colonel John R. Kane, Medal of Honor, U.S.A.A.F.

Colonel Neel E. Kearby, Medal of Honor, U.S.A.A.F.

2nd Lieutenant David R. Kingsley, Medal of Honor, U.S.A.A.F.

1st Lieutenant Roymond L. Knight, Medal of Honor, U.S.A.A.F.

1st Lieutenant William R. Lawley, Jr., Medal of Honor, U.S.A.A.F.

Captain Darrell R. Lindsey, Medal of Honor, U.S.A.A.F.

Sergeant Archibald Mathies, Medal of Honor, U.S.A.A.F.

Major Thomas B. McGuire, Jr., Medal of Honor, U.S.A.A.F.

2nd Lieutenant William E. Metzger, Jr., Medal of Honor, U.S.A.A.F.

1st Lieutenant Edward S. Michael, Medal of Honor, U.S.A.A.F.

First Officer John C. Morgan, Medal of Honor

Captain Harl Pease, Jr., Medal of Honor, U.S.A.A.F.

1st Lieutenant Donald D. Pucket, Medal of Honor, U.S.A.A.F.

2nd Lieutenant Joseph R. Sarnoski, Medal of Honor, U.S.A.A.F.

Major William A. Shomo, Medal of Honor, U.S.A.A.F.

Sergeant Maynard H. Smith, Medal of Honor, U.S.A.A.F.

2nd Lieutenant Walter E. Truemper, Medal of Honor, U.S.A.A.F.

Lieutenant-Colonel Leon R. Vance, Jr., Medal of Honor, U.S.A.A.F.

Top Sergeant Forrest L. Vosler, Medal of Honor, U.S.A.A.F.

Brigadier General Kenneth N. Walker, Medal of Honor, U.S.A.A.F.

Major Raymond H. Wilkins, Medal of Honor, U.S.A.A.F.

Major Jay Zeamer, Jr., Medal of Honor, U.S.A.A.F.

Post-Second World War

Brigadier General William C. Mitchell, Congressional Medal of Honor, late U.S.A.A.C.

The Korean War

Major George A. Davis, Jr., Medal of Honor, U.S.A.F.

Major Charles J. Loring, Jr., Medal of Honor, U.S.A.F.

Major Louis J. Sebille, Medal of Honor, U.S.A.F.

Captain John S. Walmsley, Jr., Medal of Honor, U.S.A.F.

The Vietnam War

Major Merlyn H. Dethlefsen, Medal of Honor, U.S.A.F.

Major Barnard F. Fisher, Medal of Honor, U.S.A.F.

Captain James P. Fleming, Medal of Honor, U.S.A.F.

Lieutenant-Colonel William A. Jones, III, Medal of Honor, U.S.A.F.

Sergeant John L. Levitow, Medal of Honor, U.S.A.F.

Captain Hilliard A. Wilbanks, Medal of Honor, U.S.A.F.

Captain Gerald O. Young, Medal of Honor, U.S.A.F.

GERMANY

First World War

Leutnant K. Allmenröder, *Pour le Mérite*

Oberleutnant H. Auffahrt, *Pour le Mérite*

Oberleutnant E. Freiherr von Althaus, *Pour le Mérite*

Leutnant P. Bäumer, *Pour le Mérite*

Leutnant O., Freiherr von Beaulieu-Marconnay, *Pour le Mérite*

Leutnant H. Becker, *Pour le Mérite*

Oberleutnant F. Bernert, *Pour le Mérite*

Oberleutnant H. Berr, *Pour le Mérite*

Hauptmann R. Berthold, *Pour le Mérite*

Oberleutnant H. Bethge, *Pour le Mérite*

Leutnant P. Billik, *Pour le Mérite*

Leutnant W. Blume, *Pour le Mérite*

Leutnant E. Böhme, *Pour le Mérite*

Hauptmann O. Boelcke, *Pour le Mérite*

Rittmeister K. Bolle, *Pour le Mérite*

Oberleutnant O. Freiherr von Boenigk, *Pour le Mérite*

Leutnant H. Bongartz, *Pour le Mérite*

Major E. von Brandenburg, *Pour le Mérite*

Leutnant F. Büchner, *Pour le Mérite*

Leutnant J. Buckler, *Pour le Mérite*

Hauptmann H. J. Buddecke, *Pour le Mérite*

Leutnant W. von Bülow, *Pour le Mérite*

Kapitän Leutnant Freiherr von Buttlar-Brandenfeld, *Pour le Mérite*

Oberleutnant F. Christiansen, *Pour le Mérite*

Leutnant K. Degelow, *Pour le Mérite*

Leutnant G. Dörr, *Pour le Mérite*

Leutnant A. Dossenbach, *Pour le Mérite*

Germany (*continued*)

Oberleutnant E. Ritter von Dostler, *Pour le Mérite*
Leutnant W. Fankl, *Pour le Mérite*
Leutnant H. von Freden, *Pour le Mérite*
Hauptmann H. Fricke, *Pour le Mérite*
Leutnant F. Friedrichs, *Pour le Mérite*
Vizefeldwebel O. Fruhner, *Pour le Mérite*
Oberleutnant H. Göring, *Pour le Mérite*
Leutnant H. Gontermann, *Pour le Mérite*
Oberleutnant R. Ritter von Greim, *Pour le Mérite*
Leutnant W. Greibsch, *Pour le Mérite*
Hauptmann J. von Grone, *Pour le Mérite*
Leutnant G. von Hantelmann, *Pour le Mérite*
Leutnant W. Höhndorf, *Pour le Mérite*
Oberleutnant E. Homberg, *Pour le Mérite*
General W. von Hoeppner, *Pour le Mérite*
Oberleutnant H. J. Horn, *Pour le Mérite*
Oberleutnant M. Immelmann, *Pour le Mérite*
Leutnant J. Jacobs, *Pour le Mérite*
Major A. Keller, *Pour le Mérite*
Leutnant H. Kirschstein, *Pour le Mérite*
Leutnant O. Kissenberth, *Pour le Mérite*
Leutnant H. Klein, *Pour le Mérite*
Kapitän Leutnant R. Kleine, *Pour le Mérite*
Hauptmann H. Kohl, *Pour le Mérite*
Leutnant O. Koennecke, *Pour le Mérite*
Leutnant H. Kroll, *Pour le Mérite*
Leutnant A. Laumann, *Pour le Mérite*
Leutnant G. Leffers, *Pour le Mérite*
Hauptmann L. Leonhardy, *Pour le Mérite*
Hauptmann B. Loerzer, *Pour le Mérite*
Oberleutnant E. Loewenhardt, *Pour le Mérite*
Leutnant J. Mai, *Pour le Mérite*
Hauptmann K. Menckhoff, *Pour le Mérite*
Leutnant G. Meyer, *Pour le Mérite*
Oberleutnant Ritter von Müller, *Pour le Mérite*
Oberleutnant A. Muller-Kahle, *Pour le Mérite*
Leutnant M. Ritter von Mulzer, *Pour le Mérite*

Leutnant M. Näther, *Pour le Mérite*
Leutnant U. Neckel, *Pour le Mérite*
Leutnant F. Nielebock, *Pour le Mérite*
Leutnant F. Noltenius, *Pour le Mérite*
Leutnant K. Odebrett, *Pour le Mérite*
Leutnant T. Osterkamp, *Pour le Mérite*
Leutnant O. Parschau, *Pour le Mérite*
Hauptmann P. Freiherr von Pechmann, *Pour le Mérite*
Leutnant W. Preuss, *Pour le Mérite*
Leutnant F. Pütter, *Pour le Mérite*
Leutnant W. Preuss, *Pour le Mérite*
Oberleutnant L. Freiherr von Richthofen, *Pour le Mérite*
Rittmeister M. Freiherr von Richthofen, *Pour le Mérite*
Hauptmann W. Reinhard, *Pour le Mérite*
Leutnant P. Rieper, *Pour le Mérite*
Oberleutnant F. Ritter von Röth, *Pour le Mérite*
Leutnant F. Rumey, *Pour le Mérite*
Oberleutnant G. Sachsenberg, *Pour le Mérite*
Leutnant K. Schaefer, *Pour le Mérite*
Hauptmann E. Ritter von Schleich, *Pour le Mérite*
Oberleutnant F. Schleiff, *Pour le Mérite*
Oberleutnant Doktor O. Schmidt, *Pour le Mérite*
Leutnant W. P. Schreiber, *Pour le Mérite*
Korvette Capitän P. Strasser, *Pour le Mérite*
Leutnant K. Thom, *Pour le Mérite*
Major H. von der Lieth-Thomsen, *Pour le Mérite*
Leutnant E. Thuy, *Pour le Mérite*
Hauptmann A. Ritter von Tutschek, *Pour le Mérite*
Oberleutnant E. Udet, *Pour le Mérite*
Leutnant J. Veltjens, *Pour le Mérite*
Leutnant W. Voss, *Pour le Mérite*
Hauptmann F. Walz, *Pour le Mérite*
Leutnant R. Windisch, *Pour le Mérite*
Leutnant H. Weiss, *Pour le Mérite*
Leutnant K. Wintgens, *Pour le Mérite*
Oberleutnant K. Wolff, *Pour le Mérite*
Leutnant K. Wüsthoff, *Pour le Mérite*

The Second World War

(*Only holder of the Golden Oakleaves with Swords and Diamonds of the Knight's Cross of the Iron Cross*)

Oberst Hans-Ulrich Rudel

(*Holders of the Oakleaves, Swords and Diamonds of the Knight's Cross of the Iron Cross, in addition to the above holder*)

Oberst Adolf Galland
Major Gordon Gollob
Major Hermann Graf
Oberleutnant Erich Hartmann

Oberstleutnant Helmut Lent
Hauptmann Hans-Joachim Marseille
Oberst Werner Mölders

Hauptmann Walter Nowotny
Hauptmann Heinz-Wolfgang Schnaufer

(*Holders of the Oakleaves and Swords of the Knight's Cross of the Iron Cross, in addition to the above holders*)

Hauptmann Heinrich Bär
Hauptmann Gerhard Barkhorn
Hauptmann Werner Baumbach

Major Alwin Boerst
Major Kürt Bühlingen
Oberfeldwebel Helmut Dörner

Hauptmann Alfred Druschel
Generaloberst Robert Ritter von Greim

Major Anton Häckl
Hauptmann Joachim Helbig
Oberst Hajo Herrmann
Hauptmann Herbert Ihlefeldt
Oberleutnant Otto Kittel
Oberst Doktor Ernst Kupfer
Major Friedrich Lang
Major Günther Lützow
Oberstleutnant Egon Mayer
Hauptmann Joachim Müncheberg

Major Theo Nordmann
Hauptmann Walter Oesau
Oberleutnant Max-Helmut Ostermann
Oberst Friedrich Peltz
Hauptmann Hans Philipp
Oberstleutnant Josef Priller
Hauptmann Günter Rall
Oberleutnant Ernst-Wilhelm Reinert

Major Heinrich Prinz zu Sayn-Wittgenstein
Oberstleutnant Adalbert Schulz
Oberfeldwebel Leopold Steinbatz
Oberstleutnant Johannes Steinhoff
Major Werner Streib
Oberst Theodor Tolsdorff
Major Wolf-Dieter Wilcke
Hauptmann Josef Wurmheller

(Holders of the Oakleaves of the Knight's Cross of the Iron Cross, in addition to the above holders)

Hauptmann Horst Adameit
Oberstleutnant Willi Antrup
Hauptmann Wilhelm Balthasar
Major Hansgeorg Bätcher
Hauptmann Wilhelm Batz
Hauptmann Herbert Bauer
Oberleutnant Viktor Bauer
Hauptmann Ludwig Becker
Oberfeldwebel Hans Beerenbrock
Leutnant Hans Beisswenger
Oberstleutnant Freiherr Hans-Henning Freiherr von Beust
Hauptmann Werner Brändle
Hauptmann Joachim Brendle
Hauptmann Helmut Bruck
Feldwebel Wilhelm Crinius
Oberstleutnant Walter Dahl
Generaloberst Otto Dessloch
Leutnant Adolf Dickfeld
Hauptmann Bruno Dilley
Oberstleutnant Oskar Dinort
Leutnant Otto Dommeratzky
Hauptmann Georg Dörffel
Major Werner Dörnbrack
Hauptmann Franz Eckerle
Hauptmann Georg Eder
Hauptmann Heinrich Ehrler
Oberstleutnant Volprecht Freiherr Riedesel von Eisenbach
Oberleutnant Wolf-Udo Ettel
Generalleutnant Martin Fiebig
Hauptmann Erwin Fischer
Hauptmann Hans-Dieter Frank
Oberleutnant Heinz Frank
Oberfeldwebel Rudolf Frank
Hauptmann August Geiger
Oberleutnant Friedrich Geisshardt
Oberleutnant Paul Gildner
Leutnant Adolf Glunz
Leutnant Hermann Graf
Major Hartmann Grasser
Oberstleutnant Sigmar-Ulrich Freiherr von Gravenreuth
Hauptmann Alfred Grislawski
Major Reinhard Günzel

Leutnant Anton Hafner
Oberstleutnant Walter Hagen
Hauptmann Hans (Assi) Hahn
Leutnant Horst Hannig
Major Jürgen Harder
Oberstleutnant Martin Harlinghausen
Hauptmann Jochen Helbig
Major Karl Henze
Major Wilhelm Herget
Major Rolf Hermichen
Major Hubertus Hitschold
Major Karl-Heinrich Höfer
Oberfeldwebel Heinrich Hoffmann
Major Günther Hoffmann-Schoenborn
Hauptmann Hermann Hogeback
Oberstleutnant Paul-Werner Hozzel
Oberstleutnant Dietrich Hrabak
Hauptmann Herbert Huppertz
Oberleutnant Wolf-Dieter Huy
Hauptmann Hans-Joachim Jabs
Major Georg Jacob
Major Bernhard Jope
Hauptmann Hermann-Friedrich Joppien
Oberleutnant Erbo Graf von Kageneck
Hauptmann Rolf Kaldrack
Major Horst Kaubisch
Hauptmann Karl Kennel
Oberleutnant Willy Kientsch
Hauptmann Franz Kieslich
Oberleutnant Joachim Kirschner
Hauptmann Reinhold Knacke
Major Gerhard Kollewe
Feldwebel Gerhard Köppen
Hauptmann Walter Krauss
Oberleutnant Walter Krupinski
Hauptmann Andreas Kuffner
Major Doktor Ernst Kupfer
Oberleutnant Emil Lang
Hauptmann Friedrich Lang
Major Helmut Leicht
Hauptmann Wilhelm Lemke

Hauptmann Prinz zur Lippe-Weissenberger
Hauptmann Dieter Lukesch
Hauptmann Wilhelm von Malachowski
Hauptmann Robert-Georg Freiherr von Malapert Neufville
Major Günther Freiherr von Maltzan
Hauptmann Kurt Meier
Hauptmann Manfred Meurer
Major Gerhard Michalski
Major Klaus Mietusch
Major Martin Möbus
Oberleutnant Karl-Friedrich Müller
Leutnant Leopold Münster
Oberleutnant Karl-Gottfried Nordmann
Major Doktor Maximilian Otte
Hauptmann Heinrich Paepcke
General der Flieger Kurt Pflugbeil
Hauptmann Hubert Pölz
Hauptmann Gustav Pressler
Hauptmann Gerhard Raht
Oberstleutnant Günther Radusch
Feldwebel Ernst-Wilhelm Reinert
General der Flieger Wolfram Freiherr von Richthofen
Major Gustav Roedel
Hauptmann Heinz Rökker
Leutnant Herbert Rollwage
Major Erich Rudorfer
Oberleutnant Georg Sattler
Leutnant Konrad Sauer
Leutnant Günther Schack
Oberleutnant Hans Schalanda
Hauptmann Wolfgang Schenck
Leutnant Heinz Schmidt
Major Wilhelm Schmitter
Leutnant Siegfried Schnell
Major Rudolf Schönert
Oberleutnant Herbert Schramm
Hauptmann Werner Schröer
Oberleutnant Gustav Schubert
Leutnant Walter Schuck

Germany (*continued*)

Generalmajor Ludwig Schulz
Hauptmann Heinrich Schweickhardt
Major Reinhard Seiler
Oberleutnant Heinrich Setz
Oberstleutnant Walter Sigel
Hauptmann Eduard Skrzipek
Oberleutnant Wolfgang Späte
Hauptmann Wilhelm Speiss
Oberleutnant Hendrik Stahl
Leutnant Hans-Arnold Stahlschmidt
Oberstleutnant Hans-Karl Stepp
Hauptmann Hans-Christian Stock

Major Walter Storp
Oberfeldwebel Max Stotz
Leutnant Hans Strelow
Hauptmann Heinz Strüning
General der Flieger Kurt Student
Hauptmann Hans Thurner
Oberleutnant Gerhard Thyben
Major Günther Tonne
Oberleutnant Wolfgang Tonne
Hauptmann Eduard Tratt
Hauptmann Kurt Ubben
Oberfeldwebel Heinz Vinke

Hauptmann Karl-Heinz Weber
Major Johannes Weise
Hauptmann Robert Weiss
Oberleutnant Theodor
    Weissenberger
Oberleutnant Kurt Welter
Oberleutnant Otto Wessling
Major Herbert Wittmann
Leutnant Albin Wolf
Hauptmann Johann Zemsky
Hauptmann Paul Zorner
Oberfeldwebel Josef Zwernemann

(*A total of 1,404 members of the Luftwaffe* (*excluding Flak units*) *were awarded the Knight's Cross of the Iron Cross, as well as the holders of the above decorations*)

~INDEX~

Note: In the interests of space the following Index does not include the military airfields of Great Britain and the United States of America, which are shown in the maps on pages 81 and 91 respectively, nor the towns and cities of the U.S.S.R., shown in the map on page 115 – except where otherwise mentioned in the body of the text.

Military airfields are marked thus*, and non-military airfields (or military airfields with commercial facilities) thus †.

Military recipients of decorations for outstanding gallantry, who are otherwise listed in alphabetical order in the Appendix on pages 222–226, are omitted from this Index, except where otherwise referred to in the body of the text.

227